⇥THE⇤

NORTON SAMPLER

TENTH EDITION

ALSO BY THOMAS COOLEY

Back to the Lake:
A Reader and Guide

The Norton Guide to Writing

Adventures of Huckleberry Finn,
A Norton Critical Edition

The Ivory Leg in the Ebony Cabinet:
Madness, Race, and Gender in Victorian America

Educated Lives:
The Rise of Modern Autobiography in America

THE NORTON SAMPLER

SHORT ESSAYS FOR COMPOSITION

TENTH EDITION

THOMAS COOLEY

THE OHIO STATE UNIVERSITY

W. W. NORTON & COMPANY

Independent Publishers Since 1923

W. W. Norton & Company has been independent since its founding in 1923, when William Warder Norton and Mary D. Herter Norton first published lectures delivered at the People's Institute, the adult education division of New York City's Cooper Union. The firm soon expanded its program beyond the Institute, publishing books by celebrated academics from America and abroad. By midcentury, the two major pillars of Norton's publishing program—trade books and college texts—were firmly established. In the 1950s, the Norton family transferred control of the company to its employees, and today—with a staff of five hundred and hundreds of trade, college, and professional titles published each year—W. W. Norton & Company stands as the largest and oldest publishing house owned wholly by its employees.

Editor: Erica Wnek

Project Editor: Maura Gaughan

Assistant Editor: Edwin Jeng

Managing Editor, College: Marian Johnson

Production Manager: Jeremy Burton

Media Editor: Joy Cranshaw

Media Project Editor: Cooper Wilhelm

Assistant Media Editor: Katie Bolger

Managing Editor, College Digital Media: Kim Yi

Marketing Manager, Composition: Michele Dobbins

Designer: JoAnn Metsch

Director of College Permissions: Megan Schindel

Permissions Clearing: Joshua Garvin

Photo Editor: Stephanie Romeo

Photo Researcher: Fay Torresyap

Composition: Westchester Publishing Services

Manufacturing: LSC Communications

Permission to use copyrighted material is included in the Permissions Acknowledgements beginning on p. 626.

Library of Congress Cataloging-in-Publication Data

Names: Cooley, Thomas, 1942– editor.
Title: The Norton sampler : short essays for composition / Thomas Cooley.
Description: Tenth edition. | [New York] : W. W. Norton & Company, [2021] | Includes bibliographical references and index.
Identifiers: LCCN 2020025723 | **ISBN 9780393427639 (paperback)** | ISBN 9780393537093 (epub)
Subjects: LCSH: College readers. | English language—Rhetoric. | Essays.
Classification: LCC PE1417 .N6 2021 | DDC 808/.0427—dc23
LC record available at https://lccn.loc.gov/2020025723

W. W. Norton & Company, Inc., 500 Fifth Avenue, New York, NY 10110
wwnorton.com

W. W. Norton & Company Ltd., 15 Carlisle Street, London W1D 3BS

2 3 4 5 6 7 8 9 0

CONTENTS

1 ✳ READING AS A WRITER, WRITING AS A READER 1

Getting Started • Reading Closely and Critically • Responding to a Text • Identifying Common Patterns • Reading the Essays in this Book

E. B. WHITE | Once More to the Lake   19

I felt the same damp moss covering the worms in the bait can, and saw the dragonfly alight on the tip of my rod. . . . It was the arrival of this fly that convinced me beyond any doubt that everything was as it had always been, that the years were a mirage and that there had been no years.

2 ✳ ELEMENTS OF THE ESSAY 29

Topic • Thesis • Coherence • Tone and Style • Putting It All Together

3 ✳ THE WRITING PROCESS 44

Planning • Generating Ideas • Organizing and Drafting • Revising • Editing and Proofreading

4 ✳ WRITING PARAGRAPHS 61

Supporting the Main Point • Developing Paragraphs • Introductory Paragraphs • Concluding Paragraphs

5 ✳ DESCRIPTION 77

The simplicity of the structure gives it its power—power that can be seen at the memorial every day through the tears shed by veterans taking in their fallen brothers' names. Its lack of ornament gives it a solemn feel that facilitates reflection on those we have lost and the sacrifice they made.

When the quilt was finished, one could see that the edges of each panel didn't quite match, that the soft lavender and deep crimson from one sari clashed slightly with the brilliant yellow and green from another, that the stitches were crude and uneven. Yet beheld in unison, these imperfections fashioned something only I could have created, beautiful in its own way.

Dreamland could fit hundreds of people, and yet, magically, the space around it kept growing and there was always room for more.

"He's mostly silver, but the silver is somehow made up of all the colors, if you know what I mean." I stopped. "Do you know what I mean by colors?"

Miss Dennis always wore a variation of one outfit—a dark-colored, flared woolen skirt, a tailored white blouse and a cardigan sweater, usually black, thrown over her shoulders and held together by a little pearl chain.

   Can you see her? I can. And the image of her makes me smile. Still.

At first glance, there is nothing about this hot dog that looks special, but once you take a bite, you know you've touched the nirvana of hot dogs. That first bite tells you everything.

*Annotated Student Example

To say my grandmother loved Elvis would be like describing the ceiling of the Sistine Chapel as a nice little mural.

Most Americans have never had to live with terror. I had had to live with it all my life—the psychological terror of segregation, in which there was a special set of laws governing your movements. You violated them at your peril. . . .

I was with my teacher, and in a while I was going to sit at my desk, with my crayons and pencils and books and classmates all around me, and for the next six hours I was going to enjoy a thoroughly secure, warm and stable world. It was a world I absolutely relied on. Without it, I don't know where I would have gone that morning.

The trouble began when I decided to be dangerously ambitious. Which is to say, I decided to write a poem.

Suddenly Alan's hand clamped my shoulder, communicating everything in a grip. Do not speak. Do not move. Adrenaline shot through me. We were in a clearing surrounded by bush and shadow and, well, something else. Something not-giraffe. Silence, for the blind, is often the most terrifying sound.

My daughter often follows up on the stories she half-hears. There is one story that obsesses her, a story I only tell her in pieces and for which I have not yet been able to offer a real ending. It begins with two girls in the courtroom.

7 ✳ EXAMPLE

*EDUARDO MEDINA | A Prayer in the Night   190
This is Zacarías—a father. But in the evening, after he's tucked in his kids and kissed his wife goodnight, he sits in bed and prays and remembers what else he is. With clenched fists, he begs God that this night not be his last. He prays and prays for a tomorrow, for another cool, serene evening. . . . Zacarías prays for this because of what else he is—an immigrant.

THE ONION | All Seven Deadly Sins Committed at Church Bake Sale   196
In total, 347 individual acts of sin were committed at the bake sale, with nearly every attendee committing at least one of the seven deadly sins as outlined by Gregory the Great in the Fifth Century.

RICHARD LEDERER | English Is a Crazy Language   201
Sometimes you have to believe that all English speakers should be committed to an asylum for the verbally insane. In what other language do people drive in a parkway and park in a driveway? . . . In what other language can your nose run and your feet smell?

MATTHEW DESMOND | Cold City   207
Even in the most desolate areas of American cities, evictions used to be rare. They used to draw crowds. . . . These days, there are sheriff squads whose full-time job is to carry out eviction and foreclosure orders.

CHIMAMANDA NGOZI ADICHIE | Dear Ijeawele   214
At the checkout counter, the cashier said mine was the perfect present for the new boy. I said it was for a baby girl. She looked horrified. "Blue for a girl?"

JOHN McWHORTER | Why "Redskins" Is a Bad Word   220
Words have not only core meanings, but resonances of the kind that may not make it into the dictionary but are deeply felt by all of us.

8 ✳ CLASSIFICATION...................................226

9 ✳ PROCESS ANALYSIS...275

14 ✳ CLASSIC ESSAYS AND SPEECHES

JONATHAN SWIFT | A Modest Proposal   546

I have been assured by a very knowing American of my acquaintance in London, that a young healthy child well nursed is at a year old a most delicious, nourishing, and wholesome food, whether stewed, roasted, baked, or boiled. . . .

THOMAS JEFFERSON | The Declaration of Independence   556

We hold these truths to be self-evident, that all men are created equal, that they are endowed by their Creator with certain unalienable Rights, that among these are Life, Liberty and the pursuit of Happiness.

SOJOURNER TRUTH | Ain't I a Woman?   561

If my cup won't hold but a pint, and yours holds a quart, wouldn't you be mean not to let me have my little half measure full?

ZORA NEALE HURSTON | How It Feels to Be Colored Me   563

But I am not tragically colored. There is no great sorrow dammed up in my soul, nor lurking behind my eyes. I do not mind at all.

GEORGE ORWELL | Politics and the English Language   569

A man may take to drink because he feels himself to be a failure, and then fail all the more completely because he drinks. It is rather the same thing that is happening to the English language. It becomes ugly and inaccurate because our thoughts are foolish, but the slovenliness of our language makes it easier for us to have foolish thoughts. The point is that the process is reversible.

MARTIN LUTHER KING JR. | The Other America   576

The struggle today is much more difficult. It's more difficult today because we are struggling now for genuine equality. It's much easier to integrate a lunch counter than it is to guarantee a livable income and a good solid job. It's much easier to guarantee the right to vote than it is to guarantee the right to live in sanitary, decent housing conditions. It is much easier to integrate a public park than it is to make genuine, quality, integrated education a reality.

APPENDIX: USING SOURCES IN YOUR WRITING

Finding and Evaluating Sources • Incorporating Source Materials into Your Text • Acknowledging Sources and Avoiding Plagiarism • Documentation • MLA In-Text Documentation • MLA List of Works Cited • Sample Research Paper

CONTENTS BY THEME

HOME AND FAMILY

HUMOR AND SATIRE

IDENTITY

LANGUAGE

LIFE AND DEATH

MEDIA

MEMORIES OF YOUTH

MORALITY AND ETHICS

NATURE AND THE ENVIRONMENT

OVERCOMING ADVERSITY

PUBLIC POLICY

SOCIOLOGY AND ANTHROPOLOGY

SPORTS AND LEISURE

STUDENT WRITING

WRITERS AND WRITING

PREFACE

◦▸━━━━━━━━━━━━━━━◂◦

T*HE NORTON SAMPLER* is a collection of short essays for composition students; it illustrates the basic rhetorical patterns of description, narration, example, classification, process analysis, comparison and contrast, definition, cause and effect, and argument.

Like the cloth samplers of colonial America that young people made in order to practice their stitches and ABC's, *The Norton Sampler* assumes that writing is a practical art and that its fundamental patterns and devices can be learned by studying and applying them. Thus each chapter focuses on a single pattern of development and includes six or so readings organized primarily around that pattern. Each selection is followed by study questions and writing prompts.

In addition to the fundamentals of reading and writing, this collection also samples the work of many different kinds of writers on a wide variety of topics. Nature and the self, politics and language, race and racism, finance, school, the lessons of adversity, and many other essential subjects are covered here by familiar authorities, from E. B. White, Martin Luther King Jr., and Zora Neale Hurston to Amy Tan, Deborah Tannen, and Sonia Sotomayor.

In this tenth edition of *The Norton Sampler*, however, many selections— on topics ranging from soul food, equal pay, and first poems to premature burial, digital advertising, and the official government CDIB (Certificate of Degree of Indian Blood)—are the work of newer writers. These include, for example, the professional chefs Carla Hall and Edward Lee; the Vietnamese American poet Ocean Vuong; the blogger (and licensed mortician) Caitlin Doughty; and the Native American writer Tommy Orange. Along with these fresh voices—and new essays on *whose* voices get heard—this edition of the *Sampler* introduces a style change that's grown out of the important, ongoing conversation about adopting terms for race and ethnicity that better reflect the realities of social and economic inequality. In accord with new APA (2020) guidelines, when "racial and ethnic groups" are identified in the context or discussion of an essay in this collection, they are "designated by proper nouns and are capitalized." This includes "Black" and "White" for groups that are defined in part by skin color. (The APA advises, however, to "not use colors to refer to other human groups; doing so is considered pejorative.") *Within* individual selections themselves, however, the author's own style is preserved.

Though the chapters and essays in *The Norton Sampler* can be taken up in any order, the expanded first chapter focuses on critical reading—with an eye to understanding both what a text means and how the writer uses common rhetorical strategies and structures to convey that meaning. To this end, chapter 1 includes a detailed critical analysis of E. B. White's classic essay, "Once More to the Lake," showing students not only how a great writer stitches a piece together but how to read and analyze any text, including the essays in this book. Next come a chapter on the elements of the essay, a chapter on the writing process, and a chapter on writing paragraphs.

The rest of the book takes up the patterns of writing in greater detail. Chapters 5 and 6 are devoted, respectively, to the basic techniques of description and narration. These are followed by six chapters of exposition, ranging from the simpler techniques of exemplification and classification to the more complex strategies of process analysis, comparison, definition, and cause and effect. Then there is an extended chapter on argument, followed by a chapter of classic essays that demonstrate how the rhetorical patterns work in combination. Finally, there is an appendix on research and documentation, and a glossary/index.

HIGHLIGHTS

- **Short essays—classic and contemporary—by a diverse group of writers.** There are 65 readings in all with 25 titles new to this edition. Selections cover a variety of topics that should spur students' interests, from recent pieces such as Trevor Noah's account of his childhood experiences in segregated South Africa and Tommy Orange's essay on what it means to be Native American "enough," to old favorites by Zora Neale Hurston and Sojourner Truth.

- **A revised and expanded chapter on reading critically and actively** provides concrete advice for strong reading habits (previewing, annotating, summarizing, responding); innovative templates for previewing and annotating texts; and plenty of examples modeling effective reading strategies.

- **One student essay in each chapter of readings.** Essays by student writers are annotated to show how they illustrate the principles discussed in the chapter and are the length of papers that students will write themselves.

- **Navigation features** make the book especially easy to use. Notes in the margins explicitly link the readings with writing instructions, and a combined glossary/index provides full definitions of key terms and concepts, serving as an easy reference point for students.

- **Help for students who can use more support,** including glosses for unfamiliar terms and expressions, templates to help students get started writing and reading, and grammar tips.

- **Everyday examples** that show how the patterns taught in this book play an important role across media—from book covers and billboards to packaged goods and road signs.

- **Updated coverage of argument,** with one new cluster of readings featuring different perspectives on whose voices get heard and why it matters, and another cluster on the effects of recent technologies on human minds, hearts, and habits.

WHAT'S ONLINE?

- **Ebook.** Searchable, portable, and interactive. The complete textbook for a fraction of the price. The ebook can be viewed on—and synced between—all computers and mobile devices.

- **InQuizitive for Writers** offers game-like activities to help you become a more confident, prepared writer and researcher. Practice sentence-editing and working with sources in adaptive activities.

- **LMS Resources.** Easily add high-quality Norton resources to your online, hybrid, or lecture course—all at no cost. Norton resources work within your existing learning management system; there's no new system to learn, and access is free and easy. Deploy reading quizzes, worksheets on revising, model student essays, and multimodal readings—one for each pattern in the book, and more.

- **A PDF instructor's manual** includes brief answers to study questions in the book.

Find it all at **digital.wwnorton.com/sampler10.**

ACKNOWLEDGMENTS

There are three people above all whom I want to thank for their work and support on this new edition of *The Norton Sampler*: Barbara Cooley, a superb technical writer, editor, and blogger who also happens to be my wife; my general editor, Erica Wnek, whose skill and guidance not only led the ship to port but took us through new waters along the way; and my hands-on editor, Edwin Jeng, who kept a constant lookout for low spots, red herrings, and floating debris. Then there is Julia Reidhead, a great supporter of the book since she helped to launch it in the first place, and all the other generous people at Norton who have made possible this and earlier editions, including editors Marilyn Moller and Sarah Touborg; project and developmental editor Rebecca Homiski; managing editor Marian Johnson; Maura Gaughan, who project edited the book and made sure every detail—big and small—got the attention it needed; Jeremy Burton, who is a masterful production manager; Michele Dobbins, who helped spread the word about the book; Josh Garvin, who cleared the permissions; Stephanie Romeo, who edited all photos; Fay Torresyap who researched the photos; and Joy Cranshaw and Katie Bolger who managed the ebook and all other digital resources that support this book. I'm also grateful to Michal Brody for her excellent work on the instructor's notes and quizzes and to JoAnn Metsch for her superb design.

I am indebted to Richard Bullock of Wright State University for allowing me to draw from his research and experience in the research appendix, and to Gerald Graff and Cathy Birkenstein, whose work inspired the writing templates in this book.

Among the teachers and composition experts across the country who reviewed this edition in progress and gave me advice on the selections and pedagogy, I wish especially to thank Margaret E. Altizer, Suffolk County Community College—Eastern Campus; Debra Benedetti, Pierpont Community &

Technical College; Michon Benson, Texas Southern University; Kristin Bivens, Harold Washington College; Katt Blackwell-Starnes, Lamar University; Sarah Davis, Iowa State University; Sean Epstein-Corbin, Merced College; Susan Grine, Sandhills Community College; Geraldine Gutwein, Harrisburg Area Community College; David Henry, El Paso Community College; Judy H. Hevener, Blue Ridge Community College; Ruth Holmes, Lord Fairfax Community College; Christopher Krietsch, Suffolk County Community College; Iris Lancaster, Texas Southern University; Eric Lee, Arizona Western College; Jen Malia, Norfolk State University; Tonja McCurdy-Jennings, Georgia Northwestern Technical College; Mary McGlone, Suffolk County Community College; Phillip E. Mitchell, University of North Georgia; Trishena Nieveen-Phegley, Southeast Missouri State University; Susan Ryan, Point University; Jennifer Schaefer, Lord Fairfax Community College; Joanna Scott, Temple College; S. Melissa Steinhardt, Hillsborough Community College; Ian Thomas-Bignami, Diablo Valley College; Betsy Tollefson, Southwest Wisconsin Technical College; Gail Upchurch-Mills, Dutchess Community College; Jeanine Williams, University of Maryland—University College.

Many thanks, too, to my colleagues in composition at Ohio State over the years, including the late Edward P. J. Corbett, who influenced a generation of scholars and teachers of writing; and to Roy Rosenstein, distinguished professor of comparative literature at the American University of Paris.

Thomas Cooley

⇥1⇤

READING AS A WRITER,
WRITING AS A READER

WRITING is a little like sewing or weaving. The end product is a written text that may appear seamless but is actually constructed thread by thread using common patterns of writing that good writers follow all the time in their work. In fact, the root meaning of *text*, like *textile*, is something *woven*—a fabric of words.

As with any practical art, we learn to write by writing. Many of the fundamental patterns and strategies of writing that we all must master if we're to construct tightly woven texts of our own, however, can best be learned by *reading* the work of other writers. Good writers are good readers. They read a text carefully and critically, mindful not only of *what* the text says but also of *how* it says it—and how those techniques can be used in their own writing. They read as writers. They also read as readers—in order to learn interesting things about the world, to engage with the thoughts of others, and to be good citizens. Reading well, after all, is an end in itself.

GETTING STARTED

Reading mindfully is a little like investigating a crime scene. You're looking for the writer's motives. The clues lie mainly in the text itself—the words on the page or screen before you. You're also looking for the writer's methods. You want to know not only *why* the text was committed but also *how*. With a crime scene investigation, the goal is to identify the perpetrators and bring them to justice. Your ultimate goal in reading a text—and exactly how you go

1

about achieving it—will depend on your purpose for reading—on *why* you're examining the text in the first place.

Considering Your Purpose

Consider the words of a great essayist:

> Some books are to be tasted, others to be swallowed, and some few to be chewed and digested; that is, some books are to be read only in parts; others to be read, but not curiously; and some few are to be read wholly, and with diligence and attention.
>
> —Francis Bacon, "On Studies" (1597)

Why would anyone read a book or essay "wholly, and with diligence and attention"? One reason would be if you were assigned a reading in a course and expected to be tested on the material in it. Another would be if you were writing a paper, and your research indicated that a particular article was essential reading in the field. Or you might read a book wholly and with attention (but not necessarily so much diligence) if you were reading it—a novel, say—largely for pleasure, for what Bacon called "delight."

When your purpose is to read for pleasure, read any way you like. But when you're reading to gather information and develop ideas, there is no better way than by *chewing and digesting*—that is, by thinking carefully and critically ("with diligence and attention") about the meat of what you're reading as you read it. Before you consume an entire text, however, there is a proven way—like a taste before swallowing—to see whether or not a particular text will fit your purpose: you can *preview* it.

Previewing a Text

Before you delve "wholly" into a text only to discover that you're totally on the wrong track, take a few minutes to survey the territory. Prereading a text will give you a rough idea of what the text is about and where it's going. It's your chance to anticipate, to make educated guesses—perhaps a false start or two. So let yourself be surprised; no harm will come of a little early exploration. You can always change your mind when you have more information—and are sure you're on the right track now because you've gotten your bearings before you start. Here are some tips for previewing before reading:

- *Think about your purpose for reading.* Is it to verify facts, obtain basic information on a subject, look for ideas, investigate a claim? Will you be citing (or even directly responding to) the text in your own writing? Are you hoping the text will put you onto other sources you can use? Whatever it may be, your purpose in reading will affect what you look for and focus on as you read.

- *Consider the context.* Before you dig deeply into the text, read any prefatory material that accompanies it, such as a headnote or abstract. Who is the author (or authors)? Do they appear to have an agenda—or an ax to grind? When and where (an academic journal, a magazine or newspaper, a blog) was the text originally published, and what do these facts suggest about the text?

- *Think about the title.* What does it reveal about the topic and TONE* of the text? Does the title make a direct statement or claim? Is it intended to provoke the reader? Poke fun at its subject? Something else?

- *Skim the text for other design elements* that may help guide your reading. Note headings, boldfaced words, lists, and other features that highlight important information and suggest how the text is organized.

- *Read the introductory paragraph(s) and the conclusion.* What do they imply (or tell you directly) about the topic, purpose, and main message of the text?

- *Think about the overall form and method of the text.* Does the writer seem mainly to be giving an explanation, conducting an analysis, drawing comparisons, constructing an argument, telling a story? How might this strategy offer clues to what the writer has to say?

---

*Words printed in **SMALL CAPITALS** are defined in the Glossary/Index.

Templates for Prereading

Every text is different, and no piece of writing that is worth reading can be reduced to a simple formula. However, the following templates can help you apply these strategies of prereading as you survey almost any text:

> ► My ultimate purpose in reading X is _____.
>
> ► Judging from the context and title, I would say the main subject of X is _____.
>
> ► Skimming the headings and other design elements in X, I see that it is organized by/as/into _____, perhaps indicating _____.
>
> ► About the general subject of X, the introductory and concluding paragraphs suggest that the writer is saying, specifically, _____ and/but _____.
>
> ► This reading is supported by the overall form and method of the text, which appears to be basically a _____ developed largely by _____.

To see how these templates can help you preview a specific text, let's apply them to a classic American essay, "Once More to the Lake" by E. B. White. The full text of White's essay begins on p. 19. Turn to it now, and read the introductory note for information about the circumstances, or "context," in which the essay was written. Then preview the text itself, using the templates above—and the advice on which they're based—as your guide. Hopefully, they'll lead you to something like this:

As indicated on p. 19, White's essay appeared shortly before the United States entered WWII.

> ► My ultimate purpose in reading "Once More to the Lake" is to <u>understand the essay and learn more about the reading process</u>.
>
> ► Judging from the context and title, I would say the main subject of the essay is <u>a fishing trip the writer takes with his young son to a remote lake in Maine where he himself vacationed as a boy</u>.
>
> ► Skimming the headings and other design elements, I see that it is organized as <u>a single essay</u>—perhaps indicating <u>a sharp focus on the scene at the lake</u>.

▶ About the general subject of "Once More to the Lake," the introductory and concluding paragraphs suggest that White is saying, specifically, <u>that everything seems the same at first</u> but <u>this sense of timelessness turns out to be an illusion.</u>

▶ This reading is supported by the overall form and method of the text, which appears to be basically a <u>personal narrative</u> developed largely by <u>comparing and contrasting the scene now with how it was in the past.</u>

READING CLOSELY AND CRITICALLY

Once you've previewed a text and have a general idea of what you think it's about, the next step is to probe more deeply into the meaning of the text—and how the author gets that meaning across to the reader.

Questioning a Text to Understand What It Means

Whether you're reading just a few paragraphs or an entire book, the key to understanding what any text has to say (and how) is to "interrogate" the text by asking—and jotting down your answers to—certain leading questions along the way. (You can record your responses on a separate page or directly in the margins as you read.) Here are some fundamental questions to ask (and respond to) as you interrogate a text:

- *What is the writer's main point (or* THESIS)*?* Is it clearly stated? If so, where? If the main point is not stated directly, where is it most clearly implied?

- *Where and how does the text support its main point?* Look for specific details, facts, examples, expert testimony, and other forms of evidence.

- *Is the evidence sufficient?* Or does it fail to convince you? Why? Are sources clearly identified so you can tell where cited material is coming from?

- *Does the text introduce opposing points of view?* What are they? Are they represented fairly and accurately? Where and how?

- **What seems to be the main purpose of the text?** To provide information? Describe something or someone? Tell a story? Argue a point of view?

- **What is the general TONE of the text?** Serious? Informal? Inspirational? Which specific passages illustrate this tone of voice most clearly?

- **Who is the intended audience?** Readers who are familiar with the topic? Those who know little about it? People who are inclined to agree—or disagree? How can you tell?

Templates for Questioning a Text

Again, every text is different, and no piece of writing that is worth reading can be reduced to a simple formula. However, the following templates can help you answer these fundamental questions as you probe more deeply into the meaning and form of any text:

> ▸ On the general subject of _____, the main point of the text seems to be that _____.

> ▸ The text supports this thesis mainly through _____ and _____.

> ▸ As further evidence for this view, the text also offers _____.

> ▸ The ultimate purpose of the text would seem to be _____.

> ▸ The overall tone of the text can be described as _____.

> ▸ The intended audience for the text is apparently _____.

Turn again to White's "Once More to the Lake" (p. 19–25), and read it closely from beginning to end, using these templates to question the text as you go. Plunging more deeply into White's essay with these templates in mind, we might come up with something like the following:

White makes this point most explicitly in the final paragraph of his essay, p. 25.

> ▸ On the general subject of <u>time and change</u>, the main point of this text seems to be that <u>both are inevitable in human life</u>.

▶ The text supports this thesis mainly through <u>a detailed description of the altered scene</u> and <u>a narrative of the events that lead the writer to feel his own mortality.</u>

▶ As further evidence for this view, the text also offers <u>a comparison and contrast between the place as it seems and as it actually is.</u>

▶ The ultimate purpose of the text would seem to be <u>showing the folly of believing that time can stand still.</u>

▶ The overall tone of the text can be described as <u>nostalgic.</u>

▶ The intended audience for the text is apparently <u>readers whose dreams of a more innocent time are soon to be clouded by war.</u>

Applying the "Questioning" Templates to an Academic Essay

In the following passage from a *Wikipedia* article, the authors (including the Oxford University philosopher Martin Poulter), examine the origins of a new area of study within the field of psychology. The marginal comments show how the "questioning" templates can be used to probe an example of more formal academic writing:

Heuristics in Judgment and Decision-Making

Heuristics are simple strategies to form judgments and make decisions by focusing on the most relevant aspects of a complex problem. . . . In the early 1970s, psychologists Amos Tversky and Daniel Kahneman linked heuristics to cognitive biases. Their typical experimental setup consisted of a rule of logic or probability, embedded in a verbal description of a judgment problem, and demonstrated that people's intuitive judgment deviated from the rule. The "Linda problem" is an example.

Tversky and Kahneman gave subjects a short character sketch of a woman called Linda, describing her as "31 years old, single, outspoken, and very bright. She majored in philosophy. As a student, she was deeply concerned with issues of discrimination and social justice, and also participated in anti-nuclear demonstrations." People reading this description then ranked the likelihood of different statements about Linda.

Among others, these included *Linda is a bank teller* and *Linda is a bank teller and is active in the feminist movement.* People showed a strong tendency to rate the latter, more specific statement as more likely, even though a conjunction of the form "Linda is both *X* and *Y*" can never be more probable than the more general statement "Linda is *X*." The explanation in terms of heuristics is that the judgment was distorted because, for the readers, the character sketch was representative of the sort of person who might be an active feminist but not of someone who works in a bank.

Margin notes:

On the general subject of heuristics, the main point of the text seems to be that heuristics are strategies for making judgments and decisions.

The text supports this thesis mainly through references to the work of two psychologists named Tversky and Kahneman and . . .

. . . by giving the specific example of statements about a person called "Linda."

As further evidence for this view, the text also offers a basic rule of logic having to do with "conjunction."

The ultimate purpose of the text would seem to be explaining that heuristics can often be linked to cognitive biases.

The overall tone of the text can be described as critical yet sympathetic, both toward the subjects and the experimenters.

The intended audience for the text is apparently people whose intuitive judgments don't always follow the rules of logic.

Annotating

By asking leading questions of a text and then using the "questioning" templates to help you find answers, you open a sort of dialogue with the text. That dialogue is ongoing because each time you revisit the text (or a part of it), you may think of new questions to ask—or additional answers to your original questions. How do you keep track of this "conversation"—your observations, reactions, and ideas in response to a reading? You do it by *annotating* the text.

When you annotate a text you mark it up, either by hand or by using digital annotation tools, in order to note your immediate reactions to the text and any further questions it raises in your mind as you read. In much academic writing, the writer makes a point by stating it directly and then doing something to back up that statement, such as giving examples, making comparisons, or offering logical reasons. One useful way to annotate a text, in part, therefore, is by following the "says/does approach."

With the says/does approach, you mark the text to indicate when and where the writer makes a significant statement or claim, either direct or implied. You also mark the text in some way to indicate each time the writer does something to support this statement or claim. One benefit of annotating a text by using this approach is that it helps you distinguish what a writer has to say (the "content" of the text) from how the writer says it (the "form" of the text). The ultimate purpose of the approach is to enable you to recognize the basic patterns of writing outlined in this book so that you can use them in your own writing.

So, beginning with the says/does approach, here are some tips for annotating a text as you read:

- *Mark what the text* **says.** Underscore or otherwise indicate THESIS STATEMENTS, TOPIC SENTENCES, RHETORICAL QUESTIONS (questions that are actually statements), key terms, and other places in the text where the writer says, or directly implies, what the text is about. You can even tag these elements by writing "says" in the margin next to them. This practice will help you identify the main claims and other "content" of what you're reading—focusing your attention more on *what* the text says than *how* it says it. Wherever you make a "says" notation, try restating the passage in your own words in the margin to make sure you understand it. If time permits, you might try reading through the entire text and concentrate on making "says" annotations alone.

- *Mark what the text* **does.** Underscore or otherwise indicate where the writer introduces facts, figures, logical reasoning (including LOGICAL FALLACIES), claims of special knowledge or authority, ANECDOTES (or longer stories), physical descriptions, comparisons, analyses of cause and effect, and FIGURES OF SPEECH—or makes any other move—as a way of giving proof or support for what the text has to say. Tag these elements by writing "does" in the margin next to them. This practice will help you identify the specific rhetorical strategies and patterns of organization that shape the "form" of whatever you're reading—focusing your attention more on *how* the text works than *what* it says. If feasible, try reading through the entire text again, concentrating this time on "does" annotations.

- *Jot down your immediate reactions.* Mark places in the text where you agree, disagree—or both—with the author(s), and note why. If you have an emotional reaction to the text, or it reminds you of a personal experience, indicate that and describe your feelings or recollections. Log any counterarguments or related sources that you want to check out.

- *Tag passages you find confusing or hard to understand.* Circle or underline unfamiliar words and phrases, and write down what they mean in your own words after you've looked them up. Use question marks to indicate difficult passages, and ask specific leading questions of your own about the text as you go. Be persistent when reading a difficult passage. Simply noting tough spots and admitting that they're difficult can help you deal with them later.

- *Reread the text and answer, alter, or add to your earlier annotations.* If you've found an answer to a question you posed when reading the text earlier, jot it down now. If you misunderstood something before, correct yourself; but don't erase your original thought—your annotations are like a diary of your travels back and forth through the text.

Following these tips and procedures, here's how a deeply engaged reader might annotate a page from "Once More to the Lake":

<u>We went fishing the first morning</u>. I felt the same damp moss covering the worms in the bait can, and saw the dragonfly alight on the tip of my rod as it hovered a few inches from the surface of the water. It was the arrival of this fly that convinced me beyond any doubt that <u>everything was as it always had been</u>, that the years were a mirage and there had been <u>no years. The small waves were the same,</u> (chucking the rowboat under the chin) as we fished at anchor, and the boat was the same boat, the same color green and the ribs broken in the same places, and under the floorboards <u>the same fresh-water leavings and debris</u>—the (dead helgrammite,) the <u>wisps of moss</u>, <u>the rusty discarded fishhook</u>, <u>the dried blood from yesterday's catch</u>. We stared silently at the tips of our rods, at the dragonflies that came and went. I lowered the tip of mine into the water, tentatively, pensively dislodging the fly, which darted two feet away, poised, darted two feet back, and came to rest again a little farther up the rod. There had been no years between the ducking of this (dragonfly) and <u>the other one</u>—the one that was <u>part of memory</u>. I looked at the boy, who was silently watching his fly, and it was my hands that held his rod, my eyes watching. I felt dizzy and didn't know which rod I was at the end of.

- DOES: tells a story
- SAYS: nothing has changed here since he was a boy
- Figuratively—like with a child
- Great bait for bass!
- DOES: describes the scene in minute detail
- What helgrammite worm turns into: a transformation
- DOES: compares the lake now with the lake as it was
- SAYS: the essay is about a state of mind

RESPONDING TO A TEXT

After you have read and reread a text closely, "re-view" it once more: think about your general experience in reading the text, and record your response in writing, perhaps in a notebook or file set aside for that purpose. This step in the reading process will serve you well when it comes time to recall what you've learned and put it to use on an exam, in a paper, or in other critical reading that you do. Here are a few tips for reflecting on and responding to a text as you review it:

- *Summarize what you've read in your own words.* If you can write a brief, accurate SUMMARY of a writer's main points, you probably have a good grasp of what you read. Looking back at your notes on previewing, questioning, and annotating the text may help.

- *Think about and record your lasting impressions of the text.* After reading the text in full, where are you most inclined to accept the writer's ideas? Least inclined? Aren't sure?

- *Consider what you've learned about writing.* Looking back at your annotations—particularly those indicating what the writer "does"—ask yourself which moves, methods, devices, and patterns you most want to try in your own writing. Also, consider which ones you think didn't work so well and that, consequently, you want to avoid.

IDENTIFYING COMMON PATTERNS

How a writer structures a piece of writing is often your best clue to what the writer has to say. Consider the following passage from a language experiment:

> The procedure is actually quite simple. First you arrange things into different groups. Of course, one pile may be sufficient depending on how much there is to do. If you have to go somewhere else due to lack of facilities, that is the next step. Otherwise you are pretty well set. . . . After the procedure is completed, one arranges the materials into different groups again. Then they can be put into their appropriate places. Eventually they will be used once more, and the whole cycle will then have to be repeated. However, that is part of life.
>
> —JOHN D. BRANSFORD AND MARCIA K. JOHNS, "Contextual Prerequisites for Understanding"

Although the authors of this little passage never utter the words "doing the laundry," that is clearly (or at least dimly) what it is about. We know this because the passage has the overall form of a **PROCESS ANALYSIS**. In other words, this would seem to be a set of instructions for doing something. We may not be told what that something is at first; but by the time we get to the end of the "procedure" and learn that the "cycle" starts over again once the things are "used," we can likely guess just what the writers are asking us to sort out.

When you read a text for meaning (what the text says), sometimes your best guide is the form, structure, or underlying pattern of the text (how the text says it) rather than any direct statement of meaning within the text itself. In the case of our dirty laundry example, the authors deliberately relied on the form of the passage to convey its meaning because it was part of a study about how learning is affected by using abstract language—"things," "lack of facilities," "part of life"—instead of more concrete words like "jeans," "socks," and "dirty towels." Sorting your laundry, it would seem, is good practice for other, more stubborn forms of analysis because they, too, require putting "things into different groups."

Four Basic Types of Writing

All the essays you'll read in this collection can be divided into four fundamental types of writing: description, narration, exposition, and argument. These basic writing strategies can be defined as follows:

- **DESCRIPTION** appeals to the reader's senses. Descriptive writing tells what something looks, feels, sounds, smells, or tastes like ("nice here but buggy"). Patterns and methods of description are discussed in Chapter 5.

- **NARRATION** is storytelling. Narrative writing focuses on events; it tells what happened ("pitched tent, launched canoe, caught two bass"). Patterns and methods of narration are discussed in Chapter 6.

- **EXPOSITION** is informative writing ("the fish are bigger this year than they were last year"), and it is the form of writing you are likely to use most often. Exposition explains by giving examples (Chapter 7), by classifying (Chapter 8), by analyzing a process (Chapter 9), by comparing and contrasting (Chapter 10), by defining (Chapter 11), and by analyzing causes and effects (Chapter 12). Exams, research papers, job applications, sales reports, insurance claims—in fact, almost every kind of practical writing you do over a lifetime, including your last will and testament—will require expository skills.

- **ARGUMENT** is persuasive writing. It makes a claim and offers evidence that the writer hopes will be sufficient to convince the reader to accept that claim—and perhaps even to act on it ("it's very relaxing here; you should come"). Patterns, methods, and strategies of argument are discussed in detail in Chapter 13.

Identifying Common Patterns of Writing in E. B. White's "Once More to the Lake"

Assuming that you've read "Once More to the Lake" carefully now—using the various reading strategies discussed in this chapter—let's return yet again to White's essay for a final read. This time our focus is on how a great writer like White weaves together, in a single essay, strands from the four most basic forms of writing. If we can see how White uses these common patterns to create such a fine piece of work, we'll be well on our way to using them in our own writing.

RECOGNIZING DESCRIPTION. "Once More to the Lake" is a superb piece of **DESCRIPTIVE** writing. You can recognize description because it focuses on aspects of people, places, and things that appeal directly to the five senses. For example, White writes about:

- "the fearful cold of the sea water" (1)
- "the wet woods whose scent entered through the screen" (2)
- "the first glimpse of the smiling farmer" (9)
- "the shouts and cries of the other campers" (9)
- "the pop [that] would backfire up our noses and hurt" (11)

White describes the lake itself as "fairly large and undisturbed" (3). Its shores are "heavily wooded," and the whole place feels remote, despite some cottages "sprinkled around" the water (3). When White goes fishing the first morning, he pictures the boat in vivid, **CONCRETE** detail: "the dead helgrammite, the wisps of moss, the rusty discarded fishhook, the dried blood from yesterday's catch" (5). And, of course, there are the dragonflies: "We stared silently at the tips of our rods, at the dragonflies that came and went" (5). The **DOMINANT IMPRESSION** we get of the lake and its surroundings here is one of tranquility and timelessness—at first.

RECOGNIZING NARRATION. White begins his essay with a phrase pertaining to time: "One summer along about 1904." He might as well have written "Once upon a time," as the opening paragraph takes place long ago and is almost pure narrative. **NARRATIVE** writing tells what happened to someone or something. You can recognize a narrative because it deals with events, such as:

- taking the family to a camp on a lake in Maine
- getting ringworm and having to apply Pond's Extract
- rolling over in a canoe with clothes on
- returning year after year

White's essay focuses on a particular occasion "a few weeks ago" when he took his young son to fish for the first time on the freshwater lake in Maine where White himself vacationed when he was a boy (1). What follows is an account of the ordinary events that take place during that brief visit, leading to a **CLIMAX** in the **PLOT** at the end of the week when a storm gathers over the lake and the writer suddenly feels older as his son pulls on his wet bathing suit.

RECOGNIZING EXPOSITION. White is not only telling a story about what happened at the lake and giving a description of the place, but he is also explaining the meaning and significance of those events and that setting. Writing that explains is called **EXPOSITION**; expository writing makes direct statements about the nature and significance of its subject, such as:

- "This was the American family at play" (8).
- "[T]hose times and those summers had been infinitely precious and worth saving" (9).
- "I had trouble making out which was I, the one walking at my side, the one walking in my pants" (11).

Among the many strategies of exposition that writers draw on to support statements like these, one of the main methods that White uses is COMPARISON AND CONTRAST. In particular, White is comparing his perceptions of the lake in the present with his memories of it in the past. At first, everything seems "pretty much the same as it had been before" (4). The water is still "cool and motionless"; the bedroom still smells "of the lumber it was made of" (2); and the rowboat is "the same boat, the same color green and the ribs broken in the same places" (5). White's comparison shades into contrast, however, as the tranquil scene is interrupted by the "unfamiliar nervous sound of the outboard motors" (10). In the past, White explains, the sound of the motors was peaceful. Now, however, the boats are more powerful and "whine . . . like mosquitoes" in the night (10). At the end of the essay, the peace and tranquility of the lake are interrupted by a thunderstorm.

Using various SIMILES and METAPHORS, White likens the gathering storm to a scene in a drama: the thunder sounds at first like a "kettle drum"; then comes "the snare, then the bass drum and cymbals"; lightning flashes against the dark sky; and, as in a Greek tragedy, "the gods" grin from "the hills" (12). Why this sudden turn of events in an otherwise tranquil scene from the life of the American family on vacation? Are the gods grinning, perhaps, at the swimmers' sense of security?

RECOGNIZING ARGUMENT. By comparing his past and present experiences at the lake, White is constructing an ARGUMENT about time and change. Arguments make claims that require discussion and further proof. For instance:

> It was the arrival of this fly that convinced me beyond any doubt that everything was as it had always been, that the years were a mirage, and that there had been no years. (5)

"Once More to the Lake" was published just a few months before the United States entered World War II, and in the idyllic background of his essay lurks the author's nagging suspicion that the world is about to change forever. As the boy prepares to go swimming in the lake in the rain, White cannot escape the realization that a number of years have actually passed since he last visited this place. As he feels suddenly older (and war lies just around the corner), White concludes that the generations are bound not only by the "return of light and hope and spirits" after a storm but also by the reality of change and "the chill of death" (12, 13). The dream of "summer without end," no matter how warmly inspired by nature and fond memories of childhood, White concludes, is just that—a dream (8).

White makes this key point by weaving together various strands of narrative, description, exposition, and argument. When you compose a text, let yourself be guided by the work of the great writers you have read. In the end, however, you must plunge in and choose the techniques and patterns of development (or likely a single pattern) that best fit your specific topic and the particular point you want to make about it—as well as your singular audience and purpose in writing.

READING THE ESSAYS IN THIS BOOK

In *The Norton Sampler*, you'll be reading and analyzing numerous essays by many different writers on a variety of topics. The essays are grouped into chapters according to the principal methods of development they use: **DESCRIPTION, NARRATION, EXAMPLE, CLASSIFICATION, PROCESS ANALYSIS, COMPARISON AND CONTRAST, DEFINITION, CAUSE AND EFFECT,** and **ARGUMENT.** Your main goal in reading the essays in this book is to master the methods of development they demonstrate so that you can use those methods in your own writing.

Most of the essays in this book are introduced with headnotes that give you at least some basic information about the context in which each essay was written; these should be helpful for previewing and questioning the text. Following each essay is a set of study questions and writing prompts. These are intended to help you understand—and adapt in your own writing—the specific methods and patterns of development that each writer uses. For each text, use the headnotes and study questions as tools for reading—to help you preview, question, annotate, and respond to the text and its context.

Using the Study Questions to
Focus Your Reading

The study questions and writing prompts for each essay in this book ask you to focus your attention on specific details and issues worth noticing and considering in each specific text. Even though the study questions appear after the reading, scan them quickly before you dive into the text in order to get a clearer sense of what's most important—and worth your closest attention. The study questions and writing prompts are the teaching heart of this book; don't underestimate their importance. They will enable you to read and understand the sample essays in the following ways:

- *For Discussion.* These questions are intended to help you look at the text as an exchange of ideas between a writer and a reader. They prompt you to read in order to understand *what* the text is saying and to discover your own views on the subject under discussion. In other words, these are questions that will help you think about what the author is saying and then consider what you think, and why.

- *Strategies and Structures.* These questions will help you recognize and understand *how* the text is constructed—to think about what patterns and techniques the author has used to organize their ideas and present them to an audience and to imagine how you might use those same patterns in your own writing.

- *Words and Figures of Speech.* These questions focus on the language and style of the text. They're designed to help you think about both the literal and figurative meanings of specific words and phrases.

- *For Writing.* These are prompts that will help you start writing, in some cases by suggesting topics to write about and in other instances by asking questions to help you respond to whatever the author of the reading has said.

E. B. WHITE

ONCE MORE TO THE LAKE

ELWYN BROOKS WHITE (1899–1985) was born in Mount Vernon, New York. After graduating from Cornell University in 1921, he worked as a journalist and advertising copywriter before joining the staff of the *New Yorker* in 1926. He also wrote a regular column for *Harper's*. White's numerous books include the children's classics *Stuart Little* (1945) and *Charlotte's Web* (1952), as well as *The Elements of Style* (1959), a guide to writing that updates the work of his teacher William Strunk. "Once More to the Lake," which originally appeared in *Harper's*, was written in August 1941, just a few months before the United States entered World War II. The lake described here is Great Pond, one of the Belgrade Lakes in Maine. When White returns to the familiar scene, it seems unchanged—at first.

ONE SUMMER, ALONG ABOUT 1904, my father rented a camp on a lake in Maine and took us all there for the month of August. We all got ringworm from some kittens and had to rub Pond's Extract on our arms and legs night and morning, and my father rolled over in a canoe with all his clothes on; but outside of that the vacation was a success and from then on none of us ever thought there was any place in the world like that lake in Maine. We returned summer after summer—always on August 1 for one month. I have since become a salt-water man, but sometimes in summer there are days when the restlessness of the tides and the fearful cold of the sea water and the incessant wind that blows across the afternoon and into the evening make me wish for the placidity of a lake in the woods. A few weeks ago this feeling got so strong I bought myself a couple of bass hooks and a spinner and returned to the lake where we used to go, for a week's fishing and to revisit old haunts.

I took along my son, who had never had any fresh water up his nose and 2
who had seen lily pads only from train windows. On the journey over to the lake I began to wonder what it would be like. I wondered how the time would have marred this unique, this holy spot—the coves and streams, the hills that the sun set behind, the camps and the paths behind the camps. I was sure that the tarred road would have found it out, and I wondered in what other ways it would be desolated. It is strange how much you can remember about places like that once you allow your mind to return into the grooves that lead back. You remember one thing, and that suddenly reminds you of another thing. I guess I remembered clearest of all the early mornings, when the lake was cool and motionless, remembered how the bedroom smelled of the lumber it was made of and of the wet woods whose scent entered through the screen. The partitions in the camp were thin and did not extend clear to the top of the rooms, and as I was always the first up I would dress softly so as not to wake the others, and sneak out into the sweet outdoors and start out in the canoe, keeping close along the shore in the long shadows of the pines. I remembered being very careful never to rub my paddle against the gunwale for fear of disturbing the stillness of the cathedral.

The lake had never been what you would call a wild lake. There were 3
cottages sprinkled around the shores, and it was in farming country although the shores of the lake were quite heavily wooded. Some of the cottages were owned by nearby farmers, and you would live at the shore and eat your meals at the farmhouse. That's what our family did. But although it wasn't wild, it was a fairly large and undisturbed lake and there were places in it that, to a child at least, seemed infinitely remote and primeval.

I was right about the tar: it led to within half a mile of the shore. But 4
when I got back there, with my boy, and we settled into a camp near a farm-

house and into the kind of summertime I had known, I could tell that it was going to be pretty much the same as it had been before—I knew it, lying in bed the first morning, smelling the bedroom and hearing the boy sneak quietly out and go off along the shore in a boat. I began to sustain the illusion that he was I, and therefore, by simple transposition, that I was my father. This sensation persisted, kept cropping up all the time we were there. It was not an entirely new feeling, but in this setting, it grew much stronger. I seemed to be living a dual existence. I would be in the middle of some simple act, I would be picking up a bait box or laying down a table fork, or I would be saying something, and suddenly it would be not I but my father who was saying the words or making the gesture. It gave me a creepy sensation.

We went fishing the first morning. I felt the same damp moss covering   5
the worms in the bait can, and saw the dragonfly alight on the tip of my rod as it hovered a few inches from the surface of the water. It was the arrival of this fly that convinced me beyond any doubt that everything was as it always had been, that the years were a mirage and that there had been no years. The small waves were the same, chucking the rowboat under the chin as we fished at anchor, and the boat was the same boat, the same color green and the ribs broken in the

> Pages 82–83 explain how concrete physical details like this can bring abstract ideas down to earth.

same places, and under the floorboards the same freshwater leavings and débris—the dead helgrammite,[1] the wisps of moss, the rusty discarded fishhook, the dried blood from yesterday's catch. We stared silently at the tips of our rods, at the dragonflies that came and went. I lowered the tip of mine into the water, tentatively, pensively dislodging the fly, which darted two feet away, poised, darted two feet back, and came to rest again a little farther up the rod. There had been no years between the ducking of this dragonfly and the other one—the one that was part of memory. I looked at the boy, who was silently watching his fly, and it was my hands that held his rod, my eyes watching. I felt dizzy and didn't know which rod I was at the end of.

We caught two bass, hauling them in briskly as though they were mack-   6
erel, pulling them over the side of the boat in a businesslike manner without any landing net, and stunning them with a blow on the back of the head. When we got back for a swim before lunch, the lake was exactly where we had left it,

---

1. Larvae of the dobsonfly.

the same number of inches from the dock, and there was only the merest suggestion of a breeze. This seemed an utterly enchanted sea, this lake you could leave to its own devices for a few hours and come back to, and find that it had not stirred, this constant and trustworthy body of water. In the shallows, the dark, water-soaked sticks and twigs, smooth and old, were undulating in clusters on the bottom against the clean ribbed sand, and the track of the mussel was plain. A school of minnows swam by, each minnow with its small individual shadow, doubling the attendance, so clear and sharp in the sunlight. Some of the other campers were in swimming, along the shore, one of them with a cake of soap, and the water felt thin and clear and unsubstantial. Over the years there had been this person with the cake of soap, this cultist, and here he was. There had been no years.

See p. 84 on the importance of stating your point directly, as White does here.

Up to the farmhouse to dinner through the teeming, dusty field, the road   7 under our sneakers was only a two-track road. The middle track was missing, the one with the marks of the hooves and the splotches of dried, flaky manure. There had always been three tracks to choose from in choosing which track to walk in; now the choice was narrowed down to two. For a moment I missed terribly the middle alternative. But the way led past the tennis court, and something about the way it lay there in the sun reassured me; the tape had loosened along the backline, the alleys were green with plantains and other weeds, and the net (installed in June and removed in September) sagged in the dry noon, and the whole place steamed with midday heat and hunger and emptiness. There was a choice of pie for dessert, and one was blueberry and one was apple, and the waitresses were the same country girls, there having been no passage of time, only the illusion of it as in a dropped curtain—the waitresses were still fifteen; their hair had been washed, that was the only difference—they had been to the movies and seen the pretty girls with the clean hair.

Summertime, oh, summertime, pattern of life indelible, the fade-proof   8 lake, the woods unshatterable, the pasture with the sweetfern and the juniper forever and ever, summer without end; this was the background, and the life along the shore was the design, the cottages with their innocent and tranquil design, their tiny docks with the flagpole and the American flag floating against the white clouds in the blue sky, the little paths over the roots of the trees leading from camp to camp and the paths leading back to the outhouses and the can of lime for sprinkling, and at the souvenir counters at the store the miniature birch-bark canoes and the postcards that showed things looking a little better than they looked. This was the American family at play, escaping the city heat, wondering whether the newcomers in the camp at the head of the cove were "common" or "nice," wondering whether it was true that the people who drove up for Sunday dinner at the farmhouse were turned away because there wasn't enough chicken.

It seemed to me, as I kept remembering all this, that those times and those summers had been infinitely precious and worth saving. There had been jollity and peace and goodness. The arriving (at the beginning of August) had been so big a business in itself, at the railway station the farm wagon drawn up, the first smell of the pine-laden air, the first glimpse of the smiling farmer, and the great importance of the trunks and your father's enormous authority in such matters, and the feel of the wagon under you for the long ten-mile haul, and at the top of the last long hill catching the first view of the lake after eleven months of not seeing this cherished body of water. The shouts and cries of the other campers when they saw you, and the trunks to be unpacked, to give up their rich burden. (Arriving was less exciting nowadays, when you sneaked up in your car and parked it under a tree near the camp and took out the bags and in five minutes it was all over, no fuss, no loud wonderful fuss about trunks.)

Peace and goodness and jollity. The only thing that was wrong now, really, was the sound of the place, an unfamiliar nervous sound of the outboard motors. This was the note that jarred, the one thing that would sometimes break the illusion and set the years moving. In those other summertimes all motors were inboard; and when they were at a little distance, the noise they made was a sedative, an ingredient of summer sleep. They were one-cylinder and two-cylinder engines, and some were make-and-break and some were jump-spark, but they all made a sleepy sound across the lake. The one-lungers throbbed and fluttered, and the twin-cylinder ones purred and purred, and that was a quiet sound, too. But now the campers all had outboards. In the daytime, in the hot mornings, these motors made a petulant, irritable sound; at night, in the still evening when the afterglow lit the water, they whined about one's ears like mosquitoes. My boy loved our rented outboard, and his great desire was to achieve single-handed mastery over it, and authority, and he soon learned the trick of choking it a little (but not too much), and the adjustment of the needle valve. Watching him I would remember the things you could do with the old one-cylinder engine with the heavy flywheel, how you could have it eating out of your hand if you got really close to it spiritually. Motorboats in those days didn't have clutches, and you would make a landing by shutting off the motor at the proper time and coasting in with a dead rudder. But there was a way of reversing them, if you learned the trick, by cutting the switch and putting it on again exactly on the final dying revolution of the flywheel, so that it would kick back against compression and begin reversing. Approaching a dock in a strong following breeze, it was difficult to slow up sufficiently by the ordinary coasting method, and if a boy felt he had complete mastery over his motor, he was tempted to keep it running beyond its time and then reverse it a few feet from the dock. It took a cool nerve, because if you threw the switch a twentieth of a second too soon you would catch the flywheel when it still had speed enough to go up past center, and the boat would leap ahead, charging bull-fashion at the dock.

We had a good week at the camp. The bass were biting well and the sun 11 shone endlessly, day after day. We would be tired at night and lie down in the accumulated heat of the little bedrooms after the long hot day and the breeze would stir almost imperceptibly outside and the smell of the swamp drift in through the rusty screens. Sleep would come easily and in the morning the red squirrel would be on the roof, tapping out his gay routine. I kept remembering everything, lying in bed in the mornings—the small steamboat that had a long rounded stern like the lip of a Ubangi, and how quietly she ran on the moonlight sails, when the older boys played their mandolins and the girls sang and we ate doughnuts dipped in sugar, and how sweet the music was on the water in the shining night, and what it had felt like to think about girls then. After breakfast, we would go up to the store and the things were in the same place— the minnows in a bottle, the plugs and spinners disarranged and pawed over by the youngsters from the boys' camp, the Fig Newtons and the Beeman's gum. Outside, the road was tarred and cars stood in front of the store. Inside, all was just as it had always been, except there was more Coca-Cola and not so much Moxie[2] and root beer and birch beer and sarsaparilla. We would walk out with the bottle of pop apiece and sometimes the pop would backfire up our noses and hurt. We explored the streams, quietly, where the turtles slid off logs and dug their way into the soft bottom; and we lay on the town wharf and fed worms to the tame bass. Everywhere we went I had trouble making out which was I, the one walking at my side, the one walking in my pants.

One afternoon while we were there at that lake a thunderstorm came up. It 12 was like the revival of an old melodrama that I had seen long ago with childish awe. The second-act climax of the drama of the electrical disturbance over a lake in America has not changed in any important respect. This was the big scene, still the big scene. The whole thing was so familiar, the first feeling of oppression and heat and a general air around camp of not wanting to go very far away. In midafternoon (it was all the same) a curious darkening of the sky, and a lull in everything that had made life tick; and then the way the boats suddenly swung the other way at their moorings with the coming of a breeze out of the new quarter, and the premonitory rumble. Then the kettle drum, then the snare, then the bass drum and cymbals, then crackling light against the dark, and the gods grinning and licking their chops in the hills. Afterward the calm, the rain steadily rustling in the calm lake, the return of light and hope and spirits, and the campers running out in joy and relief to go swimming in the rain, their bright cries perpetuating the deathless joke about how they were getting simply drenched, and the children screaming with delight at the new sensation of bathing in the rain, and the joke about getting drenched linking the generations in a strong indestructible chain. And the comedian who waded in carrying an umbrella.

When the others went swimming, my son said he was going in, too. He 13 pulled his dripping trunks from the line where they had hung all through the shower and wrung them out. Languidly, and with no thought of going in, I watched him, his hard little body, skinny and bare, saw him wince slightly as he pulled up around his vitals the small, soggy, icy garment. As he buckled the swollen belt, suddenly my groin felt the chill of death.

2. Brand name of an old-fashioned soft drink.

FOR DISCUSSION

1. When and why did E. B. White return with his young son to the lake he himself had visited as a boy?
2. In paragraph 2, is White describing the lake as it was in the past, or as it is in the present time of his essay? How about in paragraphs 4–6? And in paragraph 11? Explain your answers.
3. In addition to the lake, White is also describing "the American family at play" (8). What qualities and attributes does he identify as particularly "American"?
4. Do American families still take summer vacations "at the lake"? How has the pattern of family play—on a lake or elsewhere—changed since White wrote his classic essay? How has it remained the same?

STRATEGIES AND STRUCTURES

1. In his description of the "primeval" lake, what qualities does White emphasize (3)? Point out particular details in his description that you find especially effective. What is his main point in citing them?
2. Is White's description of the lake more **OBJECTIVE** or **SUBJECTIVE**? Or both at different times? Explain.
3. What **DOMINANT IMPRESSION** does White's description create? How?
4. When he returned to the lake with his young son, the two of them, says White, went fishing "the first morning" (5). Point out other direct references to time in White's essay. How does he use chronology and the passing of time to organize his entire description?
5. One way in which the lake of his childhood has definitely changed, says White, is in its sounds. What new sounds does he describe? How does he incorporate this change into his description of the lake as a timeless place?
6. How would White's essay be different without the last paragraph, in which he watches his young son get ready to go swimming?

WORDS AND FIGURES OF SPEECH

1. What's the difference between an "illusion" and a "mirage" (4, 5)? Which is White describing here at times? Explain.
2. When he describes the lake as not only "constant" but "trustworthy" (6), White has **PERSONIFIED** the natural scene. Where else does he use this figure of speech and why?
3. Why does White repeat the word "same" in paragraph 5?

4. As a boy on the lake, White did not want to disturb the "stillness of the cathedral" (2). What are the implications of this phrase? In what ways is White's son depicted as a chip off the old block?

5. How does White's reference to "a dropped curtain" (7) anticipate his description of the storm at the end of his essay?

FOR WRITING

1. Think back to a memorable family vacation or other outing. What do you recall most clearly about it and why? Make a list of the details—objects, sounds, smells, tastes, colors, textures—that you remember.

2. Using your list of details as a basis, write a few paragraphs describing the vacation or outing and where you went and what you did there. Consider describing how the place has changed since you first visited and how it remains the same.

3. Read the letter from White on p. 28, and write a critical essay arguing why the author's reluctance to explain how he wrote "Once More to the Lake" is (or is not) justified—based on what you've learned about critical reading (and about writing) in this chapter.

Letter from E. B. White to Thomas Cooley

I'm not an expert on what goes on under my hood, but I'll try to answer your questions.

When I wrote "Once More to the Lake," I was living year round in this place on the coast of Maine and contributing a monthly department to *Harper's*. I had spent many summers as a boy on Great Pond—one of the Belgrade Lakes. It's only about 75 miles from here and one day I felt an urge to revisit the lake and have a week of freshwater life, which is very different from saltwater. So I went over with my small son and we did some fishing. I simply started with a desire to see again and experience again what I had seen and experienced as a boy. During our stay over there, the "idea of time" naturally insinuated itself into my thoughts, because my son was the age *I* had been in the previous life at the lake, and so I felt a sort of mixed-up identity. I don't recall whether I had the title from the start. Probably not. I don't believe the title had anything to do with the composing process. The "process" is probably every bit as mysterious to me as it is to some of your students—if that will make them feel any better. As for the revising I did, it was probably quite a lot. I always revise the hell out of everything. It's the only way I know how to write. I came up with the "chilling ending" simply because I was describing a bodily sensation of my own. When my son drew on his wet bathing trunks, it was as though I were drawing them on myself. I was old enough to feel the chill of death. I guess.

Sorry I can't be more explicit. Writing, for me, is simply a matter of trying to find out and report what's going on in my head and get it down on paper. I haven't any devices, shortcuts, or tricks.

January 22, 1984

⇒ 2 ⇐

ELEMENTS OF THE ESSAY: TOPIC, THESIS, COHERENCE, TONE, AND STYLE

LIKE many other things, an essay is composed of certain fundamental elements. Works of art, for example, have form, line, color, space, and texture; musical compositions are made up of rhythm, pitch, tempo, and volume; and in the field of chemistry, a compound like water (H_2O) is a combination of such physical elements as hydrogen and oxygen.

Essays are made up of ideas, and ideas are not substances in the same sense as those that make up chemical compounds. With any essay you write, however, we can speak of both its content (what you have to say) and its form (how you say it). Most essays have an introduction, a body, and a conclusion as part of their basic form. In this chapter, we'll focus on the elements of the essay that will be most important for communicating what you have to say, whether you're telling a story, drawing comparisons, analyzing a process, making an argument, or doing something else.

There are no simple formulas for writing a good essay. Fortunately, however, the basic elements that you can use to make meaning in an essay are far fewer than the 118 chemical elements in the standard periodic table. In this chapter, we'll boil them down to just five: topic, thesis, coherence, tone, and style.

TOPIC

Although we often lump the two together, the **TOPIC*** of an essay is not the same as the **SUBJECT**. A subject is a broad field of inquiry; a topic is a specific area within that field. For example, if you're writing about the use of drugs in professional baseball, "baseball" is your subject and "the use of drugs in baseball" is your topic. The following subjects, for instance, are too broad to be manageable topics in an essay: education, college sports, science, pets.

A good topic focuses on a particular aspect of your general subject. It is your subject narrowed down to a manageable scope and size for the length of the composition you're writing. The following are more specific areas within general fields and would make more manageable topics for an essay:

- The advantages of attending a community college rather than a university
- The rewards of college sports
- Studying science as a profession
- Choosing a pet

Here's a template that can help you get started as you look for a meaningful topic to write about in an essay:

> ▶ Within the general subject of _____, what I want to write about specifically is _____.

Here's just one way you might fill in the blanks, for example:

> ▶ Within the general subject of <u>higher education</u>, what I want to write about specifically is <u>the advantage of attending a community college</u>.

*Words printed in **SMALL CAPITALS** are defined in the Glossary/Index.

THESIS

In any essay you write, your topic is the specific aspect of your subject you plan to focus on. Your **THESIS** is what you have to say about that topic—the main point you want to make about it. That point is usually set forth in a thesis statement. Here are some examples taken from essays in this book:

> I believe the community college system to be one of America's uniquely great institutions.
>
> —LIZ ADDISON, "Two Years Are Better Than Four"

> So even if you disdain young people who can't find the will or time to vote . . . you should want to fix this problem.
>
> —JAMELLE BOUIE, "Why Don't Young People Vote?"

> Whether it's serious illness, financial hardship, or the simple constraint of parents who speak limited English, difficulty can tap unsuspected strengths.
>
> —SONIA SOTOMAYOR, *My Beloved World*

The following template can help get you started as you figure out the main point you want to make (the thesis) about your topic in an essay:

▶ The main point I want to make about _____ is that _____.

You might fill in the blanks like this:

▶ The main point I want to make about <u>competitive college sports</u> is that <u>the players should be paid</u>.

Once you've come up with a thesis that makes a particular point about a specific topic, you may need to limit it further by using such qualifiers as "possibly," "may be," "often," "for most people," and "in this situation." Liz Addison qualifies her thesis about the unique value of community colleges, for example, by saying "I believe" it to be true. The purpose of qualifying a thesis is to make it narrower and thus easier to support. Addison's thesis would be pretty strong even if she just said "The community college system is a uniquely great institution"; by qualifying this statement with "one of America's" and "I believe," however, she defines the scope of her argument more explicitly.

Where to Position a Thesis Statement

THESIS STATEMENT AT THE BEGINNING OF THE ESSAY. A direct statement of your thesis can appear anywhere in your essay. Most often, however, it should come near the beginning to help set up the rest of what you have to say, as in this example from the beginning of a humorous piece on the English language:

> English is the most widely spoken language in the history of our planet, used in some way by at least one out of every seven human beings around the globe. Half of the world's books are written in English, and the majority of international phone calls are made in English. . . .
>
> Nonetheless, it is now time to face the fact that English is a crazy language.
>
> —RICHARD LEDERER, "English Is a Crazy Language"

From this statement, Lederer goes on to provide one example after another of linguistic "craziness" to support his claim: "no egg in eggplant, no grape in grapefruit . . . and no ham in hamburger."

THESIS STATEMENT IN THE BODY OF THE ESSAY. Building up to a thesis is almost as common a pattern in essay writing as building down from one. Consider the following thesis statement from an essay on reading (and writing) personal narratives:

> But perhaps the deepest challenge in articulating and considering the stories of our lives is not that they force us to admit our privileges but that they force us to admit our suffering. Some realities hurt to look at.

Therefore, our harshest critics are often those with whom we share the most common ground.

—SARAH SMARSH, "Believe It"

This statement about the pain of telling (and hearing) the stories of our lives comes more than two-thirds of the way into Smarsh's essay. To lead up to it, she cites the personal narratives of Sojourner Truth and Harriet Jacobs, two writers who not only endured the evils of slavery—from which they escaped—but who also suffered the indignity of defending themselves to White readers as credible witnesses of their own experience. The harsh critic of her personal story that Smarsh anticipates here is her grandmother.

THESIS STATEMENT AT THE END OF THE ESSAY. When your thesis statement comes at the end of an essay, it can both sum up what you have to say and also give your reader a satisfying sense of closure. See how a professional mortician (and humor writer) soothes the reader's fears of premature burial:

But I feel confident saying that this is not going to happen to you. On your list of "Freaky Ways to Die," you can move "buried alive—coma" down to just below "terrible gopher accident."

—CAITLIN DOUGHTY, "What If They Bury Me
When I'm Just in a Coma?"

How likely is a terrible gopher accident that would be fatal to anyone but the gopher? That's Doughty's point: coroners and morticians really know when people are dead—or not.

IMPLIED THESIS. In the following passage, by a physician and writer, the message is only implied rather than stated explicitly. The writer, who died in 2015 at age 82, is speaking about a chemical element on his desk:

Bismuth is element 83. I do not think I will see my 83rd birthday, but I feel there is something hopeful, something encouraging, about having "83" around. Moreover, I have a soft spot for bismuth, a modest gray metal, often unregarded, ignored, even by metal lovers. My feeling as a doctor for the mistreated or marginalized extends into the inorganic world and finds a parallel in my feeling for bismuth.

—OLIVER SACKS, "My Periodic Table"

Sacks is writing about bismuth most explicitly, but he is also making a larger point about the importance of passion in the pursuit of science and medicine.

When Diane Guerrero restates her thesis at the end of her essay, p. 491, she also offers a solution to the problem.

However you choose to develop your thesis, it's probably always a good idea to restate it at the end of an essay. Sacks himself did this in an essay he wrote at the end of his life when he noted that it "has been an enormous privilege and adventure" to be "a sentient being, a thinking animal, on this beautiful planet" ("My Own Life," 2015).

COHERENCE

COHERENCE in writing has to mainly do with meaning, with what you have to say. A piece of writing is coherent when every idea in the text is clear—and clearly related to every other idea.

Consider the following example from one student's response to a writing prompt that "the best way for a society to prepare its young people for leadership in government, industry, or other fields is by instilling in them a sense of cooperation, not competition":

Some may argue that competition is not needed. That those that are meant to be leaders will not become complacent, because they have their own internal drive to lead. If there was no competition, there would be no world records. Michael Phelps may not be a leader of government or industry, but he is certainly educated on the technique of swimming, and a leader in his field. Would he be as good as he is today if there was not competition? Would the leaders of Microsoft have been motivated to create Bing if there was no Google?

—EDUCATIONAL TESTING SERVICE, GRE Practice General Test in Analytical Writing

Although the ideas expressed in this passage may be related in the writer's mind, the passage lacks coherence because those ideas are not clearly and explicitly tied together in ways that are immediately evident to a reader.

See how this passage can be edited to make it more coherent.

> Some may argue that competition is not needed *and* that those *of us who* ~~that~~ are meant to be leaders *in any field* will not become complacent, because ~~they~~ *we* have ~~their~~ *our* own internal drive to lead. If there was no competition, *however,* there would be, *for example,* no world records *in athletics. The Olympic swimmer* Michael Phelps may not be a leader of government or industry, but he is certainly ~~educated on the technique of swimming, and~~ a leader in ~~his field~~ *the pool.* Would he be as good *a swimmer* as he is today if there was not competition *from other world-class swimmers? Or, to take an example from the field of business,* would the leaders of Microsoft have been motivated to create Bing if there was no Google?

This edited version is hardly perfect, but it is more coherent than the original. Simply adding the word "however" in the second sentence, for instance, makes it clear that the example of Michael Phelps is intended to challenge the idea of cooperation, not uphold it. And by indicating that the writer is talking about leadership in "other fields" besides industry and government, the new language helps justify comparing an athlete with "the leaders of Microsoft."

Adding connecting words and phrases like "because," "however," and "for example" is one of the best ways to make your writing more coherent; but be careful to choose transitions that actually lend unity to your paragraph. Otherwise, your paragraph is just longer and more wordy. (See Chapter 4 for more on tying sentences together into coherent paragraphs and tying paragraphs together into coherent essays.)

> Chimamanda Adichie uses "but," "instead," and other transition words throughout her essay, p. 214.

Using Rhetorical Patterns to Make Your Ideas Coherent

You can use any of the rhetorical patterns discussed in this book—description, narrative, example, and so on—to help you achieve coherence in an essay.

Here are five examples of how these patterns can help you tie your ideas together into a coherent whole and make clear what you have to say:

Using DESCRIPTION to show how physical characteristics are related

> These steep, verdant hills carved out of prehistoric violence have had an eternity to become smooth. They roll and undulate like fairy-tale landscapes. The homes sit far apart, isolated. A church stands alone on a hill.
>
> —EDWARD LEE, "Slaw Dogs and Pepperoni Rolls"

Lee is a chef, and a key idea in his essay is that even in the most apparently isolated places, food brings people together to celebrate a common culture.

Using NARRATIVE to show how events are related in time

> When the Supreme Court outlawed segregation in the public schools in 1954, I was twenty-one. When Congress passed the Civil Rights Act of 1964, permitting blacks free access to public places, I was thirty-one.
>
> —MARY MEBANE, "The Back of the Bus"

The main point in Mebane's essay is that her personal life is historically important because she was "part of the last generation born into a world of total legal segregation in the Southern United States." Mebane makes that point by linking public events with personal ones in time.

Using COMPARISON AND CONTRAST to show similarities and differences

> It is not that older Disney films lacked adoptive families—on the contrary, the majority of the classics are populated by orphans and stepmothers. But crucially, films such as *Cinderella* (1950) hardwired our collective conception of step-parents as Bad News. . . . By contrast, in *Maleficent* and *Finding Dory*, living with adoptive parents or self-crafted families is not a misfortune for our heroines to overcome, but a happy ending for them to achieve.
>
> —SOPHUS HELLE, "Love Isn't What It Was"

Helle's main point is that love, as defined in Disney films, has changed over the years; some of these differences, as he explains here, can be seen in the contrasting views of family depicted in earlier Disney films as compared with newer ones.

Using CAUSE AND EFFECT to explore consequences

> In time, of course, doctors realized the scale of their error. Between 2010 and 2015, opioid prescriptions declined by 18 percent. But if it was a huge, well-intended mistake to create this army of addicts, it was an even bigger one to cut them off from their supply.
>
> —ANDREW SULLIVAN, "The Poison We Pick"

Sullivan is not just analyzing the causes of the opiate epidemic in America and its immediate effects (an "army of addicts"). He is using this analysis to lead into an examination of what happens down the road when this army is cut off from its "supply."

Using ARGUMENT to make logical connections among ideas

> . . . I spoke with more than three hundred teens and young adults about their online lives. I saw a generation settle into a new way of dealing with silence from other people: namely, deny that it hurts and put aside your understanding that if you do it to others, it will hurt them as well. . . .
>
> This style of relating is part of a larger pattern. You learn to give your parents a pass when they turn to their phones instead of responding to you. You learn to give your friends a pass when they drop in and out of conversations to talk with friends on their phones.
>
> —SHERRY TURKLE, "Romance: Where Are You? Who Are You? Wait,
> What Just Happened?"

Here, Turkle argues that what she observed in her conversations with teens is related to a greater trend, "a larger pattern," about texting culture. When we text people and they don't text back, after a while we start to do the same to others and then begin to expect the same behavior from our friends and family.

TONE AND STYLE

The ideas you express in an essay can be meaningful and logically coherent;
yet readers still may not fully understand what you have to say, or accept your
conclusions, if your ideas do not reflect a clear and consistent **POINT OF VIEW**.
The elements of writing that most directly convey your stance toward your
topic are **TONE** and **STYLE**. Tone may be defined as your attitude toward your
subject or audience. Style refers to the kind of language you use to present
yourself in a piece of writing. In practice, tone and style are closely intertwined
because both are directly affected by your **AUDIENCE** and **PURPOSE** in writing.

Tone

Let's suppose you have an essay due before noon. You've been working on it
for days, and you've gotten up at 6:45 a.m. to add the finishing touches. In
your neighborhood, local ordinances prohibit excessive noise before 8:00 a.m.
As you begin to write, however, a jackhammer starts up outside your window,
making it impossible for you to concentrate. Exasperated, you text the following message to a friend who lives in the same building:

> wow these ppl drilling outside really don't care huh? ugh

In this example, your audience is your friend and your purpose is to express
your frustration. Your tone here is one of annoyance, suggesting a certain
animosity toward your subject—those who persist in disturbing the peace
when you have an assignment to complete. As for your style of writing: it
might be called informal and personal ("wow," "ppl," "ugh"), as befits one
aggrieved friend texting another.

    Now assume a different audience for your grievances and a different
purpose in writing. Logging on to your city's official website, you discover a
suggestion form and file the following complaint:

> As a concerned citizen, I would like to report a violation of the city noise
> ordinance this morning at 7:00 a.m. outside 907 Whitehead Street. I

found it impossible to concentrate when, as I sat down to finish an important writing assignment . . .

Writing to a different audience (city officials) with a different purpose in mind (to inform them of a violation of a law) so that they can address the problem, your tone and style have changed considerably. Your tone is now more measured and detached; your style is more formal and impersonal (with terms like "violation" and "ordinance") in keeping with the role (concerned citizen) that you've adopted in your text.

The range of tones you have to choose from as a writer is virtually limitless—for example, you can sound annoyed and angry, patient and rational, or sympathetic and enthusiastic. Since tone is a reflection of your attitude toward your subject, a useful way to think about the tone you might adopt in an essay is simply to consider whether you want to sound largely positive, neutral, or negative toward your subject and then to choose words to suit your audience and purpose.

John McWhorter's tone (p. 220) is measured, even as he makes clear what he finds troubling about the name "Redskins."

In our jackhammer examples, the indignant text to a friend clearly adopts a negative tone toward the noisemakers. The message to city hall, on the other hand, is more neutral in tone. You can probably imagine a written message that would be positive in its attitude toward construction noise, and thus more enthusiastic in tone, but that would require a different audience, perhaps the readers of a trade publication for paving companies, and a different purpose, let's say to sell jackhammers or other equipment.

As you look for the right tone to use in an essay, try the following template to help you get started:

> ► On the topic of _____, my attitude is _____; my purpose in writing is _____ to an audience of _____. My tone, therefore, should be _____.

You might fill in the blanks this way:

> ► On the topic of <u>why young people sometimes don't vote</u>, my attitude is <u>there's no excuse</u>; my purpose in writing is <u>to explain the importance of voting</u>

to an audience of <u>fellow students, some of whom have had trouble with the</u> <u>voting system</u>. My tone, therefore, should be <u>understanding</u>.

Style

As with tone, there are almost as many possible variations in style as there are writers. As in our jackhammer examples, however, a useful way to think about the style you want to adopt in a particular piece of writing is to consider whether you want to come across as formal or informal, personal or impersonal—or something else. Let's look at two examples from the work of Ernest Hemingway. In the following passage from his novel *A Farewell to Arms*, the narrator comes across as impersonal, a detached observer.

> In the late summer of that year we lived in a house in a village that looked across the river and the plain to the mountains. In the bed of the river there were pebbles and boulders, dry and white in the sun, and the water was clear and swiftly moving and blue in the channels. Troops went by the house and down the road and the dust they raised powdered the leaves of the trees.
>
> —ERNEST HEMINGWAY, *A Farewell to Arms*

Contrast this style of writing with the style in the next passage, which includes part of a letter that Hemingway wrote for *Esquire* magazine when the town of Key West, where he was living at the time, went bankrupt. To deal with this economic crisis, the authorities introduced tourism as the main industry in the town and published a tourist guide that included Hemingway's house.

> The house at present occupied by your correspondent is listed as number eighteen in a compilation of the forty-eight things for a tourist to see in Key West. So there will be no difficulty in a tourist finding it or any other of the sights of the city, a map has been prepared by the local . . . authorities to be presented to each arriving visitor. Your correspondent is a modest and retiring chap with no desire to compete

with the Sponge Lofts (number 13 of the sights), the Turtle Crawl (number 3 on the map), the Ice Factory (number 4), the Tropical Open Air Aquarium containing the 627 pound jewfish (number 9), or the Monroe County Courthouse (number 14). . . . Yet there your correspondent is at number 18 between Johnson's Tropical Grove (number 17) and Lighthouse and Aviaries (number 19). This is all very flattering to the easily bloated ego of your correspondent but very hard on production.

—ERNEST HEMINGWAY, "The Sights of Whitehead Street:
A Key West Letter"

In this journalistic passage, Hemingway adopts a writing style that is different from the celebrated "plain style" of his fiction. In much of Hemingway's fiction, the language is informal; yet the plain-speaking narrator comes across as impersonal, a detached observer. In his letter, the style is the reverse. The language of the passage is deferential and formal: "modest and retiring chap"; "your correspondent" (as opposed to "this reporter"); "no desire to compete"; "all very flattering." And the implied author is a self-consciously personable "chap" who claims to have an "easily bloated ego." This difference in style suggests a difference in audience and purpose.

As a famous writer living in a small town, Hemingway may well have felt overwhelmed and annoyed by the hordes of tourists at his door. His purpose in writing here, however, is not to produce great literature or even to register a complaint about a public nuisance that, in this case, has been officially promoted by the authorities. His main purpose is to entertain the knowing and sophisticated readers of *Esquire*, a men's general interest magazine. For this audience, Hemingway the journalist adopts a different style of writing from that of Hemingway the novelist and short-story writer.

Zora Neale Hurston unveils a similar let-me-entertain-you purpose in the first part of her essay on p. 563.

The point of this example, however, is not that you should write like Hemingway or any other particular writer, though imitating the various styles of writers whose work you admire is a good way of developing a style of your own. The point, rather, is that your writing style—how you present yourself through the kind of language you use—will depend not only on who you are but also on your audience and your specific purpose in writing.

As you think about the most appropriate writing style to use in an essay, try this template to help you get started:

> ► In this essay on _____, I want to present myself as _____; my purpose in writing is _____ to an audience of _____. My style of writing, therefore, should be _____.

Here's one way to fill in the blanks:

> ► In this essay on <u>Hemingway's journalism of the 1930s</u>, I want to present myself as <u>an informed reader</u>; my purpose in writing is <u>to explain the novelist's role as a reporter</u> to an audience of <u>my classmates and teacher</u>. My style of writing, therefore, should be <u>formal enough for an academic paper but still fun to read</u>.

PUTTING IT ALL TOGETHER

Here's a template you can use to check that any essay you write includes all the basic elements outlined in this chapter:

> ► Within the general subject of _____, I focus in this essay on the specific TOPIC of _____.
>
> ► My THESIS is that _____.
>
> ► To present what I have to say as COHERENTLY as I can, I have used the following rhetorical strategies: _____, _____, and _____.
>
> ► My general attitude toward this subject is _____; so my TONE, overall, is _____.
>
> ► Since I am writing largely to an audience of _____ with the purpose of _____, my STYLE is _____.

Here's one way that Liz Addison might have filled in the blanks:

- ► Within the general subject of <u>higher education</u>, I focus in this essay on the specific TOPIC of <u>the advantages of going to a community college.</u>

- ► My THESIS is that <u>community colleges are often a better choice, particularly economically, than four-year universities.</u>

- ► To present what I have to say as COHERENTLY as I can, I have used the following rhetorical strategies: <u>my own example, a point-by-point comparison of the two kinds of schools</u>, and <u>logical argument.</u>

- ► My general attitude toward this subject is <u>very positive</u>; so my TONE, overall, is <u>enthusiastic and encouraging.</u>

- ► Since I am writing largely to an audience of <u>students and potential students</u> with the purpose of <u>making a recommendation</u>, my STYLE is <u>direct and personal.</u>

With any essay you write, if you can't fill in all of the blanks, consider the possibility that some important element may be missing.

⥽ 3 ⥼

THE WRITING PROCESS

U NLIKE flying from Seattle to Hawaii, writing is not a linear process. We plan, we draft, we revise; we plan, we draft, we revise again. In addition, we tend to skip around as we write, perhaps going back and completely rewriting what we've already written before plunging in again. This chapter is about the various stages of the writing process that you will typically go through in order to get from a blank page or screen to a final draft.

PLANNING

Before you plunge headlong into any writing assignment, think about the nature of the assignment, the length and scope of the text you're supposed to write, and your PURPOSE* and AUDIENCE. To help budget your time, also keep in mind two things in particular: (1) *When the assignment is due.* As soon as you get an assignment, jot down the deadline. And remember that it's hard to write a good paper if you begin the night before it's due. (2) *What kind of research the assignment will require.* For many college papers, the research may take longer than the actual writing. Think about how much and what kind of research you will need to do, and allow plenty of time for it.

Considering Your Purpose and Audience

We write for many reasons: to organize and clarify our thoughts, express our feelings, remember people and events, solve problems, persuade others to act

*Words printed in **SMALL CAPITALS** are defined in the Glossary/Index.

or believe as we think they should. As you think about *why* you're writing, however, you also need to consider *who* your readers are. The following questions will help you think about your intended purpose and audience:

- **What is your reason for writing?** Do you want to tell readers something they may not know? Entertain them? Change their minds?

- **Who is going to read (or hear) what you say?** Your classmates? Your teacher? Your followers on social media? Your supervisor at work?

- **How much does your audience know about your subject?** If you are writing for a general audience, you may need to provide some background information and explain any unfamiliar terminology.

- **What should you keep in mind about the nature of your audience?** Does the gender of your audience matter? How about their age, level of education, occupation, economic status, or religion? Are they likely to be sympathetic or unsympathetic to your position? Knowing your audience will help you generate ideas and **EVIDENCE** to both support what you have to say and appeal to that audience.

Coming Up with a Subject—and Focusing on a Topic

Before you can get very far into the writing process, you will need to come up with a subject and narrow it down to a workable topic. Though we often use the words interchangeably, a **SUBJECT**, strictly speaking, is a broad field of inquiry, whereas a **TOPIC** is a specific area within that field. For example, if you are writing a paper on the health care system in the United States, your teacher will still want to know just what approach you plan to take to that general subject. A good topic focuses in on a specific area of a general subject—such as the *causes* of waste in the health care system, or *why* more Americans need health insurance, or *how* to reform Medicare—that can be adequately covered in the time you have to write about it. (See p. 30 for more examples of how to move from a subject to a topic.)

With many writing assignments, you will be given a specific topic, or choice of topics, as part of the assignment. Make sure you understand just what you are being asked to do. Look for important words like "describe," "define," "analyze," "compare and contrast," "evaluate," and "argue." Be aware that even short assignments may include more than one of these directives. For example, the same assignment may ask you not only to define Medicare and Medicaid but also to compare the two government programs.

For some assignments, you will have to find a topic, perhaps after meeting with your teacher. Let your instructor know if you're already interested in a particular topic. Ask your instructor for suggestions—and start looking on your own. In each chapter in this book, you'll find ideas for finding a topic and for developing it into an essay by using the basic patterns of writing—DESCRIPTION, NARRATION, EXAMPLE, CLASSIFICATION, PROCESS ANALYSIS, COMPARISON AND CONTRAST, DEFINITION, CAUSE AND EFFECT, and ARGUMENT—that good writers use all the time.

GENERATING IDEAS

Once you have a topic to write about, where do you look for ideas? Over the years, writing teachers have developed a number of techniques to help writers generate ideas. All the following techniques may come in handy at various points in the writing process, not just at the outset.

Freewriting

Simply put pen to paper (or fingers to keyboard) and jot down whatever pops into your head. Here are some tips for freewriting:

1. Write nonstop for five or ten minutes. If nothing comes to mind at first, just write: "Nothing. My mind is blank." Eventually the words *will* come—if you don't stop writing until time runs out.

2. Circle words or ideas that you might want to come back to, but don't stop freewriting. When your time is up, mark any passages that look promising and revisit the words and ideas you circled.

3. Freewrite again, starting with something you marked in the previous session. Do this over and over and over again until you find an idea you want to explore further.

Keeping Lists

Keeping lists is a good way to generate ideas—and to come up with interesting examples and details. Here are some tips for keeping a list:

- A list can be written anytime and anywhere: on a computer, in a notebook, on a napkin—and, of course, on your phone. Apps for keeping digital lists and notes abound, but always keep a pencil handy.

- If your lists start to get long, try grouping related items into "piles," as you would if you were sorting your laundry. Look for relationships not only *within* those piles but *among* them.

Brainstorming

When you brainstorm, you write down words and ideas in one sitting rather than over time. Here are a few tips for brainstorming:

- If you are brainstorming by yourself, start by jotting down a topic at the top of your page or screen. Then write out a list of every idea, comment, or word that comes to mind.

- Brainstorming is often more effective when you do it collaboratively, with everyone throwing out ideas and one person acting as scribe. If you brainstorm with others, make sure everyone contributes—no one person should monopolize the session.

Asking Questions

Journalists and other writers ask *who, what, where, when, why,* and *how* to uncover the basic information for a story. Here is how you might use these questions if you were writing an essay about an argument in a parking lot:

- **Who** was involved in the argument? What should I say about my brother (one of the instigators) and his friends? The police officer who investigated? The witnesses?

- **What** happened? What did the participants say to one another? What did my brother do after he was struck by one of his friends?

- *Where* did the argument occur? How much of the parking lot should I describe? What can I say about it?

- *When* did the argument take place? What time did my brother leave the party, and when did he arrive in the parking lot?

- *Why* did the argument occur? Did it have anything to do with my brother's partner?

- *How* would my brother have reacted if he hadn't been drinking? Should I write about the effects of alcohol on anger management?

Keeping a Journal

A personal journal can be a great source of raw material for your writing. Often, what you write in a journal today will help you with a piece of writing months or even years later. Here are some pointers for keeping a journal:

- Write as informally as you like, but jot down your observations as close in time to the event as possible.

- The observations in a journal do not have to deal with momentous events; record your everyday thoughts and experiences.

- Make each journal entry as detailed and specific as possible; don't just write, "The weather was awful" or "I went for a walk." Instead, write, "Rained for an hour, followed by hail the size of meatballs" or "Walked from my place to Market St."

Doing Research

Most academic writing—and especially longer assignments—will require at least some research beyond simply thinking about your topic and deciding what you want to emphasize. Finding out and taking notes on what has already been said on your topic, particularly by experts in the field, is basic to writing about anything much more complicated than how to tie your shoes. (And even there, you can find entire websites devoted to the subject.)

When you do research and writing in any field, you enter into an ongoing "conversation" with others who have preceded you in that same field of inquiry.

Quoting, paraphrasing, or otherwise referring to what they have said is common in academic writing, and you'll find copious information on how to do this in the Appendix ("Using Sources in Your Writing"). Whenever you use someone else's work, of course, you need to document your sources scrupulously and accurately, using a standard form of citation. The Appendix, which uses the style of the Modern Language Association (MLA), will help with this, too.

As with any lively conversation, the purpose of doing research is not only to learn what others are saying but also to spark ideas of your own. To keep track of those ideas (and your sources), record them in a research journal. It can reside in a section of a personal journal or, even better, in a separate research notebook or file on your computer.

ORGANIZING AND DRAFTING

Once you have an abundance of facts, details, and other raw material, your next job is to organize that material and develop it into a draft. Generally, you will want to report events in chronological order—unless you are tracing the causes of a particular phenomenon or event, in which case you may want to work backward in time. Facts, statistics, personal experience, expert testimony, and other **EVIDENCE** should usually be presented in the order of their relative importance to your topic. But more than anything else, the order in which you present your ideas on any topic will be determined by exactly what you have to say about it.

Stating Your Point

Before you actually begin writing, think carefully about the main point you want to make—your **THESIS**. You may find that your thesis changes as you draft, but starting with a thesis in mind will help you identify the ideas and details you want to include—and the order in which you present them to the reader. Often you'll want to state your thesis in a single sentence as a **THESIS STATEMENT**.

What makes a good thesis statement? First, let's consider what a thesis statement is not. A simple announcement of your topic—"In this paper I will discuss what's wrong with the US health care system"—is not a thesis statement. A good thesis statement not only tells the reader what your topic is, it also makes an interesting CLAIM *about* your topic, one that is open to further discussion. That's why statements of fact are not thesis statements, either: "More than thirty million people in the United States have no health insurance." Facts may support your thesis, but the thesis itself should say something about your topic that requires further proof. For example: "To fix health care in America, we need to develop a single-payer system of health insurance." (For more on coming up with a claim and finding effective evidence, see pp. 474–75.)

A thesis statement like this at the beginning of your essay clarifies your main point—and it helps set up the rest of the essay. In this case, the reader might expect a definition of a single-payer insurance system with an analysis of the effects of adopting such a system and an argument for why those particular effects will provide the needed fix.

Making an Informal Outline

Making an informal outline can also help you organize and develop your draft. Simply write down your thesis statement and follow it with the main subpoints you intend to cover. Here is an informal outline that one student in a medical ethics class jotted down for an essay on the US health care system:

> THESIS: The costs of health care in America can be contained by paying for medical results rather than medical services.
> —what the current fee-for-services system is
> —what the problems with the system are, such as unnecessary tests, high administrative costs
> —how to reform the system
> —how to pay for the new system

Using the Patterns Taught in This Book

As you draft, consider using the basic MODES OF WRITING taught in this book as patterns or prompts to help you think of things to say about your topic. For example:

- Use **DESCRIPTION** (pp. 77–87) to show what some aspect of your topic looks, sounds, feels, smells, or tastes like: "The pool was the size of a football field. Over the decades, generations of the town grew up at the edge of its crystal-blue water."

  —SAM QUINONES, "Dreamland"

- Use **NARRATION** (pp. 127–36) to tell a story about some aspect of your topic: "I was seven years old the first time I snuck out of the house in the dark."

  —LYNDA BARRY, "The Sanctuary of School"

- Use **EXAMPLES** (pp. 180–88) to give specific instances of your topic: "Every culture comes up with tests of a person's ability to get out of a sticky situation. The English plant mazes. Tropical resorts market those straw finger-grabbers that tighten their grip the harder you pull on them, and Viennese intellectuals gave us the concept of childhood sexuality—figure it out, or remain neurotic for life."

  —PHILIP WEISS, "How to Get Out of a Locked Trunk"

- Use **CLASSIFICATION** (pp. 226–33) to divide various aspects of your topic into categories: "If you make money with money, as some of my super-rich friends do, your [tax] percentage may be a bit lower than mine. But if you earn money from a job, your percentage will surely exceed mine—most likely by a lot."

  —WARREN BUFFETT, "Stop Coddling the Super-Rich"

- Use **PROCESS ANALYSIS** (pp. 275–86) to explain how some aspect of your topic works or is made: "When you go to a website and load a page, . . . there are real-time auctions running in the background that determine which ads to load on *your* page."

  —DINA SRINIVASAN, "How Digital Advertising Works"

- Use **COMPARISON AND CONTRAST** (pp. 322–31) to point out similarities and differences in various aspects of your topic: "The classroom is a different environment for those who feel comfortable putting them-selves forward in a group than it is for those who find the prospect of doing so chastening, or even terrifying."

  —DEBORAH TANNEN, "Gender in the Classroom"

- Use **DEFINITION** (pp. 371–79) to explain what some aspect of your topic is or is not: "Should I explain . . . that I am Guatemalan by birth but *pura gringa* by circumstance?"

  —TANYA MARIA BARRIENTOS, "Se Habla Español"

- Use **CAUSE AND EFFECT** (pp. 423–32) to explain why some aspect of your topic happened or what effects it might have: "There are uses to adversity, and they don't reveal themselves until tested. Whether it's serious illness, financial hardship, or the simple constraint of parents who speak limited English, difficulty can tap unsuspected strengths."

  —SONIA SOTOMAYOR, "My Beloved World"

- Use **ARGUMENT** (pp. 469–83) to make and support your thesis: "[Technology] encourages us to feel that we have infinite choice in romantic partners, a prospect that turns out to be as stressful as it is helpful in finding a mate."

  —SHERRY TURKLE, "Romance: Where Are You? Who Are You?
  Wait, What Just Happened?"

Templates for Getting Started

The following templates outline ways to use the common patterns of writing, or rhetorical modes, to get started with almost any topic ("X"). Don't take these as formulas where you just have to fill in the blanks; there are no easy formulas for good writing. However, these templates can help you get started with some of the basic moves you'll need to make as you draft:

> ► X can be described as having the following characteristics: _____, _____, and _____.
>
> ► What has happened to X is _____, _____, and _____.
>
> ► Some examples of X are _____, _____, and _____.
>
> ► X can be divided into the following categories: _____, _____, and _____.

- ► The process of X can be broken down into the following steps: _____, _____, and _____.

- ► X is like Y in that both are _____ and _____; however, X is different from Y in _____ and _____.

- ► X can be defined as a(n) _____ with the following characteristics: _____ and _____.

- ► X was caused by _____ and _____; the effects of X are _____ and _____.

- ► What should be done about X is _____, _____, and _____.

The Three Parts of a Draft

As you construct a draft, think of it as having essentially three parts: a beginning, a middle, and an ending. Each of these parts should be shaped with your potential readers in mind.

Your beginning is the introduction, the first thing the reader sees. It should grab—and hold—the reader's attention. The introduction should also tell the reader exactly what you're writing about and, most of the time, should include a clear statement of your thesis. Occasionally, you may want to build up to your thesis statement, but generally it's best to state your thesis right off the bat. (For more on drafting an introduction, see p. 73.)

The middle of your draft is the body, and it may run anywhere from a few paragraphs to many pages. This is the part in which you present your best commentary and EVIDENCE in support of your main point. That evidence can include facts and figures, examples, the testimony of experts (usually in the form of citations from sources that you carefully acknowledge), and perhaps your own personal experience. How much evidence will you need?

The amount of evidence you'll need will depend in part on how broad or narrow your thesis is. A broad thesis on how to combat climate change would obviously require more—and more detailed—evidence than a thesis about the cost of textbooks at a campus bookstore. Ultimately, it is the reader who determines whether or not your evidence is sufficient. So as you draft, ask yourself questions like these about the details you should include:

- **What is the best example I can give to illustrate my main point?** Is one example enough, or should I give several?

- **Of all the facts I could cite, which ones support my thesis best?** What additional facts will the reader expect or need to have?

- **Of everything I've read on my topic, which sources are absolutely indispensable?** What sources were particularly clear or authoritative on the issue? How do I cite my sources appropriately? (For more information on using and documenting sources, see the Appendix.)

- **Is my personal experience truly relevant to my point?** Or would I be better off staying out of the picture? Is there someone I should cite whose experience or knowledge is even more compelling than mine?

The ending of your draft is the conclusion, a SUMMARY of what you have to say, often by restating the thesis—but with some variation based on the evidence you have just cited. For instance, you can make a recommendation ("more research is needed to show which frequently prescribed medical tests actually work") or explain the larger significance of your topic ("lowering health care costs for individuals will allow more people to be covered without incurring additional outlays"). (For more on drafting a conclusion, see p. 75.)

Using Visuals

Illustrations such as graphs and charts can be especially effective for presenting or comparing data, and photographs or drawings can help readers "see" things you describe in your written text. For example, if you were writing about the legend of Elvis Presley, you might want to include a photo of an Elvis figurine like the one on p. 141. But remember that visuals should never be mere decoration or clip art. When considering any kind of illustration, here are a few guidelines to follow:

- **Visuals should be relevant to your topic and support your thesis** in some way. In this book, for example, you'll notice that most of the chapters include an illustrated example, such as a sign or cartoon, showing how the pattern of writing discussed in that chapter is used in an everyday writing situation.

- *Any visuals should be appropriate for your audience and purpose.* You might add a detailed medical drawing of a lung to an essay on the effects of smoking directed at respiratory specialists, but not to an essay about smoking aimed at a general audience who wouldn't necessarily need—or want—to see all the details.

- *Refer to any visuals in the text* by numbering them so readers can find them regardless of where the visuals are located ("see fig. 1").

- *Position each visual close to the text it illustrates,* if possible, and consider adding a caption explaining the point of the visual.

- *If you use a visual you have not created yourself,* identify the source. Both MLA and APA provide guidelines for when and how to cite visuals.

REVISING

Revising is a process of *re-vision*, of looking again at your draft and fixing problems in content, organization, or both. Sometimes revising requires some major surgery: adding new EVIDENCE, cutting out paragraphs or entire sections, rewriting the beginning, and so on.

Many writers try to revise far too soon. To avoid this pitfall, put aside your draft for a few hours—or better still, for a few days—before revising. Start by reading your draft carefully, and then try to get someone else to look it over—a classmate, a friend, your aunt. Whoever it is, be sure they are aware of your intended audience and purpose. Here's what you and the other person should look for:

- *Title.* Does the title pique the reader's interest and accurately indicate the topic of the essay?

- *Thesis.* What is the main point of the essay? Is it clearly stated in a thesis statement? If not, should it be? Is the thesis sufficiently narrow?

- *Audience.* Is there sufficient background information for the intended readers? Are there clear definitions of terms and concepts they might not know? Will they find the topic interesting?

- *Support.* What evidence supports the thesis? Is the evidence convincing and the reasoning logical? Are more facts or specific details needed? Are the facts accurate? Do they come from reliable sources? If in doubt, try running them through an online fact-checker (or two).

- *Organization.* Is the draft well organized, with a clear beginning, middle, and ending? Does each paragraph contribute to the main point, or are some paragraphs off topic?

- *Patterns of Writing.* What is the main pattern the writer uses to develop the essay? For example, is the draft primarily a NARRATIVE? A DESCRIPTION? An ARGUMENT? Should other patterns be introduced? For instance, would more EXAMPLES or a COMPARISON be beneficial?

- *Sources.* If there is material from other sources, how are those sources incorporated? Are they quoted? Paraphrased? Summarized? Are sources clearly acknowledged following appropriate guidelines for documentation, so readers know whose words or ideas are being used? Do sources effectively support the main point? (For tips on using sources and citing them properly, see the Appendix.)

- *Paragraphs.* Does each paragraph focus on one main idea and, often, state it directly in a clear topic sentence? Do your paragraphs vary in structure, or are they too much alike? Should any long or complex paragraphs be broken into two? Should short paragraphs be combined with other paragraphs or developed more fully? How well does the draft flow from one paragraph to the next? If any paragraph seems to break the flow, should it be cut—or are transitions needed to help the reader follow the text? (For more help with paragraphs, see Chapter 4.)

- *Sentences.* If all the sentences are about the same length, should some be varied? A short sentence in the midst of long sentences can provide emphasis. On the other hand, too many short sentences in a row can sound choppy. Some of them might be combined.

- *Visuals.* If the draft includes visuals, are they relevant to the topic and thesis? If there are no visuals, would any of the text be easier to understand if accompanied by a diagram or drawing?

After you analyze your own draft carefully and get advice from another reader, you may decide to make some fairly drastic changes, such as adding more examples, writing a more effective conclusion, or dropping material that doesn't support your thesis. All such moves are typical of the revision process. In fact, it is not unusual to revise a draft more than once to get it to a near-final form.

EDITING AND PROOFREADING

When you finish revising your essay, you've blended all the basic ingredients, but you still need to put the icing on the cake. That is, you need to edit and proofread your final draft before presenting it to the reader.

When you edit, you add finishing touches and correct errors in grammar, sentence structure, punctuation, and word choice. When you proofread, you take care of misspellings, typos, problems with margins and format, and other minor blemishes. Here are some tips that can help you check your drafts for some common errors.

Editing Sentences

Check that each sentence expresses a complete thought

Each sentence should have a subject (someone or something) and a verb performing an action or indicating a state of being. (The Civil War started in 1861.)

Check capitalization and end punctuation

Be sure each sentence begins with a capital letter and ends with a period, a question mark, or an exclamation point.

Look for sentences that begin with "it" or "there"

Often such sentences are vague or boring, and they are usually easy to edit. For example, if you've written "There is a security guard on duty at every entrance," you could edit it to "A security guard is on duty at every entrance."

Check for parallelism

All items in a list or series should have parallel grammatical forms—nouns (Lincoln, Grant, Lee), verbs (dedicate, consecrate, hallow), phrases (of the people, by the people, for the people), and so on. For example: "This year's Brighton Naked Bike Ride will also include swimming, running for five miles, and throwing the javelin."

Editing Words

"There," "their"

Use "there" to refer to a place or direction or to introduce a sentence. (Was he there? There was no evidence.) Use "their" as a possessive. (Their plans fell apart.)

Use "it's" to mean "it is." (It's often difficult to apologize.) Use "its" to mean "belonging to it." (Each dog has its own personality.)

Use "lie" when you mean "recline." (She's lying down because her back hurts.) Use "lay" when you mean "put" or "place." (Lay the blanket on the bed.)

Use concrete words

If some of your terms are too ABSTRACT (Lake Superior is so amazing and incredible), choose more CONCRETE terms (Lake Superior is so cold and choppy that swimming in it often seems like swimming in the ocean).

Avoid filler words like "very," "quite," "really," and "truly"

You could write that "John Updike was truly a very great novelist," but it's stronger to say, "John Updike was a great novelist."

Editing Punctuation

Check for commas after introductory elements in a sentence

► After that day, it was as if Miss Dennis and I shared something.

—ALICE STEINBACH, "The Miss Dennis School of Writing"

Check for commas before "and," "but," "or," "nor," "so," or "yet" in compound sentences

► Book sales are down, but creative writing enrollments are booming.

—ALLEGRA GOODMAN, "So, You Want to Be a Writer? Here's How."

Check for commas in a series

► Where you live, where you go to school, your job, your profession, who you interact with, how people interact with you, your treatment in the healthcare and justice system are all affected by your race.

—ROBERT WALD SUSSMAN, "The Myth of Race"

Put quotation marks at the beginning and end of a quotation

► Finally he said, "Once you get to be thirty, you make your own mistakes."

—PHILIP WEISS, "How to Get Out of a Locked Trunk"

► "Do it," I finally commanded myself. So I did.

—PRIYA CHANDRASEKARAN, "Cutting Our Grandmothers' Saris"

Check your use of apostrophes with possessives

Singular nouns should end in 's, whereas plural nouns should end in s'. The possessive pronouns "hers," "his," "its," "ours," "yours," and "theirs" should not have apostrophes.

► But to me, my mother's English is perfectly clear, perfectly natural.

—AMY TAN, "Mother Tongue"

► The allure of opiates' joys are filling a hole in the human heart and soul today as they have done since the dawn of civilization. But this time . . . they are agents of an enveloping and eternal darkness.

—ANDREW SULLIVAN, "The Poison We Pick"

Proofreading and Formatting

Proofreading is the only stage in the writing process where you are *not* primarily concerned with meaning. Of course you should correct any substantive errors you find, but your main concern is the surface appearance of your text: misspellings, margins that are too narrow or too wide, unindented paragraphs, and missing page numbers.

It is a good idea to slow down as you proofread. Use a ruler or piece of paper to guide your eye line by line; or read your entire text backward a sentence at a time; or read it aloud word by word. Use a spellchecker, too, but don't rely on it: a spellchecker doesn't always know the difference, for example, between "their" and "there" or "human" and "humane."

Also check the overall format of your document to make sure it follows any specific instructions that you may have been given. If your instructor does not have particular requirements for formatting, here are some guidelines:

Heading and title. Put your name, your instructor's name, the name and number of the course, and the date on separate lines in the upper-left corner of your first page. Center your title on the next line, but do not underline it or put it in quotation marks. Double-space the heading and title.

Typeface and size. Use ten- or twelve-point type in an easy-to-read typeface, such as Times New Roman or Arial.

Spacing and margins. Double-space your document. Leave one-inch margins on each side and at the top and bottom of your text.

Paragraph indentation and page numbers. Indent the first line of each paragraph five spaces, preferably by using the Tab key on your keyboard. Number pages consecutively and include your last name and the page number with each page, usually in the upper-right corner, half an inch from the top. Most word processors have a "Header" function that will do this for you.

⇒ 4 ⇐

WRITING PARAGRAPHS

T HIS chapter is about writing paragraphs. A paragraph is a group of closely related sentences on the same topic. In any piece of writing longer than a few sentences, paragraphs are necessary to indicate when the discussion shifts from one topic to another. Just because a group of sentences is on the same topic, however, doesn't mean they're all closely related. All the following sentences, for example, are about snakes:

> There are no snakes in Ireland. Ounce for ounce, the most deadly snake in North America is the coral snake. Snakes are our friends; never kill a snake. North America is teeming with snakes, including four venomous species. Snakes also eat insects.

Although they make statements about the same topic, these sentences do not form a coherent paragraph because they're not closely related to each other: each one snakes off in a different direction. In a coherent paragraph, all the sentences work together to support the main point.

SUPPORTING THE MAIN POINT

Suppose the main point we wanted to make in a paragraph about snakes was that, despite their reputation for evil, snakes should be protected. We could still mention snakes in North America, even the deadly coral snake. We could say that snakes eat insects. But the sentence about snakes in Ireland would have to go. Of course, we could introduce additional facts and figures about snakes and snakebites—so long as we made sure that every statement in our paragraph worked together to support the idea of conservation. For example, we might write:

> Snakes do far more good than harm, so the best thing to do if you encounter a snake is to leave it alone. North America is teeming with snakes, including four venomous species. (Ounce for ounce, the most deadly snake in North America is the coral snake.) The chances of dying from any variety of snakebite, however, are slim—less than 1 in 25,000,000 per year in the United States. Snakes, moreover, contribute to a healthy ecosystem. They help to control the rodent population, and they eat insects. (Far more people die each year from the complications of insect bites than from snakebites.) Snakes are our friends and should be protected. Never kill a snake.

This is a coherent paragraph because every sentence contributes to the main point, which is that snakes should be protected.

Don't Go Off on a Tangent

Anytime the subject of snakes comes up, it is tempting to recall the legend of Saint Patrick, the patron saint of Ireland who, in the second half of the fifth century, is said to have driven the snakes from the land with his walking stick. Beware, however, of straying too far from the main point of your paragraph, no matter how interesting the digression may be. That is, be careful not to go off on a tangent. The term "tangent," by the way, comes from geometry and refers to a line that touches a circle at only one point—on the periphery, not the center.

Every sentence in Richard Lederer's essay, p. 201, supports the point made in his title, "English Is a Crazy Language."

And, incidentally, did you know that St. Patrick used a three-leaf clover to explain the Christian doctrine of the Trinity to the Irish people? Which is why shamrocks are associated with St. Patrick's Day. Also, there's another really interesting legend about St. Patrick's walking stick. . . . But we digress.

Topic Sentences

To help you stay on track in a paragraph, state your main point in a **TOPIC SENTENCE*** that identifies your subject (snakes) and makes a clear statement about it ("should be protected"). Usually your topic sentence will come at the beginning, as in this paragraph from an essay about the benefits of working at McDonald's:

> Working at McDonald's has taught me a lot. The most important thing I've learned is that you have to start at the bottom and work your way up. I've learned to take this seriously—if you're going to run a business, you need to know how to do all the other jobs. I also have more patience than ever and have learned how to control my emotions. I've learned how to get along with all different kinds of people. I'd like to have my own business someday, and working at McDonald's is what showed me I could do that.
>
> —MARISSA NUÑEZ, "Climbing the Golden Arches"

When you put the topic sentence at the beginning of a paragraph like this, every other sentence in your paragraph should follow from it.

Sometimes you may put your topic sentence at the end of the paragraph. Then, every other sentence in the paragraph should lead up to the topic sentence. Consider this example from an essay on how to be happy:

> . . . What matters is friends and family, and human relationships: what you did for other people, what they did for you. How you helped and were helped. Where you cared and were cared for. That's the heart of happiness, and all the rest is commercial hustle. Don't buy it. Make the world a better place and you make your life worthwhile. Make your life worthwhile and you'll be happy. You don't need to buy anything or ask anybody for advice. You can just go do it.
>
> —MICHAEL CRICHTON, "Happiness"

*Words printed in **SMALL CAPITALS** are defined in the Glossary/Index.

All of the statements in this paragraph are about the nature of happiness, leading up to the topic sentence at the end, which tells the reader how to actually achieve it.

Sometimes the main point of a paragraph will be implied from the context, and you won't need to state it explicitly in a topic sentence. This is especially true when you're making a point by telling a story or describing a scene. In the following description of a region that he is just getting to know, a chef explains why he has been traveling around and tasting the local cuisine:

> Along my journey, through Appalachia or any of the small towns I've traveled to, the most insightful moments have been quiet and unseasoned. This has made me question myself and my expectations. I'm owed nothing by the people and the culture of this place. I have neither the right to judge nor the history to comment on them. If the pepperoni roll seems bland to me, it is a fault in my own palate, which is unable to detect the value of its plainness.
>
> —EDWARD LEE, "Slaw Dogs and Pepperoni Rolls"

Lee does not have to say directly in a topic sentence that his purpose in sampling regional foods goes well beyond simply looking for new recipes. That point is clearly implied in observations like these from the closing paragraph of his essay.

Topic sentences not only tell your reader what the rest of a paragraph is about; however, they also help, collectively, to tie all your ideas together in support of the main point of your essay. The main point of Lee's entire essay is to show what he learned on his road trip about the people and culture of the regions he traveled through—and about himself and his "expectations" (15). That point is clear by the end of the "journey" because, all along the way his topic sentences, whether stated or implied, point in this direction.

Using Parallel Structures

Many of the topic sentences in Lee's essay have basically the same grammatical form: Subject+Verb+Phrase. (For example: "A West Virginia hot dog is a regional specialty that starts with a soft commercial hot dog bun.") Parallel structures like this are a good way to help readers see the connections between your sentences and your ideas.

Using parallel structures can help you link ideas within paragraphs as well as between or among them. Michael Crichton used them in his paragraph about happiness: "Make the world a better place and you make your life worthwhile. Make your life worthwhile and you'll be happy." The similarities in form in these two sentences tie them together in support of the topic sentence to come: "You can just do it."

"Love Isn't What It Was," p. 365, uses parallel structures to define different kinds of love in Disney films.

Parallel structures indicate key elements in a paragraph or even in an entire essay. They do not, however, tell the reader exactly how those pieces of the puzzle fit together. For this we need transitions.

Using Transitions

Paragraphs are all about connections. The following words and phrases can help you to make **TRANSITIONS** that clearly connect one statement to another—within a paragraph and also between paragraphs:

- **When describing place or direction:** across, across from, at, along, away, behind, close, down, distant, far, here, in between, in front of, inside, left, near, next to, north, outside, right, south, there, toward, up

- **When narrating events in time:** at the same time, during, frequently, from time to time, in 2030, in the future, now, never, often, meanwhile, occasionally, soon, then, until, when

- **When giving examples:** for example, for instance, in fact, in particular, namely, specifically, that is

- **When comparing:** also, as, in a similar way, in comparison, like, likewise

- **When contrasting:** although, but, by contrast, however, on the contrary, on the other hand

- **When analyzing cause and effect:** as a result, because, because of, consequently, so, then

- **When using logical reasoning:** accordingly, hence, it follows, therefore, thus, since, so

- *When tracing sequence or continuation:* also, and, after, before, earlier, finally, first, furthermore, in addition, last, later, next

- *When summarizing:* in conclusion, in summary, in the end, consequently, so, therefore, thus, to conclude

Consider how transitional words and phrases like these work together in the following paragraph about a new trend in shopping; the transitions are indicated in **bold**:

We are awakening to a dollar-store economy. **For years** the dollar store has **not only** made a market out of the leftovers of a global manufacturing system, **but** it has **also** made it appealing—by making it amazingly cheap. **Before** the market meltdown of 2008 **and** the stagnant, jobless recovery that followed, the conventional wisdom about dollar stores—**whether** one of the three big corporate chains (Dollar General, Family Dollar, and Dollar Tree) **or** any of the smaller chains (**like** "99 Cents Only Stores") **or** the world of independents—was that they appeal to only poor people. **And while** it's true that low-wage earners still make up the core of dollar-store customers (42 percent earn $30,000 or less), what has turned this sector into a nearly recession-proof corner of the economy is a new customer base. "What's driving the growth," says James Russo, a vice president with the Nielsen Company, a consumer survey firm, "is affluent households."

—Jack Hitt, "The Dollar-Store Economy"

Without transitions, the statements in this paragraph would fall apart like beads on a broken string. Transitions indicate relationships: they help tie the writer's ideas together—in this case by showing how they are related in time ("for years, before"), by contrast ("not only," "but also"; "whether," "or"), and in comparison ("like, "and while").

DEVELOPING PARAGRAPHS

There are many ways—in addition to supporting a topic sentence and using parallel structures and transitions—to develop coherent paragraphs. In fact, all of the basic patterns of writing discussed in this book work just as well for organizing paragraphs as they do for organizing entire essays. Here are some examples.

Describing

A common way of developing a paragraph, especially when you're writing about a physical object or place, is to give a detailed **DESCRIPTION** (Chapter 5) of your subject. When you describe something, you show the reader how it looks, sounds, feels, smells, or tastes, as in the following description of a tarpon that has just been caught by a blind boy; the point of the paragraph is to help the reader (and the boy) picture the fish:

> Okay. He has all these big scales, like armor all over his body. They're silver too, and when he moves they sparkle. He has a strong body and a large powerful tail. He has big round eyes, bigger than a quarter, and a lower jaw that sticks out past the upper one, and is very tough. His belly is almost white and his back is a gunmetal gray. When he jumped, he came out of the water about six feet, and his scales caught the sun and flashed it all over the place.
>
> —CHEROKEE PAUL MCDONALD, "A View from the Bridge"

Descriptions of physical objects are often organized by the configuration of the object. Here, the object is a fish, and the writer develops this descriptive paragraph by moving from one part of the fish to another (scales, tail, eyes, jaw, belly, back), ending up with an overall view of the whole tarpon glinting in the sun.

In "Dreamland," p. 100, Sam Quinones uses the contours of the local swimming pool to organize his description of life in a small town.

Narrating

One of the oldest and most common ways of developing a paragraph on almost any subject is by narrating a story about it. When you construct a **NARRATIVE** (Chapter 6), you focus on events: you tell what happened. In the following paragraph, a writer tells how he learned to use the English language:

> My family immigrated to the U.S. from Vietnam in 1990, when I was two. We lived, all seven of us, in a one-bedroom apartment in Hartford, Connecticut, and I spent my first five years in America surrounded, inundated, by the Vietnamese language. When I entered kindergarten, I was, in a sense, immigrating all over again, except this time into English.
>
> —OCEAN VUONG, "Immigrating into English"

Narratives are usually organized by time, presenting events in chronological order. However briefly, this narrative reports on events that unfolded over a five-year period as the author moved from his native language into his adoptive one.

Giving Examples

When you use **EXAMPLES** (Chapter 7) to develop a paragraph, you give specific instances of the point you're making. In the following tongue-in-cheek paragraph, a linguist uses multiple examples to show how "unreliable" the English language can be:

> In this unreliable English tongue, greyhounds aren't always grey (or gray); panda bears and koala bears aren't bears (they're marsupials); a woodchuck is a groundhog, which is not a hog; a horned toad is a lizard; glowworms are fireflies, but fireflies are not flies (they're beetles); ladybugs and lightning bugs are also beetles (and to propagate, a significant proportion of ladybugs must be male); a guinea pig is neither a pig nor from Guinea (it's a South American rodent); and a titmouse is neither mammal nor mammaried.
>
> —RICHARD LEDERER, "English Is a Crazy Language"

Although the language and punctuation of this paragraph are playfully complex, the organization is simple: it is a series, or list, of brief examples in more or less random order.

Classifying

When you **CLASSIFY** (Chapter 8), you divide your subject into categories. In the following passage, a writer classifies different kinds of English:

> Fortunately, for reasons I won't get into today, I later decided I should envision a reader for the stories I would write. And the reader I decided upon was my mother, because these were stories about mothers. So with this reader in mind—and in fact she did read my early drafts—I began to write stories using all the Englishes I grew up with: the English I spoke to my mother, which for lack of a better term might be described as "simple"; the English she used with me, which for lack of a better term might be described as "broken"; my translation of her Chinese, which could certainly be described as "watered down"; and what I imagined to be her translation of her Chinese if she could speak in perfect English, her internal language, and for that I sought to preserve the essence, but neither an English nor a Chinese structure. I wanted to capture what language ability tests can never reveal: her intent, her passion, her imagery, the rhythms of her speech and the nature of her thought.
>
> Jennine Capó Crucet tells another story about mothers and languages on p. 337.
>
> —AMY TAN, "Mother Tongue"

This is a complex paragraph; but the heart of it is the author's classification of her various "Englishes" into four specific types. The opening statements in the paragraph explain how this classification system came about, and the closing statement explains the purpose it serves.

Analyzing a Process

When you use **PROCESS ANALYSIS** (Chapter 9) to develop a paragraph, you tell the reader how to do something—or how something works or is made—by breaking the process into steps. In the following paragraph, a writer explains what she sees as the first steps in learning to be a writer:

> To begin, don't write about yourself. I'm not saying you're uninteresting. I realize that your life has been so crazy no one could make this stuff up. But if you want to be a writer, start by writing about other people. Observe their faces, and the way they wave their hands around. Listen to the way they talk. Replay conversations in your mind—not just the words, but the silences as well. Imagine the lives of others. If you want to be a writer, you need to get over yourself. This is not just an artistic choice; it's a moral choice. A writer attempts to understand others from the inside.
>
> —ALLEGRA GOODMAN, "So, You Want to Be a Writer? Here's How."

In a process analysis, the steps of the process are usually presented in the order in which they occur in time. Here, the first step ("To begin") is something not to do: "don't write about yourself"; it is followed by five more steps in order: start, observe, listen, replay, imagine. At the end of the paragraph comes the end result of the process: (you will) "understand others from the inside."

Comparing

With a **COMPARISON** (Chapter 10) of two or more subjects, you point out their similarities and differences. In the following paragraph, a Stanford professor of neurosurgery compares the behavior of adolescents and older adults under peer pressure:

> These traits are exacerbated when adolescents are around peers. In one study, Laurence Steinberg of Temple University discovered that adolescents and adults, when left on their own, don't differ in the risks they take in a driving simulator. Add peers egging them on and rates don't budge in adults but become significantly higher in teens. When the study is carried out in a brain scanner, the presence of peers (egging on by intercom) lessens frontal cortical activity and enhances activity in the limbic dopamine system in adolescents, but not in adults.
>
> —ROBERT SAPOLSKY, "Dude, Where's My Frontal Cortex?"

Here, the writer examines both of the subjects he is comparing in a single paragraph, moving systematically from the characteristics of one to those of the other.

Often, when comparing or contrasting two subjects, you will focus first on one of them in one paragraph and on the other in another paragraph, as in this comparison of sports and academics at the University of Texas, Austin:

> Football is the most popular spectator sport in the state of Texas without rival. The sport's importance to our heritage is well known and documented.
>
> *Vietnamese is the third-most-spoken language in the state of Texas behind English and Spanish. This is a fact that is not well known or documented.*
>
> —DAN TREADWAY, "Football vs. Asian Studies"

In the first brief paragraph, the writer focuses on two characteristics of his first subject (college football): (1) its popularity and (2) its importance to Texas's heritage, which is well known. In the second paragraph, which Treadway has italicized to indicate the change in subject, he focuses on similar characteristics of his second subject (the Vietnamese language): (1) its popularity and (2) how, in contrast to football, its importance to Texas is not well known.

Defining

A **DEFINITION** (Chapter 11) explains what something is—or is not. According to the author of this paragraph from an essay on the "brilliance" of blue-collar workers, how we define intelligence depends on a number of factors:

> I couldn't have put it in words when I was growing up, but what I observed in my mother's restaurant defined the world of adults, a place where competence was synonymous with physical work. I've since studied the working habits of blue-collar workers and have come to understand how much my mother's kind of work demands of both body and brain. A waitress acquires knowledge and intuition about the ways and the rhythms of the restaurant business. Waiting on seven to nine tables, each with two to six customers, Rosie devised memory strategies

so that she could remember who ordered what. And because she knew the average time it took to prepare different dishes, she could monitor an order that was taking too long at the service station.

—MIKE ROSE, "Blue-Collar Brilliance"

In this paragraph, the writer first presents an overly simplified definition of "competence" among "blue-collar workers" as the ability to do physical labor.

A photo of Rosie is on p. 402.
He then redefines this key term to include a mental component ("knowledge and intuition"), concluding the paragraph by observing how his mother's work as a waitress demonstrates these defining traits.

Analyzing Causes and Effects

One of the most fundamental ways of developing a paragraph is to examine what caused your subject, or what effects it may have (Chapter 12). In the following paragraph, from an essay about the power of words, the author speculates about the effects, among other subsequent events, of two public speeches—by Robert Kennedy on April 4, 1968, the night Martin Luther King Jr. was killed, and by King himself in Memphis the night before that:

After King's assassination, riots broke out in more than 100 U.S. cities— the worst destruction since the Civil War. But neither Memphis nor Indianapolis experienced that kind of damage. To this day, many believe that was due to the words spoken when so many were listening.

—TIM WENDEL, "King, Kennedy, and the Power of Words"

In a cause-and-effect analysis, the writer can proceed from cause to effect, or effect to cause. This brief but efficient paragraph does both, moving first from a known cause ("King's assassination") to a known effect ("destruction" in many U.S. cities), and then from a known effect (no destruction in two cities) to a possible cause ("words spoken when so many were listening").

INTRODUCTORY PARAGRAPHS

A well-constructed essay has a beginning, middle, and ending. Every paragraph plays an important role, but introductory paragraphs are particularly important because they represent your first chance to engage the reader.

In an introductory paragraph, you tell the reader what your essay is about—and seek to earn the reader's interest. The following introductory paragraph to an important document is as clear and stirring today as it was in 1776:

> When in the Course of human events, it becomes necessary for one people to dissolve the political bands which have connected them with another, and to assume among the powers of the earth, the separate and equal station to which the Laws of Nature and of Nature's God entitle them, a decent respect to the opinions of mankind requires that they should declare the causes which impel them to the separation.
>
> —THOMAS JEFFERSON, *The Declaration of Independence*

This paragraph tells the reader exactly what's coming in the text to follow: an inventory of the reasons for the colonies' rebellion. It also seeks to justify the writer's cause and win the sympathy of the reader by invoking a higher authority: the "Laws" of God and nature trump those of Britain's King George III. Here are a few other ways to construct an introductory paragraph that may entice your readers to read on.

Tell a story that leads into what you have to say

This introductory paragraph, from a report about research on technology and literacy, begins with two stories about how today's students read and write:

> Two stories about young people, and especially college-age students, are circulating widely today. One script sees a generation of twitterers and texters, awash in self-indulgence and narcissistic twaddle, most of it riddled with errors. The other script doesn't diminish the effects of technology, but it presents young people as running a rat race that is fueled by the Internet and its toys, anxious kids who are inundated with mountains of indigestible information yet obsessed with making the

grade, with success, with coming up with the "next big thing" but who lack the writing and speaking skills they need to do so.

> —ANDREA LUNSFORD, "Our Semi-Literate Youth? Not So Fast"

The author of this paragraph considers both stories she is reporting to be inaccurate; so after introducing them here, she goes on in the rest of the essay to tell alternative stories based on her own research.

Start with a quotation

In this example, the quotation is very short:

> Our leaders have asked for "shared sacrifice." But when they did the asking, they spared me. I checked with my mega-rich friends to learn what pain they were expecting. They, too, were left untouched.
>
> —WARREN BUFFETT, "Stop Coddling the Super-Rich"

The brief quotation in this paragraph is a reference to the following statement on the deficit by then president Barack Obama on July 16, 2011: "Simply put, it will take a balanced approach, shared sacrifice, and a willingness to make unpopular choices on all our parts." Warren Buffett could have quoted this entire statement in his introductory paragraph, of course, but Buffett's main rhetorical strategy here is to be direct and to the point.

Ask a question—or questions

This strategy should be used sparingly, but it works especially well when you want to begin with a touch of humor—or otherwise suggest that you don't have all the answers. In this opening paragraph, a mortician asks the reader for clarification before proceeding:

> Okay, so to be clear, you *don't* want to be buried alive, is that correct? Got it.
>
> —CAITLIN DOUGHTY, "What If They Bury Me When I'm Just in a Coma?"

Even if your subject doesn't exactly appeal to everyone, a strong opening paragraph like this can leave your readers eager for more—or at least willing to hear you out.

CONCLUDING PARAGRAPHS

The final paragraph of an essay should be just as satisfying as the opening paragraph. The conclusion of your essay is your last chance to drive home your point and to leave the reader with a sense of closure. Here are a few ways this is commonly done.

Restate your main point

Remind the reader what you've said, but don't just repeat your point. Add a little something new. In this passage from the closing paragraph of an essay on becoming a scientist, the writer explicitly restates the point he has been making throughout the essay—and then concludes with a qualification:

> My confessional instead is intended to illustrate an important principle I've seen unfold in the careers of many successful scientists. It is quite simple: put passion ahead of training. . . . But don't just drift through courses in science hoping that love will come to you. Maybe it will, but don't take the chance. As in other big choices in your life, there is too much at stake. Decision and hard work based on enduring passion will never fail you.
> —EDWARD O. WILSON, "First Passion, Then Training"

Throughout his essay, Wilson's point has to do with the power of passion; after repeating it in this closing paragraph, however, he adds the qualification that "decision and hard work" are also necessary to ensure success in any profession.

Show the broader significance of your subject

In an essay lamenting the death of a student at the University of South Carolina, the president of the university concludes with a broad appeal for caution when using Uber, Lyft, and other ride-hailing services:

> The country has witnessed the power and effectiveness of other public-health and safety campaigns, such as those regarding smoking and the

use of seat belts. The campaigns work and have saved countless lives. A new safety campaign—and not just for college students—is needed as ride-hailing gains in popularity. We owe it to Samantha Josephson.

—HARRIS PASTIDES, "Three Words"

The three-word question that Pastides recommends asking the driver before you get in a car you think you've ordered is, "What's my name?"

End with a recommendation

This strategy is especially appropriate when you're concluding an argument. Before recommending the following experiment, the author has argued that social media can take away the user's freedom of the will:

> But whatever form your self-exploration takes, do at least one thing: detach from the behavior-modification empires for a while—six months, say? . . . After you experiment, you'll know yourself better. Then decide.
>
> —JARON LANIER, "You Are Losing Your Free Will"

What if you decide in the end that Lanier is wrong about social media? Follow his advice and cut yourself off from the influence of algorithms for six months, he would seem to claim, and you'll be a wiser person anyway.

⇥ 5 ⇤

DESCRIPTION

D ESCRIPTION* is the pattern of writing that appeals most directly to the senses by showing us the physical characteristics of a subject—what it looks like or how it sounds, smells, feels, or tastes. A good description *shows* us such characteristics; it doesn't just tell us about them. Description is especially useful for making an **ABSTRACT** or vague subject—such as freedom or truth or death—more **CONCRETE** or definite.

For example, if you were describing an old cemetery, you might say that it was a solemn and peaceful place. In order to show the reader what the cemetery actually looked or sounded like, however, you would need to focus on the physical aspects of the scene that evoked these more abstract qualities—the marble gravestones, the earth and trees, and perhaps the mourners at the site of a new grave.

Such concrete, physical details are the heart of any description. Those details can be presented either objectively or subjectively. Consider the following caption for a photograph from the website of Arlington National Cemetery:

> Six inches of snow blanket the rolling Virginia hillside as mourners gather at a fresh burial site in Arlington National Cemetery outside Washington, D.C. Rows of simple markers identify the more than 250,000 graves that make up the military portion of the cemetery. Visited annually by more than four million people, the cemetery conducts nearly 100 funerals each week.

In an **OBJECTIVE** description like this, the author stays out of the picture. The description shows what a detached observer would see and hear—snow, roll-

*Words printed in **SMALL CAPITALS** are defined in the Glossary/Index.

ing hills, graves, and mourners—but it does not say what the observer thinks or feels *about* those things.

A **SUBJECTIVE** description, on the other hand, presents the author's thoughts and feelings along with the physical details of the scene or subject, as in this description by novelist John Updike of a cemetery in the town where he lived:

> The stones are marble, modernly glossy and simple, though I suppose that time will eventually reveal them as another fashion, dated and quaint. Now, the sod is still raw, the sutures of turf are unhealed, the earth still humped, the wreaths scarcely withered. . . . I remember my grandfather's funeral, the hurried cross of sand the minister drew on the coffin lid, the whine of the lowering straps, the lengthening, cleanly cut sides of clay, the thought of air, the lack of air forever in the close dark space lined with pink satin. . . .
>
> —JOHN UPDIKE, "Cemeteries"

This intimate description is far from detached. Not only does it give us a close-up view of the cemetery itself, but it also reports the sensations that the newly dug graves evoke in the author's mind.

Whether the concrete details of a description are presented from a subjective or an objective **POINT OF VIEW**, every detail should contribute to some **DOMINANT IMPRESSION** that the writer wants the description to make on the reader. The dominant impression we get from Updike's description, for example, is of the "foreverness" of the place. Consequently, every detail in Updike's description—from the enduring marble of the headstones to the dark, satin-lined interior of his grandfather's coffin—contributes to the sense of airless eternity that Updike recalls from his grandfather's funeral.

Joseph Krivda's description of the Vietnam War memorial on p. 89 is both subjective and objective.

Updike's references to the "raw" sod and to unhealed "sutures" in the turf show how such figures of speech as **METAPHOR, SIMILE,** and **PERSONIFICATION** can be used to make a description more vivid and concrete. This is because we often describe something by telling what it is like. A thump in your closet at night sounds like a fist hitting a table. A friend's sharp words cut like a knife. The seams of turf on new graves are like the stitches closing a wound.

As Updike's description narrows in on his grandfather's grave, we get a feeling of suffocation that directly supports the main point that the author is making about the nature of death. Death, as Updike conceives it, is no abstraction; it is the slow extinction of personal life and breath.

Updike's painful reverie is suddenly interrupted by his young son, who is learning to ride a bicycle in the peaceful cemetery. As Updike tells the story of their joyful afternoon together, the gloom of the cemetery fades into the background—as descriptive writing often does. Description frequently plays a supporting role within other **PATTERNS OF WRITING**; it may serve, for example, to set the scene for a **NARRATIVE** (as in Updike's essay), or it may provide the background for an **ARGUMENT** about the significance of a national cemetery.

Almost as important as the physical details in a description is the order in which those details are presented. Beginning with the glossy stones of the cemetery and the earth around them, Updike's description comes to focus on the interior of a particular grave. It moves from outside to inside and from the general to the specific. A good description can proceed from outside in, or inside out, top to bottom,

The dominant impression of a description of a swimming pool, p. 101, is one of nostalgia.

front to back, or in any other direction—so long as it moves systematically in a way that is in keeping with the dominant impression it is supposed to give and that supports the main point the description is intended to make.

In the following description of a boy's room, the writer is setting the stage for the larger narrative—in this case, a fairy tale:

> The room was so spare one could see everything at a glance: a closet door with a lock on it, a long table with five perfect constructions— three ships, two dragons—nothing else on the table but a neat stack of stainless-steel razor blades. What defined all the rest, of course, was that immense desk and chair. They made it seem that the room itself was from a picture book, or better yet, a stage-set, for across one end hung a dark green curtain. Beyond that, presumably, the professor's son crouched, hiding. My gaze stopped and froze on an enormous bare foot that protruded, unbeknownst to its owner, no doubt, from behind the curtain. It was the largest human foot I'd ever seen or imagined. . . .
>
> —JOHN GARDNER, *Freddy's Book*

This description of the lair of a boy giant is pure fantasy, of course. What makes it appear so realistic is the systematic way in which Gardner presents the objects in the room. First we see the closet door, a feature we might find in any boy's bedroom. Next comes the lock. Even an ordinary boy might keep the contents of his closet under lock and key. The long table with the models and razor blades is the first hint that something unusual may be at play. And when we see the oversized desk and chair, we truly begin to suspect that this is no ordinary room and no ordinary boy. But it is not until our gaze falls upon the enormous foot protruding from beneath the curtain that we know for sure we have entered the realm of make-believe.

Fanciful as the details of Gardner's description may be, his systematic method of presenting them is instructive for composing more down-to-earth descriptions. Also, by watching how Gardner presents the details of Freddy's room from a consistent VANTAGE POINT, we can see how he builds up to a dominant impression of awe and wonder.

A BRIEF GUIDE TO WRITING A DESCRIPTION

As you write a description, you need to identify who or what you're describing, say what your subject looks or feels like, and indicate the traits you plan to focus on. Cherokee Paul McDonald makes these basic moves of description in the beginning of his essay in this chapter:

> He was a lumpy little guy with baggy shorts, a faded T-shirt and heavy sweat socks falling down over old sneakers. . . . Covering his eyes and part of his face was a pair of those stupid-looking '50s-style wraparound sunglasses.
>
> —CHEROKEE PAUL MCDONALD, "A View from the Bridge"

McDonald identifies what he's describing (a "little guy"); says what his subject looks like ("lumpy," "with baggy shorts, a faded T-shirt and heavy sweat socks"); and hints at characteristics (his "stupid-looking" sunglasses) that he might focus on. Here is one more example from this chapter:

> But the center of it all was that gleaming, glorious swimming pool. Memories of Dreamland, drenched in the smell of chlorine, Coppertone, and french fries, were what almost everyone who grew up in Portsmouth took with them as the town declined.
>
> —SAM QUINONES, "Dreamland"

The following guidelines will help you to make these basic moves as you draft a description—and to come up with your subject; consider your purpose and audience; generate ideas; state your point; create a dominant impression of your subject; use figurative language; and arrange the details of your description effectively.

Coming Up with a Subject

A primary resource for finding a subject is your own experience. You will often want to describe something familiar from your past—the lake in which you learned to swim, the neighborhood where you grew up, a person from

your hometown. Also consider more recent experiences or less familiar subjects that you might investigate further, such as crowd behavior
at a hockey game, an unusual T-shirt, or a popular bookstore.
Whatever subject you choose, be sure that you will be able to
describe it vividly for your readers by appealing to their senses.

Edward Lee discov-
ered "slaw dogs"
(described on
p. 123) while on
a road trip.

Considering Your Purpose and Audience

Your **PURPOSE** in describing something—whether to view your subject objectively, express your feelings about it, convince the reader to visit it (or not), or
simply amuse your reader—will determine the details you include. Before you
start composing, decide whether your purpose will be primarily objective (as
in a lab report) or subjective (as in a personal essay about your grandmother's
cooking). Although both approaches provide information, an **OBJECTIVE**
description presents its subject impartially, whereas a **SUBJECTIVE** description conveys the writer's personal response to the subject.

Whatever your purpose, you need to take into account how much your
AUDIENCE already knows (or does not know) about your subject. For example,
if you happen to attend a large state university and you want to describe to
someone who has never been on your campus the mad rush that takes place
when classes change, you're going to have to provide some background: the
main quadrangle with its sun worshippers, the brick-and-stone classroom
buildings on either side, the library looming at one end. On the other hand, if
you were to describe this same locale to fellow students, you could skip the
background description and go directly to the mob scene.

Generating Ideas: Asking What Something
Looks, Sounds, Feels, Smells, and Tastes Like

Good descriptive writing is built on **CONCRETE** particulars rather than
ABSTRACT qualities. So don't just write, "It was a dark and stormy night";
make your reader see, hear, and feel the wind and the rain, as E. B. White does
at the end of "Once More to the Lake," pp. 19–25. To come up with specific
details, observe your subject, ask questions, and take notes. Experience

your subject as though you were a reporter on assignment or a traveler in a strange land.

One of your richest sources of ideas for a description—especially if you are describing something from the past—is memory. Ask friends or parents to help you remember details accurately and truthfully. Jog your own memory by asking, "What *did* the place (or object) look like exactly? What did it sound like? What did it smell or taste like?" Recovering the treasures of your memory is a little like fishing: think back to the spots you knew well; bait the hook by asking these key sensory questions; weigh and measure everything you pull up. Later on, you can throw back the ideas you can't use.

In "The Miss Dennis School of Writing," p. 112, Alice Steinbach draws upon her memories of a favorite teacher.

Templates for Describing

The following templates can help you generate ideas for a description and then start drafting. Don't take these as formulas where you just have to fill in the blanks. There are no easy formulas for good writing. But these templates can help you plot out some of the key moves of description and thus may serve as good starting points.

> ▶ The main physical characteristics of X are _____, _____, and _____.
>
> ▶ From the perspective of _____, however, X could be described as _____.
>
> ▶ In some ways, namely _____, X resembles _____; but in other ways, X is more like _____.
>
> ▶ X is not at all like _____ because _____.
>
> ▶ Mainly because of _____ and _____, X gives the impression of being _____.
>
> ▶ From this description of X, you can see that _____.

For more techniques to help you generate ideas and start writing a descriptive essay, see Chapter 3.

Stating Your Point

E. B. White makes his point about time and mortality with a single chilling phrase (p. 25, par. 13).

We usually describe something to someone for a reason. Why are you describing bloody footprints in the snow? You need to let the reader know, either formally or informally. One formal way is to include an explicit **THESIS STATEMENT:** "This description of Washington's ragged army at Yorktown shows that the American general faced many of the same challenges as Napoleon in the winter battle for Moscow, but Washington turned them to his advantage."

Or your reasons can be stated more informally. If you are writing a descriptive travel essay, for example, you might state your point as a personal observation: "Chicago is an architectural delight in any season, but I prefer to visit from April through October because of the city's brutal winters."

Creating a Dominant Impression

Some descriptions appeal to several senses: the sight of fireflies, the sound of crickets, the touch of a hand—all on a summer evening. Whether you appeal to a single sense or several, make sure they all contribute to the **DOMINANT IMPRESSION** you want your description to make on the reader. For example, if you want an evening scene on the porch to convey an impression of danger, you probably won't include details about fireflies and crickets. Instead, you might call the reader's attention to dark clouds in the distance, the rising wind, crashing thunder, and the sound of footsteps drawing closer. In short, you will choose details that play an effective part in creating your dominant impression: a sense of danger and foreboding.

Even though you want to create a dominant impression, don't begin your description with a general statement of what that impression is sup-

E. B. White's description of a lake, p. 20, gives a sense of tranquility and timelessness.

posed to be. Instead, start with descriptive details, and let your readers form the impression for themselves. A good description doesn't *tell* readers what to think or feel; it *shows* them point by point. The dominant impression that John Gardner creates in his systematic description of Freddy's room, for instance, is a growing sense of awe and wonder. But he does so by taking us step by step into unfamiliar territory. If you were describing an actual room or other place—and you wanted to create a similar dominant impression in your reader's mind—you would likewise direct the reader's gaze to more familiar objects first (table, chairs, fireplace) and then to increasingly unfamiliar ones (a shotgun, polar bear skins on the floor, an elderly lady mending a reindeer harness).

Using Figurative Language

Figures of speech can help make almost any description more vivid or colorful. The three figures of speech you are most likely to use in composing a description are similes, metaphors, and personification.

SIMILES tell the reader what something looks, sounds, or feels like, using *like* or *as*: "Either way, or both, he died like a bug under a microscope" (Stephen King, *The Long Walk*).

METAPHORS make implicit comparisons, without *like* or *as*: "All the world's a stage" (William Shakespeare, *As You Like It*). Like similes, metaphors have two parts: the subject of the description ("world") and the thing ("stage") to which that subject is being implicitly compared.

PERSONIFICATION assigns human qualities to inanimate objects, as Sylvia Plath does in her poem "Mirror," in which she has the mirror speak as a person would: "I have no preconceptions. / Whatever I see I swallow immediately."

Arranging the Details from a Consistent Vantage Point

The physical configuration of whatever you're describing will usually suggest a pattern of organization. Descriptions of places are often organized by direction—north to south, front to back, left to right, inside to outside, near to far, top to bottom. If you were describing a room, for example, you might use an outside-to-inside order, starting with the door or the doorknob.

An object or person can also suggest an order of arrangement. If you were describing a large fish, for instance, you might let the anatomy of the fish guide your description, moving from its glistening scales to the mouth, eyes, belly, and tail. When constructing a description, you can go from whole to parts, or parts to whole; from most important to least important features (or vice versa); from largest to smallest, specific to general, or concrete to abstract—or vice versa.

Whatever organization you choose, be careful to maintain a consistent VANTAGE POINT. In other words, be sure to describe your subject from one position or perspective—across the room, from the bridge, face-to-face, under the bed, and so on. Do not include details that you are unable to see, hear, feel, smell, or taste from your particular vantage point. Before you fully reveal any objects or people that lie outside the reader's line of sight—such as a boy giant behind a curtain—you will need to cross the room and fling open the door or curtain that conceals them. If your vantage point (or that of your NARRATOR) changes while you are describing a subject, be sure to let your reader know that you have moved from one location to another, as in the following description of a robbery: "After I was pushed behind the counter of the Quik-Mart, I could no longer see the three men in ski masks, but I could hear them yelling at the owner to open up the register."

EDITING FOR COMMON ERRORS IN DESCRIPTIVE WRITING

Like other kinds of writing, description uses distinctive patterns of language and punctuation—and thus invites typical kinds of errors. The following tips will help you check for and correct these common errors in your own descriptive writing.

Check descriptive details to make sure they are concrete

> ▶ When I visited Great Pond, the lake in E. B. White's essay, it was so ~~amazing and incredible~~ <u>clear and deep</u> that floating on it in a boat seemed like floating on air.

"Amazing" and "incredible" are ABSTRACT terms; "clear" and "deep" describe the water in more CONCRETE terms.

> ▶ The Belgrade region is famous for its ~~charming views~~ <u>panoramic views of green fields, rolling hills, and deep woodlands.</u>

The revised sentence says more precisely what makes the views charming.

Check for filler words like "very," "quite," "really," and "truly"

> ► The lake was ~~very much secluded~~ fifteen miles from the nearest village.

Check that adjectives appear in the right order

Subjective adjectives (those that reflect the writer's own opinion) go before objective adjectives (those that are strictly factual): write "fabulous four-door Chevrolet" rather than "four-door fabulous Chevrolet." Beyond that, adjectives usually go in the following order: number, size, shape, age, color, nationality.

> ► The streets of Havana were lined with many ~~old, big~~ big, old American cars.

Check for common usage errors

UNIQUE, PERFECT

Don't use "more" or "most," "less" or "least," or "very" before words like "unique," "equal," "perfect," or "infinite." Either something is unique or it isn't.

> ► Their house at the lake was a ~~very~~ unique place.

AWESOME, COOL, INCREDIBLE

Not only are these modifiers too abstract, they're overused. You probably should delete them or replace them with fresher words no matter how grand the scene you're describing.

> ► The Ohio River is ~~an awesome river~~ approximately 981 miles long.

A Cheesy Label

When you describe something, you tell what its main attributes and characteristics are. A cheese, for instance, can be strong or mild in taste, hard or soft in texture, white or yellow in color—and anywhere in between. Made in Wisconsin, the Italian-style cheese described on this label is moderately strong, hard, and white. It also costs $6.39. An effective description emphasizes the most distinctive qualities of its subject, however. The folks in the marketing department at the Sartori Company ("Established 1939") recognize this. Inspired by the name of their product *MontAmoré*, which means "Mount Love" in French, they skip over the cheese's more common features and go to the seductive specifics. This cheese is "sweet, creamy, and fruity." It also has a spicy aftertaste ("finishes with a playful bite"). As the label warns, "Prepare to fall in love."

JOSEPH KRIVDA

THE WALL

JOSEPH KRIVDA is from Kensington, Maryland; his parents and three siblings have all served in the military or are about to. When he wrote "The Wall," Krivda was an ROTC cadet at the University of Notre Dame with a major in biological sciences and a minor in philosophy. His long-term plan is to become a physician in the US Army Medical Corps. "The Wall," which was published in *Fresh Writing*, University of Notre Dame's journal of student writing, was inspired by Krivda's visits to the National Mall in Washington, DC, combined with his family's military background and interest in military history. In this essay, Krivda describes the Vietnam Veterans Memorial and makes a larger point about the way memorials reflect our complex and sometimes conflicting feelings about war itself.

The Wall

The Vietnam War Memorial on the National Mall in   1
Washington, D.C., stands out from the structures surrounding it, but not because it actually stands out.[1] In
fact, this monument is not very monumental at all. While
the World War II Memorial lies in the center of the Mall
with complex fountains and wreathed pillars representing
the fifty states, the Vietnam War Memorial is a singular,
long, black wall built into the ground, bearing the names
of the war's dead. There is no victory being celebrated, no
commemoration of defended freedom, but a simple display
of respect to those who gave their lives for a country's
broken call.

The Vietnam War was hugely controversial, with   2
much of America opposing it. American men were fighting and dying to "stop the spread of communism," but to
many Americans, we were losing thousands upon thousands of American lives to protect a country we had no
business protecting (Ankony). The war was also rampant
with drug abuse, a problem that greatly affected its veterans. There were no systems in place to help Vietnam veterans like there were after World War II, and many
returned to a place with an antiwar culture. These vets
often ended up homeless and in dire conditions (Ankony).

Why would we, as a nation, build a memorial for   3
this? The answer is simple. American soldiers gave their
lives for their country. No matter what the context was
surrounding the war, brave people gave the ultimate sacrifice and deserve to be remembered for it. Maya Lin, as

1. Any opinions present in this essay belong to the author and do not
represent the views of the United States Army [Krivda's note].

Margin note beside paragraph 1: A single sentence provides CONCRETE details about the memorial's appearance

Margin note beside paragraph 2: This paragraph describes the "controversial" nature of the Vietnam War itself

an undergraduate student, understood this perfectly
when she submitted her "nihilistic slab of stone," as it
was called by James Webb, a decorated Vietnam veteran
and politician (Wills), for a design contest commissioned
by the United States government in 1981.[2] After it was
announced that her design had won the contest, it
immediately received strong opposition from many,
including James Webb. Despite this opposition, Lin held
firm to her design.

While Lin is paying tribute to the casualties of the   4
Vietnam War, Lin's design and the way it contrasts with
other war memorials captures America's general dislike of
the war. The wall was not constructed on a hill for all to

2. Webb was a Marine lieutenant and a platoon leader who was
awarded the Navy Cross, Silver Star, two Bronze Stars, and two Purple Hearts for his heroism in Vietnam. He then graduated from
Georgetown Law School and went on to become the Secretary of the
Navy and a senator of Virginia (Drew).

see, nor is it freestanding. Lin designed it to be built into the ground, like a common retaining wall one would see in a suburban backyard, making it very insignificant compared to the Washington Monument, Lincoln Memorial, and World War II Memorial that surround it. All three of these monuments are in the center of the Mall while the Vietnam Memorial is off to the north side, away from a tourist's typical walking path.

The contrast between the Vietnam and World War II　5 Memorials is telling. The World War II Memorial has an elaborate structure that seems to glorify the war. It celebrates our victory over fascism, making anyone who walks around it feel proud to be an American; the Vietnam Memorial, on the other hand, has quite a different effect. When one walks down that black wall, reading the names of those who sacrificed themselves for a battle that they ultimately lost, one feels a wave of sadness sap the excitement out of a day visiting the monuments. The simplicity of the structure gives it its power—power that can be seen at the memorial every day through the tears shed by veterans taking in their fallen comrades' names. Its lack of ornament gives it a solemn feel that facilitates reflection on those we have lost and the sacrifice they made. It does not glorify war, but pressures one to ponder why we were even in Vietnam and why those people had to die.

It's hard to drive through downtown Washington,　6 D.C., without passing an old man with a scraggly beard and camo jacket holding a brown cardboard sign with something like "Homeless. Vietnam Vet. Please Help. God Bless" written on it in black Sharpie. After World War II, new systems like the G.I. Bill, which provided

Uses COMPARISON (Chapter 10) to capture the "simplicity" of the memorial

Moves from an objective point of view to a more subjective (p. 82) one

veterans with money for education, home loans, health care, and unemployment benefits, were put in place to help veterans, and hiring veterans was highly encouraged. But apparently we forgot about this after the Vietnam War. Not much changed in these veteran benefit programs to account for the differences between the two wars, both in terms of what veterans experienced while in combat and society's attitudes toward the war. Maya Lin's memorial design recognizes this in its color scheme. The wall is black the whole way down, representing the war and how it was a dark time for those involved, but the names of the ones who were lost appear in white. This shows how those who served are the ones meant to be remembered. It shows veterans that they and their fallen comrades are being memorialized, not the war itself. The color white suggests that each soldier was a light in a time of darkness, and because every name is the same color, that light includes all veterans whether they are senators or people begging on a street corner.

To explain the colors of the wall, Krivda uses the SIMILE of light and darkness

While the majority of the details on the memorial suggest an antiwar perspective, there is one subtle detail that cannot be ignored. The memorial is in the shape of a wide "V." This wide "V" is positioned so that one leg points at the Lincoln Memorial and the other at the Washington Monument. This addresses the war's complexity. Even though there will always inevitably be casualties of war, when it comes down to it, war is often a necessary evil to protect the values that George Washington and Abraham Lincoln fought to put in place: our freedom and equality. As the World War II Memorial shows, victories against oppression and genocide, coupled with

7

the upholding of freedom and equality, can justify war. The Vietnam War Memorial silently shouts this at us, as if to say the original intentions of the war justified it, but as the war progressed, the accumulation of white names pulled it out of the main section of the Mall and into the ground.

The Vietnam War Memorial makes many arguments as to what constitutes a truly great memorial. Maya Lin went through with her design despite opposition because she knew that it was something special. The memorial being built into the ground and off to the side of the National Mall's main drag shows America's opposition to troops in Vietnam. The white names on a black surface testify that the soldiers were the ones to be memorialized, not the war itself or anything the war could have gained for us as a nation. Finally, its wide "V" shape pointing to the Washington Monument and the Lincoln Memorial remind us that if freedom and equality are in jeopardy, fighting can be necessary. The Vietnam War Memorial shows us that even on a national level, we can recognize our mistakes and attempt to heal our wounds.

Krivda combines description and ARGUMENT (Chapter 13) to conclude that the wall is a "truly great" memorial

8

Works Cited

Ankony, Robert. "Perspectives." *Vietnam Magazine*, 13 June 2015, www.robertankony.com/publications /perspectives. Accessed 12 Oct. 2014.

Drew, Elizabeth. "The Jim Webb Story." Review of *A Time to Fight: Reclaiming a Fair and Just America*, by Jim Webb. *The New York Review of Books*, 26 June 2008, www.nybooks.com/articles/2008/06/26/the-jim -webb-story. Accessed 7 Dec. 2014.

United States, Department of Veterans Affairs. "VA History." *U.S. Department of Veterans Affairs*, United States Government, 17 Nov. 2014, www.va.gov/about _va/vahistory.asp. Accessed 7 Dec. 2014.

Wills, Denise Kersten. "The Vietnam Memorial's History." *The Washingtonian*, 1 Nov. 2007, www.washingtonian .com/2007/11/01/the-vietnam-memorials-history, Accessed 12 Oct. 2014.

PRIYA CHANDRASEKARAN

CUTTING OUR GRANDMOTHERS' SARIS

PRIYA CHANDRASEKARAN teaches environmental studies at Hamilton College in Clinton, New York. She is a graduate of Cornell University and holds advanced degrees from the University of Mississippi, the New School, and the City University of New York, where she earned a PhD in cultural anthropology. Formerly a college writing teacher and a field researcher throughout the global South, she now focuses her research on women farmers and small-scale agriculture in India. In 2019, she was awarded a fellowship by the American Association of University Women. "Cutting Our Grandmothers' Saris," written when Chandrasekaran was still in graduate school, describes not only the colorful, flowing *saris*—from the Sanskrit "strip of cloth"—that her grandmother bequeathed to her; it describes the dilemma that such an inheritance poses—and what the granddaughter made of it.

I'M NO SEAMSTRESS, but when my aunt showed me my grandmother's saris, 1
I knew I was going to make something. The saris, new and old, were stacked
high in two columns of brilliant colors. When I told my aunt of my intention
to make a quilt, she was incredulous. These saris were valuable, meant to be
worn, not cut.

Until then, I'd never seen my grandmother in anything but a sari. As a 2
child visiting India, I couldn't understand how she could sleep comfortably on
sweltering nights wrapped in six yards of material, or how she could still look
impeccable when she woke. Now, bedridden and on oxygen, blind in one eye,
and having recently had a stroke, she wore nothing but a loose nightshirt that
flapped open, exposing a degree of nakedness I'd never imagined she had.

When I began the project well after her death, I didn't wash the saris. 3
The stains and scents were evidence of the life she had lived, so different from
my own. Hers was a life of cooking curries, wearing turmeric, walking barefoot on dusty floors, participating in Hindu rituals, drinking milky coffee
after afternoon naps, and clutching loved ones fiercely to her chest.

But when it came time to cut the cloth, I found myself resistant. It 4
wasn't my mother's allegations of blasphemy, so much as the fact that this
fabric—so soft, so luxurious—had caressed my grandmother's skin, reflected
her modesty, embodied her womanhood, shielded her from the sun, and made
her feel beautiful. That her hand had pleated the folds of seamless silk countless times, and that my cut, once made, would forever alter that sari's potential to live a similar life.

"Do it," I finally commanded myself. So I did. 5

After that, the work became straightforward. When the quilt was fin- 6
ished, one could see that the edges of each panel didn't quite match, that the
soft lavender and deep crimson from one sari clashed slightly with the brilliant yellow and green from another, that the stitches were crude and uneven.
Yet beheld in unison, these imperfections fashioned something only I could
have created, beautiful in its own way.

I believe we are entitled to cut our grandmothers' saris, that they were 7
not meant to hang in dark closets collecting dust. I believe that
what we create from them should make us proud, and also humble
us. I believe that not every stain needs to be rubbed out, and that
cutting the cloth can help maintain its integrity.

Parallel structures
(pp. 64–65) help to
pull the writer's
ideas together as
she builds up to a
conclusion.

I believe that to love, and to bare the boundless depth of our love, we must   8
have the courage to reshape what we inherit.

FOR DISCUSSION

1. At first, Priya Chandrasekaran hesitates to cut up the colorful garments she has inherited from her grandmother simply for the purpose of making a quilt. Why is she so reluctant to do so?
2. Chandrasekaran decides to make the quilt anyway. Is she right to overcome her hesitation, or should she have listened to her aunt who thinks the saris are "to be worn, not cut" (1)? Why do you think so?
3. "I'm no seamstress," Chandrasekaran says at the beginning of her essay (1). Judging from her description of her work in paragraph 6, how accurate is this disclaimer, and why might she have included it?
4. In addition to being a writer and a writing teacher, Chandrasekaran was trained as a cultural anthropologist. How might her descriptive essay also be seen as a cultural study?

STRATEGIES AND STRUCTURES

1. Although she refers to "six yards of material," Chandrasekaran never actually says what a sari is (2). Should she have included a formal **DEFINITION** of this form of dress, or is she right just to let her description carry the weight? Explain.
2. In addition to **DESCRIBING** her grandmother's clothes, Chandrasekaran also describes her grandmother's life. Where and how does she do this most effectively?
3. In paragraph 6, Chandrasekaran describes the quilt she made. What specific qualities and characteristics does she ascribe to it? What does the quilt have in common with the other things she has been describing?
4. At the end of her description, Chandrasekaran makes a claim about the nature of inheritance. What's the point of this **ARGUMENT**, and how does she support it?

WORDS AND FIGURES OF SPEECH

1. When she proposes to make a quilt out of the saris, says Chandrasekaran, her aunt was "incredulous" (1). How does Chandrasekaran's use of this word, which means "disbelieving," help prepare for what comes later in her essay?
2. "Blasphemy" is speech that profanes something sacred (4). Why does Chandrasekaran's mother appropriate the term to describe what her niece plans to do with the saris?

3. When Chandrasekaran first uses the word "stain," she is referring to literal stains in her grandmother's clothes (3). What is she talking about by the end of her essay when she says that "not every stain needs to be rubbed out" (7)? Explain the **METAPHOR**.

4. **METONYMY** is a figure of speech that identifies something by giving it the name of one of its parts or attributes—for example, calling a businessman a "suit." How might "seamstress" be considered an example of metonymy (1)?

FOR WRITING

1. In a paragraph, describe an article of clothing or other object that has been handed down to you or someone you know. Be sure to explain how and why the object is significant.

2. Write a brief essay that captures someone's character and personality by describing that person's clothes, car, truck, other valued possessions, workplace, or home. Include **CONCRETE**, physical details as well as more **ABSTRACT** qualities and traits.

3. Write an essay in which you argue that "we must have the courage to reshape what we inherit" (8). Describe in specific detail both something inherited and how it is to be reshaped—even if the inheritance is a general condition or way of thinking. Give particular reasons and examples to support your claim.

SAM QUINONES

DREAMLAND

SAM QUINONES (b. 1958) is a journalist known for his reporting on Mexico and the many intersections of Mexican and American culture. A native of Claremont, California, Quinones graduated from the University of California, Berkeley, before becoming a journalist at the *Orange County Register*, a daily newspaper in California, and later the *Los Angeles Times*. His books, beginning with *True Tales from Another Mexico* (2001), combine reportage and storytelling. In *Dreamland: The True Tale of America's Opiate Epidemic* (2015), Quinones uses Portsmouth, Ohio, to illustrate how a once-idyllic small-town America has been devastated in recent decades by both economic decline and an epidemic of addiction to opiates. In the following selection, which is the prologue to the book, Quinones uses abstract and concrete details to describe Dreamland, the "gleaming, glorious swimming pool" that for many was the place of "chlorine, Coppertone, and french fries."

I N 1929, three decades into what were the great years for the blue-collar town 1 of Portsmouth, on the Ohio River, a private swimming pool opened and they called it Dreamland.

The pool was the size of a football field. Over the decades, generations of 2 the town grew up at the edge of its crystal-blue water.

Dreamland was the summer babysitter. Parents left their children at the 3 pool every day. Townsfolk found respite from the thick humidity at Dreamland and then went across the street to the A&W stand for hot dogs and root beer. The pool's french fries were the best around. Kids took the bus to the pool in the morning, and back home in the afternoon. They came from schools all over Scioto County and met each other and learned to swim. Some of them competed on the Dreamland Dolphins swim team, which practiced every morning and evening. WIOI, the local radio station, knowing so many of its listeners were sunbathing next to their transistor radios at Dreamland, would broadcast a jingle—"Time to turn so you won't burn"—every half hour.

The vast pool had room in the middle for two concrete platforms, from 4 which kids sunned themselves, then dove back in. Poles topped with floodlights rose from the platforms for swimming at night. On one side of the pool was an immense lawn where families set their towels. On the opposite side were locker rooms and a restaurant.

Dreamland could fit hundreds of people, and yet, magically, the space 5 around it kept growing and there was always room for more. Jaime Williams, the city treasurer, owned the pool for years. Williams was part owner of one of the shoe factories that were at the core of Portsmouth's industrial might. He bought more and more land, and for years Dreamland seemed to just get better. A large picnic area was added, and playgrounds for young children. Then fields for softball and football, and courts for basketball and shuffleboard, and a video arcade.

For a while, to remain white only, the pool became a private club and the 6 name changed to the Terrace Club. But Portsmouth was a largely integrated town. Its chief of police was black. Black and white kids went to the same schools. Only the pool remained segregated. Then, in the summer of 1961, a black boy named Eugene McKinley drowned in the Scioto River, where he was swimming because he was kept out of the pool. The Portsmouth NAACP pushed back, held a wade-in, and quietly they integrated the pool. With integration, the pool was rechristened Dreamland, though blacks were never made to feel particularly comfortable there.

Dreamland did wash away class distinctions, though. In a swimming 7
suit, a factory worker looked no different from the factory manager or clothing-shop owner. Wealthy families on Portsmouth's hilltop donated money to a fund that would go to pay for summer passes for families from the town's East End, down between the tracks and the Ohio River. East End river rats and upscale hilltoppers all met at Dreamland.

California had its beaches. Heartland America spent its summers at 8
swimming pools, and, down at a far end of Ohio, Dreamland took on an out-

Page 85 explains sized importance to the town of Portsmouth. A family's season
how to describe
something from a pass was only twenty-five dollars, and this was a prized posses-
consistent vantage sion often given as a Christmas present. Kids whose families
point like this.
couldn't afford that could cut a neighbor's grass for the fifteen

cents that a daily pool pass cost.

Friday swim dances began at midnight. They hauled out a jukebox and 9
kids spent the night twisting by the pool. Couples announced new romances by walking hand in hand around Dreamland. Girls walked home from those dances and families left their doors unlocked. "The heat of the evening combined with the cool water was wonderful," one woman remembered. "It was my entire world. I did nothing else. As I grew up and had my own children, I took them, too."

In fact, the cycle of life in Portsmouth was repeated over and over at 10
Dreamland. A toddler spent her first years at the shallow end watched by her parents, particularly her mother, who sat on a towel on the concrete near the water with other young moms. When the child left elementary school, she migrated out to the middle section of Dreamland as her parents retreated to the grass. By high school, she was hanging out on the grass around the pool's ten-foot deep end, near the high dive and the head lifeguard's chair, and her parents were far away. When she married and had children, she returned to the shallow end of Dreamland to watch over her own children, and the whole thing began again.

"My father, a Navy Vet from WWII, insisted that his 4 children learn 11
not only how to swim but how not to be afraid of water," one man wrote. "My younger sister jumped off the 15-foot high diving board at age 3. Yes, my

father, myself & brother were in the water just in case. Sister pops up out of the water and screams . . . 'Again!'"

For many years, Dreamland's manager, Chuck Lorentz, a Portsmouth High School coach and strict disciplinarian, walked the grounds with a yardstick, making sure teenagers minded his "three-foot rule" and stayed that far apart. He wasn't that successful. It seems half the town got their first kiss at the pool, and plenty lost their virginity in Dreamland's endless grass.   12

Lorentz's son, meanwhile, learned to swim before he could walk and became a Dreamland lifeguard in high school. "To be the lifeguard in that chair, you were right in the center of all the action, all the strutting, all the flirting," said John Lorentz, now a retired history professor. "You were like a king on a throne."   13

Through these years, Portsmouth also supported two bowling alleys, a JCPenney, a Sears, and a Montgomery Ward[1] with an escalator, and locally owned Marting's Department Store, with a photo studio where graduating seniors had their portraits taken. Chillicothe Street bustled. Big U.S.-made sedans and station wagons lined the street. People cashed their checks at the Kresge's[2] on Saturdays, and the owners of Morgan Brothers Jewelry, Herrmann's Meats, Counts' Bakery, and Atlas Fashion earned a middle-class living. Kids took the bus downtown to the movie theater or for cherry Cokes at Smith's Drugstore and stayed out late trick-or-treating on Halloween. On Friday and Saturday nights, teenagers cruised Chillicothe Street, from Staker's Drugs down to Smith's, then turned around and did it again.   14

Throughout the year, the shoe factories would deduct Christmas Club money from each worker's paycheck. Before Christmas, they issued each worker a check and he would cash it at the bank. Chillicothe Street was festive then. Bells rang as shoppers went shoulder to shoulder, watching the mechanical puppets in displays in store windows painted with candy canes, Christmas trees, and snowmen. Marting's had a Santa on its second floor.   15

So, in 1979 and 1980, Portsmouth felt worthy to be selected an All-American City. The town had more than forty-two thousand people then.   16

1. A national chain of department stores in business from 1872 to 2001.
2. A national chain of stores no longer in business, known for selling merchandise at low prices.

Very few were wealthy, and the U.S. Labor Department would have gauged
many Portsmouthians poor. "But we weren't aware of it, nor did we care," one

Using memory to
generate ideas for
a description is
discussed on p. 83.
woman recalled. Its industry supported a community for all. No
one had pools in their backyards. Rather, there were parks, tennis
and basketball courts, and window-shopping and levees to slide
down. Families ice-skated at Millbrook Park in winter and picnicked at Roosevelt Lake in summer, or sat late into the evening as their kids played Kick
the Can in the street.

"My family used to picnic down by the Ohio River in a little park, where   17
my dad would push me so high on the swings I thought I'd land in Kentucky,"
another woman said.

All of this recreation let a working-class family feel well-off. But the center   18
of it all was that gleaming, glorious swimming pool. Memories of Dreamland,
drenched in the smell of chlorine, Coppertone, and french fries, were what almost
everyone who grew up in Portsmouth took with them as the town declined.

Two Portsmouths exist today. One is a town of abandoned buildings at   19
the edge of the Ohio River. The other resides in the memories of thousands in
the town's diaspora who grew up during its better years and return to the
actual Portsmouth rarely, if at all.

When you ask them what the town was back then, it was Dreamland.   20

FOR DISCUSSION

1. After its opening in Portsmouth, Ohio, in 1929, Dreamland, the immense swimming pool described in detail by Sam Quinones, "took on an outsized importance to the town" (8). Why? What was so significant about the pool to the townspeople—and to Quinones himself as a reporter writing about "Heartland America" (8)?

2. What were some of the sources of the "industrial might" of a town like Portsmouth in the years leading up to its designation in 1979 as an "All-American City" (5, 16)? How and why has the region changed since then?

3. How and how well did the town of Portsmouth adapt to the racial integration of Dreamland in 1961 (6), according to Quinones?

4. According to Quinones, how did a members-only swimming pool "wash away class distinctions" in the town (7)? What other places can you think of that might have a similar effect?

STRATEGIES AND STRUCTURES

1. In its heyday, says Quinones, the pool at Dreamland was "vast" (4). Point to some of the specific details in his description that convey the pool's immense size and any other physical attributes of the pool that you noticed.

2. What other **ABSTRACT** qualities—for example, a sense of timelessness—do Quinones and the townspeople associate with Dreamland? Cite details in the text that you find particularly effective at capturing these less **CONCRETE** aspects of the place.

3. Most of Quinones's description is devoted to the pool. Where does he describe other parts of the town? What **DOMINANT IMPRESSION** of the place does he convey here? What do all the names of stores and businesses (14) contribute to this impression? Why is it relevant, for example, that one department store had an escalator?

4. Quinones is not only describing a place and time but also the inhabitants' *recollections* of that place and time. Which particular memories and associations do you find most compelling? Why?

5. How and how well do the specific physical details and memories in Quinones's description contribute to the idea of Portsmouth as a place in a dream? Why might Quinones seek to give this impression?

WORDS AND FIGURES OF SPEECH

1. For purposes of capturing a place and region as they were "back then," why is "Dreamland" a more descriptive name than, say, "Terrace Club" (6, 20)?

2. The manager of Dreamland often carried a yardstick to enforce his "three-foot rule" (12). Explain the **PUN** on "rule" here. How well did the rule work?

3. "Time to turn so you won't burn" (3)—whose slogan was this, according to Quinones? What does it tell the reader about life in the summer during Portsmouth's heyday?

4. For many of the townspeople, their memories of Dreamland are "drenched in the smell of chlorine, Coppertone, and french fries" (18). How and how well do these three terms sum up Quinones's description?

5. The word "diaspora" (19) usually refers to the movement or migration of an entire people from their ancestral homeland. By using this term in a description of present-day Portsmouth, what is Quinones suggesting about the scope and scale of the town's decline?

FOR WRITING

1. In a single paragraph, Quinones describes an entire "cycle of life" in Portsmouth of an earlier day (10). Write a paragraph describing such a cycle of a place in your past. Organize it by time, as Quinones does—and give it a beginning, middle, and ending that circles back to the beginning.

2. Write a description of a swimming pool, amusement park, or other place of recreation that you particularly associate with growing up. Choose details that convey not only what the place meant to you but also to the larger community. Be sure to indicate how it has changed over the years.

3. Based on Quinones's description (and your own experience), write an essay explaining why a town like Portsmouth, Ohio, is (or is not) representative of what has happened to "Heartland America" (8) in recent decades. In place of Portsmouth, feel free to focus on a town or other place that is more familiar to you—or that you think is an even better **EXAMPLE**.

CHEROKEE PAUL MCDONALD

A VIEW FROM THE BRIDGE

CHEROKEE PAUL MCDONALD (b. 1949) is a fiction writer and journalist. His memoir, *Into the Green* (2001), recounts his months of combat as a US Army lieutenant in Vietnam. One of the themes of the book, says McDonald, "is hate the war, but don't hate the soldier." After Vietnam, McDonald served for ten years on the police force of Fort Lauderdale, Florida, an experience that he has drawn upon in several crime novels and that he describes graphically in *Blue Truth* (1991). McDonald is also a fisherman and the father of three children, roles that come together in the following descriptive essay about a boy who helps the author see familiar objects in a new light. The essay was first published in 1989 in the *South Florida Sun-Sentinel*.

I WAS COMING UP ON THE LITTLE BRIDGE in the Rio Vista neighborhood of   1
Fort Lauderdale, deepening my stride and my breathing to negotiate the slight incline without altering my pace. And then, as I neared the crest, I saw the kid.

He was a lumpy little guy with baggy shorts, a faded T-shirt, and heavy 2
sweat socks falling down over old sneakers.

Details in this
description are
arranged in the
order of their
significance, as
suggested on p. 85. Partially covering his shaggy blond hair was one of those 3
blue baseball caps with gold braid on the bill and a sailfish patch
sewn onto the peak. Covering his eyes and part of his face was a
pair of those stupid-looking '50s-style wrap-around sunglasses.

He was fumbling with a beat-up rod and reel, and he had a little bait bucket 4
by his feet. I puffed on by, glancing down into the empty bucket as I passed.

"Hey, mister! Would you help me, please?" 5

The shrill voice penetrated my jogger's concentration, and I was deter- 6
mined to ignore it. But for some reason, I stopped.

With my hands on my hips and the sweat dripping from my nose I asked, 7
"What do you want, kid?"

"Would you please help me find my shrimp? It's my last one and I've 8
been getting bites and I know I can catch a fish if I can just find that shrimp.
He jumped outta my hand as I was getting him from the bucket."

Exasperated, I walked slowly back to the kid, and pointed. 9

"There's the damn shrimp by your left foot. You stopped me for *that*?" 10

As I said it, the kid reached down and trapped the shrimp. 11

"Thanks a lot, mister," he said. 12

I watched as the kid dropped the baited hook down into the canal. Then 13
I turned to start back down the bridge.

That's when the kid let out a "Hey! Hey!" and the prettiest tarpon I'd 14
ever seen came almost six feet out of the water, twisting and turning as he fell
through the air.

"I got one!" the kid yelled as the fish hit the water with a loud splash and 15
took off down the canal.

I watched the line being burned off the reel at an alarming rate. The kid's 16
left hand held the crank while the extended fingers felt for the drag setting.

"No, kid!" I shouted. "Leave the drag alone . . . just keep that damn rod 17
tip up!"

Then I glanced at the reel and saw there were just a few loops of line left 18
on the spool.

"Why don't you get yourself some decent equipment?" I said, but before 19
the kid could answer I saw the line go slack.

"Ohhh, I lost him," the kid said. I saw the flash of silver as the fish turned. 20

"Crank, kid, crank! You didn't lose him. He's coming back toward you. 21
Bring in the slack!"

The kid cranked like mad, and a beautiful grin spread across his face. 22

"He's heading in for the pilings," I said. "Keep him out of those pilings!" 23

The kid played it perfectly. When the fish made its play for the pilings, he 24
kept just enough pressure on to force the fish out. When the water exploded and
the silver missile hurled into the air, the kid kept the rod tip up and the line tight.

As the fish came to the surface and began a slow circle in the middle of 25
the canal, I said, "Whooee, is that a nice fish or what?"

The kid didn't say anything, so I said, "Okay, move to the edge of the 26
bridge and I'll climb down to the seawall and pull him out."

When I reached the seawall I pulled in the leader, leaving the fish lying 27
on its side in the water.

"How's that?" I said. 28

"Hey, mister, tell me what it looks like." 29

"Look down here and check him out," I said. "He's beautiful." 30

But then I looked up into those stupid-looking sunglasses and it hit me. 31
The kid was blind.

"Could you tell me what he looks like, mister?" he said again. 32

"Well, he's just under three, uh, he's about as long as one of your arms," 33
I said. "I'd guess he goes about 15, 20 pounds. He's mostly silver, but the silver
is somehow made up of *all* the colors, if you know what I mean." I stopped.
"Do you know what I mean by colors?"

The kid nodded. 34

"Okay. He has all these big scales, like armor all over his body. They're 35
silver too, and when he moves they sparkle. He has a strong body and a large
powerful tail. He has big round eyes, bigger than a quarter, and a lower jaw
that sticks out past the upper one and is very tough. His belly is almost white
and his back is a gunmetal gray. When he jumped he came out of the water
about six feet, and his scales caught the sun and flashed it all over the place."

By now the fish had righted itself, and I could see the bright-
red gills as the gill plates opened and closed. I explained this to
the kid, and then said, more to myself, "He's a beauty." 36

See p. **84** for
tips on creating
a dominant
impression of
beauty—or any
other sensation.

"Can you get him off the hook?" the kid asked. "I don't want to kill him." 37

I watched as the tarpon began to slowly swim away, tired but still 38
alive.

By the time I got back up to the top of the bridge the kid had his line 39
secured and his bait bucket in one hand.

He grinned and said, "Just in time. My mom drops me off here, and she'll 40
be back to pick me up any minute."

He used the back of one hand to wipe his nose. 41

"Thanks for helping me catch that tarpon," he said, "and for helping me 42
to see it."

I looked at him, shook my head, and said, "No, my friend, thank you for 43
letting *me* see that fish."

I took off, but before I got far the kid yelled again. 44

"Hey, mister!" 45

I stopped. 46

"Someday I'm gonna catch a sailfish and a blue marlin and a giant tuna 47
and all those big sportfish!"

As I looked into those sunglasses I knew he probably would. I wished I 48
could be there when it happened.

FOR DISCUSSION

1. Which of the five senses does Cherokee Paul McDonald appeal to in his **DESCRIP-TION** of the tarpon (35)? In this essay as a whole?
2. How much does the jogger seem to know about fish and fishing?
3. What is the attitude of the jogger toward the "kid" before he realizes the boy is blind (31)? As a reader, what is your attitude toward the jogger? Why?
4. How does the jogger feel about the kid when they part? How do you feel about the jogger? What, if anything, changes your view of the jogger?
5. How does meticulously describing a small piece of the world help the grumpy jogger to see the world anew?

STRATEGIES AND STRUCTURES

1. McDonald serves as eyes for the boy (and us). Which physical details in his description of the scene at the bridge do you find to be visually most effective?

2. McDonald's description is part of a **NARRATIVE**. At first, the **NARRATOR** seems irritable and in a hurry. What makes him slow down? How does his behavior change? Why?

3. The narrator does not realize the boy is blind until paragraph 31, but we figure it out much sooner. What descriptive details lead us to realize that the boy is blind?

4. McDonald, of course, knew when he wrote this piece that the boy couldn't see. Why do you think he wrote from the **POINT OF VIEW** of the jogger, who doesn't know at first? How does he restrict the narrator's point of view in paragraph 6? Elsewhere in the essay?

5. How does the narrator's physical **VANTAGE POINT** change in paragraph 27? Why does this alter the way he sees the boy?

6. "No, my friend," says the jogger, "thank you for letting *me* see that fish" (43). So who is helping whom to see in this essay? How? Cite examples.

WORDS AND FIGURES OF SPEECH

1. **METONYMY** is a **FIGURE OF SPEECH** in which a word or object stands in for another associated with it. How might the blind boy's cap or sunglasses be seen as examples of metonymy?

2. Point out words and phrases in this essay—for example, "sparkle"—that refer to sights or acts of seeing (35).

3. What possible meanings are suggested by the word "view" in McDonald's title?

4. Besides its literal meaning, how else might we take the word "bridge" here? Who or what is being "bridged"?

FOR WRITING

1. Suppose you had to describe a bird, snake, thunderstorm, or other natural phenomenon to someone who hadn't seen it before. In a paragraph, describe the thing—its colors, smell, texture, movement, how the light strikes it—in sufficient detail so that the person could form an accurate mental picture of what you are describing.

2. Write an extended description of a scene in which you see a familiar object, person, or place in a new light because of someone else who brings a fresh viewpoint to the picture. For example, you might describe the scene at the dinner table when you bring home a new significant other. Or you might describe taking a tour of your campus, hometown, neighborhood, or workplace with a friend or relative who has never seen it before.

THE MISS DENNIS
SCHOOL OF WRITING

ALICE STEINBACH (1933–2012) was a teacher of writing and the author of *Without Reservations: The Travels of an Independent Woman* (2000) and *Educating Alice: Adventures of a Curious Woman* (2004). As a reporter for the *Baltimore Sun*, where she won a Pulitzer Prize for feature writing in 1985, Steinbach wrote a column about her ninth-grade creative writing teacher. It became the title piece in a collection of personal essays, *The Miss Dennis School of Writing* (1996). Here the "lesson" is both a writing lesson and a life lesson. Miss Dennis taught that good descriptive writing (her specialty) makes the reader see what the writer sees. She also taught her students to find their unique personal voices. Steinbach's distinctive voice can be heard in her vivid descriptions of her former teacher. It is a perspective, she has said, that "tends to look at people with a child's eye."

"WHAT KIND OF WRITING DO YOU DO?" asked the novelist sitting to my left at a writer's luncheon.

"I work for a newspaper in Baltimore," he was told.

"Oh, did you go to journalism school?"

"Well, yes."

"Columbia?" he asked, invoking the name of the most prestigious journalism school in the country.

"Actually, no," I heard myself telling him. "I'm one of the lucky ones. I am a graduate of the Miss Dennis School of Writing."

Unimpressed, the novelist turned away. Clearly it was a credential that did not measure up to his standards. But why should it? He was not one of the lucky ones. He had never met Miss Dennis, my ninth-grade creative writing teacher, or had the good fortune to be her student. Which meant he had never experienced the sight of Miss Dennis chasing Dorothy Singer around the classroom, threatening her with a yardstick because Dorothy hadn't paid attention and her writing showed it.

"You want to be a writer?" Miss Dennis would yell, out of breath from all the running and yardstick-brandishing. "Then pay attention to what's going on around you. Connect! You are not Switzerland—neutral, aloof, uninvolved. Think Italy!"

Miss Dennis said things like this. If you had any sense, you wrote them down.

"I can't teach you how to write, but I can tell you how to look at things, how to pay attention," she would bark out at us, like a drill sergeant confronting a group of undisciplined, wet-behind-the-ears[1] Marine recruits. To drive home her point, she had us take turns writing a description of what we saw on the way to school in the morning. Of course, you never knew which morning would be your turn so— just to be on the safe side—you got into the habit of looking things over carefully every morning and making notes: "Saw a pot of red geraniums sitting in the sunlight on a white stucco porch; an orange-striped cat curled like a comma beneath a black van; a dark gray cloud scudding across a silver morning sky."

Concrete details (p. 82) help drive home the point of any description.

1. Young and inexperienced.

It's a lesson that I have returned to again and again throughout my writ- 11
ing career. To this day, I think of Miss Dennis whenever I write a certain kind
of sentence. Or to be more precise, whenever I write a sentence that actually
creates in words the picture I want readers to see.

Take, for instance, this sentence: Miss Dennis was a small, compact 12
woman, about albatross height—or so it seemed to her students—with short,
straight hair the color of apricots and huge eyeglasses that were always slipping down her nose.

Or this one: Miss Dennis always wore a variation of one outfit—a dark- 13
colored, flared woolen skirt, a tailored white blouse and a cardigan sweater,
usually black, thrown over her shoulders and held together by a little pearl
chain.

Can you see her? I can. And the image of her makes me smile. Still. 14

But it was not Miss Dennis's appearance or her unusual teaching 15
method—which had a lot in common with an out-of-control terrier—that
made her so special. What set her apart was her deep commitment to liberating the individual writer in each student.

"What lies at the heart of good writing," she told us over and over again, 16
"is the writer's ability to find his own unique voice. And then to use it to tell
an interesting story." Somehow she made it clear that we were interesting
people with interesting stories to tell. Most of us, of course, had never even
known we had a story to tell, much less an interesting one. But soon the stories just started bubbling up from some inner wellspring.

Finding the material, however, was one thing; finding the individual 17
voice was another.

Take me, for instance. I arrived in Miss Dennis's class trailing all sorts 18
of literary baggage. My usual routine was to write like Colette on Monday, one
of the Brontë sisters on Wednesday, and Mark Twain[2] on Friday.

Right away, Miss Dennis knocked me off my high horse. 19

---

2. Sidonie-Gabrielle Colette (1873–1954), French novelist known for her depictions of
female sexuality; Charlotte Brontë (1816–1855), Emily Brontë (1818–1848), and Anne Brontë
(1820–1849), British writers of early Romantic novels; Mark Twain (1835–1910), American
novelist and essayist known for his works of wit and satire.

"Why are you telling other people's stories?" she challenged me, peering 20
up into my face. (At fourteen I was already four inches taller than Miss Dennis.) "You have your own stories to tell."

I was tremendously relieved to hear this and immediately proceeded to 21
write like my idol, E. B. White.[3] Miss Dennis, however, wasn't buying.

"How will you ever find out what you have to say if you keep trying to 22
say what other people have already said?" was the way she dispensed with my
E. B. White impersonation. By the third week of class, Miss Dennis knew my
secret. She knew I was afraid—afraid to pay attention to my own inner voice
for fear that when I finally heard it, it would have nothing to say.

What Miss Dennis told me—and I have carefully preserved these words 23
because they were then, and are now, so very important to me—was this:
"Don't be afraid to discover what you're saying in the act of saying it." Then,
in her inimitably breezy and endearing way, she added: "Trust me on this
one."

From the beginning, she made it clear to us that it was not "right" or 24
"wrong" answers she was after. It was thinking.

"Don't be afraid to go out on a limb,"[4] she'd tell some poor kid strug- 25
gling to reason his way through an essay on friendship or courage. And
eventually—once we stopped being afraid that we'd be chopped
off out there on that limb—we needed no encouragement to say   Miss Dennis used
figurative language
what we thought. In fact, after the first month, I can't remember   (p. 85) to bring her
own description
ever feeling afraid of failing in her class. Passing or failing didn't   down to earth.
seem to be the point of what she was teaching.

Miss Dennis spent as much time, maybe more, pointing out what was 26
right with your work as she did pointing out what was wrong. I can still hear
her critiquing my best friend's incredibly florid essay on nature. "You are a
very good observer of nature," she told the budding writer. "And if you just
write what you see without thinking so much about adjectives and comparisons, we will see it through your attentive eyes."

3. American essayist and children's author (1899–1985), admired for his elegant style and
attention to descriptive detail. A critical analysis of White's classic essay, "Once More to
the Lake," appears on pp. 14–17, followed by the complete text on pp. 19–25.
4. Miss Dennis's point to writers, of course, is that the greater the risk, the greater the
potential reward—up to a point.

By Thanksgiving vacation I think we were all a little infatuated with   27
Miss Dennis. And beyond that, infatuated with the way she made us feel
about ourselves—that we were interesting people worth listening to.

I, of course, fancied I had a special relationship with her. It was certainly   28
special to me. And, to tell the truth, I knew she felt the same way.

The first time we acknowledged this was one day after class when I   29
stayed behind to talk to her. I often did that and it seemed we talked about
everything—from the latest films to the last issue of the *New Yorker*. The one
thing we did not talk about was the sadness I felt about my father's death. He
had died a few years before and, although I did not know it then, I was still
grieving his absence. Without knowing the details, Miss Dennis somehow
picked up on my sadness. Maybe it was there in my writing. Looking back I
see now that, without my writing about it directly, my father's death hovered
at the edges of all my stories.

But on this particular day I found myself talking not about the movies   30
or about writing but instead pouring out my feelings about the loss of my
father. I shall never forget that late fall afternoon: the sound of the vanilla-
colored blinds flap, flap, flapping in the still classroom; sun falling in shafts
through the windows, each ray illuminating tiny galaxies of chalk dust in the
air; the smell of wet blackboards; the teacher, small with apricot-colored hair,
listening intently to a young girl blurting out her grief. These memories are
stored like vintage photographs.

The words that passed between the young girl and the attentive teacher   31
are harder to recall. With this exception. "One day," Miss Dennis told me, "you
will write about this. Maybe not directly. But you will write about it. And you
will find that all this has made you a better writer and a stronger person."

After that day, it was as if Miss Dennis and I shared something. We never   32
talked again about my father but spent most of our time discussing our mutual
interests. We both loved poetry and discovered one afternoon that each of
us regarded Emily Dickinson[5] with something approaching idolatry. Right
then and there, Miss Dennis gave me a crash course in why Emily Dickinson's
poems worked. I can still hear her talking about the "spare, slanted beauty" in

---

5. American poet (1830–1886) who wrote almost 1,800 poems (and many letters). In later
years, Dickinson seldom left her family home in Amherst, Mass.

Dickinson's unique choice of words. She also told me about the rather clois-
tered life led by this New England spinster, noting that nonetheless Emily
Dickinson knew the world as few others did. "She found her world within the
word," is the way I remember Miss Dennis putting it. Of course, I could be
making that part up.

That night, propped up in bed reading Emily Dickinson's poetry, I won- 33
dered if Miss Dennis, a spinster herself, identified in some way with the
woman who wrote:

> Wild nights—Wild nights!
> Were I with thee
> Wild Nights should be
> Our luxury!

It seems strange, I know, but I never really knew anything about Miss Dennis' 34
life outside of the classroom. Oh, once she confided in me that the initial "M"
in her name stood for Mildred. And I was surprised when I passed by the
teachers' lounge one day and saw her smoking a cigarette, one placed in a long,
silver cigarette holder. It seemed an exceedingly sophisticated thing to do and
it struck me then that she might be more worldly than I had previously thought.

But I didn't know how she spent her time or what she wanted from life 35
or anything like that. And I never really wondered about it. Once I remember
talking to some friends about her age. We guessed somewhere around fifty—
which seemed really old to us. In reality, Miss Dennis was around forty.

It was Miss Dennis, by the way, who encouraged me to enter some writ- 36
ing contests. To my surprise, I took first place in a couple of them. Of course,
taking first place is easy. What's hard is being rejected. But Miss Dennis
helped me with that, too, citing all the examples of famous writers who'd been
rejected time and time again. "Do you know what they told George Orwell[6]
when they rejected *Animal Farm*?" she would ask me. Then without waiting for
a reply, she'd answer her own question: "The publisher told him, 'It is impossible to sell animal stories in the U.S.A.'"

6. British novelist and essayist (1903–1950). Much of his major work, including the novel
Animal Farm (1945), reflects his opposition to repressive governments. Orwell's classic
essay, "Politics and the English Language," is reprinted on pp. 569–74.

When I left her class at the end of the year, Miss Dennis gave me a pre-   37
sent: a book of poems by Emily Dickinson. I have it still. The spine is cracked
and the front cover almost gone, but the inscription remains. On the inside
flyleaf, in her perfect Palmer Method handwriting,[7] she had written: "Say
what you see. Yours in Emily Dickinson, Miss Dennis."

She had also placed little checks next to two or three poems. I took this   38
to mean she thought they contained a special message for me. One of those
checked began this way:

> Hope is the thing with feathers
> That perches in the soul . . .

I can remember carefully copying out these lines onto a sheet of paper, one
which I carried around in my handbag for almost a year. But time passed, the
handbag fell apart and who knows what happened to the yellowing piece of
paper with the words about hope.

The years went by. Other schools and other teachers came and went. But   39
one thing remained constant: My struggle to pay attention to my own inner
life; to hear a voice that I would recognize finally as my own. Not only in my
writing but in my life.

Only recently, I learned that Miss Dennis had died at the age of fifty.   40
When I heard this, it occurred to me that her life was close to being over when
I met her. Neither of us knew this, of course. Or at least I didn't. But lately I've
wondered if she knew something that day we talked about sadness and my
father's death. "Write about it," she said. "It will help you."

And now, reading over these few observations, I think of Miss Dennis.   41
But not with sadness. Actually, thinking of Miss Dennis makes me smile. I
think of her and see, with marked clarity, a small, compact woman with
apricot-colored hair. She is with a young girl and she is saying something.

She is saying: "Pay attention."   42

---

7. A form of standardized handwriting that was popular around 1900 but is rarely taught
today.

FOR DISCUSSION

1. When some teachers say, "Pay attention," they mean "Pay attention to what I am saying." According to her former pupil, Alice Steinbach, what did Miss Dennis mean when she told students to pay attention (8)?

2. It was neither Miss Dennis's appearance nor her teaching methods that made her so special as a teacher of writing, says Steinbach, but "her deep commitment to liberating the individual writer in each student" (15). How did Miss Dennis accomplish this feat in Steinbach's case?

3. Steinbach poses a direct question to the reader in paragraph 14: "Can you see her?" Well, can you? And if so, what exactly do you see—and hear? For example, what color was Miss Dennis's hair?

4. Steinbach thinks of her old teacher whenever she writes a sentence "that actually creates in words the picture I want readers to see" (11). This is precisely what good **DESCRIPTIVE** writing does, although it may appeal to other senses as well as sight. How did Miss Dennis teach this kind of writing?

5. Writing about old teachers who die can be an occasion for sentimentality or excessively emotional writing. Do you think Steinbach's tribute to her former teacher is overly emotional, or does she successfully avoid sentimentality? If she avoids it, in your opinion, explain how she does so. If not, explain why you think she doesn't. Find places in her essay that support your view.

STRATEGIES AND STRUCTURES

1. Point out several descriptive passages in Steinbach's essay that follow her principle of creating in words what she wants the reader to see.

2. Why do you think Steinbach, looking back over her recollections of Miss Dennis, refers to them as "observations" (41)?

3. Description seldom stands alone. Often it shades into **NARRATION**, as here. Thus Miss Dennis, who greatly valued the writer's eye, urged the student, once she found her unique way of looking at the world, to use it "to tell an interesting story" (16). Besides Miss Dennis's, whose story is Steinbach telling? How interesting do you find *that* narrative?

4. What **DOMINANT IMPRESSION** of Miss Dennis do we get from Steinbach's description of her in paragraphs 12 through 14 and 41? Of Steinbach herself?

5. How informative do you find Steinbach's essay as a lesson on how to write, particularly on how to write good description? Where does Steinbach **ANALYZE THE PROCESS**?

WORDS AND FIGURES OF SPEECH

1. Which is more **CONCRETE**, to say that a woman has "hair the color of apricots" or to say that she has red or blond hair (12)? Which is more specific?
2. The orange-striped cat in young Steinbach's description of her walk to school is "curled like a comma" beneath a van (10). Such stated **COMPARISONS**, frequently using "like" or "as," are called **SIMILES**. Implied comparisons, without "like" or "as," are called **METAPHORS**. What metaphoric comparison does Steinbach make in the same description? What is she comparing to what?
3. Steinbach compares Miss Dennis to an "albatross" and "an out-of-control terrier" (12, 15). Besides describing Miss Dennis, what do these fanciful comparisons tell you about Steinbach?
4. Steinbach arrived in Miss Dennis's class "trailing all sorts of literary baggage" (18). To what is she comparing herself here?
5. How would you describe the words that Steinbach uses in paragraph 30 to describe the afternoon? Concrete or **ABSTRACT**? Specific or general?

FOR WRITING

1. On your next walk to or around school, pay close attention to your surroundings. Take notes, as young Steinbach does in paragraph 10. Describe what you see in a paragraph that "creates in words the picture" you want your reader to see (11). Make it as free of literary or other baggage as you can, and try to select details that contribute to a single dominant impression.
2. Write a profile—a description of a person that not only tells but also shows a piece of that person's life story—of one of your favorite (or least favorite) teachers or coaches. Try to give your reader a clear sense of what that person looks like; of what they wear, say, and do; and of the dominant impression they make on others. Be sure to show how you interact with that person and what they have (or have not) taught you.

SLAW DOGS AND PEPPERONI ROLLS

EDWARD LEE (b. 1972) is an award-winning chef, restaurant owner, and writer. The son of Korean parents, Lee was born and raised in Brooklyn, New York. He graduated from New York University with a degree in literature but began cooking professionally at age 22. In 2002 Lee moved to Louisville, Kentucky, and opened several successful restaurants. Lee's cuisine blends the flavors and ingredients of Korean food with those of the southern United States, such as sorghum, ham, and bourbon. His cookbook, *Smoke and Pickles* (2013), offers "Recipes and Stories from a New Southern Kitchen." In 2017, Lee founded an organization to promote diversity and growth in the restaurant industry. "Slaw Dogs and Pepperoni Rolls" is a selection from Lee's 2018 book, *Buttermilk Graffiti: A Chef's Journey to Discover America's New Melting-Pot Cuisine*. This essay describes, in delicious detail, not only the local cuisine that Lee consumed on his travels in West Virginia but the landscape and culture of the region as well. Lee's traveling companion in this selection is the chef and cookbook writer—and West Virgina resident—Ronni Lundy.

I MEET RONNI at the Asheville airport. She is a small, sprightly woman in her   1
sixties who glows with energy. The first thing I notice when I jump into her
van is an oversize Rand McNally road atlas. It is so big that she is completely
hidden behind it, except for her fingers curled around the edges of the cover.
Her singsong voice echoes from the driver's seat. I start to laugh involun-
tarily. I ask her if she wants to use my GPS.

"Mr. Lee, are you making fun of my maps?"   2

"No, ma'am." I snap back to attention.   3

And so begins our road trip through Appalachia.   4

The van sputters as we crest over a ridge. These steep, verdant hills   5
carved out of prehistoric violence have had an eternity to become smooth.
They roll and undulate like fairy-tale landscapes. The homes sit far apart,
isolated. A church stands alone on a hill. Through a clearing, we see an abandoned covered bridge spanning a shallow stream flanked by hulking lime-
stone rocks. It is hard not to fall in love with this land. It is hard to look at this
place and not believe in God. The roads through the valleys are lined with
poplar and ash trees, dense and emerald green. You can drive for miles without feeling sunlight on your cheeks. When we arrive at another vista, Ronni
slows the van to a crawl so we can breathe in the view. She points to where the
pasture meets the heavens. Her coral green eyes fall on me like sunlight on a
dewy morning. Her short white hair hugs the curves of her temples. She starts
every new sentence like the lyrics of a love song: "You are never far from
death and darkness even when you are standing in the light."

For our first stop, we find a small roadside diner that sells sandwiches   6
and pies. Ronni talks to me about the pickles of this region, about bread and
pigs and why pork became the major source of protein—cattle were not a
viable industry in the steep landscape of Appalachia. I'm embarrassed to
interrupt her discussion of salt-risen bread with a request for a processed hot
dog. I sheepishly ask her if we can stop off at a few places if they're not too far
out of the way.

"Well, buddy, why didn't you say so earlier? You're talking my language."   7

My heart nearly explodes.   8

A West Virginia hot dog is a regional specialty that starts with a soft   9
commercial hot dog bun. Yellow mustard is slathered on first. A boiled beef
wiener is placed in the bun next. Ground beef chili without beans is added to

that. The kind of chili will differ from place to place, but it is commonly a tomato-rich variety easy on the spice. On top of the chili is placed chopped cabbage slaw held together with mayo and vinegar, creamy and tart. Finally, a light smattering of finely chopped raw onion gets put on top. You can find this dog almost everywhere in the region, from roadside diners to gas stations and local bars. In Virginia, it's called a slaw dog. In West Virginia, it's simply a West Virginia hot dog, though in the northern parts, folks tend to serve it without the coleslaw. At the famous Umberger's in Wytheville, Virginia, they call them Skeeter Dogs and sell them for two bucks apiece, but at most places, you can find them for two dollars for a pair. At first glance, there is nothing about this hot dog that looks special, but once you take a bite, you know you've touched the nirvana of hot dogs. That first bite tells you everything. The structure of the chili is critical, because if it's too tight, it doesn't collapse in your mouth with the other ingredients. Too loose, and the chili dog falls apart after the first bite, dissolving into a sloppy mess in your hands. The same goes for the slaw. When it's done right, there is harmony and balance. I don't think Ronni truly trusted me as a person until she witnessed me take down two slaw dogs with a slug of hot black coffee before 8:00 a.m.

The West Virginia hot dog is a regional celebrity. There are websites 10 devoted to it. Though the wiener and bun are almost always factory made, there is pride in the slaw and enough technique and variation in the chili that a lively debate rages about who makes it best. Skeenies or King Tut? Skeeter's or Buddy B's? No one knows the precise origin of this dog. Ronni traces it back to the chili buns served in the pool halls that littered the railroad towns of the region. Another plausible story tells of the struggling immigrant families, many of whom grew vegetables in their backyards to supplement their humble diets. Cabbage was easy to grow, so families started to make slaw—lots of it. The slaw found its way into many dishes, including the hot dog. The first place to sell the slaw dog was the Stopette Drive-In in the 1920s, but many argue that home cooks in the region started eating their hot dogs with slaw well before that. One thing is for sure: the slaw dog is a celebration and a source of pride.

The slaw dog stands in stark contrast to West Virginia's other regional 11 specialty: the pepperoni roll. A humble food of Italian origin, it was invented by immigrant Italian coal miners who needed a hearty snack that was both portable and easy to eat. D'Annunzio's,

Lee is using the subject-by-subject method of comparison and contrast (p. 328).

a landmark bakery in Clarksburg, has been making it for decades. The preparation couldn't be simpler: pepperoni cut into sticks about four inches long and baked into a soft, sweet roll. Nothing else: just dough and pepperoni baked together.

I arrive at D'Annunzio's at 8:00 a.m., when the rolls are just coming out of the oven. I stand in a line of polite locals, many of whom are buying the rolls by the dozen. I take a bite of mine. The dough is soft and forgiving, the pepperoni lukewarm. All I taste is powdered paprika, dry and unbalanced. It takes a few chews to loosen the fat from the sausage and for flavors to develop in my mouth, but even then, it is bland and monotonous. I am underwhelmed, to say the least.

Ronni tells me that the pepperoni roll is the food of the working class. It is about making connections. When your entire day is spent deep in a coal mine, that little bit of pepperoni may be all that connects you to the sanity of family and your identity and life aboveground.

I buy a dozen rolls and decide to carry them with me for the next few days.

So many of my assumptions about food come from a desire to tell a neatly packaged story, one that has a happy ending of climactic flavors and rewarded chefs. But that tidy story is rarely the case. Along my journey, through Appalachia or any of the small towns I've traveled to, the most insightful moments have been quiet and unseasoned. This has made me question myself and my expectations. I'm owed nothing by the people and the culture of this place. I have neither the right to judge nor the history to comment on them. If the pepperoni roll seems bland to me, it is a fault in my own palate, which is unable to detect the value of its plainness. I chew another bite and try to think of someone who has been working at a physically grueling job since dawn. This pepperoni roll is the one pleasure he may have been looking forward to all morning long. This pepperoni roll may be all he has to eat until he sits down to supper late in the evening. Slowly, I get it. The darkness of the room is suffocating, and I've been here only twenty minutes. The pepperoni roll suddenly tastes like the best thing I've ever eaten.

For tips on stating the point of your description, see p. 84.

FOR DISCUSSION

1. Edward Lee offers two explanations of the possible origins of the slaw in slaw dogs. What are they, and which one do you find more plausible? Why?

2. According to Lee, there seems to be little question about where pepperoni rolls came from. What is their origin story, according to him? How about the origin of the Appalachian Mountains, as Lee describes them at the beginning of his trip (5)?

3. From the first bite, Lee worships the slaw dog. The pepperoni roll, however, he finds bland at first. What changes his mind (or palate) about this "humble food" (11)? Where does he describe the change most fully—and how?

4. According to Lee, why does the cuisine of Appalachia often feature pork instead of beef? Why wasn't beef a "viable" alternative in the region (6)? Explain.

STRATEGIES AND STRUCTURES

1. When Lee first meets Ronni Lundy, she is "completely hidden" behind a book of maps (1). What does Lee's initial description of his traveling companion show about her as a person?

2. As soon as the road trip starts, Lee describes the landscape he and Ronni will be traveling through. What **DOMINANT IMPRESSION** of the region does he convey? Point to specific details in the text that contribute to this impression.

3. Lee devotes two long paragraphs (9 and 10) to a detailed description of the West Virginia hot dog. What are the main distinguishing features of this "celebrity" dog (10)? According to Lee, which attribute in particular sets it apart from all other hot dogs?

4. By contrast with slaw dogs, says Lee, pepperoni rolls could not be "simpler" (11); yet he devotes about as much space to one as to the other. What exactly is Lee describing in the last third of his essay (11–13), if not the pepperoni rolls themselves? Explain.

5. Lee admits that he likes a "neatly packaged story," even if circumstances don't always provide "a happy ending" (15). Point out places throughout his description where Lee incorporates elements of **NARRATIVE**, such as dialogue and suspense into his description.

WORDS AND FIGURES OF SPEECH

1. As they reach the mountains, Lee and Ronni stop to "breathe in the view" (5). Is this literally possible? As a chef, why might Lee be inclined to such blended impressions?

2. Lee asks "sheepishly" if they can stop the van and get a hot dog (6). What is "sheepish" about this request?

3. "My heart nearly explodes" (8). Why might Lee indulge in such **HYPERBOLE** here? Point out other places in his essay where he seems to be particularly enthusiastic about his subject.

4. After he eats the first slaw dog, Lee reaches "the nirvana of hot dogs" (9). What is Nirvana, and how does applying this word (though without the capital letter) fit in with the **TONE** and language of the rest of Lee's description, particularly of the "fairy-tale" landscape (5)?

5. On their road trip, says Lee, "the most insightful moments have been quiet and unseasoned" (15). What are the implications of this **METAPHOR** in an essay by a chef? How might this insight apply specifically to the writer's description of the pepperoni rolls at the end?

FOR WRITING

1. Write a paragraph describing a hot dog, burger, shake, candy bar, or other indulgent item of food in "delicious" detail.

2. When the last McDonald's closed in Iceland more than ten years ago, a local citizen purchased the final burger and fries to come off the line; a short time later, he donated them to the National Museum of Iceland. The original burger and fries are still being streamed "live" online. Do a little research on these national treasures, and write a description of their condition and history.

3. Write a review describing a meal you had recently. Focus on the food, but also try to convey a sense of the place itself and of the other people in it. Be sure to comment on the overall quality of the dining experience—and whether or not you would recommend it to the reader.

4. Give an account of a trip you have taken to an isolated (or other) region where the **DOMINANT IMPRESSION** you had was one of awe and wonder. Tell how the place affected you, but also describe what it looked, smelled, tasted, sounded, and felt like by referring to particular features of the place.

⇒ 6 ⇐

NARRATIVE

NARRATIVE* writing tells a story; it reports "what happened." All the essays in this chapter are narratives, telling about what happened to a young American poet who immigrated from Vietnam, for example, and to one Black man when he refused to give up his seat on a bus in North Carolina in the 1940s. There is a big difference, however, between having something "happen" and writing about it, between an event and telling about an event.

In real life, events often occur randomly or chaotically. But in a narrative, they must be told or shown in some orderly sequence (the **PLOT**), by a particular person (the **NARRATOR**), from a particular perspective (the **POINT OF VIEW**), within a definite time and place (the **SETTING**). Let's look more closely at each of these elements.

Suppose we wanted to tell a story about a young woman sitting alone eating a snack. Our opening line might go something like this:

Little Miss Muffet sat on a tuffet, eating her curds and whey.

Here, in the first line of a well-known nursery rhyme, we have someone (Miss Muffet) who is doing something (eating) at a particular time (the past) in a particular place (on a tuffet). The problem with our narrative is that it isn't very interesting. We have a character and a setting, but we don't really have a plot.

A good plot requires more than just sitting and eating. Plot can be achieved by introducing a conflict into the action, bringing the tension to a high point

---

*Words printed in **SMALL CAPITALS** are defined in the Glossary/Index.

(the **CLIMAX**), then releasing the tension—in other words, by giving the action of the story a beginning, middle, and end. In our story about Miss Muffet, we could achieve the necessary conflict by introducing an intruder:

> Along came a spider and sat down beside her . . .

You know what's coming next, but you can still feel the tension building up before we resolve the conflict and release the rising tension in the final line of our story:

> And frightened Miss Muffet away.

Well, that's better. We have a sequence of events now. Moreover, those events occur in our narrative in some sort of order—chronologically. But the events also have to be linked together in some meaningful way. In this case, the appearance of the intruder actually *causes* the departure of the heroine. There are many ways to connect the events in a narrative, but **CAUSE AND EFFECT** is one good approach (see Chapter 12).

Mary Mebane, p. 145, tells how segregation laws caused her to "live with terror."

We said earlier that a narrative must have a narrator. That narrator may be directly involved in the action of the narrative or may only report it. Do we have one here? Yes, we do; it is the narrator who refers to Miss Muffet as "her." But this narrator is never identified and plays no part in the action. Let's look at a narrator who does—Stephen King, in a passage from a narrative about an accident that almost killed him some years ago:

> Most of the sight lines along the mile-long stretch of Route 5 that I walk are good, but there is one place, a short steep hill, where a pedestrian heading north can see very little of what might be coming his way. I was three-quarters of the way up this hill when the van came over the crest. It wasn't on the road; it was on the shoulder. My shoulder. I had perhaps three-quarters of a second to register this.
>
> —STEPHEN KING, "On Impact"

Notice that the "I" in this piece is King himself, and he is very much involved in the action of the story he is telling. In fact, he is about to be hit by the van coming over the crest of the hill. That would introduce a conflict into his walk along Route 5, wouldn't it?

By narrating this story from a **FIRST-PERSON** point of view, King is putting himself in the center of the action. If he had said instead, "The van was closing in on him fast," we would have a **THIRD-PERSON** narrative, and the narrator would be reporting the action from the sidelines instead of bearing the brunt of it. What makes a chilling story here is that King is not only showing us what happened to him, but he is also showing us what he was thinking as he suddenly realized that the van was almost on top of him: "It wasn't on the road; it was on the shoulder. My shoulder." We look in as the narrator goes, in a few swift phrases, from startled disbelief to horrified certainty.

Another way in which King creates a compelling story is by using direct speech, or **DIALOGUE**. When King tells about his first day back at work, he lets his wife speak to us directly: "I can rig a table for you in the back hall, outside the pantry. There are plenty of outlets—you can have your Mac, the little printer, and a fan." Quoting direct speech like this helps readers to imagine the characters as real people.

But why does King end his narrative back at the writing desk? Because he knows that stories serve a larger **PURPOSE** than just telling what happened. The larger purpose of King's story is to make a point about writing and the writer's life. The van almost killed him, but writing, King demonstrates, helped him recover and keeps him going.

> Valeria Luiselli, p. 172, uses dialogue to make a point about children and immigration law.

Well-told stories are almost always told for some reason. The searing tale you heard earlier about Miss Muffet, for example, was told to make a point about narrative structure. A brief, illustrative story like this is called an **ANECDOTE**. All stories should have a point, but anecdotes in particular are used in all kinds of writing to give examples and to illustrate the greater subject at hand—writing, for instance.

When you use a story to make a point, don't forget to remind the reader exactly what that point is. When Ryan Knighton narrates his close encounter with an elephant in "Blind Safari," he is also making a point about being open to new perceptions. "Being blind," says Knighton, "I'm a bit of a connoisseur"— and then an unusual guide shows him what he's been missing. Don't keep your reader in the dark. When your purpose is to explain something, don't get so caught up in telling a good story that you forget to say what the point is.

A BRIEF GUIDE TO WRITING A NARRATIVE

As you write a **NARRATIVE,** you need to say who or what the narrative is about, where it takes place, and what is happening. Mary Mebane makes these basic moves of narration in the following lines from her essay in this chapter:

> On this Saturday morning Esther and I set out for town for our music lesson. We were going on our weekly big adventure, all the way across town. . . . We walked the two miles from Wildwood to the bus line.
>
> —MARY MEBANE, "The Back of the Bus"

Mebane says *who* her story is about ("Esther and I"), *where* it takes place (on the bus line), and *what* is happening as the story opens (the two teenagers are heading for a "big adventure").

The following guidelines will help you to make these basic moves as you draft a narrative—and to come up with a subject for your story, consider your purpose and audience, state your point, and organize the specific details and events of your story into a compelling plot by using chronology, transitions, verb tenses, and dialogue.

Coming Up with a Subject

When you enjoy a well-told story, it is often because the author presents an event in an interesting or even dramatic way. To come up with a subject for a story of your own, think of events, both big and small, that you have experienced. You might write a good story about a perfectly ordinary occurrence, such as riding a bus, applying for a job, arguing with a friend—or even just doing your homework.

"No, no, no," the writer Frank McCourt, author of *Angela's Ashes*, used to say to his students when they complained that nothing had happened to them when they got home the night before. "What did you do when you walked in?" McCourt would ask. "You went through a door, didn't you? Did you have anything in your hands? A book bag? You

Lynda Barry builds a narrative around the ordinary events of a school day (p. 154).

didn't carry it with you all night, did you? Did you hang it on a hook? Did you throw it across the room and your mom yelled at you for it?" Even mundane details like these can provide the material for a good story if you use them to show what people said and did—and exactly where, why, and how they said and did it.

Considering Your Purpose and Audience

As you compose a narrative, think hard about the audience you want to reach and the **PURPOSE** your narrative is intended to serve. Suppose you are paid to tweet about a visit to an electronics store in order to convince your followers to take advantage of the great deals you found there. You might tell your story this way: "When I walked into Best Buy, I couldn't believe my eyes. Smart speakers everywhere! And the cheap prices! I went home with a speaker under each arm." Or suppose you are writing a column in a technology magazine, and the purpose of your story is to show readers how to shop for a smart speaker. You might write: "The first hurdle I encountered was the numbing variety of brands and models."

Whatever your purpose, think about how much your audience is likely to know about your subject so you can judge how much background information you need to give, what terms you need to **DEFINE**, and so on. If you are writing an **ANECDOTE**, make sure it is appropriate for your audience and illustrates your larger point.

Generating Ideas: Asking What Happened—and Who, Where, When, How, and Why

How do you come up with the raw materials for a narrative? To get started, ask yourself the questions that journalists typically ask when developing a story: who, what, where, when, how, and why? Your immediate answers will give you the beginnings of a narrative, but keep asking the questions over and over again. Try to recall lots of particular details, both visual and auditory. As the writer John Steinbeck once advised, "Try to remember [the situation] so clearly that you can see things: what colors and how warm or cold and how you got there . . . what people looked like, how they walked, what they wore, what they ate."

You will also want your readers to know *why* you're telling this particular story, so it's important to select details that support your point. For example, if you're trying to show why your sister is the funniest person in your family, your story might include specific, vivid details about the sound of her voice, her amusing facial expressions, and a practical joke she once pulled.

Templates for Narrating

The following templates can help you generate ideas for a narrative and then start drafting. Don't take these as formulas where you just have to fill in the blanks. There are no easy formulas for good writing. But these templates can help you plot out some of the key moves of narration and thus may serve as good starting points:

> ▶ This is a story about _____.
>
> ▶ My story takes place in _____ when _____.
>
> ▶ As the narrative opens, X is in the act of _____.
>
> ▶ What happened next was _____, followed by _____ and _____.
>
> ▶ At this point, _____ happened.
>
> ▶ The climax of these events was _____.
>
> ▶ When X understood what had happened, he/she/they said, "_____."
>
> ▶ The last thing that happened to X was _____.
>
> ▶ My point in telling this story is to show that _____.

For more techniques to help you generate ideas and start writing a narrative essay, see Chapter 3.

Stating Your Point

If you are writing a personal story about your sister, you might reveal your point implicitly through the details of the story. However, in much of the narrative writing you do as a student, you will want to state your point explicitly. If you are writing about information technology for a communications class, for example, you might include a story about visiting an online retailer, and you would probably want to explain why in a **THESIS STATEMENT** like this: "Go to any online store today, and you will discover that information technology is the main product of American business."

Developing a Plot Chronologically

As a general rule, arrange events in chronological order so your readers don't have to figure out what happened when. Chronology alone, however, is insufficient for organizing a good narrative. Events need to be related in such a way that one leads directly to, or causes, another. Taken together, the events should have a beginning, middle, and end. Then your narrative will form a complete action: a **PLOT**.

One of the best ways to plot a narrative is to set up a situation; introduce a conflict; build up the dramatic tension until it reaches a high point, or **CLIMAX**; and then release the tension and resolve the conflict. Even the little horror story about Miss Muffet is satisfying because it's tightly plotted with a clear sense of completion at the close.

Using Transitions and Verb Tenses

When you write a narrative, you will often incorporate direct references to time: "first," "last," "immediately," "not long after," "next," "while," "then," "once upon a time." References like these can be boring in a narrative if they become too predictable, as in "first," "second," "third." But used judiciously, such **TRANSITIONS** provide smooth links from one event to another, as do other connecting words and phrases like "thus," "therefore," "consequently," "what happened next," "before I knew it," and so on.

Ocean Vuong, p. 160, switches between present and past as he tells how he wrote one of his first poems.

In addition to clear transitions, your verb tenses can help you connect events in time. Remember that all actions that happen more or less at the same time in your narrative should be in the same tense: "I *was* three-quarters of the way up this hill when the van *came* over the crest. It *wasn't* on the road; it *was* on the shoulder." Don't shift tenses needlessly; but when you *do* need to indicate that one action happened before another, be sure to change tenses accordingly and accurately. If you need to shift out of chronological order altogether—you might shift back in time in a FLASHBACK or shift forward in time in a FLASH-FORWARD—be sure to make the leap clear to your readers.

Maintaining a Consistent Point of View

As you construct a narrative, you need to maintain a logical and consistent POINT OF VIEW. In a narrative written in the FIRST PERSON ("I" or "we"), like Stephen King's, the NARRATOR can be both an observer of the scene ("Most of the sight lines along the mile-long stretch of Route 5 that I walk are good") *and* a participant in the action ("I had perhaps three-quarters of a second to register this"). In a narrative written in the THIRD PERSON ("he," "she," "it," or "they"), as is the case in most articles and history books, the narrator is often merely an observer, though sometimes an all-knowing one.

Whether you write in the first or third person, don't attribute perceptions to yourself or your narrator that are physically impossible. If you are narrating a story from the front seat of your car, don't pretend to see what is going on three blocks away. If you claim to see (or know) more than you reasonably can from where you sit, your credibility with the reader will be strained.

Adding Dialogue

You can introduce the points of view of other people into a story by using DIALOGUE. In a story about her childhood, for example, Annie Dillard lets her mother speak for herself: "Lie on your back," her mother tells young Dillard. "Look at the clouds and figure out what they look like."

As a first-person narrator, Dillard might have written, "My mother told me to look at the clouds and figure out what they look like." But these words would be a step removed from the person who said them and so would lack the immediacy of direct dialogue. If you let people in your narrative speak for themselves, your characters will come to life, and your whole narrative will have a greater dramatic impact.

EDITING FOR COMMON ERRORS IN NARRATIVE WRITING

Like other kinds of writing, narrative uses distinctive patterns of language and punctuation—and thus invites typical kinds of errors. The following tips will help you check for and correct these errors in your narrative writing.

Check that verb tenses accurately indicate when actions occur

Because narrative writing focuses on actions and events, it relies heavily on verbs. Make sure verb tenses accurately indicate when actions take place. Don't get confused about when to use the simple past (She *arrived* at school), the present perfect (She *has arrived* at school), and the past perfect (She *had arrived* at school).

Use the simple past to indicate actions that were completed at a specified time in the past.

- ▶ He ~~has~~ completed the assignment this morning.

Use the present perfect to indicate actions begun and completed at some unspecified time in the past, or actions begun in the past and continuing into the present.

- ▶ The recession ~~comes~~ <u>has come</u> to an end.
- ▶ The recession ~~goes~~ <u>has gone</u> on for more than five years now.

Use the past perfect to indicate actions completed by a specific time in the past or before another past action occurred.

▶ The alligators arrived next, but by then the palm rats <u>had</u> moved out.

Check dialogue to be sure it's punctuated correctly

Narrative writing often includes the direct quotation of what people say. Punctuating dialogue can be challenging because you have to deal with the punctuation in the dialogue itself and also with any punctuation necessary to integrate the dialogue into the text.

Commas and periods always go inside the quotation marks.

▶ "Perspective is hard to define," my art history professor said.

▶ She noted that in a painting by Jacob Lawrence "perspective means one thing."

Semicolons and colons always go outside the quotation marks.

▶ But in a Cubist painting by Picasso, she said, "it means quite another"; then she went on to explain the differences.

▶ The painting presents the landscape "in layers": from the tops of mountains to the undersides of leaves in the same picture.

Question marks, exclamation points, and dashes go *inside* the quotation marks if they are part of the quoted text but *outside* if they are not part of the quoted text.

▶ The teacher asked, "Sam, how would you define perspective in art?"

▶ Did you say, "Divine perspective"?

A Book Cover

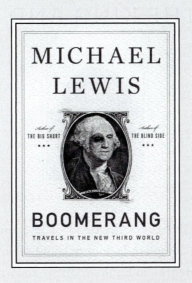

When you write a narrative, you tell what happened in a particular time and place. In the narrative illustrated on the cover of this book by best-selling author Michael Lewis, somebody has given George Washington a black eye. Lewis's title, *Boomerang*, implies that the wound is self-inflicted. Has George done something that's coming back to hit him in the face? Since the mug shot on this book cover is from a dollar bill, the offense must have been economic. A good narrative does more than simply tell what happened; it gives the story a plot with a beginning, middle, and end. Lewis traces the rise and fall of the global economy before and after 2008. How will the story end? As indicated on this book cover, Lewis concludes that the boomerang effect of excessive borrowing and lending by the United States is harming the economy and may leave the dollar with a semiperma-nent black eye. A boom in the economy, on the other hand, would likely keep the dollar strong—and the boomerang from coming back to hit George.

MELISSA UNBANKES

THE KING AND I

As a child, MELISSA UNBANKES dreamed of becoming a rock star—or a librarian. However, a complete lack of musical talent, she says, led her as an adult to pursue a degree in English. Unbankes wrote this essay for her first-year writing course at Yuba Community College in Marysville, California, when she was assigned to write a brief memoir about a person or event of particular significance to her. In this essay, which was nominated for the Norton Writer's Prize, Unbankes tells the story of her relationship with her grandmother—and of her grandmother's relationship with Elvis Presley, or at least with an Elvis figurine.

The King and I

"I want you to have this," said my grandmother, hold-   1
ing out to me a rectangular purple box. "I bought it at
Graceland." Her voice was quiet, almost reverent. I'd
heard her talk of her trip before. My grandmother loved to
travel, but Graceland always had a special significance for
her. I had the sense that she considered it a pilgrimage,
the trip that every true Elvis fan must take at least once.
"It's numbered, see? It's a limited edition." She opened
the box as she spoke, sliding out the styrofoam shell. "I
bought it at the gift shop." She paused for a moment
before separating the styrofoam, her movements slow and
careful. There was a feeling in the room like a held breath.
"You want to make sure to keep the certificate. That's
how you prove it's real." I nodded eagerly. I would have
promised anything, including carrying the certificate at
all times, if it meant I could see what was in the box. She
reached into the packaging, lifting out a figurine. "I knew
you would like it, because it's porcelain, and it's Elvis."

I collected dolls, a hobby I shared with my grand-   2
mother; she had given me my first porcelain doll years
before. She turned the figurine so I could see it, and my
heart sank. It was Elvis, there was no doubt about that,
but it wasn't the Elvis I admired. This was Elvis in a white
jumpsuit. Fat Elvis. The Elvis of velvet paintings. Tacky
Elvis. She handed me the figurine and I stared down at it,
noting that Elvis had almost perfect circles of rouge on
each cheek. Like a clown, I thought glumly. I handed it
back to her as quickly as I thought was polite, muttering
something about how cool it was. She admired it for a
moment longer before placing it back into the box. "You
can put it in your corner cabinet."

DIALOGUE captures the grandmother's character

First-person POINT OF VIEW reveals Unbankes's thoughts and feelings as a teenager

I protested immediately, telling her I could never   3
accept the responsibility for displaying such a precious
object. It should be put away, I explained, somewhere safe.
In fact, I told her, I was probably much too irresponsible
to even keep something that valuable in my possession. It
was no use. In the end I left with a cardboard box containing the Elvis figurine and several other pieces of
memorabilia she thought I would like. I placed the box on
the top shelf of my closet, hoping my grandmother would
never ask where it was.

Unbankes develops the PLOT by retelling a series of events

To say my grandmother loved Elvis would be like   4
describing the ceiling of the Sistine Chapel[1] as a nice little
mural. She was devoted, and she shared her devotion with
me on Friday afternoons. My grandmother was a school-
bus driver, and on Fridays, instead of going to day care, I
would ride her bus until the end of her route. One by one
the other passengers would leave, until it was just me and
my grandmother. Then she would turn on the radio. It
was district policy not to use the radio if students were
on the bus, so being there in the empty bus with the
music blaring gave me a kind of subversive thrill.

My grandmother always chose the oldies station,   5
"greatest hits of the '50s and '60s." I would lie across the
bench seat, feeling the bus engine rumbling underneath
me, singing along to Buddy Holly and Little Richard, the
Platters and the Drifters, and of course, Elvis. It always
came back to Elvis. My grandmother would talk between
songs, telling stories from her childhood, intertwined

1. Considered to be one of the greatest examples of Renaissance art,
the ceiling of the Sistine Chapel was painted by the artist Michelan-
gelo. The chapel is part of the Vatican in Rome, Italy.

with bits of trivia about the music. Some of the stories
she told me were probably not age-appropriate. My favorite was how she would sneak out to concerts, enlisting her
sisters to help push my great-grandfather's car down the
road so she could race it (starting the engine in front of
the house would have gotten her caught immediately, she
told me). I thought that was the smartest thing I had ever
heard, and filed it away for future use. As a child I was
used to being talked *at* instead of *to*, but I never felt like
that with her. My grandmother talked the same way to
everyone; she had no filter.

Valta Jean, or "Jeannie," as she was usually called, was   6
my best friend in those years, but by the time she gave me
the Elvis figurine we had grown apart. When I was   •······
younger, I had admired how unconventional she was; now

FLASHBACKS bring
narrative back to
Unbankes's
teenage years

those same qualities were deeply embarrassing. I had loved listening to her talk. Now it seemed as if she talked too much, asking embarrassing questions in front of my friends. Her spontaneity grated. I never knew when she would show up, carrying a bag of thrift store finds or items she had "rescued" from the side of the road. She went barefoot all the time, carrying a pair of shoes in her purse if she needed them. She smoked constantly and wore stretchy nylon pants and brightly patterned shirts. She was, in a word, tacky. While I loved her very much, I sometimes wished I could keep her hidden away like my Elvis albums.

Like most teenagers, my sense of self was very much a public production, something that had to be carefully maintained. My own love for Elvis was something that didn't fit, a tiny crack in the facade of cool, and my grandmother threatened to blow it wide open. I eventually got over my grandiose sense of teenage self-interest, but my relationship with my grandmother was never as close as it was in my childhood. I no longer found her embarrassing, only frustrating. Why, I wondered, couldn't she just *act* like a normal person? But that was never her way. She had no need to hide away pieces of herself.

There is a Japanese practice of repairing pottery, called *kintsugi*, where broken pieces of pottery are mended with gold or a gold lacquer. It's an art form that is meant to call attention to the breaks instead of hiding them, making the repair part of the history of the object. When I first read about it, I could not understand why anyone would want to display a broken cup or bowl. How could something so obviously flawed be an object of beauty? Then a few years ago at a small gallery, I saw a collection

Explicit COMPARISON (Chapter 10) of Unbankes's grandmother with the Elvis figurine

Reference to "pieces" anticipates DEFINITION of *kintsugi* in next paragraph

7

8

of kintsugi pottery and I finally understood. While the original pottery was beautiful, the repaired pottery had been transformed into something unique. After seeing the kintsugi pieces, the perfect pieces of pottery seemed somehow unfinished, blank canvases. I saw many beautiful pieces of art on display that day, but the "flawed" pieces are the ones that linger in my memory.

My grandmother died recently, and while looking for old photos of her, I found the box she had given me so many years ago. Tacky Elvis was in there. Officially, he's "Mississippi Benefit Elvis in Concert, number 1551 of a limited edition of 20,000" (I kept the certificate), but he'll always be Tacky Elvis in my mind. My memory of his appearance was fairly accurate, and my tastes haven't changed so much that I can appreciate it as a work of art. But there is something about Elvis in all his jumpsuited glory that recalls my grandmother like none of the more tasteful, classically beautiful porcelain dolls she gave me over the years ever could. 9

There were other items in the box. There was a matching commemorative plate; either my grandmother never showed it to me or my mind had blocked out the horror for all these years. Along with some books and magazines, I found two empty candy boxes with Elvis on the cover, a reproduction gold record, a golden watch with Elvis on the face, and, at the very bottom of the box, a *TV Guide* celebrating Elvis as entertainer of the century. I had to laugh at the strange collection, so imperfectly assembled, so perfectly my grandmother. 10

Tacky Elvis now has a place of honor on my bookshelf—no more hiding in the closet. I play my Elvis albums proudly (in digital form now), singing along loudly 11

Conclusion resolves conflict between Unbankes and her grandmother in the car. My oldest daughter finds it slightly embarrassing; she's getting to the age where anything I do is increasingly uncool. "It's okay," I tell her. "Someday, these will be the things you miss." She shakes her head, unconvinced. "Heartbreak Hotel" comes on, and I tell her about the first time I heard this song, about the bus, about my grandmother and her wild stories, and of course, I tell her about Elvis. It always comes back to Elvis.

THE BACK OF THE BUS

MARY MEBANE (1933–1992) was born outside Durham, North Carolina; her father was a farmer and her mother worked in a tobacco factory. She earned a PhD from the University of North Carolina and became a professor of English at the University of Wisconsin–Milwaukee. In 1971 on the op-ed page of the *New York Times*, Mebane told the story of a bus ride from Durham, North Carolina, to Orangeburg, South Carolina, that "realized for me the enormousness of the change" that had occurred since the passage of the Civil Rights Act of 1964. That bus ride was the germ of two autobiographical volumes, *Mary* (1981) and *Mary Wayfarer* (1983). The essay reprinted here is a complete chapter from the first book, which won a Coretta Scott King Book Award in 1982. It is a personal narrative of another, earlier bus ride that Mebane had taken during the 1940s, when the segregation laws were still in place. Mebane said she wrote this piece because she "wanted to show what it was like to live under legal segregation *before* the Civil Rights Act of 1964."

HISTORICALLY, MY LIFETIME IS IMPORTANT because I was part of the last generation born into a world of total legal segregation[1] in the Southern United States. When the Supreme Court outlawed segregation in the public schools in 1954, I was twenty-one. When Congress passed the Civil Rights Act of 1964, permitting blacks free access to public places, I was thirty-one. The world I was born into had been segregated for a long time—so long, in fact, that I never met anyone who had lived during the time when restrictive laws were not in existence, although some people spoke of parents and others who had lived during the "free" time. As far as anyone knew, the laws as they then existed would stand forever. They were meant to—and did—create a world that fixed black people at the bottom of society in all aspects of human life. It was a world without options.

Most Americans have never had to live with terror. I had had to live with it all my life—the psychological terror of segregation, in which there was a special set of laws governing your movements. You violated them at your peril, for you knew that if you broke one of them, knowingly or not, physical terror was just around the corner, in the form of policemen and jails, and in some cases and places white vigilante mobs formed for the exclusive purpose of keeping blacks in line.

It was Saturday morning, like any Saturday morning in dozens of Southern towns.

The town had a washed look. The street sweepers had been busy since six o'clock. Now, at eight, they were still slowly moving down the streets, white trucks with clouds of water coming from underneath the swelled tubular sides. Unwary motorists sometimes got a windowful of water as a truck passed by. As it moved on, it left in its wake a clear stream running in the gutters or splashed on the wheels of parked cars.

Homeowners, bent over industriously in the morning sun, were out pushing lawn mowers. The sun was bright, but it wasn't too hot. It was morning and it was May. Most of the mowers were glad that it was finally getting warm enough to go outside.

---

1. Government policies that barred Black people from White neighborhoods, schools, and other facilities and required Black people to sit in separate sections from White people in public spaces like buses and movie theaters.

Traffic was brisk. Country people were coming into town early with their 6
produce; clerks and service workers were getting to the job before the stores
opened at ten o'clock. Though the big stores would not be open for another
hour or so, the grocery stores, banks, open-air markets, dinettes, were already
open and filling with staff and customers.

Everybody was moving toward the heart of Durham's downtown, which 7
waited to receive them rather complacently, little knowing that in a decade
the shopping centers far from the center of downtown Durham would create a
ghost town in the midst of the busiest blocks on Main Street.

Some moved by car, and some moved by bus. The more affluent used 8
cars, leaving the buses mainly to the poor, black and white, though there were
some businesspeople who avoided the trouble of trying to find a parking place
downtown by riding the bus.

I didn't mind taking the bus on Saturday. It wasn't so crowded. At night 9
or on Saturday or Sunday was the best time. If there were plenty of seats, the
blacks didn't have to worry about being asked to move so that a white person
could sit down. And the knot of hatred and fear didn't come into my
stomach.

I knew the stop that was the safety point, both going and coming. Leav- 10
ing town, it was the Little Five Points, about five or six blocks north of the
main downtown section. That was the last stop at which four or five people
might get on. After the stop, the driver could sometimes pass two See pp. 131–32
or three stops without taking on or letting off a passenger. So the for more on the "who, where, and
number of seats on the bus usually remained constant on the trip when."
from town to Braggtown. The nearer the bus got to the end of the line, the
more I relaxed. For if a white passenger got on near the end of the line, often
to catch the return trip back and avoid having to stand in the sun at the bus
stop until the bus turned around, he or she would usually stand if there were
not seats in the white section, and the driver would say nothing, knowing that
the end of the line was near and that the standee would get a seat in a few
minutes.

On the trip to town, the Mangum Street A&P[2] was the last point at which 11
the driver picked up more passengers than he let off. These people, though

---

2. Chain of supermarkets; originally called the Great Atlantic & Pacific Tea Company.

they were just a few blocks from the downtown section, preferred to ride the bus downtown. Those getting on at the A&P were usually on their way to work at the Duke University Hospital—past the downtown section, through a residential neighborhood, and then past the university, before they got to Duke Hospital.

So whether the driver discharged more passengers than he took on near   12
the A&P on Mangum was of great importance. For if he took on more passengers than got off, it meant that some of the newcomers would have to stand. And if they were white, the driver was going to have to ask a black passenger to move so that a white passenger could sit down. Most of the drivers had a rule of thumb, though. By custom the seats behind the exit door had become "colored" seats, and no matter how many whites stood up, anyone sitting behind the exit door knew that he or she wouldn't have to move.

The disputed seat, though, was the one directly opposite the exit door.   13
It was "no-man's-land." White people sat there, and black people sat there. It all depended on whose section was fuller. If the back section was full, the next black passenger who got on sat in the no-man's-land seat; but if the white section filled up, a white person would take the seat. Another thing about the white people: they could sit anywhere they chose, even in the "colored" section. Only the black passengers had to obey segregation laws.

On this Saturday morning Esther[3] and I set out for town for our music   14
lesson. We were going on our weekly big adventure, all the way across town, through the white downtown, then across the railroad tracks, then through the "colored" downtown, a section of run-down dingy shops, through some fading high-class black neighborhoods, past North Carolina College, to Mrs. Shearin's house.

We walked the two miles from Wildwood to the bus line. Though it was   15
a warm day, in the early morning there was dew on the grass and the air still had the night's softness. So we walked along and talked and looked back constantly, hoping someone we knew would stop and pick us up.

I looked back furtively, for in one of the few instances that I remembered   16
my father criticizing me severely, it was for looking back. One day when I was walking from town he had passed in his old truck. I had been looking back and

3. Mebane's sister.

had seen him. "Don't look back," he had said. "People will think that you want them to pick you up." Though he said "people," I knew he meant men—not the men he knew, who lived in the black community, but the black men who were not part of the community, and all of the white men. To be picked up meant that something bad would happen to me. Still, two miles is a long walk and I occasionally joined Esther in looking back to see if anyone we knew was coming.

Esther and I got to the bus and sat on one of the long seats at the back   17 that faced each other. There were three such long seats—one on each side of the bus and a third long seat at the very back that faced the front. I liked to sit on a long seat facing the side because then I didn't have to look at the expressions on the faces of the whites when they put their tokens in and looked at the blacks sitting in the back of the bus. Often I studied my music, looking down and practicing the fingering. I looked up at each stop to see who was getting on and to check on the seating pattern. The seating pattern didn't really bother me that day until the bus started to get unusually full for a Saturday morning. I wondered what was happening, where all these people were coming from. They got on and got on until the white section was almost full and the black section was full.

There was a black man in a blue windbreaker and a gray porkpie hat sit-   18 ting in no-man's-land, and my stomach tightened. I wondered what would happen. I had never been on a bus on which a black person was asked to give a seat to a white person when there was no other seat empty. Usu-   See p. 128 for tips on introducing conflict and building up tension in a narrative. ally, though, I had seen a black person automatically get up and move to an empty seat farther back. But this morning the only empty seat was beside a black person sitting in no-man's-land.

The bus stopped at Little Five Points and one black got off. A young   19 white man was getting on. I tensed. What would happen now? Would the driver ask the black man to get up and move to the empty seat farther back? The white man had a businessman's air about him: suit, shirt, tie, polished brown shoes. He saw the empty seat in the "colored" section and after just a little hesitation went to it, put his briefcase down, and sat with his feet crossed. I relaxed a little when the bus pulled off without the driver saying anything. Evidently he hadn't seen what had happened, or since he was just a few stops from Main Street, he figured the mass exodus there would solve all the problems. Still, I was afraid of a scene.

The next stop was an open-air fruit stand just after Little Five Points, [20] and here another white man got on. Where would he sit? The only available seat was beside the black man. Would he stand the few stops to Main Street or would the driver make the black man move? The whole colored section tensed, but nobody said anything. I looked at Esther, who looked apprehensive. I looked at the other men and women, who studiously avoided my eyes and everybody else's as well, as they maintained a steady gaze at a far-distant land.

Just one woman caught my eye; I had noticed her before, and I had been [21] ashamed of her. She was a stringy little black woman. She could have been forty; she could have been fifty. She looked as if she were a hard drinker. Flat black face with tight features. She was dressed with great insouciance in a tight boy's sweater with horizontal lines running across her flat chest. It pulled down over a nondescript skirt. Laced-up shoes, socks, and a head rag completed her outfit. She looked tense.

The white man who had just gotten on the bus walked to the seat in no- [22] man's-land and stood there. He wouldn't sit down, just stood there. Two adult males, living in the most highly industrialized, most technologically advanced nation in the world, a nation that had devastated two other industrial giants in World War II[4] and had flirted with taking on China in Korea. Both these men, either of whom could have fought for the United States in Germany or Korea, faced each other in mutual rage and hostility. The white one wanted to sit down, but he was going to exert his authority and force the black one to get up first. I watched the driver in the rearview mirror. He was about the same age as the antagonists. The driver wasn't looking for trouble, either.

"Say there, buddy, how about moving back," the driver said, meanwhile [23] driving his bus just as fast as he could. The whole bus froze—whites at the front, blacks at the rear. They didn't want to believe what was happening was really happening.

The seated black man said nothing. The standing white man said [24] nothing.

"Say, buddy, did you hear me? What about moving on back." The driver [25] was scared to death. I could tell that.

4. The United States and its allies defeated "industrial giants" Germany and Japan, as well as Italy, in World War II (1939–45).

"These is the niggers' seats!" the little lady in the strange outfit started 26
screaming. I jumped. I had to shift my attention from the driver to the frieze
of the black man seated and white man standing to the articulate little woman
who had joined in the fray.

"The government gave us these seats! These is the niggers' seats." I was 27
startled at her statement and her tone. "The president said that these are the
niggers' seats!" I expected her to start fighting at any moment.

Evidently the bus driver did, too, because he was driving faster and 28
faster. I believe that he forgot he was driving a bus and wanted desperately to
pull to the side of the street and get out and run.

"I'm going to take you down to the station, buddy," the driver said. 29

The white man with the briefcase and the polished brown shoes who 30
had taken a seat in the "colored" section looked as though he might die of
embarrassment at any moment.

As scared and upset as I was, I didn't miss a thing. 31

By that time we had come to the stop before Main Street, and the black 32
passenger rose to get off.

"You're not getting off, buddy. I'm going to take you downtown." The 33
driver kept driving as he talked and seemed to be trying to get downtown as
fast as he could.

"These are the niggers' seats! The government plainly said these are the 34
niggers' seats!" screamed the little woman in rage.

I was embarrassed at the use of the word "nigger" but I was proud of the 35
lady. I was also proud of the man who wouldn't get up.

The bus driver was afraid, trying to hold on to his job but plainly not 36
willing to get into a row with the blacks.

The bus seemed to be going a hundred miles an hour and everybody was 37
anxious to get off, though only the lady and the driver were saying anything.

The black man stood at the exit door; the driver drove right past the 38
A&P stop. I was terrified. I was sure that the bus was going to the police station to put the black man in jail. The little woman had her hands on her hips
and she never stopped yelling. The bus driver kept driving as fast as he could.

Then, somewhere in the back of his mind, he decided to forget the whole 39
thing. The next stop was Main Street, and when he got there, in what seemed
to be a flash of lightning, he flung both doors open wide. He and his black

antagonist looked at each other in the rearview mirror; in a second the wind-breaker and porkpie hat were gone. The little woman was standing, preaching to the whole bus about the government's gift of these seats to the blacks; the man with the brown shoes practically fell out of the door in his hurry; and Esther and I followed the hurrying footsteps.

We walked about three doors down the block, then caught a bus to the   40 black neighborhood. Here we sat on one of the two long seats facing each other, directly behind the driver. It was the custom. Since this bus had a route from a black neighborhood to the downtown section and back, passing through no white residential areas, blacks could sit where they chose. One minute we had been on a bus in which violence was threatened over a seat near the exit door; the next minute we were sitting in the very front behind the driver.

The people who devised this system thought that it was going to last   41 forever.

FOR DISCUSSION

1. Why does the bus driver threaten to drive to the police station, according to Mary Mebane? What was his official duty under segregation?

2. Why does the businessman with the briefcase and brown shoes take the separate seat in the back of the bus instead of the place on the bench across from the exit? Was he upholding or violating segregation customs by doing so?

3. What is the main confrontation of the **NARRATIVE**? What emotion(s) does it arouse in young Mebane and her sister as witnesses?

4. Who are the "people" to whom Mebane refers in paragraph 41?

5. Why does Mebane claim a national significance for the events of her private life as narrated here? Is her **CLAIM** justified? How does this claim relate to her **PURPOSE** for writing?

STRATEGIES AND STRUCTURES

1. In which paragraph does Mebane begin telling the story of the bus ride? Why do you think she starts with the routine of the street sweepers and the homeowners doing yard work?

2. List several passages in Mebane's text that seem to be told from young Mary's POINT OF VIEW. Then list others that are told from the point of view of the adult author looking back at an event in her youth. Besides time, what is the main difference in their perspectives?

3. Why does Mebane refer to the Black passenger who confronts the bus driver as "the windbreaker and porkpie hat" (39)? Whose point of view is she capturing? Is she showing or telling here—and what difference does it make in her essay?

4. How does Mebane use the increasing speed of the bus to show rather than tell about the precariousness of the segregation system?

5. Mebane interrupts her narrative of the events of that Saturday morning in paragraphs 10 through 13. What is she explaining to her AUDIENCE, and why is it necessary that she do so? Where else does she interrupt her narrative with EXPOSITION?

WORDS AND FIGURES OF SPEECH

1. Why does Mebane refer to the seat across from the exit as a "no-man's-land" (13)? What does this term mean?

2. Mebane COMPARES the seated Black man and the standing White man to a "frieze," a decorative horizontal band, often molded or carved, along the upper part of a wall (26). Why is the METAPHOR appropriate here?

3. Look up "insouciance" in a dictionary (21). Does the use of this word prepare you for the rebellious behavior of the "stringy" little woman (21)? How?

4. What are the two possible meanings of "scene" (19)? How might Mebane's personal narrative be said to illustrate both kinds?

5. Which of the many meanings of "articulate" in your dictionary best fits the woman who screams back at the bus driver (26)?

FOR WRITING

1. In a brief ANECDOTE, recount a ride you have taken on a bus, train, plane, roller coaster, boat, or other vehicle. Focus on the vehicle itself and the people who were on it with you.

2. Write a personal narrative about an experience you had with racial tension in a public place. Be sure to describe the physical place and tell what you saw and heard and did there.

LYNDA BARRY

THE SANCTUARY OF SCHOOL

LYNDA BARRY (b. 1956) is a cartoonist, novelist, and teacher of writing. She was born in Wisconsin but spent most of her adolescence in Seattle, where she supported herself at age 16 as a janitor. As a student at Evergreen State College in Olympia, Washington, Barry began drawing *Ernie Pook's Comeek*, the comic strip for which she is perhaps best known. Her first novel, *Cruddy* (2000), was about a teenager and her troubled family life "in the cruddiest part of town." In "The Sanctuary of School," which first appeared in the Education section of the *New York Times* in January 1992, Barry tells how she first discovered the therapeutic value of art—and of good teachers. This narrative about her early school days also carries a pointed message for those who would cut costs in the public school system by eliminating art from the curriculum. In 2019, Barry was the recipient of a MacArthur Fellows "Genius" Grant.

I WAS SEVEN YEARS OLD the first time I snuck out of the house in the dark. It 1 was winter and my parents had been fighting all night. They were short on money and long on relatives who kept "temporarily" moving into our house because they had nowhere else to go.

My brother and I were used to giving up our bedroom. We slept on the couch, something we actually liked because it put us that much closer to the light of our lives, our television.

At night when everyone was asleep, we lay on our pillows watching it with the sound off. We watched Steve Allen's[1] mouth moving. We watched Johnny Carson's[2] mouth moving. We watched movies filled with gangsters shooting machine guns into packed rooms, dying soldiers hurling a last grenade, and beautiful women crying at windows. Then the sign-off finally came and we tried to sleep.

The morning I snuck out, I woke up filled with a panic about needing to get to school. The sun wasn't quite up yet but my anxiety was so fierce that I just got dressed, walked quietly across the kitchen and let myself out the back door.

It was quiet outside. Stars were still out. Nothing moved and no one was in the street. It was as if someone had turned the sound off on the world.

I walked the alley, breaking thin ice over the puddles with my shoes. I didn't know why I was walking to school in the dark. I didn't think about it. All I knew was a feeling of panic, like the panic that strikes kids when they realize they are lost.

That feeling eased the moment I turned the corner and saw the dark outline of my school at the top of the hill. My school was made up of about 15 nondescript portable classrooms set down on a fenced concrete lot in a run-down Seattle neighborhood, but it had the most beautiful view of the Cascade Mountains. You could see them from anywhere on the playfield and you could see them from the windows of my classroom—Room 2.

I walked over to the monkey bars and hooked my arms around the cold metal. I stood for a long time just looking across Rainier Valley. The sky was beginning to whiten and I could hear a few birds.

1. American actor and musician (1921–2000) best known for his work on late-night television.
2. American comedian and television personality (1924–2005) who hosted *The Tonight Show* for thirty years.

In a perfect world my absence at home would not have gone unnoticed. I would 9
have had two parents in a panic to locate me, instead of two parents in a panic
to locate an answer to the hard question of survival during a deep financial
and emotional crisis.

But in an overcrowded and unhappy home, it's incredibly easy for any child 10
to slip away. The high levels of frustration, depression, and anger in my house
made my brother and me invisible. We were children with the sound turned off.
And for us, as for the steadily increasing number of neglected children in this
country, the only place where we could count on being noticed was at school.

"Hey there, young lady. Did you forget to go home last night?" It was 11
Mr. Gunderson, our janitor, whom we all loved. He was nice and
he was funny and he was old with white hair, thick glasses and an
unbelievable number of keys. I could hear them jingling as he
walked across the playfield. I felt incredibly happy to see him.

By adding
dialogue (p. 134),
you can introduce
different points of
view into a
narrative.

He let me push his wheeled garbage can between the different porta- 12
bles as he unlocked each room. He let me turn on the lights and raise the
window shades and I saw my school slowly come to life. I saw Mrs. Holman,
our school secretary, walk into the office without her orange lipstick on yet.
She waved.

I saw the fifth-grade teacher, Mr. Cunningham, walking under the 13
breezeway eating a hard roll. He waved.

And I saw my teacher, Mrs. Claire LeSane, walking toward us in a red 14
coat and calling my name in a very happy and surprised way, and suddenly my
throat got tight and my eyes stung and I ran toward her crying. It was something that surprised us both.

It's only thinking about it now, 28 years later, that I realize I was crying 15
from relief. I was with my teacher, and in a while I was going to sit at my desk,
with my crayons and pencils and books and classmates all around me, and for
the next six hours I was going to enjoy a thoroughly secure, warm and stable
world. It was a world I absolutely relied on. Without it, I don't know where I
would have gone that morning.

Mrs. LeSane asked me what was wrong and when I said "Nothing," she 16
seemingly left it at that. But she asked me if I would carry her purse for her, an
honor above all honors, and she asked if I wanted to come into Room 2 early
and paint.

She believed in the natural healing power of painting and drawing for trou- 17
bled children. In the back of her room there was always a drawing table and an
easel with plenty of supplies, and sometimes during the day she would come
up to you for what seemed like no good reason and quietly ask if you wanted
to go to the back table and "make some pictures for Mrs. LeSane." We all had
a chance at it—to sit apart from the class for a while to paint, draw and silently
work out impossible problems on 11×17 sheets of newsprint.

Drawing came to mean everything to me. At the back table in Room 2, I 18
learned to build myself a life preserver that I could carry into my home.

We all know that a good education system saves lives, but the people of 19
this country are still told that cutting the budget for public
schools is necessary, that poor salaries for teachers are all we can
manage and that art, music and all creative activities must be the
first to go when times are lean.

> When you tell a story, it should have a point (p. 133).

Before- and after-school programs are cut and we are told that public schools 20
are not made for baby-sitting children. If parents are neglectful temporarily
or permanently, for whatever reason, it's certainly sad, but their unlucky
children must fend for themselves. Or slip through the cracks. Or wander in a
dark night alone.

We are told in a thousand ways that not only are public schools not 21
important, but that the children who attend them, the children who need
them most, are not important either. We leave them to learn from the blind
eye of a television, or to the mercy of "a thousand points of light"[3] that can be
as far away as stars.

I was lucky. I had Mrs. LeSane. I had Mr. Gunderson. I had an abundance 22
of art supplies. And I had a particular brand of neglect in my home that
allowed me to slip away and get to them. But what about the rest of the kids
who weren't as lucky? What happened to them?

By the time the bell rang that morning I had finished my drawing and 23
Mrs. LeSane pinned it up on the special bulletin board she reserved for draw-

---

3. In his inaugural address on January 20, 1989, President George H. W. Bush used this
phrase to refer to "all the community organizations that are spread like stars throughout
the Nation, doing good."

ings from the back table. It was the same picture I always drew—a sun in the corner of a blue sky over a nice house with flowers all around it.

Mrs. LeSane asked us to please stand, face the flag, place our right hands 24 over our hearts and say the Pledge of Allegiance. Children across the country do it faithfully. I wonder now when the country will face its children and say a pledge right back.

FOR DISCUSSION

1. As a seven-year-old leaving home in the dark in a fit of panic and anxiety, why did young Lynda Barry instinctively head for her school?

2. Why does Barry say, "We were children with the sound turned off" (10)? Who fails to hear them?

3. Barry always drew the same picture when she sat at the art table in the back of Mrs. LeSane's classroom. What's the significance of that picture? Explain.

4. Why does Barry refer to the Pledge of Allegiance in the last paragraph of her essay?

STRATEGIES AND STRUCTURES

1. Why does Barry begin her NARRATIVE with an account of watching television with her brother? Where else does she refer to watching TV? Why?

2. Most of Barry's narrative takes place at her school, which she pictures in some detail. Which of these physical details do you find most revealing, and how do they help to present the place as a "sanctuary"?

3. Point out several places in her narrative where Barry characterizes Mrs. LeSane, Mr. Gunderson, and others through their gestures and bits of DIALOGUE. What do these small acts and brief words reveal about the people Barry is portraying?

4. What does young Barry's sense of panic and anxiety contribute to the PLOT of her narrative?

5. Where and how does Barry's narrative morph into an ARGUMENT about public schools in America? What's the point of that argument, and where does she state it most directly?

WORDS AND FIGURES OF SPEECH

1. Is Barry speaking literally or metaphorically (or both) when she refers to children who "wander in a dark night alone" (20)? How and how well does she pave the way for this statement at the end of her narrative?

2. What does Barry mean when she says that the "points of light" in a child's life can be "as far away as stars" (21)? How and where does the idea of "light" take on different implications during the course of her narrative?

3. Barry characterizes her old school as a "sanctuary" instead of, for example, a "haven" or "safehouse." Why do you think she chooses this term? Is it apt? Why or why not?

4. Why does Barry refer to the "blind eye" of television (21)?

FOR WRITING

1. In a few paragraphs, tell about a time when you found school to be a sanctuary, or the opposite. Be sure to DESCRIBE the physical place and what people said and did there.

2. Write a narrative essay in which you use your experience at school to make a point about the importance of some aspect of the school curriculum that you fear may be changed or lost. If possible, expand your argument to include schools in general, not just your own.

OCEAN VUONG

IMMIGRATING INTO ENGLISH

OCEAN VUONG (b. 1988) is a poet, essayist, and best-selling novelist. He was born in Ho Chi Minh City, Vietnam, and immigrated to the United States in 1990 after spending a year as a refugee in the Philippines. He is the first person in his family to learn how to read. A graduate of Brooklyn College, where he majored in British literature, Vuong earned an MFA from New York University and teaches creative writing at the University of Massachusetts–Amherst. His collection of poems, *Night Sky with Exit Wounds* (2016), won the T. S. Eliot Prize, along with numerous other awards. In the same year that he received a MacArthur Fellows "Genius" Grant, Vuong published the best-selling novel *On Earth We're Briefly Gorgeous* (2019). "Immigrating into English," first published in the *New Yorker* magazine, is a literacy narrative that tells the story of Vuong's early experiences with learning English and writing one of his first poems.

R EADING AND WRITING, like any other crafts, come to the mind slowly, in pieces. But for me, as an E.S.L.[1] student from a family of illiterate rice farmers, who saw reading as snobby, or worse, the experience of working through a book, even one as simple as "Where the Wild Things Are,"[2] was akin to standing in quicksand, your loved ones corralled at its safe edges, their arms folded in suspicion and doubt as you sink.

My family immigrated to the U.S. from Vietnam in 1990, when I was two. We lived, all seven of us, in a one-bedroom apartment in Hartford, Connecticut, and I spent my first five years in America surrounded, inundated, by the Vietnamese language. When I entered kindergarten, I was, in a sense, immigrating all over again, except this time into English. Like any American child, I quickly learned my ABCs, thanks to the age-old melody (one I still sing rapidly to myself when I forget whether "M" comes before "N"). Within a few years, I had become fluent—but only in speech, not in the written word.

One early-spring afternoon, when I was in fourth grade, we got an assignment in language-arts class: we had two weeks to write a poem in honor of National Poetry Month. Normally, my poor writing abilities would excuse me from such assignments, and I would instead spend the class mindlessly copying out passages from books I'd retrieved from a blue plastic bin at the back of the room. The task allowed me to camouflage myself; as long as I looked as though I were doing something smart, my shame and failure were hidden. The trouble began when I decided to be dangerously ambitious. Which is to say, I decided to write a poem.

How to develop an interesting plot out of ordinary events is discussed on p. 133.

"Where is it?" the teacher asked. He held my poem up to the fluorescent classroom lights and squinted, the way one might examine counterfeit money. I could tell, by the slowly brightening room, that it had started to snow. I pointed to my work dangling from his fingers. "No, where is the poem you plagiarized? How did you even write something like this?" Then he tipped my desk toward me. The desk had a cubby attached to its underside, and I watched as the contents spilled from the cubby's mouth: rectangular pink erasers, crayons, yellow pencils, wrinkled worksheets where dotted letters were filled in, a

---

1. Refers to students learning English as a "second language," in addition to their own native language(s). Today, the acronym "ELL," short for "English Language Learner," is more commonly used.
2. Classic children's book by Maurice Sendak, first published in 1963.

lime Dum Dum lollipop. But no poem. I stood before the rubble at my feet. Little moments of ice hurled themselves against the window as the boys and girls, my peers, stared, their faces as unconvinced as blank sheets of paper.

Weeks earlier, I'd been in the library. It was where I would hide during   5 recess. Otherwise, because of my slight frame and soft voice, the boys would call me "pansy" and "fairy" and pull my shorts around my ankles in the middle of the schoolyard. I sat on the floor beside a tape player. From a box of cassettes, I chose one labeled "Great American Speeches." I picked it because of the illustration, a microphone against a backdrop of the American flag. I picked it because the American flag was one of the few symbols I recognized.

Page 135 explains when to use the past perfect ("had been") instead of the simple past ("was").

Through the headset, a robust male voice surged forth, emptying into   6 my body. The man's inflections made me think of waves on a sea. Between his sentences, a crowd—I imagined thousands—roared and applauded. I imagined their heads shifting in an endless flow. His voice must possess the power of a moon, I thought, something beyond my grasp, my little life. Then a narrator named the man as a Dr. Martin Luther King Jr. I nodded, not knowing why a doctor was speaking like this. But maybe these people were ill, and he was trying to cure them. There must have been medicine in his words—can there be medicine in words? "I have a dream," I mouthed to myself as the doctor spoke. It occurred to me that I had been mouthing my grandmother's stories as well, the ones she had been telling me ever since I was born. Of course, not being able to read does not mean that one is empty of stories.

For a selection from a major speech by King, read "The Other America," pp. 576–84.

My poem was called "If a Boy Could Dream." The phrases "promised   7 land" and "mountaintop" sounded golden to me, and I saw an ochre-lit field, a lushness akin to a spring dusk. I imagined that the doctor was dreaming of springtime. So my poem was a sort of ode to spring. From the gardening shows my grandmother watched, I'd learned the words for flowers I had never seen in person: foxglove, lilac, lily, buttercup. "If a boy could dream of golden fields, full of lilacs, tulips, marigolds . . ."

I knew words like "if" and "boy," but others I had to look up. I sounded   8 out the words in my head, a dictionary in my lap, and searched the letters. After a few days, the poem appeared as gray graphite words. The paper a white flag. I had surrendered, had written.

Looking back, I can see my teacher's problem. I was, after all, a poor stu- 9
dent. "Where is it?" he said again.

"It's right here," I said, pointing to my poem pinched between his fingers. 10

I had read books that weren't books, and I had read them using every- 11
thing but my eyes. From that invisible "reading," I had pressed my world onto
paper. As such, I was a fraud in a field of language, which is to say, I was a
writer. I have plagiarized my life to give you the best of me.

FOR DISCUSSION

1. A quick preview of Ocean Vuong's essay would suggest that he is writing an
   immigration story. How does the **NARRATIVE** develop the basic idea of moving
   from one territory to another? Explain.

2. "Where is it?" asks Ocean Vuong's fourth-grade teacher (4). Vuong's teacher
   assumes that his pupil's poem is plagiarized and that he is hiding the source. Should
   the teacher have handled the situation differently? Why or why not? Explain.

3. "Reading and writing, like any other crafts, come to the mind slowly, in pieces"
   (1). Based on your experience, is Vuong right about this? What are some specific
   examples, in your case, of the process of learning to read and write "slowly" and
   "in pieces"—or otherwise?

4. "Of course, not being able to read," says Vuong, "does not mean that one is empty
   of stories" (6). Writing is only about 5,000 years old. How long have people been
   telling stories? What kinds of stories?

5. As a child, Vuong was fluent in both Vietnamese and English—"but only in
   speech, not in the written word" (2). Why does learning to read and write a language take children longer than learning to speak it?

STRATEGIES AND STRUCTURES

1. "Literacy narratives" tell the story of some aspect of the author's experience with
   reading and writing. In Vuong's narrative, what specific aspects of literacy is he
   writing about?

2. The **CLIMAX** of Vuong's story is not the moment of discovery, when the teacher
   accuses him of plagiarism; it is the act of writing the poem, which came earlier.
   The climax of a story usually comes near the end. How and how well does Vuong
   solve this problem of chronology in telling his story?

3. In Vuong's narrative, what event leads to the climactic writing of "If a Boy Could Dream"? How did Vuong's experience with his grandmother's stories prepare him (and his readers) for this sequence of events?

4. At the end of his narrative, Vuong speaks directly to his audience. How effective is this strategy? Why might he use it, and who is his intended audience?

WORDS AND FIGURES OF SPEECH

1. Vuong says his decision to write a poem was "dangerously ambitious" (3). Why was it ambitious? Why was it dangerous?

2. What is the function of the phrase "Weeks earlier" in Vuong's narrative (5)? How does it help him to solve the problem of telling a story out of chronological order?

3. Throughout his narrative, Vuong uses terms that are related to war and the military, for example: "camouflage" (3), "rubble" (4), "white flag" (8), "surrendered" (8). How appropriate is this language? What sort of battle is he telling about?

4. Point out places in his essay where Vuong uses FIGURES OF SPEECH such as METAPHOR ("moments of ice") and SIMILE ("as blank sheets of paper") in the last sentence in paragraph 4. How and how well does the use of such figurative language fit in with Vuong's account of the first poem he wrote?

5. Plagiarism is the use of another person's words or ideas without acknowledgment, as if they were one's own. Wrongly accused of plagiarism by his fourth-grade teacher, Vuong nevertheless says at the end of his essay that he has "plagiarized" (11). What does he mean by this, and what is he implying about the nature of writing as he sees it?

FOR WRITING

1. Do some research on Vuong, and in a paragraph or two, tell the story of how he came to be called "Ocean."

2. If your first language isn't English, write a narrative telling the story of how you "immigrated" into English. If immigration isn't the metaphor you would use for your English learning process, how would you describe it instead? Why? Be sure to give examples of particular words and phrases that inspired (or intimidated) you.

3. Whatever language(s) you consider your native language, you learned to think in that language before you learned to read and write it. Write a preliteracy narrative about some aspect of your early language acquisition or of that of somebody you

know, such as a younger sibling. Again, cite specific examples of words and phrases that you (or they) learned—and how.

4. Children generally take longer to learn to read and write in Chinese than in languages like English, Greek, or Albanian. Do some research on the differences between learning alphabetical, syllabic, and logographic writing systems, and write an essay explaining why children the world over learn to speak at more or less the same age but not to read and write.

RYAN KNIGHTON

BLIND SAFARI

RYAN KNIGHTON (b. 1972) teaches English and creative writing at Capilano University in British Columbia, Canada. He is a native of Vancouver and a graduate of Simon Fraser University. On his 18th birthday, Knighton was diagnosed with a degenerative eye disease that has left him totally blind, a condition he writes about, often humorously, in books like *Cockeyed: A Memoir* (2006) and *C'mon Papa: Dispatches from a Dad in the Dark* (2010). In this selection from a 2017 essay written for *Afar* magazine, Knighton and his wife go on a safari in Zimbabwe in southern Africa, a region known for its diverse wildlife. At first, Knighton does not expect much to happen on the trip; or rather, he expects to miss what most of the others get to see. Thanks, in part, to a creative guide named Alan, he is wrong about this. "Blind Safari" is such a vivid narrative that it won the Society for American Travel's competition for best piece of foreign travel writing in 2018.

A s OUR LAND CRUISER NOSED THROUGH THE BRUSH, cicadas buzzed above 1
us like power lines. My wife and I had been in Zimbabwe[1] only a few
hours. So far, our guide on our first safari drive, Alan, had already
spotted several species of fleet antelope, and I was already concerned that for me—as a blind man—yes, this was going to kind of
suck. I might as well be at a drive-in movie.

Maintaining a consistent point of view in a narrative (p. 134) helps the reader see as you do.

Here, you try: Close your eyes. Over there is a kudu, what- 2
ever a kudu is.[2]

Welcome to a blind safari. 3

Dharmesh, the driver, stopped the vehicle. Alan suggested in his lovely 4
baritone voice that we step out and stretch our legs on the dusty path and have
a drink, or "sundowner." Robert, our animal tracker, dismounted from his seat
on the vehicle's grill to pass around beer and snacks. In the distance, apparently, a giraffe could be seen slipping into the trees. Tracy, my wife, watched
quietly as Alan began his work, describing the animal and its behavior and its
place in the ecosystem of the locale, the Malilangwe Wildlife Reserve.[3]

My can of lager, because I could taste it, was more real to me than a 5
giraffe.

How a blind man can be guided, how I might connect with unseen sights 6
in an unseen place, would be Alan's challenge for the next seven days. A few
years earlier, he had guided his first blind client through a game reserve on the
western boundary of South Africa's Kruger National Park.[4] The experience
had radically enriched his approach.

"Whether you're sighted or not, the bush is overwhelming and confus- 7
ing when you first arrive. It's an onslaught of stimuli," Alan told me. "But
guiding a blind person helped me realize the significance, the depth, of our
other senses. I could use them to enhance my voice as a guide. A taste, a
sound, touching or holding something, these slow everything down to a different focus."

---

1. Located in southeastern Africa, the Republic of Zimbabwe has a population of about
fifteen million.
2. A *kudu* is a species of striped antelope that can weigh up to 700 pounds.
3. A natural wilderness of approximately 130,000 acres that is home to an endangered
species of rhinos as well as more than eighty ancient rock-painting sites.
4. One of the largest game reserves in Africa, covering approximately 7,500 square miles.

A safari, by cliché and assumption, is overwhelmingly driven by photogra- 8
phy. Tourists survey a living museum of wild animals and, as their primary experience, merely look at Africa through cameras and screens. But with Alan at the
helm, here I was, ready not only to experience what a safari might reveal to the
full spectrum of sensory input, but also to try to deepen my own understanding
of what it means, or can mean, to be guided. Being blind, I'm a bit of a connoisseur. Daily, I'm dragged and steered and told where and how to move, perpetually
hitched like a wagon to the elbows of strangers. You could say I live in a chronic
state of guidance. But getting around without getting killed isn't anything like
having a sense of place. Perhaps a professional guide could impart some of that.

So far, I'd heard rumors of a giraffe and nursed a beer. 9

Suddenly Alan's hand clamped my shoulder, communicating everything 10
in a grip. Do not speak. Do not move. Adrenaline shot through me. We were in
a clearing surrounded by bush and shadow and, well, something else. Something not-giraffe.

Silence, for the blind, is often the most terrifying sound. Alan's grip 11
firmed and pivoted me a few degrees to the right, aiming my attention like a
satellite dish. At what?

"Elephant," he whispered. "Twenty-five meters." 12

I strained to hear it. To hear something. Was it moving? Had it seen us? 13
Alan's hand gently squeezed my shoulder, then again, and again, as if count-
ing the animal's steps.

"Fifteen meters," he whispered. 14

I couldn't hear my wife. I couldn't sense where our vehicle was, or how 15
far we were from its safety. Alan's hand assured me we were fine for now, but
it also implied, by its constant grip, everything could change in an instant.

"Ten meters." 16

Finally, a faint noise. The plodding of a six-ton bull. Something I had never 17
heard. An elephant's loose-structured feet expand, landing with a small, dispir-
ited squish, like the sound of spiking a semi-deflated football. Now I could
understand how something so large could glide so quietly through the bush.
Squish, squish, it lumbered toward us, deciding whether it would charge, or not.

Alan's hand clenched harder. The animal had stopped. I could sense its 18
stare, Alan angling my body toward its gaze. Neither I nor the bull knew what
to make of the other.

Then, squish, squish, it stepped off into the bush and was gone. An odor 19
followed. Wet earth, like parched land after a first rain. Later,
Alan would explain that I had smelled the elephant's method of
cooling and hygiene. Mud retains moisture, so elephants coat
themselves to stay cool. When it dries, they'll scrape themselves
against leadwood or baobab trees, the hardened earth taking par-
asites from their skin. An elephant waxing. I hadn't seen that, but I'd smelled
my way into something.

> After introducing conflict into the narrative, you need to resolve it (p. 128) before ending the story.

Alan's grip on my shoulder finally loosened, and a quick pat of assurance 20
told me everything was OK now. Nothing to see here. I was, in a word, awestruck.

"Well," he chirped, "that doesn't happen every day." 21

FOR DISCUSSION

1. "Blind Safari" is about Ryan Knighton's adventures while on safari in Zimbabwe. It is also, he says, about being "guided" (8). What does he mean by this?

2. When "tourists" go on safari in Africa, according to Knighton, what is usually their main goal (8)? Should they stay home instead? Why or why not?

3. Once upon a time, unfortunately, the driving motive for going on a safari to Africa was big-game hunting. What role, "by cliché and assumption," would Alan, the guide, traditionally have played in such an expedition (8)?

4. Knighton's whole attitude toward going on a safari changes during the course of his narrative. Why and how does it change? Is the change justified? Explain.

STRATEGIES AND STRUCTURES

1. The first animals to appear in Knighton's **NARRATIVE** are a species of antelope. How and how effectively does Knighton use their presence to dramatize his fears of what is going to happen (or not happen) to him on the safari? Explain.

2. Once Knighton and his party descend from the Land Cruiser, their part in the action of the narrative comes to a halt. How does the writer nevertheless intro-duce further action and conflict into the **PLOT** of his narrative?

3. In this episode of Knighton's adventures in Zimbabwe, the elephant glides off into the bush. The story could have ended differently, he implies. Where and how does the author entertain an alternative conclusion to his narrative?

4. **POINT OF VIEW** is an important element in any narrative. How and where does Knighton demonstrate that this critical aspect of his story is hardly limited to sight alone?

5. How does Knighton use the presence of Alan, the safari guide, to help him control the "focus" of his **POINT OF VIEW**, particularly with regard to the approaching elephant (10)? Explain.

6. Later in the essay, Knighton states that "everything around us is a living, working system, not just a view." How and how well does Knighton use his narrative of going on a safari in Zimbabwe to support this observation? Explain.

WORDS AND FIGURES OF SPEECH

1. If you look up the etymology, or word history, of "safari," you'll find that it means "journey or expedition" in Swahili, one of the principal languages of East Africa. Where did the Swahili word come from, according to the dictionary?

2. Why might Knighton invoke the term "cliché" when writing about going on a safari to Africa for readers of a travel magazine published in English (8)?

3. Knighton compares the sound of the elephant's foot to that of "spiking a semi-deflated football" (17). How effective do you find this **SIMILE**? Explain.

4. Near the end of his narrative, Knighton describes an elephant "waxing" (19). What does the term mean, and why might it be called this?

5. "Nothing to see here," writes Knighton before giving Alan the last word in this selection (20). Explain the **IRONY** of this statement.

FOR WRITING

1. Instead of letting his guide explain, in his own words, why the departing elephant smells of wet earth, Knighton reports the explanation in indirect discourse. Imagine what Alan and Knighton might have said to each other on the subject of "an elephant waxing," and write out their conversation in the form of a brief dialogue (19).

2. Imagine that you and your companion(s) are on safari. Write a narrative of your adventures. Base it on "cliché and assumption," but indicate the limitations of this perspective (8).

3. Write a critical analysis of "Blind Safari." Consider what happens to the writer's **POINT OF VIEW** as the elephant gets closer and closer—as well as the implica-

tions of Knighton's statement, "Everything around us is a living, working system, not just a view" (14).

4. Read Ernest Hemingway's "The Snows of Kilimanjaro" (1936)—google the title to find it online—and then write a critical analysis of Hemingway's story as an ironic tale of a big-game hunter in Tanzania. Include a discussion of how Hemingway handles the central character's **POINT OF VIEW** as he is dying.

5. Do some research on the effects of poaching in the wildlife preserves of Zimbabwe and other regions of Africa, and write an essay describing—and suggesting how to deal with—some aspect of the problem.

VALERIA LUISELLI

TELL ME HOW IT ENDS

VALERIA LUISELLI (b. 1983) is a fiction writer and essayist who teaches literature and creative writing at Bard College. A native of Mexico City, Luiselli moved at age two with her family to Madison, Wisconsin, where her father was in graduate school. From there, his work as a diplomat took the family to Costa Rica, South Korea, and South Africa. Luiselli moved back to Mexico when she was 16 and studied philosophy at the National Autonomous University of Mexico. After returning to the United States to study dance, she switched to comparative literature and earned a PhD from Columbia University. Luiselli published her first novel in Spanish in 2011. The story of a young mother living in Mexico City who is writing a novel, the book was translated into English as *Faces in the Crowd* (2014). Luiselli's fifth novel, *Lost Children Archive* (2019), was her first to be written in English. "Tell Me How It Ends" is a selection from Luiselli's 2017 essay collection by that title based on her volunteer work as an interpreter for children seeking asylum in the United States. A narrative within a narrative, it deals with the writer's frustration at not being able to control the stories she is telling that may determine the children's fates.

OFTEN, MY DAUGHTER ASKS ME:　　　　1

So, how does the story of those children end?　　　　2

I don't know how it ends yet, I usually say.　　　　3

My daughter often follows up on the stories she half-hears. There is 4
one story that obsesses her, a story I only tell her in pieces and for which
I have not yet been able to offer a real ending. It begins with two girls in the
courtroom. They're five and seven years old, and they're from a small
village in Guatemala.[1] Spanish is their second language, but the older girl
speaks it well. We sit around the mahogany table in the room where the
interviews take place, and their mother observes from one of the benches in
the back. The little girl concentrates on her coloring book, a crayon in her
right hand. The older one has her hands crossed as an adult might, and she
answers my questions one by one. She is a little shy but tries to be clear and
precise in her answers, delivering all of them with a big smile, toothless
here and there.

Why did you come to the United States?　　　　5

I don't know.　　　　6

How did you travel here?　　　　7

A man brought us.　　　　8

A coyote?[2]　　　　9

No, a man.　　　　10

Was he nice to you?　　　　11

Yes, he was nice, I think.　　　　12

And where did you cross the border?　　　　13

I don't know.　　　　14

Texas? Arizona?　　　　15

Yes! Texas Arizona.　　　　16

I realize it's impossible to go on with the interview, so I ask the 17
lawyers to make an exception and allow the mother to meet with us, at least
for a while. We go back to question one, and the mother responds for the

1. Guatemala is the largest country in Central America, with a population of over 17 million.
Most Guatemalans speak Spanish; there are also 21 Mayan and two other indigenous languages in the country.
2. Slang term for a paid guide who smuggles immigrants into the United States.

girls, filling holes, explaining things, and also telling her own version of the story.

When the younger of her daughters turned two, she decided to migrate 18 north and left them in the care of their grandmother. She crossed two national borders with no documents. She wasn't detained by Border Patrol and managed to cross the desert with a group of people. After a few weeks she arrived in Long Island, where she had a cousin. That's where she settled. Years passed, and the girls grew up. Years passed, and she remarried. She had another child.

One day she called her mother—the grandmother of the girls—and told 19 her that the time had come: she had saved enough money to bring the girls over. I don't know how the grandmother responded to the news of her granddaughters' imminent departure, but she noted the instructions down carefully and later explained them to the girls: in a few days, a man was going to come for them, a man who would help them get back to their mother. She told them that it would be a long trip, but that he would keep them safe. The man had taken many other girls from their village safely across the two borders to their mothers, and everything had gone well. So everything would go well this time, too.

The day before they left, their grandmother sewed a ten-digit telephone 20 number on the collars of the dress each girl would wear throughout the entire trip. It was a ten-digit number the girls had not been able to memorize, as hard as she tried to get them to, so she had decided to embroider it on their dresses and repeat, over and over, a single instruction: they should never take this dress off, not even to sleep, and as soon as they reached America, as soon as they met the first American policeman, they were to show the inside of the dress's collar to him. He would then dial the number and let them speak to their mother. The rest would follow.

The rest did follow: they made it to the border, were kept in custody, in 21 the hielera,[3] for an indefinite time period (they didn't remember how many days, but they said that they were colder there than they had ever been). After that they went to a shelter, and a few

How events in a narrative follow one another is discussed on p. 133.

3. Detention center, from the Spanish word for "icebox" or "cooler."

weeks later they were put on a plane and flown to JFK, where their mother, baby brother, and stepfather were waiting for them.

That's it? my daughter asks.   22

That's it, I tell her.   23

That's how it ends?   24

Yes, that's how it ends.   25

But of course it doesn't end there. That's just where it begins, with a   26
court summons: a first Notice to Appear.[4] . . .

If the child answers the [intake] questionnaire "correctly," he or she is more   27
likely to have a case strong enough to increase the chances of being placed
with a pro bono attorney.[5] An answer is "correct" if it strengthens the child's
case and provides a potential avenue of relief. So, in the warped world of
immigration, a correct answer is when, for example, a girl reveals that her
father is an alcoholic who physically or sexually abused her, or when a boy
reports that he received death threats or that he was beaten repeatedly by
several gang members after refusing to acquiesce to recruitment at school and
has the physical injuries to prove it. Such answers—more common than
exceptional—may open doors to potential immigration relief and, eventually,
legal status in the United States. When children don't have enough battle
wounds to show, they may not have any way to successfully defend their cases
and will most likely be "removed" back to their home country, often without
a trial. . . .

If the children are very young, in addition to translating from one language to   28
another, the interpreters have to reconfigure the questions, shift them from
the language of adults to the language of children. When I interviewed the
girls with the dresses, for example, I had to break many of the intake questions up into simpler, shorter phrasings, until I was finally able to find a bridge
to communicate with them. . . .

4. Document ordering an immigrant to appear in court as the first step in the deportation
process.
5. One who is donating legal services for the public good (*pro bono publico*).

What kinds of things did you do when you lived with your grandmother? 29

We played. 30

But besides playing? 31

Nothing. 32

Did you work? 33

Yes. 34

What did you do? 35

I don't remember. 36

I went on to questions thirty, thirty-one, thirty-two, and thirty-three. 37
The older girl answered them while the little one undressed a crayon and
scratched its trunk with her fingernail.

Did you ever get in trouble at home when you lived in your home 38
country?

No. 39

Were you punished if you did something wrong? 40

No. 41

How often were you punished? 42

Never. 43

Did you or anyone in your family have an illness that required special 44
attention?

What? 45

The girl's answers weren't really working. They weren't working in their 46
favor, that is. What I needed to hear, though I didn't want to hear it, was that
they had been doing hard labor, labor that put their safety and integrity in danger; that they were being exploited, abused, punished, maybe threatened with
death by gangs. If their answers didn't align with what the law considers reason
enough for the right to protection, the only possible ending to their story was
going to be a deportation order. It was going to be very hard, with the answers I
was getting, to even find them a lawyer willing to take their case. The girls were
so young, and even if they had a story that secured legal intervention in their
favor, they didn't know the words necessary to tell it. For children of that age,
telling a story—in a second language, translated to a third—a round
and convincing story that successfully inserts them into legal proceedings working up to their defense, is practically impossible.

When and where
should a story
end? See p. 129.

But how does the story about those girls end? my daughter asks. 47

I don't know how it ends, I say.   48

She comes back to this question often, demanding a proper conclusion   49
with the insistence of very small children:

But what happens next, Mamma?   50

I don't know.   51

FOR DISCUSSION

1. Valeria Luiselli's young daughter "obsesses" over the story her mother tells about two young girls from Guatemala in an immigration courtroom (4). Why might this particular story be of special interest to her daughter?

2. Luiselli's narrative of the two girls begins in the courtroom; and she knows that if their backstory is not grim enough to require protection under the law, "the only possible ending" of their story is going to be deportation (46). Yet Luiselli repeatedly tells her daughter she doesn't know how the story ends. Why might she do this?

3. As a skilled novelist, Luiselli could easily tell the court a tale of horror and abuse that might get protection for the girls. Why does she refrain from such a narrative strategy?

4. Luiselli says she does not know how the grandmother of the two Guatemalan girls responded to the news of their "imminent departure" (19). So why does she bring up the issue? What does her show of interest suggest about the writer herself, both as a person and as a consumer of stories?

5. In your opinion, how *should* the story of the two girls end? Why do you think so?

STRATEGIES AND STRUCTURES

1. How and how well does Luiselli use the introductory **DIALOGUE** with her daughter to set up the story she is going to tell about her young daughter's interest in the plight of the two girls from Guatemala? Explain.

2. How and how well does Luiselli use the fourth paragraph of her narrative to set up the story she is going to tell about the girls themselves? Which details in her account do you find particularly effective—and why?

3. Storytellers typically use dialogue to advance a story, and Luiselli sprinkles dialogue throughout her narrative. How do the spoken words in her narrative help (or hinder) Luiselli as she struggles to tell the story she wants to tell?

4. The writer's role in Luiselli's **NARRATIVE** is essentially that of a reporter. How and why does this role resemble (or differ from) the one she might play as the writer of a novel or short story?

5. Before the girls set out on their journey, their grandmother tells them the story of what she expects to happen. "The rest," she says, "would follow" (20). "The rest did follow," says Luiselli, but not quite as the grandmother had imagined. How and how well does this episode confirm what Luiselli herself has to say about the difficulties, in real life, of telling "a round and convincing story" with a happy ending (19, 46)?

WORDS AND FIGURES OF SPEECH

1. Why is a person who is hired to take would-be immigrants from Mexico or South America to the United States often called a "coyote" (9)?

2. In Spanish, a *hielera* is a cooler or ice bucket (21). Why might the term be used by immigrants and immigration authorities to refer to a detention center?

3. What are the implications of Luiselli's ascribing "battle wounds" to children (27)? Explain the **METAPHOR**.

4. Luiselli says her daughter demands a "proper conclusion" to the story (49). The girl likely is calling for a happy ending. How else might the phrase be defined in the context of how to write a narrative?

FOR WRITING

1. "But how does the story about those girls end? my daughter asks" (47). Write an alternative ending to Luiselli's essay that answers her daughter's question. Try using dialogue, as Luiselli does.

2. The questions that Luiselli asks throughout her narrative are prescribed by the court; but imagine for a moment that you are in an immigration courtroom in the role of interpreter for a young person who is likely to be deported. Make a list of the questions you would ask that person.

3. Using your own "questionnaire" as a basis, write out some of the dialogue you might expect to hear between an interpreter (you or someone else) and the person(s) being interviewed in an immigration courtroom.

4. Write a narrative in which someone tells you a story of how events are going to go and then says, in effect, "The rest would follow" (20). Then pick up the story by saying, in effect, "The rest did follow" (21)—and give the narrative an unexpected direction and ending, as demanded by reality (or your imagination).

⋗7⋖

EXAMPLE

I T'S difficult to write about any subject, however familiar, without giving
EXAMPLES.* Take hiccups, for example. The most prolonged case of hiccups
in a human being is that of an Iowa man who hiccupped from 1922 to 1990.
We know this is a true case because it is documented in the *Guinness World
Records*, which is a compendium of examples, however unique. A typical entry
consists of a category (largest pizza, oldest cat, longest bout of hiccups) and a
person or thing that fits that category.

This is what examples are and do: they're individuals (a man from Iowa
who hiccupped for 68 years) taken out of a larger category or group (serious
cases of hiccupping) to represent the whole group. Nobody knows for sure
the evolutionary purpose of hiccups—one hypothesis is that they help infants
clear air from their stomachs—but why we use examples in writing is pretty
clear.

For most of us, it is easier to digest a piece of pie than the whole pie at
once. The same goes for examples. Good examples are *representative*: they
exhibit all of the main, important characteristics of the group
they exemplify. That is, they give the flavor of the whole subject
in a single bite. This makes it easier for the reader to grasp (if not
swallow) what we have to say—assuming, of course, that our
examples are interesting and compelling. Or at least vivid.

Through one
family's eviction,
Matthew Desmond
(p. 207) comments
on poverty in
America.

Good examples vivify—or give life to—a subject by making general
statements ("cats can live a long time") more specific ("the oldest cat on record is Creme Puff of Austin, Texas, who lived to be 38 years old"). They also
help make **ABSTRACT** concepts more **CONCRETE**.

*Words printed in **SMALL CAPITALS** are defined in the Glossary/Index.

Example 181

In the following passage, the author is explaining the abstract idea that specific characteristics make individuals seem more "representative" of a group than they actually are:

> People were blind to logic when it was embedded in a story. Describe a very sick old man and ask people: Which is more probable, that he will die within a week or die within a year? More often than not, they'll say, "He'll die within a week." Their mind latches on to a story of imminent death, and the story masks the logic of the situation.
>
> —MICHAEL LEWIS, *The Undoing Project*

Abstractions are concepts, such as "representativeness," that are more or less detached from our five senses. Concrete examples, such as Lewis's "very sick old man," make abstractions more immediately perceptible, especially to our eyes and ears.

As the *Guinness World Records* demonstrates, concrete examples can be interesting in their own right. In most kinds of writing, however, we do not use examples for their own sake but to make a point. Lewis's point here has to do with logical thinking. In terms of pure logic, no matter how sick a person is, they are more likely to live between 0 and 365 days than to live exactly 7 days or less. The first scenario is more probable because it includes every possibility in the second scenario and more—staying alive for 8 days, a month, half a year, and so on. What leads human judgment "astray" in such cases, Lewis explains, is the power of stories to reinforce people's preconceptions. People hear a story about someone who is very sick, says Lewis, and it "represents" the idea of imminent death that they already "had in their mind about that thing."

How many examples are sufficient to prove your point? As with other kinds of evidence, that will depend on the complexity of your subject, the nature of your audience, and your purpose in writing. Are you speaking mainly to an audience of statisticians and psychologists who will immediately recognize the representative **FALLACY** in operation, despite the complexity of the idea? Or is your audience made up of people who like a good story and are likely to need further proof when you claim that they can't always trust a tale to be true just because it is well told?

Sometimes a single example can suffice—and even provide a focal point for an essay or an entire book—if it is truly representative and appealing enough to your audience. Take the example of J. P. Morgan's nose, for instance. In her introduction to *Morgan, American Financier* (1999), the biographer Jean Strouse discusses the difficulties she faced in writing a life of the banker who almost single-handedly ran the American economy a hundred years ago. In addition to the sheer bulk of biographical material, there were countless stories and legends that had grown up around Morgan.

Strouse did not solve the problem of organizing all this material by focusing on Morgan's unusual nose; but she did effectively use the nose example to introduce the legendary nature of her subject to her readers:

> Even Morgan's personal appearance gave rise to legend. He had a skin disease called rhinophyma that in his fifties turned his nose into a hideous purple bulb. One day the wife of his partner Dwight Morrow reportedly invited him to tea. She wanted her daughter Anne to meet the great man, and for weeks coached the girl about what would happen. Anne would come into the room and say good afternoon; she would not stare at Mr. Morgan's nose, she would not say anything about his nose, and she would leave.

That "one day" came, as Strouse tells the story, and the Morrows' young daughter, Anne, played her part flawlessly. Mrs. Morrow, however, had more difficulty:

> Mrs. Morrow and Mr. Morgan sat on a sofa by the tea tray. Anne came in, said hello, did not look at Morgan's nose, did not say anything about his nose, and left the room. Sighing in relief, Mrs. Morrow asked, "Mr. Morgan, do you take one lump or two in your nose?"

The usefulness of this story as a way to show how examples can help organize and focus our writing is enhanced only by the fact that this story never actually happened.

When she grew up, Anne Morrow went on to become a successful writer and aviator who charted new intercontinental flight routes with her husband, Charles Lindbergh. "This ridiculous story has not a grain of truth in it," Mrs. Lindbergh told Morgan's biographer many years later; but "it is so funny I am sure it will continue."

Example 183

Brief **NARRATIVES**, or **ANECDOTES**, such as the story of Mrs. Morrow and J. P. Morgan's nose, often make good organizing examples because they link generalities or abstractions—logical fallacies, principles of biography—to specific people and concrete events. By citing just this one story among the many inspired by Morgan's appearance and personality, Strouse accomplishes several things with one stroke: she paints a clear picture of how his contemporaries regarded the man whose life story she is introducing; she shows how difficult it was to see her controversial subject through the legends that enshrouded him; and she finds a focal point for organizing the introduction to her entire book. Evidently, Strouse has a good nose for examples.

A BRIEF GUIDE TO WRITING
AN ESSAY BASED ON EXAMPLES

As you write an essay based on examples, you need to identify your subject, say what its main characteristics are, and give specific instances that exhibit those characteristics. The editors of the *Onion* make these basic moves in the following tongue-in-cheek passage from an essay in this chapter:

> In total, 347 individual acts of sin were committed at the bake sale, with nearly every attendee committing at least one of the seven deadly sins as outlined by Gregory the Great in the Fifth Century.
> —THE ONION, "All Seven Deadly Sins Committed at Church Bake Sale"

The editors of the *Onion* identify their subject ("the seven deadly sins"), define it or state its main characteristics ("as outlined by Gregory the Great"), and give specific instances that exhibit these characteristics ("347 individual acts of sin").

The following guidelines will help you make these basic moves as you draft an exemplification essay. They will also help you ensure that your examples fit your purpose and audience, are sufficient to make your point, are truly representative of your subject, and are effectively organized with appropriate transitions.

Coming Up with a Subject

To come up with a subject for your essay, take any subject you're interested in—the presidency of Abraham Lincoln, for example—and consider whether it can be narrowed down to focus on a specific aspect of the subject (such as Lincoln's humor in office) for which you can find a reasonable number of examples. Then choose examples that show the characteristics of that narrower topic. In this case, a good example of the presidential humor might be the time a well-dressed lady visited the White House and inadvertently sat on Lincoln's hat. "Madame," the president is supposed to have responded, "I could have told you it wouldn't fit."

Eduardo Medina gets the examples he needs for his essay, p. 190, by conducting a personal interview.

If you have personal knowledge of your topic, you may already have many exemplary facts or stories about it. Or you may need to do some research. As you look for examples, choose ones that represent the qualities and characteristics you're trying to illustrate—and that are most likely to appeal to your **AUDIENCE**.

Considering Your Purpose and Audience

Before you begin writing, think about your **PURPOSE**. Is it to entertain? Inform? Persuade? For instance, the purpose of "All Seven Deadly Sins Committed at Church Bake Sale" on page 196 is to entertain, so the writer offers humorous examples of incidents at the bake sale. But if you were writing about the bake sale in order to persuade others to participate next time, you might offer examples of the money earned at various booths, how much fun participants had, and the good causes the money will be used for. In every case, your purpose determines the kinds of examples you use.

Before you select examples, you need to take into account how much your **AUDIENCE** already knows about your topic and how sympathetic they are likely to be to your position. If you are writing to demonstrate that the health of Americans has declined over the past decade, and your audience consists of doctors and nutritionists, a few key examples would probably suffice. For a general audience, however, such as your classmates, you would need to give more background information and cite more (and more basic) examples. And

Example 185

if your readers are unlikely to view your topic as you do, you will have to work even harder to come up with convincing examples.

Generating Ideas: Finding Good Examples

Try to find examples that display as many of the typical characteristics of your topic as possible. Suppose you were writing an essay on the seven deadly sins, and you decided to focus on wrath. Getting angry is a basic characteristic of wrath, but anger and wrath are not the same thing. Wrath is habitual anger that is often directed toward someone or something in particular; therefore, a good example of wrath would need to display this quality. As a superhero, the Hulk not only gets angry, he gets angry often; and he goes after whomever or whatever is making him angry. Thus, the Hulk would probably be a good example of wrath.

Templates for Exemplifying

The following templates can help you generate ideas for an exemplification essay and then start drafting. Don't take these as formulas where you just have to fill in the blanks. There are no easy formulas for good writing. But these templates can help you plot out some of the key moves of exemplification and thus may serve as good starting points.

▶ About X, it can generally be said that _____; a good example would be _____.

▶ The main characteristics of X are _____ and _____, as exemplified by _____, _____, and _____.

▶ For the best example(s) of X, we can turn to _____.

▶ Additional examples of X include _____, _____, and _____.

▶ From these examples of X, we can conclude that _____.

For more techniques to help you generate ideas and start writing with examples, see Chapter 3.

Stating Your Point

In an exemplification essay, you usually state your point directly in a **THESIS STATEMENT** in your introduction. For example:

> College teams depend more on teamwork than on star athletes for success.

> The health of most Americans has declined in the last ten years.

> The Italian army's desert campaign of World War II was the result of a number of tactical errors.

Each of these thesis statements calls for specific examples to support it. How many examples do you need—and what kinds?

Using Sufficient Examples

As you select examples to support a thesis, you can use either multiple brief examples or one or two extended examples. The approach you take will depend, in part, on the kind of generalization you're making. Multiple examples work well when you are dealing with different aspects of a large topic (battle strategy in a world war) or with trends involving large numbers of people (college athletes, Americans' declining health). Extended examples work better when you are writing about a particular case, such as a single scene in a novel.

For an essay made up almost entirely of brief examples, see p. 201.

Keep in mind that sufficiency isn't strictly a matter of numbers. Often a few good examples will suffice, which is what sufficiency implies: enough to do the job, and no more. In other words, whether or not your examples are sufficient to support your thesis is not determined by the number of examples but by how persuasive those examples seem to your readers. Choose examples that you think they will find vivid and convincing.

Example 187

Using Representative Examples

Be sure that your examples fairly and accurately support the point you're making. In an essay on how college athletic teams depend on teamwork, for instance, you would want to choose examples from several teams and sports. Similarly, if you are trying to convince readers that a general made many tactical errors in a strategic battle, you would need to show a number of errors from different points in the battle. And if you're exemplifying an **ABSTRACT** concept, such as wrath, be sure to choose **CONCRETE** examples that possess all its distinguishing characteristics.

It is also good to avoid using highly unusual examples. In an essay about the benefits of swimming every day, for instance, Katie Ledecky might not be the best example since she is not a typical swimmer. Better to cite several swimmers who have more typical routines to demonstrate the benefits of swimming.

Organizing Examples and Using Transitions

Once you have stated your thesis and chosen your examples, you need to put them in some kind of order. You might present them in order of increasing importance or interest, perhaps saving the best for last. Or if you have a large number of examples, you might organize them into categories. Or you might arrange them chronologically, if you are citing errors made during a political campaign, for example.

Regardless of the organization you choose, you need to relate your examples to each other and to the point you're making by using clear **TRANSITIONS** and other connecting words and phrases. You can always use the phrases "for example" and "for instance." But consider using other transitions as well, such as "more specifically," "exactly," "precisely," "thus," "namely," "indeed," "that is," "in other words," "in fact," and "in particular": "Better health care, in fact, has led to a dramatic improvement in the general treatment of diabetes." Or try using a **RHETORICAL QUESTION**, which you then answer with an example: "So what factor has contributed the most to the declining health of Americans?"

EDITING FOR COMMON ERRORS IN EXEMPLIFICATION

Exemplification invites certain typical errors, especially with lists or series of examples. The following tips will help you check and correct your writing for these common problems.

When you list a series of examples, make sure they are parallel in structure

▶ Animals avoid predators in many ways. They travel in groups, move fast, blending in with their surroundings, and looking threatening.

Edit out "etc.," "and so forth," or "and so on" when they don't add useful information to your sentence

▶ Animals typically avoid predators by traveling in groups, moving fast, <u>and</u> blending in with their surroundings, etc.

Check your use of "i.e." and "e.g."

These abbreviations of Latin phrases are often used interchangeably to introduce examples, but they do not mean the same thing: "i.e." means "that is" and "e.g." means "for example." For most academic papers, it is more appropriate to simply give the English equivalents:

▶ The tree sloth is an animal that uses protective coloring to hide—i.e. <u>that is</u>, it lets green algae grow on its fur in order to blend in with the tree leaves.

▶ Some animals, e.g. <u>for example</u>, the tree sloth, use protective coloring to hide.

Food Fakes

This tempting dish may look good enough to eat, but it's actually a plastic model of an item on the menu of a restaurant in Japan. Actual samples of real food would look (and smell) a little less than perfect after a few hours in a warm display case. By contrast, food model displays like this—called *sampuru* in Japanese, from the English word "sample"—stay flawless-looking (if odorless and tasteless) almost indefinitely, requiring nothing more than a little dusting from time to time. Visual examples of the most popular dishes a restaurant has to offer, *sampuru* are designed to entice customers off the street and inside the store to eat the real food they represent. In academic writing, likewise, well-selected and appealing examples can help the reader "see" the broader ideas that the writer is explaining and convince the reader that the writer's argument—like a delicious meal—is worth buying. Unlike *sampuru*, however, the best written examples tend to be those served fresh.

EDUARDO MEDINA

A PRAYER IN THE NIGHT

EDUARDO MEDINA (b. 1997) is from Birmingham, Alabama. At Auburn University, he served as editor in chief of the award-winning student newspaper, the *Auburn Plainsman*. "A Prayer in the Night" is part of a series that Medina wrote in his junior year while he was an assistant editor of the paper; it won top honors in the news feature category from the Alabama Press Association in 2019. Medina's essay reports on the experience of a young man from Guatemala whose name is given simply as Zacarías, which in Spanish means one who is "remembered by God." Here is one immigrant's story of the hazards of coming to the United States—and of trying to stay here.

A Prayer in the Night

Zacarías loves pineapple Jarritos. He's a husband, a
forward for his two-and-five soccer team, a construction
worker, a tan-complexioned, boot-wearing, ramen-for-
dinner kind of man. "But above all," he says as he pauses
and points with his chin at the little girl and boy, before
getting cut off by his daughter: "I'm a dad, a dad for these
beautiful, smart, amazing—"

"Papi," she exclaims. "That's a lot of things."

This is Zacarías—a father. But in the evening, after
he's tucked in his kids and kissed his wife goodnight, he
sits in bed and prays and remembers what else he is. With
clenched fists, he begs God that this night not be his last.
He prays and prays for a tomorrow, for another cool,
serene evening with his family. He wants nightfall to
come endlessly, he says, to flow like a river and drown his
worries of being taken. Zacarías prays for this because of
what else he is—an immigrant.

But before earning that label, before Auburn and kids
and life, Zacarías' story began as a little boy abandoned
by his father and left at his grandfather's coffee farm in
Guatemala. He remembers "the first day of hell" perfectly.
It was the early '90s when grandpa gave five-year-old
Zacarías a machete. "You're old enough now," his grand-
father said to him. "Go on and get to work." Little
Zacarías grabbed the machete and with all his scrawny,
malnourished strength, hacked away at the coffee plants.
"My grandfather worked with the sun," Zacarías says.
"When it rose, we worked. When it fell, we went home.
That's how it was."

At age 13, Zacarías packed his sack and left. His
family's goodbyes felt like those given at a funeral, he

1

2

3

4

5

Medina intro-
duces the central
figure of his essay

Suggests that this
is going to be a
story about immi-
gration with
Zacarías as the
chief example

An example of a
typical day in
Zacarías's early
life helps explain
why he ultimately
leaves

says. He trekked across Mexico for three weeks in buses and on foot. Finally, he made it to a small town in Sonora. The place was controlled by drug dealers, and they'd torture those who refused to pay when asked. Most times, people did pay because on the other side was their destination—Arizona. The guide responsible for taking Zacarías gathered everyone together.

"Buy water for five days. We leave at night," Zacarías   6
remembers the guide telling the group. All Zacarías could do was look out to the barren desert and pray. With the first batch of peeking stars, they picked up their bags and ran, knowing full well the likelihood of detection and—if their prayers and saints failed them—death. . . .

"We walked for such a long time until, finally, we saw   7
three white trucks on a dirt road," Zacarías says. The men driving the trucks had been hired to transport the migrants to a haven in Tucson, Arizona, where they would get situated to board the bus of their choosing. One by one, the men tied up Zacarías' group by the hands as they placed them in the back of the pickup. No one made any fuss of being tied. They were too weary and dehydrated to care. "Thank you, God," Zacarías thought to himself. "I made it." People were crammed on top of Zacarías. In the bumpy, three-hour ride, Zacarías gasped through dusty, sweat-smelling pockets of air. But he didn't mind. The journey felt like it was over.

The truck suddenly came to a halt. They were here.   8
"Everyone stay where you are," the men driving the truck ordered. Zacarías felt himself get dragged to the floor. He managed to see the name of the apartment complex and room number as he looked up. "What the hell is the matter with you?" Zacarías asked the men. "You shut the

Exemplifies the desperation and false hopes that drive Zacarías and provides an excellent example of IRONY

hell up, or we'll toss you back to el desierto," one of the men barked. Zacarías saw the guns tucked inside each man's jeans and realized what was going on. They looked nervous and high and ready to kill if need be, he said. "Once I saw that, I knew we had just been kidnapped." . . .

> An example of another hazard for many on the Guatemala-U.S. migrant journey: kidnapping

9

As Zacarías readjusts in his couch to continue, his daughter turns off the television and stares at her father intently as if a ghost were in front of her. "Y qué te pasó?" she asks. What happened to you?

He knew an uncle who was crossing to the United States around this time and had his number memorized. He repeated those seven digits quietly to himself. He also remembered the name of the apartment complex and room number they were held in. . . .

10

The only captor in the apartment lay on the couch in a cocaine-infused haze. The rest of the men were out. The man's back was facing them, but his heavy breathing sig-naled he was asleep. In his pocket was a cellphone. Zacarías couldn't see well from his battered eyes, and his hands were tied. One of the women, however, wasn't tied up. She rose from the wall and tiptoed closer and closer, until her hands could reach the cellphone. . . .

11

> Exemplifies yet another common hazard in the migrants' path: torture

At around 5 a.m., he dialed his uncle. After explain-ing their situation, his uncle said something that Zacarías says made him believe in God: "Sobrino, esta-mos 30 minutos de Tucson." Nephew, we're 30 minutes away from Tucson. His uncle had just crossed the desert and was in a van with other migrants. Zacarías told them the apartment complex and room number, and his uncle demanded they be ready. "We're getting there in 30 minutes," Zacarías recalls his uncle saying. "When

12

we push the door open, you run as fast as you can to this car."

The half hour passed. Four knocks on the door. The man got up, still groggy, reached for the handle and opened. Immediately, Zacarías said, a man at the door hurled a hand, clenched around a rock, at the kidnapper. The kidnapper fell, letting out a loud scream, and Zacarías got to his feet and sprinted, chasing the white van's back door.   13

He heard his uncle yell, "Hurry, hurry!" as the vehicle rolled and readied for takeoff. The roar of the revving engine whirred in his ear as he jumped inside, landing on his rib cage. He looked back and saw his bloodied captor aim with his gun—but he didn't fire. The women were in the van as well. They sped onto the road, and Zacarías said he heard them yell, "Tenemos todos?" Do we have everyone? They did, so they rode onto the American highway with tension still in their throats and prayers stuck to their minds.   14

Soon enough, life unfolded for Zacarías in Auburn. He married, had kids, but always, even in the best of times, there is fear, he says. Recently, he's been discussing with his wife if they should return to Guatemala, where she is also from. They argue, he says, because they are drained from this fear. A fear that ICE[1] will take him or his wife away.   15

"She wants us, or at least she wanted us, to go back to Guatemala with the kids, together, but—" Zacarías says before cutting himself off. He looks at his daughter and asks that she go upstairs with her brother. She nods and   16

Fortunately—or more than one immigrants' story might have ended here

This FLASH-FORWARD brings the narrative into the present

1. US Immigration and Customs Enforcement, a federal agency that enforces US immigration laws.

walks up, and he continues. "It's difficult. The life of an immigrant is not like the life of those that will read this." . . .

But he says he loves America—loves it powerfully. Even as a kid, walking in the coffee fields of Guatemala, he loved America. "I remember I would get on top of a hill, and I'd think, 'Where is the United States?' and then I'd point to where I thought it was, and I would smile," Zacarías said. And then he'd pick up his machete.

For now, he picks up his kids and tucks them in. Softly, he says, he whispers in their ears each night that he loves them. Then, he goes to his bed and prays. He likes to look up at "las estrellas" when he's done, he said. It's as if a bucketful of jewels has been tossed across the sky, each flickering a little light. Each waiting to be found. "I just want to work, and I want to love my children," Zacarías said. "That's all I pray for."

17

18

The intended audience for Zacarías's story, apparently, is not his fellow immigrants

Reminds us of how the story began—and why Zacarías and others like him risk such hazardous journeys

Gives final examples of what immigrants like Zacarías might hope and pray for

ALL SEVEN DEADLY SINS COMMITTED AT CHURCH BAKE SALE

THE *ONION* is a **SATIRICAL** newspaper that originated in Madison, home of the University of Wisconsin. In a typical issue, the paper pokes fun at everything from politics ("Nation's Bison Hold Lavish Fundraiser in Effort to Get 2020 Candidates to Support Environment") and American lifestyles ("TV Helps Build Valuable Looking Skills") to medicine ("Colonoscopy Offers Non-Fantastic Voyage through Human Body") and religion (which is what this selection is about—sort of). According to the Roman Catholic Church, there are basically two types of sins: "venial" ones that are easily forgiven and "deadly" ones that, well, are not. In the sixth century, Pope Gregory the Great identified what he took to be the seven worst of the worst: pride, envy, wrath, sloth, avarice (or greed), gluttony, and lust. In this tongue-in-cheek news release from a church bake sale in Gadsden, Alabama, the *Onion* reporter finds concrete, specific examples of each of them.

G ADSDEN, AL—The seven deadly sins—avarice, sloth, envy, lust, gluttony, 1 pride, and wrath—were all committed Sunday during the twice-annual bake sale at St. Mary's of the Immaculate Conception Church.

Page 186 explains how to state the point of your examples.

In total, 347 individual acts of sin were committed at the bake sale, with 2 nearly every attendee committing at least one of the seven deadly sins as outlined by Gregory the Great in the Fifth Century.

"My cookies, cakes, and brownies are always the highlight of our church 3 bake sales, and everyone says so," said parishioner Connie Barrett, 49, openly committing the sin of pride. "Sometimes, even I'm amazed by how well my goodies turn out."

Fellow parishioner Betty Wicks agreed. 4

"Every time I go past Connie's table, I just have to buy something," said 5 the 245-pound Wicks, who commits the sin of gluttony at every St. Mary's bake sale, as well as most Friday nights at Old Country Buffet. "I simply can't help myself—it's all so delicious."

The popularity of Barrett's mouth-watering wares elicited the sin of 6 envy in many of her fellow vendors.

"Connie has this fantastic book of recipes her grandmother gave her, 7 and she won't share them with anyone," church organist Georgia Brandt said. "This year, I made white-chocolate blondies and thought they'd be a big hit. But most people just went straight to Connie's table, got what they wanted, and left. All the while, Connie just stood there with this look of smug satisfaction on her face. It took every ounce of strength in my body to keep from going over there and really telling her off."

While the sins of wrath and avarice were each committed dozens of 8 times at the event, Barrett and longtime bake-sale rival Penny Cox brought them together in full force.

"Penny said she wanted to make a bet over whose table would make the 9 most money," said Barrett, exhibiting avarice. "Whoever lost would have to sit in the dunk tank at the St. Mary's Summer Fun Festival. I figured it's for such a good cause, a little wager couldn't hurt. Besides, I always bring the church more money anyway, so I couldn't possibly lose."

Moments after agreeing to the wager, Cox became wrathful when Barrett, 10 the bake sale's co-chair, grabbed the best table location under the pretense of

having to keep the coffee machine full. Cox attempted to exact revenge by reporting an alleged Barrett misdeed to the church's priest.

"I mentioned to Father Mark [O'Connor] that I've seen candles at Con-   11
nie's house that I wouldn't be surprised one bit if she stole from the church's storage closet," said Cox, who also committed the sin of sloth by forcing her daughter to set up and man her booth while she gossiped with friends. "Perhaps if he investigates this, by this time next year, Connie won't be co-chair of the bake sale and in her place we'll have someone who's willing to rotate the choice table spots."

An extended exam-   The sin of lust also reared its ugly head at the bake sale, largely
ple (p. 186) may rear   due to the presence of Melissa Wyckoff, a shapely 20-year-old red-   12
its head throughout
several paragraphs.   head whose family recently joined the church. While male attendees ogled Wyckoff, the primary object of lust for females was the personable, boyish Father Mark.

Though attendees' feelings of lust for Wyckoff and O'Connor were never   13
acted on, they did not go unnoticed.

"There's something not right about that Melissa Wyckoff," said envious   14
and wrathful bake-sale participant Jilly Brandon, after her husband Craig
offered Wyckoff one of her Rice Krispie treats to "welcome [her] to the parish." "She might have just moved here from California, but that red dress of
hers should get her kicked out of the church."

According to St. Mary's treasurer Beth Ellen Coyle, informal church-   15
sponsored events are a notorious breeding ground for the seven deadly sins.

"Bake sales, haunted houses, pancake breakfasts . . . such church events   16
are rife with potential for sin," Coyle said. "This year, we had to eliminate the
'Guess Your Weight' booth from the annual church carnival because the envy
and pride had gotten so out of hand. Church events are about glorifying God,
not violating His word. If you want to do that, you're no better than that
cheap strumpet Melissa Wyckoff."

FOR DISCUSSION

1. The *Onion* reporter gives bake-sale-specific **EXAMPLES** for each of the deadly
   sins. How well do you think these examples represent the sins they're meant to
   illustrate?

2. Statistics is the science of analyzing numerical examples. In all, says the *Onion*
   reporter, parishioners at the St. Mary's bake sale committed "347 individual acts of
   sin" (2). Anything suspicious about these stats? How do you suppose they were
   determined?

3. All of the seven deadly sins are identified in the first paragraph of the *Onion*'s
   spoof. In what order are they explained after that? Which one does the watchful
   reporter come back to at the end?

4. Which specific deadly sin is the only one unacted on at the bake sale? Who
   inspired it?

STRATEGIES AND STRUCTURES

1. Pope Gregory might object that the *Onion*'s examples are a bit trivial. But how
   CONCRETE and specific are they?

2. **SATIRE** is writing that makes fun of vice or folly for the **PURPOSE** of exposing and
   correcting it. To the extent that the *Onion* is satirizing the behavior of people at
   "church-sponsored events," what less-than-truly-deadly "sins" is the paper actually making fun of (15)?

3. A spoof is a gentle parody or mildly satirical imitation. What kind of writing or reporting is the *Onion* spoofing here? Who is the AUDIENCE for this spoof?

4. As a Catholic priest, "boyish Father Mark" would probably say that all the other deadly sins are examples of pride (12). How might pride be thought of as the over-archingly general "deadly sin"?

5. As a "news" story, this one has elements of NARRATIVE. What are some of them, specifically?

WORDS AND FIGURES OF SPEECH

1. What, exactly, is a "strumpet" (16)? What sin might Coyle herself be committing by labeling Wyckoff with this term?

2. Deadly (or "mortal") sins are to be distinguished from *venial* sins. According to your dictionary, what kind of sins would be venial sins? Give several examples.

3. Give a SYNONYM for each of the following words: "avarice," "sloth," "gluttony," and "wrath" (1).

4. Another word for pride is "hubris." What language does the latter derive from? What's the distinction between the two?

5. Hypocrisy is not one of the seven deadly sins, but how would you DEFINE it? Which of the St. Mary's parishioners might be said to commit *this* sin?

FOR WRITING

1. Imagine a strip mall called the Seven Deadly Sins Shopping Center, where each item on Pope Gregory's list is represented by a store selling ordinary products and services. Draw up a list of store names that would exemplify each of the seven deadlies—for example, Big Joe's Eats for gluttony. You might also compose some signs or other advertising to place in the windows of each shop.

2. Using examples, write an essay titled "All Seven Deadly Sins Committed at _____." Fill in the blank with any venue you choose—"School Cafeteria," for example, or "College Library." Give at least one example for each offense.

RICHARD LEDERER

ENGLISH IS A CRAZY LANGUAGE

RICHARD LEDERER (b. 1938) taught for many years at St. Paul's, a boarding school in New Hampshire. He retired in 1989 to carry on his "mission as a user-friendly English teacher" by writing and speaking extensively and humorously about the peculiarities of the English language. He coined the term "verbivore" to describe those who, like himself, "devour words." Lederer is the author of *Get Thee to a Punnery* (1988) and *Anguished English* (1989), among other books. This essay, made up of one example after another, is the opening chapter of his best-selling *Crazy English* (1989).

•>————————————————————————————————<•

ENGLISH IS THE MOST WIDELY SPOKEN LANGUAGE in the history of our planet, used in some way by at least one out of every seven human beings around the globe. Half of the world's books are written in English, and the majority of international telephone calls are made in English. English is the language of over 60 percent of the world's radio programs, many of them beamed, ironically, by the Russians, who know that to win friends and influence nations, they're best off using English. More than 70 percent of international mail is written and addressed in English, and 80 percent of all computer text is stored in English. English has acquired the largest vocabulary of all the world's languages, perhaps as many as two million words, and has generated one of the noblest bodies of literature in the annals of the human race.

Nonetheless, it is now time to face the fact that English is a crazy language. 2

In the crazy English language, the blackbird hen is brown, blackboards 3 can be blue or green, and blackberries are green and then red before they are ripe. Even if blackberries were really black and blueberries really blue, what are strawberries, cranberries, elderberries, huckleberries, raspberries, boysenberries, mulberries, and gooseberries supposed to look like?

For tips on when and how to use multiple examples like these, see pp. 187.

To add to the insanity, there is no butter in buttermilk, no egg in egg- 4 plant, no grape in grapefruit, neither worms nor wood in wormwood, neither pine nor apple in pineapple, neither peas nor nuts in peanuts, and no ham in a hamburger. (In fact, if somebody invented a sandwich consisting of a ham patty in a bun, we would have a hard time finding a name for it.) To make matters worse, English muffins weren't invented in England, french fries in France, or danish pastries in Denmark. And we discover even more culinary madness in the revelations that sweetmeat is candy, while sweetbread, which isn't sweet, is made from meat.

In this unreliable English tongue, greyhounds aren't always grey (or 5 gray); panda bears and koala bears aren't bears (they're marsupials); a woodchuck is a groundhog, which is not a hog; a horned toad is a lizard; glowworms are fireflies, but fireflies are not flies (they're beetles); ladybugs and lightning bugs are also beetles (and to propagate, a significant proportion of ladybugs must be male); a guinea pig is neither a pig nor from Guinea (it's a South American rodent); and a titmouse is neither mammal nor mammaried.

Language is like the air we breathe. It's invisible, inescapable, indispens- 6 able, and we take it for granted. But when we take the time, step back, and listen to the sounds that escape from the holes in people's faces and explore the paradoxes and vagaries of English, we find that hot dogs can be cold, darkrooms can be lit, homework can be done in school, nightmares can take place in broad daylight, while morning sickness and daydreaming can take place at night, tomboys are girls, midwives can be men, hours—especially happy hours and rush hours—can last longer than sixty minutes, quicksand works *very* slowly, boxing rings are square, silverware can be made of plastic and tablecloths of paper, most telephones are dialed by being punched (or pushed?), and most bathrooms don't have any baths in them. In fact, a dog can go to the bathroom under a tree—no bath, no room; it's still going to the bathroom. And doesn't it seem at least a little bizarre that we go to the bathroom in order to go to the bathroom?

Why is it that a woman can man a station but a man can't woman one, 7 that a man can father a movement but a woman can't mother one, and that a king rules a kingdom but a queen doesn't rule a queendom? How did all those Renaissance men reproduce when there don't seem to have been any Renaissance women?

A writer is someone who writes, and a stinger is something that stings. 8 But fingers don't fing, grocers don't groce, hammers don't ham, and humdingers don't humding. If the plural of *tooth* is *teeth*, shouldn't the plural of *booth* be *beeth*? One goose, two geese—so one moose, two meese? One index, two indices—one Kleenex, two Kleenices? If people ring a bell today and rang a bell yesterday, why don't we say that they flang a ball? If they wrote a letter, perhaps they also bote their tongue. If the teacher taught, why isn't it also true that the preacher praught? Why is it that the sun shone yesterday while I shined my shoes, that I treaded water and then trod on soil, and that I flew out to see a World Series game in which my favorite player flied out?

If we conceive a conception and receive at a reception, why don't we 9 grieve a greption and believe a beleption? If a horsehair mat is made from the hair of horses and a camel's hair brush from the hair of camels, from what is a mohair coat made? If a vegetarian eats vegetables, what does a humanitarian eat? If a firefighter fights fire, what does a freedom fighter fight? If a weightlifter lifts weights, what does a shoplifter lift? If *pro* and *con* are opposites, is congress the opposite of progress?

Sometimes you have to believe that all English speakers should be com- 10 mitted to an asylum for the verbally insane. In what other language do people drive in a parkway and park in a driveway? In what other language do people recite at a play and play at a recital? In what other language do privates eat in the general mess and generals eat in the private mess? In what other language do men get hernias and women get hysterectomies? In what other language do people ship by truck and send cargo by ship? In what other language can your nose run and your feet smell?

And when can a question be a statement? See p. 187.

How can a slim chance and a fat chance be the same, "what's going on?" and "what's coming off?" be the same, and a bad licking and a good licking be the same, while a wise man and a wise guy are opposites? How can sharp speech and blunt speech be the same and *quite a lot* and *quite a few* the same, while *overlook* and *oversee* are opposites? How can the weather be hot as hell one day and cold as hell the next?

If *button* and *unbutton* and *tie* and *untie* are opposites, why are *loosen* and *unloosen* and *ravel* and *unravel* the same? If *bad* is the opposite of *good*, *hard* the opposite of *soft*, and *up* the opposite of *down*, why are *badly* and *goodly*, *hardly* and *softly*, and *upright* and *downright* not opposing pairs? If harmless actions are the opposite of harmful actions, why are shameless and shameful behavior the same and pricey objects less expensive than priceless ones? If appropriate and inappropriate remarks and passable and impassable mountain trails are opposites, why are flammable and inflammable materials, heritable and inheritable property, and passive and impassive people the same and valuable objects less treasured than invaluable ones? If *uplift* is the same as *lift up*, why are *upset* and *set up* opposite in meaning? Why are *pertinent* and *impertinent*, *canny* and *uncanny*, and *famous* and *infamous* neither opposites nor the same? How can *raise* and *raze* and *reckless* and *wreckless* be opposites when each pair contains the same sound?

Why is it that when the sun or the moon or the stars are out, they are visible, but when the lights are out, they are invisible, and that when I wind up my watch, I start it, but when I wind up this essay, I shall end it?

English is a crazy language.

FOR DISCUSSION

1. Most of the time, Richard Lederer is illustrating his main point that "English is a crazy language" (2). But what does he say about its widespread influence? What **EXAMPLES** does he give?

2. Do you think English is as crazy as Lederer says it is? Why or why not? Give several examples to support your opinion.

3. How seriously do you think Lederer actually intends for us to take the general proposition of his essay? Why do you think he gives so many crazy examples?

4. In paragraph 6, Lederer refers to two related aspects of the English language that all of his examples might be said to illustrate. What are these aspects? Where else in his essay does Lederer actually name the aspects of English he is exemplifying?

5. Lederer begins by providing statistics about the English language, but this essay was written more than thirty years ago. Fact check some of those statistics—has anything changed?

STRATEGIES AND STRUCTURES

1. What is the **PURPOSE** of the opening paragraph of Lederer's essay? How does the opening paragraph color the rest of what he says about the craziness of the English language?

2. Lederer's essay is made up almost entirely of clusters of examples. What do the examples in paragraph 3 have in common? Are the examples in paragraph 4 more like those in paragraph 3 or paragraph 5? Explain.

3. In paragraph 8, Lederer pretends to be upset with irregular verbs and irregular plurals of nouns. Which are examples of which? Make a list of his examples for both categories.

4. Which examples have to do primarily with gender? What connects all the examples in paragraph 12?

5. Lederer gives his essay the form of a logical **ARGUMENT**. The proposition he intends to prove is stated in paragraph 2. Where does he state it again as a conclusion? Is the argument in between primarily **INDUCTIVE** (reasoning from specific examples to a general conclusion) or **DEDUCTIVE** (reasoning from general principles to a more specific conclusion)? Explain.

WORDS AND FIGURES OF SPEECH

1. In American English, a "rant" is a form of vehement speech; in British English, a rant can also mean an outburst of wild merriment. Which meaning or meanings apply to Lederer's essay?

2. A "misnomer" is a term that implies a meaning or interpretation that is actually untrue or inaccurate—"koala bears," for example, are marsupials (5). Choose one

of the following misnomers that Lederer mentions and explain why you think the object it refers to has this inaccurate name—and why the name persists: "eggplant," "peanut," "french fries," "horned toad," "firefly," and "guinea pig" (4, 5).

3. Look up the definition of the word "vagaries" (6)? How is it related to the word "vagabonds"?

4. Lederer "winds up" his essay in paragraph 13. Could he have said, just as accurately, to "wind it down"?

FOR WRITING

1. Write an essay illustrating the craziness of a variety of English or some language other than English—one you speak and/or have studied. For example, one way to say you're welcome in French is "Je vous en prie," which means, literally, "I beg of you."

2. For all its "craziness," Lederer asserts that "English is the most widely spoken language in the history of our planet" (1). Write an essay that supports or contests this proposition. Be sure to include sufficient examples of who uses the language, where, and for what purposes.

3. If you're familiar with a language other than English, write an essay giving copious examples of why it is (or is not) a "crazy" language. Be sure to explain how and why your examples illustrate your point.

MATTHEW DESMOND

COLD CITY

MATTHEW DESMOND (b. 1979) is a professor of urban sociology at Princeton University and the author of numerous books and articles on race,
social class, educational inequality, and poverty in America. Desmond
grew up in San Jose, California, and graduated from Arizona State University in 2002 with a degree in communications and justice studies. In 2010,
he earned a PhD in sociology from the University of Wisconsin–Madison.
Evicted: Poverty and Profit in the American City (2016), which won both
the Pulitzer Prize and the National Book Critics Circle Award for general
nonfiction, examines why an increasing number of people—more than one
in eight renters during the worst years of the economic recession that
began in 2007—are being forced from their homes in Milwaukee, Wisconsin, and similar cities. Displaying their typical "vulnerability and desperation, as well as their ingenuity and guts," the people in "Cold City," which
forms the prologue to *Evicted*, are representative examples of those hit
hardest by the housing crisis.

J ORI AND HIS COUSIN WERE CUTTING UP, tossing snowballs at passing cars. 1
From Jori's street corner on Milwaukee's near South Side, cars driving on
Sixth Street passed squat duplexes with porch steps ending at a sidewalk
edged in dandelions. Those heading north approached the Basilica of
St. Josaphat, whose crowning dome looked to Jori like a giant overturned
plunger. It was January of 2008, and the city was experiencing the snowiest
winter on record. Every so often, a car turned off Sixth Street to navigate
Arthur Avenue, hemmed in by the snow, and that's when the boys would take
aim. Jori packed a tight one and let it fly. The car jerked to a stop, and a man
jumped out. The boys ran inside and locked the door to the apartment where
Jori lived with his mother, Arleen, and younger brother, Jafaris. The lock was

Page 183 explains
how you can use a
brief narrative to
exemplify a compli-
cated situation.
cheap, and the man broke down the door with a few hard-heeled
kicks. He left before anything else happened. When the landlord
found out about the door, she decided to evict Arleen and her boys.
They had been there eight months.

The day Arleen and her boys had to be out was cold. But if she waited 2
any longer, the landlord would summon the sheriff, who would arrive with a
gun, a team of boot-footed movers, and a folded judge's order saying that her
house was no longer hers. She would be given two options: truck or curb. "Truck"
would mean that her things would be loaded into an eighteen-footer and later
checked into bonded storage. She could get everything back after paying $350.
Arleen didn't have $350, so she would have opted for "curb," which would
mean watching the movers pile everything onto the sidewalk. Her mattresses.
A floor-model television. Her copy of *Don't Be Afraid to Discipline*. Her nice
glass dining table and the lace tablecloth that fit just-so. Silk plants. Bibles.
The meat cuts in the freezer. The shower curtain. Jafaris's asthma machine.

Arleen took her sons—Jori was thirteen, Jafaris was five—to a homeless 3
shelter, which everyone called the Lodge so you could tell your kids, "We're
staying at the Lodge tonight," like it was a motel. The two-story stucco building could have passed for one, except for all the Salvation Army signs. Arleen
stayed in the 120-bed shelter until April, when she found a house on Nineteenth and Hampton, in the predominantly black inner city, on Milwaukee's
North Side, not far from her childhood home. It had thick trim around the
windows and doors and was once Kendal green, but the paint had faded and
chipped so much over the years that the bare wood siding was now exposed,

making the house look camouflaged. At one point someone had started repainting the house plain white but had given up mid-brushstroke, leaving more than half unfinished. There was often no water in the house, and Jori had to bucket out what was in the toilet. But Arleen loved that it was spacious and set apart from other houses. "It was quiet," she remembered. "And five-twenty-five for a whole house, two bedrooms upstairs and two bedrooms downstairs. It was my favorite place."

After a few weeks, the city found Arleen's favorite place "unfit for human habitation," removed her, nailed green boards over the windows and doors, and issued a fine to her landlord. Arleen moved Jori and Jafaris into a drab apartment complex deeper in the inner city, on Atkinson Avenue, which she soon learned was a haven for drug dealers. She feared for her boys, especially Jori—slack-shouldered, with pecan-brown skin and a beautiful smile—who would talk to anyone.

Arleen endured four summer months on Atkinson before moving into a bottom duplex unit on Thirteenth Street and Keefe, a mile away. She and the boys walked their things over. Arleen held her breath and tried the lights, smiling with relief when they came on. She could live off someone else's electricity bill for a while. There was a fist-sized hole in a living-room window, the front door had to be locked with an ugly wooden plank dropped into metal brackets, and the carpet was filthy and ground in. But the kitchen was spacious and the living room well lit. Arleen stuffed a piece of clothing into the window hole and hung ivory curtains.

The rent was $550 a month, utilities not included, the going rate in 2008 for a two-bedroom unit in one of the worst neighborhoods in America's fourth-poorest city. Arleen couldn't find a cheaper place, at least not one fit for human habitation, and most landlords wouldn't rent her a smaller one on account of her boys. The rent would take 88 percent of Arleen's $628-a-month welfare check. Maybe she could make it work. Maybe they could at least stay through winter, until crocuses and tulips stabbed through the thawed ground of spring, Arleen's favorite season.

There was a knock at the door. It was the landlord, Sherrena Tarver. Sherrena, a black woman with bobbed hair and fresh nails, was loaded down with groceries. She had spent $40 of her own money and picked up the rest at a food pantry. She knew Arleen needed it.

Arleen thanked Sherrena and closed the door. Things were off to a good   8
start.

Even in the most desolate areas of American cities, evictions used to be rare.   9
They used to draw crowds. Eviction riots erupted during the Depression,[1]
even though the number of poor families who faced eviction each year was a
fraction of what it is today. A *New York Times* account of community resistance to the eviction of three Bronx families in February 1932 observed,
"Probably because of the cold, the crowd numbered only 1,000." Sometimes
neighbors confronted the marshals directly, sitting on the evicted family's
furniture to prevent its removal or moving the family back in despite the
judge's orders. The marshals themselves were ambivalent about carrying out
evictions. It wasn't why they carried a badge and a gun.

These days, there are sheriff squads whose full-time job is to carry out   10
eviction and foreclosure orders. There are moving companies specializing in
evictions, their crews working all day, every weekday. There are hundreds of
data-mining companies that sell landlords tenant screening reports listing
past evictions and court filings. These days, housing courts swell, forcing
commissioners to settle cases in hallways or makeshift offices crammed with
old desks and broken file cabinets—and most tenants don't even show up.
Low-income families have grown used to the rumble of moving trucks, the
early-morning knocks at the door, the belongings lining the curb.

Families have watched their incomes stagnate, or even fall, while their   11
housing costs have soared. Today, the majority of poor renting families in
America spend over half of their income on housing, and at least one in four
dedicates over 70 percent to paying the rent and keeping the lights on. Millions of Americans are evicted every year because they can't make rent. In
Milwaukee, a city of fewer than 105,000 renter households, landlords evict
roughly 16,000 adults and children each year. That's sixteen families evicted
through the court system daily. But there are other ways, cheaper and
quicker ways, for landlords to remove a family than through court order.

---

1. The "Great Depression," which began with a stock market crash in 1929 and lasted about
a decade, was the most severe economic depression of the 20th century in the United
States (and many other parts of the world).

Some landlords pay tenants a couple hundred dollars to leave by the end of the week. Some take off the front door. Nearly half of all forced moves experienced by renting families in Milwaukee are "informal evictions" that take place in the shadow of the law. If you count all forms of involuntary building condemnations—you discover that between 2009 and 2011 more than 1 in 8 Milwaukee renters experienced a forced move.

There is nothing special about Milwaukee when it comes to eviction. 12 The numbers are similar in Kansas City, Cleveland, Chicago, and other cities. In 2013, 1 in 8 poor renting families nationwide were unable to pay all of their rent, and a similar number thought it was likely they would be evicted soon. . . .

See p. 187 for the importance of using representative examples.

The evictions [of families like Arleen's] take place throughout the city, 13 embroiling not only landlords and tenants but also kin and friends, lovers and ex-lovers, judges and lawyers, dope suppliers and church elders. Eviction's fallout is severe. Losing a home sends families to shelters, abandoned houses, and the street. It invites depression and illness, compels families to move into degrading housing in dangerous neighborhoods, uproots communities, and harms children. Eviction reveals people's vulnerability and desperation, as well as their ingenuity and guts.

Fewer and fewer families can afford a roof over their head. This is among 14 the most urgent and pressing issues facing America today, and acknowledging the breadth and depth of the problem changes the way we look at poverty. For decades, we've focused mainly on jobs, public assistance, parenting, and mass incarceration. No one can deny the importance of these issues, but something fundamental is missing. We have failed to fully appreciate how deeply housing is implicated in the creation of poverty. Not everyone living in a distressed neighborhood is associated with gang members, parole officers, employers, social workers, or pastors. But nearly all of them have a landlord.

FOR DISCUSSION

1. In "Cold City," Arleen and her two sons are presented as a typical example of "poor renting families in America" who often get evicted from their homes (11). How common, according to Matthew Desmond, are cases like theirs? Why do they occur?

2. Decades ago, according to Desmond, evictions "used to draw crowds" of supporters for the evictees (9). How and why have things changed since then?

3. Arleen and her family get evicted, on one occasion, as the indirect result of the boys' throwing snowballs at cars. Does the punishment fit the crime here? Why or why not?

4. When Arleen moves the family to Atkinson Avenue, she "feared for her boys, especially Jori" (4). Why is she afraid? How justified are her fears?

5. "Cold City" is the prologue to an entire book on the subject of eviction. Judging from this introduction, what do you think the methods and point of view of the book are likely to be? Does this sampling make you want to read the book? Why or why not?

STRATEGIES AND STRUCTURES

1. Desmond divides his essay into two parts: the specific case of Arleen, Jori, and Jafaris (1–8)—followed by his own general observations on the issue of eviction in America (9–14). Is this a good strategy? Why do you think he adopts this order instead of, say, presenting his observations first and then the example?

2. A good example exhibits the typical characteristics of the group it exemplifies. What are some of the main characteristics Desmond ascribes to Arleen and her family?

3. Desmond uses an example (Arleen and family) within an example (Milwaukee). What group does the city of Milwaukee exemplify? Is it a good example? Why or why not?

4. Why do you think Desmond ends his narrative of Arleen's troubles with the appearance of a new landlord bearing gifts for her and her family (7–8)?

5. Desmond uses a mix of strategies in addition to exemplification. Where and how does he analyze CAUSE AND EFFECT? The PROCESS of eviction itself?

WORDS AND FIGURES OF SPEECH

1. Since Milwaukee, in Desmond's essay, is experiencing its "snowiest winter on record," "Cold City" is a reference to the weather (1). What else does this PUN refer to?

2. Desmond never gives Arleen's last name. Should he have? Why or why not?

3. Evictees, according to Desmond, can either "truck" or "curb" (2). How appropriate are these terms for the options they designate? How does the list of examples at the end of paragraph 2 help to make Desmond's explanation more concrete?

4. Among Arleen's possessions is a book titled *Don't Be Afraid to Discipline* (2). Why do you think Desmond makes an **ALLUSION** to Arleen's reading? What does this example tell us about her as a mother?

5. At one point, Arleen takes her boys to a homeless shelter. Why is it called "the Lodge" (3)?

6. As Desmond draws to a close, he addresses the reader directly as "you" (11). Why might he switch to the second-person here instead of sticking with the third-person **POINT OF VIEW** ("he," "she," "they") he has been using?

FOR WRITING

1. Do you know someone who has been evicted? Write a case study of that person or persons that gives numerous examples of their experience. Be sure to get your subject's permission before sharing their story.

2. Desmond's broader subject here is not just eviction but also poverty in America. Write a case history of someone you know whose experience exemplifies this larger subject.

3. Have you ever had difficulty finding appropriate housing? What were some of the causes of those difficulties? Write an essay about this experience—and its causes and conditions—including examples of what you went through.

DEAR IJEAWELE

CHIMAMANDA NGOZI ADICHIE (b. 1977) is an award-winning writer who grew up in Nigeria. At age 19, she came to the United States to attend college, first at Eastern Connecticut State University and then at Yale, where she earned a master's degree in African studies, and at Johns Hopkins University, where she earned a master's in creative writing. Her third novel, *Americanah,* about a young woman from Nigeria who struggles with what it means to be Black but not American while studying in the United States, won the 2013 National Book Critics Circle Award for fiction. *Dear Ijeawele, or A Feminist Manifesto in Fifteen Suggestions* (2017) is addressed to a childhood friend in Nigeria who has asked Adichie for advice on how to raise her baby daughter as a feminist. Here are Adichie's third, fifth, and sixth "Suggestions"—with numerous examples of the principles of parenting that they embody.

D EAR IJEAWELE,   1
What joy. And what lovely names: Chizalum Adaora. She is so beautiful.   2
Only a week old and she already looks curious about the world. What a
magnificent thing you have done, bringing a human being into the world.
"Congratulations" feels too slight.

Your note made me cry. You know how I get foolishly emotional some-   3
times. Please know that I take your charge—how to raise her feminist—very
seriously. And I understand what you mean by not always knowing what the
feminist response to situations should be. For me, feminism is always
contextual. . . .

I have some suggestions for how to raise Chizalum. But remember that   4
you might do all the things I suggest, and she will still turn out to be different
from what you hoped, because sometimes life just does its thing. What
matters is that you try. And always trust your instincts above all else, because
you will be guided by your love for your child.

Here are my suggestions: . . .   5

Third Suggestion

Teach her that the idea of "gender roles" is absolute nonsense. Do not ever tell   6
her that she should or should not do something because she is a girl.

"Because you are a girl" is never a reason for anything. Ever.   7

I remember being told as a child to "bend down properly   8
while sweeping, like a girl." Which meant that sweeping was   Examples
about being female. I wish I had been told simply, "bend down   replace abstrac-
                                                                 tions like "gender
and sweep properly because you'll clean the floor better." And I roles" with more
wish my brothers had been told the same thing. . . .   concrete ideas
                                                                 (p. 181) like sweep-
                                                                 ing the floor.

It is interesting to me how early the world starts to invent gender roles.   9
Yesterday I went to a children's shop to buy Chizalum an outfit. In the girls'
section were pale creations in washed-out shades of pink. I disliked them.
The boys' section had outfits in vibrant shades of blue. Because I thought
blue would be adorable against her brown skin—and photograph better—I
bought one. At the checkout counter, the cashier said mine was the perfect
present for the new boy. I said it was for a baby girl. She looked horrified. "Blue
for a girl?" . . .

I looked at the toy section, which was also arranged by gender. Toys for   10
boys are mostly active, and involve some sort of doing—trains, cars—and
toys for girls are mostly passive and are overwhelmingly dolls. I was struck by
this. I had not quite realized how early society starts to invent ideas of what a
boy should be and what a girl should be.

I wished the toys had been arranged by type, rather than by gender.   11

Did I ever tell you about going to a US mall with a seven-year-old Nige-   12
rian girl and her mother? She saw a toy helicopter, one of those things that fly
by wireless remote control, and she was fascinated and asked for one. "No,"
her mother said. "You have your dolls." And she responded, "Mummy, is it
only dolls I will play with?" . . .

Gender roles are so deeply conditioned in us that we will often follow   13
them even when they chafe against our true desires, our needs, our happiness.
They are very difficult to unlearn, and so it is important to try to make sure
that Chizalum rejects them from the beginning. Instead of letting her internalize the idea of gender roles, teach her self-reliance. . . .

Fifth Suggestion

Teach Chizalum to read. Teach her to love books. The best way is by casual   14
example. If she sees you reading, she will understand that reading is valuable.
If she were not to go to school, and merely just read books, she would arguably
become more knowledgeable than a conventionally educated child. Books will
help her understand and question the world, help her express herself, and help
her in whatever she wants to become—a chef, a scientist, a singer, all benefit
from the skills that reading brings. I do not mean schoolbooks. I mean books
that have nothing to do with school, autobiographies and novels and histories.
If all else fails, pay her to read. Reward her. I know this remarkable Nigerian
woman, Angela, a single mother who was raising her child in the United
States; her child did not take to reading so she decided to pay her five cents
per page. An expensive endeavor, she later joked, but a worthy investment.

Sixth Suggestion

Teach her to question language. Language is the repository of our prejudices,   15
our beliefs, our assumptions. But to teach her that, you will have to question

your own language. A friend of mine says she will never call her daughter "princess." People mean well when they say this, but "princess" is loaded with assumptions, of a girl's delicacy, of the prince who will come to save her, etc. This friend prefers "angel" and "star."

So decide for yourself the things you will not say to your child. Because 16 what you say to your child matters. It teaches her what she should value. You know that Igbo joke, used to tease girls who are being childish—"What are you doing? Don't you know you are old enough to find a husband?" I used to say that often. But now I choose not to. I say "You are old enough to find a job." Because I do not believe that marriage is something we should teach young girls to aspire to.

If you're using a culturally specific example, you may need to give your audience the context they need to understand it (p. 184).

Try not to use words like "misogyny" and "patriarchy" too 17 often with Chizalum. We feminists can sometimes be too jargony, and jargon can sometimes feel too abstract. Don't just label something misogynistic; tell her why it is, and tell her what would make it not be. . . .

Remember the mechanic in Lagos who was described as a "lady mechanic" 18 in a newspaper profile? Teach Chizalum that the woman is a mechanic, not a "lady mechanic."

Point out to her how wrong it is that a man who hits your car in Lagos 19 traffic gets out and tells you to go and bring your husband because he "can't deal with a woman."

Instead of merely telling her, show her with examples that misogyny can 20 be overt and misogyny can be subtle and that both are abhorrent. . . .

May she be healthy and happy. May her life be whatever she wants it to be. 21

Do you have a headache after reading all this? Sorry. Next time don't ask 22 me how to raise your daughter feminist.

With love, oyi gi,

Chimamanda

FOR DISCUSSION

1. In her *Feminist Manifesto*, Chimamanda Ngozi Adichie gives advice to a friend about how to raise her daughter. Why might the friend be consulting Adichie in particular?

2. Among the many specific suggestions that Adichie offers for raising a "feminist" (3), which ones do you think are most important? least important? Why?

3. How and how well does Adichie's suggestion about reading books fit with what you learned about close reading in Chapter 1 of this book? Explain.

4. What does Adichie mean when she says, "For me, feminism is always contextual" (3)? Point to specific examples in the text that illustrate this statement.

STRATEGIES AND STRUCTURES

1. Adichie's manifesto is written as a personal letter (originally, an email). As a means of explaining the writer's specific ideas about feminism and parenting, how effective is this epistolary form? Explain.

2. Point out places in her "Suggestions" where Adichie exemplifies the conviction that various kinds of work should not be gendered. Are the examples well chosen? Why or why not?

3. Point out places where Adichie gives examples of the idea that "gender roles" are "invented" (9) and "conditioned" (13). How effective do you find these examples? Explain.

4. When giving examples of stereotypes, Adichie is explaining how not to conform to them. Point to specific passages in her manifesto where she uses **PROCESS ANALYSIS** to achieve this purpose.

WORDS AND FIGURES OF SPEECH

1. Adichie's manifesto includes an entire section on language. Why is language important in a discussion of stereotypes and how to avoid them?

2. The terms "feminine" and "feminist" come up throughout Adichie's essay. How is she defining these key terms?

3. Adichie warns against using "words like 'misogyny' and 'patriarchy' too often" (17). Are her objections valid? Why or why not?

4. A manifesto is a statement of principles, often political and sometimes expressed as rules or commands. (In *The Communist Manifesto*, for instance, Karl Marx proclaims, "Workers of the World, Unite!") Adichie offers "Suggestions." Judging from the examples she gives, what is the difference between a suggestion and a rule?

FOR WRITING

1. Visit a shop or department store (or a store's website) that sells toys or children's clothing. Take detailed notes on items that appear to be marketed specifically for girls, for boys, and for both or either. Write several paragraphs giving specific examples of the differences.

2. Do some additional research and write an essay explaining how the marketing of consumer items for children reinforces (or doesn't reinforce) gender stereotypes. Give plenty of examples.

3. Adichie concludes by advising her friend to teach "with examples that misogyny can be overt and misogyny can be subtle and that both are abhorrent" (20). On the basis of your own experience and reading, write an essay, with examples, that makes an **ARGUMENT** about this issue.

4. Write an open letter to your classmates setting forth what you consider to be the most important principles of good parenting. Use lots of examples.

JOHN MCWHORTER

WHY "REDSKINS" IS A BAD WORD

JOHN MCWHORTER (b. 1965) is an associate professor of English and comparative literature at Columbia University, specializing in creole languages as well as the philosophy and sociology of language. A Philadelphia native, McWhorter holds degrees from Simon's Rock College, Rutgers University, New York University, and Stanford University. In addition to his teaching and appearances as a commentator on radio and television programs, he is a prolific writer, with many essays and books on linguistics and race relations, among them *Losing the Race: Self-Sabotage in Black America* (2000) and *Words on the Move: Why English Won't—and Can't—Sit Still (Like, Literally)* (2017). He is also the host of Lexicon Valley, "a podcast about language, from pet peeves to syntax" on Slate.com. In 2015, McWhorter wrote the essay "Why 'Redskins' Is a Bad Word" for *Time* magazine. Discussing the controversy surrounding this common name for athletic teams, McWhorter argues that the connotations of the word make it inherently insulting to Native Americans—a clear example of "a slur despite not being a literal insult." "As always," he writes, "life is more than the literal."

C ALIFORNIA'S BAN OF THE USE OF THE NAME "REDSKINS" by schools is likely   1
the beginning of a trend.¹ Native Americans have been decrying the
term "Redskin" as a slur for a good while now, and Washington Redskins
owner Dan Snyder's refusal to change the name of the team is looking increasingly callous and antique.² Many will celebrate that "Redskin" is likely starting to go the way of "Oriental" and—well, you know.

Yet some may quietly be harboring another question: What's so terrible   2
about referring to the fact that many Native Americans have a reddish skin
tone compared to other people? It's not as if having "red" skin is a negative or
even humorous trait. It isn't illogical to wonder, deep down, whether Native
Americans are fashioning a controversy.

They aren't, though, because words can come to have mean-   3
ings quite different from their literal ones, and when it comes to
matters of insult and dignity, meaning counts.

Page 18 explains why almost every essay in this book has study questions dealing with this issue.   4

For example, the term "Oriental" for Asians became impolite
25 years ago. Yet it's true that Asian heritage, for Chinese, Japanese and
Korean people, is in "the Orient," traditionally a Western word for Asia. One
now and then hears someone, usually of a certain age, grousing that "Well,
now they want to be called Asians" with an air of dismissal, as if people go
around willfully creating confusion and feigning hurt.

But actually, "Oriental" came to be associated with stereotypes of the   5
people in question, such that it was felt that a new term was necessary. Long
ago, the same thing happened to "Chinaman." What's wrong with calling a
man from China a "Chinaman"? Nothing, in the literal sense—but as always,
life is more than the literal. "Chinaman" signifies the subservient, exotified
"Ah, sohhh!" figure from Charlie Chan³ movies; out it went and few miss it.
"Oriental" was next.

1. In 2016, the California General Assembly passed a bill banning "racially derogatory or
discriminatory" names for athletic teams and their mascots in the state's public schools.
2. "We'll never change the name," Snyder said in 2013. "It's that simple. NEVER — you
can use caps." In 2020, under pressure from corporate sponsors, the team announced that
it would change the name.
3. A fictional detective of mystery novels in the 1920s and, later, of more than 50 films.
Chan was presented as a positive, sympathetic character, but he also displayed stereotypical qualities and was the object of light mockery.

A detail view of a Washington Redskins helmet. In 2016, the state of California passed a bill banning its public schools from using "derogatory" terms like "Redskins" as names for athletic teams and mascots.

These things can be subtle. I once had to inform a foreign student 6 that in class discussion it was unseemly to refer to another person directly as "a Jew," rather than as "a Jewish person." To be American is to internalize that "a Jew" has an air of accusation and diminishment (ironically the student was from Israel!). That makes no literal sense, but it is a reality, as it is that to many, "blacks" sounds abrupt and hostile compared to "black people."

We are faced with something analogous to what Steven Pinker has art- 7 fully called the "euphemism treadmill."[4] When something has negative asso-

4. A professor of psychology at Harvard University, Pinker wrote in "The Game of the Name" (1994): "People invent new `polite' words . . . but the euphemism becomes tainted by association and the new one that must be found acquires its own negative connotations."

ciations, the word referring to it gradually takes on implied meanings connected with that contempt. This happens under the radar, but after about a generation, the reality becomes impossible to ignore.

What was once called "home relief" became more politely called "welfare" after a while, for example. But it's easy to forget what a positive and even warm word "welfare" is, given the associations it had amassed by the 1970s. Today one increasingly speaks of "cash assistance," and that term will surely have the same bad odor about it among many sooner rather than later. Yet all of these terms mean the same thing literally. The literal is but one part of language as we actually live it.

"Crippled," for example, is in itself a neutral, descriptive term—taken literally, it even harbors an element of sympathy. However, the realities of discrimination meant that "crippled" had a less neutral connotation after a while, upon which "handicapped" was a fine substitute. But after a while, we needed "disabled," and of course now there is "differently abled," and indeed there will likely be something else before long.

This, then, is why "Redskins" qualifies as a slur despite not being a literal insult. Words have not only core meanings, but resonances of the kind that may not make it into the dictionary but are deeply felt by all of us. Sometimes we need to get back down to cases[5] with a new word.

For an extended example of how to base an argument on examples, see p. 471.

It may not be mean to tell someone their skin happens to be reddish. But it's mean to call someone a Redskin. There's a difference.

FOR DISCUSSION

1. It is a "slur," John McWhorter argues, to call someone a name like "Redskin" just because "their skin happens to be reddish" (1, 11). Why does McWhorter think so? Is he right, being politically correct, or some combination of both? Explain your view.

2. Many linguists would agree that no words are inherently "bad," since words take their meanings from the people who use them. To what extent would you say McWhorter's ARGUMENT is (or is not) based on this premise? Explain.

3. So, should the Washington Redskins change their name? Why or why not?

5. "Back down to cases": that is, back to particular instances (or examples).

4. Give several examples of other common words or names for people or groups that, in your opinion, clearly constitute slurs even though they may not be intended as insults.

STRATEGIES AND STRUCTURES

1. How and how effectively does McWhorter anticipate and counter the argument that it's not "so terrible" to call people a name based on the color of their skin (2)? Explain.

2. To support his argument that a particular word is disrespectful and offensive—and, therefore, not to be used—McWhorter cites **EXAMPLES** of several other words that have taken on negative **CONNOTATIONS** over time. Which examples do you find particularly effective? Why?

3. Are the examples that McWhorter gives *sufficient* to prove his point about how the implications of words change over time? Or should he have given more examples or different kinds of examples? Explain.

4. McWhorter concludes by saying, "It may not be mean to tell someone their skin happens to be reddish. But it's mean to call someone a Redskin. There's a difference" (11). Is this an effective summary of his argument? Is it a good way to end the essay? Why or why not?

WORDS AND FIGURES OF SPEECH

1. McWhorter calls the owner of the Washington Redskins "callous and antique" for his refusal to change the name of the team (1). Do these words constitute a slur by McWhorter's **DEFINITION**? Why or why not?

2. In what sense is McWhorter using the term "mean" (11)? What else can "mean" mean (in the adjective form)? Which, if any, of these other definitions relate to McWhorter's argument?

3. McWhorter refers to a "euphemism treadmill" (7). Explain the implications of this **METAPHOR**.

4. Is McWhorter choosing his words carefully when he says that changes in meaning occur "under the radar"; or should he have edited out this **CLICHÉ** (7)? How about "bad odor" (8)? Explain.

FOR WRITING

1. At Florida State University, football fans root avidly for the "Seminoles" (or "Noles"), the historical designation (in English) of an actual tribe of Native Americans. In a paragraph or two, outline the main points you would make to support the argument that there is (or is not) "a difference" between this case and that of the Redskins fans.

2. In 2016, the *Washington Post* conducted a telephone poll with 504 self-identifying Native Americans; nine out of ten said they were not offended by the name "Redskins." Look up the details of the survey, and, based on those findings, write an argument for (or against) the use of "Redskins" as a name for the football team. Be sure to consider the survey's methodology and how likely its respondents are to be representative of the broader Native American population.

3. Choose one of the following terms and write an essay explaining how it exemplifies the concept of the "euphemism treadmill" (7): "mental retardation," "water closet," "garbage collector," "house maid," "political correctness."

8

CLASSIFICATION

WHEN WE CLASSIFY* things, we say what categories they belong to. Dogs, for instance, can be classified as Basset hounds, Labrador retrievers, Chihuahuas, and so on. A category is a group with similar characteristics. Thus, to be classified as a Labrador, a dog must be sturdily built, have soft jaws, and have a yellow, black, or chocolate coat—these are the characteristics, among others, that distinguish its group or breed.

Dogs, like anything else, can be classified in more than one way. We can also classify dogs as working dogs, show dogs, and mutts that make good family pets. Or simply as small, medium, and large dogs—or as males and females. The categories into which we divide any subject will depend on the basis on which we classify it. In the case of dogs, our principle of classification is often by breed, but it can also be by role, size, sex, or some other principle.

No matter your subject or your principle of classification, the categories in your system must be inclusive and not overlap. You wouldn't classify dogs as hunting dogs, show dogs, or retrievers, because some dogs, such as most family pets, would be left out—while others, such as Irish setters, would belong to more than one category, since setters are both hunting dogs and retrievers.

Robert Sussman shows how one classification system *does not* work for humans on p. 254.

The categories in any classification system will vary with who is doing the classifying and for what **PURPOSE**. A teacher divides 30 students according to the quality of the work they do in class: A, B, C. A basketball coach might divide the same group of students into forwards, guards, and centers. The director of a student drama group would have another set of criteria. Yet

*Words printed in **SMALL CAPITALS** are defined in the Glossary/Index.

all three systems are valid for the purposes they are intended to serve. And classification must serve some larger purpose, or it becomes an empty game.

Systems of classification can help us organize our thoughts about the world around us. They can also help us organize our thoughts in writing, whether in a single paragraph or a whole essay. For example, you might organize a paragraph by introducing your subject, dividing it into types, and then giving the distinguishing features of each type. Here is a paragraph about lightning that follows such a pattern:

> There are several types of lightning named according to where the discharge takes place. Among them are intracloud lightning, by far the most common type, in which the flash occurs within the thundercloud; air-discharge lightning, in which the flash occurs between the cloud and the surrounding air; and cloud-to-ground lightning, in which the discharge takes place between the cloud and the ground.
>
> —RICHARD ORVILLE, "Bolts from the Blue"

This short paragraph could be the opening of an essay that goes on to discuss each of the three types of lightning in order, devoting a paragraph or more to each type. If the author's purpose were simply to help us understand the different types, he would probably spend more time on the first kind of lightning—perhaps coming back to it in detail later in his essay—because "intracloud lightning" is the most common variety.

In this case, however, Richard Orville, a meteorologist at Texas A&M University, chose to develop his essay by writing several additional paragraphs on the third type of lightning, "in which the discharge takes place between the cloud and the ground." Why emphasize this category?

Meteorologists classify storms—especially hurricanes, tornadoes, and thunderstorms—not only to understand them but also to predict where they are most likely to occur. As Orville says, his main point in classifying lightning is to "tell what parts on the ground will be most threatened by the lightning activity." Based on this information, the meteorologist can then warn people to take shelter. He can also alert the power companies, so they can deploy power crews more effectively or reroute electricity away from a power plant even before it is hit.

Given this purpose—to predict weather activity so he can issue accurate warnings and advisories—Orville first classifies his subject into types based on the location of the electrical discharge, or "flash." He then devotes most of his essay to the third type of lightning (cloud to ground) because it is the most dangerous kind—to property, to natural resources such as forests, and to people.

Meteorologists divide the subject of lightning into groups or kinds—intracloud, air discharge, cloud to ground. This is the equivalent of classifying dogs by dividing them into distinct breeds. Meteorologists also sort individual bolts of lightning according to the group or kind they belong to: "The bolt of lightning that just destroyed the oak tree in your yard was the cloud-to-ground kind." This is the equivalent of saying that a particular dog is a Lab or a husky or a Portuguese water dog. In this chapter, we will use the term "classification" whether we are dividing a subject into groups or sorting individuals according to the group they belong to—because in either case we are organizing a subject into categories.

A BRIEF GUIDE TO WRITING
A CLASSIFICATION ESSAY

As you write a classification essay, you need to identify your subject and explain the basis on which you're classifying it. Trevor Noah makes these basic moves of classification in the second paragraph of an essay about his childhood in South Africa:

> In my class we had all kinds of kids. Black kids, white kids, Indian kids, colored kids. Most of the white kids were pretty well off. Every child of color pretty much wasn't.
>
> —Trevor Noah, "Chameleon"

Noah identifies his subject (kids in his class), divides them into four "kinds" (based mainly on skin color), and then explains that they can be further classified into just two basic categories on the basis of economic status.

The following guidelines will help you make these basic moves as you draft a classification essay. They'll also help you come up with your subject and select categories that fit your purpose and audience, are effectively organized, support your main point, and are sufficiently inclusive yet don't overlap.

Coming Up with a Subject

Almost any subject—lightning, convertibles, TV dramas—can be classified in some way. As you consider subjects to classify, think about what you might learn from doing so—your PURPOSE for classifying. For example, you might want to classify something in order to evaluate it (Which dog breeds are appropriate for families with young children?); to determine causes (Was the crash due to mechanical failure, weather, or pilot error?); or to make sense of events (What kinds of economic recessions has the United States historically experienced?). Choose a subject that interests you, but also ask yourself, "Why is this subject worth classifying?"

Considering Your Purpose and Audience

The specific traits you focus on and the categories you divide your subject into will be determined largely by your purpose and audience. Suppose the roof of your town's city hall blows off in a hurricane, and your PURPOSE is to write an article for your neighborhood newsletter explaining what kind of roof will stay on best in the next hurricane. In this case, you'd look closely at such traits as weight and wind resistance and pay less attention to such traits as color or energy efficiency.

Once you've determined the kind of roof that has the highest wind rating, you probably will not have a hard time convincing your AUDIENCE (some of whom also lost their roofs) that this is the kind to buy. However, since your audience of homeowners may not be experts in roofing materials, you'll want to DEFINE any technical terms and use language they're familiar with. Keep in mind that readers will not always agree with the way you classify a subject. So you may need to explain why they should accept the criteria you've used.

Generating Ideas:
Considering What Categories There Are

Once you have a subject in mind and a reason for classifying it, consider what categories there are and choose the ones that best suit your purpose and audience. For example, if your purpose is to evaluate different kinds of movies for a film course, you might classify them by genre—drama, comedy, romance, horror, thriller, or musical. But if you are reviewing movies for the campus newspaper, you would probably base your classification on quality, perhaps dividing them into these five categories: "must see," "excellent," "good," "mediocre," and "to be avoided at all costs."

When you devise categories for a classification essay, make sure they adhere to a consistent principle (or basis) of classification. For example, if the basis of your movie classification is "movies appropriate for young children," you might use categories such as "good for all ages," "preschool," "six and up," and "not suitable for children." But you should avoid mixing such categories with those based on genre or quality. In other words, you wouldn't use "drama," "excellent," and "not suitable for children" as the categories.

Templates for Classifying

The following templates can help you generate ideas for a classification essay and then start drafting. Don't take these as formulas where you just have to fill in the blanks. There are no easy formulas for good writing. But these templates can help you plot out some of the key moves of classification and thus may serve as good starting points.

> ► X can be classified on the basis of _____.
>
> ► Classified on the basis of _____, some of the most common types of X are _____, _____, and _____.
>
> ► X can be divided into two basic types, _____ and _____.
>
> ► Experts in the field typically divide X into _____, _____, and _____.

► This particular X clearly belongs in the _____ category, since it is _____,
_____, and _____.

► _____ and _____ are examples of this type of X.

► By classifying X in this way, we can see that _____.

For more techniques to help you generate ideas and start writing a classification essay, see Chapter 3.

Organizing a Classification Essay

In the opening paragraphs of your essay, tell the reader what you're classifying and why, and explain your classification system. If you were using classification in an opinion piece on public transportation for your school newspaper, for example, you might start with an introduction like this:

> If the city council is serious about reducing pollution, it needs to replace our old fleet of diesel buses with more sustainable vehicles. Buses that run on alternative fuels can be classified as follows: hybrid-electric buses, all-electric buses, natural gas buses, and biodiesel buses. The council should study the benefits and drawbacks of each type in order to ensure that taxpayer money is spent on public transportation that reduces air pollution and greenhouse gas emissions.

Typically, the body of a classification essay is devoted to a point-by-point discussion of each of the categories that make up your classification system. If you are classifying buses on the basis of fuel types (and thus emissions levels), for example, you would spend a paragraph, or at least several sentences, explaining the most important characteristics of each type, particularly as they affect the environment.

Once you've laid out the categories in some detail, remind the reader of the point you are making. The point of classifying buses by fuel type in our example is to *reduce* emissions and air pollution—and to spend public money wisely.

Stating Your Point

When you compose a classification essay, you should have in mind what you learned about your subject by classifying it in a particular way. Tell the reader in a **THESIS STATEMENT** what your main point is and why you're dividing up your subject as you do. Usually, you'll want to state your main point in the introduction as you explain your classification system. In the opening paragraph of the essay on sustainable buses, for instance, the main point is stated in the last sentence: "The council should study the benefits and drawbacks of each type in order to ensure that taxpayer money is spent on public transportation that reduces air pollution and greenhouse gas emissions."

Choosing Significant Characteristics

Whatever classification system you use, base your categories on the most significant characteristics of your subject—ones that explain something important about it. For example, you probably would not discuss color when classifying environmentally friendly buses because this attribute does not tell the reader much about a bus's impact on the environment. After all, every kind of bus comes in more or less the same colors. Instead, you would probably use such attributes as fuel type, miles per gallon, and types of emissions—traits that differentiate, say, an electric bus from other kinds of buses.

"If you're brain-dead," says Caitlin Doughty, p. 271, "you're dead. There is no gray area."

Choosing Categories That Are Inclusive and Don't Overlap

When you divide your subject into categories, those categories must be inclusive enough to cover most cases, and they must not overlap. For example, classifying ice cream into chocolate and vanilla alone isn't very useful because this system leaves out many other important kinds, such as strawberry, pistachio, and rum raisin. The categories in a good classification system include all kinds: for instance, no-fat, low-fat, and full-fat ice cream. And they should not overlap. Thus, chocolate, vanilla, homemade, and Ben and Jerry's do not make a good classification system because the same scoop of ice cream could fit into more than one category.

EDITING FOR COMMON ERRORS IN A CLASSIFICATION ESSAY

Classification invites problems with listing groups or traits. Here are some common errors to check for and correct when you write a classification essay.

When you list categories or traits in a classification system, make sure they are parallel in form

► How much income tax you pay each year depends largely on whether your income is taxed as wages or ~~you have a lot of~~ capital gains.

► Capital gains are classified according to whether the earnings are long term (more than a year) or ~~are produced over the~~ short term (a year or less).

Check that traits used to describe or define categories are in the following order: size, age, color, region

► His preferred type of headgear was ~~Panama, old, big, white~~ <u>big, old, white Panama</u> hats.

Potato Proverb

When you classify things, you tell what categories they fall into. According to this inscription on a blackboard outside the Perfect Potato restaurant in Brooklyn, New York, all things "in this world" can be classified as those that are potatoes and those that are not potatoes. A binary (two-part) system like this can be useful when you want to classify individuals and groups according to whether they exhibit a particular trait—being a potato, for example, or being tall (basketball players), having a high concentration of fluoride (toothpaste), or allowing pets (hotel rooms).

Depending on your purpose and audience, however, your classification system may need to include a number of different categories, each defined by a variety of traits. Suppose you're writing about the best potato varieties to use for making not only french fries but also potato salad and other dishes. For this purpose, you might classify potatoes according to the following system from the *Huffington Post* in the article "A Guide to Every Type of Potato You Need to Know": starchy (Idaho Russet, for example), waxy (Red Bliss), and all-purpose (Yukon Gold).

ERIC A. WATTS

THE COLOR OF SUCCESS

ERIC A. WATTS wrote the following essay about racial stereotyping when he was a sophomore at Brown University. In it, Watts argues that African Americans who criticize one another for "acting white" and who say that success based on academic achievement is "not black" are misclassifying themselves as "victims." After tracing the historical roots of this "outdated" system, Watts assesses its damaging effects and examines more recent ways of classifying and achieving success that are based more on economics than race. "The Color of Success" originally appeared in the *Brown Alumni Monthly.*

The Color of Success

When I was a black student at a primarily white high   1
school, I occasionally confronted the stereotypes and
prejudice that some whites aimed at those of my race.
These incidents came as no particular surprise—after all,
prejudice, though less prevalent than in the past, is ages
old.

What did surprise me during those years was the   2
profound disapproval that some of my black peers
expressed toward my studious behavior. "Hitting the
books," expressing oneself articulately, and, at times, displaying more than a modest amount of intelligence—
these traits were derided as "acting white."

Once, while I was traveling with other black students,   3
a young woman asked me what I thought of one of our
teachers. My answer, phrased in what one might call
"standard" English, caused considerable discomfort
among my audience. Finally, the young woman exploded:
"Eric," she said, "stop talking like a white boy! You're
with us now!"

Another time, again in a group of black students, a   4
friend asked how I intended to spend the weekend. When
I answered that I would study, my friend's reaction was
swift: "Eric, you need to stop all this studying; you need
to stop acting so white." The others laughed in
agreement.

Signithea Fordham's 1986 ethnographic study of a   5
mostly black high school in Washington, D.C., *Black Students' School Success,* concluded that many behaviors associated with high achievement—speaking standard
English, studying long hours, striving to get good
grades—were regarded as "acting white." Fordham further

Introduces the general topic of the essay: false categories

Identifies the particular false category that he will emphasize

Gives the first in a series of traits that define "acting white"

concluded that "many black students limit their academic success so their peers won't think they are 'acting white.'"

Frankly, I never took the "acting white" accusation seriously. It seemed to me that certain things I valued—hard work, initiative, articulateness, education—were not solely white people's prerogative.

6

Rejects "acting white" as a valid category

Trouble begins, however, when students lower their standards in response to peer pressure. Such a retreat from achievement has potentially horrendous effects on the black community.

7

Watts's purpose in examining a false classification system is to examine its harm-ful effects

Even more disturbing is the rationale behind the "acting white" accusation. It seems that, on a subconscious level, some black students wonder whether success—in particular, academic success—is a purely white domain.

8

In his essay "On Being Black and Middle Class," in *The Content of Our Character* (1990), Shelby Steele, a black scholar at San Jose State University, argues that certain "middle-class" values—the work ethic, education, initiative—by encouraging "individualism," encourage identification with American society, rather than with race. The ultimate result is integration.

9

But, Steele argues, the racial identification that emerged during the 1960s, and that still persists, urges middle-class blacks to view themselves as an embattled minority: to take an adversarial stance toward the mainstream. It emphasizes ethnic consciousness over individualism.

10

Analyzes CAUSES that led to self-stereotyping

Steele says that this form of black identification emerged in the civil rights effort to obtain full racial equality, an effort that demanded that blacks present themselves (by and large) as a racial monolith: a single

11

mass with the common experience of oppression. So blackness became virtually synonymous with victimization and the characteristics associated with it: lack of education and poverty.

I agree with Steele that a monolithic form of racial   12
identification persists. The ideas of the black as a victim and the black as inferior have been too much entrenched in cultural imagery and too much enforced by custom and law not to have damaged the collective black psyche.

This damage is so severe that some black adolescents   13
still believe that success is a white prerogative—the white "turf." These young people view the turf as inaccessible, both because (among other reasons) they doubt their own abilities and because they generally envision whites as, if not outspoken racists, people who are mildly interested in "keeping blacks down."

States the main
damaging effect ·······•   The result of identifying oneself as a victim can be,   14
of believing in the   "Why even try? It's a white man's world."
stereotypes

Several years ago I was talking to an old friend, a   15
black male. He justified dropping out of school and failing to look for a job on the basis of one factor: the cold, heart-less, white power structure. When I suggested that such a

Gives an example
from personal ·······•   power structure might indeed exist, but that opportunity
experience   for blacks was at an unprecedented level, he laughed. Doomed, he felt, to a life of defeat, my friend soon eased his melancholy with crack.

The most frustrating aspect of the "acting white" accu-   16
sation is that its main premise—that academic and subse-quent success are "white"—is demonstrably false. And so is the broader premise: that blacks are the victims of whites.

Attacks the
premises of the ·······•   That academic success is "not black" is easily seen as   17
"victims"   false if one takes a brisk walk through the Brown University
argument

campus and looks at the faces one passes. Indeed, the most comprehensive text concerning blacks in decades, *A Common Destiny* (1989), states, "Despite large gaps . . . whether the baseline is the 1940s, 1950s, or 1960s, the achievement outcomes . . . of black schooling have greatly improved." That subsequent success in the world belongs to blacks as well as whites is exemplified today by such blacks as Jesse Jackson, Douglas Wilder, Norman Rice, Anne Wortham, Sara Lawrence Lightfoot, David Dinkins, August Wilson, Andrew Young . . .

The idea of a victimized black race is slowly becoming outdated. Today's black adolescents were born after the *Brown v. Board of Education* decision of 1954; after the passage of the Civil Rights Act; after the Economic Opportunity Act of 1964. With these rulings and laws, whites' attitudes toward blacks have also greatly improved. Although I cannot say that my life has been free of racism on the part of whites, good racial relations in my experience have far outweighed the bad. I refuse to apologize for or retreat from this truth. 18

The result of changes in policies and attitudes has been to provide more opportunities for black Americans than at any other point in their history. As early as 1978, William Julius Wilson, in *The Declining Significance of Race,* concluded that "the recent mobility patterns of blacks lend strong support to the view that economic class is clearly more important than race in predetermining . . . occupational mobility." 19

> Argues that racial conditions in America have changed

There are, of course, many factors, often socioeconomic, that still impede the progress of blacks. High schools in black neighborhoods receive less local, state, and federal support than those in white areas; there is 20

> Anticipates objections to his position

evidence that the high school diplomas of blacks are little valued by employers.

We should rally against all such remaining racism,   21 confronting particularly the economic obstacles to black success. But we must also realize that racism is not nearly as profound as it once was, and that opportunities for blacks (where opportunity equals jobs and acceptance for the educated and qualified) have increased. Furthermore, we should know that even a lack of resources is no excuse for passivity.

As the syndicated columnist William Raspberry (who   22 is black) says, it is time for certain black adolescents to "shift their focus": to move from an identity rooted in victimization to an identity rooted in individualism and hard work.

Simply put, the black community must eradicate the   23 "you're-acting-white" syndrome. Until it does, black Americans will never realize their potential.

> Concludes by
> saying what
> should be done

MOTHER TONGUE

Amy Tan (b. 1952) is a native of Oakland, California. She attended high school in California and Switzerland and graduated with bachelor's and master's degrees from San Jose State University. After the death of her father, an electrical engineer and Baptist minister who immigrated to the United States during a period of civil war in China, Tan discovered that her mother had four children in China by a previous marriage. This discovery was the basis of her first novel, *The Joy Luck Club* (1989), which was a finalist for the National Book Award. Tan has written several other novels—including *The Kitchen God's Wife* (1991), *The Bonesetter's Daughter* (2001), and *The Valley of Amazement* (2013)—and a "writer's memoir," *Where the Past Begins* (2017). In "Mother Tongue," which first appeared in the *Threepenny Review* (1990), Tan uses all the various forms of the English language she has spoken since childhood with her mother, whose native language is Chinese. She also classifies these different "Englishes" into their various types and explains how each type lends itself to a particular form of communication.

I AM NOT A SCHOLAR of English or literature. I cannot give you much more than personal opinions on the English language and its variations in this country or others.

I am a writer. And by that definition, I am someone who has always loved language. I am fascinated by language in daily life. I spend a great deal of my time thinking about the power of language—the way it can evoke an emotion, a visual image, a complex idea, or a simple truth. Language is the tool of my trade. And I use them all—all the Englishes I grew up with.

When you define something, you tell what general cat-egory it belongs to (p. 374).

Recently, I was made keenly aware of the different Englishes I do use. I was giving a talk to a large group of people, the same talk I had already given to half a dozen other groups. The nature of the talk was about my writing, my life, and my book, *The Joy Luck Club.* The talk was going along well enough, until I remembered one major difference that made the whole talk sound wrong. My mother was in the room. And it was perhaps the first time she had heard me give a lengthy speech, using the kind of English I have never used with her. I was saying things like, "The intersection of memory upon imagi-nation" and "There is an aspect of my fiction that relates to thus-and-thus"—a speech filled with carefully wrought grammatical phrases, burdened, it sud-denly seemed to me, with nominalized forms, past perfect tenses, conditional phrases, all the forms of standard English that I had learned in school and through books, the forms of English I did not use at home with my mother.

Just last week, I was walking down the street with my mother, and I again found myself conscious of the English I was using, the English I do use with her. We were talking about the price of new and used furniture and I heard myself saying this: "Not waste money that way." My husband was with us as well, and he didn't notice any switch in my English. And then I realized why. It's because over the twenty years we've been together I've often used the same kind of English with him, and sometimes he even uses it with me. It has become our language of intimacy, a different sort of English that relates to family talk, the language I grew up with.

So you'll have some idea of what this family talk I heard sounds like, I'll quote what my mother said during a recent conversation which I videotaped and then transcribed. During this conversation, my mother was talking about a political gangster in Shanghai who had the same last name as her family's,

Du, and how the gangster in his early years wanted to be adopted by her family, which was rich by comparison. Later, the gangster became more powerful, far richer than my mother's family, and one day showed up at my mother's wedding to pay his respects. Here's what she said in part:

"Du Yusong having business like fruit stand. Like off the street kind. He 6 is Du like Du Zong—but not Tsung-ming Island people. The local people call putong, the river east side, he belong to that side local people. That man want to ask Du Zong father take him in like become own family. Du Zong father wasn't look down on him, but didn't take seriously, until that man big like become a mafia. Now important person, very hard to inviting him. Chinese way, came only to show respect, don't stay for dinner. Respect for making big celebration, he shows up. Mean gives lots of respect. Chinese custom. Chinese social life that way. If too important won't have to stay too long. He come to my wedding. I didn't see, I heard it. I gone to boy's side, they have YMCA dinner. Chinese age I was nineteen."

You should know that my mother's expressive command of English 7 belies how much she actually understands. She reads the *Forbes*[1] report, listens to *Wall Street Week*, converses daily with her stockbroker, reads all of Shirley MacLaine's[2] books with ease—all kinds of things I can't begin to understand. Yet some of my friends tell me they understand 50 percent of what my mother says. Some say they understand 80 to 90 percent. Some say they understand none of it, as if she were speaking pure Chinese. But to me, my mother's English is perfectly clear, perfectly natural. It's my mother tongue. Her language, as I hear it, is vivid, direct, full of observation and imagery. That was the language that helped shape the way I saw things, expressed things, made sense of the world.

Lately, I've been giving more thought to the kind of English my mother speaks. 8 Like others, I have described it to people as "broken" or "fractured" English. But I wince when I say that. It has always bothered me that I can think of no way to describe it other than "broken," as if it were damaged and needed to be fixed, as if it lacked a certain wholeness and soundness. I've heard other terms

1. Business magazine.
2. American film actress (b. 1934) who has written a number of memoirs.

used, "limited English," for example. But they seem just as bad, as if everything is limited, including people's perceptions of the limited English speaker.

I know this for a fact, because when I was growing up, my mother's "limited" English limited *my* perception of her. I was ashamed of her English. I believed that her English reflected the quality of what she had to say. That is, because she expressed them imperfectly her thoughts were imperfect. And I had plenty of empirical evidence to support me: the fact that people in department stores, at banks, and at restaurants did not take her seriously, did not give her good service, pretended not to understand her, or even acted as if they did not hear her. 9

My mother has long realized the limitations of her English as well. When I was fifteen, she used to have me call people on the phone to pretend I was she. In this guise, I was forced to ask for information or even to complain and yell at people who had been rude to her. One time it was a call to her stockbroker in New York. She had cashed out her small portfolio and it just so happened we were going to go to New York the next week, our very first trip outside California. I had to get on the phone and say in an adolescent voice that was not very convincing, "This is Mrs. Tan." 10

And my mother was standing in the back whispering loudly, "Why he don't send me check, already two weeks late. So mad he lie to me, losing me money." 11

And then I said in perfect English, "Yes, I'm getting rather concerned. You had agreed to send the check two weeks ago, but it hasn't arrived." 12

Then she began to talk more loudly. "What he want, I come to New York tell him front of his boss, you cheating me?" And I was trying to calm her down, make her be quiet, while telling the stockbroker, "I can't tolerate any more excuses. If I don't receive the check immediately, I am going to have to speak to your manager when I'm in New York next week." And sure enough, the following week there we were in front of this astonished stockbroker, and I was sitting there red-faced and quiet, and my mother, the real Mrs. Tan, was shouting at his boss in her impeccable broken English. 13

We used a similar routine just five days ago, for a situation that was far less humorous. My mother had gone to the hospital for an appointment, to find out about a benign brain tumor a CAT scan had revealed a month ago. She said she had spoken very good English, her best English, no mistakes. Still, 14 she said, the hospital did not apologize when they said they had lost the CAT scan and she had come for nothing. She said they did not seem to have any sympathy when she told them she was anxious to know the exact diagnosis, since her husband and son had both died of brain tumors. She said they would not give her any more information until the next time and she would have to make another appointment for that. So she said she would not leave until the doctor called her daughter. She wouldn't budge. And when the doctor finally called her daughter, me, who spoke in perfect English—lo and behold—we had assurances the CAT scan would be found, promises that a conference call on Monday would be held, and apologies for any suffering my mother had gone through for a most regrettable mistake.

I think my mother's English almost had an effect on limiting my possibilities in life as well. Sociologists and linguists probably will tell you that a person's developing language skills are more influenced by peers. But I do think that the language spoken in the family, especially in immigrant families which are more insular, plays a large role in shaping the language of the child. And I believe that it affected my results on achievement tests, IQ tests, and the SAT. While my English skills were never judged as poor, compared to math, English could not be considered my strong suit. In grade school I did moderately well, getting perhaps B's, sometimes B-pluses, in English and scoring perhaps in the sixtieth or seventieth percentile on achievement tests. But those scores were not good enough to override the opinion that my true abilities lay in math and science, because in those areas I achieved A's and scored in the ninetieth percentile or higher.

This was understandable. Math is precise; there is only one correct answer. Whereas, for me at least, the answers on English tests were always a judgment call, a matter of opinion and personal experience. Those tests were constructed around items like fill-in-the-blank sentence completion, such as, "Even though Tom was _____, Mary thought he was _____." And the correct answer always seemed to be the most bland combinations of thoughts, for example, "Even though Tom was shy, Mary thought he was charming," with the grammatical structure "even though" limiting the correct answer to some sort of semantic opposites, so you wouldn't get answers like, "Even though Tom was foolish, Mary thought he was ridiculous." Well, according to my mother, there were very

See p. 232 on choosing categories that don't overlap.

15

16

few limitations as to what Tom could have been and what Mary might have thought of him. So I never did well on tests like that.

The same was true with word analogies, pairs of words in which you 17 were supposed to find some sort of logical, semantic relationship—for example, "*Sunset* is to *nightfall* as _____ is to _____." And here you would be presented with a list of four possible pairs, one of which showed the same kind of relationship: *red* is to *stoplight, bus* is to *arrival, chills* is to *fever, yawn* is to *boring*. Well, I could never think that way. I knew what the tests were asking, but I could not block out of my mind the images already created by the first pair, "*sunset* is to *nightfall*"—and I would see a burst of colors against a darkening sky, the moon rising, the lowering of a curtain of stars. And all the other pairs of words—red, bus, stoplight, boring—just threw up a mass of confusing images, making it impossible for me to sort out something as logical as saying: "A sunset precedes nightfall" is the same as "a chill precedes a fever." The only way I would have gotten that answer right would have been to imagine an associative situation, for example, my being disobedient and staying out past sunset, catching a chill at night, which turns into feverish pneumonia as punishment, which indeed did happen to me.

I have been thinking about all this lately, about my mother's English, about 18 achievement tests. Because lately I've been asked, as a writer, why there are not more Asian Americans represented in American literature. Why are there few Asian Americans enrolled in creative writing programs? Why do so many Chinese students go into engineering? Well, these are broad sociological questions I can't begin to answer. But I have noticed in surveys—in fact, just last week—that Asian students, as a whole, always do significantly better on math achievement tests than in English. And this makes me think that there are other Asian-American students whose English spoken in the home might also be described as "broken" or "limited." And perhaps they also have teachers who are steering them away from writing and into math and science, which is what happened to me.

Fortunately, I happen to be rebellious in nature and enjoy the challenge 19 of disproving assumptions made about me. I became an English major my first year in college, after being enrolled as pre-med. I started writing nonfiction as a freelancer the week after I was told by my former boss that writing was my worst skill and I should hone my talents toward account management.

But it wasn't until 1985 that I finally began to write fiction. And at first 20 I wrote using what I thought to be wittily crafted sentences, sentences that would finally prove I had mastery over the English language. Here's an example from the first draft of a story that later made its way into *The Joy Luck Club*, but without this line: "That was my mental quandary in its nascent state." A terrible line, which I can barely pronounce.

Fortunately, for reasons I won't get into today, I later decided I should 21 envision a reader for the stories I would write. And the reader I decided upon was my mother, because these were stories about mothers. So with this reader in mind—and in fact she did read my early drafts—I began to write stories using all the Englishes I grew up with: the English I spoke to my mother, which for lack of a better term might be described as "simple"; the English she used with me, which for lack of a better term might be described as "broken"; my translation of her Chinese, which could certainly be described as "watered down"; and what I imagined to be her translation of her Chinese if she could speak in perfect English, her internal language, and for that I sought to preserve the essence, but neither an English nor a Chinese structure. I wanted to capture what language ability tests can never reveal: her intent, her passion, her imagery, the rhythms of her speech and the nature of her thoughts.

Apart from what any critic had to say about my writing, I knew I had 22 succeeded where it counted when my mother finished reading my book and gave me her verdict: "So easy to read."

FOR DISCUSSION

1. Into what two basic categories does Amy Tan CLASSIFY all the Englishes that she uses in writing and speaking?

2. How many Englishes did Tan learn at home from conversing with her mother, a native speaker of Chinese? How does she distinguish among them?

3. According to Tan, what are the significant characteristics of "standard" English (3)? How and where did she learn standard English?

4. Tan tells us that she envisions her mother as the AUDIENCE for her stories, using "all the Englishes I grew up with" in writing them (21). For what audience did Tan write this essay? How would you classify the English she uses in it?

STRATEGIES AND STRUCTURES

1. Why do you think Tan begins her essay with the disclaimer that she is "not a scholar" of the English language (1)? How does she otherwise establish her **CREDIBILITY** on the subject? How well does she do it?

2. Tan first gives **EXAMPLES** of "family talk" and only later classifies them (4, 21). Why do you think she follows this order? Why not give the categories first, then the specific examples?

3. What specific kind of English, by Tan's classification, is represented by paragraph 6 of her essay?

4. Besides classifying Englishes, Tan also includes **NARRATIVES** about using them. What do the narratives contribute to her essay? How would the essay be different without the stories?

5. In which paragraphs is Tan advancing an **ARGUMENT** about achievement tests? What is her point here, and how does she use her different Englishes to support that point?

WORDS AND FIGURES OF SPEECH

1. Explain the **PUN** in Tan's title. What does it tell us about the essay?

2. By what standards, according to Tan, is "standard" English established and measured (3)? Where and how did she learn these standards?

3. What are some of the implications of using such terms as "broken" or "fractured" to refer to nonstandard forms of speech or writing (8)?

4. Do you find "simple" to be better or worse than "broken" for describing forms of English other than the "standard" variety taught in schools? How about "watered down" (21)? Explain.

5. Tan does not give a term for the kind of English she uses to represent her mother's "internal language" (21). What name would you give it? Why?

FOR WRITING

1. Many families have private jokes, code words, gestures, even family whistles. In a paragraph or two, give examples of your family's private speech or language. How does each function within the family? In relation to the family and the outside world?

2. How many different Englishes (and other languages) do you use at home, at school, among friends, and elsewhere? Write an essay classifying them, giving the characteristics of each, and explaining how and when each is used.

WARREN BUFFETT

STOP CODDLING THE SUPER-RICH

WARREN BUFFETT (b. 1930) is the CEO of Berkshire Hathaway, a holding company headquartered in Omaha, Nebraska. One of the richest people in the world and widely regarded as the most successful investor of his generation, the "Sage of Omaha" has pledged to donate approximately 99 percent of his wealth to charitable causes. He once said, "I want to give my kids just enough so that they would feel that they could do anything, but not so much that they would feel like doing nothing." In "Stop Coddling the Super-Rich" (*New York Times,* 2011), Buffett uses a classification system based on income (and equity) to argue for an increase in taxes for the wealthiest Americans, classifying them in general as "those making more than $1 million." A version of this "Buffett rule" was considered by the US Senate as part of the Paying a Fair Share Act of 2012, but it failed to attract enough votes to move forward.

O UR LEADERS HAVE ASKED FOR "SHARED SACRIFICE." But when they did the asking, they spared me. I checked with my mega-rich friends to learn what pain they were expecting. They, too, were left untouched.   1

While the poor and middle class fight for us in Afghanistan, and while ₂ most Americans struggle to make ends meet, we mega-rich continue to get our extraordinary tax breaks. Some of us are investment managers who earn billions from our daily labors but are allowed to classify our income as "carried interest," thereby getting a bargain 15 percent tax rate. Others own stock index futures for 10 minutes and have 60 percent of their gain taxed at 15 percent, as if they'd been long-term investors.[1]

These and other blessings are showered upon us by legislators in Wash- ₃ ington who feel compelled to protect us, much as if we were spotted owls or some other endangered species. It's nice to have friends in high places.

To belong to a particular species, one must exhibit *all* its significant traits, p. 232. Billionaires are rare but not endangered.

Last year my federal tax bill—the income tax I paid, as well ₄ as payroll taxes paid by me and on my behalf—was $6,938,744.

That sounds like a lot of money. But what I paid was only 17.4 percent of my taxable income—and that's actually a lower percentage than was paid by any of the other 20 people in our office. Their tax burdens ranged from 33 percent to 41 percent and averaged 36 percent.

If you make money with money, as some of my super-rich friends do, ₅ your percentage may be a bit lower than mine. But if you earn money from a job, your percentage will surely exceed mine—most likely by a lot.

To understand why, you need to examine the sources of government ₆ revenue. Last year about 80 percent of these revenues came from personal income taxes and payroll taxes. The mega-rich pay income taxes at a rate of 15 percent on most of their earnings but pay practically nothing in payroll taxes. It's a different story for the middle class: typically, they fall into the 15 percent and 25 percent income-tax brackets, and then are hit with heavy payroll taxes to boot.

Back in the 1980s and 1990s, tax rates for the rich were far higher, and ₇ my percentage rate was in the middle of the pack. According to a theory I

---

1. Carried interest is the pay that investment managers receive for making a profit with a client's investment. Such profits are taxed at a lower rate than ordinary wages. Stock index futures are speculative contracts to buy or sell stocks at a fixed price on a set date in the future.

sometimes hear, I should have thrown a fit and refused to invest because of the elevated tax rates on capital gains and dividends.

I didn't refuse, nor did others. I have worked with investors for 60 years and I have yet to see anyone—not even when capital gains rates were 39.9 percent in 1976–77—shy away from a sensible investment because of the tax rate on the potential gain. People invest to make money, and potential taxes have never scared them off. And to those who argue that higher rates hurt job creation, I would note that a net of nearly 40 million jobs were added between 1980 and 2000. You know what's happened since then: lower tax rates and far lower job creation.

8

Since 1992, the I.R.S. has compiled data from the returns of the 400 Americans reporting the largest income. In 1992, the top 400 had aggregate taxable income of $16.9 billion and paid federal taxes of 29.2 percent on that sum. In 2008, the aggregate income of the highest 400 had soared to $90.9 billion—a staggering $227.4 million on average—but the rate paid had fallen to 21.5 percent.

9

The taxes I refer to here include only federal income tax, but you can be sure that any payroll tax for the 400 was inconsequential compared to income. In fact, 88 of the 400 in 2008 reported no wages at all, though every one of them reported capital gains. Some of my brethren may shun work but they all like to invest. (I can relate to that.)

10

I know well many of the mega-rich and, by and large, they are very decent people. They love America and appreciate the opportunity this country has given them. Many have joined the Giving Pledge, promising to give most of their wealth to philanthropy. Most wouldn't mind being told to pay more in taxes as well, particularly when so many of their fellow citizens are truly suffering.

11

A class or category ("mega-rich") is a group with similar characteristics, p. 226.

Twelve members of Congress will soon take on the crucial job of rearranging our country's finances.[2] They've been instructed to devise a plan that reduces the 10-year deficit by at least $1.5 trillion. It's vital, however, that they achieve far more than that. Americans are rapidly losing

12

2. Reference to the Congress's Joint Select Committee on Deficit Reduction (popularly known as the "Supercommittee"), which was unable to come to an agreement on how best to handle the US budget deficit and disbanded in November 2011.

faith in the ability of Congress to deal with our country's fiscal problems. Only action that is immediate, real, and very substantial will prevent that doubt from morphing into hopelessness. That feeling can create its own reality.

Job one for the 12 is to pare down some future promises that even a rich America can't fulfill. Big money must be saved here. The 12 should then turn to the issue of revenues. I would leave rates for 99.7 percent of taxpayers unchanged and continue the current 2-percentage-point reduction in the employee contribution to the payroll tax. This cut helps the poor and the middle class, who need every break they can get. 13

But for those making more than $1 million—there were 236,883 such households in 2009—I would raise rates immediately on taxable income in excess of $1 million, including, of course, dividends and capital gains. And for those who make $10 million or more—there were 8,274 in 2009—I would suggest an additional increase in rate. 14

My friends and I have been coddled long enough by a billionaire-friendly Congress. It's time for our government to get serious about shared sacrifice. 15

FOR DISCUSSION

1. Why does Warren Buffett think legislators in Washington should stop "coddling" the country's richest taxpayers? Do you agree? Why or why not?

2. According to Buffett, how has the federal tax system changed since the 1980s? Should he have said more about the causes of those changes, or is he wise to leave them largely unspecified? Explain.

3. What economic "theory" is Buffett referring to in paragraph 7? Why does he think this view of investment is incorrect? What **EVIDENCE** does he give?

4. According to Buffett, what specific actions should Congress take in order to do "the crucial job of rearranging our country's finances" (12)? Why does Buffett think these steps are especially needed now?

STRATEGIES AND STRUCTURES

1. An income tax system is, by definition, a **CLASSIFICATION** system. As laid out by Buffett, what are some of the primary categories of the present system of classifying taxpayers and their incomes in the United States?

2. How and how well does Buffett use these various categories to support his **ARGUMENT** that the system needs to be changed? Point out specific **EXAMPLES** in the text that you find particularly effective.

3. When and where does Buffett use mainly **ANECDOTAL** evidence to make his case? When does he turn to statistics? Should he have included more (or fewer) numbers? Explain.

4. Many wealthy people, says Buffett, "classify our income as 'carried interest'" (2). How and how well does this example support Buffett's claim that such a classification system is faulty?

5. "I know well many of the 'mega-rich' and, by and large, they are very decent people" (11). How and how well does Buffett establish his **CREDIBILITY** as someone qualified to speak authoritatively about each of these categories? Explain.

WORDS AND FIGURES OF SPEECH

1. If the "mega-rich," according to Buffett's classification system, are "those who make $10 million or more" (14), how does the system **DEFINE** the merely "super-rich"?

2. "Coddled" is a word usually reserved for children. What does it mean, and why does Buffett use the term to refer to a particular economic class (or classes)?

3. In Buffett's accounting of the traits and conditions that define the super-rich, what are the implications of the word "blessings" (3)? Of "showered" (3)?

4. Why does Buffett put "shared sacrifice" in quotation marks at the beginning of his essay but not at the end (1, 15)?

FOR WRITING

1. Check out the Internal Revenue Service's website at www.irs.gov. Make a list of the main categories of information and services on the site.

2. Many banks and lending institutions in the United States identify a category of customers whom they call the "mass affluent." Write a classification essay about this socioeconomic group that explains its common traits and divides this general category into subgroups. Be sure to explain why bankers and stockbrokers might be particularly interested in this segment of the American population.

ROBERT WALD SUSSMAN

THE MYTH OF RACE

ROBERT WALD SUSSMAN (1941–2016) was a primatologist and anthropologist who devoted decades to studying macaques—a primate group that includes more than 23 species of monkeys—and lemurs. A native of Brooklyn, New York, Sussman completed his PhD at Duke University in 1972 and then joined the anthropology department at Washington University in St. Louis. Among his principal interests was, as he put it, "the evolution of human and nonhuman primate behavior and the ways in which the study of primates can help us understand the biological basis of human behavior." Sussman is best remembered for his book *The Myth of Race: The Troubling Persistence of an Unscientific Idea* (2014), in which he asserts that the commonly understood notion of race is a social construct. In the following excerpt, he explains that classification of human beings by race is a cultural myth, not a biological fact.

⊷————————————————————————————⊷

R ACISM IS A PART OF OUR EVERYDAY LIVES. Where you live, where you go to   1
school, your job, your profession, who you interact with, how people interact with you, your treatment in the healthcare and justice systems are all

affected by your race. For the past 500 years people have been taught how to interpret and understand racism. We have been told that there are very specific things that relate to race, such as intelligence, sexual behavior, birth rates, infant care, work ethics and abilities, personal restraint, life span, law-abidingness, aggression, altruism, economic and business practices, family cohesion, and even brain size. We have learned that races are structured in a hierarchical order and that some races are better than others. Even if you are not a racist, your life is affected by this ordered structure. We are born into a racist society.

What many people do not realize is that this racial structure is not based **2** on reality. Anthropologists have shown for many years now that there is no biological reality to human race. There are no major complex behaviors that directly correlate with what might be considered human "racial" characteristics. There is no inherent relationship between intelligence, law-abidingness, or economic practices and race, just as there is no relationship between nose size, height, blood group, or skin color and any set of complex human behaviors. However, over the past 500 years, we have been taught by an informal, mutually reinforcing consortium of intellectuals, politicians, statesmen, business and economic leaders, and their books that human racial biology is real and that certain races are biologically better than others. These teachings have led to major injustices to Jews and non-Christians during the Spanish Inquisition;[1] to blacks, Native Americans, and others during colonial times; to African Americans during slavery and reconstruction; to Jews and other Europeans during the reign of the Nazis in Germany; and to groups from Latin America and the Middle East, among others, during modern political times.

I am not going to dwell upon all of the scientific information that has been gathered by anthropologists, biologists, geneticists, and other scientists concerning the fact that there are no such things as human biological races. This has been done by many people over the past fifty or so years. What I am going to do is describe the history of our myth of race and racism. . . .

The categories **3** you use to classify a subject will depend on your purpose and audience, p. 229.

1. A campaign in 15th-century Spain to enforce and maintain Catholic orthodoxy. Its history is controversial, but it is associated with the persecution, expulsion, and murder of thousands of people, principally Jews and Muslims, but many others as well.

Before beginning this story, however, it is important to understand how   4
scientists define the concept of race. How is race defined in *bio-*

As defined on
p. 226, a general
category—such as
"race," "class," or
"species"—is simply
a group with similar
characteristics.

logical terms? What do we mean by the term *race* when describing
population variation in large mammals such as humans? Do the
criteria used in describing these variations hold when we examine human population variation? In biological terms, the concept
of race is integrally bound to the process of evolution and the origin of species. It is part of the process of the formation of new species and is
related to subspecific differentiation. However, because conditions can change
and subspecies can and do merge (Alan Templeton, personal communication,
2013), this process does not necessarily lead to the development of new species. In biology, a species is defined as a population of individuals who are able
to mate and have viable offspring; that is, offspring who are also successful in
reproducing. The formation of new species usually occurs slowly over a long
period of time. For example, many species have a widespread geographic distribution with ranges that include ecologically diverse regions. If these regions
are large in relationship to the average distance of migration of individuals
within the species, there will be more mating, and thus more exchange of
genes, within than between regions. Over very long periods of time (tens of
thousands of years), differences would be expected to evolve between distant
populations of the same species. Some of these variations would be related to
adaptations to ecological differences within the geographic range of the populations, while others might be purely random. Over time, if little or no mating
(or genetic exchange) occurs between these distant populations, genetic (and
related morphological)[2] differences will increase. Ultimately, over tens of
thousands of years of separation, if little or no mating takes place between
separate populations, genetic distinctions can become so great that individuals
of the different populations could no longer mate and produce viable offspring.
The two populations would now be considered two separate species. This is
the process of speciation. However, again, none of these criteria require that
speciation will ultimately occur.

2. When Sussman uses the word "genetic," he is referring to the actual genes or DNA that
determine the characteristics of a living thing. The term "morphological" refers to the study
of the form and structure of a living thing, which is determined by its genetic makeup.

Since speciation develops very slowly, it is useful to recognize interme- 5 diate stages in this process. Populations of a species undergoing differentiation would show genetic and morphological variation due to a buildup of genetic differences but would still be able to breed and have offspring that could successfully reproduce. They would be in various stages of the process of speciation but not yet different species. In biological terminology, it is these populations that are considered "races" or "subspecies" (Williams 1973; Amato and Gatesy 1994; Templeton 1998, 2013). Basically, subspecies within a species are geographically, morphologically, and genetically distinct populations but still maintain the possibility of successful interbreeding (Smith, Chiszar, and Montanucci 1997). Thus, using this biological definition of race, we assume that races or subspecies are populations of a species that have genetic and morphological differences due to barriers to mating. Furthermore, little or no mating (or genetic exchange) between them has persisted for extremely long periods of time, thus giving the individuals within the population a common and separate evolutionary history.

Given advances in molecular genetics, we now have the ability to exam- 6 ine populations of species and subspecies and reconstruct their evolutionary histories in an objective and explicit fashion. In this way, we can determine the validity of the traditional definition of human races "by examining the patterns and amount of genetic diversity found within and among human populations" (Templeton 1998, 633) and by comparing this diversity with other large-bodied mammals that have wide geographic distributions. In other words, we can determine how much populations of a species differ from one another and how these divergences came about.

A commonly used method to quantify the amount of within- to among- 7 group genetic diversity is through examining molecular data, using statistics measuring genetic differences within and between populations of a species. Using this method, biologists have set a minimal threshold for the amount of genetic differentiation that is required to recognize subspecies (Smith, Chiszar, and Montanucci 1997). Compared to other large mammals with wide geographic distributions, human populations do not reach this threshold. In fact, even though humans have the widest distribution, the measure of human genetic diversity (based on sixteen populations from Europe, Africa, Asia, the Americas, and the Australia-Pacific region) falls well below the threshold used to recognize races for other species and is among the lowest value known for large mammalian species. This is true even if we compare humans to chimpanzees (Templeton 2013).

Using a number of molecular markers, Templeton (1998, 2013), further, [8] has shown that the degree of isolation among human populations that would have been necessary for the formation of biological subspecies or races never occurred during the 200,000 years of modern human evolution. Combined genetic data reveal that from around one million years ago to the last tens of thousands of years, human evolution has been dominated by two evolutionary forces: (1) constant population movement and range expansion; and (2) restrictions on mating between individuals only because of distance. Thus, there is no evidence of fixed, long-term geographic isolation between populations. Other than some rare, temporary isolation events, such as the isolation of the aborigines of Australia, for example, the major human populations have been interconnected by mating opportunities (and thus genetic mixture) during the last 200,000 years (as long as modern humans, *Homo sapiens*, have been around). As summarized by Templeton (1998, 647), who is among the world's most recognized and respected geneticists,

> because of the extensive evidence for genetic interchange through population movements and recurrent gene flow going back at least hundreds of thousands of years ago, there is only one evolutionary lineage of humanity and there are no subspecies or races. . . . Human evolution and population structure has been and is characterized by many locally differentiated populations coexisting at any given time, but with sufficient contact to make all of humanity a single lineage sharing a common, long-term evolutionary fate.

Thus, given current scientific data, biological races do not exist among [9] modern humans today, and they have never existed in the past. Given such clear scientific evidence as this and the research data of so many other biologists, anthropologists, and geneticists that demonstrate the nonexistence of biological races among humans, how can the "myth" of human races still persist? If races do not exist as a biological reality, why do so many people still believe that they do? In fact, even though biological races do not exist, the concept of race obviously is still a reality, as is racism. These are prevalent and persistent elements of our everyday lives and generally accepted aspects of our culture. Thus, the concept of human races is real. It is not a biological reality, however, but a cultural one. Race is not a part of our biology, but it is definitely a part of our culture. Race and racism are deeply ingrained in our history.

References

Amato, G., and J. Gatesy. 1994. PCR Assays of Variable Nucleotide Sites for Identification of Conservation Units. In *Molecular Ecology and Evolution: Approaches and Applications*, edited by B. Schierwater, B. Streit, G. P. Wagner, and R. DeSalle, 215–226. Basel: Birkhäser Verlag.

Smith, H. M., D. Chiszar, and R. R. Montanucci. 1997. Subspecies and Classification. *Herpetological Review* 28:13–16.

Templeton, A. R. 1998. Human Races: A Genetic and Evolutionary Perspective. *American Anthropologist* 100:632–650.

———. 2013. Biological Races in Humans. *Studies in History and Philosophy of Science Part C: Studies in History and Philosophy of Biological and Biomedical Sciences* 44:262–271.

Williams, B. J. 1973. *Evolution and Human Origins: An Introduction to Physical Anthropology*. New York: Harper & Row.

FOR DISCUSSION

1. "The formation of new species," says Robert Wald Sussman, "usually occurs slowly over a long period of time" (4). How long? Why is the process so slow?

2. According to Sussman, what conditions allow new species to form?

3. Over the last 200,000 years, modern humans have been separated by distance and other factors. Why have humans nevertheless remained a single species?

4. "Taxonomy" (or the science of **CLASSIFICATION**) divides all living things into six general categories. What are they, and how are modern human beings (*Homo sapiens*) classified within this general system?

STRATEGIES AND STRUCTURES

1. To develop his **THESIS** that race is a cultural myth rather than a scientific fact, Sussman launches immediately into a scientific **DEFINITION** of "the concept of race" (4). Why might he begin this way?

2. The concept of race is closely related to that of species. How and where does Sussman define this term in the scientific classification of living things?

3. As the basis for a biological classification system, how significant and distinctive is being "able to mate and have viable offspring" (4)? Explain.

4. In scientific classification systems, races are not species but "subspecies" (5). Where and how does Sussman develop this distinction?

5. Where and how does Sussman use **PROCESS ANALYSIS** to support his thesis about the misclassification of human beings?

WORDS AND FIGURES OF SPEECH

1. Sussman is writing about both "race" and "racism" (1). What's the difference between these two closely related terms?

2. Charles Darwin's *On the Origin of Species* (1859) laid the foundation for the field of modern evolutionary biology. Where and why does Sussman **ALLUDE** to Darwin's work?

3. The word "taxonomy" derives from a Greek term meaning, in part, "arrangement." How might this ancient meaning help explain the modern one?

4. What is a "myth," and why might Sussman use the term when writing that there is "no biological reality to human race" (2)?

FOR WRITING

1. To many people, says, Sussman, "the concept of race" is a "reality" (9). In a few paragraphs, explain why this is (or is not) the case.

2. Look up the terms "hominid" and "hominin," and write an essay explaining why one has replaced the other in the scientific classification of human beings.

3. Citing Sussman and other sources, write an essay on the role(s) of science and myth in discussions of race and racism.

TREVOR NOAH

CHAMELEON

Trevor Noah (b. 1984) is a comedian, writer, producer, television personality, and host, since 2015, of *The Daily Show* on Comedy Central. Noah is a native of Johannesburg, South Africa; his father is of Swiss and German ancestry, and his mother is Xhosa, a branch of the second-largest ethnic group in South Africa, after the Zulu. In addition to English and German, therefore, Noah grew up speaking several African languages. "If you spoke to me in Zulu," he writes in *Born a Crime: Stories from a South African Childhood* (2016), "I replied to you in Zulu. If you spoke to me in Tswana, I replied to you in Tswana." Noah thus became a "chameleon," as demonstrated in this selection from the chapter by that name in his memoir of childhood. When he enters a new school, Noah does not change his color; he changes his *perception* of color—both as a basis for defining himself and for understanding how he is classified by others—and he changes how he talks depending on his audience.

AS APARTHEID WAS COMING TO AN END,[1] South Africa's elite private schools started accepting children of all colors. My mother's company offered bursaries, scholarships, for underprivileged families, and she managed to get me into Maryvale College, an expensive private Catholic school. Classes taught by nuns. Mass on Fridays. The whole bit. I started preschool there when I was three, primary school when I was five.

In my class we had all kinds of kids. Black kids, white kids, Indian kids, colored kids.[2] Most of the white kids were pretty well off. Every child of color pretty much wasn't. But because of scholarships we all sat at the same table. We wore the same maroon blazers, the same gray slacks and skirts. We had the same books. We had the same teachers. There was no racial separation. Every clique was racially mixed.

Kids still got teased and bullied, but it was over usual kid stuff: being fat or being skinny, being tall or being short, being smart or being dumb. I don't remember anybody being teased about their race. I didn't learn to put limits on what I was supposed to like or not like. I had a wide berth to explore myself. I had crushes on white girls. I had crushes on black girls. Nobody asked me what I was. I was Trevor.

It was a wonderful experience to have, but the downside was that it sheltered me from reality. Maryvale was an oasis that kept me from the truth, a comfortable place where I could avoid making a tough decision. But the real world doesn't go away. Racism exists. People are getting hurt, and just because it's not happening to you doesn't mean it's not happening. And at some point, you have to choose. Black or white. Pick a side. You can try to hide from it. You can say, "Oh, I don't pick sides," but at some point life will force you to pick a side.

A scientist argues, p. 254, that racism, though real, is based on "no biological reality."

At the end of grade six I left Maryvale to go to H. A. Jack Primary, a government school. I had to take an aptitude test before I started, and, based on the results of the test, the school counselor told me, "You're going to be in the smart classes, the A classes." I showed up for the first day of school and went

---

1. Established in 1948 as an official system of racial segregation in South Africa, apartheid ended in 1994 when Nelson Mandela was elected as the country's first non-White president.
2. South Africans refer to people of mixed ethnicity as "colored."

to my classroom. Of the thirty or so kids in my class, almost all of them were white. There was one Indian kid, maybe one or two black kids, and me.

Then recess came. We went out on the playground, and black kids were 6 *everywhere*. It was an ocean of black, like someone had opened a tap and all the black had come pouring out. I was like, *Where were they all hiding?* The white kids I'd met that morning, they went in one direction, the black kids went in another direction, and I was left standing in the middle, totally confused. Were we going to meet up later on? I did not understand what was happening.

I was eleven years old, and it was like I was seeing my country for the 7 first time. In the townships you don't see segregation, because everyone is black. In the white world, any time my mother took me to a white church, we were the only black people there, and my mom didn't separate herself from anyone. She didn't care. She'd go right up and sit with the white people. And at Maryvale, the kids were mixed up and hanging out together. Before that day, I had never seen people being together and yet not together, occupying the same space yet choosing not to associate with each other in any way. In an instant I could see, I could feel, how the boundaries were drawn. Groups moved in color patterns across the yard, up the stairs, down the hall. It was insane. I looked over at the white kids I'd met that morning. Ten minutes earlier I'd thought I was at a school where they were a majority. Now I realized how few of them there actually were compared to everyone else.

I stood there awkwardly by myself in this no-man's-land in the middle 8 of the playground. Luckily, I was rescued by the Indian kid from my class, a guy named Theesan Pillay. Theesan was one of the few Indian kids in school, so he'd noticed me, another obvious outsider, right away. He ran over to introduce himself. "Hello, fellow anomaly! You're in my class. Who are you? What's your story?" We started talking and hit it off. He took me under his wing, the Artful Dodger to my bewildered Oliver.[3]

Through our conversation it came up that I spoke several African languages, and Theesan thought a colored kid speaking black languages was the 9 most amazing trick. He brought me over to a group of black kids. "Say some-

3. In the novel *Oliver Twist* (1838) by Charles Dickens (1812-1870), the young pickpocket Jack Dawkins is called the Artful Dodger because of his agility on the streets of London.

thing," he told them, "and he'll show you he understands you." One kid said something in Zulu, and I replied to him in Zulu. Everyone cheered. Another kid said something in Xhosa, and I replied to him in Xhosa. Everyone cheered. For the rest of recess Theesan took me around to different black kids on the playground. "Show them your trick. Do your language thing."

The black kids were fascinated. In South Africa back then, it wasn't common to find a white person or a colored person who spoke African languages; during apartheid white people were always taught that those languages were beneath them. So the fact that I did speak African languages immediately endeared me to the black kids. 10

"How come you speak our languages?" they asked. 11

"Because I'm black," I said, "like you." 12

"You're not black." 13

"Yes, I am." 14

"No, you're not. Have you not seen yourself?" 15

They were confused at first. Because of my color, they thought I was a colored person, but speaking the same languages meant that I belonged to their tribe. It just took them a moment to figure it out. It took me a moment, too. 16

At some point I turned to one of them and said, "Hey, how come I don't see you guys in any of my classes?" It turned out they were in the B classes, which also happened to be the black classes. That same afternoon, I went back to the A classes, and by the end of the day I realized that they weren't for me. Suddenly, I knew who my people were, and I wanted to be with them. I went to see the school counselor. 17

Why choose one category over another? Page 227 gives several reasons.

"I'd like to switch over," I told her. "I'd like to go to the B classes." 18

She was confused. "Oh, no," she said. "I don't think you want to do that." 19

"Why not?" 20

"Because those kids are . . . you know." 21

"No, I don't know. What do you mean?" 22

"Look," she said, "you're a smart kid. You don't want to be in that class." 23

"But aren't the classes the same? English is English. Math is math." 24

"Yeah, but that class is . . . those kids are gonna hold you back. You want to be in the smart class." 25

"But surely there must be some smart kids in the B class." 26

"No, there aren't." 27

"But all my friends are there." 28

"You don't want to be friends with those kids." 29

"Yes, I do." 30

We went back and forth. Finally she gave me a stern warning. 31

"You do realize the effect this will have on your future? You do under- 32
stand what you're giving up? This will impact the opportunities you'll have
open to you for the rest of your life."

"I'll take that chance." 33

I moved to the B classes with the black kids. I decided I'd rather be held 34
back with people I liked than move ahead with people I didn't know.

Being at H. A. Jack made me realize I was black. Before that recess I'd 35
never had to choose, but when I was forced to choose, I chose black. The world
saw me as colored, but I didn't spend my life looking at myself. I spent my life
looking at other people. I saw myself as the people around me, and the people
around me were black. My cousins are black, my mom is black, my gran is
black. I grew up black. Because I had a white father, because I'd been in white
Sunday school, I got along with the white kids, but I didn't *belong* with the
white kids. I wasn't a part of their tribe. But the black kids embraced me.
"Come along," they said. "You're rolling with us." With the black kids, I wasn't
constantly trying to be. With the black kids, I just was.

FOR DISCUSSION

1. At Maryvale, where Trevor Noah first went to school, "there was no racial separation" (2). What was the "downside" of this otherwise "wonderful" experience,
   according to Noah (4)?

2. When Noah transfers to H. A. Jack Primary at age 11, he is "totally confused" (6).
   Why is his new school so different from his old one?

3. At his new government school, Noah maintains that he is Black "like you" (12). To
   whom is he speaking here? Why are these "kids" skeptical of his claims but nonetheless "fascinated" by him (10)?

4. Elsewhere in *Born a Crime*, Noah says that "language, even more than color, defines
   who you are to people." Is this true in your experience? Why or why not?

5. How and where does Noah himself define who he is? What part does language play in his decision to belong to one racial category rather than another?

STRATEGIES AND STRUCTURES

1. At times, Noah divides his classmates into three groups: White, Black, and colored. In his account of "how the boundaries were drawn," what were the distinguishing features of each of these racial and social categories as constituted "back then" in South Africa (7, 10)?

2. Sometimes, instead of dividing his classmates into three categories, Noah adds a fourth ("Indian")—or uses only two (Black and White). In a good classification system, the categories do not overlap. How do the various systems that Noah cites here meet (or fail to meet) this standard?

3. If Noah uses a shifting set of categories to characterize race in "Chameleon," is he being shifty? Why or why not?

4. Noah says that "at some point life will force you to pick a side," because "the real world doesn't go away" (4). How is he DEFINING "real world" here? Is his ARGU- MENT valid? Why or why not?

5. In addition to using CLASSIFICATION to make a point about race, Noah is con- structing a NARRATIVE about his experience with race as he was growing up in South Africa. How and why does paragraph 7 represent a major turning point in the PLOT of the story?

WORDS AND FIGURES OF SPEECH

1. "Apartheid" (1) means, literally, "separateness"; it derives from the Dutch word *apart* (which means the same as in English), plus the suffix "heid." What is the English equivalent of "heid"?

2. "No-man's-land" refers to territory separating warring parties (8). Why might Noah use a military METAPHOR in a discussion of race?

3. One of the "Indian kids" in Noah's school refers to him as a "fellow anomaly" (8). What is an "anomaly"? Do Noah and Theesan Pillay qualify as such? Why or why not?

4. In paragraph 8, Noah says he played "Oliver" to Pillay's "Artful Dodger." What is the purpose of this ALLUSION to Dickens's novel, and what does it suggest about the boys' education?

5. Maryvale College, where Noah first went to school as a child, was clearly a grade school. So why was it called a "college" in the South Africa of his childhood?

6. Noah does not use the term in his narrative, but a moment of sudden revelation in a story is sometimes referred to as an "epiphany." Why? Where and how might the term be applied to Noah's account of his first day at H. A. Jack?

FOR WRITING

1. In a paragraph or two, define "apartheid" as it was practiced in the South Africa of Trevor Noah's childhood. Be sure to explain how apartheid differed from the less formal systems of racial classification that Noah talks about.

2. Do further research on the system of apartheid in South Africa and elsewhere, and write an essay explaining how the system worked, how it was enforced, and how and when it came to an end.

3. Tell the story of when you first become aware of race as a basis for putting people into categories. Describe the situation in detail.

4. Tell the story of when you first became aware of language as a way of defining (or failing to define) yourself in the eyes of other people. Give examples of specific words and phrases that you (and others) used—and how they helped you (or not) be the person you wanted to be.

CAITLIN DOUGHTY

WHAT IF THEY BURY ME WHEN I'M JUST IN A COMA?

CAITLIN DOUGHTY (b. 1984) is a writer, blogger, *YouTube* personality, and mortician. A native of Hawaii, Doughty graduated from the University of Chicago, where she majored in medieval history. After training at a crematory, Doughty studied mortuary science at Cypress College. In 2011, she founded the Order of the Good Death, which advocates for natural burial and open discussion of human mortality, and started her popular *YouTube* series, "Ask a Mortician." Doughty is the author of *Smoke Gets in Your Eyes* (2014); *From Here to Eternity* (2017); and *Will My Cat Eat My Eyeballs?* (2019). "What if they make a mistake and bury me when I'm just in a coma?" is one of 35 questions Doughty raises in this last book. Her answer is *not to worry*: death professionals today are expert classifiers with strict scientific criteria for identifying different states of human mortality, such as merely being in a coma or being "good and dead."

O KAY, SO TO BE CLEAR, you *don't* want to be buried alive, is that correct? 1
Got it.

Lucky for you, you don't live in Ye Olden Times! During Ye Olden Times 2
(before the twentieth century), doctors had a less-than-flawless track record when
it came to declaring people dead. The tests they used to determine if someone
was honest-to-God-really-dead were not just low-tech, they were horrifying.

For your enjoyment, here's a fun sample of the death tests: 3

- Shoving needles under the toenails, or into the heart or stomach.

- Slicing the feet with knives or burning them with red-hot pokers.

- Smoke enemas for drowning victims—someone would literally "blow
  smoke up your ass" to see if it would warm you up and make you breathe.

- Burning the hand or chopping off a finger.

And, my personal favorite:

- Writing "I am really dead" in invisible ink (made from acetate of lead) on
  a piece of paper, then putting the paper over the corpse-in-question's
  face. According to the inventor of this method, if the body was putrefy-
  ing, sulfur dioxide would be emitted, thus revealing the message. Unfortunately, sulfur dioxide can also be emitted by living people, like those
  with decaying teeth. So, it's possible there were a few false positives.

If you woke up, breathed, or visibly responded to these "tests"—hallelujah!—
you weren't dead. But you might be maimed. And that needle stuck in your
heart could actually kill you.

But what about the poor souls who weren't put through the battery of 4
stabs, slices, and enemas, but were just assumed to be 100 percent dead and
sent to the grave?

Take the tale of Matthew Wall, a man living (yes, *living*) in Braughing, 5
England, in the sixteenth century. Matthew was thought to be dead, but was
lucky enough to have his pallbearers slip on wet leaves and drop the coffin on
the way to his burial. As the story goes, when the coffin was dropped, Matthew awakened and knocked on the lid to be released. To this day, every
October 2nd is celebrated as Old Man's Day to commemorate Matthew's
revival. He lived, by the way, *for twenty-four more years.*

With stories like that, it's no wonder that certain cultures had extreme   6
taphophobia, or the fear of being buried alive. Matthew Wall was lucky that
his "body" never reached his grave, but Angelo Hays was not.

In 1937—true, 1937 is not quite Ye Olden Times, but at least it's way   7
before you were born—Angelo Hays of France was in a motorcycle accident.
When doctors couldn't find his pulse, he was pronounced dead. He was buried
quickly and his own parents were not allowed to see his disfigured body.
Angelo would have remained buried if it wasn't for the life insurance company's suspicions of foul play.

Two days after Angelo was buried, he was exhumed for an investigation.   8
Upon inspecting the "corpse," examiners found that it was still warm, and
that Angelo was alive.

The theory is that Angelo had been in a very deep coma which slowed   9
his breathing way, way down. It was that slow breathing that allowed him to
stay alive while buried.* Angelo recovered, lived a full life, and even invented a
"security coffin" with a radio transmitter and a toilet.

Luckily, if you fall into a coma today, in the twenty-first century, there   10
are many, many ways to make sure that you are good and dead before you're
moved on to burial. But while the tests may show that you are technically
alive, your new status may be small comfort to you and your kin.

Media and TV shows often throw around terms like "coma" and "brain-   11
dead" interchangeably. "Chloe was my true love, and now she will never wake
from her coma. I must decide whether to pull the plug." This Hollywood version of medicine can make it seem like those conditions are the same, just one
step away from death. Not true!

Of the two, the one you really don't want to be is brain-dead. (I mean, nei-   12
ther is great, let's be honest.) But once you're brain-dead, there is no coming
back. Not only have you lost all the upper brain functions that create your memories and behaviors and allow you to think and talk, but you have also lost all the
involuntary stuff your lower brain does to keep you alive, like controlling your

---

* If you're buried alive and breathing normally, you're likely to die from suffocation. A
person can live on the air in a coffin for a little over five hours, tops. If you start hyperven-
tilating, panicked that you've been buried alive, the oxygen will likely run out sooner
[author's note].

heart, respiration, nervous system, temperature, and reflexes. There are gobs of biological actions controlled by your brain so that you don't have to constantly remind yourself, "Stay alive, stay alive . . ." If you are brain-dead, these functions are being performed by hospital equipment like ventilators and catheters.

You cannot recover from brain death. If you're brain-dead, you're dead. 13 There is no gray area (brain matter joke): either you are brain-dead or you are not. If you are in a coma, on the other hand, you are legally very much alive. In a coma, you still have brain function, which doctors can measure by observing electrical activity and your reactions to external stimuli. In other words, your body continues to breathe, your heart beats, etc. Even better, you can, potentially, recover from a coma and regain consciousness.

This either-or condition is true of any "binary" classification system (p. 234).

Okay, but what if I fall into a deep, deep coma? Will someone eventually 14 pull the plug and send me off to the mortuary? Will I be trapped in both a casket and in the *prison of my mind*?

No. We now have a whole battery of scientific tests to confirm that 15 someone is not just in a coma, but really, truly brain-dead.

These tests include but are not limited to: 16

- Seeing if your pupils are reactive. When a bright light is shined into them, do they contract? Brain-dead people's eyes don't do anything.

- Dragging a cotton swab over your eyeball. If you blink, you're alive!

- Testing your gag reflex. Your breathing tube might be moved in and out of your throat, to see if you gag. Dead people don't gag.

- Injecting ice water into your ear canal. If doctors do this to you and your eyes don't flick quickly from side to side, it's not looking good.

- Checking for spontaneous respiration. If you are removed from a ventilator, CO_2 builds up in your system, essentially suffocating you. When blood CO_2 levels reach 55 mm Hg, a living brain will usually tell the body to spontaneously breathe. If that doesn't happen, your brain stem is dead.

- An EEG, or electroencephalogram, which is an all-or-nothing test. Either there is electrical activity in your brain or there isn't. Dead brains have zero electrical activity.

- A CBF, or cerebral blood flow, study. A radioactive isotope is injected into your bloodstream. After a period of time, a radioactive counter is held over your head to see if blood is flowing to your brain. If there is blood flow to the brain, the brain cannot be called dead.

- Administering atropine IV. A living patient's heart rate will accelerate, but a brain-dead patient's heartbeat will not change.

A person has to fail *a lot* of tests to be declared brain-dead. And more   17
than one doctor has to confirm brain death. Only after countless tests and an in-depth physical exam will you go from "coma patient" to "brain-dead" patient. Nowadays, it's not just some dude with a needle poised over your heart and "I am really dead" scrawled on a scrap of paper.

It is highly unlikely that your living brain will slip through the cracks   18
and that you'll be sent away from the hospital in a coma. Even if

As page 227   you were, there is no funeral director or medical examiner I know
explains, we classify
things in order to   who can't tell the difference between a living person and a corpse.
make sense of the
world around us.   Having seen thousands of dead bodies in my career, let me tell
                        you—dead people are very dead in a very predictable way. Not that

my words sound all that comforting. Or scientific. But I feel confident saying that this is not going to happen to you. On your list of "Freaky Ways to Die" you can move "buried alive—coma" down to just below "terrible gopher accident."

FOR DISCUSSION

1. Is Caitlin Doughty right to say that the tests that even doctors once used to determine whether or not a person was dead were "less-than-flawless" ones (2)? Why or why not?

2. What about the "battery of scientific tests" that doctors use today (15)? How reliable are they, according to Doughty; and what, precisely, are they used to determine?

3. On anyone's list of "Freaky Ways to Die," just how far down *is* "terrible gopher accident" likely to be: *not very, more than halfway, off the charts* (18)? Explain.

4. "I must decide whether to pull the plug" (11). Why does Doughty describe this as a "Hollywood version of medicine" (11)?

5. Do you think Doughty's essay is in bad taste? Why or why not?

STRATEGIES AND STRUCTURES

1. "Okay, so to be clear, you *don't* want to be buried alive, is that correct?" (1) Would this qualify as a **RHETORICAL QUESTION**? Is it an effective way for Doughty to begin her essay? Explain.

2. Doughty presents her first list of dead-or-alive tests "for your enjoyment" (3). To whom is she speaking here? What assumptions is she making about her intended audience, especially about their capacity for **IRONY**?

3. Doughty studied history in college. Why does she tell the ancient "tale" of Matthew Wall (5)? How about the more recent (but still "way before you were born") story of the Frenchman Angelo Hays (7–9)? Are they good historical **EXAMPLES**? Why or why not?

4. In the first part of her essay, Doughty uses a binary classification system (comatose or dead); what "new status" does she introduce in paragraph 10? What are the main distinguishing features of this third category, as established by the second set of tests that Doughty outlines?

5. According to Doughty, what is the most important difference between being "in a coma" and being "brain-dead" (13)? Doughty is an advocate of mortuary reform; what **ARGUMENT** is she implying here, especially when referring to "equipment like ventilators and catheters" (12)?

6. How would you describe the overall **TONE** of Doughty's essay: "sharp as a needle," "lighthearted," heavy-handed," "deadpan," all of these, or other? Explain.

WORDS AND FIGURES OF SPEECH

1. Doughty defines "Ye Olden Times" as the period "before the twentieth century" (2). Did she likely learn this binary (then and now) system of classifying historical events in college, or is she sharing a joke with her audience? Explain.

2. Doughty defines "taphaphobia" as "the fear of being buried alive" (6). The common suffix "phobia" means "fear of." What is the literal meaning of "taphos" in Greek?

3. With brain death, says Doughty, there is no "gray area" (13). Is this an insufferable **PUN**—or welcome levity in a serious discussion of a difficult topic? Explain.

4. "Will I be trapped in both a casket and in the *prison of my mind*?" (14) In addition to being buried alive, what other condition would have to be met for a person to suffer from the second, more **METAPHORICAL** of these unlikely horrors?

FOR WRITING

1. Make a "Freaky Ways to Die" list that includes possibilities even more irrational and unlikely than being buried alive or killed in a terrible gopher accident.

2. "Ye Olden Times. Ye Olde Gifte Shoppe." Do a little research on spelling and printer's conventions in early modern English, and write a paragraph or two explaining the extra letters in words like these—and how "Y" came to be used at times for "Th."

3. In college, Doughty wrote and directed a play based, in part, on the work of Edgar Allan Poe (1809–1849). Read Poe's late short story "The Premature Burial," and write a critical analysis of it as a psychological tale of terror. You can find the story online by googling the title.

4. Write an essay defining "brain death" as a medical condition and ARGUING that patients who meet all the standard criteria for this condition should (or should not) be taken off life support.

9

PROCESS ANALYSIS

THE essays in this chapter are examples of **PROCESS ANALYSIS*** or "how to" writing. Basically, there are two kinds of process analysis: *directive* and *explanatory*. A directive process analysis explains how to make or do something—for instance, how to throw a boomerang. ("Bring the boomerang back behind you and snap it forward as if you were throwing a baseball."— howstuffworks.com) An explanatory process analysis explains how something works; it tells you what makes the boomerang come back.

Both kinds of analysis break a process into the sequence of actions that lead to its end result. In her sassy memoir *Bossypants*, for example, the comedian Tina Fey explains how to do improvisational comedy by breaking the process into four basic rules. "The first rule of improvisation," Fey writes, "is AGREE. Always agree and SAY YES." Then "add something of your own" (rule 2), continue to make positive statements (rule 3), and treat all "mistakes" as "opportunities" (rule 4).

The end result of improvisational comedy is the audience's laughter. Here's an example of how Fey follows her own "rules" to achieve this end:

> If I start a scene as what I think is very clearly a cop riding a bicycle, but you think I am a hamster in a hamster wheel, guess what? Now I'm a hamster in a hamster wheel. I'm not going to stop everything to explain that it was really supposed to be a bike. Who knows? Maybe I'll end up being a police hamster who's been put on "hamster wheel" duty because I'm "too much of a loose cannon" in the field. In improv there are no mistakes, only beautiful happy accidents. And many of the world's

*Words printed in **SMALL CAPITALS** are defined in the Glossary/Index.

greatest discoveries have been by accident. I mean, look at the Reese's
Peanut Butter Cup, or Botox.

—Tina Fey, *Bossypants*

In a directive process analysis, you typically use the second-person pronoun
("you") because you're giving instructions directly to the reader. Sometimes
the "you" is understood, as in a recipe: "[You] combine the milk
with the eggs, then add a pinch of salt and the juice of one lemon."
In an explanatory process analysis, you typically use third-person
pronouns ("he," "she," "it," "they") because you're giving information *about* something:

Allegra Goodman,
p. 298, uses
second-person
point of view to tell
you how to be a
writer.

> The uneven force caused by the difference in speed between the two
> wings applies a constant force at the top of the spinning boomerang. . . .
> Like a leaning bicycle wheel, the boomerang is constantly turning to the
> left or right, so that it travels in a circle and comes back to its starting
> point.
>
> —HOWSTUFFWORKS.COM

Sometimes a process is best explained by *showing* how it works, so you may
want to add diagrams or drawings to the written text. An analysis of how to
throw a boomerang, for example, might benefit from a clearly labeled
diagram.

Bring behind head, then snap forward.

Most processes that you analyze will be linear rather than cyclical. Even if the process is repeatable, your analysis will proceed chronologically step by step, stage by stage to an end result that is different from the starting point. Consider this explanatory analysis of how fresh oranges are turned into orange juice concentrate:

> As the fruit starts to move along a concentrate plant's assembly line, it is first culled. . . . Moving up a conveyer belt, oranges are scrubbed with detergent before they roll on into juicing machines. There are several kinds of juicing machines, and they are something to see. One is called the Brown Seven Hundred. Seven hundred oranges a minute go into it and are split and reamed on the same kind of rosettes that are in the centers of ordinary kitchen reamers. The rinds that come pelting out the bottom are integral halves, just like the rinds of oranges squeezed in a kitchen. Another machine is the Food Machinery Corporation's FMC In-line Extractor. It has a shining row of aluminum teeth. When an orange tumbles in, the upper jaw comes crunching down on it while at the same time the orange is penetrated from below by a perforated steel tube. As the jaws crush the outside, the juice goes through the perforations in the tube and down into the plumbing of the concentrate plant. All in a second, the juice has been removed and the rind has been crushed and shredded beyond recognition.
>
> From either machine, the juice flows on into a thing called the finisher, where seeds, rag, and pulp are removed. The finisher has a big stainless-steel screw that steadily drives the juice through a fine-mesh screen. From the finisher, it flows on into holding tanks.
>
> —JOHN MCPHEE, *Oranges*

John McPhee divides the process of making orange juice concentrate from fresh fruit into five stages: (1) culling, (2) scrubbing, (3) extracting, (4) straining, (5) storing. When you plan an essay that analyzes a process, make a list of all the stages or phases in the process you are analyzing. Make sure that they are separate and distinct and that you haven't left any out. When you are satisfied that your list is complete, you are ready to decide on the order in which you will present the steps.

The usual order of process analysis is chronological, beginning with the earliest stage of the process (the culling of the split and rotten oranges from the rest) and ending with the last, or with the finished product (concentrated orange juice in holding tanks). Notice that after they leave the conveyer belt, McPhee's oranges come to a fork in the road. They can go in different directions, depending on what kind of juicing machine is being used. McPhee briefly follows the oranges into one kind of juicer and then comes back to the other. He has stopped time and forward motion for a moment. Now he picks them up again and proceeds down the line: "From either machine, the juice flows on into a thing called the finisher," where it is strained. From the straining stage, the orange concentrate goes into the fifth (and final) holding stage, where it is stored in large tanks.

An early stage in becoming a man, says Jon Katz, p. 292, is learning to show no fear.

Another lesson to take away from McPhee: if the order of the process you are analyzing is controlled by a piece of machinery or other mechanism, let it work for you. McPhee, in fact, lets several machines—conveyor belt, extractor, and finisher—help him organize his analysis.

Some stages in a process analysis may be more complicated than others. Suppose you are explaining to someone how to replace a light switch. You might break the process down into six stages: (1) select and purchase the new switch; (2) turn off the power at the breaker box; (3) remove the switch plate; (4) disconnect the old switch and install the new one; (5) replace the switch plate; (6) turn the power back on. Obviously, one of these stages—"disconnect the old switch and install the new one"—is more complicated than the others. When this happens, you can break down the more complicated stage into smaller steps, as McPhee does with his analysis of the production of orange juice concentrate.

The most complicated stage in McPhee's process analysis is the third one, extracting. He breaks it into the following steps: (1) an orange enters the extractor; (2) it is crushed by the extractor's steel jaws; (3) at the same time, the orange is "penetrated from below by a perforated steel tube"; (4) the extracted juice flows on to the next stage of the process. All of this happens "in a second," says McPhee; but for purposes of analysis and explanation, the steps must be presented in sequence, using such **TRANSITIONS** as "when," "while at the same time," "all in a second," "from . . . to," "next," and "then."

McPhee's process analysis is explanatory; it tells how orange juice concentrate is made. When you are telling someone how to do something (a directive process analysis), the method of breaking the process into steps and stages is the same. Here's how our analysis of how to change a light switch might break down the most complicated step in the process, the one where the old switch is removed and replaced. The transitions and other words that signal the order and timing of the steps *within* this stage are underlined:

Harris Pastides uses directive process analysis to explain how to hail a ride safely, p. 303.

> To remove the old switch, <u>first</u> unscrew the two terminal screws on the sides. <u>If</u> the wires are attached to the back of the switch, <u>instead</u> clip off the old wires as close to the switch as possible. As necessary, strip the insulation from the ends of the wires <u>until</u> approximately half an inch is exposed. <u>Next</u>, unscrew the green grounding screw, <u>and</u> disconnect the bare wire attached to it. You are <u>now</u> ready to remove the old switch and replace it with the new one. <u>Either</u> insert the ends of the insulated wires into the holes on the back of the new switch, <u>or</u> bend the ends of the wires around the terminal screws <u>and</u> tighten the screws. <u>Reattach</u> the bare wire to the green terminal. <u>Finally</u>, secure the new switch by tightening the two long screws at top and bottom into the ears on the old switch box.

Explaining this stage in our analysis is further complicated because we have to stop the flow of information (with "if . . . instead"; "either . . . or . . . and") to go down a fork in the road—the wires can be attached either to the screws on the sides of the switch or to holes in the rear—before getting back on track. And we now have to signal a move on to the next stage: "Once the new switch is installed, replacing the switch plate is a snap."

Actually, this simple next-to-last stage (before turning the power back on) requires a *twist* of the little screw in the center of the switch plate, which can serve to remind us that the forward movement of a process analysis, step by step, from beginning to end, is much like the twisting and turning of the **PLOT** in a **NARRATIVE**—a process is a sequence of events or actions. You are the **NARRATOR,** and you are telling the exciting story of how something is made or done or how it works. Also as with a narrative, you will want your process analysis to make a point so the reader knows why you're analyzing the process and what to expect. When Tina Fey analyzes how to do improv, for example, she is also careful to explain that "the rules of improvisation appealed to me not only as a way of creating comedy, but as a worldview."

You may simply conclude your story with the product or end result of the process you've been analyzing. But you may want to round out your account by summarizing the stages you have just gone through or by encouraging the reader to follow your directions—"Changing a light switch yourself is easy, and it can save money"—or by explaining why the process is important. The production of orange juice concentrate, for example, transformed Florida's citrus industry. In what is called "the old fresh-fruit days," 40 percent of the oranges grown in Florida were left to rot in the fields because they couldn't travel well. "Now," as McPhee notes, "with the exception of split and rotten fruit, all of Florida's orange crop is used." This is not exactly the end product of the process McPhee is analyzing, but it is an important consequence and one that makes technical advances in the citrus industry seem more worth reading about.

One other detail, though a minor one, in McPhee's analysis that you may find interesting: when all that fresh fruit was left to rot on the ground because it couldn't be shipped and local people couldn't use it all, the cows stepped in to help. Thus McPhee notes that in the days before orange juice concentrate, "Florida milk tasted like orangeade." Details like this may not make the process you are analyzing clearer or more accurate, but they may well make the reader more interested in the process itself.

A BRIEF GUIDE TO WRITING
A PROCESS ANALYSIS

As you write a **PROCESS ANALYSIS,** you need to say what process you're analyzing and to identify some of its most important steps. These moves are fundamental to any process analysis. Allegra Goodman makes these basic moves in her essay in this chapter:

Forthwith, some advice for those of you who have always wanted to write. . . . To begin, don't write about yourself. . . . [I]f you want to be a writer, start by writing about other people. . . . Find a peaceful place to work. . . . Read widely. . . . value your own time.

—ALLEGRA GOODMAN, "So, You Want to Be a Writer? Here's How."

Goodman identifies the process she's analyzing (how "to be a writer") and indicates the most important steps that make up the process (write "about other people," "find a peaceful place to work," "read widely," "value your own time").

The following guidelines will help you make these basic moves as you draft a process analysis. They will also help you choose a process to analyze, divide it into steps, and put those steps in order, using appropriate transitions and pronouns.

Coming Up with a Subject

Your first challenge is to find a process worth analyzing. You might start by considering processes you are already familiar with, such as running a marathon, training a puppy, or playing a video game. Or you might think about processes you are interested in and want to learn more about. Do you wonder how bees make honey, how to tune a guitar, how to change the oil in a car engine, or how the oil and gas in your car are produced and refined? Whatever process you choose, you will need to understand it fully yourself before you can explain it clearly to your readers.

Considering Your Purpose and Audience

When your **PURPOSE** is to tell readers how to do something, a basic set of instructions will usually do the job, as when you give someone the recipe for your Aunt Ana's famous empanadas. When, however, you want your **AUDIENCE** to understand, not duplicate, a complicated process—such as the chemistry that makes dough form—your analysis should be explanatory. So instead of giving instructions ("add flour and salt to the water"), you would go over the inner workings of the process in some detail, telling readers, for example, what happens when they add lard to the dough mixture.

The nature of your audience will also influence the information you include. How much do your intended readers already know about the process? Why might they want to know more, or less? If you are giving a set of instructions, will they require any special tools or equipment? What problems are they likely to encounter? Will they need to know where to find more information on your topic? Asking questions like these will help you select the appropriate steps and details.

Generating Ideas: Asking How Something Works

When you analyze a process, the essential question to ask yourself is *how*. How does a cake rise? How do I back out of the garage? To get started, ask yourself a *how* question about your subject, research the answer (if necessary), and write down all the steps involved. For instance, "How do I back out of the garage?" might result in a list like this: put the car in reverse, step on the gas, turn the key in the ignition, look in the rearview mirror. Although this list includes all the essential steps for backing a car out of a garage, you wouldn't want your reader to follow them in this order. Once you have a complete list of steps, think about the best order in which to present them to your reader. Usually it will be chronological: turn the key in the ignition, put the car in reverse, look in the rearview mirror, and step lightly on the gas pedal.

Or pick a lock (p. 307)? Or understand digital advertising (p. 315)?

Also think about whether you should demonstrate the process—or a complex part of it—visually. If you decide to include one or more diagrams or drawings, make sure there are words to accompany each visual. Either DESCRIBE what the visual shows, or label the parts of a diagram (the parts of an engine, for instance).

Templates for Analyzing a Process

The following templates can help you generate ideas for an essay that analyzes a process and then start drafting. Don't take these as formulas where you just have to fill in the blanks. There are no easy formulas for good writing. But these templates can help you plot out some of the key moves of process analysis and thus may serve as good starting points.

> ▸ In order to understand how process X works, we can divide it into the following steps: _____, _____, and _____.
>
> ▸ The various steps that make up X can be grouped into the following stages: _____, _____, and _____.
>
> ▸ The end result of X is _____.
>
> ▸ In order to repeat X, you must first _____; then _____ and _____; and finally _____.
>
> ▸ The tools and materials you will need to replicate X include _____, _____, and _____.
>
> ▸ The most important reasons for understanding/repeating X are _____, _____, and _____.

For more techniques to help you generate ideas and start writing a process analysis, see Chapter 3.

Putting the Steps in Order

When you write about a process, you must present its main steps in order. If the process is a linear one, such as backing out of a garage or driving to a particular address in Dallas, you simply start at the earliest point in time and move forward chronologically, step by step, to the end result. If the process is cyclical, such as what's happening in your car engine as you drive, you will have to pick a logical point in the process and then proceed through the rest of the cycle. If, however, the process you are analyzing does not follow a chronology, try arranging the steps from most important to least important, or the other way around.

Stating Your Point

A good process analysis should have a point to make, and that point should be clearly expressed in a **THESIS STATEMENT**. Make sure your thesis statement identifies the process, indicates its end result, and tells the reader why you're analyzing it. For example:

> You cannot understand how the Florida citrus industry works without understanding how fresh orange juice gets processed into "concentrate."
>
> —JOHN McPHEE, *Oranges*

McPhee's thesis statement clearly tells the reader what process he's analyzing (making "concentrate" from fresh oranges), its end result (orange juice concentrate), and why he is analyzing it (to understand the Florida citrus industry).

Using Appropriate Transitions

As you move from one step to another, include clear **TRANSITIONS**, such as "next," "from there," "after five minutes," and "then." Because the actions and events that make up a process are repeatable, you will frequently use expressions such as "usually," "normally," "in most cases," and "whenever." Also, use transitions like "sometimes," "rarely," and "in one instance" to note any deviations from the normal order.

Using Appropriate Pronouns

In addition to appropriate transition words, be careful to use pronouns that fit the kind of analysis you are writing. In an explanatory process analysis, you will focus on the things (oranges) and activities (culling and scrubbing) that make up the process. Thus, you will usually write about the process in the third person ("he," "she," "it," "they"), as John McPhee does: "Moving up a conveyor belt, oranges are scrubbed with detergent before <u>they</u> roll on into the juicing machines." In a directive process analysis, by contrast, you are telling the reader directly how to do something as when Tina Fey tells readers how to do improv comedy. So you should typically use the second person ("you"): "When <u>you</u>'re improvising . . . <u>you</u> are required to agree with whatever your partner has created."

Concluding a Process Analysis

A process analysis is not complete until it explains how the process ends—and the significance of that result. For example, in concluding a process analysis about training a puppy, you might say not only what the result will be but why it is important or desirable: "A well-trained dog will behave when guests visit, won't destroy your carpeting and furniture, and will make less work for you in the long run." In the case of processing oranges into concentrate, John McPhee concludes his essay by telling readers not only that the process yielded a new, concentrated form of orange juice, but that it also totally changed the Florida citrus industry and saved much of the crop from going to waste—or winding up as orange-flavored milk.

EDITING FOR COMMON ERRORS
IN A PROCESS ANALYSIS

Like other kinds of writing, process analysis uses distinctive patterns of language and punctuation—and thus invites typical kinds of errors. The following tips will help you check for (and correct) these common errors when you analyze a process in your own writing.

Check to ensure you've used the right pronouns

When you're explaining how something works or is done, make sure you use mostly third-person pronouns ("he," "she," "it," "they"). When you're explaining how to do something, make sure you emphasize the second-person pronoun ("you").

Here, readers are being told how oranges are processed by others:

▶ When fresh oranges are turned into concentrate, ~~you first scrub them~~ <u>they are first scrubbed</u> with detergent.

Here, readers are being told how to make orange concentrate for themselves:

▶ To turn fresh oranges into concentrate, ~~they are first scrubbed~~ <u>you must first scrub them</u> with detergent.

Check your verbs to make sure you haven't shifted needlessly between the indicative and the imperative moods

▶ According to my mother's recipe, ~~add~~ the nuts <u>are added</u>, and then the cinnamon is sprinkled on top.

▶ According to my mother's recipe, add the nuts, and then <u>sprinkle</u> the cinnamon ~~is sprinkled~~ on top.

How to Wash Your Hands

When you analyze a process, you explain how to do something, usually by breaking the process down into a set of steps. In this general set of instructions for washing your hands, there are only six steps. A more detailed analysis—in a hospital setting, for example—might include a dozen or more, especially when combating particularly virulent pathogens, such as a coronavirus. How can the same, relatively simple process require six steps by one analysis and twice that many by another? The answer lies in step 3 in the shorter version illustrated here: "WASH YOUR HANDS FOR 20 SECONDS." Obviously, this "step" is far more complicated than the others. That's because it's not actually a step but a *stage* in the entire hand-washing process. A stage is a process within a process, and to analyze a more complicated stage in any process made up largely of simple steps (wet hands, apply soap), you break the more complicated stage (the actual washing) into further steps, such as: "Rub Your Palms," "Rub the Back of Your Palms," "Clean Between Fingers," "Clean the Back of Each Finger," "Clean Thumb," "Clean Fingertips and Nails." And while you're doing this, don't forget to sing ["Happy Birthday" twice to time yourself.]

PEGAH MORADI

SPLITTING HAIRS

PEGAH MORADI is from Haymarket, Virginia. She attended Thomas Jefferson High School and Cornell University, graduating in 2019 with a degree in politics and technology—and with the career goal of working for a telecommunications firm or the federal government. Moradi has curly hair, as indicated in "Splitting Hairs," which she wrote in her sophomore year for the *Cornell Daily Sun*. So does her mother. "Combating our curls was our shared language," she says in this humorous analysis of the various stages of hair combat from straightening and slashing to styling and accepting. The process, says Moradi, was also one of vocabulary building: "The new word I learned was *free*." As her mother's "permanent" hair straightener wears off, Moradi hopes to pass on this lesson.

Splitting Hairs

I started straightening my own hair when I was in the seventh grade. Before then, I would ask my mother to do it for me. We started when I was just six, sitting cross-legged on our out-of-place Tabriz rugs in our quaint little Boise home. My mother would plug in a thick, two-inch ironing wand. While we waited for it to warm, she would pull my hair out from its elastic prison and begin to torture away its tangles. She would brush. I would scream.

1

> Introduces straightening, the first phase of the hair-care process

I hated my hair. That's an uncomfortable thing for me to think, let alone write. I think it's accurate though; I hated it. Once I was old enough to take care of it myself, I tied it up in as tight of a ponytail as possible until my curls were flattened by sheer tension. When it got long enough, I would force the ponytail into a Professor McGonagall—style bun,[1] hiding as much of it as possible. I used to brush through it right after I showered, when it was sopping wet, watching as it would straighten out with every brush, then squirm its way back into coils, sort of like how a worm contorts its smooth body into kinks and knots.

2

> This SIMILE provides a clear picture of what her hair looked like

Straightening my hair became a skill. My mother and I moved on from the wand to a flat iron. We learned words like *anti-frizz* and *heat-protectant*. We were told about the pricier names like *Chi* and *Biolage*.[2] We traded secrets and shampoos. I'm told I have the same hair as my

3

---

1. In the *Harry Potter* series, Professor Minerva McGonagall is head-mistress of Hogwarts School; she wears her hair in a bun beneath her witch's hat.
2. Hair-care products sold, respectively, under the brand names Ultra and Matrix.

father, but at this point he hardly has any hair at all. I feel as though I have the same hair as my mother, if you think about hair in a more abstract sense, as in, we don't have the same curl type, but we have the same hair history. My mother told me how she resented her hair growing up, how her mother sat her down and brushed her hair just like my mother brushed mine. How she would cry, but how mothers in 1970s Iran were far less tolerant of whining kids.

An important part of the process, especially for a writer, is learning the language of hair care

Combating our curls was our shared language. My mother is graceful, while I have walked into a pole more than once in the past month. She is conventionally feminine, while I spent most of my childhood eating dirt and wearing cargo capris. Nevertheless, I would watch as my mother spent an hour with her arms up in the air, parting her hair and brushing down her tightly wound spirals.

Moradi figures out how to straighten her hair by watching her mother do it

Near the end of my sophomore year of high school, I walked into my mom's hair salon of choice like a man with a plan, clutching a photo of Carey Mulligan[3] that I printed off of the Internet and a book I had to read for world history class. I was going to get a keratin treatment and make my hair permanently straight, then cut it like Mulligan in the hit 2011 crime drama *Drive*. A few important notes: this plan seemed absolutely horrible to everyone who knew me, I have never seen the movie *Drive*, and my stylist found out I was friends with one of her clients and kept noting how handsome he was the entire time she was doing my hair. Despite these minor setbacks, I left the salon that night running my fingers through my new

4

5

3. As Irene in *Drive* (2011), the British actress Carey Mulligan wears her hair in a blond bob.

off-brand—Carey Mulligan hair and feeling a resounding sense of victory. After I had had straight hair for several months, my mother decided to get the treatment too.

Over a year ago I stopped straightening my hair, partly because I was bored of it, partly because I felt fake. I didn't want to hate my hair anymore. Why did I even hate it so much? I cut off the permanently straight parts and I read an entire book on curly hair. I took up a new skill. I figured out how curls should be cut. I googled videos on how to style spirals straight out of the shower. I read about what foods to eat for shinier hair. It's a different kind of language, I think. It's easier to speak.

The new word I learned was *free*. As in, *sulfate-free* and *paraben-free*. My mother asks if I want to go back to the keratin treatment anytime soon. I say no. Her permanent straightener is wearing off. You can start to see her curls again.

6

Entering a new phase of the process—self-acceptance

7

JON KATZ

HOW BOYS BECOME MEN

JON KATZ (b. 1947) is a mystery writer and media critic. A former executive producer for *CBS Morning News*, he has also written a number of books about animals, including *Katz on Dogs* (2005), *Soul of a Dog* (2009), and *Saving Simon* (2014), as well as columns for *Rolling Stone*, *Slate*, and *HotWired* (an early web magazine that is now Wired.com). In "How Boys Become Men," which was first published in 1993 in *Glamour*, a magazine for women, Katz analyzes the male maturation process. It can be "ruthless," he writes; and, unfortunately, it may be a long time "before male culture evolves to the point that boys can learn more from one another than how to hit curve balls."

•———————————————————————————•

T WO NINE-YEAR-OLD BOYS, neighbors and friends, were walking home   1
from school. The one in the bright blue windbreaker was laughing and
swinging a heavy-looking book bag toward the head of his friend, who kept

ducking and stepping back. "What's the matter?" asked the kid with the bag, whooshing it over his head. "You chicken?"[1]

His friend stopped, stood still and braced himself. The bag slammed 2 into the side of his face, the thump audible all the way across the street where I stood watching. The impact knocked him to the ground, where he lay mildly stunned for a second. Then he struggled up, rubbing the side of his head. "See?" he said proudly. "I'm no chicken."

No. A chicken would probably have had the sense to get out of the 3 way. This boy was already well on the road to becoming a *man*, having learned one of the central ethics of his gender: Experience pain rather than show fear.

Women tend to see men as a giant problem in need of solution. They tell 4 us that we're remote and uncommunicative, that we need to demonstrate less machismo and more commitment, more humanity. But if you don't understand something about boys, you can't understand why men are the way we are, why we find it so difficult to make friends or to acknowledge our fears and problems.

Telling the reader why you're analyzing a particular process is discussed on p. 284.

Boys live in a world with its own Code of Conduct, a set of ruthless, 5 unspoken, and unyielding rules:

Don't be a goody-goody.

Never rat.[2] If your parents ask about bruises, shrug.

Never admit fear. Ride the roller coaster, join the fistfight, do what you have to do. Asking for help is for sissies.

Empathy is for nerds. You can help your best buddy, under certain circumstances. Everyone else is on his own.

Never discuss anything of substance with anybody. Grunt, shrug, dump on teachers, laugh at wimps, talk about comic books. Anything else is risky.

1. Slang term in American English that means "coward" or "afraid."
2. Slang term in American English for informing the authorities (parent, teacher, police) about another person's activities.

Boys are rewarded for throwing hard. Most other activities—reading, befriending girls, or just thinking—are considered weird. And if there's one thing boys don't want to be, it's weird.

More than anything else, boys are supposed to learn how to handle 6 themselves. I remember the bitter fifth-grade conflict I touched off by elbowing aside a bigger boy named Barry and seizing the cafeteria's last carton of chocolate milk. Teased for getting aced out by a wimp, he had to reclaim his place in the pack. Our fistfight, at recess, ended with my knees buckling and my lip bleeding while my friends, sympathetic but out of range, watched resignedly.

When I got home, my mother took one look at my swollen face and 7 screamed. I wouldn't tell her anything, but when my father got home I cracked and confessed, pleading with them to do nothing. Instead, they called Barry's parents, who restricted his television for a week.

The following morning, Barry and six of his pals stepped out from 8 behind a stand of trees. "It's the rat," said Barry.

I bled a little more. *Rat* was scrawled in crayon across my desk. 9

They were waiting for me after school for a number of afternoons to fol- 10 low. I tried varying my routes and avoiding bushes and hedges. It usually didn't work.

I was as ashamed for telling as I was frightened. "You did ask for it," said 11 my best friend. Frontier Justice has nothing on Boy Justice.

In panic, I appealed to a cousin who was several years older. He followed 12 me home from school, and when Barry's gang surrounded me, he came barreling toward us. "Stay away from my cousin," he shouted, "or I'll kill you."

After they were gone, however, my cousin could barely stop laughing. 13 "You were afraid of *them*?" he howled. "They barely came up to my waist."

Men remember receiving little mercy as boys; maybe that's why it's 14 sometimes difficult for them to show any.

"I know lots of men who had happy childhoods, but none who have 15 happy memories of the way other boys treated them," says a friend. "It's a macho marathon from third grade up, when you start butting each other in the stomach."

"The thing is," adds another friend, "you learn early on to hide what you 16 feel. It's never safe to say, 'I'm scared.' My girlfriend asks me why I don't talk more about what I'm feeling. I've gotten better at it, but it will *never* come naturally."

You don't need to be a shrink to see how the lessons boys learn affect 17 their behavior as men. Men are being asked, more and more, to show sensitivity, but they dread the very word. They struggle to build their increasingly uncertain work lives but will deny they're in trouble. They want love, affection, and support but don't know how to ask for them. They hide their weaknesses and fears from all, even those they care for. They've learned to be wary of intervening when they see others in trouble. They often still balk at being stigmatized as weird.

Some men get shocked into sensitivity—when they lose their jobs, their 18 wives, or their lovers. Others learn it through a strong marriage, or through their own children.

It may be a long while, however, before male culture evolves to the 19 point that boys can learn more from one another than how to hit curve balls. Last month, walking my dog past the playground near my house, I saw three boys encircling a fourth, laughing and pushing him. He was skinny and rumpled, and he looked frightened. One boy knelt behind him while another pushed him from the front, a trick familiar to any former boy. He fell backward.

A process analysis is not complete (p. 285) until it tells how the process ends (or doesn't end).

When the others ran off, he brushed the dirt off his elbows and walked 20 toward the swings. His eyes were moist and he was struggling for control.

"Hi," I said through the chain-link fence. "How ya doing?" 21

"Fine," he said quickly, kicking his legs out and beginning his swing. 22

FOR DISCUSSION

1. In order to explain how boys become men, Jon Katz must first explain how boys become boys. By what specific "rules" does this process occur, according to him (5)?

2. Is Katz right, do you think, in his **PROCESS ANALYSIS** of how boys are brought up? Why or why not?

3. The end result of how they learn to behave as boys, says Katz, is that men find it difficult "to make friends or to acknowledge our fears and problems" (4). They lack "sensitivity" (18). Do you agree? In your experience, is Katz's analysis accurate or inaccurate? Explain.

4. According to Katz, women are puzzled by "male culture" (19). How, in his view, do women regard men? Do you agree or disagree with this analysis? Why?

5. What evidence, if any, can you find in Katz's essay to indicate that the author has learned as an adult male to behave in ways he was not taught as a boy? By what processes, according to Katz, do men sometimes learn such new kinds of behavior?

STRATEGIES AND STRUCTURES

1. Katz tells the story in paragraphs 1 and 2 of a boy who prefers to get knocked down rather than be called a "chicken." Why do you think he begins with this incident? What stage or aspect of the boy-training process is he illustrating?

2. The longest of the **ANECDOTES** that Katz tells to show how boys learn to behave is the one about himself. Where does it begin and end? By what process or processes is he being taught here?

3. What is the role of the older cousin in the **NARRATIVE** Katz tells about himself as a boy? How does the cousin's response in paragraph 13 illustrate the process Katz is analyzing?

4. Where else in his essay does Katz tell a brief story to illustrate what he is saying about how boys are trained? How do these stories support his main point? What would the essay be like without any of the stories?

5. "If you don't understand something about boys, you can't understand why men are the way we are . . ." (4). To whom is Katz speaking here? What **PURPOSES** might he have for explaining the male maturation process to this particular **AUDIENCE**?

6. Besides analyzing the processes by which boys learn to behave according to a rigid "Code of Conduct," Katz's essay also analyzes the lasting effects caused by this early training (5). What are some of these effects?

WORDS AND FIGURES OF SPEECH

1. How does your dictionary define "machismo" (4)? What language(s) does it derive from?

2. To feel sympathy for someone means to have feelings and emotions similar to theirs. What does "empathy" mean (5)?

3. How does Katz's use of the various meanings of the words "chicken" and "rat" help him to make his point about how boys become men (1–3, 5, 8–9)?

4. Verbal **IRONY** is the use of one word or phrase to imply another with a quite different meaning. What's ironic about the boy's reply to Katz's question in paragraph 22?

FOR WRITING

1. Write a brief code of conduct like the one in paragraph 5 that lays out the unspoken rules of the "culture," regardless of gender, in which you grew up.

2. Katz says "it may be a long while . . . before male culture evolves" into something better (19). Write an essay arguing that, in the years since Katz made this observation, "male culture," particularly as transmitted among boys, has or has not become more nurturing and compassionate.

3. Write an essay that analyzes the process of how boys become men, as *you* see it. Or, alternatively, write an analysis of the process(es) by which *girls* are typically socialized to become women in America or somewhere else you specify. Draw on your own personal experience, or what you know from others, or both. Feel free to use **ANECDOTES** and other elements of narrative as appropriate to illustrate your analysis.

ALLEGRA GOODMAN

SO, YOU WANT TO BE A WRITER? HERE'S HOW.

ALLEGRA GOODMAN (b. 1967) is a novelist and short-story writer who wrote and illustrated her first novel at the age of seven. After growing up in Honolulu, she studied at Harvard, then earned a PhD in English from Stanford University. Her most recent novels include *The Other Side of the Island* (2008), *The Cookbook Collector* (2010), and *The Chalk Artist* (2017). "If there's one thing I've learned over the years," says Goodman, who is fascinated by the writing process, "it's the value of revision. I write draft after draft, rereading, rethinking, rephrasing every step of the way." In the following essay, published in the *Boston Globe* in 2008, Goodman gives advice on the process of becoming a writer.

WHEN PEOPLE HEAR THAT I'M A NOVELIST, I get one comment more than any other. "I'm a physician (or a third-grade teacher, or a venture capitalist) but what I really want to do is write." A mother of three muses: "I've always loved writing since I was a little girl." A physicist declares, "I've got a great idea for a mystery-thriller-philosophical-love story—if I only had the time." I nod, resisting the temptation to reply: "And I have a great idea for a unified field theory—if I just had a moment to work it out on paper."

Book sales are down, but creative writing enrollments are booming. The 2 longing to write knows no bounds. A lactation consultant[1] told me, "I have a story inside of me. I mean, I know everybody has a story, but I really have a story."

Forthwith, some advice for those of you who have always wanted to 3 write, those with best-selling ideas, and those who really have a story.

To begin, don't write about yourself. I'm not saying you're uninterest- 4 ing. I realize that your life has been so crazy no one could make this stuff up. But if you want to be a writer, start by writing about other people. Observe their faces, and the way they wave their hands around. Listen to the way they talk. Replay conversations in your mind—not just the words, but the silences as well. Imagine the lives of others. If you want to be a writer, you need to get over yourself. This is not just an artistic choice; it's a moral choice. A writer attempts to understand others from the inside.

Find a peaceful place to work. Peace does not necessarily entail an art- 5 ists' colony or an island off the coast of Maine. You might find peace in your basement, or at a cafe in Davis Square,[2] or amid old ladies rustling magazines at the public library. Peace is not the same as quiet. Peace means you avoid checking your e-mail every ten seconds. Peace means you are willing to work offline, screen calls, and forget your to-do list for an hour. If this is difficult, turn off your Web browser, or try writing without a computer altogether. Treat yourself to pen and paper and make a mess, crossing out sentences, crumpling pages, inserting paragraphs in margins. Remember spiral-bound notebooks, and thank-you notes with stamps? Handwriting is arcane in all the best ways. Writing in ink doesn't feel like work; it feels like secret diaries and treasure maps and art.

Let readers know when they will need special equipment, as in the fifth template on p. 283.

---

1. Someone who advises mothers about nursing their infants.
2. Central intersection in Somerville, Massachusetts, a city north of Boston.

Read widely, and dissect books in your mind. What, exactly, makes 6
David Sedaris[3] funny? How does George Orwell[4] fill us with dread? If you want
to be a novelist, read novels new and old, satirical, experimental, Victorian,

For example, a biographer of the banker J. P. Morgan points out, p. 182, that he had a "hideous purple" nose.

American. Read nonfiction as well. Consider how biographers
select details to illuminate a life in time. If you want to write
nonfiction, study histories and essays, but also read novels and
think about narrative, and the novelist's artful release of information. Don't forget poetry. Why? Because it's good to go where
words are worshipped, and essential to remember that you are not a poet.
Lyric poets linger on a mood or fragmentary phrase; prose writers must move
along to tell their story, and catch their train.

And this is true for everyone, but especially for women: If you don't value 7
your own time, other people won't either. Trust me, you can't write a novel in
stolen minutes outside your daughter's tap class. Virginia Woolf[5] declared that
a woman needs a room of her own. Well, the room won't help, if you don't shut
the door. Post a note. "Book in progress, please do not disturb unless you're
bleeding." Or these lines from Samuel Taylor Coleridge,[6] which I have adapted
for writing mothers: ". . . Beware! Beware! / Her flashing eyes, her floating hair!
Weave a circle round her thrice, / And close your eyes with holy dread, / For she
on honey-dew hath fed, / and drunk the milk of Paradise."

FOR DISCUSSION

1. Why, according to Allegra Goodman, should aspiring writers write about other
   people instead of themselves? Do you think this is sensible advice? Why or why not?

2. What **PROCESS** is Goodman **ANALYZING** exactly—how to write or how to become
   a writer? Is her analysis explanatory or directive? Explain.

3. Best-selling American author (b. 1956), known for his witty autobiographical writing.
4. British novelist and essayist (1903–1950), whose novel *1984* is a foreboding story of a
repressive totalitarian government. "Politics and the English Language," Orwell's classic
essay on being a lucid writer, is reprinted in Chapter 14.
5. British novelist and essayist (1882–1941). In her book *A Room of One's Own* (1929), Woolf
noted that "a woman must have money and a room of her own if she is to write fiction."
6. British Romantic poet and critic (1772–1834). Goodman adapts lines from his poem
"Kubla Khan" (1816), which Coleridge claimed he was unable to complete after being interrupted by a knock at the door during its composition.

3. Why does Goodman recommend writing by hand in ink? Is she right? Why or why not?

4. Why does Goodman think all writers should study poetry? Is she right? Why or why not?

5. What special advice does Goodman have for women writers? Why, in her view, do they need such advice even more than men do?

STRATEGIES AND STRUCTURES

1. What is the end result of the process that Goodman is analyzing? Where and how does she first introduce it?

2. In the beginning of her essay, Goodman tells about all the people she has met who want to be writers. Is this an effective way to begin? Why or why not?

3. Goodman tells us early on who she has in mind as her main AUDIENCE for the advice she gives. Who is it? In what ways is her essay directed toward this audience? Explain.

4. Goodman divides the process that she is analyzing into four basic stages. What are they? Does she use chronology to organize them? If not, how are they organized?

5. Into what steps is the reading stage of the process further broken down? What about the other stages? Why does Goodman break them down in this way?

6. Why does Goodman end her analysis with the words of another writer? Is this an effective strategy? Why or why not?

7. In paragraph 6, Goodman COMPARES the writer of prose to the writer of poetry. Which kind of writer—or aspiring writer—is her advice aimed at? How does she DEFINE the kind of writer she has in mind?

WORDS AND FIGURES OF SPEECH

1. Why is writing about other people rather than oneself a "moral" choice, according to Goodman (4)? What's moral about it?

2. The writer, says Goodman, needs "a peaceful place to work" (5). How does she define "peaceful"?

3. Why does Goodman use the word "arcane" instead of "old-fashioned" or "outmoded" to DESCRIBE handwriting (5)?

4. What does Goodman mean by "artful" when she uses it to describe how the novelist releases information in a **NARRATIVE** (6)?

5. Explain the **ALLUSION** to Virginia Woolf in the last paragraph of Goodman's essay. What **PURPOSE** does it serve in her analysis?

FOR WRITING

1. In a paragraph or two, analyze the process you follow for managing your time when you write.

2. Write an essay analyzing the process you have gone through so far in learning how to be a writer. Be sure to say how much further you have to go in order to reach your goal and what advice you have for other writers.

HARRIS PASTIDES

THREE WORDS TO HELP AVOID TRAGEDY

HARRIS PASTIDES (b. 1954) was the president of the University of South Carolina from 2008 to 2019. He grew up in New York City, the son of immigrants from Cyprus. The first member of his family to go to college, he is a graduate of the State University of New York–Albany and of Yale University, where he earned a PhD in epidemiology. In "Three Words," first published in the *Washington Post* in 2019, Pastides describes a simple procedure of "ride-hailing safety" that might well help students (and others) avoid the fate of Samantha Josephson, a 21-year-old senior at the University of South Carolina, who was murdered by a stranger whom she may have taken to be the driver of her Uber ride.

"WHAT'S MY NAME?"   1
These three words have the power to save lives and must   2
become as automatic to every college student getting into a ride-hailing vehicle

as putting on a seatbelt. The policy would probably be worthwhile for *anyone* who uses ride-hailing companies such as Uber and Lyft, but I have a particu-

You may want to begin a process analysis by putting the most important step first, as explained on p. 283.

lar, and urgent, reason to try to persuade college students to make "What's my name?" a habit.

Samantha Josephson, a student at the University of South Car- 3
olina, where I am president, was buried last week, the victim of a senseless crime that tears at the heart of every parent and has shaken me and our university family. The death of any student is hard to comprehend, but that is especially true of Samantha, a 21-year-old senior who was majoring in political science, eager to commit herself to helping change the world.

According to police here in Columbia, S.C., Samantha ordered an Uber to 4
pick her up at 2 a.m. on March 29 in the Five Points district, a nightlife area near campus, and mistakenly got into a black Chevrolet Impala, thinking it was her ride. A heartbreaking surveillance video released by law enforcement officials shows the vehicle pulling up beside her as people walk past; Samantha opens the door, slips into the back seat and closes the door. The same scene, of trusting young people getting into ride-hailing vehicles, no doubt played out countless times near college campuses early that Friday morning all over America.

Later that day, hunters found Samantha's body, about 70 miles away in 5
rural South Carolina. Police said she had been stabbed to death. They soon made an arrest, charging the suspect with murder and kidnapping. What happened to Samantha was not the first time that someone has mistaken a vehicle for a ride-hailing pickup and then been attacked by a driver who seemed to be prowling for victims. The *New York Times* on April 4 reported on "a rash of kidnappings, sexual assaults and robberies carried out largely against young women by assailants posing as ride-share drivers." Publicly reported cases indicate that there have been "at least two dozen such attacks in the past few years," the paper said.

In South Carolina, lawmakers have introduced the Samantha L. Joseph- 6
son Ridesharing Safety Act, which would require ride-hailing drivers to display illuminated signs when their vehicles are in service, and to turn off the sign when off-duty. Any steps to improve safety are welcome, but illuminated signs for ride-hailing companies can be easily purchased online.

In recent days, I've heard from many students, public-safety officials 7
and parents, including Samantha's own family, about the importance of ride-

hailing safety. We have discussed many ways to improve the transportation options for students, including traveling in groups on nights out.

For ride-hailing safety, students should first ensure that the license 8 plate, make, model and color of the vehicle match the details provided by the app used to hail the ride. But I think one of the best safety measures of all would be for customers, every time they use a ride-hailing service, to stop before entering the vehicle and ask the driver plainly: What's my name? A legitimate driver will have that information; someone with criminal intent will not.

As a college president for more than a decade, I recognize that the exu- 9 berant and trusting nature of our students—characteristics that make them such wonderful people—also make them vulnerable targets for those who seek to do harm. On campuses across the country, administrators have put great effort into safety programs, includ- ing education about drugs and alcohol. Ride-hailing safety infor- mation is a new frontier, but I urge my fellow administrators to devise a program and put it into practice as soon as possible.

A neurologist ana- lyzes these same opposing charac- teristics in "Dude, Where's My Frontal Cortex?" on p. 358.

The country has witnessed the power and effectiveness of other public- 10 health and safety campaigns, such as those regarding smoking and the use of seatbelts. The campaigns work and have saved countless lives. A new safety campaign—and not just for college students—is needed as ride-hailing gains in popularity. We owe it to Samantha Josephson.

FOR DISCUSSION

1. Harris Pastides recommends a simple procedure to avoid getting into a predator's car instead of your Uber driver's. Will it work? Explain.

2. Pastides says that students are generally "exuberant and trusting" in nature (9). Is he right about this? Why or why not?

3. The downside of being exuberant and trusting, says Pastides, is that it can make people "vulnerable targets" (9). What's the upside, in his view?

4. Requiring drivers to display illuminated signs when they're on duty does not go far enough, according to Pastides, to guarantee the rider's safety. Why not?

STRATEGIES AND STRUCTURES

1. Along with an audience of "fellow administrators," whom else is Pastides addressing throughout much of his essay (9)? Explain.

2. In addition to speaking the "three words," what other steps should you take, according to Pastides, to avoid harm when you hail a ride?

3. Pastides is analyzing a process and giving advice as part of a larger **ARGUMENT**. What claim is he making, and what evidence does he give to support it?

4. How and where does Pastides indicate that Samantha Josephson's death is not an isolated case? Why does he need to do this?

5. Why does Pastides describe the "heartbreaking surveillance video" in which Samantha Josephson gets into a car and closes the door (4)?

WORDS AND FIGURES OF SPEECH

1. Pastides speaks of students as "exuberant and trusting" (9). What other terms might he have used? Why do think he settled on these?

2. "What's in a name?" Under what circumstances does Shakespeare pose this question in *Romeo and Juliet*, and for what purpose?

3. As an *epidemiologist*, why might Pastides be especially interested in "safety programs" even when they do not have to do with disease (9)?

4. Do words really have "power" (2)? When and how—or why not?

FOR WRITING

1. What steps, if any, did Pastides leave out of his analysis? Make a list of additional actions and precautions you would advise ride-sharers to take.

2. Write an essay analyzing the potential hazards of a trip you make regularly, whether by walking, biking, taking public transit, or driving. Explain the steps you follow to ensure your safety from beginning to end of the process.

3. The person whose untimely death Pastides writes about was a political science major "eager to commit herself to helping change the world" (3). Write an essay explaining the methodology of political science as a field of study and how it might be applied to help change the world for the better.

PHILIP WEISS

HOW TO GET OUT OF
A LOCKED TRUNK

PHILIP WEISS (b. 1955) is an investigative journalist who has written for the *Jewish World Review, Esquire,* and the *New York Observer,* where he began the blog *Mondoweiss,* a now independent website that covers developments in Israel, Palestine, and relevant American foreign policy. Weiss is the author of the political novel *Cock-A-Doodle-Doo* (1995) and the investigative work *American Taboo: A Murder in the Peace Corps* (2004). About to be married when he wrote "How to Get Out of a Locked Trunk" for *Harper's* (1992), Weiss obsessively analyzes his way out of the trunks of locked cars, a strange fixation that suggests his bachelor self may be carrying some extra baggage. The essay also analyzes how Weiss got out of his condition.

ON A HOT SUNDAY LAST SUMMER my friend Tony and I drove my rental   1
car, a '91 Buick, from St. Paul to the small town of Waconia, Minnesota,
forty miles southwest. We each had a project. Waconia is Tony's boyhood
home, and his sister had recently given him a panoramic postcard of Lake
Waconia as seen from a high point in the town early in the century. He wanted
to duplicate the photograph's vantage point, then hang the two pictures
together in his house in Frogtown. I was hoping to see Tony's father, Emmett,
a retired mechanic, in order to settle a question that had been nagging me: Is
it possible to get out of a locked car trunk?

We tried to call ahead to Emmett twice, but he wasn't home. Tony 2
thought he was probably golfing but that there was a good chance he'd be back
by the time we got there. So we set out.

I parked the Buick, which was a silver sedan with a red interior, by the 3

Setting out on a
process analysis,
p. 279, is similar to
setting out on a
journey or
investigation.

graveyard near where Tony thought the picture had been taken.
He took his picture and I wandered among the headstones, reading the epitaphs. One of them was chillingly anti-individualist. It
said, "Not to do my will, but thine."

Trunk lockings had been on my mind for a few weeks. It 4
seemed to me that the fear of being locked in a car trunk had a particular hold
on the American imagination. Trunk lockings occur in many movies and
books—from *Goodfellas* to *Thelma and Louise* to *Humboldt's Gift*.[1] And while the
highbrow national newspapers generally shy away from trunk lockings, the
attention they receive in local papers suggests a widespread anxiety surrounding the subject. In an afternoon at the New York Public Library I found
numerous stories about trunk lockings. A Los Angeles man is discovered,
bloodshot, banging the trunk of his white Eldorado following a night and a
day trapped inside; he says his captors went on joyrides and picked up women.
A forty-eight-year-old Houston doctor is forced into her trunk at a bank ATM
and then the car is abandoned, parked near the Astrodome.[2] A New Orleans
woman tells police she gave birth in a trunk while being abducted to Texas.
Tests undermine her story, the police drop the investigation. But so what if
it's a fantasy? That only shows the idea's hold on us.

Every culture comes up with tests of a person's ability to get out of a 5
sticky situation. The English plant mazes. Tropical resorts market those
straw finger-grabbers that tighten their grip the harder you pull on them, and
Viennese intellectuals[3] gave us the concept of childhood sexuality—figure it
out, or remain neurotic for life.

At least you could puzzle your way out of those predicaments. When 6
they slam the trunk, though, you're helpless unless someone finds you. You

1. *Humboldt's Gift* (1975), a novel by Saul Bellow about a spiritually empty writer whose life
is reawakened by a mob member; *Goodfellas* (1990), a gangster movie; *Thelma and Louise*
(1991), a road movie about two women trying to escape oppressive marriages.
2. A large sports arena in Houston, Texas.
3. These would include the founder of psychoanalysis, Sigmund Freud (1856–1939).

would think that such a common worry should have a ready fix, and that the secret of getting out of a locked trunk is something we should all know about.

I phoned experts but they were very discouraging.   7

"You cannot get out. If you got a pair of pliers and bat's eyes, yes. But   8
you have to have a lot of knowledge of the lock," said James Foote at Automotive Locksmiths in New York City.

Jim Frens, whom I reached at the technical section of *Car and Driver*[4] in   9
Detroit, told me the magazine had not dealt with this question. But he echoed the opinion of experts elsewhere when he said that the best hope for escape would be to try and kick out the panel between the trunk and the backseat. That angle didn't seem worth pursuing. What if your enemies were in the car, crumpling beer cans and laughing at your fate? It didn't make sense to join them.

The people who deal with rules on auto design were uncomfortable with   10
my scenarios. Debra Barclay of the Center for Auto Safety, an organization founded by Ralph Nader,[5] had certainly heard of cases, but she was not aware of any regulations on the matter. "Now, if there was a defect involved—" she said, her voice trailing off, implying that trunk locking was all phobia. This must be one of the few issues on which she and the auto industry agree. Ann Carlson of the Motor Vehicle Manufacturers Association became alarmed at the thought that I was going to play up a non-problem: "In reality this very rarely happens. As you say, in the movies it's a wonderful plot device," she said. "But in reality apparently this is not that frequent an occurrence. So they have not designed that feature into vehicles in a specific way."

When we got to Emmett's one-story house it was full of people. Tony's sister,   11
Carol, was on the floor with her two small children. Her husband, Charlie, had one eye on the golf tournament on TV, and Emmett was at the kitchen counter, trimming fat from meat for lunch. I have known Emmett for fifteen years. He looked better than ever. In his retirement he had sharply changed his diet and lost a lot of weight. He had on shorts. His legs were tanned and muscular. As always, his manner was humorous, if opaque.

---

4. A monthly magazine for car enthusiasts.
5. American attorney and political activist (b. 1934) who was an early advocate of automobile safety.

Tony told his family my news: I was getting married in three weeks. 12
Charlie wanted to know where my fiancée was. Back East, getting everything
ready. A big-time hatter was fitting her for a new hat.

Emmett sat on the couch, watching me. "Do you want my advice?" 13

"Sure." 14

He just grinned. A gold tooth glinted. Carol and Charlie pressed him to 15
yield his wisdom.

Finally he said, "Once you get to be thirty, you make your own mistakes." 16

He got out several cans of beer, and then I brought up what was on my 17
mind.

Emmett nodded and took off his glasses, then cleaned them and put 18
them back on.

We went out to his car, a Mercury Grand Marquis, and Emmett opened 19
the trunk. His golf clubs were sitting on top of the spare tire in a green golf
bag. Next to them was a toolbox and what he called his "burglar tools," a set
of elbowed rods with red plastic handles he used to open door locks when
people locked their keys inside.

Tony and Charlie stood watching. Charlie is a banker in Minneapolis. 20
He enjoys gizmos and is extremely practical. I would describe him as unflap-
pable. That's a word I always wanted to apply to myself, but my fiancée had
recently informed me that I am high-strung. Though that surprised me, I
didn't quarrel with her.

For a while we studied the latch assembly. The lock closed in much the 21
same way that a lobster might clamp on to a pencil. The claw portion, the jaws
of the lock, was mounted inside the trunk lid. When you shut the lid, the jaws
locked on to the bend of a U-shaped piece of metal mounted on the body of
the car. Emmett said my best bet would be to unscrew the bolts. That way the
U-shaped piece would come loose and the lock's jaws would swing up with it
still in their grasp.

"But you'd need a wrench," he said. 22

It was already getting too technical. Emmett had an air of endless 23
patience, but I felt defeated. I could only imagine bloodied fingers, cracked
teeth. I had hoped for a simple trick.

Charlie stepped forward. He reached out and squeezed the lock's jaws. 24
They clicked shut in the air, bound together by heavy springs. Charlie now

prodded the upper part of the left-hand jaw, the thicker part. With a rough flick of his thumb, he was able to force the jaws to snap open. Great.

Unfortunately, the jaws were mounted behind a steel plate the size of 25 your palm in such a way that while they were accessible to us, standing outside the car, had we been inside the trunk the plate would be in our way, blocking the jaws.

This time Emmett saw the way out. He fingered a hole in the plate. It 26 was no bigger than the tip of your little finger. But the hole was close enough to the latch itself that it might be possible to angle something through the hole from inside the trunk and nudge the jaws apart. We tried with one of my keys. The lock jumped open.

It was time for a full-dress test. Emmett swung the clubs out of the 27 trunk, and I set my can of Schmidt's on the rear bumper and climbed in. Everyone gathered around, and Emmett lowered the trunk on me, then pressed it shut with his meaty hands. Total darkness. I couldn't hear the people outside. I thought I was going to panic. But the big trunk felt comfortable. I was pressed against a sort of black carpet that softened the angles against my back.

I could almost stretch out in the trunk, and it seemed to me I could 28 make them sweat if I took my time. Even Emmett, that sphinx, would give way to curiosity. Once I was out he'd ask how it had been and I'd just grin. There were some things you could only learn by doing.

It took a while to find the hole. I slipped the key in and angled it to one 29 side. The trunk gasped open.

Emmett motioned the others away, then levered me out with his big 30 right forearm. Though I'd only been inside for a minute, I was disoriented—as much as anything because someone had moved my beer while I was gone, setting it down on the cement floor of the garage. It was just a little thing, but I could not be entirely sure I had gotten my own beer back.

Charlie was now raring to try other cars. We examined the latch on his 31 Toyota, which was entirely shielded to the trunk occupant (i.e., no hole in the plate), and on the neighbor's Honda (ditto). But a 1991 Dodge Dynasty was doable. The trunk was tight, but its lock had a feature one of the mechanics I'd phoned described as a "tailpiece": a finger-like extension of the lock mechanism itself that stuck out a half inch into the trunk cavity; simply by twisting the tailpiece I could free the lock. I was even faster on a 1984 Subaru that had a little lever device on the latch.

We went out to my rental on Oak Street. The Skylark was in direct sun   32
and the trunk was hot to the touch, but when we got it open we could see that its latch plate had a perfect hole, a square in which the edge of the lock's jaw appeared like a face in a window.

The trunk was shallow and hot. Emmett had to push my knees down   33
before he could close the lid. This one was a little suffocating. I imagined being trapped for hours, and even before he had got it closed I regretted the decision with a slightly nauseous feeling. I thought of Edgar Allan Poe's live burials,[6] and then about something my fiancée had said more than a year and a half before. I had been on her case to get married. She was divorced, and at every opportunity I would reissue my proposal—even during a commercial. She'd interrupted one of these chirps to tell me, in a cold, throaty voice, that she had no intention of ever going through another divorce: "This time, it's death out." I'd carried those words around like a lump of wet clay.

As it happened, the Skylark trunk was the easiest of all. The hole was   34
right where it was supposed to be. The trunk popped open, and I felt great satisfaction that we'd been able to figure out a rule that seemed to apply about 60 percent of the time. If we publicized our success, it might get the attention it deserved. All trunks would be fitted with such a hole. Kids would learn about it in school. The grip of the fear would relax. Before long a successful trunk-locking scene would date a movie like a fedora[7] dates one today.

"As it happened" is one example of Weiss's use of transitions, p. 284.

When I got back East I was caught up in wedding preparations. I live in New   35
York, and the wedding was to take place in Philadelphia. We set up camp there with five days to go. A friend had lent my fiancée her BMW, and we drove it south with all our things. I unloaded the car in my parents' driveway. The last thing I pulled out of the trunk was my fiancée's hat in its heavy cardboard

6. American author (1809–1849) known for his eerie short stories and poems; his story "The Premature Burial" recounts the terror of a man buried alive.
7. Brimmed men's hat popular from the 1920s through the 1950s, often worn by gangsters and detectives in movies from that era.

shipping box. She'd warned me I was not allowed to look. The lid was free but I didn't open it. I was willing to be surprised.

When the trunk was empty it occurred to me I might hop in and give it 36
a try. First I looked over the mechanism. The jaws of the BMW's lock were shielded, but there seemed to be some kind of cable coming off it that you might be able to manipulate so as to cause the lock to open. The same cable that allowed the driver to open the trunk remotely . . .

I fingered it for a moment or two but decided I didn't need to test out the 37
theory.

FOR DISCUSSION

1. So, according to Philip Weiss, how *do* you get out of a locked trunk? How, according to his fiancée, do you get out of a marriage? What is the implication of Weiss's addressing these two problems in the same essay?

2. Of the cars he tests, which one alarms Weiss most yet turns out to be the easiest to get out of? Why is he so alarmed, do you think? Why is he so anxious to find a "simple trick" that will fit all instances (23)?

3. Why does Weiss say, "There were some things you could only learn by doing" (28)? What might some of them be?

4. Why do you think Weiss refrains from taking a peek at his fiancée's new hat, since the lid is "free" and the box would be so easy to open (35)? Incidentally, how does Weiss know that the lid is free?

STRATEGIES AND STRUCTURES

1. What is Weiss's PURPOSE in ANALYZING THE PROCESS of getting out of a locked trunk? What AUDIENCE does Weiss think will be interested in his analysis? Why?

2. Weiss's essay is divided into three parts—paragraphs 1–10, 11–34, and 35–37. In which section does Weiss most fully analyze the process of getting out of a locked car trunk? Is his analysis explanatory or directive? Explain.

3. Why do you think the last section of Weiss's essay is the shortest? How and how effectively does it bring the essay to a satisfying conclusion?

4. What is Weiss's purpose in citing several "experts" in paragraphs 7–10? What is Emmett's role in the big experiment?

5. "It's a wonderful plot device," Weiss quotes one expert as saying about being locked in a car trunk (10). Is she right? Where in his essay is Weiss telling a story, and where is he analyzing a process? Give specific **EXAMPLES** from the text.

6. Like **NARRATIVES**, which often report events chronologically, process analyses are often organized in the chronological order of the steps or stages of the process that is being analyzed. Where does Weiss use chronology either to tell a story or to analyze a process? Give specific examples from the text.

WORDS AND FIGURES OF SPEECH

1. The lock on the trunk of Emmett's Mercury Grand Marquis, says Weiss, "closed in much the same way that a lobster might clamp on to a pencil" (21). How effective do you find this **SIMILE** for explaining how this particular trunk locks? Where else does Weiss use **FIGURES OF SPEECH** as a tool of process analysis?

2. A phobia is an irrational fear (10). Point out specific **EXAMPLES** in his essay where Weiss (or his persona) might be said to exhibit phobic behavior. What's he afraid of?

3. To whom is Weiss referring when he mentions "Viennese intellectuals" (5)? Why is he **ALLUDING** to them? Why does he allude to Poe in paragraph 33?

4. "Not to do my will, but thine" (3). What are the implications of this inscription, which Weiss reads on a tombstone at the beginning of his essay?

5. "Case," "reissue," "chirp," and "death out" (33): why does Weiss use these words in the **ANECDOTE** about his proposals? What about "willing" (35)?

FOR WRITING

1. Has anyone you know ever exhibited phobic behavior? Explain how the phobia manifested itself and what specific steps the victim took to deal with it.

2. "Every culture," writes Weiss, "comes up with tests of a person's ability to get out of a sticky situation" (5). Have you ever been in such a situation? How did you get out of it? Write an essay analyzing the process.

DINA SRINIVASAN

DINA SRINIVASAN
HOW DIGITAL ADVERTISING WORKS

DINA SRINIVASAN (b. 1980) is a consultant on the economics of digital advertising markets. She has written about media and antitrust issues for many publications and is a Fellow at the Thurman Arnold Project at Yale University, from which she holds a law degree. A former advertising executive, Srinivasan is the author of "The Antitrust Case against Facebook," which appeared in the *Berkeley Business Law Journal* (2018) and has been cited by several members of Congress who argue Facebook should be broken up. (The company for which Srinivasan formerly worked was the British ad agency WPP, one of the largest advertising and public relations companies in the world.) Part of a longer 2019 study published in the *American Prospect* magazine, "How Digital Advertising Works" analyzes the process by which the "Big Tech duopoly" (Facebook and Google) turns users' private data into billions of advertising dollars through a behind-the-scenes auction market based, in Srinivasan's view, "on who can better track users and invade their privacy more thoroughly."

A DVERTISING CAMPAIGNS USED TO BE PLANNED AND MANAGED by media   1
buyers—usually 22-year-old, newly graduated communications majors.
If that media buyer needed to help a car manufacturer reach men looking to buy
a car, she might place an ad in *Car and Driver,* or in the automotive
section of the newspaper. Advertising used to be something you
could place, count, then see in the front cover spread of a magazine.

Philip Weiss speaks
directly to the
experts at *Car and
Driver* magazine on
p. 309.

But this is not digital advertising today. Digital advertising   2
is automated, data-driven, and opaque in its mechanics. That 22-year-old
communications major has had to make way for data scientists, mathemati-
cians, and computer programmers who, behind the scenes, use statistics, calculus, and linear algebra to optimize advertising campaigns by microtargeting
users and constantly tweaking algorithms.[1]

Does that car manufacturer still want to reach men looking to buy a car?   3
A data scientist may tell them the optimal target is a 39-year-old man, carrying on an extramarital affair, who's on the brink of divorce. They can model
this hypothesis (and prove it works), and advertising companies like Google
and Facebook can put that into execution, finding ways to home in and target
those types of people online.

When you go to a website and load a page, in the milliseconds that it takes   4
for that page to load, there are real-time auctions running in the background that
determine which ads to load on *your* page. Almost all online ads are delivered in
this way, where highly complex auction markets make their money by competing on who can better track users and invade their privacy more thoroughly.

The targeting begins the moment you as a reader visit any website. Typ-   5
ically, your IP address, your location, and the URL of the page you are on are
swiped from your browser without your explicit knowledge and shared with
advertising companies that run these ad auctions. The goal, of course, is to
build as specific a portrait about you as possible—by linking your device with
your identity—and cookies are a common tool for doing so.

A "cookie" is a small text file that a site can install on your computer   6
when you visit. The text file fingerprints your device with a unique identifier,
or "cookie ID" (such as 12345qwert). If the website knows your real identity
(for example, if you log on to the site with your real name), the company can

---

1. As a set of steps to be followed (usually by a computer) when making calculations or solving problems, an *algorithm* can be seen as a specific form of process analysis.

link it to your cookie (here, 12345qwert) and begin to gain an advantage in determining which ads to load onto your page.

For example, if you're on the hypothetical URL newspaper.com/how-to -fight-melanoma, this probably means you're reading an article about melanoma. Companies might use that information to make a prediction about whether you or someone you love may have cancer. And they most certainly use that information to determine which ads to load onto your page. 7

The prices that any company is able to fetch for its ads depend on two crucial factors: the ability to identify *who* is loading the page, and the ability to then connect the user's identity with more information about the user. 8

Imagine a person visits espn.com to read an article about the upcoming Super Bowl. Assume first he doesn't log on to the site, and blocks his browser cookies, so maybe the website he is visiting can't know who he really is. An advertiser can nonetheless bid on the opportunity to display an ad to this anonymous reader. Maybe the slot goes to a beer brand that wants to generally reach people who like football. Perhaps the going price is a $2 CPM (cost per thousand) and the ad gets sold at this price (meaning, this is the clearing auction price). 9

Using the imperative mood when you give directions is discussed on p. 286.

But you're not usually anonymous when you're online, even when you think you are. Again, advertising companies might know your identity because you log in or because you are using a browser that allows tracking. Now it's not simply an anonymous person loading a page about the Super Bowl, it's "Michael Greenberg," of Wichita, Kansas. 10

Now, companies can combine Michael's identity with other commercially available datasets in real time. For example, they might stitch Michael's identity with the fact that he makes $1 million-plus per year, which means that they can match Michael with an ad for a private jet service instead of a Bud Light. The private jet ad might sell at a $200 CPM as opposed to the $2 CPM beer ad targeted to an anonymous user. 11

"The exact same ad, on the same website, at the same time, could be worth vastly different amounts to two different buyers depending on how much they know about the consumer being targeted," explains Ari Paparo, now founder and CEO of advertising company Beeswax and a former Google exec. "User data is everything." 12

Advertisers gain an even better advantage when they're able to track what users do as they move from site to site, app to app, site to app, and vice 13 versa, which is exactly how Facebook and Google operate (and exactly the type of information traditional publishers don't have).

If a company that sells online ads can know what their readers are read-   14 ing on *other* sites, then they can target the users based on that information when the user returns to their own site. For example, say Michael visits CNBC's website in the mornings and reads about the markets, but visits the *New York Times* in the evenings and only reads the book review section. CNBC[2] knows Michael is someone who follows the markets, and might monetize his view at a $30 CPM. The *Times* knows that Michael is someone who likes to read books so might only monetize Michael at a $10 CPM. If the *Times* can somehow find out that Michael is reading CNBC in the mornings, then when Michael visits the *Times* book section in the evening, the *Times* can target him as someone who follows the markets and monetize him at $30, too.

Would CNBC want to share with the *Times* what Michael reads on cnbc   15 .com? Of course not. The two are competitors on the advertising side of the

Milliseconds before this advertisement appeared above the front-page news on the website of the New York Times, *computer algorithms at LVMH (the Paris-based purveyor of luxury goods, such as expensive watches) vied with those at other high-end companies for this coveted digital space.*

2. A provider of financial and business news and information, CNBC was founded in 1989 as the Consumer News and Business Channel. It is owned by Comcast.

market. If CNBC is selling its audience of financial readers at a cost of $30, and the *Times* can copy CNBC's readers and their reading patterns, then the *Times* could theoretically undercut CNBC and sell ads targeted to CNBC financial readers for, say, $20 instead of $30.

But publishers like the *Times* and CNBC have no choice but to share this   16
information with Facebook and Google. How, might you ask, does Facebook currently get this data from news publishers that are also advertising competitors? Well, Facebook has a number of derivative products that flow from the social network, including "Like" buttons and log-in tools. Facebook licenses Like buttons to publishers so that their readers can "like" and then "share" news stories across the Facebook social network. But Facebook now conditions these licenses on the ability to track publishers' readers, whether the readers click the Like buttons or not, and Facebook can now use publishers' reader data to sell its own ads.

Google, which now tracks users on over 70 percent of the top one mil-   17
lion sites, also uses its ability to track users across the internet to extract an advantage in advertising markets. Google tracks users via its analytics and ad-serving products, which Google consolidated and rebranded last summer as the Google Marketing Platform. Google was actually the first of the two companies to consolidate products under a rubric of privacy.

The implication of all this is that the money that Google and Facebook   18
can make selling advertising goes well beyond what other ad sellers can demand in the market. The Big Tech duopoly can track billions of users across millions of sites and mobile apps, creating longitudinal profiles[3] on users. News publishers simply cannot compete with that kind of an informational advantage.

> To fully explain the end result of a process, you may need to explain the *significance* of that result, p. 285.

But there is another thing going on in these markets that   19
explains the duopoly in the advertising market. When most people think about Google and Facebook, they think the companies make so much money by selling ads on their own properties—*Google* search, *Gmail*, the *Facebook* social network, *Instagram*, and so on. This is partly true. Google and Facebook also run auctions through which publishers now sell their own advertising.

---

3. A *longitudinal profile* in marketing consists of information gathered about a potential customer over an extended period of time.

Unlike in finance, there are several auction markets where digital ads   20
trade. Anyone can create one. But Google and Facebook make sure their own
advertising inventory (*YouTube, Facebook*) can only be bought through their
own, proprietary auctions. Google made almost $20 billion last year from selling
other companies' ads. This is why Google today is the largest seller of advertising, globally, period.

FOR DISCUSSION

1. Not so long ago, says Dina Srinivasan, the process of advertising a product in
   print and related media was relatively simple. How did it work?

2. According to Srinivasan, how has the job market in the field of advertising
   changed drastically as a result of digital advertising? Who has been particularly
   hard hit by the changes?

3. Agencies that sell online advertising, says Srinivasan, can charge far more to
   some companies than to others for "the exact same [type of] ad, on the same
   website, at the same time" (12). When and how does this happen?

4. The profit that Google and Facebook make from the sale of advertising, says
   Srinivasan, "goes well beyond what other ad sellers can demand in the market"
   (18). Why is this the case, in her analysis?

5. If Srinivasan is right that other advertising agencies can't compete with Facebook
   and Google, should this "duopoly" be more highly regulated by government (18)?
   Why or why not?

STRATEGIES AND STRUCTURES

1. Digital advertising works, says Srinivasan, "by using statistics, calculus, and linear algebra"; by "microtargeting"; and by "tweaking algorithms" (2). Should
   Srinivasan have been more specific about the "mechanics" of digital advertising
   here (2)? What type of **AUDIENCE** does she appear to have in mind? Explain.

2. "The targeting begins," says Srinivasan, "the moment you as a reader visit any
   website" (5). According to Srinivasan's analysis, what are the next steps in the
   targeting process?

3. When a reader visits a website and gets targeted by competing sellers of advertising, what other, related process is going on in the background? Where and how
   does Srinivasan analyze *this* process most clearly?

4. The immediate goal of the targeting process that takes place when a consumer
   visits a website, according to Srinivasan, is "to build as specific a portrait . . . as

possible" of that person (5). How and how well does her **EXAMPLE** of "Michael Greenberg" serve to explain how this goal is achieved?

5. As an attorney, Srinivasan uses her analysis of how digital advertising works as the basis for a legal **ARGUMENT**. What claim is she making, and what additional evidence does she cite? How and how well does all her evidence, taken together, support her claim?

6. Why might Srinivasan conclude her analysis with the statement that Google is the world's largest purveyor of advertising "period" (20)? Explain.

WORDS AND FIGURES OF SPEECH

1. The mechanics of digital advertising, says Srinivasan, are "opaque" (2). Is this an **UNDERSTATEMENT**? Why or why not?

2. An *algorithm* is a process or set of rules to be followed, especially by a computer, when making calculations or solving problems (2). What specific, historical person are algorithms named after?

3. Srinivasan defines a "cookie" as a small text file that gets installed on your computer when you visit a website (6). Witches and evil stepmothers often hand out cookies and other goodies in fairy tales. Why? Is there any linguistic carryover here?

4. Srinivasan makes up an example of a "cookie ID" (12345qwert) by combining five numbers and five letters (6). The numbers are in sequence beginning with 1. What sequence do the letters follow? (Hint: look at your computer keyboard.)

5. Is it a **CLICHÉ** to end a sentence by saying "period" (20)? Why or why not?

FOR WRITING

1. For two or three days, make notes on the advertisements that crop up on your social media feed or as you visit different websites. Pay special attention to the kinds of products they're selling and the frequency with which those products are offered.

2. Based on your notes about the advertisements you encounter online, write an essay confirming (or contesting) what Srinivasan says about how companies profile and target particular customers with specific products. Give lots of examples.

3. Write a summary of Srinivasan's "The Antitrust Case against Facebook." (Her article, published in 2018 in the *Berkeley Business Law Journal*, is readily available online.)

4. Are internet giants like Facebook and Google invading our privacy as "thoroughly" as Srinivasan suggests (4)? Do some research on the subject, and write an essay analyzing what happens to our personal data when we use the internet. Be sure to include what you think can be done about it (or not in this situation).

⇥10⇤

COMPARISON AND CONTRAST

I F you're thinking of buying a new or used car, you'll probably want to do some **COMPARISON*** shopping. You might compare the Honda Accord to the Toyota Camry, for example. Both are midsize sedans with similar features in about the same price range. If you're in the market for a sporty convertible, however, you would be wasting your time getting a quote on a van or pickup. That would be comparing apples to oranges, and true comparisons can be made only among like kinds. Your final decision, however, will be based more on differences (in acceleration, fuel economy, trunk space) than on the similarities. Your comparison, that is, will also entail **CONTRAST**. Strictly speaking, a *comparison* looks at both the similarities and the differences between two subjects, whereas a *contrast* looks mainly at the differences.

Drawing comparisons in writing is a lot like comparison shopping. It points out similarities in different subjects and differences in similar ones. Consider the following comparison between two items we might normally think of as identical:

> The common yo-yo is crudely made, with a thick shank between two widely spaced wooden disks. The string is knotted or stapled to the shank. With such an instrument nothing can be done except the simple up-down movement. My yo-yo, on the other hand, was a perfectly balanced construction of hard wood, slightly weighted, flat, with only a sixteenth of an inch between the halves. The string was not attached to the shank, but looped over it in such a way as to allow the wooden part

*Words printed in **SMALL CAPITALS** are defined in the Glossary/Index.

to spin freely on its own axis. The gyroscopic effect thus created kept the yo-yo stable in all attitudes.

—FRANK CONROY, *Stop-Time*

Why is Frank Conroy comparing yo-yos here? He is not going to buy one, nor is he telling the reader what kind to buy. Conroy is making a larger point: all yo-yos are not created equal. They may look alike and they may all go up and down on a string, but he points out meaningful differences between them. There are good yo-yos, Conroy is saying, and bad yo-yos.

Once Conroy has brought together like kinds (apples to apples, yo-yos to yo-yos) and established in his own mind a basis for comparing them (the "common" kind versus "my" kind), he can proceed in one of two ways. He can dispense his information in "chunks" or in "slices" (as when selling bologna). These basic methods of organizing a comparison or contrast are sometimes called the subject-by-subject and the point-by-point methods. The subject-by-subject method treats several aspects of one subject, then discusses the same aspects of the other. So the author provides chunks of information all about one subject before moving on to the other subject. Point-by-point organization shifts back and forth between each subject, treating each point of similarity and difference before going on to the next one.

Dan Treadway uses the subject-by-subject method in "Football vs. Asian Studies," p. 333.

In his comparison, Conroy uses the subject-by-subject method. He first gives several traits of the inferior, "common" yo-yo ("crudely made," string fixed to the shank, only goes up and down); then he gives contrasting traits of his superior yo-yo ("perfectly balanced," string loops over the shank, "spins freely on its own axis"). Now let's look at an example of a comparison that uses the point-by-point method to compare two great basketball players, Wilt ("the Stilt") Chamberlain and Bill Russell:

Russell has been above all a team player—a man of discipline, self-denial and killer instinct; in short, a *winner*, in the best American Calvinist tradition. Whereas Russell has been able somehow to squeeze out his last ounce of ability, Chamberlain's performances have been marked by a seeming nonchalance—as if, recognizing his Gigantistic fate, he were more concerned with personal style than with winning. "I never want to set records. The only thing I strive for is perfection," Chamberlain has said.

—JAMEY LARNER, "David vs. Goliath"

Paragraph by paragraph, Jamey Larner goes on like this, alternating "slices" of information about each player: Chamberlain's free throws were always uncertain; Russell's were always accurate in the clutch. Chamberlain was efficient; Russell was more so. Chamberlain was fast; Russell was faster. Chamberlain was Goliath at seven feet three inches tall; Russell was David at six feet nine. The fans expected Chamberlain to lose; they expected Russell to win.

Point by point, Larner goes back and forth between his two subjects, making one meaningful (to basketball fans) distinction after another. But why, finally, is he bringing these two players together? What's his reason for comparing them at all? Larner has a point to make, just as Conroy does when he compares two yo-yos and just as you should when you draw comparisons in your writing. The author compares these two in order to ARGUE that although the giant Chamberlain was "typecast" by the fans to lose to Russell the giant-killer, it was Wilt "the Stilt," defying all expectations, who arguably became the greatest basketball player ever. (This decision was made without consulting Kobe Bryant or LeBron James.)

Whether you use chunks or slices, you can take a number of other hints from Conroy and Larner. First, choose subjects that belong to the same general class or category: two toys, two athletes, two religions, two mammals. You might point out many differences between a mattress and motorcycle, but any distinctions you make between them are not likely to be meaningful because there is little logical basis for comparing them.

Gary Soto compares his family's perceptions of ethnic groups, p. 343, when he tries to figure out whom to marry.

Even more important, you need to have a good reason for bringing your subjects together in the first place—and a main point to make about them. Then, whether you proceed subject by subject or point by point, stick to two and only two subjects at a time.

And, finally, don't feel that you must always give equal weight to similarities and differences. You might want to pay more attention to the similarities if you wish to convince your parents that a two-seater convertible actually has a lot in common with the big, safe SUV they want you to consider—they both have wheels, brakes, and an engine, for example. But you might want to emphasize the differences between your two subjects if the similarities are readily apparent, as between two yo-yos and two basketball stars.

A BRIEF GUIDE TO WRITING
A COMPARISON-AND-CONTRAST ESSAY

As you begin to write a comparison, you need to identify your subjects, state the basis on which you're comparing them, and indicate whether you plan to emphasize their similarities or their differences. Jennine Capó Crucet makes these basic moves of comparison in the second paragraph of her essay in this chapter:

> I was a first-generation college student as well as the first in our family to be born in America—my parents were born in Cuba—and we didn't yet know that families were supposed to leave pretty much right after they unloaded your stuff from the car.
>
> —JENNINE CAPÓ CRUCET, "Taking My Parents to College"

Crucet identifies her subjects (families), states the basis on which she is comparing them (knowledge of the unstated rules for sending a kid off to college), and indicates that she is planning to emphasize their differences ("we didn't yet know").

Here is one more example from this chapter:

> Today, Disney no longer expects us to expect a knight in shining armor, but rather to forgive our siblings and make peace with our parents. Consider the gulf that separates *Sleeping Beauty* (1950) from its remake *Maleficent* (2014).
>
> —SOPHUS HELLE, "Love Isn't What It Was"

The following guidelines will help you make these basic moves as you draft a comparison. They will also help you come up with two subjects to compare, present their similarities and differences in an organized way, and state your point in comparing them.

Coming Up with Your Subjects

The first thing you need to do when composing a comparison essay is to choose two subjects that are different in significant ways but that also have enough in common to provide a solid basis of comparison. A bus and a jet, for instance, are very different machines; but both are modes of transportation, and that shared characteristic can become the basis for comparing them.

When you look for two subjects that have shared characteristics, don't stretch your comparison too far. The Duchess in Lewis Carroll's *Alice in Wonderland* compares mustard to flamingos because they "both bite." In the real world, however, there's no point in bringing two subjects together when the differences between them are far more significant than the similarities. Better to compare mustard and ketchup or flamingos and roseate spoonbills (another type of pink bird).

Considering Your Purpose and Audience

Suppose that you are comparing smartphones because the screen cracked on your old one and you need to replace it. In this case, your **PURPOSE** is to evaluate them and decide which smartphone fits your needs best. However, if you were writing the comparison for *CNET*, you would be comparing and contrasting smartphones in order to inform readers about their various functions and capabilities.

With comparisons, one size does not fit all. Whether you're writing a comparison to inform, to evaluate, or for some other purpose, always keep the specific needs of your **AUDIENCE** in mind. How much do your readers already know about your topic? Why should they want or need to know more? What distinctions can you make that they haven't already thought of?

Deborah Tannen's audience is teachers in her essay "Gender in the Classroom," p. 349.

Generating Ideas: Asking How Two Things Are Alike or Different

Once you have a clear basis for comparing two subjects—flamingos and rose-ate spoonbills are both large pink birds; mustard and ketchup are both condi-ments; buses and jets are both modes of transportation—look for specific points of comparison between them. Ask yourself: How, specifically, are my two subjects alike? How are they different?

As you answer these questions, make a point-by-point list of the simi-larities and differences between your subjects. When you draw up your list, make sure you look at the same elements in both subjects. For example, if you are comparing two smartphone models, you might list such elements as the price, size, and camera quality for each one. Preparing such a list will help you determine whether your two subjects are actually worth comparing—and will also help you get the similarities and differences straight in your own mind before attempting to explain them to your audience.

Templates for Comparing

The following templates can help you generate ideas for a comparison and then start drafting. Don't take these as formulas where you just have to fill in the blanks. There are no easy formulas for good writing. But these templates can help you plot out some of the key moves of comparison and contrast and thus may serve as good starting points.

> ► X and Y can be compared on the grounds that both are _____.
>
> ► Like X, Y is also _____, _____, and _____.
>
> ► Although X and Y are both _____, the differences between them far out-weigh the similarities. For example, X is _____, _____, and _____, while Y is _____, _____, and _____.
>
> ► Unlike X, Y is _____.
>
> ► Despite their differences, X and Y are basically alike in that _____.

▶ At first glance, X and Y seem _____; however, a closer look reveals
_____.

▶ In comparing X and Y, we can see that _____.

For more techniques to help you generate ideas and start writing a comparison
essay, see Chapter 3.

Organizing a Comparison

As we discussed earlier, there are fundamentally two ways to organize a
comparison: point by point or subject by subject. With a point-by-point
organization (like Larner's comparison of Wilt Chamberlain and Bill Russell), you discuss each point of comparison (or contrast) between your two
subjects before going on to the next point. With the subject-by-subject
method, you discuss each subject individually, making a number of points
about one subject and then covering more or less the same points about the
other subject. This is the organization Conroy follows in his comparison of
yo-yos.

Which method of organization should you use? You will probably find
that the point-by-point method works best for beginning and ending an essay,
while the subject-by-subject method serves you well for longer stretches in
the main body.

One reason for using the subject-by-subject method to organize most of
your essay is that the point-by-point method, when relentlessly applied, can
make the reader a little seasick as you jump back and forth from your first
subject to your second. With the subject-by-subject method, you do not have

<aside>Robert Sapolsky
uses the point-by-
point method to
compare adoles-
cents and adults,
p. 358.</aside>

to give equal weight to both subjects. The subject-by-subject
method is, thus, indispensable for treating a subject in depth,
whereas the point-by-point method is an efficient way to establish a basis of comparison at the beginning, to remind readers
along the way why two subjects are being compared, and to sum up your essay
at the end.

Stating Your Point

Your main point in drawing a comparison will determine whether you emphasize similarities or differences. For instance, if your thesis is that there are certain fundamental qualities that all successful coaches share—and you're comparing the best coaches from your own high school days to make this point—you will focus on the similarities among them. However, if you're comparing blind dates to make the point that it's difficult to be prepared for a blind date because no two are alike, you would focus on the differences among the blind dates you've had.

Whatever the main point of your comparison might be, state it clearly right away in an explicit **THESIS STATEMENT**: "Blind dates are inherently unpredictable; since no two are alike, the best way to go into one is with no expectations at all." Be sure to indicate to readers which you are going to emphasize—the similarities or differences between your subjects. Then, in the body of your essay, use specific points of comparison to show those similarities or differences and to prove your main point.

Providing Sufficient Points of Comparison

No matter how you organize a comparison essay, you will have to provide a sufficient number of points of comparison between your subjects to demonstrate that they are truly comparable and to justify your reasons for comparing them. How many points of comparison are enough to do the job?

Sufficiency isn't strictly a matter of numbers. It depends, in part, on just how inclined your audience is to accept (or reject) the main point your comparison is intended to make. If you are comparing subjects that your readers are not familiar with, you may have to give more examples of similarities or differences than you would if your readers already knew a lot about your subjects. For instance, if you were comparing different brands of pasta, readers who don't know the difference between spaghetti and angel hair (pasta, that is) are going to require more (and more basic) points of comparison than those who do a lot of cooking.

To determine how many points of comparison you need to make, consider your intended readers, and choose the points of comparison you think they will find most useful, interesting, or otherwise convincing. Then give a sufficient number to get your larger point across, but not so many that you run the comparison into the ground.

EDITING FOR COMMON ERRORS
IN COMPARISONS

Like other kinds of writing, comparison uses distinctive patterns of language and punctuation—and thus invites typical kinds of errors. The following tips will help you check for (and correct) these common errors when you make comparisons in your own writing.

Make sure all comparisons are complete

Comparisons examine at least two things at once. Check to make sure you've identified both of them; otherwise, readers may not fully understand what is being compared.

▶ When you enter a chapel, there is more solitude and calm <u>than in the world outside</u>.

▶ Most public chapels are not as quiet <u>as those attached to monasteries</u>.

Check that all comparisons are grammatically consistent

When you compare items, they should be grammatically parallel—that is, similar in grammatical form. The original version of this sentence unintentionally compares churches to a country.

▶ In Italy the churches seemed even older than <u>those in</u> France.

Check for common errors in usage

GOOD, WELL, BETTER

"Good" is an adjective; "well" is the adverb form. "Better" can be either an adjective or an adverb.

> ► Celeste plays the clarinet ~~good~~ <u>well</u>, but Angela plays it even <u>better</u> because she is generally a <u>better</u> musician.

BETWEEN, AMONG

Use "between" when you're comparing individuals, usually two at a time; use "among" when you're comparing parts of a larger whole:

> ► <u>Between</u> France and Germany, Germany has the larger economy.

> ► <u>Among</u> all the countries in the euro zone, Germany has the largest economy.

> ► <u>Between</u> a rock and a hard place, choose the rock; it may be a diamond.

> ► <u>Among</u> rocks, diamonds are some of the hardest.

Buses, Bikes, and Cars

When you compare and contrast, you show the similarities and differences among related subjects. Buses, cars, and bikes are related subjects—all are common means of transportation—and in this visual comparison from the website of the Cycling Promotion Fund, an organization that promotes cycling across communities in Australia, they're shown as transporting the same number of passengers. The big difference here, of course, is in the number of vehicles that appear with the large group of people in each photo: at least 100 cars, just as many bicycles, but only one long bus. We draw comparisons in order to make a larger point, and in this case, the one here aligns with the fund's mission: to make cities biker friendly, to fight climate change, and to reduce congestion. If more people used public transit and rode bikes, we could save fuel and leave a smaller carbon footprint.

DAN TREADWAY

FOOTBALL VS. ASIAN STUDIES

DAN TREADWAY wrote "Football vs. Asian Studies" as a senior majoring in communication studies at the University of Texas–Austin. Far from comparing apples to oranges, his essay uses strategies of comparison to uncover unexpected similarities between sports and academics at a large state university. "Sadly," argues Treadway, an associate editor of the *Daily Texan* at the time, those similarities are generally ignored. "Football vs. Asian Studies" was a finalist in a student writing contest sponsored in 2010 by the *Nation* magazine.

Football vs. Asian Studies

The University of Texas football team is among the best in the nation. It has been a beloved part of the university since 1894, and has grown each year since its inception. The program is seemingly larger than life, making more money last year than any other athletic program in history. Its place at this university is defined and unquestioned. If one attends the University of Texas, it's impossible to not know about the importance of the football team. [1]

The University of Texas Asian Studies program is one of the best in the nation. It's been a part of the university since 1994, and is already among the most distinguished academic departments of its kind. Its place at this university is defined to those who know about the major, but it's quite possible to study on campus for four years and never become aware of the fact that the Asian Studies program even exists. [2]

The football team is comprised of eighty-five student-athletes who receive full scholarships to attend the university. [3]

While there is limited funding for those who study abroad, the Department of Asian Studies does not have the funds to offer scholarships specifically aimed at students within the major to help them pay for classes at UT. [4]

To bolster the team's defense, the University recently recruited Will Muschamp, the former defensive coordinator at Auburn University, to stabilize the shaky unit. Muschamp was offered a salary of $425,000 annually to bring his unique services to the program. Entering only his third year at the University, Muschamp has already become a team favorite among players and fans alike. [5]

Italics indicate change from subject A (football) to subject B (Asian Studies)

Covers the same points in the same order, here and throughout, for each subject

To bolster an incomplete Asian Studies program, students 6
along with faculty lobbied tirelessly for the university to adopt
a class that would teach the Vietnamese language. After two
years of diligent campaigning, the university decided to add
the language to the curriculum in the Department of Asian
Studies in 2006. Dr. Hoang Ngo was selected to teach both the
regular and advanced Vietnamese courses at the University. He
was offered a salary of a little more than $45,000 for his
unique services. Ngo quickly became a favorite among his stu-
dents for his knowledge and patience.

Football is the most popular spectator sport in the 7
state of Texas without rival. The sport's importance to
our heritage is well known and documented.

Vietnamese is the third-most-spoken language in the state 8
of Texas behind English and Spanish. This is a fact that is not
well known or documented.

Under head coach Mack Brown, the Longhorns foot- 9
ball program has soared to new heights. In the past
decade, the Longhorns have won more games than in any
other ten-year stretch in the program's history. Brown's
smart coaching and savvy recruiting have built a seemingly unstoppable athletic machine in the city of Austin.
His success has distinguished this era of Texas football as
the golden age, unmatched by teams from past
generations.

Under Dr. Hoang Ngo, the Vietnamese language course 10
had grown quite popular in a short period of time. According
to Nickie Tran, a former student in Ngo's class, "[Teaching the
Vietnamese language] is important because if you talk to a lot
of second-generation Asian-Americans, you hear it's hard for
them to retain their native language." Teaching Vietnamese at
the University of Texas has enabled this generation of

> Frequent repetition of phrases estab- lishes a firm basis of COMPARISON

Vietnamese-Americans to develop a special connection to generations past.

Mack Brown recently received a $2.1 million pay raise 11
on his $3 million base salary to reward all of his success.
The University of Texas's football program is thriving—
last year it generated $120 million in revenue.

Dr. Ngo has now moved back to Vietnam to seek new 12
employment. The Vietnamese language program at UT has
been discontinued. A casualty of budget cuts, the administra-
tion felt that the program was expendable because of its small
size—its absence will save the university approximately
$50,000 a year.

A 2009 study revealed that less than 50 percent of 13
football players at the University of Texas ultimately
graduated and received a degree.

With the elimination of the Vietnamese language pro- 14
gram, dozens of students will be forced to take courses in a
different foreign language so that they may fulfill their aca-
demic requirement and graduate with a degree.

Come September, when students come back to cam- 15
pus, the most popular sport in Texas will be put on display before an ecstatic crowd of more than 100,000
screaming people in Darrell K. Royal-Texas Memorial
Stadium, which recently received $179 million in
renovations.

Come September, when students come back to campus, the 16
third most spoken language in Texas will no longer be taught
due to budgetary constraints and sadly, hardly anybody will ask
questions or even notice.

Sidebar notes:

Frames Asian Studies as a bargain by comparison

Conclusion emphasizes points of contrast between the two subjects

JENNINE CAPÓ CRUCET

TAKING MY PARENTS TO COLLEGE

JENNINE CAPÓ CRUCET (b. 1981) is a writer of fiction and essays and a professor of English and ethnic studies at the University of Nebraska–Lincoln. Crucet grew up in Hialeah, Florida, just north of Miami. She majored in English and in feminist, gender, and sexuality studies at Cornell University and earned an MFA in creative writing from the University of Minnesota. In both her first story collection, *How to Leave Hialeah* (2009), and her first novel, *Make Your Home among Strangers* (2015), Crucet writes about a young woman whose life "has been shaped by South Florida, its people and its landscape, and by the stories of Cuba repeated to me almost daily by my parents and *abuelos*." In "Taking My Parents to College," Crucet compares her experience of going off to college with that of her peers at an Ivy League school who are not the first in their families to go to college—or the first to be born in America. Originally published in the *New York Times* in 2015, this essay also forms the basis of Crucet's introduction to her collection of essays called, with tongue in cheek, *My Time among the Whites* (2019).

I T WAS A SIMPLE QUESTION, but we couldn't find the answer in any of the paperwork the college had sent. How long was my family supposed to stay for orientation? This was 1999, so Google wasn't really a verb yet, and we were a low-income family (according to my new school) without regular Internet access.

I was a first-generation college student as well as the first in our family to be born in America—my parents were born in Cuba—and we didn't yet know that families were supposed to leave pretty much right after they unloaded your stuff from the car.

We all made the trip from Miami, my hometown, to what would be my new home at Cornell University. Shortly after arriving on campus, the five of us—my parents, my younger sister, my abuela and me—found ourselves listening to a dean end his welcome speech with the words: "Now, parents, please: Go!"

Almost everyone in the audience laughed, but not me, and not my parents. They turned to me and said, "What does he mean, *Go*?" I was just as confused as they were: We thought we *all* needed to be there for freshman orientation—the whole family, for the entirety of it. My dad had booked their hotel through the day after my classes officially began. They'd used all their vacation days from work and had been saving for months to get me to school and go through our orientation.

> Crucet is emphasizing the *differences* between her subjects rather than their similarities, p. 324–25.

Every afternoon during that week, we had to go back to the only department store we could find, the now-defunct Ames, for some stupid thing we hadn't known was a necessity, something not in our budget: shower shoes, extra-long twin sheets, mesh laundry bags. Before the other families left, we carefully watched them—they knew what they were doing—and we made new shopping lists with our limited vocabulary: *Those things that lift up the bed*, we wrote. *That plastic thing to carry stuff to the bathroom.*

My family followed me around as I visited department offices during course registration. *Only four classes?* they asked, assuming I was mistakenly taking my first semester too easy. They walked with me to buildings I was supposed to be finding on my own. They waited outside those buildings so that we could all leave from there and go to lunch together.

The five of us wandered each day through the dining hall's doors. "You guys are still here!" the over-friendly person swiping ID cards said after day three. "They sure are!" I chirped back, learning via the cues of my hallmates that I was supposed to want my family gone. But it was an act: We sat together at meals—amid all the other students, already making friends—my mom placing a napkin and fork at each place, setting the table as we did at home.

I don't even remember the moment they drove away. I'm told it's one of those instances you never forget, that second when you realize you're finally on your own. But for me, it's not there—perhaps because, when you're the first in your family to go to college, you never truly feel like they've let you go.

They did eventually leave—of course they did—and a week into classes, I received the topics for what would be my first college paper, in an English course on the modern novel. I might as well have been my non-English-speaking grandmother trying to read and understand them: The language felt that foreign. I called my mom at work and in tears told her that I had to come home, that I'd made a terrible mistake.

She sighed into the phone and said: "Just read me the first question. We'll go through it a little at a time and figure it out."

I read her the topic slowly, pausing after each sentence, waiting for her to say something. The first topic was two paragraphs long. I remember it had the word *intersectionalities* in it. And the word *gendered*. And maybe the phrase *theoretical framework*. I waited for her response and for the ways it would encourage me, for her to tell me I could do this, that I would eventually be the first in my family to graduate from college.

"You're right," she said after a moment. "You're screwed."

Other parents—parents who have gone to college themselves—might have known at that point to encourage their kid to go to office hours, or to the writing center, or to ask for help. But my mom thought I was as alone as I feared.

"I have no idea what any of that means," she said. "I don't even know how it's a *question*."

While my college had done an excellent job recruiting me, I had no road map for what I was supposed to do once I made it to campus. I'd already embarrassed myself by doing things like asking my R.A. what time the dorm closed for the night. As far as I knew, there'd been no mandatory meeting geared toward first-generation students like me: Aside from a check-in with my financial aid officer when she explained what work-study was (I didn't know and worried it meant I had to join the army or something) and where she had me sign for my loans, I was mostly keeping to myself to hide the fact that I was a very special kind of lost. I folded the sheet with the paper topics in half and put it in my desk drawer.

"I don't know what you're gonna do," my mom almost laughed. "Maybe— 16 have you looked in the dictionary?"

I started crying harder, my hand over the receiver.   17

"You still there?" she eventually asked, clearly hiding her own tears. I   18 murmured *Mmmhmm.*

"Look, just stick it out up there until Christmas," she said. "We have no 19 more vacation days this year. We can't take off any more time to go get you."

"O.K.," I swallowed. I started breathing in through my nose and out   20 through my mouth, calming myself. "I can do that," I said.

My mom laughed for real this time and said, "Mamita, you don't really 21 have a choice."

She didn't say this in a mean way. She was just telling me the truth. 22 "This whole thing was your idea, remember?" she said. Then she told me she had to go, that she needed to get back to work.

So I got back to work, too, and *Get back to work* became a sort of mantra for 23 me. I tackled the paper with the same focus that had landed me, to everyone's surprise—even my own—at Cornell in the first place. I did O.K. on it, earning a "B−/C" (I never found out how a grade could have a slash in it, but now that I'm an English professor I understand what he was trying to say). The professor had covered the typed pages with comments and questions, and it was in his end-note that he listed the various campus resources available to me.

My mom didn't ask outright what grade I earned—she eventually 24 stopped asking about assignments altogether—and I learned from my peers

Sometimes a single point of comparison is sufficient, p. 329. that grades were something that I didn't have to share with my parents the way I had in high school.

My grades were the first of many elements of my new life 25 for which they had no context and which they wouldn't understand. With each semester, what I was doing became, for them, as indecipherable as that paper topic; they didn't even know what questions to ask. And that, for me, is the quintessential quality of the first-generation college student's experience. It's not even knowing what you don't know.

FOR DISCUSSION

1. When Jennine Capó Crucet went off to college, she didn't know that her family was not supposed to come and stay through the entire orientation period. Was she the only one to blame? Why or why not?

2. Crucet started college in 1999. By contrast, she implies, first-generation students today would likely have a better idea of what to expect than she did. Do you agree? Explain.

3. Crucet tells us that she succeeded at her studies in time. How did she do with regard to the strange language that was such a source of anxiety to her in the beginning? How do we know?

4. In Crucet's comparison, what are some of the main differences between her parents and those of many of her fellow classmates? What strengths (if any) does Crucet ascribe to her family (particularly her mother)?

STRATEGIES AND STRUCTURES

1. Crucet begins her essay by COMPARING AND CONTRASTING her family, including herself, with those families that "knew what they were doing" (5). By the end of her essay, who is she mostly contrasting with whom? Where and why does her focus shift during the course of her essay?

2. Where does Crucet explicitly compare her subsequent life in college to the set of topics she was given for her first college paper? What is her point in making the comparison? Is it effective for this purpose? Why or why not?

3. When Crucet's English professor returns her first paper, he has covered it "with comments and questions" and given her a grade of "B−/C" (23). What else does her professor provide in his endnote? Why and how is this relevant to the story she is telling?

4. Crucet's essay includes many elements of NARRATIVE. Do these elements support (or fail to support) the comparisons she is making? Be sure to comment on her use of DIALOGUE, particularly in the phone conversation with her mother.

5. Crucet ends her essay with a DEFINITION: "And that, for me, is the quintessential quality of the first-generation college student's experience. It's not even knowing what you don't know" (25). She notes that her definition is particular to her

experience with the addition of "for me." Does this make her definition more or less persuasive? Explain.

WORDS AND FIGURES OF SPEECH

1. "Abuela" (3) is the word for grandmother in Spanish. Should Crucet have given an English translation when she first uses the term in her essay? Why or why not?

2. "Indecipherable" (25) is usually applied to forms of writing, often in code, that the reader cannot understand. To whom or what is Crucet applying it? Is this an apt use of the term? Why or why not?

3. Throughout her college years, says Crucet, "Get back to work" became her "mantra" (23). Look up the term in a dictionary. How and how well does it apply to Crucet's trials and tribulations—and to those of college in general?

4. In ancient Greek philosophy, the word "quintessence" referred to a "fifth essence" in addition to earth, air, fire, and water, which were thought to be the four essential elements of the physical universe. Look up the term and explain what Crucet means by a "quintessential quality" (25).

FOR WRITING

1. Crucet begins her essay with a "simple" question: "How long was my family supposed to stay for orientation?" In a paragraph or two, answer this question and explain how and why you think so.

2. In a brief essay, compare your experience of first-year "orientation" (or that of somebody you know) with Crucet's and her family's experience. Whether you focus on the similarities or differences, give several specific **EXAMPLES** of both.

3. At the other end of the spectrum from first-year orientation lies graduation. Write an essay comparing the purposes and ceremonies, as you understand them, of the two occasions (whether in college or high school). Consider, for example, that one might be aimed largely at students—"Now, parents, please: Go!"—while the other might be conceived as a reward for those who helped along the way.

LIKE MEXICANS

GARY SOTO (b. 1952) is a poet and novelist and the author of numerous books for children and young adults. His memoir, *Living up the Street* (1985) won an American Book Award. Soto grew up in Fresno, California; as a teenager and college student, he chopped beets and picked cotton and grapes in the fields of the San Joaquin Valley. After graduating from the University of California–Fresno, Soto earned an MFA in creative writing at the University of California–Irvine. He has taught at both the Berkeley and Riverside campuses of the university. Soto's latest collections of poetry are *You Kiss by th' Book* (2016) and *Meatballs for the People* (2017). In "Like Mexicans," from *Small Faces* (1986), another collection of reminiscences of growing up in the *barrio*, Soto compares his future wife's Japanese American family with his own Mexican American one.

M Y GRANDMOTHER GAVE ME BAD ADVICE AND GOOD ADVICE when I was in my early teens. For the bad advice, she said that I should become a barber because they made good money and listened to the radio all day. 1

"Honey, they don't work como burros," she would say every time I visited her. She made the sound of donkeys braying. "Like that, honey!" For the good advice, she said that I should marry a Mexican girl. "No Okies, hijo"—she would say—"Look, my son. He marry one and they fight every day about I don't know what and I don't know what." For her, everyone who wasn't Mexican, black, or Asian were Okies. The French were Okies, the Italians in suits were Okies. When I asked about Jews, whom I had read about, she asked for a picture. I rode home on my bicycle and returned with a calendar depicting the important races of the world. "Pues si, son Okies tambien!"[1] she said, nodding her head. She waved the calendar away and we went to the living room where she lectured me on the virtues of the Mexican girl: first, she could cook and, second, she acted like a woman, not a man, in her husband's home. She said she would tell me about a third when I got a little older.

I asked my mother about it—becoming a barber and marrying Mexican. 2 She was in the kitchen. Steam curled from a pot of boiling beans, the radio was on, looking as squat as a loaf of bread. "Well, if you want to be a barber— they say they make good money." She slapped a round steak with a knife, her glasses slipping down with each strike. She stopped and looked up. "If you find a good Mexican girl, marry her of course." She returned to slapping the meat and I went to the backyard where my brother and David King were sitting on the lawn feeling the inside of their cheeks.

"This is what girls feel like," my brother said, rubbing the inside of his 3 cheek. David put three fingers inside his mouth and scratched. I ignored them and climbed the back fence to see my best friend, Scott, a second-generation Okie. I called him and his mother pointed to the side of the house where his bedroom was, a small aluminum trailer, the kind you gawk at when they're flipped over on the freeway, wheels spinning in the air. I went around to find Scott pitching horseshoes.

I picked up a set of rusty ones and joined him. While we played, we talked 4 about school and friends and record albums. The horseshoes scuffed up dirt, sometimes ringing the iron that threw out a meager shadow like a sundial. After three argued-over games, we pulled two oranges apiece from his tree and started down the alley still talking school and friends and record albums. We

1. Well yes, they're Okies, too.

pulled more oranges from the alley and talked about who we would marry. "No offense, Scott," I said with an orange slice in my mouth, "but I would never marry an Okie." We walked in step, almost touching, with a sled of shadows dragging behind us. "No offense, Gary," Scott said, "but I would *never* marry a Mexican." I looked at him: a fang of orange slice showed from his munching mouth. I didn't think anything of it. He had his girl and I had mine. But our seventh-grade vision was the same: to marry, get jobs, buy cars and maybe a house if we had money left over.

> By making comparisons, we often discover unexpected similarities, p. 326.

We talked about our future lives until, to our surprise, we were on the downtown mall, two miles from home. We bought a bag of popcorn at Penney's and sat on a bench near the fountain watching Mexican and Okie girls pass. "That one's mine," I pointed with my chin when a girl with eyebrows arched into black rainbows ambled by. "She's cute," Scott said about a girl with yellow hair and a mouthful of gum. We dreamed aloud, our chins busy pointing out girls. We agreed that we couldn't wait to become men and lift them onto our laps. 5

But the woman I married was not Mexican but Japanese. It was a surprise to me. For years, I went about wide-eyed in my search for the brown girl in a white dress at a dance. I searched the playground at the baseball diamond. When the girls raced for grounders, their hair bounced like something that couldn't be caught. When they sat together in the lunchroom, heads pressed together, I knew they were talking about us Mexican guys. I saw them and dreamed them. I threw my face into my pillow, making up sentences that were good as in the movies. 6

But when I was twenty, I fell in love with this other girl who worried my mother, who had my grandmother asking once again to see the calendar of the Important Races of the World. I told her I had thrown it away years before. I took a much-glanced-at snapshot from my wallet. We looked at it together, in silence. Then Grandma reclined in her chair, lit a cigarette, and said, "Es pretty." She blew and asked with all her worry pushed up to her forehead: "Chinese?" 7

I was in love and there was no looking back. She was the one. I told my mother who was slapping hamburger into patties. "Well, sure if you want to marry her," she said. But the more I talked, the more concerned she became. Later I began to worry. Was it all a mistake? "Marry a Mexican girl," I heard my mother say in my mind. I heard it at breakfast. I heard it over math problems, between Western Civilization and cultural geography. But then one afternoon 8 while I was hitchhiking home from school, it struck me like a baseball in the back: my mother wanted me to marry someone of my own social class—a poor girl. I considered my fiancée, Carolyn, and she didn't look poor, though I knew she came from a family of farm workers and pull-yourself-up-by-your-bootstraps ranchers. I asked my brother, who was marrying Mexican poor that fall, if I should marry a poor girl. He screamed "Yeah" above his terrible guitar playing in his bedroom. I considered my sister who had married Mexican. Cousins were dating Mexican. Uncles were remarrying poor women. I asked Scott, who was still my best friend, and he said, "She's too good for you, so you better not."

I worried about it until Carolyn took me home to meet her parents. We   9
drove in her Plymouth until the houses gave way to farms and ranches and finally her house fifty feet from the highway. When we pulled into the drive, I panicked and begged Carolyn to make a U-turn and go back so we could talk about it over a soda. She pinched my cheek, calling me a "silly boy." I felt better, though, when I got out of the car and saw the house: the chipped paint, a cracked window, boards for a walk to the back door. There were rusting cars near the barn. A tractor with a net of spiderwebs under a mulberry. A field. A bale of barbed wire like children's scribbling leaning against an empty chicken coop. Carolyn took my hand and pulled me to my future mother-in-law who was coming out to greet us.

We had lunch: sandwiches, potato chips, and iced tea. Carolyn and her   10
mother talked mostly about neighbors and the congregation at the Japanese Methodist Church in West Fresno. Her father, who was in khaki work clothes, excused himself with a wave that was almost a salute and went outside. I heard a truck start, a dog bark, and then the truck rattle away.

Carolyn's mother offered another sandwich, but I declined with a shake   11
of my head and a smile. I looked around when I could, when I was not saying over and over that I was a college student, hinting that I could take care of her daughter. I shifted my chair. I saw newspapers piled in corners, dusty cereal boxes and vinegar bottles in corners. The wallpaper was bubbled from rain that had come in from a bad roof. Dust. Dust lay on lamp shades and window sills. These people are just like Mexicans, I thought. Poor people.

> Soto's basis, p. 326, for comparing his two subjects is their economic condition.

Carolyn's mother asked me through Carolyn if I would like a *sushi*. A   12
plate of black and white things were held in front of me. I took one, wide-eyed,

and turned it over like a foreign coin. I was biting into one when I saw a kitten crawl up the window screen over the sink. I chewed and the kitten opened its mouth of terror as she crawled higher, wanting in to paw the leftovers from our plates. I looked at Carolyn who said that the cat was just showing off. I looked up in time to see it fall. It crawled up, then fell again.

We talked for an hour and had apple pie and coffee, slowly. Finally, we got up with Carolyn taking my hand. Slightly embarrassed, I tried to pull away but her grip held me. I let her have her way as she led me down the hallway with her mother right behind me. When I opened the door, I was startled by a kitten clinging to the screen door, its mouth screaming "cat food, dog biscuits, *sushi*. . . ." I opened the door and the kitten, still holding on, whined in the language of hungry animals. When I got into Carolyn's car, I looked back: the cat was still clinging. I asked Carolyn if it were possibly hungry, but she said the cat was being silly. She started the car, waved to her mother, and bounced us over the rain-pocked drive, patting my thigh for being her lover baby. Carolyn waved again. I looked back, waving, then gawking at a window screen where there were now three kittens clawing and screaming to get in. Like Mexicans, I thought. I remembered the Molinas and how the cats clung to their screens— cats they shot down with squirt guns. On the highway, I felt happy, pleased by it all. I patted Carolyn's thigh. Her people were like Mexicans, only different.

13

FOR DISCUSSION

1. After COMPARING his future wife's family to his own, Gary Soto concludes that they are much alike, "only different" (13). How and how well does this conclusion summarize the main point of Soto's comparison? Explain.

2. How does Soto's grandmother DEFINE an "Okie" (1)? Why doesn't she want him to marry one?

3. Why does Soto say that his grandmother gave him bad and good advice (1)? Which is which, and why?

4. "It was a surprise to me," says Soto about marrying a girl of Japanese descent (6). Why didn't he marry a Mexican girl, as his grandmother advised?

5. What does Soto imply about ethnic and racial stereotypes when he refers to the calendar showing the "Important Races of the World" (1, 7)? Why does his grandmother ask for the calendar again?

STRATEGIES AND STRUCTURES

1. Before comparing them with Japanese Americans, Soto explains what Mexican Americans are "like." What are some of the specifics by which he characterizes himself and his family? What is his **PURPOSE** for citing these particular traits?

2. We meet Carolyn's family in paragraph 10. How has Soto already prepared us to expect more similarities than differences between the two families? Cite details by which Soto explains what Carolyn's people are "like."

3. Why does Soto refer so often to the kittens of Carolyn's family's house? What role do they play in his comparison?

4. Besides giving advice, Soto's grandmother, like all the other adult women in the essay, is engaged in what activity? Why do you think Soto focuses on this?

5. Soto's comparison of two American families has many elements of **NARRATIVE**. Who is the **NARRATOR**: a young man growing up in a Mexican American neighborhood, an older man looking back at him, or both? Explain.

WORDS AND FIGURES OF SPEECH

1. What is the effect of Soto's **DESCRIPTION** of the orange slice in Scott's mouth as a "fang" (4)? Why do you think he says, "I didn't think anything of it" (4)?

2. What does Soto mean by the term "social class" in paragraph 8?

3. Why do you think Soto compares sushi to a foreign coin (12)? Give examples of other **SIMILES** like this one in his essay.

4. What is the derivation of Soto's grandmother's favorite ethnic slur, "Okies"?

FOR WRITING

1. Write a paragraph comparing and contrasting your family with that of a close friend, spouse, or partner. Choose one specific point of comparison—how or what they eat, how they interact within their family, how they celebrate special occasions, and so forth.

2. Whether or not you grew up in a racially or ethnically diverse neighborhood, you may recall friends and acquaintances who differed from each other in social, economic, cultural, religious, or other ways. Choose a person or family that, at first glance, would appear to closely resemble (or starkly contrast with) you and your family. In an essay comparing the two subjects, show, point by point, how and why the two people or groups are actually not so similar to (or different from) each other after all.

DEBORAH TANNEN

GENDER IN THE CLASSROOM

DEBORAH TANNEN (b. 1945) is a professor of linguistics at Georgetown University who specializes, as she says, in "the language of everyday conversation." Although Tannen's latest book, *You're the Only One I Can Tell* (2017), focuses on the language of women's friendships, the following selection from the *Chronicle of Higher Education* (1991), grew out of her earlier research on the conversational styles of both men and women. In the United States, says Tannen, the sexes bond differently. Women do it by talking with each other about their troubles; men do it by exchanging "playful insults." In "Gender in the Classroom," Tannen compares and contrasts the various behaviors that result, in her view, from gender-related styles of talking and then explains how she adjusts her teaching methods to accommodate these behaviors.

WHEN I RESEARCHED AND WROTE MY LATEST BOOK, *You Just Don't Understand: Women and Men in Conversation*, the furthest thing from my mind was reevaluating my teaching strategies. But that has been one of the direct benefits of having written the book. 1

The primary focus of my linguistic research always has been the language of everyday conversation. One facet of this is conversational style: how different regional, ethnic, and class backgrounds, as well as age and gender, result in different ways of using language to communicate. *You Just Don't Understand* is about the conversational styles of women and men. As I gained more insight into typically male and female ways of using language, I began to suspect some of the causes of the troubling facts that women who go to single-sex schools do better in later life, and that when young women sit next to young men in classrooms, the males talk more. This is not to say that all men talk in class, nor that no women do. It is simply that a greater percentage of discussion time is taken by men's voices.

The research of sociologists and anthropologists such as Janet Lever, Marjorie Harness Goodwin, and Donna Eder has shown that girls and boys learn to use language differently in their sex-separate peer groups. Typically, a girl has a best friend with whom she sits and talks, frequently telling secrets. It's the telling of secrets, the fact and the way that they talk to each other, that makes them best friends. For boys, activities are central: Their best friends are the ones they do things with. Boys also tend to play in larger groups that are hierarchical. High-status boys give orders and push low-status boys around. So boys are expected to use language to seize center stage: by exhibiting their skill, displaying their knowledge, and challenging and resisting challenges.

A good example would be Gary Soto's relationship with his friend Scott, p. 344.

These patterns have stunning implications for classroom interaction. Most faculty members assume that participating in class discussion is a necessary part of successful performance. Yet speaking in a classroom is more congenial to boys' language experience than to girls', since it entails putting oneself forward in front of a large group of people, many of whom are strangers and at least one of whom is sure to judge speakers' knowledge and intelligence by their verbal display.

Another aspect of many classrooms that makes them more hospitable to most men than to most women is the use of debate-like formats as a learning tool. Our educational system, as Walter Ong[1] argues persuasively in his book *Fighting for Life* (Cornell University Press, 1981), is fundamentally male in that

1. Cultural historian, philosopher, and Jesuit priest (1912–2003).

the pursuit of knowledge is believed to be achieved by ritual opposition: public display followed by argument and challenge. Father Ong demonstrates that ritual opposition—what he calls "adversativeness" or "agonism"—is fundamental to the way most males approach almost any activity. (Consider, for example, the little boy who shows he likes a little girl by pulling her braids and shoving her.) But ritual opposition is antithetical to the way most females learn and like to interact. It is not that females don't fight, but that they don't fight for fun. They don't *ritualize* opposition.

Anthropologists working in widely disparate parts of the world have 6 found contrasting verbal rituals for women and men. Women in completely unrelated cultures (for example, Greece and Bali) engage in ritual laments: spontaneously produced rhyming couplets that express their pain, for example, over the loss of loved ones. Men do not take part in laments. They have their own, very different verbal ritual: a contest, a war of words in which they vie with each other to devise clever insults.

When discussing these phenomena with a colleague, I commented that I 7 see these two styles in American conversation: Many women bond by talking about troubles, and many men bond by exchanging playful insults and put-downs, and other sorts of verbal sparring. He exclaimed: "I never thought of this, but that's the way I teach: I have students read an article, and then I invite them to tear it apart. After we've torn it to shreds, we talk about how to build a better model."

This contrasts sharply with the way I teach: I open the discussion of 8 readings by asking, "What did you find useful in this? What can we use in our own theory building and our own methods?" I note what I see as weaknesses in the author's approach, but I also point out that the writer's discipline and purposes might be different from ours. Finally, I offer personal anecdotes illustrating the phenomena under discussion and praise students' anecdotes as well as their critical acumen.

These different teaching styles must make our classrooms wildly differ- 9 ent places and hospitable to different students. Male students are more likely to be comfortable attacking the readings and might find the inclusion of personal anecdotes irrelevant and "soft." Women are more likely to resist discussion they perceive as hostile, and, indeed, it is women in my classes who are most likely to offer personal anecdotes.

A colleague who read my book commented that he had always taken for   10
granted that the best way to deal with students' comments is to challenge
them: this, he felt, was self-evident, sharpens their minds and helps them
develop debating skills. But he had noticed that women were relatively silent
in his classes, so he decided to try beginning discussion with relatively open-
ended questions and letting comments go unchallenged. He found, to his
amazement and satisfaction, that more women began to speak up.

Though some of the women in his class clearly liked this better, perhaps   11
some of the men liked it less. One young man in my class wrote in a questionnaire about a history professor who gave students questions to think about
and called on people to answer them: "He would then play devil's advocate . . .
i.e., he debated us. . . . That class *really* sharpened me intellectually. . . . We as
students do need to know how to defend ourselves." This young man valued
the experience of being attacked and challenged publicly. Many, if not most,
women would shrink from such a "challenge," experiencing it as a public
humiliation.

A professor at Hamilton College told me of a young man who was upset   12
because he felt his class presentation had been a failure. The professor was
puzzled because he had observed that class members had listened attentively
and agreed with the student's observations. It turned out that it was this very
agreement that the student interpreted as failure: Since no one had engaged
his ideas by arguing with him, he felt they had found them unworthy of
attention.

So one reason men speak in class more than women is that many of   13
them find the "public" classroom setting more conducive to speaking, whereas
most women are more comfortable speaking in private to a small group of
people they know well. A second reason is that men are more likely to be
comfortable with the debate-like form that discussion may take. Yet another
reason is the different attitudes toward speaking in class that typify women
and men.

Students who speak frequently in class, many of whom are men, assume   14
that it is their job to think of contributions and try to get the floor to express
them. But many women monitor their participation not only to get the floor
but to avoid getting it. Women students in my class tell me that if they have
spoken up once or twice, they hold back for the rest of the class because they

don't want to dominate. If they have spoken a lot one week, they will remain silent the next. These different ethics of participation are, of course, unstated, so those who speak freely assume that those who remain silent have nothing to say, and those who are reining themselves in assume that the big talkers are selfish and hoggish.

When I looked around my classes, I could see these differing ethics and 15 habits at work. For example, my graduate class in analyzing conversation had twenty students, eleven women and nine men. Of the men, four were foreign students: two Japanese, one Chinese, and one Syrian. With the exception of the three Asian men, all the men spoke in class at least occasionally. The biggest talker in the class was a woman, but there were also five women who never spoke at all, only one of whom was Japanese. I decided to try something different.

I broke the class into small groups to discuss the issues raised in the 16 readings and to analyze their own conversational transcripts. I devised three ways of dividing the students into groups: one by the degree program they were in, one by gender, and one by conversational style, as closely as I could guess it. This meant that when the class was grouped according to conversational style, I put Asian students together, fast talkers together, and quiet students together. The class split into groups six times during the semester, so they met in each grouping twice. I told students to regard the groups as examples of interactional data and to note the different ways in which they participated in the different groups. Toward the end of the term, I gave them a questionnaire asking about their class and group participation.

I could see plainly from my observation of the groups at work that 17 women who never opened their mouths in class were talking away in the small groups. In fact, the Japanese woman commented that she found it particularly hard to contribute to the all-woman group she was in because "I was overwhelmed by how talkative the female students were in the female-only group." This is particularly revealing because it highlights that the same person who can be "oppressed" into silence in one context can become the talkative "oppressor" in another. No one's conversational style is absolute; everyone's style changes in response to the context and others' styles.

Some of the students (seven) said they preferred the same-gender 18 groups; others preferred the same-style groups. In answer to the question

"Would you have liked to speak in class more than you did?" six of the seven who said yes were women; the one man was Japanese. Most startlingly, this response did not come only from quiet women; it came from women who had indicated they had spoken in class never, rarely, sometimes, and often. Of the eleven students who said the amount they had spoken was fine, seven were men. Of the four women who checked "fine," two added qualifications indicating it wasn't completely fine: One wrote in "maybe more," and one wrote, "I have an urge to participate often but feel I should have something more interesting/relevant/wonderful/intelligent to say!"

I counted my experiment a success. Everyone in the class found the 19
small groups interesting, and no one indicated he or she would have preferred that the class not break into groups. Perhaps most instructive, however, was the fact that the experience of breaking into groups, and of talking about participation in class, raised everyone's awareness about classroom participation. After we had talked about it, some of the quietest women in the class made a few voluntary contributions, though sometimes I had to insure their participation by interrupting the students who were exuberantly speaking out.

Americans are often proud that they discount the significance of cul- 20
tural differences: "We're all individuals," many people boast. Ignoring such issues as gender and ethnicity becomes a source of pride: "I treat everyone the same." But treating people the same is not equal treatment if they are not the same.

The classroom is a different environment for those who feel comfortable 21
putting themselves forward in a group than it is for those who find the prospect of doing so chastening, or even terrifying. When a professor asks, "Are there any questions?," students who can formulate statements the fastest have the greatest opportunity to respond. Those who need significant time to do so have not really been given a chance at all, since by the time they are ready to speak, someone else has taken the floor.

In a class where some students speak out without raising hands, those 22
who feel they must raise their hands and wait to be recognized do not have equal opportunity to speak. Telling them to feel free to jump in will not make them feel free; one's sense of timing, of one's rights and obligations in a classroom, are automatic, learned over years of interaction. They may be changed over time, with motivation and effort, but they cannot be changed on the

spot. And everyone assumes his or her own way is best. When I asked my students how the class could be changed to make it easier for them to speak more, the most talkative woman said she would prefer it if no one had to raise hands, and a foreign student said he wished people would raise their hands and wait to be recognized.

My experience in this class has convinced me that small-group interaction should be part of any class that is not a small seminar. I also am convinced that having the students become observers of their own interaction is a crucial part of their education. Talking about ways of talking in class makes students aware that their ways of talking affect other students, that the motivations they impute to others may not truly reflect others' motives, and that the behaviors they assume to be self-evidently right are not universal norms. 23

The goal of complete equal opportunity in class may not be attainable, but realizing that one monolithic classroom-participation structure is not equal opportunity is itself a powerful motivation to find more diverse methods to serve diverse students—and every classroom is diverse. 24

Stating why a comparison is important is discussed on p. 329.

FOR DISCUSSION

1. According to Deborah Tannen, speaking up in class is typically more "congenial" to whom, women or men (4)? What accounts for this difference, according to her **COMPARISON** of the "language experience" (4)?

2. Men, says Tannen, "ritualize opposition"; women don't (5). Why not? What is the difference, according to the authorities she cites, between how men fight and how women fight? Do you agree?

3. One of Tannen's colleagues teaches by asking students to read an article and then "tear it apart" (7). How does Tannen say this compares with the way she teaches?

4. Tannen **CONTRASTS** the "ethics of [class] participation" by men with those of women (14). What differences does she find? What are the consequences of their being "unstated" (14)?

5. In paragraph 18, Tannen presents the results of her questionnaire about class and group participation. What are some of those results? What do you think of her findings?

6. Tannen says that her research in the conversation of men and women caused her to change her classroom teaching strategies. What are some of the changes she made? How compelling do you find her reasons for making them?

STRATEGIES AND STRUCTURES

1. Tannen's title announces that she is comparing men and women on the basis of their classroom behavior. Where does she first indicate the aspects of behavior she will focus on? What are some of them?

2. This essay appeared in the *Chronicle of Higher Education*, a periodical read mostly by educators. How does Tannen tailor her essay to suit this **AUDIENCE**? How might this essay be different if she had written it for first-year college students?

3. In paragraph 13, Tannen sums up two of the points of comparison that she has previously made. What are they, and why do you think she summarizes them here? What new point of comparison does she then introduce, and how does she develop it in the next paragraph(s)?

4. "No one's conversational style is absolute," says Tannen; "everyone's style changes in response to the context and others' styles" (17). How does the **EXAMPLE** of the Japanese woman in her class illustrate the principle that people have different styles of conversation in different situations?

5. Tannen is advancing an **ARGUMENT** about equal opportunity in the classroom (24). What is her main point? How and how well does she support her position?

6. "I broke the class into small groups," says Tannen (16). Where else in her essay do you find Tannen introducing an **ANECDOTE**? How do the **NARRATIVE** elements in her essay support the comparison she is making?

WORDS AND FIGURES OF SPEECH

1. Roughly speaking, one's "sex" is biological while one's "gender" is not, or not entirely. Why do you think Tannen uses the second term rather than the first?

2. "Behavior" usually functions as a collective noun, as in the sentence "Their behavior last night was atrocious." Why do you suppose social scientists like Tannen often use the plural form, "behaviors," in their writing (23)?

3. Tannen's writing style is peppered with compound nouns and nouns used as adjectives—for example, "single-sex schools" and "sex-separate peer groups" (2, 3). Point out other expressions like these.

4. What is the meaning of the word "hierarchical" (3), and why does Tannen use it to refer to boys?

5. What is the difference between "ritual opposition" as Tannen uses the term and just plain opposition (5)? What other behaviors does Tannen cite that might be considered rituals?

FOR WRITING

1. How do Tannen's observations on gender in the classroom compare with your own? Make a list of specific classroom events and conversations you have observed that may (or may not) indicate differences in behavior based on gender identity.

2. In an essay comparing and contrasting specific **EXAMPLES** on your list, make the **ARGUMENT** that they do, in fact, confirm (or contradict) Tannen's claim that people talk and behave in substantially different ways according to their gender identities.

3. Tannen comments on the different ways, as she sees them, in which men and women use language to make friends. Write an essay comparing and contrasting your experiences in making friends with Tannen's. Give specific examples and include **ANECDOTES** (with dialogue) when possible.

R O B E R T   S A P O L S K Y

DUDE, WHERE'S MY FRONTAL CORTEX?

ROBERT SAPOLSKY (b. 1957) is a professor of biology and neurology at Stanford University and a research associate in primatology at the National Museums of Kenya. He grew up in New York City, the son of Orthodox Jewish parents who emigrated from the Soviet Union. Sapolsky taught himself to read Swahili, one of the major languages in Kenya, where he would later study the social behavior of baboons in the wild. He graduated from Harvard University with a major in biological anthropology, and earned a PhD from Rockefeller University in neuroendocrinology. Sapolsky's research, which focuses on the effects of stress on the brain, has been published in both academic studies—such as *Stress, the Aging Brain, and the Mechanisms of Neuron Death* (1992)—and more popular works, such as *Behave: The Biology of Humans at Our Best and Worst* (2017). "Dude, Where's My Frontal Cortex?" originally appeared in *Nautilus* magazine in 2014. It compares and contrasts (but mostly contrasts) the social and neurological behavior of young adult humans (and other primates) with that of persons who have survived to reach a 30th birthday.

I N THE FOOTHILLS OF THE SIERRA MOUNTAINS, a few hours east of San Fran-   1
cisco, are the Moaning Caverns, a cave system that begins, after a narrow,
twisting descent of 30-some feet, with an abrupt 180-foot drop. The Park Service has found ancient human skeletons at the bottom of the drop. Native
Americans living there at the time didn't make human sacrifices. Instead,
these explorers took one step too far in the gloom. The skeletons belonged to
adolescents. . . .

So adolescents are lousy at risk assessment and take more risks. But there's   2
more to the story of those skeletons in Moaning Caverns. It's not the case that
adolescents and adults have an equal desire to do the same dumb-ass thing,
and the sole difference is that the fully mature frontal cortex in the latter prevents them from doing so. Adolescents *feel* the allure of jumping off things.
Middle-aged adults just recklessly cheat on their diets. Adolescents not only
take more risks, they seek more novelty. . . .

These [novelty-seeking] traits are exacerbated when adolescents are   3
around peers. In one study, Laurence Steinberg of Temple University discovered that adolescents and adults, when left on their own, don't differ in the
risks they take in a driving simulator. Add peers egging them on and rates
don't budge in adults but become significantly higher in teens. When the
study is carried out in a brain scanner, the presence of peers (egging on by
intercom) lessens frontal cortical activity and enhances activity in the limbic
dopamine system in adolescents, but not in adults.

This teenage vulnerability to peer pressure is worsened by the fact that   4
such pressure rarely takes the form of hesitant adolescents coerced into
joining in the fun of committing random acts of kindness. Instead, pressure
disproportionately takes the form of "deviance training," increasing the likelihood of risky sexual behavior, poor health habits, substance abuse, and violence. As has been said, the greatest crime-fighting tool available to society is
a 30th birthday.

But adolescence isn't always as dark as it's made out to be. There's a feature of   5
adolescence that makes up for the stupid risk-taking and hideous
fashion decisions. And that's an adolescent's frenzied, agitated,
incandescent ability to feel someone else's pain, to feel the pains

Page 329 explains
when a single
important feature
can be *sufficient*
for drawing a
comparison.

of the entire world, to want to right all its wrongs. Adolescents are nature's most wondrous example of empathy, where the forcefulness of feeling as the other can border on nearly *being* the other.

This intensity is at the intersection of so many facets of adolescence. 6 With the highs higher and lows lower, the empathic pain scalds and the glow of having done the right thing makes it seem plausible that we are here for a purpose. Another factor is the openness to novelty. An open mind is a prerequisite for an open heart, and the adolescent hunger for the new readily presents opportunities to walk a mile in someone else's shoes. And there is the egoism of adolescence. There was a period during my late adolescence where I hung out with Quakers. They'd often say, "All God has is thee." This is God of limited means, not just a God who needs the help of humans to right a wrong, but who needs *your* help most of all. Egoism is tailor-made for adolescents. Throw in inexhaustible energy and the sense of omnipotence and it seems possible to make the world whole.

A few years ago, I saw a magnificent example of the empathy that a slug- 7 gish frontal cortex can produce in teenagers. My daughter is seriously into theater and at the time she was in a production of a superb, searing play about the Bosnian genocide, Stefanie Zadravec's *Honey Brown Eyes*. She played a 12-year-old Bosnian girl for whom things don't go so great, and whose life-or-death fate is ambiguous as the play ends.

Some high school kids had come to a performance as a group outing for 8 an English class. About halfway through the play, my daughter's character appears for the first time, cautiously emerging from a ventilation duct in her kitchen where she'd been hiding, unaware that the soldier who had just left the apartment after killing her mother was going to return. Up until that point, she had only been hinted at as a character. The soldier had his ethnic-cleansing to-do list of names of Bosnians in the building to kill, and kept demanding of the mother, "Where's your daughter? It says you have a daughter." "I don't have a daughter," the mother repeated up until her death. So as the girl begins to emerge from the ventilation duct, the realization sweeps through the audience: there is a daughter. As my daughter began to crawl out, the teenagers in the audience did something you're not supposed to do in a theater, something no adult with a developed frontal cortex would do. After a moment of hushed

When you're comparing two subjects, use examples that display their most important characteristics (p. 185).

silence, two or three voices called out, "No!" Another called, "Go back in, it's not safe!," another, "He's coming back!" After the play, the teenagers clustered around my little girl when she came out of the stage door, hugging her, reassuring themselves that both she and her character were OK.

This is the picture of adolescents with their hearts on their sleeves, limbic systems going full blast, and their frontal cortices straining to catch up with some emotional self-regulation. When I see the best of my university students in that agitated, optimistic state, I always have the same thought: It used to be so much easier to be like this. Having this adult frontal cortex of mine probably enables me to do good in a more efficacious, detached way. The trouble, though, is the same detachment makes it so much easier to decide that it's really not my problem.

So what is the adaptive advantage of human brain development evolving this way?

I think that the genetic program of brain development has evolved to help free the frontal cortex from the straightjacket of genes. If the frontal cortex is the last part of the brain to fully mature, it is by definition the brain region least shaped by that genome and most sculpted by experience. With each passing day, the frontal cortex is more the creation of what life has thrown at you, and thus who you become. . . .

Why is this [brain development during young adulthood] important? One answer comes from recent studies of intelligence in education. Some educators stress that a student's "emotional intelligence" or "social intelligence" (as measured various ways) is a better predictor of adult success and happiness than their IQ or SAT scores. It's all about social memory rather than memory of vocabulary words, about emotional perspective-taking, impulse control, empathy, ability to work with others, self-regulation.

There's a parallel in other primates, with their big, slow-maturing frontal cortexes. What makes a "successful" male baboon in a world of dominance interactions? Attaining a high rank is all about muscle, sharp canines, well-timed aggression. But once alpha status has been achieved, maintaining it is all about social smarts—which potential coalitions to form, which to stay away from, how to cow a rival through psychological intimidation, having sufficient impulse control to walk away from provocations, and avoiding displacing aggression onto everyone else when you're having a bad hair day. This is the realm where doing the right thing is often the harder thing, and adult life is filled with consequential forks in the road where intelligence lights the way forward.

This is all worth keeping in mind the next time you find yourself being   14
an adolescent, or dealing with one who has the volume up to 11 in every domain. Sure, adolescence has its down sides, but it has its abundant pluses— the inventiveness, the optimism, the empathy. Its biggest plus is that it allows the frontal cortex time to develop. There's no other way we could navigate the ever-increasing complexity of our social world.

FOR DISCUSSION

1. "Native Americans living there at the time didn't make human sacrifices" (1). Why does Robert Sapolsky include this curious bit of information in the opening paragraph of his essay?

2. What distinction, exactly, is Sapolsky making when he says, "Adolescents *feel* the allure of jumping off things. Middle-aged adults just recklessly cheat on their diets" (2)? Explain.

3. Peer pressure, says Sapolsky, seldom takes the form of urging people to commit "random acts of kindness" (4). What form *does* it usually take, in his view?

4. "An open mind is a prerequisite for an open heart" (6). What does Sapolsky mean by this statement? What particular characteristics of typical adolescent behavior does he have in mind; and how, according to him, do they work together to embody this principle?

5. For all its "stupid risk-taking and hideous fashion decisions," says Sapolsky, adolescence has many "pluses" (5, 14), one of the biggest of which is "that it allows the frontal cortex time to develop" (14). Why is this such a big deal? Explain.

STRATEGIES AND STRUCTURES

1. The question in Sapolsky's title would seem to be posed by a person whose frontal cortex is not yet fully developed. What is Sapolsky's implied answer to this **RHETORICAL QUESTION**, and to whom is he addressing it?

2. On what basis is Sapolsky **COMPARING AND CONTRASTING** the brains and behaviors of human primates? Are the differences significant enough to warrant study? Why or why not?

3. In the human brain, says Sapolsky, physical differences translate into social and behavioral differences. Which particular distinguishing characteristics does he emphasize, and where does he identify them most clearly and directly? Point to specific passages in the text.

4. What is the purpose of Sapolsky's reference to his daughter's performance in a play about "genocide" in Bosnia (7)? Is it an effective **EXAMPLE**? Why or why not?

5. "So what is the adaptive advantage of human brain development evolving this way?" (10) This is a question about **CAUSE AND EFFECT**. How does Sapolsky answer it, and how is his analysis related to the comparison he has been developing up to this point in his essay? Explain.

WORDS AND FIGURES OF SPEECH

1. Sapolsky might have titled his essay "Sir, Where's My Frontal Cortex?" Why do you think he chose "Dude" instead?

2. "Lousy" means, literally, "infested with lice" (2). Explain the **METAPHOR** in Sapolsky's description of risk assessment among teenagers. (Why, by the way, is focusing on fine points in a discussion sometimes called "nitpicking"?)

3. Sapolsky uses the term "egoism" instead of the more familiar "egotism" (6). What's the difference, and why might he have chosen one rather than the other?

4. Sapolsky refers to "adolescents with their hearts on their sleeves" (9). Explain the **METAPHOR** he is using here. Does this figure of speech enhance his comparison, or is it a **CLICHÉ**?

5. Figuratively speaking, what might constitute "a bad hair day" for a baboon (13)?

FOR WRITING

1. In a paragraph or two, define "adolescence" and compare and contrast it with "childhood," "early adulthood," or some other generally recognized stage of human development. Be sure to identify the main characteristics that distinguish one stage from the other.

2. *Adolescence* (1904), by the American psychologist G. Stanley Hall, was one of the first major studies of the teenage years as a distinct period in human life. Do some research on the field of developmental psychology, as pioneered by Hall and others, and write an essay on the concept of adolescence and how it grew.

3. For most of human history, children have been regarded as miniature adults. Look up images of babies in typical medieval paintings of Mary and Jesus, and in a critical essay, compare and contrast them with the somewhat later images of children in typical paintings from the Renaissance.

4. "Adaptive advantage" is a term from evolutionary biology (10). In a comparative essay, use this fundamental concept to explain how evolutionary biology both resembles and differs from other areas of study within the field of biology as a whole.

SOPHUS HELLE

LOVE ISN'T WHAT IT WAS

SOPHUS HELLE (b. 1993) is a scholar specializing in ancient literature. His research interests include authorship and early forms of writing such as cuneiform, the wedge-shaped characters inscribed on clay tablets in ancient cultures of the near East. In "Love Isn't What It Was," published in the digital magazine *Aeon* in 2019 and composed while he was a PhD student studying comparative literature at Aarhus University in Denmark, Helle writes about recent trends in animated film, but his focus is still on how stories are told. Comparing earlier Disney films like *Cinderella* (1950) and *Sleeping Beauty* (1959) with more recent ones like *Frozen* (2013) and *Moana* (2016), Helle finds that "the story arc" of a Disney tale is "the same as of old": we still expect Disney to deliver happy endings where true love prevails. However, the meaning of "love" in Disney films "has changed" in just the past few years, Helle writes. So has the meaning of "family."

L OVE, IN THE WORLD OF WALT DISNEY FILMS, has changed. Between *Tangled*   1
(2010) and *Moana* (2016), the ideal of heterosexual romance has been
dethroned by a new ideal: family love. The happy ending of our most-watched
childhood stories is no longer a kiss. Today, Disney films end with two siblings reconciled despite their differences, as in *Frozen* (2013); or a mother and
a daughter making amends, as in *Brave* (2012) and *Inside Out* (2015); or a child
reunited with long-lost parents, as in *Tangled, Finding Dory* (2016) and *Coco*
(2017). Love remains the all-important linchpin of these stories: love is supposed to bring us joy, solve our problems, and get us to our happy ending. We
are told to love love, for love will always save us in the end. But over the past
10 years, we have been told to love a new kind of love.

Today, Disney no longer expects us to expect a knight in shining armor,   2
but rather to forgive our siblings and make peace with our parents. Consider
the gulf that separates *Sleeping Beauty* (1959) from its remake *Maleficent* (2014).
Both are based on Charles Perrault's *La Belle au bois dormant* (1829), but in
Maleficent the story has been updated for the times. The princess is still told
that only a "true love's kiss" will end her magic sleep. The prince's lips, however, have now lost their power. We see him kiss the princess and the music
swells—and nothing happens. But when the fairy godmother then realizes her
mistake in cursing the princess and bends down to kiss her forehead in

On the left, Prince Phillip kisses Princess Aurora in Sleeping Beauty *(1959). On
the right, Maleficent kisses Aurora, her adopted daughter, in* Maleficent *(2014).*

remorse, she wakes. The story arc is still the same as of old, but the words "true love" now mean something new.

The tipping point was *Tangled*. There were intimations to be found already in   3
Finding Nemo (2003) and *Lilo and Stitch* (2002), but it was *Tangled* that first showed us how dramatic the shift away from romance would end up being. The plot pits the two forms of love against each other. One thread of the story is about Rapunzel's ambiguous relation with her adoptive parent, Mother Gothel, while the other is about her romance with the swashbuckling bandit Flynn Rider. At first, it seems as if romance wins the day. Rapunzel and Rider abscond, and Gothel falls to her death, leaving Rapunzel free to find her way home to her biological parents. But in the end, the romantic relationship that is supposed to be the center of the story falls curiously flat. Rider is just too perfect. His romance with Rapunzel is simple and light-hearted—sweet, but hardly the stuff of great passion. Rapunzel's bond with Gothel, on the other hand, is far more complex and far more interesting. The relation- ship is by turns abusive and nurturing, exploitative and caring, terrifying and funny, and all the more entertaining for the way it takes well-worn clichés about overprotective mothers and their teenage daughters, and turns them into the psychotic manipula- tions of an evil witch. With *Tangled*, romance might have won the battle, but it lost the war. Even if Gothel had to die in the end, she showed just how much narrative gold could be mined from family love.

Using parallel grammatical forms like this, p. 330, gives equal weight to your points of comparison.

It's not just the word "love" that has changed meaning over the past   4
10 years of Disney. The word "family" has done the same. Neither Mother Gothel nor the fairy godmother of *Maleficent* are the biological parents of the films' main characters, but they still end up taking emotional center-stage because the actual biological parents are either cruel and psychotic, as in *Maleficent*, or distant and idealized, as in *Tangled*. Parenthood is determined by one's emotional bonds. As a result, the very question of what counts as a "family" in Disney has become more ambiguous and more modern. In *Finding Dory*, an overjoyed Dory finally gets what she always wanted: a family. But that family is a rather patchwork affair, a mixture of biological, adoptive and indeterminate relations. The happily-ever-after scene includes Dory and her parents, but also Marlin, Dory's friend, surrogate brother and not-quite

romantic partner, as well as Marlin's son Nemo and a coterie of various friends and their relatives. Dory hasn't only found a nuclear family. She has crafted an extended family out of bits and pieces of emotional attachment.

It is not that older Disney films lacked adoptive families—on the contrary, the majority of the classics are populated by orphans and stepmothers. But crucially, films such as *Cinderella* (1950) hardwired our collective conception of step-parents as Bad News. For the main characters, living with a parent to whom they are not biologically related seems just a step short of a prison sentence. Biological parenthood was the golden ideal against which our orphaned heroine's fate could be held up as an unbearable misery. By contrast, in *Maleficent* and *Finding Dory*, living with adoptive parents or self-crafted families is not a misfortune for our heroines to overcome, but a happy ending for them to achieve. The shift toward family love has also made "family" a far more capacious concept. That is both the main advantage of this new development and, as it turns out, its most insidious threat. . . .

When you end a comparison, consider explaining its broader significance p. 75.

In the end, the question of what we see as true love is related to the question of who can be part of that "we." As *Frozen*'s cross-clipping between Elsa's and Anna's monologues reminds us, love and the state are flip sides of the same coin. Those who live in the same nation are expected to love that nation.

As a result, when the ideal of love changes, so does the relation between the state and its borders. It is not only that everyone in a community is expected to love that community, everyone is also expected to share a basic understanding of what it means to love—and if you don't, you can go live with the trolls. In *Frozen*, love draws the boundary between the nation that Elsa rules and the backward denizens of the forest outside it. Love separates those who are in the know from those who are left in the cold.

FOR DISCUSSION

1. By comparison with older Disney films, says Sophus Helle, newer ones define "love" differently. What are some of the main differences, in his view?

2. In older Disney films such as *Cinderella* (1950), says Helle, stepparents are "Bad News" (5). What do they do (or fail to do), according to him?

3. Helle notes that "what counts as a 'family' in Disney has become more ambiguous and more modern" (4). What assumptions is he making about the nature of modern families? How valid are those assumptions? Explain.

4. In *Tangled,* says Helle, "the romantic relationship that is supposed to be the center of the story falls curiously flat" (3). Why does Helle think the bond between Rapunzel and Mother Gothel is "far more interesting," by comparison, than the romantic relationship between the heroine and the traditional hero of the tale (3)?

5. According to Helle, why is Disney's redefining of true love as family love both an "advantage" and a "threat" (5)? What's so threatening about it?

STRATEGIES AND STRUCTURES

1. Helle compares and contrasts Disney films largely on the grounds of their narrative elements. Is this a valid basis of comparison? Why or why not?

2. In his introductory paragraph, Helle outlines the trajectory of his entire essay. Is this an effective strategy, or is he giving away too much of the "plot"? Explain.

3. "The tipping point was *Tangled*" (3). To what extent does this statement itself serve as a major point of transition in Helle's then-and-now comparison of Disney films, particularly that of *Sleeping Beauty* (1959) and the 2014 remake, *Maleficent*? Explain.

4. To support his **THESIS** about the changing nature of love and family in Disney, Helle summarizes the plots not only of *Tangled* but also of several other Disney films. Which events does he focus on? Why? Point to specific passages in the text.

5. Summarizing the plot of a narrative is not the same as analyzing it. In Helle's comparative analysis of various Disney films, how and how well does he go beyond mere plot summary to actually use this device in support of his **THESIS**? Explain.

WORDS AND FIGURES OF SPEECH

1. The title of Disney's *Tangled,* which is based on the Rapunzel story, is a reference to the heroine's long hair. Judging from Helle's description of the different "threads" of the story line, what else does the title refer to (3)? How so?

2. Helle's analysis hinges on the definitions (or redefinitions) of several key words. What are they, and how do the revised meanings compare with the old ones?

3. What is a "tipping point," and how appropriate is the phrase in a before-and-after (or then-and-now) comparison (3)? Explain.

4. "With *Tangled*," says Helle, "romance might have won the battle, but it lost the war" (3). Does the **METAPHOR** help to clarify the meaning of this statement, or is it a **CLICHÉ**? Explain.

5. What does Helle mean by "narrative gold" (3)? What other kinds of gold is he suggesting that Disney might spin from its updated fairy tales of love and family?

6. Classic Disney films, says Helle, do not lack "adoptive families" (5). What's the difference between an "adoptive" family or country and an "adopted" one?

FOR WRITING

1. Do some research on the story of *Sleeping Beauty* as composed by the French writer Charles Perrault (1628–1703); in a paragraph or two, write a summary of this version of the tale—or of Perrault's *Cinderella*, *Little Red Riding Hood*, or *Puss in Boots*.

2. In a critical analysis that goes well beyond plot summary, compare and contrast two classic versions of the same fairy tale by different authors (such as Perrault and the Grimm brothers); or compare and contrast two Disney versions of the same story from different eras (such as *Aladdin* in its original animated form and the 2019 live action remake).

3. In a critical analysis that goes well beyond plot summary, compare and contrast *Frozen* (2013) and *Frozen 2* (2019). With both films, be sure to discuss the issue of "love and the state" that Helle raises at the end of his essay (6).

⸎ 11 ⸎

DEFINITION

W HEN YOU DEFINE* something, you tell what it is—and what it is not—as in the following famous definitions:

Happiness is a warm puppy.
—CHARLES M. SCHULZ

Man is a biped without feathers.
—PLATO

Hope is the thing with feathers.
—EMILY DICKINSON

Golf is a good walk spoiled.
—MARK TWAIN

All of these model definitions, you'll notice, work in the same way. They place the thing to be defined (happiness, man, hope, golf) into a general class (puppy, biped, thing, walk) and then add characteristics (warm, without feathers, with feathers, spoiled) that distinguish it from others in the same class.

This is the kind of defining—by general class and characteristics—that dictionaries do. *The American Heritage Dictionary,* for example, defines the word "scepter" as "a staff held by a sovereign . . . as an emblem of authority." Here the general class is "staff," and the characteristics that differentiate it from other staffs—such as those carried by shepherds—are "held by a sovereign" and "as an emblem of authority."

* Words printed in SMALL CAPITALS are defined in the Glossary/Index.

371

The problem with a basic dictionary definition like this is that it often doesn't tell us everything we need to know. You might begin an essay with one, but you are not going to get very far with a topic unless you *extend* your definition. One way to give an extended definition is to name other similar items in the same category as the item you are defining.

Take the term "folklore," for example. A standard definition of "folklore" is "the study of traditional materials." This basic definition is not likely to enlighten anyone who is not already familiar with what those "materials" are, however. So one folklorist defines his field by listing a host of similar items that all belong to it:

> Folklore includes myths, legends, folktales, jokes, proverbs, riddles, chants, charms, blessings, curses, oaths, insults, retorts, taunts, teases, toasts, tongue-twisters, and greeting and leave-taking formulas (e.g., see you later, alligator). It also includes folk costumes, folk dance, folk drama (and mime), folk art, folk belief (or superstition), folk medicine, folk instrumental music (e.g., fiddle tunes), folksongs (e.g., lullabies, ballads), folk speech (e.g., to paint the town red), and names (e.g., nicknames and place names).
>
> —ALAN DUNDES, *The Study of Folklore*

Dundes's extended definition does not stop here; it goes on to include "latrinalia (writings on the walls of public bathrooms)," "envelope sealers (e.g., SWAK—Sealed With A Kiss)," "comments made after body emissions (e.g., after burps or sneezes)," and many others items that populate the field he is defining.

Another way to extend a basic definition is to specify additional characteristics of the item or idea you are defining. "Hydroponic tomatoes," for example, are tomatoes grown mostly in water. Food expert Raymond Sokolov further defines this kind of tomato as one that is "mass-produced, artificially ripened, mechanically picked, and long-hauled." "It has no taste," he says, "and it won't go splat" (all additional negative characteristics). "Organic tomatoes," by contrast, says Sokolov, are to be defined as tomatoes that are "squishable, blotchy, tart, and sometimes green-dappled."

Carla Hall extends the definition of "soul food" this way on p. 417.

To extend your definition further, you might give **SYNONYMS** for the word or concept you're defining, or trace its **ETYMOLOGY**, or word history. "Tomatoes," for example, are commonly defined as "vegetables," but an extended definition might point out that they are actually synonymous with "berries" or "fleshy fruits" and that they derive their name from the Nahuatl word *tomatl*. How do we know this last obscure fact? Because most standard dictionaries include etymologies along with basic definitions. Etymologies trace the origins of a word and sometimes can help organize an entire essay.

For example, here is the beginning of an essay by biologist Stephen Jay Gould on the concept of evolution:

> The exegesis [interpretation] of evolution as a concept has occupied the lifetimes of a thousand scientists. In this essay, I present something almost laughably narrow in comparison—an exegesis of the word itself. I shall trace how organic change came to be called *evolution*. The tale is complex and fascinating as a pure antiquarian exercise in etymological detection. But more is at stake, for a past usage of this word has contributed to the most common, current misunderstanding among laymen of what scientists mean by evolution.
>
> —STEPHEN JAY GOULD, *Ever Since Darwin*

The misunderstanding to which this paragraph refers is the idea that "evolution" means "progress." Among scientists, the term signifies simply "organic change," adaptation—without any implication of improvement.

Gould could make this point by tracing the history of evolution "as a concept"; but that might take another scientific lifetime, and he is only writing an essay. So he chooses the much narrower topic of tracing the origins of "the word itself." Following the etymology of a key term like this is an efficient way to reach a larger conclusion—in this case, the modern scientific understanding of evolution. And it can provide a road map for organizing the rest of an essay as a tale of "detection" that uncovers and explains how various related terms have been used in the past.

There is no set formula for writing good definitions, but there are some questions to keep in mind when you are working on one: What is the essential nature or main use of the thing you are defining? What are its distinguishing characteristics? How is it different from other things like it? And, perhaps most important, why do your readers need to know about it, and what point do you want to make?

A BRIEF GUIDE TO WRITING
A DEFINITION ESSAY

As you write a definition, you need to identify your subject, assign it to a general class, and specify particular characteristics that distinguish it from others in that same class—as novelist Michael Crichton does here:

> We're often told that happiness is an illusion, and some of us believe it, despite the experience of our own lives. Happiness is obviously not an illusion, because we've all felt it, not once but many times.
>
> —MICHAEL CRICHTON, "Happiness"

Crichton identifies the term he is defining (happiness), assigns it to a general class (realities), and specifies a particular characteristic ("we've all felt it") that distinguishes his subject from others like it (illusions that seem real but aren't).

Basic definitions like this can be useful in almost any kind of essay. To define a concept in depth, however, you will need to explain why you're defining it—Crichton's purpose in defining happiness is to explain how to achieve it—and to extend your definition by adding other distinguishing characteristics, by giving synonyms, and by tracing the etymology of key terms. The following guidelines will help you make these and other key moves of definition as you draft an essay.

Coming Up with a Subject

When you compose a definition essay, a good strategy is to look for a concept or term that you think has been defined incorrectly or inadequately—as Gould and Crichton do with "evolution" and "happiness"—or that is complex enough in meaning to leave room for discussion and debate. For example: What constitutes "racism" or "sexual harassment"? What characterizes "friendship"? What is "intelligent design"? Whatever term you choose, you will need to discover its essential characteristics (such as the trust and loyalty involved in friendship) and make a specific point about it.

Considering Your Purpose and Audience

When you define something, you may be conveying useful information, demonstrating that you understand the term's meaning, arguing for a particular definition, or just entertaining the reader. Keep your **PURPOSE** in mind as you construct your definition, and adapt the **TONE** of your essay accordingly—objective when you want to inform, persuasive when you are arguing, humorous when you want the reader to smile.

Also consider why your **AUDIENCE** might want (or be reluctant) to know more about your term and what it means. How might the reader already define the term? What information can you supply to make it easier for the reader to understand your definition or be more receptive to it? For example, a definition of "acid" in a lab manual for chemistry students would be considerably different from a definition of "acid" for readers of a cookbook. Whatever term you are defining, be sure to focus on those aspects of it that your audience is most likely to find interesting and useful.

Generating Ideas: Asking What Something Is—and Is Not

In order to define a term or concept, you need to know what its distinguishing characteristics are—what makes it different from other things in the same general class. For instance, suppose you wanted to define what a bodybuilder is. It might occur to you to say that bodybuilders are athletes who need to maintain a certain weight and to build up muscle strength. But these characteristics also apply to runners and swimmers. Among these three types of athletes, however, only bodybuilders train primarily for muscle definition and bulk. In other words, training for muscle definition and bulk is a characteristic that distinguishes bodybuilders from other athletes.

In "Blue-Collar Brilliance," p. 399, Mike Rose questions traditional definitions of intelligence.

Runners and swimmers need strong muscles, too, but what distinguishes them is their speed on the track or in the pool, characteristics that do *not* apply to bodybuilders. As you list the essential characteristics for your term, remember that definitions set up boundaries. They say, in effect: "This is the territory occupied by my concept, and everything outside these boundaries is something else."

Once you have identified the distinguishing characteristics for your term or concept, you can construct a basic definition of it—and then extend it from there. So a good basic definition of a bodybuilder might be "an athlete who trains primarily for muscle definition and bulk."

Templates for Defining

The following templates can help you generate ideas for a definition and then start drafting. Don't take these as formulas where you just have to fill in the blanks. There are no easy formulas for good writing. But these templates can help you plot out some of the key moves of definition and thus may serve as good starting points.

▶ In general, X can be defined as a kind of _____.

▶ What specifically distinguishes X from others in this category is _____.

▶ Other important distinguishing characteristics of X are _____, _____, and _____.

▶ X is often used to mean _____, but a better synonym would be _____ or _____.

▶ One way to define X is as the opposite of _____, the distinguishing characteristics of which are _____, _____, and _____.

▶ If we define X as _____, we can then define Y as _____.

▶ By defining X in this way, we can see that _____.

For more techniques to help you generate ideas and start writing effective definitions, see Chapter 3.

Stating Your Point

In any definition essay, you need to explain the point your definition is intended to make. A **THESIS STATEMENT**—usually in the introduction of your essay and perhaps reiterated with variations at the end—is a good way to do this. The following example is from an essay defining a farmer, written by Craig Schafer, a student at Ohio State who grew up on a farm in the Midwest: "By definition, a farmer is someone who tills the soil for a living, but I define a true farmer according to his or her attitudes toward the land." This is a good thesis statement because it defines the subject in an interesting way that may draw the reader in to the rest of the essay.

Adding Other Distinguishing Characteristics

Of all the ways you can extend a basic definition, perhaps the most effective is simply to specify additional characteristics that set your subject apart. To support his definition of a farmer as a person with certain attitudes toward the land, Schafer goes on to specify what those attitudes are, devoting a paragraph to each: A farmer is a born optimist, planting crops "with no assurances that nature will cooperate." A farmer is devoted to the soil, sifting it through the fingers and "sniffing the fresh clean aroma of a newly plowed field." A farmer is self-denying, with a barn that is often "more modern than the house." And so on. As you compose a definition essay, make sure you provide enough characteristics to identify your subject thoroughly and completely.

Using Synonyms and Etymologies

Another way to extend a definition is by offering **SYNONYMS**. For example, if you were defining "zine" for readers who are unfamiliar with the term, you might say that it is short for "magazine." You could then explain which characteristics of magazines apply to zines and which ones don't. Both zines and magazines, you might point out, include printed articles and artwork; but zines, unlike magazines, are typically self-published, are photocopied and bound by hand, have very small circulations and are rarely sold at newsstands, and include both original work and work appropriated from other sources.

Often you can extend the definition of a term by tracing its history, or **ETYMOLOGY**. This is what one engineer did when he asked: "Who are we who have been calling ourselves engineers since the early nineteenth century?" Here's part of his answer:

> The word *engineering* probably derives from the Latin word *ingeniatorum*. In 1325 a contriver of siege towers was called by the Norman word *engynours*. By 1420 the English were calling a trickster a *yngynore*. By 1592 we find the word *enginer* being given to a designer of phrases—a wordsmith.
>
> —JOHN H. LIENHARD, "The Polytechnic Legacy"

Knowing the history of a word and its variations can help you with a current definition. You can find the etymology of a word in most dictionaries.

EDITING FOR COMMON ERRORS IN DEFINITIONS

Like other kinds of writing, definitions use distinctive patterns of language and punctuation—and thus invite typical kinds of errors. The following tips will help you check for (and correct) these common errors in your own definitions.

Make sure that words referred to as words are in quotation marks or in italics and be consistent

- ▶ Often used as a synonym for "progress," says Gould, "evolution" simply means change.

- ▶ An expert in evolution, Gould defines the term *evolution* by explaining how it has been misused.

Be sure each basic definition includes the general class to which the term belongs

▶ Engineering <u>is a professional field that</u> applies science for practical purposes.

▶ A Thoroughbred is <u>a breed of horse</u> capable of racing at high speeds for long distances.

Without "professional field" and "breed of horse," the preceding sentences are statements about their subjects rather than definitions of them.

Check for common usage errors

IS WHERE, IS WHEN

Definitions that use "where" and "when" as general categories are not logically complete.

▶ Engineering is ~~where you put~~ <u>the practice of putting</u> science to use.

▶ A recession is ~~when~~ <u>the economic condition in which</u> both prices and sales go down.

COMPRISE, COMPOSE

"Comprise" means "to consist of." "Compose" means "to make up." The whole *comprises* the parts; the parts *compose* the whole.

▶ The federal government ~~composes~~ <u>comprises</u> three branches.

▶ Three branches ~~comprise~~ <u>compose</u> the federal government.

An Epitaph

When we define something (or someone), we identify its distinguishing characteristics. In this cartoon by Roz Chast, a frequent contributor to the *New Yorker*, the deceased's entire life is defined by his scores on a standardized test. Chast's purpose in penning the cartoon is to amuse the reader, but she is also making fun of overly narrow definitions. Test scores do not adequately define life—or death. For some people and institutions (such as college admissions offices), narrow definitions can run deep—too deep if they lose sight of the complexities of the person or thing they're defining. Like Mr. Jones's epitaph, good definitions require precision. But when constructing a definition, keep your (and the reader's) eye on the distinguishing features that actually give (or gave) life to your subject.

MATT TREACY

SHE

MATT TREACY is a media production specialist at the Virginia Department of Health Professions in Richmond. He has been a partner and engineer at production studios in Richmond and the manager of the nonprofit entertainment company Free Jambalaya, Inc. He wrote this essay in his Rhetoric 101 class at Hampden-Sydney College, a liberal arts college for men in Virginia. His teacher asked students to write about a person and to "create for your reader a sense not only of what or who the person is or was but also why the person should be of interest to your reader." Treacy writes of his mother, focusing on how she "always shingled lessons" into his mind, "leaving each one slightly raised for prying up later on."

She

Mom says, "If you go a day without using your hands, you die." It's a principle that influences the way I do things. Nothing is ever futile. The most horrible chores ever devised by the devil in the days of man do not even leave me with a gutted feeling anymore, though God knows they used to. Repainting a chicken shed or lying prostrate to the sun on a steel roof is never as bad as it sounds; you've used your hands, and at least *that's* worthwhile. My Mother has always shingled lessons into my mind, leaving each one slightly raised for prying up later on. There was never a day when we didn't do some meaningless household task just to pass the time. She always used her hands. On top of an adamant refusal to learn the first thing about technology, manual labor just fits her. She used her hands when She shot the groundhog who had one of her zucchinis in its mouth. She used her hands when crunching rabbits under the blunt end of a hatchet for some of the best stew in the Western hemisphere. She used her hands to hang the stockings, even when my sister and I knew better than to believe in a fat guy in a red suit. In the past I have questioned her claim of devotion to me, but there were always ethics to be spaded out of the dirt She was normally covered in, sandy values scraping the back of my neck during a rough hug before bed. Loving me is something She has always done, but with a sharp manner that hides the tenderness I sometimes cry for.

My Mother is not a woman so much as She is a field of energy. Mom is a force, a kind of aura that only takes human form to be that much more intimidating. An order

1

2

Defines the using-your-hands "principle" by giving EXAMPLES

Defines "My Mother" ("She") by saying what she is and what she is not

to cut the grass is not a request but an international doctrine, and She sits at the helm of an aircraft carrier just waiting for a rebellious child to give her reason for an atomic strike. Making us cut the grass is her method of control. There lies, somewhere beneath the tile of our kitchen, a proverbial bag of chores just waiting to be opened, like Pandora's Box. I am in constant fear that, one day, a refusal to mow will burst that bag wide open and spill hell into my life, so I do whatever I'm told. These responsibilities have become more of a tradition than a job, so I can't mind them; God forbid I break that custom. The sun bakes me like a scone on early August days, but smiles down on the Mother weeding eggplant, and the neighbors selling lemonade under an oak. She works like a madwoman in the garden, and still keeps an eye on whichever unlucky child has a job outside. When all is said and done, the yard has grown to the heavens, leaving me to give it the haircut of a lifetime under the omniscient eye from among the bean rows. It is a task that takes a light-year, but after three hours in the field I'll gladly accept the neighbor's lemonade, no matter what's floating in it. The common image is me standing at attention and She a drill sergeant inspecting my work, looking for any surviving dandelion to give me away. I imagine She would love to find a single uncut weed to justify beating the shag out of me with the garden hose. But then, smiling a smile that would have wilted the grass anyway, She goes to get a beer and watch me finish off the front yard.

There are some unexplainable phenomena between the two of us. These things I've grown accustomed to but have never understood. It's all to do with her. No one else

Ultimately, Treacy is
not only defining a
relationship but
saying "how weird"
it is

can really grasp just how weird our relationship is,
because no one else has ever gone through another like it.
The first clue that our mother-son bond was stronger
than most was the day I came home to a chaotic scene and
She immediately informed me, "Way to go baby, you let
the emu out." That night I did homework in electrified
silence, forcing down home-grown garden squash and
awaiting her return. Finally the door screamed and I prepared for a verbal thrashing only to be greeted with a hug.
Everything was forgotten. The homework lay strewn on
the table and the snow fell as She unfolded a story that
would eventually go down in family lore. It was not a
story like the boring epics that college professors pride
themselves on, but a *story*. It was like something told by
five different people at Thanksgiving with sporadic inter-
jections thrown in through mouthfuls of mashed potatoes
and venison. There was a plot line, rising action, a climax,
blood, and plenty of cursing. By the time She finished and
I had chewed my lip raw, the escaped emu had been recap-
tured somehow by a turkey call and something resem-
bling a German infantry tactic. I sat there in awe,
swallowing repeatedly to wet my vocal cords back into
coherence. "That's the most incredible thing I've ever
heard," I managed to gasp, unable to get the image of my
Mom pulling a tackle on a bird from the Cretaceous
period out of my mind. The amount of respect She lost
for me that night was more than made up by my amazement and overwhelming love for this woman who brought
down ostriches. Even being sentenced to double grass-
cutting duty and cooking for a week didn't really sting
that much. After all, I'd be using my hands.

Uses story of
escaped emu to
explain what a
NARRATIVE is and
how to tell one

So many times She would ruin my chances for fun. So 4
many times I was caught when it seemed I could not be,
and so many times I would be forced to dry dishes instead
of climbing hay bales in the fields. Of course there will
always be hay, and there will always be home. She will
always be there weeping me away to college and willing
me back with that same aura of power that surrounds her.
Each time I will argue, but apparently dishes will never
just dry themselves. And each time that I think I'm too
tired to get up and turn off the dorm room TV, I will
think of my Mother and stumble over in the pitch black to
use my hands at least one more time that day.

Concludes by returning to the basic principle of using your hands as defined at the essay's beginning

TANYA MARIA BARRIENTOS

SE HABLA ESPAÑOL

T<small>ANYA</small> M<small>ARIA</small> B<small>ARRIENTOS</small> (b. 1960) is a novelist, a former columnist for the *Philadelphia Inquirer*, and presently a communications director at the Robert Wood Johnson Foundation. With a journalism degree from the University of Missouri, she is the author of the novels *Frontera Street* (2002) and *Family Resemblance* (2003). "Se Habla Español" was first published in the bilingual magazine *Latina* (2004). Her title refers to the sign, often seen in store windows, announcing that "Spanish is spoken" here. In this essay, Barrientos raises a basic question of self-definition and ethnic identity: Can a woman born in Guatemala who grew up in the United States speaking English instead of Spanish be legitimately considered Latina?

T<small>HE MAN ON THE OTHER END OF THE PHONE LINE</small> is telling me the classes 1
I've called about are first-rate: native speakers in charge, no more than six students per group. I tell him that will be fine and yes, I've studied a bit of Spanish in the past. He asks for my name and I supply it, rolling the double "r" in "Barrientos" like a pro. That's when I hear the silent snag, the momentary

hesitation I've come to expect at this part of the exchange. Should I go into it again? Should I explain, the way I have to half a dozen others, that I am Guatemalan by birth but *pura gringa*[1] by circumstance?

This will be the sixth time I've signed up to learn the language my parents speak to each other. It will be the sixth time I've bought workbooks and notebooks and textbooks listing 501 conjugated verbs in alphabetical order, in hopes that the subjunctive tense will finally take root in my mind. In class I will sit across a table from the "native speaker," who will wonder what to make of me. "Look," I'll want to say (but never do). "Forget the dark skin. Ignore the obsidian eyes. Pretend I'm a pink-cheeked, blue-eyed blonde whose name tag says 'Shannon.'" Because that is what a person who doesn't innately know the difference between *corre, corra,* and *corrí*[2] is supposed to look like, isn't it?

> Asking what something is—or is not— is a key step in defining it, p. 375.

I came to the United States in 1963 at age three with my family and immediately stopped speaking Spanish. College-educated and seamlessly bilingual when they settled in west Texas, my parents (a psychology professor and an artist) wholeheartedly embraced the notion of the American melting pot. They declared that their two children would speak nothing but *inglés.* They'd read in English, write in English, and fit into Anglo society beautifully.

It sounds politically incorrect now. But America was not a hyphenated nation back them. People who called themselves Mexican Americans or Afro Americans were considered dangerous radicals, while law-abiding citizens were expected to drop their cultural baggage at the border and erase any lingering ethnic traits.

To be honest, for most of my childhood I liked being the brown girl who defied expectations. When I was seven, my mother returned my older brother and me to elementary school one week after the school year had already begun. We'd been on vacation in Washington, D.C., visiting the Smithsonian, the Capitol, and the home of Edgar Allan Poe. In the Volkswagen on the way home, I'd memorized "The Raven," and I would recite it with melodramatic

---

1. Completely non-Latina. *Pura* is Spanish for "pure"; *gringa,* the feminine form of *gringo,* is used to refer to someone of non-Latina background.
2. Verb forms of "run."

flair to any poor soul duped into sitting through my performance. At the school's office, the registrar frowned when we arrived.

"You people. Your children are always behind, and you have the nerve to 6 bring them in late?"

"My children," my mother answered in a clear, curt tone, "will be at the 7 top of their classes in two weeks."

The registrar filed our cards, shaking her head.   8

I did not live in a neighborhood with other Latinos, and the public school 9 I attended attracted very few. I saw the world through the clear, cruel vision of a child. To me, speaking Spanish translated into being poor. It meant waiting tables and cleaning hotel rooms. It meant being left off the cheerleading squad and receiving a condescending smile from the guidance counselor when you said you planned on becoming a lawyer or a doctor. My best friends' names were Heidi and Leslie and Kim. They told me I didn't seem "Mexican" to them, and I took it as a compliment. I enjoyed looking into the faces of Latino store clerks and waitresses and, yes, even our maid and saying *"Yo no hablo español."*[3] It made me feel superior. It made me feel American. It made me feel white. I thought if I stayed away from Spanish, stereotypes would stay away from me.

Then came the backlash. During the two decades when I'd worked hard 10 to isolate myself from the stereotype I'd constructed in my own head, society shifted. The nation changed its views on ethnic identity. College professors started teaching history through African American and Native American eyes. Children were told to forget about the melting pot and picture America as a multicolored quilt instead. Hyphens suddenly had muscle, and I was left wondering where I fit in.

John McWhorter explains how definitions become stereotypes on p. 221.

The Spanish language was supposedly the glue that held the new Latino 11 community together. But in my case it was what kept me apart. I felt awkward among groups whose conversations flowed in and out of Spanish. I'd be asked a question in Spanish and I'd have to answer in English, knowing this raised a mountain of questions. I wanted to call myself Latina, to finally take pride, but it felt like a lie. So I set out to learn the language that people assumed I already knew.

3. I don't speak Spanish.

After my first set of lessons, I could function in the present tense. *"Hola,* 12
Paco. ¿Qué tal? ¿Qué color es tu cuaderno? El mío es azul."[4] My vocabulary built
quickly, but when I spoke, my tongue felt thick inside my mouth—and if I
needed to deal with anything in the future or the past, I was sunk. I enrolled
in a three-month submersion program in Mexico and emerged able to speak
like a sixth-grader with a solid C average. I could read Gabriel García Márquez[5]
with a Spanish-English dictionary at my elbow, and I could follow 90 percent
of the melodrama on any given telenovela.[6] But true speakers discover my
limitations the moment I stumble over a difficult construction, and that is
when I get the look. The one that raises the wall between us. The one that
makes me think I'll never really belong. Spanish has become a litmus test
showing how far from your roots you've strayed.

My bilingual friends say I make too much of it. They tell me that my 13
Guatemalan heritage and unmistakable Mayan features are enough to legiti-
mize my membership in the Latin American club. After all, not all Poles speak
Polish. Not all Italians speak Italian. And as this nation grows more and more
Hispanic, not all Latinos will share one language. But I don't believe them.

There must be other Latinas like me. But I haven't met any. Or, I should 14
say, I haven't met any who have fessed up. Maybe they are secretly struggling
to fit in, the same way I am. Maybe they are hiring tutors and listening to
tapes behind locked doors, just like me. I wish we all had the courage to come
out of our hiding places and claim our rightful spot in the broad Latino spectrum. Without being called hopeless gringas. Without having to offer apologies or show remorse.

If it will help, I will go first. 15
Aquí estoy.[7] Spanish-challenged and *pura* Latina. 16

---

4. Hello, Paco. How are you? What color is your notebook? Mine is blue.
5. Colombian novelist and short-story writer (1928–2014).
6. Spanish-language TV soap opera.
7. Here I am.

FOR DISCUSSION

1. Tanya Maria Barrientos is not a native speaker of Spanish, though both of her parents were. Why didn't they encourage her to learn the language as a child? Should they have? Why or why not?

2. According to Barrientos, how were "hyphenated" Americans DEFINED when she and her family first came to the United States from Guatemala in 1963 (4)? How did young Barrientos define Latinos who spoke Spanish?

3. In the decades following her arrival in the United States, says Barrientos, societal views toward ethnic identity "shifted" (10). What are some of the more significant aspects of that shift, according to Barrientos?

4. In your opinion, is Barrientos a legitimate member of "the Latin American club" (13)? That is, can she and others with similar backgrounds rightfully define themselves as Latinas or Latinos? Why or why not?

STRATEGIES AND STRUCTURES

1. What is Barrientos's PURPOSE in "Se Habla Español"? To explain why she does not speak Spanish with the fluency of a native speaker? To persuade readers that she is a true Latina? To define the ambiguous condition of being both "Spanish-challenged and *pura* Latina" (16)? Explain.

2. Is Barrientos's essay aimed mainly at a multilingual AUDIENCE or a largely English-speaking one? Why do you think so?

3. How does Barrientos use the Spanish language itself to help define who and what she is? Give several examples that you find particularly effective.

4. Where and how does Barrientos construct a stereotypical definition of "Latin American"? Where and how does she reveal the shortcomings of this definition?

5. Barrientos's essay includes many NARRATIVE elements. What are some of them, and how do they help her to define herself and her condition?

WORDS AND FIGURES OF SPEECH

1. Once defined as a "melting pot," the United States, says Barrientos, is now a "multicolored quilt" (10). What are some of the implications of this shift in METAPHORS for national diversity?

2. When Barrientos refers to the Spanish language as "glue," is she avoiding CLI-CHÉS or getting stuck in one (11)? Explain.

3. In printing, a *stereotype* was a cast metal plate used to reproduce blocks of type or crude images. How does this early meaning of the term carry over into the modern definition as Barrientos uses it (10)?

4. Barrientos sometimes groups herself with other "Latinos," sometimes with other "Latinas" (9, 14). Why the difference? If this essay were written today, could she have used "Latinx" instead of either? Why or why not?

FOR WRITING

1. Write a paragraph or two about an incident in which someone defined you on the basis of your choice of words, your accent, or some other aspect of your speech or appearance.

2. Write an essay about your experience learning, or attempting to learn, a language other than your native tongue—and how that experience affected your own self-definition or cultural identity.

GEETA KOTHARI

IF YOU ARE WHAT YOU EAT, THEN WHAT AM I?

GEETA KOTHARI (b. 1962) is the nonfiction editor of the *Kenyon Review* and director of the Writing Center at the University of Pittsburgh. She is the editor of *Did My Mama Like to Dance? and Other Stories about Mothers and Daughters* (1994). Her stories and essays have appeared in various newspapers and journals, including the *Toronto South Asian Review* and the *Kenyon Review,* from which these complete sections of a longer article are taken. Kothari's essay (1999) presents a problem in personal definition. The Indian food she eats, says Kothari, is not really Indian like her mother's; nor is the American food she eats really American like her husband's. So, Kothari wonders, if we are defined by what we eat—and the culture it represents—how are she and her culture to be defined?

> To belong is to understand the tacit codes of the people you live with.
>
> —MICHAEL IGNATIEFF, *Blood and Belonging*

THE FIRST TIME MY MOTHER AND I OPEN A CAN OF TUNA, I am nine years 　1
old. We stand in the doorway of the kitchen, in semidarkness, the can tilted toward daylight. I want to eat what the kids at school eat: bologna, hot dogs, salami—foods my parents find repugnant because they contain pork and meat byproducts, crushed bone and hair glued together by chemicals and fat. Although she has never been able to tolerate the smell of fish, my mother buys the tuna, hoping to satisfy my longing for American food.

Indians, of course, do not eat such things. 　2

The tuna smells fishy, which surprises me because I can't remember 　3
anyone's tuna sandwich actually smelling like fish. And the tuna in those sandwiches doesn't look like this, pink and shiny, like an internal organ. In fact, this looks similar to the bad foods my mother doesn't want me to eat. She is silent, holding her face away from the can while peering into it like a half-blind bird.

For a good definition of the bad foods Kothari's mother has in mind, Lee's essay on p. 121–24.

"What's wrong with it?" I ask. 　4

She has no idea. My mother does not know that the tuna everyone else's 　5
mothers made for them was tuna *salad*.

"Do you think it's botulism?" 　6

I have never seen botulism, but I have read about it, just as I have read 　7
about but never eaten steak and kidney pie.

There is so much my parents don't know. They are not like other par- 　8
ents, and they disappoint me and my sister. They are supposed to help us negotiate the world outside, teach us the signs, the clues to proper behavior: what to eat and how to eat it.

We have expectations, and my parents fail to meet them, especially my 　9
mother, who works full-time. I don't understand what it means, to have a mother who works outside and inside the home; I notice only the ways in which she disappoints me. She doesn't show up for school plays. She doesn't make chocolate-frosted cupcakes for my class. At night, if I want her attention,

I have to sit in the kitchen and talk to her while she cooks the evening meal, attentive to every third or fourth word I say.

We throw the tuna away. This time my mother is disappointed. I go to   10
school with tuna eaters. I see their sandwiches, yet cannot explain the discrepancy between them and the stinking, oily fish in my mother's hand. We do not understand so many things, my mother and I.

When we visit our relatives in India, food prepared outside the house is care-   11
fully monitored. In the hot, sticky monsoon months in New Delhi and Bombay, we cannot eat ice cream, salad, cold food, or any fruit that can't be peeled. Definitely no meat. People die from amoebic dysentery, unexplained fevers, strange boils on their bodies. We drink boiled water only, no ice. No sweets except for jalebi, thin fried twists of dough in dripping hot sugar syrup. If we're caught outside with nothing to drink, Fanta, Limca, Thums Up (after Coca-Cola is thrown out by Mrs. Gandhi[1]) will do. Hot tea sweetened with sugar, served with thick creamy buffalo milk, is preferable. It should be boiled, to kill the germs on the cup.

My mother talks about "back home" as a safe place, a silk cocoon frozen   12
in time where we are sheltered by family and friends. Back home, my sister

"When" or "where" are often used in informal definitions, but see p. 379 for advice on doing so correctly.

and I do not argue about food with my parents. Home is where they know all the rules. We trust them to guide us safely through the maze of city streets for which they have no map, and we trust them to feed and take care of us, the way parents should.

Finally, though, one of us will get sick, hungry for the food we see our   13
cousins and friends eating, too thirsty to ask for a straw, too polite to insist on properly boiled water.

At my uncle's diner in New Delhi, someone hands me a plate of aloo tikki,   14
fried potato patties filled with mashed channa dal and served with a sweet and a sour chutney. The channa, mixed with hot chilies and spices, burns my tongue and throat. I reach for my Fanta, discard the paper straw, and gulp the sweet orange soda down, huge drafts that sting rather than soothe.

---

1. Coca-Cola was banned in India for 20 years beginning in the mid-1970s, when Indira Gandhi was prime minister, because the company would not reveal its formula to the government. Fanta, Limca, and Thums Up are other soft drinks popular in India.

When I throw up later that day (or is it the next morning, when a stom-   15
achache wakes me from deep sleep?), I cry over the frustration of being sin-
gled out, not from the pain my mother assumes I'm feeling as she holds my
hair back from my face. The taste of orange lingers in my mouth, and I remember my lips touching the cold glass of the Fanta bottle.

At that moment, more than anything, I want to be like my cousins.   16

In New York, at the first Indian restaurant in our neighborhood, my father   17
orders with confidence, and my sister and I play with the silverware until the
steaming plates of lamb biryani arrive.

What is Indian food? my friends ask, their noses crinkling up.   18

Later, this restaurant is run out of business by the new Indo-Pak-   19
Bangladeshi combinations up and down the street, which serve similar food.
They use plastic cutlery and Styrofoam cups. They do not distinguish between
North and South Indian cooking, or between Indian, Pakistani, and Bangladeshi cooking, and their customers do not care. The food is fast, cheap, and
tasty. Dosa, a rice flour crepe stuffed with masala potato, appears on the same
trays as chicken makhani.

Now my friends want to know, Do you eat curry at home?   20

One time my mother makes lamb vindaloo for guests. Like dosa, this is   21
a South Indian dish, one that my Punjabi[2] mother has to learn from a cookbook. For us, she cooks everyday food—yellow dal, rice, chapati, bhaji. Lentils,
rice, bread, and vegetables. She has never referred to anything on our table as
"curry" or "curried," but I know she has made chicken curry for guests. Vindaloo, she explains, is a curry too. I understand then that curry is a dish created for guests, outsiders, a food for people who eat in restaurants.

I look around my boyfriend's freezer one day and find meat: pork chops, ground   22
beef, chicken pieces, Italian sausage. Ham in the refrigerator, next to the home-
made bolognese sauce. Tupperware filled with chili made from ground beef and
pork.

He smells different from me. Foreign. Strange.   23

I marry him anyway.   24

2. Native of the state of Punjab, in northern India.

He has inherited blue eyes that turn gray in bad weather, light brown   25
hair, a sharp pointy nose, and excellent teeth. He learns to make chili with
ground turkey and tofu, tomato sauce with red wine and portobello mush-
rooms, roast chicken with rosemary and slivers of garlic under the skin.

He eats steak when we are in separate cities, roast beef at his mother's   26
house, hamburgers at work. Sometimes I smell them on his skin. I hope he
doesn't notice me turning my face, a cheek instead of my lips, my nose wrinkled at the unfamiliar, musky smell.

I have inherited brown eyes, black hair, a long nose with a crooked bridge, and   27
soft teeth with thin enamel. I am in my twenties, moving to a city far from my
parents, before it occurs to me that jeera, the spice my sister avoids, must
have an English name. I have to learn that haldi = turmeric, methi = fenugreek.
What to make with fenugreek, I do not know. My grandmother used to make
methi roti for our breakfast, cornbread with fresh fenugreek leaves served
with a lump of homemade butter. No one makes it now that she's gone, though
once in a while my mother will get a craving for it and produce a facsimile
("The cornmeal here is wrong") that only highlights what she's really missing:
the smells and tastes of her mother's house.

I will never make my grandmother's methi roti or even my mother's unsat-   28
isfactory imitation of it. I attempt chapati; it takes six hours, three phone calls
home, and leaves me with an aching back. I have to write translations down:
jeera = cumin. My memory is unreliable. But I have always known garam = hot.

If I really want to make myself sick, I worry that my husband will one   29
day leave me for a meat-eater, for someone familiar who doesn't sniff him
suspiciously for signs of alimentary infidelity.

Indians eat lentils. I understand this as absolute, a decree from an   30
unidentifiable authority that watches and judges me.

So what does it mean that I cannot replicate my mother's dal? She and   31
my father show me repeatedly, in their kitchen, in my kitchen. They coach me
over the phone, buy me the best cookbooks, and finally write down their
secrets. Things I'm supposed to know but don't. Recipes that should be, by
now, engraved on my heart.

Living far from the comfort of people who require no explanation for   32
what I do and who I am, I crave the foods we have shared. My mother con-

vinces me that moong is the easiest dal[3] to prepare, and yet it fails me every time: bland, watery, a sickly greenish yellow mush. These imperfect imitations remind me only of what I'm missing.

But I have never been fond of moong dal. At my mother's table it is the 33 last thing I reach for. Now I worry that this antipathy toward dal signals something deeper, that somehow I am not my parents' daughter, not Indian, and because I cannot bear the touch and smell of raw meat, though I can eat it cooked (charred, dry, and overdone), I am not American either.

I worry about a lifetime purgatory in Indian restaurants where I will 34 complain that all the food looks and tastes the same because they've used the same masala.

FOR DISCUSSION

1. How does Geeta Kothari DEFINE "meat byproducts" (1)? Why is she so concerned with different kinds of food? Who or what is she trying to define?

2. How do Kothari and her mother define "back home" in paragraph 12?

3. Why is Kothari angry with herself in paragraphs 15 and 16? What "rule" has she momentarily forgotten?

4. Kothari's friends ask for a definition of Indian food in paragraph 18. How does she answer them (and us)?

5. What's wrong, from Kothari's POINT OF VIEW, with the "Indo-Pak-Bangladeshi" restaurants that spring up in her neighborhood (19)?

6. Marriage is an important event in anyone's biography, but why is it especially central in Kothari's case?

STRATEGIES AND STRUCTURES

1. How does Kothari go about answering the definition question that she raises in her title? Give specific examples of her strategy. What point is she making in answering this question?

2. Why does Kothari recall the tuna incident in paragraphs 1 through 10? What does this ANECDOTE illustrate about her relationship with her mother? About her "Americanness"?

---

3. *Dal* is a common Indian dish made by simmering lentils—as with *moong* (or yellow) *dal*—or dried beans, peas, or other legumes.

3. Why does Kothari introduce the matter of heredity in paragraphs 25 and 27? How do these paragraphs anticipate the reference to "something deeper" in paragraph 33?

4. According to Kothari, is culture something we inherit or something we learn? How do paragraphs 31 and 32 contribute to her definition of culture?

5. Kothari's essay is largely made up of specific EXAMPLES, particularly culinary ones. How do they relate to the matters of personal and cultural identity she is defining? Should she have made these connections more explicit? Why?

WORDS AND FIGURES OF SPEECH

1. What is usually meant by the saying "You are what you eat"? How is Kothari interpreting this adage?

2. What does Kothari mean by "alimentary infidelity" (29)? What ANALOGY is she drawing here?

3. What is "purgatory" (34)? Why does Kothari end her essay with a reference to it?

4. *Synecdoche* is the FIGURE OF SPEECH that substitutes a part for the whole. What part does Kothari substitute for what whole when she uses the phrase "meat-eater" (29)? How important is synecdoche throughout her entire essay? Explain.

5. Kothari provides both the Indian word and its English equivalent for several terms in her essay—"garam" for "hot" in paragraph 28, for example. Why? What do these translations contribute to her definition of cultural identity? Point out several other examples in the text.

FOR WRITING

1. Write an extended definition of your favorite type of food. Be sure to relate how your food and food customs help to define who you are.

2. Food and food customs are often regional, as Kothari points out. Write an essay in which you define one of the following: New England, Southern, or Midwestern cooking; California cuisine; Tex-Mex, French, or Chinese food; fast food; or some other distinctive cuisine.

3. Write an essay about food and eating in your neighborhood. Use the food customs of specific individuals and groups to help define them—personally, ethnically, socially, or in some other way.

MIKE ROSE

BLUE-COLLAR BRILLIANCE

MIKE ROSE (b. 1944) is a professor of social research methodology in the UCLA Graduate School of Education and Information Studies. When he was seven, Rose moved with his parents from Altoona, Pennsylvania, to Los Angeles, where his mother worked as a waitress, and he "watched the cooks and waitresses and listened to what they said." After graduating from Loyola University, Rose earned advanced degrees from the University of Southern California and UCLA. His books on language, literacy, and cognition include *The Mind at Work: Valuing the Intelligence of the American Worker* (2004) and *Back to School: Second Chances at Higher Ed* (2012). Based on years of teaching and close observations of the workplace, Rose is convinced that people can be smart in many different ways. In "Blue-Collar Brilliance," from the *American Scholar* (2009), he offers a definition of intelligence that does not separate the mind from the body—a shortcoming, in his view, of more conventional definitions.

•>───<•

M Y MOTHER, ROSE MERAGLIO ROSE (ROSIE), shaped her adult identity as a waitress in coffee shops and family restaurants. When I was growing up in Los Angeles during the 1950s, my father and I would occasionally hang

1

out at the restaurant until her shift ended, and then we'd ride the bus home with her. Sometimes she worked the register and the counter, and we sat there; when she waited booths and tables, we found a booth in the back where the waitresses took their breaks.

There wasn't much for a child to do at the restaurants, and so as the hours stretched out, I watched the cooks and waitresses and listened to what they said. At mealtimes, the pace of the kitchen staff and the din from customers picked up. Weaving in and out around the room, waitresses warned *behind you* in impassive but urgent voices. Standing at the service window facing the kitchen, they called out abbreviated orders. *Fry four on two,* my mother would say as she clipped a check onto the metal wheel. Her tables were *deuces, four-tops,* or *six-tops* according to their size; seating areas also were nicknamed. The *racetrack,* for instance, was the fast-turnover front section. Lingo conferred authority and signaled know-how.

Rosie took customers' orders, pencil poised over pad, while fielding questions about the food. She walked full tilt through the room with plates stretching up her left arm and two cups of coffee somehow cradled in her right hand. She stood at a table or booth and removed a plate for this person, another for that person, then another, remembering who had the hamburger, who had the fried shrimp, almost always getting it right. She would haggle with the cook about a returned order and rush by us, saying, *He gave me lip, but I got him.* She'd take a minute to flop down in the booth next to my father. *I'm all in,* she'd say, and whisper something about a customer. Gripping the outer edge of the table with one hand, she'd watch the room and note, in the flow of our conversation, who needed a refill, whose order was taking longer to prepare than it should, who was finishing up.

I couldn't have put it in words when I was growing up, but what I observed in my mother's restaurant defined the world of adults, a place where competence was synonymous with physical work. I've since studied the working habits of blue-collar workers and have come to understand how much my mother's kind of work demands of both body and brain. A waitress acquires knowledge and intuition about the ways and the rhythms of the restaurant business. Waiting on seven to nine tables, each with two to six customers, Rosie devised memory strategies so that she could remember who ordered what. And because she knew the

Page 377 offers advice on using synonyms to start a definition.

2

3

4

average time it took to prepare different dishes, she could monitor an order that was taking too long at the service station.

Like anyone who is effective at physical work, my mother learned *to work smart*, as she put it, *to make every move count*. She'd sequence and group tasks: What could she do first, then second, then third as she circled through her station? What tasks could be clustered? She did everything on the fly, and when problems arose—technical or human—she solved them within the flow of work, while taking into account the emotional state of her co-workers. Was the manager in a good mood? Did the cook wake up on the wrong side of the bed? If so, how could she make an extra request or effectively return an order?

And then, of course, there were the customers who entered the restaurant with all sorts of needs, from physiological ones, including the emotions that accompany hunger, to a sometimes complicated desire for human contact. Her tip depended on how well she responded to these needs, and so she became adept at reading social cues and managing feelings, both the customers' and her own. No wonder, then, that Rosie was intrigued by psychology. The restaurant became the place where she studied human behavior, puzzling over the problems of her regular customers and refining her ability to deal with people in a difficult world. She took pride in *being among the public*, she'd say. *There isn't a day that goes by in the restaurant that you don't learn something.*

My mother quit school in the seventh grade to help raise her brothers and sisters. Some of those siblings made it through high school, and some dropped out to find work in railroad yards, factories, or restaurants. My father finished a grade or two in primary school in Italy and never darkened the schoolhouse door again. I didn't do well in school, either. By high school I had accumulated a spotty academic record and many hours of hazy disaffection. I spent a few years on the vocational track, but in my senior year I was inspired by my English teacher and managed to squeak into a small college on probation.

My freshman year was academically bumpy, but gradually I began to see formal education as a means of fulfillment and as a road toward making a living. I studied the humanities and later the social and psychological sciences and taught for ten years in a range of situations—elementary school, adult education courses, tutoring centers, a program for Vietnam veterans who wanted to go to college. Those students had socioeconomic and educational

Rosie solved technical and human problems on the fly.

backgrounds similar to mine. Then I went back to graduate school to study education and cognitive psychology and eventually became a faculty member in a school of education.

Intelligence is closely associated with formal education—the type of 9 schooling a person has, how much and how long—and most people seem to move comfortably from that notion to a belief that work requiring less schooling requires less intelligence. These assumptions run through our cultural history, from the post–Revolutionary War period, when mechanics were characterized by political rivals as illiterate and therefore incapable of participating in government, until today. More than once I've heard a manager label his workers as "a bunch of dummies." Generalizations about intelligence, work, and social class deeply affect our assumptions about ourselves and each other, guiding the ways we use our minds to learn, build knowledge, solve problems, and make our way through the world.

Although writers and scholars have often looked at the working class, 10 they have generally focused on the values such workers exhibit rather than on the thought their work requires—a subtle but pervasive omission. Our cultural iconography promotes the muscled arm, sleeve rolled tight against biceps, but no brightness behind the eye, no image that links hand and brain.

One of my mother's brothers, Joe Meraglio, left school in the ninth grade   11
to work for the Pennsylvania Railroad. From there he joined the Navy, returned to the railroad, which was already in decline, and eventually joined his older brother at General Motors where, over a 33-year career, he moved from working on the assembly line to supervising the paint-and-body department. When I was a young man, Joe took me on a tour of the factory. The floor was loud—in some places deafening—and when I turned a corner or opened a door, the smell of chemicals knocked my head back. The work was repetitive and taxing, and the pace was inhumane.

This famous poster by J. Howard Miller, which came to be called "Rosie the Riveter," was created to boost morale among factory workers during World War II. "Our cultural iconography," writes Mike Rose, "promotes the muscled arm, sleeve rolled tight against biceps, but no brightness behind the eye, no image that links hand and brain." With the feminist movement of the 1960s and later, however, "Rosie" came to represent what Rose himself calls "blue-collar brilliance"—a blending of muscle and intelligence.

Still, for Joe the shop floor provided what school did not; it was *like* 12
schooling, he said, a place where *you're constantly learning.* Joe learned the most
efficient way to use his body by acquiring a set of routines that were quick and
preserved energy. Otherwise he would never have survived on the line.

As a foreman, Joe constantly faced new problems and became a consum- 13
mate multi-tasker, evaluating a flurry of demands quickly, parceling out physical and mental resources, keeping a number of ongoing events in his mind,
returning to whatever task had been interrupted, and maintaining a cool head
under the pressure of grueling production schedules. In the midst of all this,
Joe learned more and more about the auto industry, the technological and
social dynamics of the shop floor, the machinery and production processes,
and the basics of paint chemistry and of plating and baking. With further
promotions, he not only solved problems but also began to find problems to
solve: Joe initiated the redesign of the nozzle on a paint sprayer, thereby eliminating costly and unhealthy overspray. And he found a way to reduce energy
costs on the baking ovens without affecting the quality of the paint. He lacked
formal knowledge of how the machines under his supervision worked, but he
had direct experience with them, hands-on knowledge, and was savvy about
their quirks and operational capabilities. He could experiment with them.

In addition, Joe learned about budgets and management. Coming off the 14
line as he did, he had a perspective of workers' needs and management's
demands, and this led him to think of ways to improve efficiency on the line
while relieving some of the stress on the assemblers. He had each worker in a
unit learn his or her co-workers' jobs so they could rotate across stations to
relieve some of the monotony. He believed that rotation would allow assemblers to get longer and more frequent breaks. It was an easy sell to the people
on the line. The union, however, had to approve any modification in job duties,
and the managers were wary of the change. Joe had to argue his case on a
number of fronts, providing him a kind of rhetorical education.

Eight years ago I began a study of the thought processes involved in 15
work like that of my mother and uncle. I catalogued the cognitive demands of
a range of blue-collar and service jobs, from waitressing and hair styling to
plumbing and welding. To gain a sense of how knowledge and skill develop, I
observed experts as well as novices. From the details of this close examination, I tried to fashion what I called "cognitive biographies" of blue-collar

workers. Biographical accounts of the lives of scientists, lawyers, entrepreneurs, and other professionals are rich with detail about the intellectual dimension of their work. But the life stories of working-class people are few and are typically accounts of hardship and courage or the achievements wrought by hard work.

Our culture—in Cartesian fashion [1]—separates the body from the mind, 16 so that, for example, we assume that the use of a tool does not involve abstraction. We reinforce this notion by defining intelligence solely on grades in school and numbers on IQ tests. And we employ social biases pertaining to a person's place on the occupational ladder. The distinctions among blue, pink, and white collars carry with them attributions of character, motivation, and intelligence. Although we rightly acknowledge and amply compensate the play of mind in white-collar and professional work, we diminish or erase it in considerations about other endeavors— physical and service work particularly. We also often ignore the experience of everyday work in administrative deliberations and policymaking.

See p. 331 for when to use "among" and "between" in making comparisons.

But here's what we find when we get in close. The plumber seeking 17 leverage in order to work in tight quarters and the hair stylist adroitly handling scissors and comb manage their bodies strategically. Though work-related actions become routine with experience, they were learned at some point through observation, trial and error, and, often, physical or verbal assistance from a co-worker or trainer. I've frequently observed novices talking to themselves as they take on a task, or shaking their head or hand as if to erase an attempt before trying again. In fact, our traditional notions of routine performance could keep us from appreciating the many instances within routine where quick decisions and adjustments are made. I'm struck by the thinking-in-motion that some work requires, by all the mental activity that can be involved in simply getting from one place to another: the waitress rushing back through her station to the kitchen or the foreman walking the line.

The use of tools requires the studied refinement of stance, grip, balance, 18 and fine-motor skills. But manipulating tools is intimately tied to knowledge of what a particular instrument can do in a particular situation and do better

1. After French philosopher René Descartes (1596–1650), who proposed the dualism of mind and body.

With an eighth-grade education, Joe (hands together)
advanced to supervisor of a G.M. paint-and-body
department.

than other similar tools. A worker must also know the characteristics of the material one is engaging—how it reacts to various cutting or compressing devices, to degrees of heat, or to lines of force. Some of these things demand judgment, the weighing of options, the consideration of multiple variables, and, occasionally, the creative use of a tool in an unexpected way.

In manipulating material, the worker becomes attuned to aspects of the   19 environment, a training or disciplining of perception that both enhances knowledge and informs perception. Carpenters have an eye for length, line, and angle; mechanics troubleshoot by listening; hair stylists are attuned to shape, texture, and motion. Sensory data merge with concept, as when an auto mechanic relies on sound, vibration, and even smell to understand what cannot be observed.

Planning and problem solving have been studied since the earliest days of   20 modern cognitive psychology and are considered core elements in Western definitions of intelligence. To work is to solve problems. The big difference between the psychologist's laboratory and the workplace is that in the former the problems are isolated and in the latter they are embedded in the real-time flow of work with all its messiness and social complexity.

Much of physical work is social and interactive. Movers determining 21 how to get an electric range down a flight of stairs require coordination, negotiation, planning, and the establishing of incremental goals. Words, gestures, and sometimes a quick pencil sketch are involved, if only to get the rhythm right. How important it is, then, to consider the social and communicative dimension of physical work, for it provides the medium for so much of work's intelligence.

The templates on p. 376 show how to add new "dimensions" to any definition.

Given the ridicule heaped on blue-collar speech, it might seem odd to 22 value its cognitive content. Yet, the flow of talk at work provides the channel for organizing and distributing tasks, for troubleshooting and problem solving, for learning new information and revising old. A significant amount of teaching, often informal and indirect, takes place at work. Joe Meraglio saw that much of his job as a supervisor involved instruction. In some service occupations, language and communication are central: observing and interpreting behavior and expression, inferring mood and motive, taking on the perspective of others, responding appropriately to social cues, and knowing when you're understood. A good hair stylist, for instance, has the ability to convert vague requests (*I want something light and summery*) into an appropriate cut through questions, pictures, and hand gestures.

Verbal and mathematical skills drive measures of intelligence in the 23 Western Hemisphere, and many of the kinds of work I studied are thought to require relatively little proficiency in either. Compared to certain kinds of white-collar occupations, that's true. But written symbols flow through physical work.

Numbers are rife in most workplaces: on tools and gauges, as measure- 24 ments, as indicators of pressure or concentration or temperature, as guides to sequence, on ingredient labels, on lists and spreadsheets, as markers of quantity and price. Certain jobs require workers to make, check, and verify calculations, and to collect and interpret data. Basic math can be involved, and some workers develop a good sense of numbers and patterns. Consider, as well, what might be called material mathematics: mathematical functions embodied in materials and actions, as when a carpenter builds a cabinet or a flight of stairs. A simple mathematical act can extend quickly beyond itself. Measuring, for example, can involve more than recording the dimensions of an object. As I watched a cabinetmaker measure a long strip of wood, he read a number off the tape out loud, looked back over his shoulder to the kitchen wall, turned back to his task, took another measurement, and paused for a moment in thought. He was solving a problem involving the molding, and the measurement was important to his deliberation about structure and appearance.

In the blue-collar workplace, directions, plans, and reference books rely 25 on illustrations, some representational and others, like blueprints, that require training to interpret. Esoteric symbols—visual jargon—depict switches and receptacles, pipe fittings, or types of welds. Workers themselves often make sketches on the job. I frequently observed them grab a pencil to sketch something on a scrap of paper or on a piece of the material they were installing.

Though many kinds of physical work don't require a high literacy level, 26 more reading occurs in the blue-collar workplace than is generally thought, from manuals and catalogues to work orders and invoices, to lists, labels, and forms. With routine tasks, for example, reading is integral to understanding production quotas, learning how to use an instrument, or applying a product. Written notes can initiate action, as in restaurant orders or reports of machine malfunction, or they can serve as memory aids.

True, many uses of writing are abbreviated, routine, and repetitive, and 27 they infrequently require interpretation or analysis. But analytic moments can be part of routine activities, and seemingly basic reading and writing can be cognitively rich. Because workplace language is used in the flow of other activities, we can overlook the remarkable coordination of words, numbers, and drawings required to initiate and direct action.

If we believe everyday work to be mindless, then that will affect the 28 work we create in the future. When we devalue the full range of everyday cognition, we offer limited educational opportunities and fail to make fresh and meaningful instructional connections among disparate kinds of skill and knowledge. If we think that whole categories of people—identified by class or occupation—are not that bright, then we reinforce social separations and cripple our ability to talk across cultural divides.

Affirmation of diverse intelligence is not a retreat to a softhearted defi- 29 nition of the mind. To acknowledge a broader range of intellectual capacity is to take seriously the concept of cognitive variability, to appreciate in all the Rosies and Joes the thought that drives their accomplishments and defines who they are. This is a model of the mind that is worthy of a democratic society.

FOR DISCUSSION

1. Is Mike Rose correct when he says that DEFINITIONS of human intelligence should not be based solely "on grades in school and numbers on IQ tests" (16)? Why or why not?

2. According to Rose, how *should* intelligence be defined, especially among workers whose tasks are not "closely associated with formal education" (9)? What would he add to more traditional definitions?

3. Why is Rose concerned with definitions of intelligence that consider "everyday work to be mindless" (28)? What EFFECTS are such misguided (in his view) conceptions likely to have on society "in the future" (28)?

4. What does Rose mean by the "concept of cognitive variability" (29), and where—aside from watching his mother wait tables in a restaurant—did he likely learn about it?

STRATEGIES AND STRUCTURES

1. Why does Rose begin his essay with an account of his mother's experience as a waitress (1–6)? Where else does he use elements of NARRATIVE to support his definition of intelligence? How effective are they? Explain.

2. What are some of the main traits of "blue-collar brilliance" as Rose defines it? Point to specific passages in the text where he identifies those traits.

3. "There wasn't much for a child to do at the restaurants," says Rose, "and so as the hours stretched out, I watched the cooks and waitresses and listened to what they said" (2). How does his childhood role as an observer at his mother's restaurant anticipate the adult role that Rose adopts as a scholar who tells "the life stories of working-class people" (15)?

4. "I couldn't have put it into words," Rose says of this early experience of the workplace (4). How *did* he learn to put his observations into words, and what kind of language does he typically use to do it? Point to specific examples in the text.

5. Rose's definition of blue-collar intelligence is based on "a model of the mind" that, he claims at the end of his essay, is "worthy of a democratic society" (29). How and how well does Rose anticipate this ARGUMENT? Should he have stated this major point more directly earlier? Why or why not?

6. Rose's essay first appeared in the *American Scholar,* a journal aimed at readers who are interested in intellectual subjects beyond their narrow fields of expertise. How appropriate are the language and writing style of his essay to this intended **AUDIENCE**? Explain.

WORDS AND FIGURES OF SPEECH

1. How and how well does Rose capture the "lingo" of the workplace (2)? Point to specific words and phrases in the text.

2. **SYNONYMS** are different words that have essentially the same meaning. What is Rose defining when he refers to "a place where competence was synonymous with physical work" (4)?

3. Look up the word "iconography" in your dictionary (10). Who or what did it pertain to before the rock stars and television celebrities of today?

4. Rose says that he has long observed blue-collar workers for the purpose of writing their "cognitive biographies" (15). Judging from the context in which he uses it, what does Rose mean by this term? Which parts of his essay (if any) would you point to as examples of this type of writing? Why?

FOR WRITING

1. Spend an hour or so watching and listening to the workers in a diner, factory, store, hair salon, or other workplace environment where you feel comfortable. Take notes on what they say and do, and write a paragraph or two capturing the scene as Rose does in the opening paragraphs of his essay.

2. Write an essay explaining how a group of workers you have observed, blue-collar or otherwise, defines some important aspect of their work. For example, you might explain how they define competency in their field—or failure, loyalty, or some other broad concept. Cite particular cases and conversations in some detail.

HOW NATIVE AMERICAN IS NATIVE AMERICAN ENOUGH?

TOMMY ORANGE (b. 1982) is a novelist and an enrolled member of the Cheyenne and Arapaho tribes of Oklahoma. Orange grew up in Oakland, California, and attended the Institute of American Indian Arts in Santa Fe, New Mexico, where he earned an MFA in creative writing. In his award-winning first novel, *There There* (2018), Orange tells the story of 12 characters, mostly urban and of Cheyenne descent, who come together at the Big Oakland Powwow, in part to define themselves. ("We've been defined by everyone else," says Orange in the prologue, "and continue to be … [with] Kevin Costner saving us, John Wayne's six-shooter slaying us, an Italian guy named Iron Eyes Cody playing our parts in movies.") "How Native American Is Native American Enough?," which first appeared on *BuzzFeed News* in 2018, is likewise an essay in definition. Having "Indian blood," of course, says Orange, is "a metaphor." However, if you're filling out an official document called a "Certificate of Degree of Indian Blood" (CDIB), the metaphor is "real"; and it defies mathematics. "I am not half of two things or made up of fractions," Orange concludes, "I am made up of whole things, things that are things unto themselves."

I'M NOT TRYING TO BE MORE NATIVE than I am. Less white than I am. I'm try- 1 ing to be honest about what I have to include. More often than not I've introduced myself as half Native. I know what people want to know as soon as I say that I'm Native: How much? I watch them wait to see what I'll say about it. They don't want to have to ask, and they know I don't want to have to say it. They're testing me that way, so when the quiet between us becomes too much for me, I mumble out the side of my mouth: *From my dad's side.* The other half of me is apparent. My skin is light and I have freckles. I'm brown around the summer months and whiter in the winter. But I look like my dad if you saw me next to him. We have the same head and body. Same barrel chest, same nose. I reference my dad when I bring up being Native because I'm always doing it, qualifying my quantity. My amount. Where it comes from. And it's

See p. 187 for advice on introducing a subject by using a rhetorical question.

never enough. Too many claim great-grandparents. People are tired of hearing about great-grandparents, and great-great-grandparents even more so. It's too much math. Do I think we shouldn't include smaller fractions in the definition of what it means to be Native? I don't know. What I do know is that if I don't include the amount that I am, people assume less. So if asked whether or not I'm Native, I say yeah, and then, maybe sadly, maybe with assertion, maybe both, I say: half.

Those with less than half lose more than half the battle at the outset. 2 One Native grandparent equals one-quarter blood quantum. Should someone with this amount not be allowed to identify as Native, if their grandmother raised them? If they didn't even know that grandparent? What about great-great-grandparents? That's an eighth—if there's only one. What equations make sense to keep doing? How come math isn't taught with stakes? There are Natives enrolled in tribes with less than a 30 second's worth of Native blood in them—as in, less than 30 seconds after hearing about that kind of low-percentage ancestry, you'll probably have dismissed them as faking. You. Everyone.

There are full-blooded Native people raised by white families in white 3 communities who don't know a thing about what it means to be Native or how to live in such a way as to be identified as such.

Walking between worlds is an old Native half-breed trope. I've never felt 4 that I've walked in two worlds. The half-world feels more like being pulled apart and told to speak in singular terms—to pick a side. Actively identifying as a Native person if you have a valid claim is important work—an act against systematically designed erasure.

A half is not a number. Mathematically speaking, it doesn't count as a number. I never did well in math, but I understand fractions better now. When I was talking to my dad recently he said, "The way I got it worked out, it's like this, you're 3/64 short of being half Cheyenne."[1]

That's about 4% less than half. According to a poll conducted by the Atlantic, 4% of Americans believe lizard people control politics.[2] So I'm that amount of crazy Americans short of being half Native American.

But I'm not half, technically. I can't, for example, technically call myself biracial. I'd have to include 1/32 Sioux* blood and 1/64 German blood. I know this because my dad knows this. Growing up they called him *Vehoe*. It means white man. It also means spider, and references a mythological trickster figure. He told me I'm less than half. He didn't mean it in any way. My dad's an engineer. Exact math matters to him. As it does to all of us who have to figure out the kind of math involved in the equation: Enough Blood times Not Enough Blood equals eligibility or ineligibility for tribal enrollment and therefore citizenship in a sovereign nation.

But I am half Native—Cheyenne—from my dad. This half of me is a cutting fraction, which cuts if I rub up against it too firmly, if I slide my finger along its edge. Halving is the beginning of erasure. I'm doing it here again. Qualifying myself. Worried about what you will think of me.

I had a son in 2011. He'd be a quarter. The last in my line to be able to call himself Cheyenne, officially. He would have been. But he is an eighth Cheyenne. An eighth nothing.

1. The Cheyenne are a group of Indigenous people who have historically lived in the Great Plains region of North America. Today, Cheyenne people may be enrolled in either the Cheyenne and Arapaho tribes in Oklahoma or the Northern Cheyenne tribe in Montana.
2. The report in the *Atlantic* magazine (April 2013) was based on a poll conducted by Public Policy Polling. The precise term used in the firm's questionnaire was "reptilian people."

* Most Lakota people I've met don't like to be called Sioux because it's the given white name, but when I asked my dad if we're Lakota or Dakota or Nakota, he just said, "The way my grandma told it to me, we're Sioux." There was an *And that's that* feel to the way he said it. [author's note.]

We are very clear with our son at home. He knows he's Native. But what 10 that will mean for him in 20 years, I don't know. And what it will mean for his children?

There is something you'd never know about if you weren't Native or had 11 a close Native relation or friend. It's called the CDIB. Certificate of Degree of Indian Blood. This is a real, actual, official piece of paper with a record writ in fraction how much "Indian blood" I have. An official document about an amount of blood in my body. Which is a metaphor. But it isn't. It's real. We don't have enough blood to keep going for our people. It stops. Ends. My son won't have a CDIB.

> Orange's use of fragments and short sentences helps to define his tone and style, p. 38.

As it is, I am an enrolled member of the Cheyenne and Arapaho Tribes 12 of Oklahoma. On my Certificate of Degree of Indian Blood it says I am one-quarter Cheyenne. One-fourth. The one indicates a person who did not die. Who was not killed. Whose blood has since thinned, and is more than probably on the way down that sloping line. To the stopping point.

My blood is not enough because my dad's dad never accepted him as a 13 son. So he is half nothing, resulting in my quarter nothingness. This is how I became biracial and bi-nihilist. My son cannot be enrolled in our tribe as a result of being an eighth nothing, as a result of not having the proper documents to prove he has the required amount of blood in his body. It has to be funny that after spilling all that blood, our blood, our government, which first imposed this blood law—that we keep such close track of it—make sure we don't lose its quantity, or quality, or, what are we talking about again? If my skin is white, that's because that's what my mom is. And if it isn't brown, it isn't because of what my dad isn't. I'm not half of two things or made up of fractions. I am made up of whole things, things that are things unto themselves.

FOR DISCUSSION

1. According to Tommy Orange, why is it important to identify as Native American if you have a "valid claim" (4)?

2. Orange mentions that his father is an engineer (7). Why is this relevant (or not) in a discussion of who he is?

3. Orange's father works out that his son is "3/64 short of being half Cheyenne" (5). What is he quantifying? Explain.

4. According to Orange, many members of the Sioux tribe do not like to be called by that name. Why not? Why does Orange himself accept the designation?

5. To "technically call myself biracial," Orange says, "I'd have to include . . . 1/64 German blood" (7). What is the point of this calculation?

6. So, given the math, does Orange qualify as "Native"? Why or why not?

STRATEGIES AND STRUCTURES

1. The longest paragraph in Orange's essay is the first one, which introduces the problem of defining how "Native" he is; it concludes with a tentative single-word answer: "half" (1). How and how well does this introduction fit the rest of the essay? Explain.

2. Orange says he's "trying to be honest about what [he has] to include" (1). Why do you think he includes all the mathematical calculations? Do they help (or not) establish his **CREDIBILITY**? Explain.

3. "Worried about what you will think of me" (8). To whom is Orange speaking here? What social (and rhetorical) situation is he imagining, and what assumptions is he making about his intended **AUDIENCE**? Explain.

4. "So he is half nothing, resulting in my quarter nothingness," says Orange of his father, whose own father "never accepted him as a son" (13). At this point in his essay, Orange is well beyond **DEFINING** the self in terms of "blood." On what basis is he defining it here? Explain.

5. In the last paragraph of his essay, Orange asks, parenthetically: "What are we talking about again?" What point is he making here? Is this an appropriate way to conclude? Why or why not?

WORDS AND FIGURES OF SPEECH

1. Both "half-breed" (4) and "biracial" (13) refer to persons of mixed race. What are the differences in **CONNOTATION**, or implied meaning, between the two terms? Is Orange's use of the more pejorative term justified? Why or why not?

2. Orange speaks of walking between worlds as a "trope," or **FIGURE OF SPEECH** (4). What kind of trope, specifically, is it? Explain.

3. An extended **METAPHOR** is sometimes called a *conceit*. Explain the "cutting fraction" conceit in Orange's definition of himself as "half Native" (8).

4. Orange speaks of "that amount of crazy Americans" (6). Should he have said "that number" instead? Why or why not?

5. "Halving is the beginning of erasure" (8). Why might a writer, in particular, be inclined to use this trope in an essay about self-definition?

6. On an official CDIB, says Orange, how much "Indian blood" one has is "writ in fraction" (11). Why might he use an antiquated form of the verb here instead of the modern form, "written"?

FOR WRITING

1. Do the math: in a paragraph or two, **SUMMARIZE** your ancestry and who you are based on what you know of your DNA; on family history, lore, or legend; on whom you imagine yourself to be—or on all these.

2. On the internet, look up a copy of the official "Bureau of Indian Affairs Certificate of Degree of Indian or Alaska Native Blood" (OMB Control #1076-0153). Study the instructions and the form itself, and write an essay explaining the apparent nature and purpose of this government document. Pay particular attention to the assumptions it makes about how people are to be defined.

3. In an essay that **DEFINES** a particular race, creed, religion, sexual orientation, or other category that you identify with, explain why "actively identifying" with that group is (or is not) important, in your view (4). Be sure to consider whether doing so is in any way "an act against systematically designed erasure" (4).

CARLA HALL AND GENEVIEVE KO

SOUL FOOD

CARLA HALL (b. 1964) is a celebrity chef and author of cookbooks. A former cohost of ABC's talk show *The Chew*, she has also appeared on Netflix's cooking competition show, *Crazy Delicious*. Born in Nashville, Tennessee, Hall graduated from the business school at Howard University and went to work in an accounting firm before switching careers to work as a runway model in Europe. She spent a few years across the Atlantic, then decided to make a career out of her love for food. As a chef, Hall trained at l'Academie de cuisine in Bethesda, Maryland, and in various hotel and restaurant kitchens in Washington, DC. "Soul Food" is part of the introduction to her 2018 cookbook by that title written with the assistance of Genevieve Ko, who is a food writer, chef consultant, and cooking editor at the *Los Angeles Times*. What is soul food, exactly? Hall is here to tell us: "I don't just know soul food. Soul food is in my soul. . . . I'm here to redefine soul food, to reclaim it."

I'VE BEEN EATING SOUL FOOD ALL MY LIFE and cooking it my whole career. I 1
don't just know soul food. Soul Food is *in* my soul.

By definition, soul food refers to the dishes of the Cotton Belt of Geor- 2
gia, Mississippi, and Alabama that traveled out to the rest of the country during the Great Migration.[1] (The term itself came around the middle

For more on defin-
ing a term by tracing
its history, see
p. 373.

of the twentieth century.) You know what travels well? Fried
chicken. Mac and cheese. Delicious, but not what anyone's meant
to eat every day. I'm here to redefine soul food, to reclaim it.

Soul food is the true food of African-Americans. 3

The roots of our cooking are in West Africa. And from there, the Ameri- 4
can South, from the slave ports along the eastern coast to the southern border. We relied on seasonal vegetables, beans, and grains, with meat on rare
occasions. Let's be clear: those were horrible times of suffering under the
most unspeakable evil. I don't want to romanticize any of it. Not even the
food. Remember, we didn't get to choose what we ate. But we made the most
delicious dishes from what little we had. And what we cooked for the slave
owners effectively became what we know as "American" food today.

After emancipation,[2] African-Americans relied on the land and water for 5
their daily meals. Collards in winter, peas through spring, tomatoes come
summer. Chickens were for laying eggs, not frying. Fish and shrimp were
abundant for coast and river folks. We lost that connection during the Great
Migration and in the decades since as industrialized convenience food has
made us unhealthy and sick. Our celebration foods—smoked whole hogs, can-
died yams, caramel cake—became what we ate all the time. We forgot about
all the amazing daily meals we created from greens and beans and grains.

You may be wondering, "What's the difference between Southern food 6
and soul food?" Easy answer: black cooks. And I'm one of them. A lot of the
dishes, seasonings, and techniques are the same, but there's an extra *oomph* in
soul food. It's like the difference between a hymn and a spiritual. Both sound
beautiful and express the same message, but the spiritual's got a groove.

1. The northern movement, between 1916 and 1970, of approximately six million African
Americans from the rural and small-town South to more urban centers in the United States.
2. Slavery was officially abolished in the United States in April 1864 with the passage of the
13th Amendment to the Constitution. The earlier (1862) Emancipation Proclamation by
President Lincoln applied only to the states not under Union control.

Southern food's delicious any which way, but when it's made in the Black-American tradition with influences from Africa and the Caribbean, it delivers the kind of warmth and joy that makes you want to get up and dance.

I got that soul food in my bones. I was born into it in the South, with   7
roots that go back generations. I grew up dunkin' cornbread into pot likker at the table, snapping green beans for church suppers, slicing chess pie at every baby shower and graduation party. At my very core, I'm always going back home to Tennessee when it comes to what I cook and eat. I've got a Nashville-born-and-bred palate, which marries heat and spice with tart and tangy and a sweetness that's not too sugary. Coming from that heritage, I got a hold on the food with the *soul* that bears its name.

African-Americans were cooking farm-to-table centuries before it was a   8
label to slap on hip restaurants. Foraging, pickling, preserving—that's how we survived. Our farms were all "organic." You think you discovered kale? Child, we've been eatin' those greens for hundreds of years. I'm going back to all that.

Granny, my greatest inspiration in the kitchen, raised me on good-for-   9
you soul food. Granny was a dietician at a hospital and prepared meals at home for her husband, who needed heart-healthy dishes. She never skimped on flavor or made anything too lean but cut back where she could.

Nashville was a great place to grow up. Maybe it'd be nice to retire there too.   10
But I needed to be somewhere else in between. To get some perspective before I could come back. Mama's from a well-respected doctor's family and raised me and my sister, Kim, on the "good" side of town. Still, I got slurs thrown at me. Some boys even spat on me.

Despite that disgusting racism and prejudice, I was comfortable with my   11
African-American identity *and* hanging out with white folks. My best friend Karen was white, and we had a grand ol' time playing together. Granny gathered my cousins, aunts, and uncles for Sunday supper each week after we spent the day at our historically black churches. My theater troupe was totally mixed, but we felt more connected to each other than to all the other kids.

Then I went to Howard for college. *Woke*.[3]   12

3. Howard University in Washington, DC. The slang term *woke*, now a synonym for being broadly aware of social justice issues, originated as as a term used by African Americans to indicate consciousness of the struggle against racism.

Then Europe to model. In London, I cured homesickness with soul food. 13

Back in Washington, D.C., I started a lunch delivery service. My soups, 14
sandwiches, and pound cakes fueled the guys at the barbershops. I found my
life's passion in the kitchen, so I went to culinary school.

Like a lot of African-Americans who go to cooking school, I couldn't run 15
fast enough from soul food as soon as I was taught European dishes. Early in
my career, I was like, "Now I'm educated and I don't need to do soul food. You
can't pigeonhole me in mac and cheese." Once I learned traditional French
techniques, I got all uppity. I stopped frying chicken and started stewing it in
red wine. With my European cooking, I rose through fancy restaurant ranks
to become executive chef, private-cheffed for the super-rich, started my own
catering company. Then I showed the world what I could do as a contestant on
Top Chef.

In the intensity of the competition, I found my way home. When the 16
pressure to win felt almost unbearable, I remembered what Granny always told
me: "It's your job to be happy, not rich. If you do that, then everything else will
follow." Nothing makes me happier than Granny's food. So I started cooking it,
working in techniques I'd learned in professional kitchens. The judges, fellow
contestants, viewers—everyone—could feel the love in my food.

Cooking soul food with love got me into the *Top Chef* finals and voted 17
fan favorite. That opened the door for me to become one of the hosts on ABC's
The Chew. Over my past six years of cooking for millions of Americans on TV,
it's been all about coming back to soul food.

Those hot spots in the nicer neighborhoods where foodies are discovering 18
"real" Southern food? Those places are built on the backs and shoulders of
African-American cooks. You may not see many African-Americans as executive chefs of Michelin-starred restaurants,[4] topping lists, or winning the big
awards. Not yet. You don't see us, but we're here. We're in hotel kitchens, at
catering companies, on the line at those starred places. We've always been
here. And we're rising.

---

4. *The Michelin Guide* (English title), published annually for more than a century by the
French tire manufacturer, uses a three-star system to rate top restaurants.

Now, I'm here to help y'all see us. Because, yes, you can see me. But I 19
don't want you to ever think that I'm better than you are, better
than any other chef out there. I certainly don't. But I've been
blessed with this platform. I'm using it to say: I want all of us to
be proud of soul food. Soul food is ours. Claim it. Reclaim it. I'm
just here to share a taste.

Welcome to my table. 20

> Hall concludes by putting a fine point on her purpose and intended audience (p. 375).

FOR DISCUSSION

1. "By definition," says Carla Hall, "soul food refers to the dishes of the Cotton Belt of Georgia, Mississippi, and Alabama" (2). In Hall's extended definition of "soul food," what else does it entail? Explain.

2. What does Hall mean by "the Great Migration" (2)? How is her definition of this social and geographical movement related to her definition of "soul food"?

3. What other key historical terms and movements does Hall define in her essay? Which ones do you find particularly relevant (or not) to her extended definition of soul food? Explain.

4. The subtitle of Hall's cookbook is *Everyday and Celebration*. How does Hall define these two different kinds of soul food, and which type does she plan to emphasize? Why?

5. Hall says she learned to cook soul food mainly from her grandmother, whose philosophy of life was "be happy, not rich" (16). How does this philosophy carry over into Hall's definition of soul food (16)?

STRATEGIES AND STRUCTURES

1. "I got that soul food in my bones" (7). How and how well does Hall establish her **CREDIBILITY** as an expert in the particular kind of cuisine she is identifying and defining here? Explain.

2. Hall often speaks directly to the reader as, for example, when she says, "You may be wondering" or "Welcome to my table" (6, 20). Point out other examples in her essay. What do they suggest about the makeup of her intended **AUDIENCE** and the relationship she hopes to establish with them?

3. To distinguish soul food from "Southern food," Hall cites "the difference between a hymn and a spiritual" (6). Is the **COMPARISON** an effective way of defining her subject? Why or why not?

4. How and how well does Hall link her personal story—growing up in Nashville as the daughter of a doctor, studying accounting at Howard University, modeling in Europe, competing on *Top Chef*—to the more general story she tells about Black cooks in America? Explain.

5. Hall's definition of soul food is also an **ARGUMENT** about the need to "redefine" and "reclaim" it (2). What are some of the main issues she raises? How and how well does she support her claim about the need for change?

WORDS AND FIGURES OF SPEECH

1. Look up the history of the term "soul food." Under what circumstances did it come into general use "around the middle of the twentieth century" (2)?

2. Hall's language and **TONE** is often folksy, as when she says, for example, "tomatoes come summer" or "I got all uppity" (5, 15). Point out other examples, and explain why they are (or are not) appropriate in an essay about food.

3. "Foodies" (18), of course, are people who're interested in food. What does the term mean exactly, and when did it come into general use? How do foodies differ from more old-fashioned food lovers, such as *gourmets, gourmands,* and *gluttons?*

4. Define *neologism* and give several examples in addition to "foodie" and "soul food."

5. As she says, Hall was "one of the hosts on ABC's *The Chew*" (17). Is this a good name for a cooking and talk show? Why or why not?

FOR WRITING

1. In a paragraph or two, define one of the following: "soul," "oomph," "groove," "industrialized convenience food."

2. Write a brief definition of a "spiritual" as a distinctive form of "hymn." Don't forget to mention the element of rhythm, or "groove."

3. Write an extended definition of what you consider to be standard "American" food. Be sure to consider the extent to which it derives (or does not derive) from "the Black-American tradition" (6).

4. In an extended definition, explain the nature and distinguishing features of French, Italian, Chinese, Indian, or some other cuisine you're interested in. Include in your definition the vocabulary and some of the history of this type of cooking.

⇥12⇤

CAUSE AND EFFECT

I F you were at home on vacation and saw on social media that the physics
building at your school had burned, your first questions would probably be
about the *effects* of the fire: "How much damage was done? Was anyone hurt?"
Once you knew what the effects were—the building burned to the ground, but
the blaze broke out in the middle of the night when nobody was in it—your
next questions would likely be about the *causes*: "What caused the fire? Lightning? A short circuit in the electrical system? An arsonist's match?"

If you went on to read the news report and learned that the fire was set
by your friend, Larry, you would probably have some more questions, such as
"Why did Larry do it? What will happen to Larry as a result of his action?"
When you write a **CAUSE-AND-EFFECT*** essay, you answer fundamental questions like these about the *what* and *why* of an event or phenomenon. The
questions may be simple, but answering them fully and adequately may require
you to consider a variety of possible causes and effects—and to distinguish
one type of cause from another.

In our example, Larry struck a match, which caused the building to catch
fire. That effect in turn caused another effect—the building burned down.
Larry's striking the match is the *immediate* cause of the fire—the one closest
to the event in time. A *remote* cause, on the other hand, might be Larry's failure on a physics test two weeks earlier. But which cause is the *main* cause, the
most important one, and which causes are less important—merely *contributing*? Was Larry angry before he took the physics test? What were his feelings
toward the physics professor? Often you will need to run through a whole

---

* Words printed in **SMALL CAPITALS** are defined in the Glossary/Index.

chain of related causes and effects like these before deciding to emphasize one or two.

How do you make sure that the causes you choose to emphasize actually account for the particular event or phenomenon you're analyzing? Two basic conditions have to be met to prove causation. A main cause has to be both *necessary* and *sufficient* to produce the effect in question. That is, it must be shown that (1) the alleged cause *always* accompanies the effect, and (2) that the alleged cause (and only the alleged cause) has the power to produce the effect. Let's look at these conditions in the following passage from an article on statistics in the *New York Times*. The author is recalling a time before the Salk vaccine defeated polio:

> For example, in the late 1940s, before there was a polio vaccine, public health experts in America noted that polio cases increased in step with the consumption of ice cream and soft drinks. . . . Eliminating such treats was even recommended as part of an anti-polio diet. It turned out that polio outbreaks were most common in the hot months of summer, when people naturally ate more ice cream. . . .
>
> —STEVE LOHR, "For Today's Graduates, Just One Word: Statistics"

The health experts who thought that ice cream and soft drinks *caused* polio failed to distinguish between causation and mere correlation.

Tim Wendel makes a distinction between causation and correlation in "King, Kennedy, and the Power of Words," p. 439.

Although outbreaks of polio always seemed to be accompanied by an increase in the consumption of cool summer treats, ice cream and soft drinks did not actually have the power to cause the disease. And though the *heat* was the clear cause of the increased consumption of ice cream and soft drinks, Jonas Salk and his colleagues suspected that normal summer weather was not sufficiently harmful to induce paralysis. Eventually they isolated the *main* cause—the poliomyelitis virus. This tiny killer met both tests for true causality: it appeared in every case, and it was the only factor capable of producing the dire effect ascribed to it. It was both necessary and sufficient.

As Dr. Salk knew from the beginning, mere sequences in time—cases of polio increase as, or immediately after, the consumption of ice cream and soft drinks increases—are not sufficient to prove causation. This mistake in causal analysis is commonly referred to as the *post hoc, ergo propter hoc* **FALLACY**, Latin for "after this, therefore because of this." Salk understood the two conditions that must be met before causation may be accurately inferred.

These two conditions can be expressed as a simple formula:

B cannot have happened without A;
Whenever A happens, B must happen.

When we are dealing with psychological and social rather than purely physical factors, the main cause may defy simple analysis. Or it may turn out that there are a number of causes working together. Suppose we looked for an answer to the following question: Why does Maria smoke? This looks like a simple question, but it is a difficult one to answer because there are so many complicated reasons a young woman like Maria might smoke. The best way to approach this kind of causal analysis might be to list as many of the contributing causes as you can turn up:

> MARIA: I smoke because I need to do something with my hands.
>
> MARIA'S BOYFRIEND: Maria smokes because she thinks it looks cool.
>
> MEDICAL DOCTOR: Because Maria has developed a physical addiction to tobacco.
>
> PSYCHOLOGIST: Because of peer pressure.
>
> SOCIOLOGIST: Because Maria is Hispanic; in recent years tobacco companies have spent billions in advertising to attract more Hispanic smokers.

When you list particular causes like this, be as specific as you can. When you list effects, be even more specific. Instead of saying "Smoking is bad for your health," be particular. In an essay on the harm of tobacco, for example, Erik Eckholm provides a grim effect. "The most potentially tragic victims," he writes, "are the infants of mothers who smoke. They are more likely than the babies of nonsmoking mothers to be born underweight and thus to encounter death or disease at birth or during the initial months of life."

In singling out the effects of smoking upon unwitting infants, Eckholm uses an **EXAMPLE** that might be just powerful enough to convince some smokers to quit. Though your examples may not be as dramatic as Eckholm's, they must be specific to be powerful. And they must be selected with your **AUDIENCE** in mind. In the previous example, Eckholm addresses young women who smoke. If he were writing for a middle-aged audience, however, he might point out that the incidence of cancer and heart disease is 70 percent higher among one-pack-a-day men and women than among nonsmokers.

Your audience needs to be taken into account when you analyze causes and effects because, among other reasons, you are usually making an **ARGU-MENT** about the causes or effects of a phenomenon or event. Thus, you must carry the reader step by step through some kind of proof. Your explanation may be instructive, amusing, or startling; but if your analysis is to make the point you want it to make, it must also be persuasive.

A BRIEF GUIDE TO WRITING A CAUSE-AND-EFFECT ESSAY

When you analyze causes or effects, you explain why something happened or what its results are. So as you write a cause-and-effect essay, you need to identify your subject and indicate which you plan to emphasize—causes or effects. Myriam Márquez makes these basic moves in the opening paragraphs of her essay in this chapter:

> When I'm shopping with my mother or standing in line with my stepdad to order fast food or anywhere else we might be together, we're going to speak Spanish. . . . Let me explain why we haven't adopted English as our official family language.
>
> —Myriam Márquez, "Why and When
> We Speak Spanish in Public"

Márquez identifies the subject of her analysis (speaking Spanish in public) and indicates that she plans to emphasize the causes of this phenomenon ("why").

Whether you emphasize causes or effects, remember that the effect of one event may become the cause of a subsequent event, forming a **CAUSAL CHAIN** that you will need to follow link by link in order to fully analyze why something happened. For example: Two cars collide, killing the driver of the second car. The first driver's excessive speed is the cause; the death of the second driver is the effect. That effect, in turn, causes another one—the children of the second driver grow up without that parent.

Elisa Gonzalez traces a chain of causes and effects in "Family History," p. 434.

The following guidelines will help you make the basic moves for analyzing cause and effect as you draft an essay. They will also help you come up with your subject, explain why you're analyzing causes and effects, distinguish between different kinds of causes, and present your analysis in an organized way.

Coming Up with a Subject

To find a subject for an essay that analyzes cause and effect, start with your own curiosity—about the physical world or about history, sociology, or any other field that interests you. Look for specific phenomena or events—climate change, President Truman's decision to drop atomic bombs on Japan in 1945, the rising cost of health care in the United States—that you find intriguing. In order to narrow your subject down into a topic that is specific enough to investigate within the time allotted by your instructor, begin by asking yourself what its main causes (or effects) are likely to be. You may need to do some research on your subject; you'll find guidelines for doing research in the Appendix of this book.

Considering Your Purpose and Audience

As you examine particular causes and effects, think about why you're analyzing them. Is your **PURPOSE** to inform your readers? Amuse them? **ARGUE** that one set of causes (or effects) is more likely than another? One writer, for example, may try to persuade readers that autism is caused by inherent biological factors, while another writer might argue for environmental causes.

You'll also need to consider the **AUDIENCE** you want to reach. Are your readers already familiar with the topic, or will you need to provide back-ground information and **DEFINE** unfamiliar terms? Are they likely to be receptive to the point you're making, or opposed to it? An article on the causes of autism may have a very different slant depending on whether the intended readers are parents of children with autism, medical doctors, psychologists, or the general public.

Myriam Márquez, p. 444, assumes a reader who knows little about her subject.

Generating Ideas: Asking *Why, What,* and *What If*

When you want to figure out what caused something, the essential question to ask is *why*. Why does a curveball drop as it crosses home plate? Why was Napoleon defeated in his invasion of Russia in 1812? If, on the other hand, you want to figure out what the effects of something are, or will be, then the basic question to ask is *what* or *what if*. What will happen if the curveball fails to drop? What effect did the weather have on Napoleon's campaign?

As you ask *why* or *what* about your subject, keep in mind that a single effect may have multiple causes, or vice versa. Be sure to write down as many causes or effects as you can think of. If you were to ask, for example, why retail sales at traditional department stores in the United States plummeted in 2020, you would need to consider a number of possible causes. The first, of course, would be the COVID-19 pandemic, which physically shut down most stores and businesses. Before the virus hit, however, brick and mortar stores in general were already losing sales to due to the growing popularity of online vendors. Similarly, if you were analyzing the *effects* of the retail crisis, you would need to consider several of them, including a sales force without jobs, shopping malls without anchors, and fashion designers without commissions.

Templates for Analyzing Causes and Effects

The following templates can help you generate ideas for a cause-and-effect essay and then start drafting. Don't take these as formulas where you just have to fill in the blanks. There are no easy formulas for good writing. But these templates can help you plot out some of the key moves to make when you analyze cause and effect—and thus may serve as good starting points.

- ▶ The main cause/effect of X is _____.

- ▶ X would also seem to have a number of contributing causes, including _____, _____, and _____.

- ▶ One effect of X is _____, which in turn causes _____.

- ▶ Some additional effects of X are _____, _____, and _____.

- ▶ Although the causes of X are not known, we can speculate that a key factor is _____.

- ▶ X cannot be attributed to mere chance or coincidence because _____.

- ▶ Once we know what causes X, we are in a position to say that _____.

For more techniques to help you generate ideas and start writing a cause-and-effect analysis, see Chapter 3.

Stating Your Point

As you draft an essay that analyzes cause and effect, tell readers at the outset whether you are going to focus on causes or effects—or both. Also make clear what your main point, or **THESIS**, is. For example, if you are analyzing the causes of the financial meltdown in the United States in 2008, you might signal your main point in a **THESIS STATEMENT** like this one:

> The main cause of the financial meltdown in the United States in 2008 was the freezing of credit, which made it impossible for anyone to borrow money.

Once you have stated your thesis, you are ready to present evidence that supports it.

Distinguishing One Type of Cause from Another

To help your reader understand how a number of causes work together to produce a particular effect, you can distinguish among causes based on their relative importance in producing the effect and on their occurrence in time.

MAIN AND CONTRIBUTING CAUSES. The *main cause* is the one that has the greatest power to produce the effect. It must be both necessary to cause the effect and sufficient to do so. On August 1, 2007, a bridge collapsed on Interstate 35W in Minneapolis, Minnesota. Most investigators now agree that the main cause of the collapse was a flaw in the bridge's design. A *contributing cause* is a secondary cause—it helps to produce the effect but is not sufficient to do it alone. In the Minnesota bridge collapse, a contributing cause was the weight of construction supplies and equipment on the bridge at the time. Although it would have been wise to locate at least some of the construction equipment off the bridge, the added weight alone did not cause the collapse. As one investigator pointed out, "If the bridge had not been improperly designed, everybody says it would have held up that weight easily."

IMMEDIATE AND REMOTE CAUSES. The *immediate cause*, often called the *proximate* cause in legal cases, is the one closest in time and most directly responsible for producing an effect. If someone is injured from a fall after stepping on a banana peel, the banana peel is the immediate cause. (Gravity plays a part, too, as with the Minnesota bridge collapse, but it was already there, unmoved by human act or motive.) *Remote causes*, as the name implies, are less apparent in producing an end result and are more removed from it in time. A remote cause of tripping on a banana peel is that someone had earlier dropped (or thrown) the peel on the sidewalk. The main cause of an effect is often a remote cause—in this case, the negligence of the person who did not toss the remains of their lunch into a garbage can. Immediate causes, though closest to the effect in time, are often merely contributing causes. Here, the slippery banana peel led directly to the fall but would not have been in a position to cause harm if not for the person who left it there.

As you link together causes and effects, be careful not to confuse causation with coincidence. Just because one event (increased sales of soft drinks) comes before another (higher incidence of polio) does not mean the first event actually caused the second.

Organizing a Cause-and-Effect Essay

One way to present the effects of a given cause is by arranging them in chronological order. If you were tracing the effects of the credit crisis of 2008, for example, you would start with the crisis itself (the freezing of credit) and then proceed chronologically, detailing its effects in the order in which they occurred: first several investment banks collapsed, then the stock market plummeted, then the federal government stepped in with a massive bailout, and so on.

Reverse chronological order, in which you begin with a known effect and work backward through the possible causes, can also be effective. In the case of the Minnesota bridge collapse, you would start with the collapse itself (the known effect) and work backward in time through all of the possible causes: heavy construction equipment overloaded the bridge; the bridge structure was already weakened by corrosion; corrosion had not been discovered because of lack of inspections and maintenance; the capacity of the bridge was reduced at the outset by an error in design.

Sonia Sotomayor travels back in time to examine the causes of adversity in her life, p. **454**.

Often you will want to organize your analysis around various types of causes or effects. You might, for instance, explore the immediate cause before moving on to the remote causes, or vice versa. Or you might explore the contributing causes before the main cause, or vice versa. Whatever method you choose, be sure to organize your analysis in a way that makes the relationship between causes and effects as clear to your reader as possible.

EDITING FOR COMMON ERRORS IN A CAUSE-AND-EFFECT ANALYSIS

Like other kinds of writing, a cause-and-effect analysis uses distinctive patterns of language and punctuation—and thus invites typical kinds of errors. The following tips will help you check for (and correct) these common errors when you analyze causes and effects in your own writing.

Check your verbs to make sure they clearly express causation

Some verbs express causation clearly and directly, whereas other verbs merely imply that one thing causes another.

VERBS THAT EXPRESS CAUSATION	VERBS THAT IMPLY CAUSATION
account for	follow
bring about	happen
cause	imply
effect	involve
make	implicate
result	influence

Using verbs that clearly express causation makes your analysis more precise.

► The collapse of the bridge on Interstate 35W ~~involved~~ <u>was caused by</u> faulty design.

Check for common usage errors

AFFECT, EFFECT

In cause-and-effect analysis, "affect" is usually a verb meaning "to influence." "Effect" is usually a noun meaning "result," but it can also be a verb meaning "to bring about." In psychology, "affect" can be a noun meaning "display of emotion" (or lack thereof).

► Failing the course did not <u>affect</u> his graduation.

► Failing the course did not have the <u>effect</u> he feared most.

► Failing the course, however, did <u>effect</u> a change in his normally smiling <u>affect</u>.

REASON IS BECAUSE, REASON WHY

Both of these expressions are redundant. In the first case, use "that" instead of "because." In the second, use "reason" alone.

► The reason the bridge collapsed was ~~because~~ <u>that</u> it was poorly designed.

► Faulty design is the reason ~~why~~ the bridge collapsed.

A "Text and Drive" Billboard

The folks at Wathan Funeral Home know something about cause and effect. For instance, they know from experience that texting while driving causes motorists to become distracted, lose control of their vehicles, and die. That's too bad for the drivers and their passengers but good for the funeral business, right? Actually, this cautionary billboard on the Gardiner Expressway in Toronto, Canada, is a public service announcement sponsored by an advertising agency. Their fake website for the nonexistent funeral home explains the ruse:

> If you're here, you've probably seen our "Text and Drive" billboard. And if you have, you probably came to this website to tell us what horrible people we are for running an ad like that. And you'd be right.
>
> It is a horrible thing for a funeral home to do.
>
> But we're not a funeral home.
>
> We're just trying to ... stop texting and driving, which is projected to kill more people ... this year than drinking and driving. That's right. More.

In their haste to make this public service announcement, the people back at the ad agency may have neglected to point out yet another benefit of keeping texting drivers out of the funeral home: it will mean more customers over time for other businesses, including advertising agencies.

ELISA GONZALEZ

FAMILY HISTORY

ELISA GONZALEZ is a poet, essayist, and writer of fiction whose work has appeared in the *New Yorker*, *Hyperallergic*, the *Harvard Review*, and elsewhere; she holds an MFA in creative writing from New York University. Gonzalez wrote "Family History" for a writing class when she was an undergraduate at Yale. In this essay, she explores the causes and effects of bipolar disorder in two members of the same family. Gonzalez does not try to determine if such psychological conditions are inherited, but she does find sufficient evidence in her family's history to suggest that the effects of one person's disorder may become causes of the same disorder in another family member. "Family History," along with other work by Gonzalez, won the 2011 Norman Mailer College Writing prize, sponsored jointly by the National Council of Teachers of English and the Norman Mailer Center and Writers Colony.

Family History

By the time I am diagnosed with bipolar disorder type II, I have known Dr. Bradley for years. I know that he is divorced with two children, that he dated a beautiful Russian nurse who quit last year under obscure circumstances, that he colors his hair to stop the gray from infringing on his catalogue-model looks. He delivered my littlest sister, now seven, and he cried when my youngest brother died after several days in an incubator, his lungs hesitantly fluttering like moth wings before they finally deflated. Dr. Bradley has spent years counseling my mother after suicide attempts. In many ways, he knows us better than my closest friends who, blithe and unsuspecting, have always accepted my selective disclosures about my family. So when he pauses, clears his throat, and asks if I have a family history of bipolar disorder, I stare at him without speaking. It seems impossible that he doesn't know about my father.

For several minutes, I have trouble comprehending what he's saying, though he's kind and clear. Based on what I've told him—that I've had to leave parties because the urge to scream was so uncontrollable I felt I might disintegrate, that I've stayed up for days without speaking or going to class, that I've frightened my boyfriend with my bursts of rage—bipolar disorder seems probable. It often manifests in people around my age, especially in creative high-achieving people. There is no blood test; he will give me medication, a combination of new antipsychotic drugs and traditional lithium pills, and see if I improve. Confirming my family history is the last piece of the diagnosis. Heredity strikes most people as soon as

1

First line introduces a serious effect of yet unknown cause(s)

Probes for possible causes of the disorder

2

Gives specific effects that might confirm the diagnosis

they look in the mirror, in how much the jawline pro-
trudes or how adamantly the earlobes crease, so I should
not be so surprised at being confronted with my own history. Studying a chart of the cardiovascular system, I
briefly wonder if I have always known that I carried with
me more than my father's curly hair and dry sense of
humor. But this is impossible, and far too mystical for the
sterility of the exam table. It is true, though, that I have
always feared my father, not just the physical reality of
him—those thick hands that have left bruises around my
throat and shoved my mother's teeth through her
cheeks—but the lingering effects of his presence.

When I was six, I went to the kitchen expecting   3
breakfast and found my father frying Sesame Street vid-
eotapes in the cast-iron skillet. The charred plastic littered the kitchen for days and smoke stained the walls for
the whole summer, until my father was released from his
month-long stay in the hospital and repainted the entire
house as penance. He also mended the holes he'd made in
the walls and bought a new couch to replace the one he'd
gutted with a butcher knife one night while we were
sleeping. To celebrate, we ate store-bought pecan pie in a
kitchen that smelled of fresh white paint. He talked about
repairing the furnace and my sister showed him the
stuffed dog named Rosie she'd gotten for her birthday.
Although this cycle—destruction, then rehabilitation—
has happened many times, I have always recalled the precision of his hands as he stood so calmly by the stove
stirring twisted plastic with a metal spatula.

A month before my diagnosis, my sister and I fought   4
about who would use the car, a typical sibling fight,
except in its escalation. I started screaming and threw a

Introduces a signifi-
cant probable cause
of the disorder

Implies that immedi-
ate effects of one
disorder may be
remote causes of
the other

book at her head, threatening to call the police on her and report the car stolen if she took it. When she moved toward the door, I got a knife from the kitchen and told her I would slash the tires before I would let her leave. She stopped arguing with me to say, disbelievingly, "You're just like Daddy." I wanted to tell her that I couldn't be like him because he is crazy and I am not. Instead, I began to weep soundlessly, collapsing to the ground, my mouth gaping and silent. Now, in the exam room, I feel that type of ache again, beyond expression because no noise can cure it. It is here that I realize my entire life has converged in a dark pattern newly revealed.

> Suggests a CAUSE-AND-EFFECT relationship between the two disorders

When my father was nineteen—the same age I am now—he cut up houseplants in precise segments and neatly ate a plateful with a fork before his brother found him and rushed him to the hospital. Later that month, after the doctors bandied around the word "schizophrenia" for a while, he received his own proper diagnosis. In 1979, lithium pharmacology had been approved for the treatment of manic depression, as bipolar disorder was called then, so his illness was manageable if he took his pills. But he never liked lithium, or the other medications his doctors prescribed. I wonder if I too will feel blunted and blurred without other forces sharpening themselves on my mind. Dr. Bradley asks if I have any questions before he writes me a prescription, and I say no. I am familiar with the required monthly checkups and learned the difference between the words "manic" and "maniac" when I was seven. Years before I grew up a little and participated in the national spelling bee, I was awed by the crucial distinction created through the addition of an *A*.

5

> Gives early symptoms of the father's disorder

> Anticipates possible future effects

> Suggests that the old name for the disorder confused cause and effect

The strangest part of hearing the diagnosis is that I   6
suddenly want something I haven't wanted in years: to
talk to my father. I know that he ran away after the doctors told him the news and his brothers found him four
days later on a beach in California, but I know nothing
else. I would like to call my father and say, "I know I've
always hated you, but as it turns out, I'm just like you."
Perhaps he would tell me how he felt when he found out,
if he slept on the beach and wandered through a shabby
town looking for the anonymity that would let him lose
his label, or if he blurted his diagnosis to people to try it
out. Mostly, I would like to know if he would have come
back, had they not found him, or if instead he would have
woken up and walked into the ocean one day, the only
person to separate the sky from all that water. The lure of
water in the lungs, of the non-breathing world, is one that
I too will face in the months after the diagnosis.

But my father and I haven't exchanged more than a   7
few words since I was fourteen, when he tried to strangle
me, saying that he had brought me into this world and he
could take me out of it. After that, he left us, hauled out
by police officers and kept away by court orders; I no longer know his number. I will not call him, nor mention
when I see him for a few minutes at Christmas that I am
also bipolar. Yet months after, when I am assigned *Paradise Lost* for a class, I will start to cry upon reading a piece
of the poet's invocation:

> *though fallen on evil days,*
> *on evil days though fallen, and evil tongues;*
> *in darkness, and with dangers compass'd round,*
> *and solitude; yet not alone.*

Confronts one of
the worst remote
effects she may
face

Ends with a positive
effect: the discovery
that her condition is
shared

TIM WENDEL

KING, KENNEDY, AND
THE POWER OF WORDS

TIM WENDEL (b. 1956) is a novelist, sportswriter, and teacher of writing. He was born in Philadelphia and grew up in Lockport, New York. After graduating from Syracuse University as a journalism major, Wendel earned an MFA from Johns Hopkins University, where he now teaches writing. His articles and essays have appeared in *Esquire, Go, Gargoyle*, the *New York Times*, the *Washington Post*, and *USA Today*. Author of *Summer of '68: The Season That Changed Baseball, and America, Forever* (2012), among other books, Wendel believes that American discourse, especially political discourse, has changed significantly in the decades since the assassinations of John F. Kennedy, Martin Luther King Jr., and Robert F. Kennedy. In "King, Kennedy, and the Power of Words" (from the website of the *American Scholar*, 2012), Wendel analyzes some of the specific causes and effects of those changes, particularly what he sees as the tendency of politicians today to slip into "passive-voice mode."

T HE NIGHT OF APRIL 4, 1968, presidential candidate Robert Kennedy received   1
the news that Martin Luther King Jr. had been assassinated. Kennedy
was about to speak in Indianapolis and some in his campaign wondered if
they should go ahead with the rally.

Moments before Kennedy climbed onto a flatbed truck to address the   2
crowd, which had gathered in a light rain, press secretary Frank Mankiewicz
gave the candidate a sheet of paper with ideas of what he might say. Kennedy
slid it into his pocket without looking at it. Another aide approached with
more notes and the candidate waved him away.

"Do they know about Martin Luther King?" Kennedy asked those gath-   3
ered on the platform. No, came the reply.

After asking the crowd to lower its campaign signs, Kennedy told his   4
audience that King had been shot and killed earlier in Memphis. Gasps went
up from the crowd and for a moment everything seemed ready to come apart.
Indianapolis might have joined other cities across America that burned on
that awful night.

But then Kennedy, beginning in a trembling, halting voice, slowly   5
brought the people back around and somehow held them together. Listening
to the speech decades later is to be reminded of the real power of words. How
they can heal, how they can still bring us together, but only if they are spoken
with conviction and from the heart.

Compare what we often hear from politicians today to what Kennedy   6
said on that tragic night in Indianapolis. He told the crowd how he "had a
member of my family killed"—a reference to his brother John, who had been
assassinated less than five years before.

Later on, Kennedy recited a poem by Aeschylus, which he had memo-   7
rized long before that trying night in Indianapolis:

Even in our sleep, pain which cannot forget
Falls drop by drop upon the heart,
Until, in our own despair, against our will,
Comes wisdom through the awful grace of God.

Kennedy's heartfelt speech came only hours after King's last address.   8
The night before, the civil rights leader had reluctantly taken to the dais at the

Martin Luther King Jr.

Mason Temple in Memphis. The weather that evening had been miserable—thunderstorms and tornado warnings. As a result, King arrived late and was just going to say a few words and then tell everyone to please go home.

Visibly tired and with no notes in hand, King stumbled at first. The shutters hitting against the temple walls sounded like gun shots to him. So much so that King's friend, the Reverend Billy Kyles, found a custodian to stop the noise. Only then, at the crowd's urging, did the words begin to come together for King.

> King identifies a number of threats to the civil rights movement in "The Other America," p. 576.

"We've got some difficult days ahead," he said that night. "But it really doesn't matter with me now. Because I've been to the mountaintop."

King closed by telling the crowd, "We as a people will get to the Promised Land. So I'm happy tonight. I'm not worried about anything. I'm not fearing any man. . . ."

Novelist Charles Baxter contends that the greatest influence on American writing and discourse in recent memory can be traced back to the phrase

9

10

11

12

"Mistakes were made." Of course, that's from Watergate and the shadowy intrigue inside the Nixon White House.[1] In his essay "Burning Down the House," Baxter compares that "quasi-confessional passive-voice-mode sentence" to what Robert E. Lee said after the battle of Gettysburg and the disastrous decision of Pickett's Charge.[2]

Remote causes are discussed on p. 430.

"All of this has been my fault," the Confederate general said. "I asked   13
more of the men than should have been asked of them."

In Lee's words, and those of King and Kennedy, we hear a refreshing can-   14
dor and directness that we miss today. In 1968, people responded to what King and Kennedy told them. During that tumultuous 24-hour period in 1968, people cried aloud and chanted in Memphis. Words struck a chord in Indianapolis, too, and decades later former mayor (and now U.S. Senator) Richard Lugar[3] told writer Thurston Clarke that Kennedy's speech was "a turning point" for his city.

After King's assassination, riots broke out in more than 100 U.S. cities—   15
the worst destruction since the Civil War. But neither Memphis nor Indianapolis experienced that kind of damage. To this day, many believe that was due to the words spoken when so many were listening.

FOR DISCUSSION

1. Beginning with the title of his essay, Tim Wendel **CLAIMS** that words have "power." Under what circumstances—and spoken by whom?

2. In Wendel's view, why did Memphis and Indianapolis largely escape destruction during the "riots" that followed the assassination of Martin Luther King Jr. in April 1968 (15)? Is his analysis correct? Why or why not?

3. "American writing and discourse," says Wendel, have changed since April 1968 (12). How have they changed? What are some of the chief causes of these effects?

1. Shortly after President Richard Nixon (1913–1994), a Republican, began his second term in office, it was discovered that operatives of his campaign had broken into offices of the Democratic Party in the Watergate office complex in June 1972. The resulting scandal, popularly known as Watergate, prompted Nixon to resign from office in 1974.
2. On July 3, 1863, Confederate commander Robert E. Lee ordered General George Pickett to lead an infantry assault against Union positions at Gettysburg, Pennsylvania. The attack failed, and the Battle of Gettysburg was lost. Many historians consider this to be the turning point of the Civil War.
3. Lugar's term as a senator ended in 2013.

4. To what extent is Wendel's essay ultimately about the art of **RHETORIC**, which can be defined as the use of words to move an audience to action or belief? Explain.

STRATEGIES AND STRUCTURES

1. Wendel's essay was written for Martin Luther King Day. How and how well do his words speak to that occasion? Explain.

2. Wendel criticizes the rhetoric of "politicians today" (6). Should he have named more names (12)? Why or why not?

3. As evidence of the power of words to heal, Wendel cites **EXAMPLES** of speech by King, Kennedy, and Robert E. Lee (15). Is this evidence sufficient to prove his claim? Explain.

4. On June 5, 1968, just two months after the death of Martin Luther King Jr., Robert Kennedy was shot while campaigning for the presidency; he died the next day. Should Wendell have mentioned this? Why or why not?

WORDS AND FIGURES OF SPEECH

1. The word "awful" comes up twice in Wendel's essay (4, 7). In what different senses does he use it?

2. Martin Luther King Jr. said he had been to the "mountaintop" (10). What mountaintop was he referring to? Explain the **ALLUSION**.

3. Look up "discourse" in a dictionary (12). In what sense is Wendel using the term here?

4. "Mistakes were made," Wendell quotes another writer as saying, is a "quasi-confessional passive-voice-mode sentence" (12)? What is passive about this verbal construction, and how does it fit in with Wendel's overall argument about the use of words by public figures?

FOR WRITING

1. Martin Luther King Jr.'s "The Other America" speech is reprinted in Chapter 14. Make a list of the words and phrases in King's speech that confirm (or call into question) the power of words when "spoken with conviction and from the heart" (5).

2. Choose one of the classic speeches or essays in Chapter 14, and write an essay analyzing where and how the author gives (or fails to give) the impression that we are listening a trustworthy person whose words deserve to be heard and even acted upon.

WHY AND WHEN WE SPEAK SPANISH IN PUBLIC

MYRIAM MÁRQUEZ (b. 1955) is the communications director and senior adviser for the mayor of Miami-Dade County, Florida. As a journalist and editor, she directed *El Nuevo Herald*, a sister publication of the *Miami Herald* and the Spanish-language daily newspaper with the largest circulation in America. Born in Cuba, Márquez fled to the United States with her parents in 1959. After graduating from the University of Maryland, where she studied journalism and political science, Márquez worked for 18 years at the *Orlando Sentinel* before joining the staff of the *Herald* in 2005. In "Why and When We Speak Spanish in Public" (*Orlando Sentinel,* 1999), Márquez examines the causes and effects of her family's decision not to adopt English as "our official family language."

WHEN I'M SHOPPING WITH MY MOTHER or standing in line with my step-dad to order fast food or anywhere else we might be together, we're going to speak to one another in Spanish.

That may appear rude to those who don't understand Spanish and over- 2
hear us in public places.

Those around us may get the impression that we're talking about them. 3
They may wonder why we would insist on speaking in a foreign
tongue, especially if they knew that my family has lived in the
United States for forty years and that my parents do understand
English and speak it, albeit with difficulty and a heavy accent.

> Assuming someone would only speak in another language if they don't speak English ignores the fact that an effect may have multiple causes (p. 430). 4

Let me explain why we haven't adopted English as our official
family language. For me and most of the bilingual people I know,
it's a matter of respect for our parents and comfort in our cultural roots.

It's not meant to be rude to others. It's not meant to alienate anyone or 5
to balkanize America.

It's certainly not meant to be un-American—what constitutes an 6
"American" being defined by English speakers from North America.

Being an American has very little to do with what language we use dur- 7
ing our free time in a free country. From its inception, this country was careful not to promote a government-mandated official language.

We understand that English is the common language of this country and 8
the one most often heard in international-business circles from Peru to Nor-
way. We know that, to get ahead here, one must learn English.

But that ought not mean that somehow we must stop speaking in our 9
native tongue whenever we're in a public area, as if we were ashamed of who
we are, where we're from. As if talking in Spanish—or any other language, for
that matter—is some sort of litmus test used to gauge American patriotism.

Throughout this nation's history, most immigrants—whether from Poland 10
or Finland or Italy or wherever else—kept their language through the first generation and, often, the second. I suspect that they spoke among themselves in
their native tongue—in public. Pennsylvania even provided voting ballots written in German during much of the 1800s for those who weren't fluent in English.

In this century, Latin American immigrants and others have fought for 11
this country in U.S.-led wars. They have participated fully in this nation's
democracy by voting, holding political office, and paying taxes. And they have
watched their children and grandchildren become so "American" that they
resist speaking in Spanish.

You know what's rude? 12

When there are two or more people who are bilingual and another person   13

To introduce a new example or topic, try using a rhetorical question, p. 187.

who speaks only English and the bilingual folks all of a sudden start speaking Spanish, which effectively leaves out the English-only speaker. I don't tolerate that.

One thing's for sure. If I'm ever in a public place with my   14
mom or dad and bump into an acquaintance who doesn't speak Spanish, I will switch to English and introduce that person to my parents. They will respond in English and do so with respect.

FOR DISCUSSION

1. Even though they have lived in the United States for many years, Myriam Márquez and her parents have not adopted English as their "official family language" (4). Should they have? Why or why not?

2. Márquez defends her family's right to speak Spanish among themselves, but she nevertheless insists that "one must learn English" (8). Why? What are the consequences of doing so—and of not doing so—in her view?

3. "I don't tolerate that," Márquez says of people who continue to speak Spanish in the presence of others who speak only English (13). Why does she think this is "rude" (12)? Do you agree? Why or why not?

STRATEGIES AND STRUCTURES

1. Márquez gives specific **EFFECTS** ("we're going to speak to one another in Spanish") before she gives particular **CAUSES** ("respect for our parents and comfort in our cultural roots") (1, 4). Is this a logical order of presentation? Why or why not?

2. Why does Márquez cite immigrants from Poland, Finland, Italy, and "wherever else" (10)? Is this additional evidence sufficient to justify her **CLAIM** that it's okay for her family to speak their native language in public? Why or why not?

3. Márquez makes a point of saying that immigrants from Latin America have "fought for this country" and "participated fully in this nation's democracy by voting, holding political office, and paying taxes" (11). What potential objection to her claim is she anticipating here?

4. How and how effectively does Márquez use elements of **NARRATIVE** to develop her analysis of causes and effects? Point to specific passages in the text that support your answer.

WORDS AND FIGURES OF SPEECH

1. To "balkanize" means to divide a region into small, less powerful states (5). Where does the meaning of this word come from, and how appropriate is Márquez's use of the term here?

2. A "litmus test" is a test in which the outcome is based on only one factor (9). Why might Márquez be reluctant to apply such an either/or test to a person's "patriotism" (9)?

3. Why does Márquez make a point of describing certain behavior as "rude" (2, 12)? How does her choice of this word affect her **CREDIBILITY** as someone who can judge when social behavior is proper or not?

FOR WRITING

1. In a paragraph or two, explain why it would or would not be rude to continue speaking rapidly in English (or some other language) in the presence of others who aren't familiar with the language being spoken.

2. Write an essay analyzing how and why you and your family (or friends) might speak or behave in a fashion that could seem exclusive to others but that is not intended to be disrespectful. Give specific circumstances under which you think such conduct would and would not be appropriate.

JAMELLE BOUIE

WHY DON'T YOUNG PEOPLE VOTE?

JAMELLE BOUIE (b. 1987) is a journalist and political analyst who writes about elections, history, and culture. Bouie grew up in Virginia Beach, Virginia, and graduated from the University of Virginia in 2009. An opinion columnist for the *New York Times*, he was chief political correspondent for *Slate*, where "Why Don't Young People Vote?" first appeared in 2018, on the eve of national midterm elections. The short answer to this question of cause and effect, says Bouie in the original subtitle of his essay, is "this system doesn't want them to." Why not? And what's to be done about it? According to Bouie's analysis, the current voting system favors "people with time, money, and property"; but more young people might vote, he concludes, if they understood that "knowledge of issues was less important than knowledge of their own interests."

T O VOTE IN THE UNITED STATES, you can't simply go cast a ballot. In most 1 states, you first have to register. If you've registered, you have to have state-issued identification to then actually vote. If you don't have identification, you might have to pay a fee to obtain it. If you don't live in an early voting state—or one with flexible absentee rules—you have to take time from work to cast your ballot. If you live in states like Georgia or Florida, you may have to wait for hours before you can step into a voting booth. If you can't drive or aren't mobile, you may have to find a ride.

If you're middle-aged with a stable job and a fixed-address, this is 2 straightforward. If you're anyone else, it's less so. And if your life is defined by *instability*—in location, in housing, in employment—any single obstacle might be enough to discourage you from voting altogether. That might be why turnout for the youngest voters in the electorate is lower than most other groups.

To define anything, look for its most distinctive characteristics, p. 375–76.

America lowered the voting age to 18 with the 26th Amendment in 1971. 3 In 1972, nearly half of eligible young people turned out to vote. Since then, the voting rate for 18- to 24-year-olds in presidential elections has hovered between 30 and 45 percent, with average turnout of about 40 percent according to data from the Census Bureau. For midterm elections, the average is closer to 20 percent.

More striking than the low averages is the consistency of the difference 4 with older Americans. In any given election year, the youngest voters *always* turn out at lower rates than their next oldest counterparts, who always turn out at lower rates than their next oldest counterparts, and so on, until you reach the oldest Americans. Since 1972, older Americans have voted at an average rate of 67 percent in presidential elections and nearly 59 percent in midterms. The fact of this pattern should obliterate any speculation about generational difference. There's either something about being young that precludes or prevents political participation, or there's something about the structure of American elections that impedes young people from participating.

It's much more likely that something is the instability that comes with 5 being young. You're less likely to have a permanent address, less likely to have secure and flexible employment, less likely to have the confidence to participate in the political process. You can see all of this in a set of interviews with young adults who say they won't vote in this week's elections, published in

New York magazine. Some respondents are cynical or simply uninspired. But others report real obstacles to their ability to participate.

Megan, age 29, says she moves too much to keep track with her registra-   6
tion. "I rent and move around quite a bit, and when I try to get absentee ballots, they need me to print out a form and mail it to them no more than 30 days before the election but also no less than seven days before the election," she said.

Anna, age 21, also says the process is too cumbersome. "I'm trying to   7
register in my hometown of Austin, Texas. It's such a tedious process to even get registered in Texas, let alone vote as an absentee," she says, adding that "if someone had the forms printed for me and was willing to deal with the post office, I'd be much more inclined to vote."

Jocelyn, age 27, also blames the process. "It was easier to get my medical-   8
marijuana card—not a right, or even federally legal—than it was to register to vote. Massachusetts had online registration but only if you have a DMV-issued ID. I don't drive, so I was like, okay, I can register in person, but I'm also dealing with a chronic illness."

Maria, age 26, doesn't want to commit the time. "The idea of leaving   9
work, forwarding all of my calls to my phone, to go stand in line for four hours, to probably get called back to work before I even get halfway through the line, sounds terrible."

With each account, we have a different example of how our voting sys-   10
tem doesn't actually encourage voting, especially among people whose lives are defined by a certain amount of instability and unpredictability. Look beyond young adults to the larger population of nonvoters and you see a significant group whose lives are marked by traits asso-ciated with a lack of stability. They are less likely to have college degrees, more likely to have family incomes below $30,000, and more likely to belong to racial and ethnic minorities, making them more likely to experience conditions associated with instability.

Cause or correla-
tion? For the differ-
ence, see p. 424.

Our system has adopted universal suffrage, which points toward open and   11
easy access to the ballot, but our heritage in political exclusivity—where voting was once a privilege reserved for property-owning white men—continues to influence our handling of elections. Voter identification laws are tied to a sordid history of discrimination and vote suppression, but even procedures as uncon-troversial as voter registration contain assumptions about who *should* participate.

(Indeed, voter registration was first developed as a method to keep recent immigrants and the poor from the ballot box in Northern cities and was used similarly against black Americans in the Jim Crow South.) Our voting system is tilted toward people with stable, conventional lives. And that, overwhelmingly, is who participates, producing a conservative bias in the status quo.

Our government is less representative than it could be because of our voter-unfriendly policies. So even if you disdain young people who can't find the will or time to vote—even if you're unsympathetic toward the uninspired or the uninterested—you should want to fix this problem. 12

It's not a difficult one to solve. Automatic, universal registration would obviate the need for any action from individual voters, who would be registered upon contact with state agencies like the DMV; pre-registration of older teenagers would prepare the youngest voters for political participation; and Election Day registration would open the doors to anyone eligible to cast a ballot. If bundled with vote by mail (with a stamp provided by the government), states could eliminate most obstacles to participation, with no obvious downsides. (Voter fraud, after all, is practically nonexistent.) 13

This isn't speculation. After Oregon passed automatic voter registration in 2016, an additional 270,000 people were added to the voter rolls. New voters were disproportionately black, Latino, and Asian American, and more likely to belong to the youngest age cohorts. Automatic registration also increased the economic diversity of the state's electorate. Likewise, in Colorado, vote by mail has boosted turnout among young and infrequent voters. 14

As long as voting is voluntary, young people will likely always vote at lower rates than their older counterparts. Instability may be the most concrete limiting factor, but there's also just something about being young—about being preoccupied with your first years of adulthood—that makes politics a secondary concern. There are cultural factors too. Several *New York* magazine interviewees felt too uninformed to responsibly cast a ballot, which suggests a discourse that puts too high a premium on arbitrary political knowledge and not enough on knowing oneself as a political actor with a legitimate claim on the state. Perhaps more young people would vote if they knew knowledge of *issues* was less important than knowledge of their own *interests*. 15

But if there is an upper bound to youth turnout under the constitutional status quo, we haven't reached it. And the reasons have everything to do with 16 how we still structure elections to advantage people with time, money, and property.

Moralism and appeal to civic virtue may move some nonvoters off the 17 sidelines in time, and if they live in states with same-day registration, they'll be able to cast a ballot. But that "if" gets us to the larger issue: We will only have a culture of voting and high turnout if we build one. And if there is apathy and disdain for political participation, we should understand that it's likely produced by institutions and systems that too often do everything they can to *keep* people from having a say in their government.

FOR DISCUSSION

1. In national elections, according to Jamelle Bouie, how does voter turnout correlate with age? Where does Bouie get his figures, and how reliable do you find them?

2. "For midterm elections," says Bouie, the average turnout among the youngest of eligible voters "is closer to 20 percent" (3). What are "midterm" elections, exactly, and why might young voters turn out for them in even fewer numbers?

3. Bouie implies that "instability" not only hinders people from voting but that it actually "defines" the lives of many young people (2). What does he mean by "instability," and how common is it, in your view? Explain.

4. Some people fail to vote, says Bouie, because they lack "the confidence to participate in the political process" (5). Is this true? Why or why not?

5. Even if they lack "knowledge of issues," says Bouie, young people should vote based on a "knowledge of their own interests" (15). How might potential voters gain this second kind of knowledge?

STRATEGIES AND STRUCTURES

1. In Bouie's view, what are some of the prior causes, both immediate and remote, of a voting system that can be overly complicated and time consuming? Point to specific passages in the text where he identifies them.

2. Among the various factors in Bouie's analysis, which ones indicate that "there's something about the structure of American elections that impedes young people from participating," and which ones indicate that there is "something about being young that precludes or prevents political participation" (4)? Explain.

3. Bouie gives several **EXAMPLES** of young people who fail to vote. How and how well do they confirm his analysis of the effects of "instability" and other life factors on the voting process?

4. Along with enlightened self-interest, what else is necessary, according to Bouie, for building "a culture of voting and high turnout" (17)? How and how well does he make the case that this can and should be done?

5. Bouie does not mention political parties by name in his essay. As a result of this apparently bipartisan approach, is his analysis stronger or weaker in your view? Why do you think so?

WORDS AND FIGURES OF SPEECH

1. The word "if" appears 20 times in Bouie's essay. Why might this particular conjunction occur frequently in an analysis of causes and effects?

2. What is "an early voting state" (1), and which particular states belong in this category?

3. "Universal suffrage" is the right of all adult citizens to vote (11). How did the 26th Amendment of 1971 change the definition of "universal" for voting purposes?

4. The history of laws pertaining to voter identification, says Bouie, is "sordid" (11). Is this **HYPERBOLE**? Why or why not?

5. In informal use, a "cohort" may be defined as a group of friends or colleagues. How is Bouie defining the term when, for example, he refers to "the youngest age cohorts" (14)?

FOR WRITING

1. A journalist has asked you why you do (or do not) expect to vote in the next general election. In a paragraph or two, write out what you would say to the interviewer about the process of casting your ballot.

2. Do some research on compulsory voting in Australia and elsewhere, and write an essay explaining how it came about, how it works (or doesn't), and why compulsory voting would (or would not) improve the voting system in the United States, especially for young adults.

3. Bouie refers to "the instability that comes with being young" as a general condition of "the youngest age cohort" (5, 14). Write an analysis of the common causes of some other important characteristic or condition that might be ascribed to your age cohort—empathy, enthusiasm for new ideas and experience, generosity, tolerance, fairness. Discuss some of the specific effects that this common "trait" might possibly have on public life.

MY BELOVED WORLD

SONIA SOTOMAYOR (b. 1954) is an associate justice of the Supreme Court of the United States, a position she has held since 2009, following her nomination by then-president Barack Obama. Sotomayor was born in the Bronx to parents who moved from Puerto Rico to New York. Her only goal when growing up, she has said, was to graduate from college. Indeed, she achieved that goal: after graduating as the valedictorian of her high school, Sotomayor attended Princeton University and Yale Law School. Her ensuing legal career has been a steady ascent: assistant district attorney, U.S. District Court judge, U.S. Court of Appeals judge, and now a justice of the Supreme Court, where she is the third woman (and the first Latina) to be appointed. This reading is the prologue to her memoir *My Beloved World* (2013)—here, Sotomayor writes about the adversity she faced in her childhood and how hardship shaped her life for the better. As she says, "difficulty can tap unsuspected strengths."

I WAS NOT YET EIGHT YEARS OLD when I was diagnosed with diabetes. To my 1 family, the disease was a deadly curse. To me, it was more a threat to the already fragile world of my childhood, a state of constant tension punctuated by explosive discord, all of it caused by my father's alcoholism and my mother's response to it, whether family fight or emotional flight. But the disease also inspired in me a kind of precocious self-reliance that is not uncommon in children who feel the adults around them to be unreliable.

There are uses to adversity, and they don't reveal themselves until 2 tested. Whether it's serious illness, financial hardship, or the simple constraint of parents who speak limited English, difficulty can tap unsuspected strengths. It doesn't always, of course: I've seen life beat people down until they can't get up. But I have never had to face anything that could overwhelm the native optimism and stubborn perseverance I was blessed with.

At the same time, I would never claim to be self-made—quite the con- 3 trary: at every stage of my life, I have always felt that the support I've drawn from those closest to me has made the decisive difference between success and failure. And this was true from the beginning. Whatever their limitations and frailties, those who raised me loved me and did the best they knew how. Of that I am sure.

The world that I was born into was a tiny microcosm of Hispanic New 4 York City. A tight few blocks in the South Bronx bounded the lives of my extended family: my grandmother, matriarch of the tribe, and her second husband, Gallego, her daughters and sons. My playmates were my cousins. We spoke Spanish at home, and many in my family spoke virtually no English. My parents had both come to New York from Puerto Rico in 1944, my mother in the Women's Army Corps, my father with his family in search of work as part of a huge migration from the island, driven by economic hardship.

My brother, now Juan Luis Sotomayor Jr., M.D., but to me forever Junior, 5 was born three years after I was. I found him a nuisance as only a little brother can be, following me everywhere, mimicking my every gesture, eavesdropping on every conversation. In retrospect, he was actually a quiet child who made few demands on anyone's attention. My mother always said that compared with me, caring for Junior was like taking a vacation. Once, when he was still tiny and I wasn't much bigger, my exasperation with him inspired me to lead him into the hallway outside the apartment and shut the door. I don't know how much later it was that my mother found him, sitting right where I'd left him, sucking his thumb. But I do know I got walloped that day.

But that was just domestic politics. On the playground, or once he started school at Blessed Sacrament with me, I watched out for him, and any bully thinking of messing with him would have to mix it up with me first. If I got beat up on Junior's account, I would settle things with him later, but no one was going to lay a hand on him except me.

Around the time that Junior was born, we moved to a newly constructed public housing project in Soundview, just a ten-minute drive from our old neighborhood. The Bronxdale Houses sprawled over three large city blocks: twenty-eight buildings, each seven stories tall with eight apartments to a floor. My mother saw the projects as a safer, cleaner, brighter alternative to the decaying tenement where we had lived. My grandmother Abuelita, however, saw this move as a venture into far and alien territory, *el jurutungo viejo* for all practical purposes. My mother should never have made us move, she said, because in the old neighborhood there was life on the streets and family nearby; in the projects we were isolated.

I knew well enough that we were isolated, but that condition had more to do with my father's drinking and the shame attached to it. It constrained our lives as far back as my memory reaches. We almost never had visitors. My cousins never spent the night at our home as I did at theirs. Even Ana, my mother's best friend, never came over, though she lived in the projects too, in the building kitty-corner from ours, and took care of my brother, Junior, and me after school. We always went to her place, never the other way around.

A single cause can have multiple effects, p. 428.

The only exception to this rule was Alfred. Alfred was my first cousin— the son of my mother's sister, Titi Aurora. And just as Titi Aurora was much older than Mami, and more of a mother to her than a sister, Alfred, being sixteen years older than I, acted more as an uncle to me than a cousin. Sometimes my father would ask Alfred to bring him a bottle from the liquor store. We counted on Alfred a lot, in part because my father avoided driving. This annoyed me, as it clearly contributed to our isolation—and what's the point of having a car if you never drive it? I didn't understand until I was older that his drinking was probably the reason.

My father would cook dinner when he got home from work; he was an 10
excellent cook and could re-create from memory any new dish he encountered
as well as the Puerto Rican standards he no doubt picked up in Abuelita's
kitchen. I loved every dish he made without exception, even his liver and
onions, which Junior hated and shoveled over to me when Papi's back was
turned. But as soon as dinner was over, the dishes still piled in the sink, he
would shut himself in the bedroom. We wouldn't see him again until he came
out to tell us to get ready for bed. It was just Junior and I every night, doing
homework and not much else. Junior wasn't much of a conversationalist yet.
Eventually, we got a television, which helped to fill the silence.

My mother's way of coping was to avoid being at home with my father. 11
She worked the night shift as a practical nurse at Prospect Hospital and often
on weekends too. When she wasn't working, she would drop us off at Abuelita's or sometimes at her sister Aurora's apartment and then disappear for
hours with another of my aunts. Even though my mother and I shared the
same bed every night (Junior slept in the other room with Papi), she might as
well have been a log, lying there with her back to me. My father's neglect made
me sad, but I intuitively understood that he could not help himself; my
mother's neglect made me angry at her. She was beautiful, always elegantly
dressed, seemingly strong and decisive. She was the one who moved us to the
projects. Unlike my aunts, she chose to work. She was the one who insisted
we go to Catholic school. Unfairly perhaps, because I knew nothing then of
my mother's own story, I expected more from her.

However much was said at home, and loudly, much also went unsaid, 12
and in that atmosphere I was a watchful child constantly scanning the adults
for cues and listening in on their conversations. My sense of security depended
on what information I could glean, any clue dropped inadvertently when they
didn't realize a child was paying attention. My aunts and my mother would
gather in Abuelita's kitchen, drinking coffee and gossiping. "*¡No me molestes!*[1]
Go play in the other room now," an aunt would say, shooing me away, but I
overheard much regardless: how my father had broken the lock on Titi Gloria's
liquor cabinet, ruining her favorite piece of furniture; how whenever Junior
and I slept over with our cousins, my father would phone every fifteen min-

---

1. Don't bother me!

utes all night long, asking, "Did you feed them? Did you give them a bath?" I knew well enough that my aunts and my grandmother were all prone to exaggeration. It wasn't really every fifteen minutes, but Papi did call a lot, as I gathered from my aunts' exasperated and mechanically reassuring side of the conversations.

The gossip would then take a familiar turn, my grandmother saying   13
something like "Maybe if Celina ever came home, he wouldn't be drinking every night. If those kids had a mother who ever cooked a meal, Juli wouldn't be worrying about them all night." As much as I adored Abuelita—and no one resented my mother's absence more than I did—I couldn't bear this constant blaming. Abuelita was unconditionally loyal to blood kin. Her sons' wives were not outside the ambit of her protection, but they didn't enjoy the same immunity from prosecution. And often my mother's efforts to please Abuelita—whether a generously chosen gift or her ready services as a nurse—went dimly acknowledged. Even being Abuelita's favorite, I felt exposed and unmoored when she criticized my mother, whom I struggled to understand and forgive myself. In fact, she and I wouldn't achieve a final reconciliation before working on it for many years.

See p. 430 for more on main and contributing causes.

My surveillance activities became family legend the Christmas that   14
Little Miss Echo arrived. I had seen the doll with its concealed tape recorder advertised on television and begged for it. It was the hottest gift of the season, and Titi Aurora had searched far and wide for a store that still had one in stock. I sent my cousin Miriam into the kitchen with the doll to bug the adults' conversation, knowing that I would have been immediately suspect. But before anything could be recorded, Miriam cracked and gave me up at the first question, and I got walloped anyway.

One overheard conversation had a lasting effect, though I now remember   15
it only dimly. My father was sick: he had passed out, and Mami took him to the hospital. Tío Vitín and Tío Benny came to get Junior and me, and they were talking in the elevator about how our home was a pigsty, with dishes in the sink and no toilet paper. They spoke as if we weren't there. When I realized what they were saying, my stomach lurched with shame. After that I washed the dishes every night, even the pots and pans, as soon as we finished dinner. I also dusted the living room once a week. Even though no one ever came over, the house was always clean. And when I went shopping with Papi

on Fridays, I made sure we bought toilet paper. And milk. More than enough milk.

The biggest fight my parents ever had was because of the milk. At dinner- 16
time, Papi was pouring a glass for me, and his hands were shaking so badly the milk spilled all over the table. I cleaned up the mess, and he tried again with the same result. "Papi, please don't!" I kept repeating. It was all I could do to keep myself from crying; I was utterly powerless to stop him. "Papi, I don't want any milk!" But he didn't stop until the carton was empty. When my mother got home from work later and there was no milk for her coffee, all hell broke loose. Papi was the one who had spilled the milk, but I was the one who felt guilty.

FOR DISCUSSION

1. As a child, Sonia Sotomayor and her family lived, she says, in "a state of constant tension punctuated by explosive discord" (1). As Sotomayor analyzes them here, what were some of the main CAUSES of that tension and discord?

2. Her father's "neglect" of her as a child, writes Sotomayor, made her "sad," but her mother's "neglect" made her "angry" (11). Why did such similar causes have such different emotional EFFECTS upon young Sotomayor?

3. As she was growing up, Sotomayor struggled with material poverty, illness, and, after the early death of her father, a mother who remained emotionally distant from her. What, according to Sotomayor, allowed her to overcome this adversity?

4. In her preface to *My Beloved World*, Sotomayor says that her main purpose in writing the book was "to make my hopeful example accessible." Is the example she offers in this reading actually "hopeful," despite all the hardships? Is it "accessible?" Explain.

5. Sotomayor says she was "a watchful child" (12). What caused her to be this way in particular? Point to specific passages in the text to support your answer.

STRATEGIES AND STRUCTURES

1. How do the first three paragraphs of Sotomayor's text serve as an introduction to the rest? In particular, how do they indicate that she is doing more here than just telling a story? Point to specific passages in the text that signal her wider intentions to the reader.

2. Sotomayor is writing about the "uses to adversity," as well as the causes of it in her early life (2). The causes she analyzes are rich in detail. Where and how does she examine the useful effects of those causes?

3. In her next-to-last paragraph, Sotomayor recalls overhearing a conversation that had a "lasting effect" on her (15). To what extent might her account of this conversation be said to represent the entire chapter? How and how well does her analysis of causes and effects in this passage serve her stated purpose of presenting a "hopeful example" to the reader?

4. "People who live in difficult circumstances need to know that happy endings are possible." Why, then, do you think she ends the chapter with a scene of tension, where "all hell broke loose" (16)?

WORDS AND FIGURES OF SPEECH

1. Given the many difficulties she had to overcome, the title of Sotomayor's book *My Beloved World* sounds like an example of **IRONY**. Is it? Explain.

2. Sotomayor writes "the world that I was born into was a tiny microcosm of Hispanic New York City" (4). The term "microcosm" means "little world." How might this entire early chapter of her book be seen as a microcosm of her entire life story?

3. Unlike her mother, says Sotomayor, her father enjoyed "immunity from prosecution" by her sometimes critical grandmother (13). Where else in her text does Sotomayor's language and perspective reflect her background as a lawyer and judge? Point to specific words and phrases.

FOR WRITING

1. In two or three paragraphs, recall a difficult relationship that affected you in your early years. What do you think caused the relationship to be difficult, and how did you achieve (or fail to achieve) a "final reconciliation" with that person (13)?

2. Write an essay about hardships in your childhood or early youth. Explain the lasting effects such adversity had on you and what you learned.

ANDREW SULLIVAN

THE POISON WE PICK

ANDREW SULLIVAN (b. 1963) is a writer, editor, and political blogger. A native of Britain, Sullivan attended Oxford University, where he earned a bachelor's degree in modern history and languages. Sullivan came to the United States in 1984 and continued his studies at Harvard University in political science, earning an MA and a PhD. A former editor of the *New Republic* and writer for the *New York Times Magazine*, he is the author of several books, including *Virtually Normal* (1996), about the politics of homosexuality, and *The Conservative Soul* (2006). In 2002, Sullivan started *The Daily Dish*, an influential political and cultural blog that he ran until 2015. Since 2016, Sullivan has been a contributing editor of *New York* magazine, where "The Poison We Pick" appeared in 2018. In this selection, Sullivan explores the causes and myriad effects of the opioid epidemic in America. The online version of this article was titled "Americans Invented Modern Life. Now We're Using Opioids to Escape It."

N O OTHER DEVELOPED COUNTRY IS AS DEVOTED to the poppy as America.   1
      We consume 99 percent of the world's hydrocodone and 81 percent of
its oxycodone.[1] We use an estimated 30 times more opioids than is medically
necessary for a population our size. And this love affair has been with us from
the start.

Based on contemporary accounts, it appears that the epidemic of the   2
late 1860s and 1870s was probably more widespread, if far less intense, than
today's—a response to the way in which the [Civil] war tore up
settled ways of life, as industrialization transformed the landscape, and as huge social change generated acute emotional distress. This aspect of the epidemic—as a response to mass social and cultural
dislocation—was also clear among the working classes in the earlier part of
the 19th century in Britain. As small armies of human beings were lured from
their accustomed rural environments, with traditions and seasons and community, and thrown into vast new industrialized cities, the psychic stress
gave opium an allure not even alcohol could match. Some historians estimate
that as much as 10 percent of a working family's income in industrializing
Britain was spent on opium. By 1870, opium was more available in the United
States than tobacco was in 1970. It was as if the shift toward modernity and a
wholly different kind of life for humanity necessitated for most working
people some kind of relief—some way of getting out of the train while it was
still moving.

Page 427 explains
how to trace the
links in a causal
chain like this.

It is tempting to wonder if, in the future, today's crisis will be seen as   3
generated from the same kind of trauma, this time in reverse. If industrialization caused an opium epidemic, deindustrialization is no small part of what's
fueling our opioid surge. It's telling that the drug has not taken off as intensely
among all Americans—especially not among the engaged, multiethnic, urban-
dwelling, financially successful inhabitants of the coasts. The poppy has instead
found a home in those places left behind—towns and small cities that owed
their success to a particular industry, whose civic life was built around a factory or a mine. Unlike in Europe, where cities and towns existed long before

---

1. Like the opiates morphine and heroin, these two narcotic drugs, usually prescribed as
painkillers, are derived from the opium poppy plant; as "opioids," however, they do not
occur in nature but are made by modifying chemicals found naturally in opium.

industrialization, much of America's heartland has no remaining preindustrial history, given the destruction of Native American societies. The gutting of that industrial backbone—especially as globalization intensified in a country where market forces are least restrained—has been not just an economic fact but a cultural, even spiritual devastation. The pain was exacerbated by the Great Recession and has barely receded in the years since. And to meet that pain, America's uniquely market-driven health-care system was more than ready. . . .

The [pharmaceutical] industry moved quickly to cash in on the opportunity: aggressively marketing the new drugs to doctors via sales reps, coupons, and countless luxurious conferences, while waging innovative video campaigns designed to be played in doctors' waiting rooms. As Sam Quinones explains in his indispensable account of the epidemic, *Dreamland*, all this happened at the same time that doctors were being pressured to become much more efficient under the new regime of "managed care."[2] It was a fateful combination: Patients began to come into doctors' offices demanding pain relief, and doctors needed to process patients faster. A "pain" diagnosis was often the most difficult and time-consuming to resolve, so it became far easier just to write a quick prescription to abolish the discomfort rather than attempt to isolate its cause. The more expensive and laborious methods for treating pain—physical and psychological therapy—were abandoned almost overnight in favor of the magic pills.

For a selection from *Dreamland*, see p. 100.

[U]nscrupulous doctors, often in poorer areas, found a way to make a literal killing from shady pill mills. So did many patients. A Medicaid co-pay of $3 for a bottle of pills, as Quinones discovered, could yield $10,000 on the streets—an economic arbitrage that enticed countless middle-class Americans to become drug dealers. One study has found that 75 percent of those addicted to opioids in the United States began with prescription painkillers given to them by a friend, family member, or dealer. As a result, the social and cultural profile of opioid users shifted as well: The old stereotype of a heroin junkie—a dropout or a hippie or a Vietnam vet—disappeared in the younger generation, especially in high schools. Football players were given opioids to

2. *Managed care* health plans seek to lower the costs of medical treatment by restricting patients to a list of doctors in the plan and capping those doctors' fees.

mask injuries and keep them on the field; they shared them with cheerleaders and other popular peers; and their elevated social status rebranded the addiction. Now opiates came wrapped in the bodies and minds of some of the most promising, physically fit, and capable young men and women of their generation. Courtesy of their doctors and coaches.

It's hard to convey the sheer magnitude of what happened. Between 2007 and   6
2012, for example, 780 million hydrocodone and oxycodone pills were delivered to West Virginia, a state with a mere 1.8 million residents. In one town, population 2,900, more than 20 million opioid prescriptions were processed in the past decade. Nationwide, between 1999 and 2011, oxycodone prescriptions increased sixfold. National per capita consumption of oxycodone went from around 10 milligrams in 1995 to almost 250 milligrams by 2012.

The quantum leap in opioid use arrived by stealth. Most previous drug   7
epidemics were accompanied by waves of crime and violence, which prompted others, outside the drug circles, to take notice and action. But the opioid scourge was accompanied, during its first decade, by a record drop in both. Drug users were not out on the streets causing mayhem or havoc. They were inside, mostly alone, and deadly quiet. There were no crack houses to raid or gangs to monitor. Overdose deaths began to climb, but they were often obscured by a variety of dry terms used in coroners' reports to hide what was really happening. When the cause of death was inescapable—young corpses discovered in bedrooms or fast-food restrooms—it was also, frequently, too shameful to share. Parents of dead teenagers were unlikely to advertise their agony.

In time, of course, doctors realized the scale of their error. Between 2010   8
and 2015, opioid prescriptions declined by 18 percent. But if it was a huge, well-intended mistake to create this army of addicts, it was an even bigger one to cut them off from their supply. That is when the addicted were forced to turn to black-market pills and street heroin. Here again, the illegal supply channel broke with previous patterns. It was no longer controlled by the established cartels in the big cities that had historically been the main source of narcotics. This time, the heroin—particularly cheap, black-tar heroin from Mexico—came from small drug-dealing operations that avoided major urban areas, instead following the trail of methadone clinics and pill mills into the American heartland.

Their innovation, Quinones discovered, was to pay the dealers a flat sal- 9
ary, rather than a cut from the heroin itself. This removed the incentives to
weaken the product, by cutting it with baking soda or other additives, and so
made the new drug much more predictable in its power and reliable in its dosage. And rather than setting up a central location to sell the drugs—like a
conventional shooting gallery or crack house—the new heroin marketers
delivered it by car. Outside methadone clinics or pill mills, they handed out
cards bearing only a telephone number. Call them and they would arrange to
meet you near your house, in a suburban parking lot. They were routinely
polite and punctual.

Buying heroin became as easy in the suburbs and rural areas as buying 10
weed in the cities. No violence, low risk, familiar surroundings: an entire system specifically designed to provide a clean-cut, friendly, middle-class high.
America was returning to the norm of the 19th century, when opiates were a
routine medicine, but it was consuming compounds far more potent, addictive,
and deadly than any 19th century tincture enthusiast could have imagined. . . .

Heroin, rather than good old-fashioned opium, became the opioid of the 11
streets.

Then came fentanyl, a massively concentrated opioid that delivers up to 12
50 times the strength of heroin.[3] Developed in 1959, it is now one of the most
widely used opioids in global medicine, its miraculous pain relief delivered
through transdermal patches, or lozenges, that have revolutionized surgery
and recovery and helped save countless lives. But in its raw form, it is one of
the most dangerous drugs ever created by human beings. A recent shipment
of fentanyl seized in New Jersey fit into the trunk of a single car yet contained
enough poison to wipe out the entire population of New Jersey and New York
City combined. That's more potential death than a dirty bomb or a small
nuke. That's also what makes it a dream for traffickers. A kilo of heroin can
yield $500,000; a kilo of fentanyl is worth as much as $1.2 million.

3. Hydrocodone and oxycodone are "semi-synthetic" opioids made by manipulating chemicals derived from poppies; fentanyl is completely synthetic: all compounds in it are made
in the lab. Fentanyl can thus be produced much faster, cheaper, and with far greater potency
than natural opiates.

The problem with fentanyl, as it pertains to traffickers, is that it is close   13
to impossible to dose correctly. To be injected at all, fentanyl's microscopic
form requires it to be cut with various other substances, and that cutting is
playing with fire. Just the equivalent of a few grains of salt can send you into
sudden paroxysms of heaven; a few more grains will kill you. It is obviously
not in the interests of drug dealers to kill their entire customer base, but keeping most of their clients alive appears beyond their skill. The way heroin kills
you is simple: The drug dramatically slows the respiratory system, suffocating
users as they drift to sleep. Increase the potency by a factor of 50 and it is no
surprise that you can die from ingesting just a half a milligram of the stuff. . . .

We have seen this story before—in America and elsewhere. The allure of opi-   14
ates' joys are filling a hole in the human heart and soul today as they have
since the dawn of civilization. But this time, the drugs are not merely laced
with danger and addiction. In a way never experienced by humanity before,
the pharmaceutically sophisticated and ever more intense bastard children of
the sturdy little flower bring mass death in their wake. This time, they are
agents of an eternal and enveloping darkness. And there is a long, long path
ahead, and many more bodies to count, before we will see any light.

FOR DISCUSSION

1. As Andrew Sullivan sees it, the opioid epidemic in America has been largely a
   matter of supply and demand. If physical pain was the immediate cause of the
   limitless demand for prescription pain killers, what was the immediate cause, in
   Sullivan's analysis, of the limitless supply? Explain.

2. Beginning in the 1990s, the opiate scourge, says Sullivan, "arrived by stealth" (7).
   What was so sneaky (and unprecedented) about its arrival and spread, especially
   in American high schools?

3. The immediate (or *proximate*) cause of death from an overdose of heroin is suffocation. "The drug," says Sullivan, "dramatically slows the respiratory system, suffocating users as they drift to sleep" (13). Why, according to Sullivan, did so many people
   nevertheless shift from prescription opiates to this much more deadly street drug?

4. "Then came fentanyl" (12). Fentanyl does not come from poppies; it is a synthetic
   opioid that "delivers up to 50 times the strength of heroin" (12). How and why, as
   reported by Sullivan, does this even greater potency make fentanyl "a dream for
   traffickers" (12)?

5. The trafficker's dream is the user's nightmare. Why do so many users of uncontrolled fentanyl die even though it is "obviously not in the interests of drug dealers to kill their entire customer base" (13)?

6. Sullivan is tempted to see "trauma" as the ultimate cause, now and earlier, of the widespread use of opioids in America and elsewhere (3). In his analysis, the pain that accompanies this trauma goes far beyond physical pain because it is the result of "a hole in the human heart and soul" (14). What is the nature of this hole, and how did it come about?

7. The opioid epidemic, says Sullivan, "has not taken off as intensely among all Americans" (3). Who has been least affected by it in his view? Why?

STRATEGIES AND STRUCTURES

1. Sullivan begins his analysis of the causes of today's opioid "epidemic" by referring to those of earlier epidemics. Is this an effective strategy? Why or why not?

2. Having glanced at the past in the second paragraph of his essay, Sullivan immediately looks ahead to "the future" (3). How does this change in perspective broaden (or fail to broaden) the scope of his analysis? Explain.

3. With its focus on supply and demand, Sullivan's account of the opioid crisis reads, in many ways, like an analysis of the ups and downs (or highs and lows) in the market for almost any commodity, whether poppies or pork bellies. Why might he take this semi-detached market-analysis approach to such a solemn subject? How and why do Sullivan's language and tone change in the conclusion of the essay?

4. As Sullivan follows the chain of cause and effect that runs through the opioid crisis, the first link is the "trauma" caused by "mass social and cultural dislocation" (2); and the final link is widespread death as a result of massive overdosing on opiates. Does Sullivan leave out any critical links in the chain, or is his analysis logically unbroken and essentially complete? Point to specific passages (or holes) in the text that confirm your reading.

5. Sullivan concludes that there is "a long, long path ahead" before the great epidemic ends (14). Should he have included a solution to the problem? Why or why not?

WORDS AND FIGURES OF SPEECH

1. America is "devoted to the poppy" (1). Explain the **METAPHOR** of the "love affair" with which Sullivan begins his analysis.

2. Drug addiction is, technically, not contagious. So why do Sullivan and others use the disease **ANALOGY** when referring to an "epidemic" of addiction? Explain.

3. Why might Sullivan compare taking drugs to getting off a "train" rather than say, a horse and buggy—or an elevator (2)?

4. What is the effect of the pileup of modifiers in the following phrase: "the engaged, multiethnic, urban-dwelling, financially successful inhabitants of the coasts" (3)?

5. "It was a fateful combination" (4). The term "fateful" does not mean "caused by fate"; it means "having far-reaching effects." Does Sullivan use the term appropriately here? Explain.

6. "Arbitrage" is a term from the field of investing and finance (5). Explain the IRONY (and humor) of Sullivan's use of the term in the context of small Medicaid copayments.

7. "This time, they are agents of an eternal and enveloping darkness" (14). Is this HYPERBOLE? Why or why not?

FOR WRITING

1. According to the official government website of the Centers for Disease Control and Prevention, almost 500,000 Americans died between 1999 and 2017 from overdoses of drugs containing opiates. Based on figures from this and other reliable sources, SUMMARIZE, in a paragraph or two, the effects of the opioid epidemic thus far as measured simply by loss of human life.

2. Read the excerpt, pages 100-06, from Sam Quinones's *Dreamland: The True Tale of America's Opiate Epidemic* (2015), a book that Sullivan calls an "indispensable account" of the opioid epidemic in America (4). Write a paragraph or two summarizing the main causes (or some other important aspect) of the epidemic as reported by Quinones.

3. "The pain was exacerbated by the Great Recession and has barely receded in the years since" (3). At the time, the recession of 2007-2009 was the most severe economic crisis in the United States since the Great Depression of the 1930s. In an essay, analyze some of the main causes of the recession and its effects on public health and morale, particularly among people "in those places left behind—towns and small cities that owed their success to a particular industry, whose civic life was built around a factory or a mine" (3).

4. Write an essay analyzing the main effects of the COVID-19 pandemic on the economy and on public health in the United States. Be sure to say how they COMPARE with those of the "Great Recession" of a decade before—or with the most significant effects of some earlier crisis.

⇒ **13** ⇐

ARGUMENT

RGUMENT* is the strategic use of language to convince an **AUDIENCE** to agree with you on an issue or to act in a way that you think is right—or at least to hear you out, even if they disagree with you. According to classical rhetoric, the ancient art of persuasion that goes back to at least Aristotle, you can convince people in three ways: (1) by appealing to their sense of reason, (2) by appealing to their emotions, and (3) by appealing to their sense of ethics (their standards of what constitutes proper behavior). The essays in this chapter illustrate all three appeals.

When you appeal to a reader's sense of reason, you don't simply declare, "Be reasonable; agree with what I say." You must supply solid **EVIDENCE** for your claim in the form of facts, examples, statistics, expert testimony, and personal experience. And you must use logical reasoning in presenting that evidence. There are basically two kinds of logical reasoning: **INDUCTION** and **DEDUCTION**. When we use induction, we reason from particulars to generalities: "You and your neighbors own guns; it's possible that many other families in the neighborhood own guns." When we deduce something, we reason from general premises to particular conclusions: "All guns are dangerous; your family is in danger because you have one in your house."

> John McWhorter, p. 220, uses induction when he concludes that words take on meanings beyond their literal definitions.

Of course, a proposition can be logically valid without necessarily being true. If it is true that "all guns are dangerous," then logically a particular gun must be dangerous as well. Given this general premise (or assumption) about guns, the conclusion about the danger of any particular gun is a valid conclusion. The same is true of the following argument: "*No* guns are dangerous; this particular gun is *not* dangerous." This is a valid argument, too; but here, again,

*Words printed in **SMALL CAPITALS** are defined in the Glossary/Index.

not everyone will accept the first (or major) premise about guns in general. Most real-life debates, in fact, take place because rational people disagree about the truth of one or more of the premises on which their conclusions are based.

Whether an argument uses induction or deduction, it must make an arguable statement or CLAIM. Take, for example, the idea that the world's leaders "should start an international campaign to promote imports from sweatshops." Nicholas D. Kristof argues in favor of this controversial proposition in "Let Them Sweat," an editorial published in the *New York Times*. Kristof's essay is an instructive example of how all the techniques of argumentation can work together.

Kristof knows that arguing in favor of sweatshops is likely to be an unpopular position. Like any writer with a point to make, especially a controversial one, he needs to win the reader's trust by establishing his CREDIBILITY. One way to do this is to anticipate objections that the reader might raise. So before anyone can accuse him of being totally out of his head for promoting sweatshops, Kristof writes: "The Gentle Reader will think I've been smoking Pakistani opium. But sweatshops are the only hope of kids like Ahmed Zia, 14, here in Attock, a gritty center for carpet weaving."

Right away, Kristof is hoping to convince his audience that they are hearing the words of an ethical person who deserves their attention. Next, he tugs at the readers' heartstrings:

> Ahmed earns $2 a day hunched over the loom, laboring over a rug that will adorn some American's living room. It is a pittance, but the American campaign against sweatshops could make his life much more wretched by inadvertently encouraging mechanization that could cost him his job.
>
> "Carpet-making is much better than farm work," Ahmed said. "This makes much more money and is more comfortable."

Underlying Kristof's emotional appeal in citing Ahmed's case is the logical claim that Ahmed's story is representative of the plight of most factory workers in poor countries. "Indeed," writes Kristof, "talk to Third World factory workers and the whole idea of 'sweatshops' seems a misnomer. It is farmers and brick-makers who really sweat under the broiling sun, while sweatshop workers merely glow."

The same claim—that other cases are like this one—also lies behind Kristof's second example: "But before you spurn a shirt made by someone like Kamis Saboor, eight, an Afghan refugee whose father is dead and who is the sole breadwinner in the family, answer this question: How does shunning sweatshop products help Kamis? All the alternatives for him are worse." Kristof is appealing to the reader's emotions and sense of ethics, and he is using logical reasoning. If we grant Kristof's premise that in really poor countries "all the alternatives" to sweatshop labor are worse, we must logically concede his main point that, for these workers, "a sweatshop job is the first step on life's escalator" and, therefore, that sweatshops are to be supported.

Kristof has not finished marshaling his reasons and evidence yet. To strengthen his argument, he introduces another, broader example, one that Americans are more likely to be familiar with:

> Nike has 35 contract factories in Taiwan, 49 in South Korea, only three in Pakistan, and none at all in Afghanistan—if it did, critics would immediately fulminate about low wages, glue vapors, the mistreatment of women.
>
> But the losers are the Afghans, and especially Afghan women. The country is full of starving widows who can find no jobs. If Nike hired them at 10 cents an hour to fill all-female sweatshops, they and their country would be hugely better off.
>
> Nike used to have two contract factories in impoverished Cambodia, among the neediest countries in the world. Then there was an outcry after BBC reported that three girls in one factory were under 15 years old. So Nike fled controversy by ceasing production in Cambodia.
>
> The result was that some of the 2,000 Cambodians (90 percent of them young women) who worked in three factories faced layoffs. Some who lost their jobs probably were ensnared in Cambodia's huge sex slave industry—which leaves many girls dead of AIDS by the end of their teenage years.

We can object to Kristof's premises. Can widows in Afghanistan find no decent jobs whatsoever? Will they actually starve if they don't? Did young women in Cambodia really die after being laid off? (Notice that Kristof qualifies this assertion with "probably.") We can even dispute Kristof's reasoning based on statistics. In statistics, when it is not possible to poll every individual in a group of people being analyzed, sound practice requires at least a representative sampling. Has Kristof given us a truly representative sampling of *all* sweatshop workers?

We can pick away at Kristof's logic—as have many of his critics since this article was first published. Michelle Chen, for example, recently reported in the *Nation* that the high-tech imports of today are often assembled under essentially the same conditions as low-tech products like shirts and shoes. Peel back "the shrink-wrap of Big Tech," she writes, based on a 2018 investigation of Samsung production facilities in Vietnam, and you "reveal an extremely vulnerable, mostly female workplace that may be sacrificing its neurological and reproductive health in digitized Dickensian workshops to make cutting-edge smartphones." If female factory workers continue to face hazardous work conditions even after technological advancement, then how valid is Kristof's logic that sweatshop jobs will eventually lead to better lives for workers? But unless it's being presented at a court of law in a criminal case, a good argument does not have to prove its point beyond a shadow of a doubt. It only has to convince the reader. Whether or not you're convinced by Kristof's argument, you can learn from the tactics he uses to support his position.

A BRIEF GUIDE TO WRITING AN ARGUMENT

When you construct an **ARGUMENT,** you take a position on an issue and then support that position with evidence. To do this, you need to identify the subject or issue you are addressing and to state the claim you're making about it. Here's how former first lady Michelle Obama made these moves in a critical evaluation of the fiction of Toni Morrison, which she first read "the summer after [her] senior year of high school":

> [S]he didn't just give us permission to share our own stories; she underlined our responsibility to do so. She showed how incomplete the world's narrative was without ours in it.
>
> —Michelle Obama, "On Reading Toni Morrison"

In what is ultimately an argument about the nature of narrative, Obama identifies the subject of her argument ("our own stories," as reflected in Morrison's fiction) and then states her claim: Morrison not only gives readers permission to tell their own diverse stories, but she also shows their "responsibility" to do so. Otherwise, Obama contends "the world's narrative" is "incomplete."

The following guidelines will help you make these basic moves as you draft an argument. They will also help you support your claim with reasoning and evidence, avoid logical fallacies, appeal to your readers' emotions and sense of ethics, and anticipate other arguments.

Coming Up with a Claim

Unlike a statement of fact (broccoli is a vegetable) or personal taste (I hate broccoli), a **CLAIM** is a statement that is debatable, that rational people can disagree with. We can all agree, for example, that pop culture has something to teach us. We might reasonably disagree, however, on what those lessons are. To come up with a claim, think of issues that are debatable: Batman is (is not) a model of ethical behavior. Broccoli provides (does not provide) more health benefits than any other vegetable. Genetic factors are (are not) the main determiners of personality. The health risks of vaping have (have not) been exaggerated by the medical community. Before you decide on a particular claim, make sure it is one you actually care enough about to argue it persuasively. If you don't care much about your topic, your readers probably won't either.

For example, see the debates on pp. 504 and 523.

Considering Your Purpose and Audience

One **PURPOSE** of an argument is to convince other people to listen thoughtfully to what you have to say—even if they don't completely accept your views. Whatever your claim, your argument is more likely to appeal to your audience if it is tailored to their particular needs and interests. Suppose, for example, that you have a friend who habitually sends text messages while driving even though she knows it's dangerous. You think your friend should put down her phone while driving—or pull over when she needs to text. Your friend might be more likely to agree with you if, in addition to citing statistics on increased traffic deaths due to driving while texting, you also pointed out that she was setting a bad example for her younger sister.

So think about what your audience's views on the particular issue are likely to be. Of all the evidence you might present in support of your case, what kind would your intended readers most likely find reasonable and, thus, convincing?

Generating Ideas: Finding Effective Evidence

Suppose you want to argue that the SAT is unfair because it is biased in favor of the wealthy. To support a claim like this effectively, you can use facts, statistics, examples, personal experience, and expert testimony.

FACTS. To argue that the SAT favors the wealthy, you might cite facts about the cost of tutors for the test: "In New York City, a company called Advantage charges $500 for 50 minutes of coaching with their most experienced tutors."

STATISTICS. You could cite statistics about income and text scores: "On the 2016 SAT, students with family incomes of more than $200,000 had an average math score of 586, while those with family incomes up to $20,000 had an average score of 453."

EXAMPLES. You could discuss a question from an actual SAT exam that might show SAT bias. The following question asks the test taker to select a pair of words whose relationship matches the relationship expressed by RUNNER : MARATHON. The choices are (A) envoy : embassy; (B) martyr : massacre; (C) oarsman : regatta; (D) referee : tournament; (E) horse : stable. The correct answer is C: an oarsman competes in a regatta, an organized boat race, in much the same way as a runner competes in a marathon. But because regattas are largely a pursuit of the wealthy, you could argue that the question favors the wealthy test taker.

PERSONAL EXPERIENCE. The following anecdote reveals, in a personal way, how the SAT favors certain socioeconomic groups: "No one in my family ever participated in a regatta—as a high school student, I didn't even know the meaning of the word. So when I took the SAT and encountered analogy questions that referred to regattas and other unfamiliar things, I barely broke 600 on the verbal aptitude section."

EXPERT TESTIMONY. You might quote a statement like this one by John A. Pérez, chair of the Board of Regents of the University of California, which suspended the SAT requirement during the COVID-19 pandemic: "By removing artificial barriers and decreasing stressors—including suspending the use of the SAT—for this unprecedented moment in time, we hope there will be less worry for our future students."

To identify your sources, use a works-cited list like the one on p. 624.

No matter what type of evidence you present, it should be pertinent to your argument and sufficient to convince your audience that your claim is worth taking seriously. (For example, citing the 2019 college admissions bribery scandal would clearly be pertinent if you're arguing that cheating on college admissions tests is not a good idea; that example might even be sufficiently serious, since a number of the parents involved in the scandal went to jail.) Your evidence should also be presented to the reader in a well-organized fashion that makes sense logically.

Templates for Arguing

The following templates can help you generate ideas for an argument and then start drafting. Don't take these as formulas where you just have to fill in the blanks. There are no easy formulas for good writing, though these templates can help you plot out some of the key moves of argumentation and thus may serve as good starting points.

> ▶ In this argument about X, the main point I want to make is _____.
>
> ▶ Others may say _____, but I would argue that _____.
>
> ▶ My contention about X is supported by the fact that _____.
>
> ▶ Additional facts that support this view of X are _____, _____, and _____.
>
> ▶ My own experience with X shows that _____ because _____.

> ▸ My view of X is supported by _____, who says that X is _____.
>
> ▸ What you should do about X is _____.

For more techniques to help you generate ideas and start writing an argument, see Chapter 3.

Organizing an Argument

Any well-constructed argument is organized around a claim and support for that claim. Here is a straightforward plan that can be effective for most argument essays. You may, of course, need to supplement or modify this plan to fit a particular topic.

1. In your *introduction*, identify your topic and state your claim clearly. Indicate why you're making this claim and why the reader should be interested in it. Make sure your topic is narrow enough to be covered in the time and space allotted.

2. In the main *body* of your argument, start with an important example or a solid piece of evidence that is likely to catch your reader's attention; then use a clear, logical organization to present the rest of your support. For example, move from your strongest point to your weakest. Or vice versa.

3. Deal with *counterarguments* at appropriate points throughout your essay.

4. In the *conclusion*, restate your claim, sum up how the evidence supports that claim, and recall the broader significance of your claim and why you're making it.

Narrowing and Stating Your Claim

State your claim clearly at the beginning of your argument—and take care not to claim more than you can possibly prove in one essay. "Sweatshops are acceptable," for example, is too broad to work as an arguable claim. Acceptable for whom? we might ask. Under what circumstances?

To narrow this claim, we could restate it as follows: "In very poor countries, sweatshops are acceptable." This claim could be even narrower, however: "In very poor countries, sweatshops are acceptable *when the alter-natives for the workers employed there are even worse.*" Because it is narrower, this is a more supportable claim than the one we started with.

Using Logical Reasoning: Induction and Deduction

In many writing situations, logical reasoning is indispensable for persuading others that your ideas and opinions are valid. As we noted in the introduction, there are two main kinds of logical reasoning: induction and deduction. Induc-tion is reasoning from particular evidence to a general conclusion. It is based on probability and draws a conclusion from a limited number of specific cases. You reason inductively when you observe the cost of a gallon of gas at half a dozen service stations and conclude that the price of gas is uniformly high. In contrast to induction, deduction moves from general principles to a particular conclusion. You reason deductively when your car stops running and—knowing that cars need fuel, that you started with half a tank and have been driving all day—you conclude that you are out of gas.

Deductive arguments can be stated as **SYLLOGISMS**, which have a major (or general) premise, a minor (or narrower) premise, and a conclusion. For example:

> *Major premise:* Science classes should teach all important scientific theories.
> *Minor premise:* Phrenology is an important scientific theory.
> *Conclusion:* Phrenology should be taught in science classes.

This is a valid syllogism, meaning that the conclusion follows logically from the premises. (Remember, however, that *validity* in a deductive argument is not the same as *truth*.)

The advantage of deduction over induction is that it deals with logical certainty rather than mere probability. As long as a deductive argument is properly constructed, the conclusion must be valid. The conclusion can still be untrue, however—as in the example above—if one or more of the premises is false. (Phrenology is, in fact, not a scientific theory, since it is based on the long-discredited notion that a person's mental and moral character can be determined by measuring the size and shape of their skull.)

What do you do when you know that some readers may disagree with your premises, but you still want to convince them to accept (or at least think seriously about) your conclusion anyway? For example, if you are arguing that a particular firearm is not dangerous because "no guns are dangerous," many readers are likely to take exception with your reasoning. What to do? One tactic would be to tone down your major premise. Your ultimate purpose in constructing any argument, after all, is to convince readers to accept your conclusion. So instead of the (obviously loaded) premise that "no guns are dangerous," you might instead restate your premise as follows: "Not all guns are dangerous." That a particular gun is safe does not necessarily follow from this premise, but more readers may be inclined to accept it—and thus more likely to take your conclusion seriously—especially if the rest of your evidence is strong.

Sherry Turkle's major premise (p. 511) is that people always have their phones with them.

An argument can be valid but untrue if one or more of the premises is false. An improperly constructed argument will be *invalid,* on the other hand, even when the premises are true (or generally acceptable to the reader). Consider the following example:

> **Major premise:** Tattoos are cool.
> **Minor premise:** Olivia and Sarah have tattoos.
> **Conclusion:** Olivia and Sarah are cool.

Even if you grant the assumption that tattoos are cool, there is a problem with the logical reasoning here. Olivia and Sarah may indeed be cool, but it's not necessarily because they have (or do not have) tattoos. Advertisers use this kind of faulty reasoning all the time to try to convince you that if you buy their products you'll be a cooler, smarter, or otherwise enhanced person. Recognizing logical fallacies like this is a big step toward avoiding them in your own writing.

Avoiding Logical Fallacies

LOGICAL FALLACIES are errors in logical reasoning. Here are some of the most common logical fallacies to watch out for:

POST HOC, ERGO PROPTER HOC. Latin for "after this, therefore because of this." This is the error of assuming that just because one event (such as rain) comes after another event (a rain dance), it therefore occurs *because* of the first event: "From 1995 to 2005, as the internet grew, the number of new babies named Jennifer grew by 30 percent." The increase in "Jennifers" may have followed the spread of the internet, but the greater internet use didn't necessarily *cause* the increase.

NON SEQUITUR. A statement that has no logical connection to the preceding statement: "The early Egyptians were masters of architecture. Thus they created a vast network of trade throughout the ancient world." Since mastering architecture has little to do with expanding trade, this second statement is a *non sequitur*.

BEGGING THE QUESTION. Taking for granted what is supposed to be proved: "Americans should be required to carry ID cards because Americans need to be prepared to prove their identity." Instead of addressing the claim that Americans should be required to prove their identity by having an ID card that verifies it, the "because" statement takes that claim for granted.

APPEAL TO DOUBTFUL AUTHORITY. Citing as expert testimony the opinions of people who are not experts on the issue: "According to my hairdresser, vaccinations cause autism." Hairdressers are not usually trained in medicine.

AD HOMINEM. Latin for "to the man," a type of fallacy where someone attacks the person making an argument instead of addressing the actual issue: "She's too young to be head of the teachers' union, so why listen to her views on wages?" Saying she's too young focuses on her as a person rather than on her views on the issue.

EITHER/OR REASONING. Treating a complicated issue as if it had only two sides: "Either you believe that God created the universe, or you believe that the universe evolved randomly." This statement doesn't allow for possibilities outside of these two options.

HASTY GENERALIZATION. Drawing conclusions based on too little evidence: "In the four stories by Edgar Allan Poe that we read, the narrator is mentally ill. Poe himself must have had a mental illness." There is not nearly enough evidence here to determine Poe's mental health.

FALSE ANALOGY. Making a faulty comparison: "Children are like dogs. A happy dog is a disciplined dog, and a happy child is one who knows the rules and is taught to obey them." Dogs and children aren't enough alike to assume that what is good for one is necessarily good for the other.

RED HERRING. Misleading readers by distracting them from the main argument: "Sure, my paper is full of spelling errors. But English is not a very phonetic language. Now if we were writing in Spanish . . ."

OVERSIMPLIFICATION. Assigning insufficient causes to explain an effect or justify a conclusion: "In a school budget crunch, art and music classes should be eliminated first because these subjects are not very practical." This argument is oversimplified because it doesn't admit that there are other reasons, besides practicality, for keeping a subject in the school curriculum.

Appealing to Your Readers' Emotions

Sound logical reasoning is hard to refute, but appealing to your readers' emotions can also be an effective way to convince them to accept—or at least listen to—your argument. In a follow-up to his argument in favor of sweatshops, Nicholas D. Kristof writes:

> The miasma of toxic stink leaves you gasping, breezes batter you with filth, and even the rats look forlorn. Then the smoke parts and you come across a child ambling barefoot, searching for old plastic cups that recyclers will buy for five cents a pound.
>
> —NICHOLAS D. KRISTOF, "Where Sweatshops Are a Dream"

Kristof is describing a gigantic garbage dump in Phnom Penh, Cambodia, where families try to make a living under inhumane conditions. Compared to this "Dante-like vision of hell," Kristof argues, "sweltering at a sewing machine" seems like an unattainable dream. By making us feel the desperation of the people he describes, Kristof is clearly tugging at the readers' heartstrings—before going on to supply more facts and examples to support his claim.

Establishing Your Own Credibility

When you construct an argument, you can use logic to show that what you have to say is valid and true. And you can appeal to your readers' emotions with genuine fervor. That might not be enough, however, if your readers don't fully trust you. Here are a few tips to help you establish trust with your readers:

- *Present issues objectively.* Acknowledge opposing points of view, and treat them fairly and accurately. If you have experience or expertise in your subject, let your readers know. For example, Kristof tells his readers, "My views on sweatshops are shaped by years living in East Asia, watching as living standards soared—including those in my wife's ancestral village in southern China—because of sweatshop jobs."

- *Pay close attention to the* TONE *of your argument.* Whether you come across as calm and reasonable or full of righteous anger, your tone will say much about your own values and motives for writing—and about you as a person.

- *Convince your readers* that you have considered their values and that you understand their concerns.

Anticipating Other Arguments

As you construct an argument, it's important to consider viewpoints other than your own, including objections that others might raise. Anticipating other arguments, in fact, is yet another way to establish your credibility. Readers are more likely to see you as trustworthy if, instead of ignoring an opposing argument, you state it fairly and accurately and then refute it. Kristof knows that many readers will disagree with his position on sweatshops, so he acknowledges the opposition up front before going on to give his evidence for his position:

> Hoping to win over skeptics, Diane Guerrero admits that "the issues are complicated" (p. 491).

> When I defend sweatshops, people always ask me: But would you want to work in a sweatshop? No, of course not. But I would want even less to pull a rickshaw. . . . I often hear the argument: Labor standards can

improve wages and working conditions, without greatly affecting the eventual retail cost of goods. That's true. But . . .

—Nicholas D. Kristof, "Where Sweatshops Are a Dream"

You still may not agree with Kristof's position that sweatshops are a good idea. But you're more likely to listen to what he, or any other writer, has to say if you think that person has thought carefully about all aspects of the issue, including points of view opposed to their own.

EDITING FOR COMMON ERRORS IN ARGUMENTS

As with other modes of writing, certain errors in punctuation and usage are common in arguments. The following guidelines will help you spot such problems and edit them appropriately.

Check to see that you've correctly punctuated connecting words

"If," "therefore," "thus," "consequently," "however," "nevertheless," and "because" are common connecting words in logical arguments. When the connecting word comes at the beginning of a sentence and links the statement you're making to earlier statements, it should be followed by a comma:

- ▶ Therefore, stronger immigration laws will not be necessary.
- ▶ Consequently, the minimum drinking age should be lowered to age 18.

When the connecting word comes at the beginning of a sentence and is part of an introductory clause—a group of words that includes a subject and a verb— the entire clause should be followed by a comma:

- ▶ Because guest workers will be legally registered, stronger immigration laws will be unnecessary.
- ▶ If people are old enough to vote and go to war, they're old enough to drink responsibly.

▶ If recent statistics from the Department of Transportation are accurate, far fewer people die when the legal drinking age is 21 instead of 18.

When the connecting word indicates a relationship—such as cause and effect, logical sequence, or comparison—between two independent clauses, it is usually preceded by a semicolon and followed by a comma:

▶ Many of the best surgeons have the highest rates of malpractice; thus, the three-strikes-and-you're-out rule for taking away a doctor's license may do more harm than good.

When the connecting word comes in the middle of an independent clause, it should usually be set off by commas:

▶ A surgeon who removes the wrong leg, however, deserves a somewhat harsher penalty than one who forgets to remove a sponge.

Check for common errors in usage

HOWEVER, NEVERTHELESS

Use "however" when you acknowledge an opposing argument but want to minimize its impact by presenting a counterargument:

▶ The surgeon was negligent in her duties; ~~nevertheless,~~ however, the patient played a larger role in the accident by lying about the dosage he was taking.

Use "nevertheless" when you acknowledge an opposing argument but wish to express that your argument is valid anyway:

▶ The surgeon was not completely at fault; ~~however,~~ nevertheless, she should lose her license because even partial responsibility for a patient's death is unacceptable.

IMPLY, INFER

Use "imply" when you mean "to state indirectly":

▶ The coach's speech ~~inferred~~ implied that he expected the team to lose the game.

Use "infer" when you mean "to draw a conclusion":

▶ From the coach's speech, I ~~implied~~ inferred that the team would lose the game.

Mysterious Warning Sign

Like many road signs—"YIELD," "STOP," "EXIT LANE ONLY"—a good argument catches our attention and is immediately clear. Let this sign, which appeared beside a narrow road on a barrier island in Florida, be a warning of the confusion that can result when you alert a reader to a problem or issue without being clear exactly what point you're making about it. The point of this ambiguous road sign might be to warn us to speed up because dangerous low-flying owls could come zooming in through the open car windows at any time. More likely, we're supposed to read the sign as saying that low-flying owls are particularly vulnerable to speeding traffic, so we should slow down to avoid them. If that's the message, the sign would be clearer if it read, for example, as follows: SLOW FOR LOW-FLYING OWLS. On a road sign, of course, there is not much room to go into detail, so the purpose of the sign needs to be apparent right away. When you construct a formal argument, you have more space and time to get your message across; but here again, the sooner you state the issue and your position on it—low-flying owls should be protected—the smoother the entire ride will be for your reader.

LIZ ADDISON

TWO YEARS ARE BETTER THAN FOUR

LIZ ADDISON argues that community colleges are "one of America's uniquely great institutions" in her essay "Two Years Are Better than Four." A graduate of Southern Maine Community College, Addison submitted her essay to a national college writing contest sponsored by the *New York Times Magazine*. The topic was to respond to "What's the Matter with College?," an opinion piece by the historian Rick Perlstein, published online by the *Times* in 2007. A graduate of an elite four-year university, Perlstein argued that colleges "seem to have lost their centrality" in American culture. Approximately 600 students from institutions across the country took up the challenge, and Addison's rebuttal was chosen as one of four runners-up.

Two Years Are Better than Four

Oh, the hand wringing. "College as America used to   1
understand it is coming to an end," bemoans Rick Perlstein and his beatnik friend of fallen face. Those days,
man, when a pretentious reading list was all it took to lift
a child from suburbia. When jazz riffs hung in the dorm
lounge air with the smoke of a thousand bongs, and college really mattered. Really mattered?

Rick Perlstein thinks so. It mattered so much to him   2
that he never got over his four years at the University of
Privilege. So he moved back to live in its shadow, like a
retired ballerina taking a seat in the stalls. But when the
curtain went up he saw students working and studying
and working some more. Adults before their time. Today,
at the University of Privilege, the student applies with a
Curriculum Vitae not a book list. Shudder.

Thus, Mr. Perlstein concludes, the college experi-   3
ence—a rite of passage as it was meant to be—must have
come to an end. But he is wrong. For Mr. Perlstein, so
rooted in his own nostalgia, is looking for himself—and
he would never think to look for himself in the one place
left where the college experience of self-discovery does
still matter to those who get there. My guess, reading
between the lines, is that Mr. Perlstein has never set foot
in an American community college.

The philosophy of the community college, and I have   4
been to two of them, is one that unconditionally allows its
students to begin. Just begin. Implicit in this belief is the
understanding that anything and everything is possible.
Just follow any one of the 1,655 road signs, and pop your
head inside—yes, they let anyone in—and there you will
find discoveries of a first independent film, a first independent thought, a first independent study. This college expe-

rience remains as it should. This college brochure is not marketing for the parents—because the parents, nor grandparents, probably never went to college themselves.

Upon entry to my first community college I had but one O'level to my name. These now disbanded qualifications once marked the transition from lower to upper high school in the Great British education system. It was customary for the average student to proceed forward with a clutch of O'levels, say eight or nine. On a score of one, I left school hurriedly at sixteen. Thomas Jefferson once wrote, "Everybody should have an education proportional to their life." In my case, my life became proportional to my education. But, in doing so, it had the good fortune to land me in an American community college and now, from that priceless springboard, I too seek admission to the University of Privilege. Enter on empty and leave with a head full of dreams? How can Mr. Perlstein say college does not matter anymore?

5

COMPARES the British system that she left with the American one

The community college system is America's hidden public service gem. If I were a candidate for office I would campaign from every campus. Not to score political points, but simply to make sure that anyone who is looking to go to college in this country knows where to find one. Just recently, I read an article in the *New York Times* describing a "college application essay" workshop for low-income students. I was strangely disturbed that those interviewed made no mention of community college. Mr. Perlstein might have been equally disturbed, for the thrust of the workshop was no different to that of an essay coach to the affluent. "Make Life Stories Shine," beams the headline. Or, in other words, prove yourself worldly, insightful, cultured, mature, before you get to college.

6

Her claim is based on an ideal of "public service"

Yet, down at X.Y.C.C. it is still possible to enter the college experience as a rookie. That is the understanding—that you will grow up a little bit with your first English class, a bit more with your first psychology class, a whole lot more with your first biology, physics, chemistry. That you may shoot through the roof with calculus, philosophy, or genetics. "College is the key," a young African American student writes for the umpteenth torturous revision of his college essay, "as well as hope." Oh, I wanted desperately to say, please tell him about community college. Please tell him that hope can begin with just one placement test.

When Mr. Perlstein and friends say college no longer holds importance, they mourn for both the individual and society. Yet, arguably, the community college experience is more critical to the nation than that of former beatnik types who, lest we forget, did not change the world. The community colleges of America cover this country college by college and community by community. They offer a network of affordable future, of accessible hope, and an option to dream. In the cold light of day, is it perhaps not more important to foster students with dreams rather than a building take-over?

I believe so. I believe the community college system to be one of America's uniquely great institutions. I believe it should be celebrated as such. "For those who find it necessary to go to a two-year college," begins one University of Privilege admissions paragraph. None too subtle in its implication, but very true. For some students, from many backgrounds, would never breathe the college experience if it were not for the community college. Yes, it is here that Mr. Perlstein will find his college years of self-discovery, and it is here he will find that college does still matter.

7

8

9

Gives an EXAMPLE of someone who might well choose a community college to get started

Conclusion restates her claim as a matter of "belief"

MY PARENTS WERE DEPORTED

DIANE GUERRERO (b. 1986) is an actress best known for her roles in the television series *Orange Is the New Black* and *Jane the Virgin*. Born in New Jersey and raised in Boston, her parents and older brother are from Colombia and came to the United States before she was born. They immigrated without documentation, and though they made every effort to obtain legal citizenship they were deported back to Colombia when Guerrero was 14 years old. In her memoir, *In the Country We Love: My Family Divided* (2016), Guerrero writes about her and her family's experience of being undocumented immigrants in the United States. In "My Parents Were Deported," which appeared in the *Los Angeles Times* (2014), Guerrero uses her family's story to argue for more justice and compassion in the immigration system.

⊷————————————————————————————————————⊶

I N *ORANGE IS THE NEW BLACK*, I play Maritza Ramos, a tough Latina from the 1
'hood. In *Jane the Virgin*, I play Lina, Jane's best friend and a funny know-it-
all who is quick to offer advice.

I love both parts, but they're fiction. My real story is this: I am the ₂ citizen daughter of immigrant parents who were deported when I was 14. My older brother was also deported.

My parents came here from Colombia during a time of great instability ₃ there. Escaping a dire economic situation at home, they moved to New Jersey, where they had friends and family, seeking a better life, and then moved to Boston after I was born.

Throughout my childhood I watched my parents try to become legal but ₄ to no avail. They lost their money to people they believed to be attorneys, but who ultimately never helped. That meant my childhood was haunted by the fear that they would be deported. If I didn't see anyone when I walked in the door after school, I panicked.

And then one day, my fears were realized. I came home from school to an ₅ empty house. Lights were on and dinner had been started, but my family wasn't there. Neighbors broke the news that my parents had been taken away by immigration officers, and just like that, my stable family life was over.

Not a single person at any level of government took any note of me. No ₆ one checked to see if I had a place to live or food to eat, and at 14, I found myself basically on my own.

While awaiting deportation proceedings, my parents remained in deten- ₇ tion near Boston, so I could visit them. They would have liked to fight depor- tation, but without a lawyer and an immigration system that rarely gives judges the discretion to allow families to stay together, they never had a

See p. 480 for ways
to appeal to your
readers' emotions.

chance. Finally, they agreed for me to continue my education at Boston Arts Academy, a performing arts high school, and the par- ents of friends graciously took me in.

I was lucky to have good friends, but I had a rocky existence. I was always ₈ insecure about being a nuisance and losing my invitation to stay. I worked a variety of jobs in retail and at coffee shops all through high school. And, though I was surrounded by people who cared about me, part of me ached with every accomplishment because my parents weren't there to share my joy.

My family and I worked hard to keep our relationships strong, but too- ₉ short phone calls and the annual summer visits I made to Colombia didn't suffice. They missed many important events in my life, including my singing recitals—they watched my senior recital on a tape I sent them instead of from the audience. And they missed my prom, my college application process, and my graduations from high school and college.

My story is all too common. Every day, children who are U.S. citizens 10
are separated from their families as a result of immigration policies that need
fixing.

I consider myself lucky because things turned out better for me than for 11
most, including some of my own family members. When my brother was
deported, his daughter was just a toddler. She still had her mother, but in a
single-parent household, she faced a lot of challenges. My niece made the wrong
friends and bad choices. Today, she is serving time in jail, living the reality that
I act out on screen. I don't believe her life would have turned out this way if her
father and my parents had been here to guide and support her.

I realize the issues are complicated. But it's not just in the interest of 12
immigrants to fix the system: It's in the interest of all Americans. Children
who grow up separated from their families often end up in foster care, or
worse, in the juvenile justice system despite having parents who love them
and would like to be able to care for them.

I don't believe it reflects our values as a country to separate children and 13
parents in this way. Nor does it reflect our values to hold people in detention
without access to good legal representation or a fair shot in a court of law. President Obama has promised to act on providing deportation relief for families
across the country, and I would urge him to do so quickly. Keeping families
together is a core American value.

Congress needs to provide a permanent, fair legislative solution, but in 14
the meantime families are being destroyed every day, and the president
should do everything in his power to provide the broadest relief possible now.
Not one more family should be separated by deportation.

FOR DISCUSSION

1. As an American citizen and the daughter of immigrant parents who were deported
   when she was 14, Diane Guerrero does not believe that "it reflects our values as a
   country to separate children and parents in this way" (13). To what extent do you
   agree or disagree with this CLAIM? Why?

2. Which do you think is more instrumental in establishing her CREDIBILITY and
   winning sympathy for her position—that Guerrero is a well-known actress or
   that she is a first-generation American? Why do you think so?

3. When her parents were deported, Guerrero could have elected to return to Colombia with them. Why might she have stayed in the United States?

STRATEGIES AND STRUCTURES

1. Why do you think Guerrero begins her **ARGUMENT** by distinguishing between "fiction" and reality (1, 2)? Is this an effective strategy? Why or why not?

2. For the most part, Guerrero's argument takes the form of a **NARRATIVE** about being separated from her parents as a teenager. At what point in her essay does Guerrero switch from "my real story" to making a larger claim? What is her claim exactly, and where does she state it most clearly and directly?

3. A fair and equitable immigration system benefits not only immigrants like her parents, Guerrero argues, but the country as a whole. What reasons does she give? How and how well do they support this aspect of her claim?

4. What point is Guerrero making when she cites the **EXAMPLE** of her niece who is in jail? How and how well does it represent the group of people it purports to exemplify? Explain.

WORDS AND FIGURES OF SPEECH

1. Her jailed niece, Guerrero says, is "living the reality that I act out on screen" (11). How do these words near the end of Guerrero's essay recall those of her opening paragraphs?

2. According to Guerrero, the immigration system in America needs "fixing" (10). What are the implications of this **METAPHOR**, and why do you think Guerrero uses it instead of simply saying that she thinks immigration policies should be changed?

3. In the final paragraph of her argument, Guerrero calls for a "solution" rather than a "fix" (14). What's the difference, if any? Is this a better choice of words? Why or why not?

FOR WRITING

1. Tell the story of someone you know, or have heard about, who faced deportation. Based on that narrative and any other **EVIDENCE** you choose, make the case that American immigration policies need to be reformed—or, alternatively, that the existing immigration system works, more or less.

2. In a carefully composed argument, support or refute this claim: "Except in cases of serious crime, separating families through deportation (or incarceration) is wrong and does more harm than good to American society." Try to include facts and figures as well as **ANECDOTAL** evidence in your proof.

WHY I'M FIGHTING FOR EQUAL PAY

CARLI LLOYD (b. 1982) is a professional soccer player and a member, since 2005, of the US Women's National Team. She is two-time World Cup Champion and a two-time Olympic gold medalist. A native of New Jersey, Lloyd graduated from Rutgers University in 2004 with a major in exercise science and sports studies. She is the author (with Wayne Coffey) of the best-selling memoir, *When Nobody Was Looking* (2016). In "Why I'm Fighting for Equal Pay" (*New York Times*, 2016), Lloyd explains why she and four other members of the US women's soccer team filed a wage-discrimination complaint with the Equal Employment Opportunity Commission in March 2016. It's a simple matter, she argues, of "what's right and what's fair." The legal fight over "equal pay for equal play" for women in soccer is ongoing. Lloyd and many other players filed a related suit in 2019. Here's Lloyd's 2016 argument in support of the players' rights.

I've WORN A U.S. SOCCER UNIFORM FOR 12 YEARS and have done so proudly. I've 1 had some of the greatest moments of my life—winning two Olympic gold medals and the 2015 Women's World Cup—wearing that uniform. So when I joined four teammates in filing a wage-discrimination complaint against U.S. Soccer late last month, it had nothing to do with how much I love to play for my country.

It had everything to do with what's right and what's fair, and with 2 upholding a fundamental American concept: equal pay for equal play.

Even if you are female. 3

Simply put, we're sick of being treated like second-class citizens. It 4 wears on you after a while. And we are done with it.

The United States women's national team is the most successful team in 5 the history of U.S. Soccer. We've won three World Cups and will try to win our fifth Olympic gold medal this summer in Brazil.[1] When we captured the Women's World Cup title in Canada in July, we drew the highest American television rating for soccer in history and, according to a financial report published by U.S. Soccer last month, helped generate $17.7 million in profit for the federation.

Yet even though U.S. Soccer's financials confirm that we are the driving 6 force that generates a majority of the revenue for the federation, when we as a team presented our proposal for increased compensation in our new collective bargaining agreement, U.S. Soccer told us, on more than one occasion, that our proposal was not rational. Essentially, the federation said that it had a certain sum of money set aside for the women's team and that our proposal was unacceptable.

We've gotten nowhere negotiating with our federation for years, and it 7 became clear to us that nothing had changed. That's why we went to the Equal Employment Opportunity Commission with our complaint.[2]

---

1. The US Women's National Soccer Team made it to the quarterfinals of the 2016 Summer Olympics before being eliminated by Sweden in a penalty shoot-out.
2. As of 2020, the litigation is still ongoing, but in May 2020, a federal judge in California dealt a serious blow to the case of the women's national team by dismissing the team's argument that they had been paid less than the men's team.

I won't bury you with numbers, but there are a few important basic facts 8 worth noting. Each year, the United States men's and women's national teams each play a minimum of 20 friendly matches. The top five players on the men's team make an average of $406,000 each year from these games. The top five women are guaranteed only $72,000 each year.

See p. 474 for advice on citing "numbers" to support an argument.

Yes, U.S. Soccer has stepped up to support the National Women's Soccer 9 League—it also subsidizes our salaries for the N.W.S.L., at roughly $54,000 per player—and yes, we can get some modest bonuses by playing for the national team. But still, the inequality is jarring.

If I were a male soccer player who won a World Cup for the United 10 States, my bonus would be $390,000. Because I am a female soccer player, the bonus I got for our World Cup victory last summer was $75,000.

The men get almost $69,000 for making a World Cup roster. As women, 11 we get $15,000 for making the World Cup team.

I understand that the men's World Cup generates vastly more money 12 globally than the women's event, but the simple truth is that U.S. Soccer projects that our team will generate a profit of $5.2 million in 2017 while the men are forecast to lose almost $1 million. Yet we get shortchanged coming and going.

I was on the road for about 260 days last year. When I am traveling 13 internationally, I get $60 a day for expenses. Michael Bradley gets $75. Maybe they figure that women are smaller and thus eat less.

When Hope Solo or Alex Morgan, say, makes a sponsor appearance for 14 U.S. Soccer, she gets $3,000. When Geoff Cameron or Jermaine Jones makes the same sort of appearance, he gets $3,750.[3]

Our beef is not with the men's national team; we love those guys, and we 15 support those guys. It's with the federation, and its history of treating us as if we should be happy that we are professional players and not working in the kitchen or scrubbing the locker room.

---

3. Star players on various professional soccer teams, Bradley, Solo, Morgan, Cameron, and Jones have also represented the men's and women's national teams as governed by the United States Soccer Federation.

The fact that women are being mistreated financially is, sadly, not a 16 breaking news story. It goes on in every field. We can't right all the world's wrongs, but we're totally determined to right the unfairness in *our* field, not just for ourselves but for the young players coming up behind us and for our soccer sisters around the world.

The Matildas—Australia's women's national team, which is currently 17 ranked fifth in the world—have battled their federation for years and went on strike last year over the federation's refusal to pay the players more than $21,000 a year. The women on the Colombian national team recently went four months without being paid at all.

When I first made the national team, there were no salaries and no 18 health benefits, so yes, we've made some progress. But we're nowhere near where we should be.

I don't think anyone would say that the women on the United States 19 national team are not great role models and ambassadors. Everywhere we go, we connect with fans, sign autographs and represent our sport and federation with class. We will continue to do that, provided that U.S. Soccer treats us in the same manner.

Two years ago, before the Algarve Cup, an important annual tourna- 20 ment in Portugal, we considered going on strike over these issues, but we weren't completely united then and wound up backing down.

We are not backing down anymore. 21

If I've learned anything in my career, it's that nothing worthwhile in life 22 comes easy. That's just the way it is. This isn't about a money grab. It's about doing the right thing, the fair thing. It's about treating people the way they deserve to be treated, no matter their gender.

Appealing to the readers' sense of ethics is discussed on p. 471.

FOR DISCUSSION

1. Carli Lloyd calls for "equal pay for equal play" (2). Is "play" really work? Should Olympic athletes get paid? Why or why not? How about college players?

2. Professional athletes do not generally get paid at, say, a simple hourly rate; instead, they tend to get salaries or bonuses or some combination of the two. If one salaried team makes more money in a season than a team that is paid largely in bonuses (for wins, etc.), is that fair? Explain.

3. The concept of equal pay for equal work assumes not only that pay can be measured on some common scale but that work can, too. Is this possible with athletes? Why or why not?

4. In general, women's teams do not make as much in salaries and benefits as men's teams do. The reason often given for this discrepancy is that men's athletic events earn more in the form of ticket revenue, advertising, endorsements, and broadcasting rights than do events featuring women's teams. Is this a valid premise? Explain.

5. Whether or not one athletic program makes more money in "sales" than another, should the star players in each program be compensated equally, regardless of gender? Or should the rate of pay depend on the sport? Why or why not?

STRATEGIES AND STRUCTURES

1. In her introductory paragraph, Lloyd mentions her accomplishments first and the discrimination suit she is defending second. Would her introduction be stronger or weaker if she had reversed the order of the two opening sentences? Explain.

2. Lloyd frames equal pay as primarily an "American concept" rather than, say, a legal or financial one (2). How effective is this strategy? Why might she have adopted it in an argument about "what's right and what's fair" in national sports (2)?

3. Lloyd adds "even if you are female," to clarify her main point—that wage discrimination *by gender* is unfair (3). Should Lloyd have mentioned gender directly in her first sentence or two; or is she wise, rhetorically, to lead up to it in steps? Explain.

4. By definition, a paragraph is a group of sentences. "Even if you are female" is not a complete sentence (3). Is Lloyd justified, logically and grammatically, in constructing an entire paragraph out of a single dependent clause here? Why or why not? What effect does she achieve by doing so?

5. "It wears on you after a while" (4). Is this a good reason for arguing against being treated "like second-class citizens" (4)? Why or why not? What other reasons does Lloyd give? Which ones do you find most convincing—and why?

6. "I won't bury you with numbers" (8). To whom is Lloyd speaking directly here? In general, how and how well does she use numbers to support her argument? Explain.

WORDS AND FIGURES OF SPEECH

1. Why are soccer matches, horse races, and other sporting events often called "cups"? Explain this use of **METONYMY**.

2. Lloyd uses the phrase "equal pay for equal play" instead of the more common "equal pay for equal work" (2). What is she suggesting about the nature of professional athletics?

3. Lloyd likens female athletes to "second-class citizens" (4). How appropriate is this **SIMILE** in an argument that addresses discrimination in sports on the basis of gender? Explain.

4. "Maybe they figure that women are smaller and thus eat less" (13). Is Lloyd being **IRONIC** here? Explain.

5. What are the implications of the phrase "money grab" (22)? Why might Lloyd use it in the conclusion of her essay instead of saying simply, "This isn't about money"?

FOR WRITING

1. In a brief essay, evaluate the basic differences between playing soccer and playing (American) football, basketball, or another team sport. Make the argument, with strong supporting reasons, that one is (or is not) more physically demanding than the other—or that the demands are simply different.

2. In recent years, the rules have changed to allow professional athletes to play on most Olympic teams. Do some research on the history of the international Olympic games; and, in a well-supported argument, make the case for (or against) this innovation.

3. Write a critical analysis based on your close reading of one of the following memoirs by soccer stars currently or formerly on the US Women's National Team: *Solo: A Memoir of Hope* (2012) by Hope Solo; *Breakaway: Beyond the Goal* (2015) by Alex Morgan; *When Nobody Was Watching* (2016) by Carli Lloyd; *Forward* (2016) by Abby Wambach.

THE CLASS POLITICS OF DECLUTTERING

STEPHANIE LAND (b. 1978) is a writer and reporter who focuses on issues of poverty in the United States. After growing up in Anchorage, Alaska, and Washington, DC, Land graduated from the University of Montana in 2014 with a major in English and creative writing. She is the author of *Maid: Hard Work, Low Pay, and a Mother's Will to Survive* (2019), based on her years as a single mother working below the poverty line. In this op-ed piece, originally published in the *New York Times* in 2016, Land assesses the class politics of the "decluttering" craze that is sweeping through the American closet. It's fine to get rid of stuff, she argues—but not if you don't have anything, not even a choice.

S UDDENLY, DECLUTTERING IS everywhere. It may have started with Marie 1 Kondo and her mega-best seller, *The Life-Changing Magic of Tidying Up,*[1] but it has exploded into a mass movement, anchored in websites, seminars and—ironically—a small library's worth of books about how to get rid of stuff.

To its advocates, decluttering, or "minimalism," is about more than just 2 maximizing space: "By clearing the clutter from life's path, we can all make room for the most important aspects of life: health, relationships, passion, growth and contribution," say Joshua Fields Millburn and Ryan Nicodemus, hosts of *The Minimalists* podcast.

The underlying structure of a deductive argument like this is syllogism (p. 477).

But minimalism is a virtue only when it's a choice, and it's 3 telling that its fan base is clustered in the well-off middle class. For people who are not so well off, the idea of opting to have even less is not really an option.

I understand why people with a lot of stuff feel burdened by it, and the 4 contrasting appeal of having less of it. I cleaned houses to put myself through college as a single mother. I spent my days in expensive homes, full of large televisions and stereo systems, fully furnished rooms that collected dust. I was alone and isolated most days, and at night, I concentrated on the three or four online classes I took through a local community college. My daughter and I had about $50 in spending money a month.

Over the course of a year, and after seeing how the other half lived, I 5 started to recognize that by having less, by trying to find joy in what little things life brings—like a 25-cent puzzle we found at a garage sale—we were living a somewhat happier life. Or, I assumed we were, after noticing while cleaning bathrooms that my clients tended to be on several medications for depression, pain and sleeplessness.

In some ways, I was practicing what minimalism preaches. But it didn't 6 make me happy. And I imagine for millions of other working-class Americans who struggle to get by, minimalism's principles don't sit well either. Buddhist belief says happiness is the freedom from want, and yet, what if your life is streamlined out of necessity, and not choice?

1. First published in English in 2014 with the subtitle *The Japanese Art of Decluttering and Organizing*; translated from the Japanese by Cathy Hirano.

I had to downsize severely several years ago when my daughter and I 7
moved into a 400-square-foot studio. I had no usable wall space, and although
my boss gave me temporary storage space in her garage over the summer, I
had to sort through and get rid of carloads of clothes, my childhood toys,
school papers, books, movies and artwork. I couldn't afford to store all of
these items, which had value to me only as a record of my history—including
mementos from my parents.

My stuff wasn't just stuff, but a reminder that I had a foundation of sup- 8
port of people who had loved me growing up: a painting I'd done as a child that
my mom had carefully framed and hung in our house, a set of antique Raggedy
Ann and Andy dolls my ferret once chewed an eye out of when I was 15, artwork my mom had collected over the decade we lived in Alaska. Giving examples to
Things I grew up with that brought me back to a time of living a support a claim is
carefree life. discussed on p. 474.

I've grown to appreciate living in a small space over the last decade, even 9
after having another child. I now keep a 667-square-foot apartment clean, and
can't imagine the responsibility of doing the same to two or three times the
space. But it would be nice for my girls to have their own rooms, and a yard to
run around in. It would be nice to have a real couch that isn't a futon I've held
on to for several years. I hunt for deals, and hurry to Walmart whenever
there's a sale.

And that's the other class element lurking behind minimalism's facade. 10
In a new documentary about the movement, "bad" consumption is portrayed
by masses of people swarming into big box stores on Black Friday, rushing
over one another for the best deals. They are, we're led to understand, slaves
to material goods, whereas the people who stay away from mass consumption
are independent thinkers, free to enjoy the higher planes of life.

But those people flocking to Walmart and other stores don't necessarily 11
see things that way. To go out and purchase furniture, or an entertainment set,
or a television bigger than an average computer monitor—let alone decide that
I can afford to get rid of such things—are all beyond my means. That those
major sales bring the unattainable items to a level of affordability is what drives
all of those people to line up and storm through doors on Black Friday.

Those aren't wealthy people who have a house full of expensive items 12
they don't need. Those are people teetering on or even below the poverty

level, desperate for comfort in their homes. To point to them as a reason to start an anti-consumerism movement is just another form of social shaming. Those aren't the people who would benefit from a minimalist life. They can't afford to do with less.

FOR DISCUSSION

1. "Ironically," says Stephanie Land, the decluttering movement has produced "a small library's worth of books about how to get rid of stuff" (1). What's so **IRONIC** about this?

2. What does the minimalistic goal of "clearing the clutter from life's path" assume about the nature and power of mere objects (2)? Are these assumptions valid? Why or why not?

3. Land and her daughter "had to downsize" into a studio apartment with 400 square feet of floor space. Is this enough living room for two people? Why or why not?

4. Is Land correct in assuming that Walmart shoppers don't have enough money to shop elsewhere? Are their motives for shopping there fundamentally different from those who shop at more expensive consumer palaces such as Sam's Club (which, of course, is a Walmart affiliate) and Costco? Explain.

STRATEGIES AND STRUCTURES

1. Land begins by citing the views of certain "advocates" of decluttering (2). Is her statement of their position fair and accurate? Why or why not?

2. As a maid working "in expensive houses," Land encounters not only excess furniture in "rooms that collected dust" but "medications for depression, pain and sleeplessness" (4, 5). What is her apparent purpose in mentioning these details? How and how well do they support her **ARGUMENT**?

3. Land lists a number of "mementos" from her childhood—including "a set of antique Raggedy Ann and Andy dolls [her] ferret once chewed an eye out of"—that she was forced to discard because she had no place to store them (7, 8). How and how well do these specific details support Land's claim that her "stuff wasn't just stuff" (8)?

4. Minimalism, says Land, "didn't make [her] happy" because she was practicing it "out of necessity" (6). This is, in part, an argument in favor of free will. Is it based largely on logic, ethics, or both? Explain.

5. Lack of choice is one of the main "class" elements in the politics of minimalism, according to Land; what is the "other" one—as indicated by the swarms of Black Friday shoppers at Walmart (10)? Taken together are these two factors sufficient to support Land's claim that minimalism has a class bias? Explain.

6. In addition to offering logical and ethical reasons for her position, Land also tells the story of her (and her daughter's) own experience. How and how well does the personal **NARRATIVE** support those parts of Land's argument that appeal to logic and ethics?

WORDS AND FIGURES OF SPEECH

1. If the word "clutter" implies disorder and overabundance, what are the implications of the terms "decluttering" and "minimalism"? Why might advocates of these practices use such terms to frame their work (2)?

2. Land says she is seeking to expose the classism behind the "facade" of minimalism (10). In this context, why might she choose an architectural term referring to the front of a building or other structure?

3. Although Land does not use the phrase, Marie Kondo and other tidy-up-your-life coaches often speak of "putting your house in order." Is the **METAPHOR** appropriate for the task? Why or why not?

4. What is "social shaming" (12)? How and how well does Land's use of the term support her claim that the decluttering "movement" is guilty of playing class politics?

FOR WRITING

1. In a brief essay, define "clutter" and explain why people should (or should not) join the decluttering "movement."

2. In *The Life-Changing Magic of Tidying Up* (2014), Marie Kondo argues that "when you put your house in order, you put your affairs and your past in order, too." In a well-reasoned **ARGUMENT**, defend (or contest) this position based on your own experience or that of someone you know.

3. Write a critical analysis of Marie Kondo's (or some other) popular book (or essay) on decluttering. Evaluate both the validity of the author's claims and how and how well those claims are presented and supported.

MIND AND MEDIA:
IS TECHNOLOGY CHANGING
OUR MINDS—AND HEARTS?

S MARTPHONES are smart, right? At a touch or swipe, they connect us to a universe of ideas and information that once would have taken ages to locate in the great libraries of the world—if they could be found at all. But access to information and access to intelligence, one might argue, are not necessarily the same. "Is Google Making Us Stupid?" is how the technology writer Nicholas Carr famously framed the question back in 2008 in a much-discussed cover article for the *Atlantic* magazine. Technology, he concluded, may be expanding our knowledge base, but it is also making us intellectually shallower.

What about our emotions—and will? If access and intelligence do not always equate, neither do access and communication. Some might say that because of technology we are able to stay in touch with our friends and family who live far away and to make new connections with people we would otherwise never meet. At the same time, we are becoming ever more glued to our devices, perhaps at the expense of genuine conversation. Are we ignoring the emotional needs of the people physically around us—not to mention our own deeper feelings—when we text each other from afar instead of engaging face-to-face? And are we doing so against our own will? Or do smartphones and other technologies keep us meaningfully connected with one another at all times as never before? Maybe both realities are true.

In the following essays, **Jaron Lanier, Sherry Turkle**, and **Andrea Lunsford** address these and other fundamental questions about the effects of digital media and technology on the human mind, heart, and will, including our capacities for engaging with other people through thoughtful conversation as well as intelligent reading and writing.

JARON LANIER

YOU ARE LOSING YOUR FREE WILL

JARON LANIER (b. 1960) is a computer scientist and pioneer in the field of virtual reality. Born in New York City, Lanier grew up in New Mexico and, at age 13, began the study of mathematical notation at New Mexico State University. He is the founder of VPL Research, a company that sold virtual reality products, and has worked for Atari, Internet2, Silicon Graphics, and Microsoft. A composer and a collector of rare musical instruments, he has also served as an assistant to a midwife. Lanier is the author of several books on technology and the internet, including *Ten Arguments for Deleting Your Social Media Accounts Right Now* (2018), from which this selection is taken. In "You Are Losing Your Free Will," Lanier argues that the internet is constantly monitoring and modifying the user's behavior, and "the person doesn't even know it." What's to be done about this situation? Instead of serving as "lab rats," Lanier advises, humans should become a different kind of animal.

L ET'S START WITH CATS.

　　Cats are everywhere online. They make the memiest memes and the cut- 2
est videos.

　　Why cats more than dogs? 3

　　Dogs didn't come to ancient humans begging to live with us; we domes- 4
ticated them. They've been bred to be obedient. They take to training and
they are predictable. They work for us. That's not to say anything against dogs.
It's great that they're loyal and dependable.

When you
compare cats
to dogs (or other
creatures), be sure
you're comparing
apples to apples
(p. 326).

　　Cats are different. They came along and partly domesticated 5
themselves. They are not predictable. Popular dog videos tend to
show off training, while the most wildly popular cat videos are
the ones that capture weird and surprising behaviors.

　　Cats are smart, but not a great choice if you want an animal 6
that takes to training reliably. Watch a cat circus online, and what's so touching is that the cats are clearly making their own minds up about whether to
do a trick they've learned, or to do nothing, or to wander into the audience.

　　Cats have done the seemingly impossible: They've integrated them- 7
selves into the modern high-tech world without giving themselves up. They
are still in charge. There is no worry that some stealthy meme crafted by
algorithms and paid for by a creepy, hidden oligarch has taken over your cat.
No one has taken over your cat; not you, not anyone.

　　Oh, how we long to have that certainty not just about our cats, but about 8
ourselves! Cats on the internet are our hopes and dreams for the future of
people on the internet.

　　Meanwhile, even though we love dogs, we don't want to *be* dogs, at least 9
in terms of power relationships with people, and we're afraid Facebook and
the like are turning us into dogs. When we are triggered to do something
crappy online, we might call it a response to a "dog whistle." Dog whistles can
only be heard by dogs. We worry that we're falling under stealthy control.

　　How can you remain autonomous in a world where you are under con- 10
stant surveillance and are constantly prodded by algorithms run by some of
the richest corporations in history, which have no way of making money
except by being paid to manipulate your behavior? How can you be a cat,
despite that? . . .

Something entirely new is happening in the world. Just in the last five or ten   11
years, nearly everyone started to carry a little device called a smartphone on
their person all the time that's suitable for algorithmic behavior modification.
A lot of us are also using related devices called smart speakers on our kitchen
counters or in our car dashboards. We're being tracked and measured constantly, and receiving engineered feedback all the time. We're being hypno-
tized little by little by technicians we can't see, for purposes we don't know.
We're all lab animals now.

Algorithms gorge on data about you, every second. What kinds of links   12
do you click on? What videos do you watch all the way through? How quickly
are you moving from one thing to the next? Where are you when you do these
things? Who are you connecting with in person and online? What facial
expressions do you make? How does your skin tone change in different situations? What were you doing just before you decided to buy something or not?
Whether to vote or not?

All these measurements and many others have been matched up with   13
similar readings about the lives of multitudes of other people through massive spying. Algorithms correlate what you do with what almost everyone
else has done.

The algorithms don't really understand you, but there is power in num-   14
bers, especially in large numbers. If a lot of other people who like the foods
you like were also more easily put off by pictures of a candidate portrayed in a
pink border instead of a blue one, then you *probably* will be too, and no one
needs to know why. Statistics are reliable, but only as idiot demons.

Are you sad, lonely, scared? Happy, confident? Getting your period?   15
Experiencing a peak of class anxiety?

So-called advertisers can seize the moment when you are perfectly   16
primed and then influence you with messages that have worked on other
people who share traits and situations with you.

I say "so-called" because it's just not right to call direct manipulation of   17
people advertising. Advertisers used to have a limited chance to make a pitch,
and that pitch might have been sneaky or annoying, but it was fleeting. Furthermore, lots of people saw the same TV or print ad; it wasn't adapted to
individuals. The biggest difference was that you weren't monitored and

assessed all the time so that you could be fed dynamically optimized stimuli—whether "content" or ad—to engage and alter you.

Now everyone who is on social media is getting individualized, continu-   18
ously adjusted stimuli, without a break, so long as they use their smartphones. What might once have been called advertising must now be understood as continuous behavior modification on a titanic scale.

Please don't be insulted. Yes, I am suggesting that you might be turning,   19
just a little, into a well-trained dog, or something less pleasant, like a lab rat or

Also be aware of what makes an analogy *false* (p. 480).

a robot. That you're being remote-controlled, just a little, by clients of big corporations. But if I'm right, then becoming aware of it might just free you, so give this a chance, okay?

A scientific movement called behaviorism arose before computers were   20
invented. Behaviorists studied new, more methodical, sterile, and nerdy ways to train animals and humans.

One famous behaviorist was B. F. Skinner.[1] He set up a methodical sys-   21
tem, known as a Skinner box, in which caged animals got treats when they did something specific. There wasn't anyone petting or whispering to the animal, just a purely isolated mechanical action—a new kind of training for modern times. Various behaviorists, who often gave off rather ominous vibes, applied this method to people. Behaviorist strategies often worked, which freaked everyone out, eventually leading to a bunch of creepy "mind control" sci-fi and horror movie scripts.

An unfortunate fact is that you can train someone using behaviorist   22
techniques, *and the person doesn't even know it*. Until very recently, this rarely happened unless you signed up to be a test subject in an experiment in the basement of a university's psychology building. Then you'd go into a room and be tested while someone watched you through a one-way mirror. Even though you knew an experiment was going on, you didn't realize *how* you were being manipulated. At least you gave consent to be manipulated in *some* way.

---

1. A psychology professor at Harvard, Burrhus Frederic Skinner (1904–1990) considered free will to be an illusion. Along with many academic studies, Skinner was the author of the utopian novel, *Walden Two* (1948). The technical name of the Skinner box was "the operant conditioning chamber."

(Well, not always. There were all kinds of cruel experiments performed on prisoners, on poor people, and especially on racial targets.)

[W]hat has become suddenly normal—pervasive surveillance and con- 23 stant, subtle manipulation—is unethical, cruel, dangerous, and inhumane. Dangerous? Oh, yes, because who knows who's going to use that power, and for what? . . .

Your goal should not necessarily be to force governments to regulate or 24 even nationalize Facebook before you'll rejoin, or to force Facebook to change its business model, even though those are achievements that must precede the long-term survival of our species. Your immediate goal is to be a cat.

It's like learning to write. You can't read well until you can write at least 25 a little. The reason we teach writing to students is not in the hopes that they'll all become professional writers. That would be too cruel. Instead, we hope they'll learn what it means to write, and to think, which will make them more thoughtful when they read. You can't use the internet well until you've confronted it on your own terms, at least for a while. This is for your integrity, not just for saving the world.

> For more good reasons to read and write well, see Chapter 1.

It's unlikely that there will be a vast wave of people quitting social media 26 all at once; the combination of mass addiction with network-effect lock is formidable. But as more people become aware of the problems, they—you—can speak to the hearts of the tech industry and have an impact. If you drop accounts even for a while, it helps.

I realize that we live in a world of stunning inequality, and not everyone has the 27 same options. Whoever you are, I hope you have options to explore what your life might be, especially if you are young. You need to make sure your own brain, and your own life, isn't in a rut. Maybe you can go explore wilderness or learn a new skill. Take risks. But whatever form your self-exploration takes, do at least one thing: detach from the behavior-modification empires for a while—six months, say? . . . After you experiment, you'll know yourself better. Then decide.

UNDERSTANDING THE ESSAY

1. Jaron Lanier begins his **ARGUMENT** with an analysis of the differences between cats and dogs. Is this **COMPARISON** an effective way to raise the issue of how the internet affects human behavior? Why or why not?

2. Lanier claims that in the last few years "something entirely new is happening in the world" (11). What's new, according to him? Is he right about this, or is he overstating the case? Why or why not?

3. An argument by **ANALOGY** says that—because a close comparison can be drawn between them—what is true of one group (pets) is true of the other group (humans). How valid is Lanier's argument that for purposes of avoiding "behavior modification" when using the internet, it is better to be a cat than a dog (18)? Explain.

4. According to Lanier, how does the "so-called" advertising we encounter on the internet today differ from the sort of advertising traditionally found in newspapers and on television? Why does Lanier think we shouldn't even call it advertising anymore (17)?

5. It would be "too cruel," says Lanier, to teach writing for the purpose of turning everybody into professional writers (25). In his view, why *do* we teach writing, and how does learning to write help people to "use the internet well" (25)?

6. Lanier says he is not arguing that people should immediately "force governments to regulate or even nationalize Facebook" and other media (24). What immediate "goal" *is* he urging readers to adopt, and how does he suggest they begin to achieve it (24)?

7. Lanier concludes his argument with the following call to action: "But whatever form your self-exploration takes, do at least one thing: detach from the behavior-modification empires for a while. . . . Then decide" (27). In order to accept the conclusion that it might be a good idea to disconnect from social media "for a while," is it logically necessary to grant Lanier's premise that the hidden purpose or goal of social media and the internet is "behavior modification"? Why or why not?

SHERRY TURKLE

ROMANCE: WHERE ARE YOU? WHO ARE YOU? WAIT, WHAT JUST HAPPENED?

SHERRY TURKLE (b. 1948) is a professor of social studies at the Massachusetts Institute of Technology and the author of nine books. Turkle was born in New York and holds degrees from Radcliffe College and Harvard University, where she earned her doctorate in sociology and personal psychology. Much of her scholarly career has been devoted to studying the relationship between people and the technology they use, especially computers. Her book *The Second Self* (1984), for example, argues that computers fundamentally alter the ways we think and act. The thesis of *Alone Together* (2011) is evident in that book's subtitle: *Why We Expect More from Technology and Less from Each Other*. In the following selection from her most recent book, *Reclaiming Conversation: The Power of Talk in a Digital Age* (2015), Turkle argues that new technologies have changed the rules of our oldest preoccupation—love.

I only ask, "How's the conversation?"

—OPERA SINGER LUCIANO PAVAROTTI, WHEN ASKED
ABOUT RAISING ONLY DAUGHTERS

True love is a lack of desire to check one's
smartphone in another's presence.

—ALAIN DE BOTTON

FOR ADULTS AS FOR TEENAGERS, it comes down to this: You always expect   1
other people to have their phones with them. You expect that no matter
what else they are doing, they will see a message you sent. So, if they care
about you, you should be getting a text back. If they care. But in romantic texting, responding to a communication with silence happens all the time. It's the
NOTHING gambit. It appeared early. As soon as texting had established itself
in flirting, there was talk about how to handle the strategy of silence. Even in
high school.

The NOTHING Gambit

In 2008, eighteen-year-old Hannah tells me that in online flirting, "the hard-   2
est thing" is that the person you text has the option of simply not responding—
that is, of responding with NOTHING, a conversational choice not really
available in face-to-face talk. Her assessment of its effects: "It is a way of driving someone crazy. . . . You don't exist."

Hannah explains that after a no-response, she feels a strong tempta-   3
tion to make things worse for herself by following the online activities of the
boy who ignored her—on *Facebook* she can see if he's been out to dinner or a
party. In the past, you could console yourself that a person ignoring you was
perhaps busy with a family emergency. You could tell yourself all manner of
improbable stories. Now, as one of Hannah's friends puts it, "You have to cope
with the reality: they are busy with everything but you." Hannah says that
this makes rejection on social media "five times as great as regular rejection."

The NOTHING gambit is not a resolved conversation or a conversation   4
that has trailed off. It is not, Hannah insists, like "someone telling you a few

times that they are busy and then you get the picture." It is more like a conversation with someone who simply looks away as if they don't understand that human beings need to be responded to when they speak. Online, we give ourselves permission to behave this way.

And when it happens to you, the only way to react with dignity is to   5
pretend it didn't happen. Hannah describes the rules: If people don't respond to you online, your job is to pretend to not notice. "I'm *not* going to be that person who goes off on people saying, 'Why don't you get back to me, blah, blah, blah.' . . . Not cool. I'm *not* going to be, like, 'Hello, are you still there? If you don't want to talk, just tell me.'"

Hannah and I are talking in a circle of seven high school seniors, boys and   6
girls. When she says, "Why don't you get back to me, blah, blah, blah," everyone breaks out laughing. Hannah is doing a perfect imitation of a pathetic loser. The behavior she describes is what no one would ever do. When someone hits you with a no-response, you meet silence with silence. Hannah is explicit: "If people want to disappear, I'll be, like, 'Okay, I'm fine with it.'" In fact, in Hannah's circle, the socially correct response to the NOTHING gambit is to get aggressively busy on social media—busy enough that your activity will be noticed by the person who has gone silent on you.

In the early days of texting, 2008–2010, I spoke with more than three   7
hundred teens and young adults about their online lives. I saw a generation settle into a new way of dealing with silence from other people: namely, deny that it hurts and put aside your understanding that if you do it to others, it will hurt them as well. We tolerate that we are not being shown empathy. And then we tolerate that we don't show it to others.

> Citing such a large sampling of opinion helps Turkle establish her credibility (p. 481).

This style of relating is part of a larger pattern. You learn to give your   8
parents a pass when they turn to their phones instead of responding to you. You learn to give your friends a pass when they drop in and out of conversations to talk with friends on their phones. And in flirtation, you learn to treat NOTHING as something to put out of your mind.

You could say that in romance, being ignored is a staple and that this is old   9
wine in new bottles. But in the past, the silent treatment was a moment. It could be the beginning of a chase or what led a suitor to abandon hope. But it was a moment. Now, as we've seen before, a moment has turned into a method.

Friction-Free

Even the apps we use to find love are in formats that make it easy to ignore   10
being ignored. On *Tinder*, a mobile dating app, rejection is no longer rejection,
it is "swiping left," and when it happens to you, you don't even know it happened. Tinder asks, "Who is available, right now, near you, to go out for a coffee or a drink, to maybe be your lover?" People who want to be considered sign
up, and their photograph and a brief bio appear on the system.

Once you have the app open, if you like the looks of someone, you swipe   11
right on your phone. If you're not interested, you swipe left. If I swipe right on
you and you swipe right on me, then we are notified that we have been "matched"
and can begin to communicate. But if I choose you with a right swipe and you
don't do the same for me, you simply don't appear in my visual field again.

This is what people mean by "friction-free," the buzzword for what a life   12
of apps can bring us. Without an app, it would not be possible to reject hundreds, even thousands of potential mates with no awkwardness. It has never
been easier to think of potential romantic partners as commodities in abundance.

In this social environment, studies show a decline in the ability to form   13
secure attachments—the kind where you trust and share your life. Ironically,
our new efficient quests for romance are tied up in behavior that discourages
empathy and intimacy. The preliminaries of traditional courtship, the dinner
dates that emphasized patience and deference, did not necessarily lead to intimacy but provided practice in what intimacy requires. The new preliminaries—
the presentation of candidates as if in a game—don't offer that opportunity.

Love talk during the chase involves new skills. You'll want a fluidity   14
with apps that will become part of your romantic game—apps for meeting,
apps for texting and messaging, apps for video chat. All of these bring the
promise of businesslike crispness to falling in love. They bring efficiency into
the realm of our intimacies. In a world where people live far away from parents
and neighborhood ties, apps bring hope that they will smooth out the hard job
of finding a partner without the community connections enjoyed by previous generations. And so, the first story that young people tell about technology
and romance is that their phones have made things more efficient. But the
first story is not the whole story.

In fact, technology brings significant complications to the conversa- 15
tions of modern romance. We feel we have permission to simply drop out. It
encourages us to feel that we have infinite choice in romantic partners, a
prospect that turns out to be as stressful as it is helpful in finding a mate. It
offers a dialogue that is often not a dialogue at all because it is not unusual for
people to come to online conversations with a team of writers.
You want a team because you feel you are working in an unfor-   For help with punc-
giving medium. Timing matters and punctuation counts!   tuating arguments,
see p. 482.

Finally, although technology offers so much to the chase—   16
new ways to meet, new ways to express interest and passion—it also makes a
false promise. It is easy to think that if you feel close to someone because of
their words on a screen, you understand the person behind them. In fact,
you may be overwhelmed with data but have little of the wisdom that comes
with face-to-face encounters.

Our new ways of communicating have an effect on every stage of romance, 17
from searching for love to presenting ourselves when we are hopeful of finding it to the new complexities we encounter as we try to make it work. In this
environment, we move from "Where are you?" (the technology-enhanced
encounter) to "Who are you?" and then to "Wait, what just happened? Did I
make you disappear?"

UNDERSTANDING THE ESSAY

1. Turkle's essay raises the question of "how to handle the strategy of silence" in
   online communication (1). What are some of the counterstrategies she mentions?
   How well do they work?

2. In Turkle's analysis, what are some of the main **EFFECTS**, in addition to not
   expecting "empathy," of being constantly online (7)?

3. Turkle draws on interviews with "more than three hundred teens and young
   adults" (7). Is this sufficient proof in your view? Why or why not?

4. What is a "gambit" in chess (4)? How and how well does this **METAPHOR** fit the
   online practice Turkle is analyzing? Explain.

ANDREA LUNSFORD

OUR SEMI-LITERATE YOUTH?
NOT SO FAST

ANDREA LUNSFORD (b. 1942) is professor emerita of English at Stanford University and is on the faculty at the Bread Loaf School of English. After graduating from the University of Florida, Lunsford taught English at Colonial High School in Orlando before earning a PhD in rhetoric from the Ohio State University. "Our Semi-Literate Youth? Not So Fast" reports on research by Lunsford and others about trends in undergraduate writing (and thinking) as a result of increased use of digital technologies. Based on their findings, Lunsford argues, writing and literacy should be redefined for the digital age—and teachers of writing, she implies, should reconsider how they teach.

T WO STORIES ABOUT YOUNG PEOPLE, and especially college-age students, 1 are circulating widely today. One script sees a generation of twitterers and texters, awash in self-indulgence and narcissistic twaddle, most of it riddled with errors. The other script doesn't diminish the effects of technology, but it presents young people as running a rat race that is fueled by the internet and its toys, anxious kids who are inundated with mountains of indigestible information yet obsessed with making the grade, with success, with coming up with the "next big thing," but who lack the writing and speaking skills they need to do so.

No doubt there's a grain of truth in both these depictions. But the doom 2 sayers who tell these stories are turning a blind eye on compelling alternative narratives. As one who has spent the last 30-plus years studying the writing of college students, I see a different picture. For those who think *Google* is making us stupid and *Facebook* is frying our brains, let me sketch that picture in briefly.

Anticipating the views of opponents, p. 481, strengthens your own claims.

In 2001, I and my colleagues began a longitudinal study of writing at 3 Stanford, following a randomly selected group of 189 students from their first day on campus through one year beyond graduation; in fact, I am still in touch with a number of the students today. These students—about 12 percent of that year's class—submitted the writing they did for their classes and as much of their out-of-class writing as they wanted to an electronic database, along with their comments on those pieces of writing. Over the years, we collected nearly 15,000 pieces of student writing: lab reports, research essays, *PowerPoint* presentations, problem sets, honors theses, email and textings (in 11 languages), blogs and journals, poems, documentaries, even a full-length play entitled *Hip-Hopera*. While we are still coding these pieces of writing, several results emerged right away. First, these students were writing A LOT, both in class and out, though they were more interested in and committed to writing out of class, what we came to call "life writing," than they were in their school assignments. Second, they were increasingly aware of those to whom they were writing and adjusted their writing styles to suit the occasion and the audience. Third, they wanted their writing to count for something; as they said to us over and over, good writing to them was performative, the kind of writing that "made something happen in the world." Finally, they increasingly saw writing as collaborative, social, and participatory rather than solitary.

So yes, these students did plenty of emailing and texting; they were 4 online a good part of every day; they joined social networking sites enthusiastically. But rather than leading to a new illiteracy, these activities seemed to help them develop a range or *repertoire* of writing styles, tones, and formats along with a range of abilities. Here's a student sending a text message to friends reporting on what she's doing on an internship in Bangladesh (she refers in the first few words to the fact that power has been going on and off ever since she arrived): "Next up: words stolen from before the power went out****~~~~Whadda-ya-know, I am back in Dhaka from the villages of Mymensingh. I'm familiar enough with the villages now that it's harder to find things that really surprise me, though I keep looking ☺." In an informal message, this students feels free to use fragments ("Next up"), slang ("whadda-ya-know"), asterisks and tildes for emphasis, and a smiley.

Now look at a brief report she sends to the faculty adviser for her intern-   5
ship in Bangladesh: "In June of 2003, I traveled to Dhaka, Bangladesh, for 9 weeks to intern for Grameen Bank. Grameen Bank is a micro-credit institution which seeks to alleviate poverty by providing access to financial capital. Grameen Bank provides small loans to poor rural women, who then use the capital to start small businesses and sustain income generating activities." Here the student is all business, using formal academic style to begin her first report. No slang, no use of special-effects markings: just the facts, ma'am.[1] In the thousands of pieces of student writing we have examined, we see students moving with relative ease across levels of style (from the most informal to the most formal): these young people are for the most part aware of the context and audience for their writing—and they make the adjustments necessary to address them effectively.

Ah, you say, but these are students at Stanford—the crème de la crème.   6
And I'll agree that these students were all very keen, very bright. But they were not all strong writers or communicators (though our study shows that they all improved significantly over the five years of the study) and they did not all come from privilege—in fact, a good number far from it. Still, they were part of what students on this campus call the "Stanford bubble." So let's look beyond that bubble to another study I conducted with researcher Karen Lunsford. About 18 months ago, we gathered a sample of first-year student writing from across all regions of the United States, from two-year and four-year schools, big schools and small schools, private and public. Replicating a

---

1. Phrase made famous by the lead detective on *Dragnet*, a 1950s TV show in which Joe Friday, a stern, no-nonsense cop, said the phrase often during witness interviews.

study I'd conducted twenty-five years ago, we read a random sample of these student essays with a fine-tooth eye, noting every formal error in every piece of writing. And what did we find? First, that the length of student writing has increased nearly three-fold in these 25 years, corroborating the fact that students today are writing more than ever before. Second, we found that while error patterns have changed in the last twenty-five years, the ratio of errors to number of words has remained stable not just for twenty-five years but for the last 100 years. In short, we found that students today certainly make errors— as all writers do—but that they are making no more errors than previous studies have documented. Different errors, yes—but more errors, no.

We found, for example, that spelling—the most prevalent error by over   7
300 percent some 25 years ago—now presents much less of a problem to writers. We can chalk up that change, of course, to spell-checkers, which do a good job overall—but still can't correct words that sound alike (to, too, two). But with technology, you win some and you lose some: the most frequent error in our recent study is "wrong word," and ironically a good number of these wrong words come from advice given by the sometimes-not-so-trusty spell-checkers. The student who seems from the context of the sentence to be trying to write "frantic," for example, apparently accepts the spell-checker's suggestion of "fanatic" instead. And finally, this recent study didn't turn up any significant interference from internet lingo—no IMHOs, no LOLs, no 2nites, no smileys. Apparently, by the time many, many students get to college, they have a pretty good sense of what's appropriate: at the very least, they know the difference between a *Facebook* friend and a college professor.

In short, the research my colleagues and I have been doing supports what   8
other researchers are reporting about digital technologies and learning. First, a lot of that learning (perhaps most of it) is taking place outside of class, in the literate activities (musical compositions, videos, photo collages, digital stories, comics, documentaries) young people are pursuing on their own. This is what Mimi Ito[2] calls "kid-driven learning." Second, the participatory nature of digital media allows for more—not less—development of literacies, as Henry Jenkins[3] argues compellingly.

2. Cultural anthropologist (b. 1968) who studies learning and new media.
3. Professor (b. 1958) and author of many books and articles about the role of media.

If we look beyond the hand-wringing about young people and literacy 9
today, beyond the view that paints them as either brain-damaged by technology or as cogs in the latest race to the top, we will see that the changes brought
about by the digital revolution are just that: changes. These changes alter the
very grounds of literacy as the definition, nature, and scope of writing are all
shifting away from the consumption of discourse to its production across a
wide range of genres and media, away from individual "authors" to participatory and collaborative partners-in-production; away from a single static standard of correctness to a situated understanding of audience and context and

For more on a situ-
ated understanding
of audience, see
p. 473.
purpose for writing. Luckily, young people are changing as well,
moving swiftly to join in this expanded culture of writing. They
face huge challenges, of course—challenges of access and of
learning ever new ways with words (and images). What students need in facing these challenges is not derision or dismissal but solid and informed
instruction. And that's where the real problem may lie—not with student
semi-literacy but with that of their teachers.

WORKS CITED

Fishman, Jenn, et al. "Performing Writing, Performing Literacy." *College Composition and Communication*, vol. 57, no. 3, 2005, pp. 224–52.

Ito, Mizuko, et al. *Living and Learning with New Media: Summary of Findings from the Digital Youth Project.* MIT P, 2009.

Ito, Mizuko, et al. *Hanging Out, Messing Around, and Geeking Out: Kids Living and Learning with New Media.* MIT P, 2009.

Jenkins, Henry. *Confronting the Challenges of Participatory Culture: Media Education for the 21st Century.* MIT P, 2009.

———. *Convergence Culture: When Old and New Media Collide.* New York UP, 2008.

Lunsford, Andrea A., and Karen J. Lunsford. "'Mistakes Are a Fact of Life': A National Comparative Study." *College Composition and Communication*, vol. 59, no. 4, 2008, pp. 781–807.

Rogers, Paul M. *The Development of Writers and Writing Abilities: A Longitudinal Study across and beyond the College-Span.* 2008. U of California, Santa Barbara, PhD dissertation.

UNDERSTANDING THE ESSAY

1. When Andrea Lunsford and her colleagues did a longitudinal study of undergraduate student writing at Sanford, she says, "several results emerged right away" (3). What were some of those preliminary results?

2. The students in Lunsford's study "did plenty of" emailing, texting, and other forms of online social networking and writing (4). These "activities," however, did not lead to "a new illiteracy," Lunsford argues (4). In her view, what did they lead to? Does Lunsford offer convincing **EVIDENCE** to support this part of her **CLAIM**? Point to specific **EXAMPLES** in her text.

3. How might the following words and phrases in Lunsford's text be said to confirm (or disprove) what she says about "a range . . . of styles, tones, and formats" as a mark of good writing: "longitudinal" (3), "just the facts, ma'am" (5), "crème de la crème" and "fine-tooth eye" (6), and "you win some and you lose some" (7)?

4. "Ah, you say, but these are students at Stanford" (6). Is Lunsford wise to bring up this counterargument at this point in her **ARGUMENT**? Why or why not?

5. A significant portion of Lunsford's argument has to do with "errors" in student writing (6). What claim is she making here? How and how well does she support that claim? Point to specific details in her argument.

6. "In short," says Lunsford near the end of her argument, "the research my colleagues and I have been doing supports what other researchers are reporting about digital technologies and learning" (8). So what larger conclusion(s) about technology and literacy do Lunsford and her colleagues come to? How and how effectively is this claim supported by her earlier, narrower conclusions about student writing at particular universities?

MIND AND MEDIA:
IS TECHNOLOGY CHANGING
OUR MINDS—AND HEARTS?

ANALYZING THE ARGUMENTS

1. Among the three writers in this debate, which ones make the strongest **ARGU-MENT** about the way digital technologies are changing the way we feel, think, and act? What makes those arguments particularly convincing?

2. Among the three arguments in this debate, which one makes the strongest argument that technology may be diminishing our capacities in some way? What makes this argument effective in your view?

3. Whether or not you agree with their conclusions, which of the writers in this cluster do you find most credible? Why? What strategies do they use to establish their **CREDIBILITY**? For example, how well do they anticipate opposing arguments? Refer to particular passages in the text.

FOR WRITING

1. Choose a **CLAIM** from one of these three arguments that you think could use more support. Write a paragraph providing additional **EVIDENCE** to support (or refute) that claim.

2. Write an argument supporting or opposing (or both) the claim that face-to-face communication is more effective and satisfying than texting or other forms of digital communication. Feel free to cite your own experience to support your argument.

3. "You can't use the internet well," writes Jaron Lanier (p. 505), "until you've confronted it on your own terms" (25). Write a "modest proposal" (see Jonathan Swift's "A Modest Proposal," p. 546) suggesting that the reader should cease to use [insert digital technology of your choice] for an entire year. Cite the specific advantages of adopting your proposal.

4. What is the role of memes on social media today? Are internet memes controlling our responses (like those of Pavlov's dogs)? Or are they part of a shared language that enhances our communication skills? Address this issue in a well-supported **ARGUMENT**.

REPRESENTATION: WHOSE STORIES GET HEARD AND WHY DOES IT MATTER?

M EG? Jo? Beth? Amy? Which of the March sisters in Louisa May Alcott's *Little Women* would you most identify with? If you are a woman and an aspiring writer, the answer is probably Jo, whether you're responding to the hit 2019 film adaptation by Greta Gerwig or to the original novel, published in 1868 and 1869. "It's simple," says Pulitzer Prize—winning journalist Anna Quindlen. "Jo wants to be a writer. . . . As a girl, that made my own highly improbable professional dreams seem possible." Seeing yourself—or the person you might someday become—on the screen or printed page may not be so simple, however, if you (and your dreams) are not typically represented in the media. Though female and relatively poor, as novelist and poet Julia Alvarez observes, "the March sisters were white New Englanders" of a social and intellectual class that is often reflected, even idealized, in American literature. What if, like Alvarez when she first picked up Alcott's book, you and your sisters spoke Spanish and "were newly arrived immigrants from a dictatorship in the Dominican Republic"? Good literature, according to Alvarez, dissolves boundaries. In today's media, however, not everyone gets fair and equal representation. Whose stories get told—and who gets to tell them? Which stories are heard and believed? Why does it matter?

In the following essays, **Zachary Wood**, **Sarah Smarsh**, and **Nancy Wang Yuen** address these and other issues of representation and credibility in the media and in government, school, work, and elsewhere.

ZACHARY WOOD

UNCENSORED

ZACHARY WOOD (B. 1995) is a writer and assistant opinion editor at the *Guardian*. He grew up living with his mother—who suffered from mental illness—in Detroit and with his estranged father in Washington, DC. Wood chronicles these and other formative experiences in *Uncensored: My Life and Uncomfortable Conversations at the Intersection of Black and White America* (2018), from which this selection is taken. Wood wrote most of the book while still an undergraduate at Williams College, where he was a political science major and president of Uncomfortable Learning, a student organization that brought "speakers who would offer different viewpoints from those we were typically exposed to on our liberal campus." Wood himself came under fire for inviting figures like Charles Murray, author of *The Bell Curve*, who contends that intelligence is heritable by race. To the question of how he became such a fierce advocate of free speech and open dialogue with people whose ideas he finds deeply "uncomfortable," Wood gives a simple answer at the end of this selection: "I wasn't exactly coddled."

"DO BLACK PEOPLE COME FROM APES?" a high school friend of mine asked, 1
looking me in the eye. His dad had told him about Charles Murray's
book *The Bell Curve*,[1] which links intelligence to race and class in America.
"You know, black people are always good at four things," my friend continued,
"running, jumping, stealing, and shooting."

At the elite private school I attended, which took two hours to get to by 2
public transportation, I sometimes heard these types of comments. These
same students would call the neighborhood I grew up in poor, and though it
was dangerous and considered by some to be one of the city's rougher areas,
it was where my father worked harder than anyone I'd ever met. So when race
came up, either subtly or overtly, his image was the one I carried of my neighborhood and my blackness.

"Zach, why are black people so athletic?" they asked me. Other times, they 3
insisted that I impersonate Obama and complained that my nose wasn't big
enough for me to really be black. Did I like this? Of course not. But did it faze me?
Please. I had been learning how to adapt to difficult circumstances since before I
could remember. Sometimes I debated race with these students;   Appealing to the
other times it seemed futile. No matter the case, I always tried my   reader's sense of
  fair play is just one
best to show through my own actions that the things they believed   of many tools for
  establishing your
about black people weren't true. But I knew that I could make a big-   credibility (p. 481).
ger impact by going to the source and learning every facet of their arguments so
that I could ultimately take them on. I filed away Charles Murray's name, but not
in order to avoid it. Rather, so that I could seek out his books and educate myself
about exactly what he was saying, and why.

Only three years later, I had an opportunity to do just that. As the presi- 4
dent of Uncomfortable Learning at Williams College, I had the job of bringing
speakers who would offer different viewpoints from those we were typically
exposed to on our liberal campus. First, I invited Suzanne Venker, a self-
described anti-feminist who claims that feminist women are waging a war on
men. Within minutes of announcing the event, my in-box, phone, and *Facebook* page were flooded with negative comments, insults, and even implicit

1. Murray, a political scientist, first published *The Bell Curve* in 1994 in collaboration with
the psychologist Richard J. Hernstein. It carried the subtitle, *Intelligence and Class Structure
in American Life.*

threats. "Zach Wood, you're a filthy misogynist," my peers said. "You're a sellout, a traitor to your race. You're worse than Ben Carson."

I was shocked. Many of these comments were coming from students who 5 knew me. They'd engaged with me on campus, and some were even my friends. Yet, based on this one event, they were characterizing me in a way that went against everything I stood for. But I was determined not to back down. When we eventually had to cancel Venker's appearance due to concerns about her personal safety, I followed up with an invitation to John Derbyshire, a divisive pop-math author and opinion journalist who'd publicly defended white supremacy, advised readers to stay away from groups of black people, and, like Murray, claimed that blacks had lower IQs than whites.

This time, the backlash was even worse. Now the topic was race. A note 6 was slipped under my door that read, "Your blood will be in the leaves," next to a picture of a tree. A comment on *Facebook* read, "We need the oil and switch to deal with him in this midnight hour." A few student activists came up to me in the cafeteria and insulted me to my face. Others whispered about me behind my back.

I tried explaining to my fellow students that I wasn't doing this because 7 I was secretly a conservative, a self-hating black man, or an anti-feminist, men's rights activist. Rather, I was sick of living in an echo cham-

For tips on delving into opposing views, see p. 481.

ber. At Williams, most of my professors taught their perspective on any given issue as if it were fact instead of delving into opposing views to create well-rounded lessons. Around campus, progressive ideas were lauded while conservative ones were shut down for being insensitive. The few conservatives at Williams were largely scared into silence, knowing that if they went against the status quo they would be labeled as biased and wrong.

I wasn't satisfied hearing only one side of things, even if it was the side I 8 agreed with. I wanted to use the education I received at Williams to create positive change in the world one day. How would I do that if I shut out the voices I disagreed with instead of engaging with them? My curiosity led me to examine issues from all sides, trying to find understanding and hopefully some common ground. It wasn't about letting a racist convince me that I was wrong or that I was less intelligent than he was. Instead, I sought to stand firmer in my convictions and become better able to defend them by thoroughly understanding the logic of my opponents.

My explanations made little difference. When the president of Williams   9
College, Adam Falk, canceled Derbyshire's talk, I was disappointed but not
deterred. Charles Murray had reached out to me, saying that he'd love to come
speak at Williams, and I decided to invite him. While some students continued to protest, this time the event went on as planned.

In his book, Murray attributed IQ disparities and achievement gaps to the   10
genetic inferiority of blacks and the behavioral impediments holding back
black communities. One of Murray's contentions was that there are cultural
problems in the black community that no amount of welfare or government
spending can possibly correct. As he was explaining some of his ideas over
dinner, I realized that the IQ discussion was just a distraction. If I focused on
the actual issues, maybe we could find some common ground. So I started by
acknowledging his side of the argument head-on.

"I am not discounting cultural problems," I told him, going on to describe   11
them better than he could: the emulation of rappers, the glorification of hip-
hop culture and violence, the broken families, and so on. "But," I continued,
"we need to address the structural issues first. You do acknowledge that they
exist, right? So how can we increase social mobility and economic opportunity for Americans living below the poverty line?"

Murray engaged thoughtfully but continued on undeterred. After the   12
event, a friend approached me to say that my argument had resonated with
him and had even made him think differently about racial disparities in
America. For me, Murray's visit to Williams was a successful example of
Uncomfortable Learning. Neither of us changed our opinions or switched
sides, but that wasn't the point. Instead, by listening to and challenging Murray, my classmates and I were forced to think more deeply about our own
beliefs and even question them.

In my mind, this type of debate is valuable and would not have been   13
possible if we did not give Murray an opportunity to share his perspective,
but my critics felt that by giving him that opportunity, I was bolstering his
misguided and often hurtful views.

Hurtful. That's the word that campus activists and others who opposed   14
Murray's invitation to speak at Williams used to describe why they were
against it. As I sat down with some of them to hear them out, just as I'd heard
out Murray, they explained why it was so painful and triggering for them.

They discussed incidents of sexual assault, police brutality, and growing up in poverty, and they explained that, to them, Williams wasn't just a learning institution—it was their home.

As the topic of free speech on college campuses has continued to cause 15 controversy, protests, and even bursts of violence across the country, the criticism most often levied against campus activists is that they're too sensitive. On campus, their feelings are coddled. Class materials that may be upsetting are given a trigger warning. Speech codes restrict many college students from talking about certain subjects. And controversial speakers such as Venker and Derbyshire are kept away. The result is millions of college students who have little tolerance for healthy debate and view someone voicing his or her opposing view as an attack on their very personhood.

Make no mistake—these subjects are extremely difficult for me to grapple 16 with, too. But I don't want to give someone like Derbyshire the satisfaction of writing me off as too sensitive when I can rise to the occasion and challenge him instead.

And, yes, of course there's more to it than that. This is something I've 17 been asked about many times. In several of the interviews I've done following the Uncomfortable Learning controversy, I've been asked why my peers are so sensitive and what makes me different.

"Your classmates are hurt by someone like Murray merely being on cam- 18 pus, and you're willing to face implicit threats in order to bring him there," one reporter remarked during a phone interview. "How have you grown such a thick skin? Are you just wired differently than the students who criticize you?"

I repeated the question, trying to think of how best to answer. This was 19 something I'd been asked many times, but not in such a pointed way. The truth is, I know full well where my thick skin comes from. It's something I've processed and moved on from, but once in a while when I'm asked a question like this, I think back to her[2] words: "You worthless punk-ass nigga." I can remember the piercing look in her eyes, the leather belt in her hand, the anger and pain that made her face quiver as she told me to take off my clothes and turn around.

"Well," I said slowly, taking a deep breath. "I wasn't exactly coddled." 20

2. Zachary Wood's mother. [Editor's note]

UNDERSTANDING THE ESSAY

1. "Do black people come from apes?" (1) Asked in an interview why he started a personal story with this question, Zachary Wood replied that he "wanted to open up with . . . a point or a question of uncomfortable learning . . . that would draw the reader in." Did his plan work? Why or why not?

2. As an undergraduate at Williams College, Wood says he "wasn't satisfied hearing only one side of things, even if it was the side [he] agreed with" (8). What reasons does Wood give for dealing with the "uncomfortable" ideas of people he disagrees with "by going to the source and learning every facet of their arguments" (3)?

3. "As the topic of free speech on college campuses has continued to cause controversy, and even bursts of violence across the country, the criticism most often levied against campus activists is that they're too sensitive" (15). What is Wood's view on the issue of campus opposition to "hurtful" speech (14)? How did he arrive at that position, and how (and how well) does he show that he understands both sides of the issue?

4. What is Wood's purpose in citing the **EXAMPLE** of his conversation with Charles Murray? How does the exchange with Murray fit in with Wood's rationale for listening to and learning about uncomfortable ideas in order "to take them on" (3)?

5. "Are you wired differently than the students who criticize you?" (18). This is a question about inheritance. What answer does Wood give, and how does it confirm what else he says about character traits like determination and open mindedness?

6. "So when race came up, either subtly or overtly," Wood says of his hardworking father, "his image was the one I carried of my neighborhood and my blackness" (2). When explaining the source of his "thick skin," Wood invokes his mother's image instead. To what extent do such glimpses of his parents' stories, however brief, contribute to the story their son is telling about himself? Explain.

BELIEVE IT

SARAH SMARSH (b. 1980) is a journalist, former writing professor, and the acclaimed author of *Heartland: A Memoir of Working Hard and Being Broke in the Richest Country on Earth* (2018). A native of Kansas, Smarsh moved at age nine from the family farm to Wichita, where her newly divorced mother sought work. "Largely owing to the chaos of poverty," she wrote in the *Guardian,* "I would attend eight schools by the time I finished ninth grade." One of these was a public elementary school in Wichita, where Smarsh was first inspired to write about her family and the region by a devoted fifth-grade teacher. By sixth grade, Smarsh had returned to farm life, where she remained until leaving home as a first-generation college student. In 2002, Smarsh graduated from the University of Kansas with a BA in English and a BS in journalism, followed in 2005 by an MFA from Columbia University. From her own storytelling, as well as her formal study of narrative, Smarsh has discerned that "narrative credibility is in the eye of the beholder." Whose stories do people tend to believe, and whose do people distrust? The answer, Smarsh argues in "Believe It," depends largely on the social and economic "class" of the storyteller.

CRYING "FICTION!" is often a convenient first line of self-defense against stories that blow the whistle on unjust structures. Men balk when women describe harassment, white people insist racism is over, and the wealthy discount tales of poverty not just because they can't fathom realities they haven't witnessed firsthand but because those narratives threaten systems from which they benefit. Belief is a choice, however unconscious, and it self-sustains: we believe what serves our purposes, and the world we're thus open to seeing validates those beliefs.

In my German Catholic farming community, we believed in Jesus. The crucifixion story, in particular, resonated: someone had given up his body for a cause. Jesus suffered on a cross for someone else's soul, and we suffered in wheat fields for someone else's bread—maybe even for the wafers we accepted on our tongues after priests transformed it into the body of Christ.

Some features of Jesus's story were more difficult to swallow—his dark skin, say, or the oil-rich deserts of a Middle East, to which we'd not yet sent our small-town children with Stealth bombers. We found ways to trust the messenger by finding in him our own likeness. Like us, Jesus came from peasants. Near the altar of our tiny country church rested a sculpted scene of carpenter Joseph, teenage Mary, and the baby Jesus. When I was very small, I thought my dad, who built houses for a living, was Joseph; my grandfather had hammered together the steeple above us and carved the Communion rail from a walnut tree on our land. Females weren't allowed to stand, let alone preach, at the altar beyond that rail; at the nearby Pietà, dusted with care by elderly women, I recognized in Mary's face the emotional anguish of my mother, who became pregnant with me at seventeen.

In memoir, too, perceived credibility of the speaker holds sway. Just as the crucifix in my childhood church required a white Jesus, Sojourner Truth's dictated testimony of slavery went to press with "Certificates of Character," provided by such upstanding white men as her former owner, John Dumont.

"This is to certify, that Isabella, this colored woman, lived with me since the year 1810, and that she has always been a good and faithful servant; and the eighteen years that she was with me, I always found her to be perfectly honest," Dumont wrote for the 1850 text dictated by Truth. "I have always heard her well spoken of by every one that has employed her."

Isabella Baumfree, also known as Sojourner Truth, speaks for herself in "Ain't I a Woman?," p. 561.

Harriet Jacobs, whose *Incidents in the Life of a Slave Girl* was, in 1861, the 6
first published "slave narrative" actually written by a black woman, knew her
burden of proof all too well. She wrote in the preface:

> *Readers be assured this narrative is no fiction. I am aware that some of*
> *my adventures may seem incredible; but they are, nevertheless, strictly*
> *true. I have not exaggerated the wrongs inflicted by Slavery; on the con-*
> *trary, my descriptions fall far short of the facts.*

Jacobs's sympathetic editor, Lydia Maria Child, forewent blurbs from male
landowners but, in her introduction, told readers that Jacobs lived for seventeen years "with a distinguished family in New York and has so supported herself as to be highly esteemed by them. . . . I believe those who know her will
not be disposed to doubt her veracity, though some incidents in her story are
more romantic than fiction." (Child, for the record, had few qualms with representing actual slavery through generalized, fictionalized accounts.)

Child's introduction went on to address another barrier to belief: negative 7
assumptions about the storyteller's capabilities. "It will naturally excite sur-

Using the testimony
of others to bolster
an argument is
discussed on
p. 475.

prise that a woman reared in slavery should be able to write so
well," she wrote. She explained that a mistress had taught Jacobs to
read and write in childhood, that Jacobs was now in the mix with
smart Northerners, and that "nature endowed her with quick
perceptions"—a bold assessment, at the time, to make of a black woman.

More than a century and a half later, memoirs from underprivileged 8
ranks continue to be questioned by the powerful. . . .

But perhaps the deepest challenge in articulating and considering the sto- 9
ries of our lives is not that they force us to admit our privileges but that they force
us to admit our suffering. Some realities hurt to look at. Therefore, our harshest
critics are often those with whom we share the most common ground.

The first person I heard say she didn't believe Anita Hill[1] was my hard- 10

---

1. On October 11, 1991, Washington attorney Anita Faye Hill testified before the US Congress
that Supreme Court nominee Clarence Thomas had sexually harassed her while he was
her supervisor in the Department of Education and the Equal Employment Opportunity
Commission. Thomas denied the allegations and was confirmed by the Senate to replace
retiring Justice Thurgood Marshall, who was the first Black justice on the court.

luck grandma, a longtime employee of the courts system, who had seen plenty of sexism—though she never spoke of it. Among Frank McCourt's few but staunch detractors, in the wake of his Pulitzer-Prize-winning 1996 memoir, *Angela's Ashes*, were the people of his native Limerick.[2]. . . .

In matters of truth, much has been said of the memoirist's responsibility   11 in wielding accuracy; much less has been said of the reader's responsibility in wielding belief. Belief is a form of reverence; disbelief, a form of rejection. Both can be destructive when unexamined: blind faith might give power where it's not due while blind doubt might strip away power where it's needed most. Whether we out our tongues to deny or savor another person's claims, the revelation is about ourselves.

For more on the writer's responsibility to be accurate, see p. 481.

In one such revelation, I decided as a young adult that Catholicism was no   12 longer for me. Around the same time, the Church changed, too: girls could serve at the altar. One needn't believe in a church's tenets to be moved by the efforts of its parishioners; even after I stopped taking Communion, I sometimes went to Mass to marvel at the new altar girls—white-robed and ponytailed, carrying gifts to an altar, where, someday, they might even be priests.

Belief and doubt are inevitably selfish things. But beyond our dubious   13 ability to judge a story is something transcendent: our ability to receive it. Memoirists aren't making an argument. They're making an offering.

UNDERSTANDING THE ESSAY

1. Sarah Smarsh begins and ends with references to her German Catholic upbringing. How and why does Smarsh's attitude toward religion and the church *change* between her childhood and the time she becomes a "young adult" (12)? How relevant is this experience to what she says about stories and belief? Explain.

2. According to Smarsh, why did the crucifix in her childhood church require "a white Jesus" (4)? In her view, what does this version of the story of Jesus have in common with the stories of people like Sojourner Truth, Harriet Jacobs, Anita Hill, and Frank McCourt's Angela? Explain.

3. "Therefore, our harshest critics are often those with whom we share the most common ground" (9). Why is this the case, according to Smarsh? What **EVIDENCE**

---

2. Limerick, where McCourt spent a portion of his childhood, is a city in midwestern Ireland with a population of around 94,000.

does she offer to back up such a conclusion, and how sufficient is it to prove her point?

4. "Belief is a form of reverence; disbelief, a form of rejection," says Smarsh (11). If this principle explains why we should believe the stories of "those with whom we share the most common ground," what does it suggest about the stories of people with whom we have *little* in common? Is Smarsh urging us to *disbelieve* them? Why or why not?

5. What does Smarsh mean when she says that memoirists who tell their own stories "aren't making an argument. They're making an offering" (13)? To what extent is this claim itself part of a larger **ARGUMENT** about **CREDIBILITY** in narrative? Explain.

NANCY WANG YUEN

REEL INEQUALITY

NANCY WANG YUEN (b. 1976) is a professor of sociology at Biola University in La Mirada, California, where she teaches Asian American Studies and popular culture. She is a graduate of the University of California at Los Angeles with a B.A. in creative writing (1997) and a Ph.D. in sociology (2008). A contributor to both academic journals and popular publications such as *Newsweek, Elle*, and *HuffPost*, Yuen is also a speaker and consultant on issues of race and representation in the Hollywood film industry. As "an immigrant kid" growing up in a racially diverse neighborhood in Southern California, Yuen watched more than her share of movies and television. She did not, however, see herself or her family represented in the media "beyond the occasional cringe-worthy Asian nerd or massage parlor worker." In *Reel Inequality: Hollywood Actors and Racism* (2016), the book from which the following selection is taken, Yuen argues that little has changed in Hollywood since her childhood, when it seemed that "only white lives mattered, and the rest of us were either marginalized or demonized." Representation (or the lack of it) in the media is still reality, Yuen concludes, not only for Asian American, Black, and Latino actors and spectators but White ones as well.

I N 2016, FOR THE SECOND CONSECUTIVE YEAR, the Academy of Motion Picture   1
Arts and Sciences nominated white actors for all acting awards. This
revived the hashtag #OscarsSoWhite, pulling back the curtain on Hollywood's
enduring race problem.[1] Despite showing talent, resilience, and bankability,
why do actors of color continue to lag white actors in numbers and prominence? At the epicenter is the industry's racial and gender homogeneity, epito-
mized by the Academy's corps of invited-only members. With a 93 percent
white and 76 percent male membership,[2] the Academy has come under pressure to diversify. In protest, Spike Lee and Jada Pinkett Smith
both announced they would not attend the [2016] Oscars ceremo-
ny.[3] The Academy's president, Cheryl Boone Isaacs, responded
quickly with promises of change. Several (white) Academy members defended the status quo. Oscar nominee Charlotte Rampling
called the protest "racist to whites" and suggested that perhaps "black actors
did not deserve to make the final list."[4] Similarly, double-Oscar winner
Michael Caine said, "In the end, you can't vote for an actor because he's black.
You can't say, 'I'm going to vote for him. He's not very good, but he's black.'"[5]
Cries of reverse racism and blaming actors of color for their own marginaliza-
tion are commonplace in Hollywood. These arguments falsely assume an

Yuen uses Chicago-style footnote documentation to cite her sources. See p. 597 for advice on using MLA-style.

1. Tre'vell Anderson, "#Oscarssowhite Creator on Oscar Noms: 'Don't Tell Me That People of Color, Women Cannot Fill Seats,'" *Los Angeles Times*, January 14, 2016, https://www .latimes.com/entertainment/envelope/la-et-mn-april-reign-oscars-so-white-diversity -20160114-story.html.

2. John Horn and Doug Smith, "Diversity Efforts Slow to Change the Face of Oscar Voters," *Los Angeles Times*, December 21, 2013, https://www.latimes.com/entertainment/movies /moviesnow/la-et-mn-diversity-oscar-academy-members-20131221-story.html.

3. David Ng, "Spike Lee and Jada Pinkett Smith to Boycott Oscars; Academy Responds," *Los Angeles Times*, January 18, 2016, https://www.latimes.com/entertainment/movies/la-et -spike-lee-to-boycott-oscars-html-20160118-htmlstory.html.

4. Ben Child, "Oscars 2016: Charlotte Rampling Says Diversity Row Is 'Racist to White People,'" *Guardian*, January 22, 2016, https://www.theguardian.com/film/2016/jan/22 /oscars-2016-charlotte-rampling-diversity-row-racist-to-white-people.

5. Yesha Callahan, "#Oscarssowhite: Michael Caine Thinks Blacks Should Be Patient; Charlotte Rampling Says Diversity Complaints Are Racist against Whites," *The Root*, Jan-uary 22, 2016, https://thegrapevine.theroot.com/oscarssowhite-michael-caine-thinks -blacks-should-be-p-1790887745.

equal playing field while dismissing institutional racial biases that privilege white actors for roles and recognition.

Hollywood's systemic exclusion of actors of color is evident in the Academy's abysmal record of nominating and awarding actors of color. In Oscar's eighty-eight-year history, actors of color received only 6.2 percent of total acting nominations and won only 7.8 percent of total acting awards. The only woman of color to ever win a best actress award was African American actor Halle Berry in 2002 for her performance in *Monster's Ball*. . . . By deeming only white actors worth honoring, the Academy reproduces Hollywood's structural racial bias.

Though public pressures have prompted the Academy to implement immediate changes to diversify its membership,[6] the impact on future nominations remains uncertain. This is because the Academy's diversity problem is not just numerical but also ideological. The Academy constrains actors of color by granting Oscars to a narrow set of stereotyped roles. David Oyelowo describes how black actors "have been celebrated more for when we are subservient . . . not just in the Academy, but in life generally. We have been slaves, we have been domestic servants, we have been criminals, we have been all of those things. But we have been leaders, we have been kings, we have been those who changed the world."[7] . . .

Though actors of color have played leaders, they rarely win Oscars for such roles. Denzel Washington won the best actor Oscar for playing a corrupt cop in *Training Day* (2001), but not for his widely lauded performance of the title character in *Malcom X* (1992). Another noteworthy performance, David Oyelowo's critically acclaimed portrayal of Martin Luther King Jr. in *Selma* (2014), did not even garner a nomination. By honoring actors of color for playing slaves, maids, and criminals rather than civil rights leaders, the Academy denies them the full breadth of accolades afforded to white actors. The Academy may or may not intentionally vote for roles that keep people of color "in

6. Janice Min, "#OscarsSoWhite: Academy Chiefs Reveal Behind-the-Scenes Drama That Led to Historic Change (Exclusive)," *Hollywood Reporter*, January 27, 2016, https://www.hollywoodreporter.com/features/oscarssowhite-academy-chiefs-reveal-behind-859693.
7. Scott Feinberg, "'Selma' Star David Oyelowo Says Academy Favors 'Subservient' Black Roles," *Hollywood Reporter*, February 2, 2015, https://www.hollywoodreporter.com/race/selma-star-david-oyelowo-says-769032.

their place," but its record reveals a pattern of bias. Consequently, the Academy will have to diversify more than just members' numbers, but their hearts and minds, as well.

#OscarsSoWhite is a symptom of Hollywood's larger race problem. The exclusion and stereotyping of actors of color extend far beyond the Academy Awards. Even though people of color made up 37.4 percent of the US population in 2013, actors of color played only 6.5 percent of lead roles in broadcast television shows and 16.7 percent of lead roles in films.[8] Furthermore, Hollywood tends to view actors of color—from the Oscar contenders to the average working actor—through a racist lens, reducing them to tokens and caricatures.

Far from neutral, mass media institutions such as Hollywood are major transmitters of racist ideologies. . . . Hollywood's dominant narratives of whites as heroes and actors of color as sidekicks or villains legitimize and reproduce the racial hierarchies existent in US society.

Though they are largely fictional, on-screen images can shape our view of reality. I witnessed this firsthand when I went to see *Skyfall* (2012), a James Bond film. Preview after preview of action films featured white male protagonists shooting and killing people, yet it was the preview for *Django Unchained* (2012) that elicited an extreme audience reaction. In one scene, Django (played by Jamie Foxx), a black slave-turned-bounty-hunter, says, "Kill white folks, and they pay you for it—what's not to like?" This statement caused two middle-aged white women sitting in my row to groan loudly, as one of them griped, "That's what's wrong with our urban areas!" Even though we were about to watch a violent James Bond film and had just sat through brutal violence enacted by Tom Cruise, Bruce Willis, and Arnold Schwarzenegger, none of those previews elicited critique. The lack of black heroes in film and television, coupled with the preponderance of white heroes and black villains, demonizes black male violence and legitimizes white male violence. Further-

8. US Population (2014 estimate): US Census, "State and County Quickfacts," http://quickfacts.census.gob/qfd/states/00000.html; lead roles in broadcast television shows (2012-2013) and lead roles in film (2011-2013): Darnell Hunt and Ana-Christina Ramon, "2015 Hollywood Diversity Report: Flipping the Script" (Los Angeles: Ralph J. Bunche Center for African American Studies at UCLA, 2015), 9, 13.

more, this extrapolation of a fictional Django to "our urban areas" demonstrates how audiences fail to distinguish between fiction and reality in racial stereotypes. Through countless reiterations in popular media, racial stereotypes can become *real* in the minds of audiences.[9]

Popular media can have a negative impact on whites' perceptions of people of color. One study found that nonverbal racial biases in facial expressions and body language, as represented on popular television shows, influence white viewers' racial biases.[10] Furthermore, a lack of contact between racial groups can lead to greater reliance on media stereotypes when formulating ideas about people outside one's race.[11] Studies show that audiences substitute stereotypes they see on screen for reality when they have not had any direct interactions with particular racial groups.[12] For instance, Latino stereotypes in the media can lead audiences negatively to associate immigration with increased unemployment and crime.[13] Film and television can also exacerbate preexisting racist fears. For example, people who perceive that they live in a neighborhood with a high percentage of blacks are more likely than those who do not hold that perception to fear crime after watching scripted crime dramas.[14]

8

To support her claim, Yuen uses all of the different forms of evidence discussed on pp. 474–75

9. Michael Omi, "In Living Color: Race and American Culture," in *Signs of Life in the USA: Readings on Popular Culture for Writers*, ed. Sonia Maasik and Jack Solomon (Boston: Bedford Books, 1997), 500.

10. Max Weisbuch et al., "The Subtle Transmission of Race Bias via Televised Nonverbal Behavior," *Science* 326 (December 18, 2009): 1711.

11. Qingwen Dong and Arthur Phillip Murrillo, "The Impact of Television Viewing on Young Adults' Stereotypes towards Hispanic Americans," *Human Communication* 19, no. 1 (2007); Robert M. Entman and Andrew Rojecki, *The Black Image in the White Mind: Media and Race in America*, Studies in Communications, Media and Public Opinion (Chicago: University of Chicago Press, 2000).

12. Joe R. Feagin, *Racist America: Roots, Current Realities, and Future Reparations* (New York: Routledge, 2000), 141-142.

13. Jeffrey M. Timberlake et al., "Who 'They' Are Matters: Immigrant Stereotypes and Assessments of the Impact of Immigration," *Social Science Quarterly* 56, no. 2 (2015): 267-299.

14. Sarah Eschholz et al., "Television and Fear of Crime: Program Types, Audience Traits, and the Mediating Effect of Perceived Neighborhood Racial Composition," *Social Problems* 50, no. 3 (2003): 395-415.

Given that whites greatly overestimate the share of crimes committed 9
by blacks,[15] media stereotypes can aggravate such misperceptions and can be
used to justify violence against people of color. Darren Wilson—the white
police officer who shot and killed Michael Brown, an unarmed black man, in
Ferguson, Missouri—characterized Brown as a "demon" and a "hulk." Journalists pointed out that Wilson's descriptors came from the "black brute"
racial stereotype, a "stock figure of white supremacist rhetoric in the lynching
era of the late 19th and early 20th centuries,"[16] as popularized in Hollywood
films.[17] . . . Racism, when packaged as entertainment, can skew the way viewers
understand and categorize people.

In addition to aggravating racial tensions, the erasure and negative por- 10
trayals of people of color can adversely affect how people of color see themselves. Prolonged television exposure predicts a decrease in self-esteem for all
girls and for black boys, and an increase in self-esteem for white boys.[18] These
differences correlate with the racial and gender biases in Hollywood, which
casts only white men as heroes, while erasing or subordinating other groups
as villains, sidekicks, and sexual objects. Studies also show how media images
of Native American mascots lower the self-esteem and affect the moods of
Native American adolescents and young adults, who have the highest suicide
rates in the United States.[19] The ubiquity of racist imagery can have cumula-

15. Ana Swanson, "Whites Greatly Overestimate the Share of Crimes Committed by Black
People," *Washington Post*, December 1, 2014, https://www.washingtonpost.com/news/wonk/wp
/2014/12/01/whites-greatly-overestimate-the-share-of-crimes-committed-by-black-people/.
16. Jamelle Bouie, "Michael Brown Wasn't a Superhuman Demon: But Darren Wilson's
Racial Prejudice Told Him Otherwise," *Slate*, November 26, 2014, https://slate.com/news-and
-politics/2014/11/darren-wilsons-racial-portrayal-of-michael-brown-as-a-superhuman
-demon-the-ferguson-police-officers-account-is-a-common-projection-of-racial-fears.html;
Frederica Boswell, "In Darren Wilson's Testimony, Familiar Theme about Black Men,"
National Public Radio (November 26, 2014).
17. Donald Bogle, *Toms, Coons, Mulattoes, Mammies, and Bucks: An Interpretive History of
Blacks in American Films* (New York: Continuum, 2001), 10.
18. N. Martins and K. Harrison, "Racial and Gender Differences in the Relationship
between Children's Television Use and Self-Esteem: A Longitudinal Panel Study," *Communication Research* 39, no. 3 (2011): 338.
19. Michael A. Friedman, "The Harmful Psychological Effects of the Washington Football
Mascot," 2013. https://www.changethemascot.org/wp-content/uploads/2013/10
/DrFriedmanReport.pdf.

tive effects on society. We cannot dismiss the media's differential portrayals of racial groups as mere entertainment if we are to take seriously their impact on our youth.

In an ideal Hollywood industry, all actors can play all ethnicities equally. 11 After all, acting is pretending to be someone else. However, Hollywood is not an equal playing field when actors of color remain invisible or sidelined to a select few shows while white actors enjoy the privilege to portray every role under the sun—even characters of color.

> The conclusion of an argument is a good place to explain the broader significance of your claim (p. 476).

UNDERSTANDING THE ESSAY

1. "Why," asks Nancy Wang Yuen, "do actors of color continue to lag white actors in numbers and prominence?" (1) What answer does Yuen give to this **RHETORICAL QUESTION?**

2. Yuen claims that Hollywood tends to reduce actors of color and the roles they play "to tokens and caricatures" (5)? To what extent does your own viewing experience bear out (or contradict) this claim? Explain.

3. What is the point of Yuen's **ANECDOTE** recalling a conversation she overheard between two women at a James Bond movie?

4. After **ARGUING** that racial stereotypes in film and television can have a negative influence on how White people regard people of color in real life, what related claim does Yuen make in paragraph 10?

5. "After all, acting is pretending to be someone else" (11). Why might Yuen end her argument with this succinct **DEFINITION** of the actor's profession? Explain.

REPRESENTATION: WHOSE STORIES
GET HEARD AND WHY DOES IT MATTER?

ANALYZING THE ARGUMENTS

1. Among the three writers in this debate, which of them make the strongest **ARGU-MENT** for representing all kinds of people and their stories in the media and society in general? What makes these arguments particularly convincing? Cite particular passages and pieces of evidence.

2. "In any social order," Sarah Smarsh writes elsewhere, "you will know the powerful by who is believed and the subjugated by who is doubted." How and how well does her essay support this observation? In seeking out speakers with whom he disagrees, does Zachary Wood appear to agree or disagree with Smarsh? How about Yuen in her claim that people of color come to doubt themselves because of media stereotypes? Explain.

3. Whether or not *you* agree with the conclusions, which of these three writers do you find most **CREDIBLE**? How is that credibility established? For example, which writers seem most **OBJECTIVE**, or best informed, or most committed to their subjects? Refer to specific passages in the texts to support your answers.

FOR WRITING

1. Choose a **CLAIM** from one of these three arguments that you think could use more support. Write a paragraph or two outlining the additional evidence you would introduce to support (or refute) that claim.

2. Write an argument that either supports or opposes one of the following claims: believe no stories or claims until they are authenticated or substantiated; believe what a writer says unless or until the writer proves to be unreliable; credibility is in the eye of the reader; credibility lies is in what a writer has to say—and how it's said; credibility derives from a mutual trust between reader and writer.

⇒14⇐

CLASSIC ESSAYS AND SPEECHES

T HE essays and speeches in this chapter are "classics"—timeless examples of good writing across the centuries. What makes them timeless? Jonathan Swift's "A Modest Proposal," for instance, is nearly 300 years old, and the speaker is a "projector," a word we don't even use anymore in the sense that Swift used it, for a person who is full of foolish projects. However, the moral and economic issues that Swift addresses are as timely today as they were in the 18th century. His greedy countrymen, Swift charges—not to mention English landlords and "a very knowing American of my acquaintance"—will do anything for money (9).

What Makes a Classic Essay or Speech?

This sense of relevance—the feeling that what the writer has to say applies directly to us and our time—is one measure of a "classic." We feel it with all the essays and speeches in this chapter, including the Declaration of Independence; Sojourner Truth's "Ain't I a Woman?"; Zora Neale Hurston's "How It Feels to Be Colored Me"; George Orwell's "Politics and the English Language"; and Martin Luther King Jr.'s "The Other America."

In addition to their timeless themes, the works in this chapter are classics because the writer of each one has a unique command of language and of the fundamental forms and patterns of written or spoken discourse. By taking apart these great essays and speeches, you will find that they are constructed using the same basic strategies and techniques of writing you have been studying throughout this book. All the basic patterns of writing are here—**NARRATION**,[*]

[*]Words printed in **SMALL CAPITALS** are defined in the Glossary/Index.

DESCRIPTION, EXPOSITION, and **ARGUMENT**—but interwoven into a single (and singular) grand design.

Let's look more closely at Zora Neale Hurston's "How It Feels to Be Colored Me" to see how a great writer combines several of the basic patterns of writing into a well-constructed essay.

Mixing the Patterns

Hurston's essay is built on a series of **DESCRIPTIONS**—of the passing parade of strangers as seen from the front porch of her childhood home in Florida; of the jazz scene at the New World Cabaret in Harlem; of a sophisticated lady sauntering down a Paris boulevard; and, finally, of the mundane contents of the "brown bag of miscellany" that, Hurston claims, made up her essential life and being (17). In addition to describing particular places, people, and objects, these passages describe Hurston's feelings about them. Taken together, Hurston is capturing the feelings she has around her own identity and her awareness of how others perceive her—as suggested by the title "How It Feels to Be Colored Me."

Written when she was in her late 30s, the essay is not only a description of what Hurston saw and felt at various times in her life, but a **NARRATIVE** that focuses on her growing awareness of race, including her memory from age 13 of "the very day I became colored" (2). At the beginning of her story, she is "unconscious Zora" (9) to whose mind "white people differed from colored" only in that they passed through her little town but didn't live there (4). By the end of her narrative, time has passed and she reflects on what it means to be "colored," both in her "heart as well as in the mirror" (5).

Writing in 1928, before the Civil Rights movement of the 1960s, Hurston cannot escape the racial and social distinctions of her day. Her narrative, in fact, is also an example of **CLASSIFICATION**. You could say that on one level, Hurston is describing a world that is divided across racial lines. At Barnard she is a "dark rock" amid "the thousand white persons" (10) and when attending a jazz concert her "pulse is throbbing like a war drum" while a White man sits "motionless in his seat, smoking calmly" (11). As she says, "He has only heard what I felt" (13). On another level, Hurston's classification system also divides the world into winners and losers: "I have seen that the world is to the strong regardless of a little pigmentation more or less" (6).

For a scientist's views on "the myth of race," see Robert Wald Sussman's essay on p. 254.

Hurston's **PURPOSE** in "How It Feels to Be Colored Me" is not, however, only to describe and classify but also to make the **ARGUMENT** that such skin-deep ways of dividing up humanity are worth challenging. Her **EVIDENCE** for this claim is both "cosmic"—if she is "a fragment of the Great Soul," then so is everyone else, regardless of color—and grounded in history (14, 15). When confronted with the legacy of slavery, for example, Hurston takes the position that White people are in a "more difficult" situation than she is because they are haunted by feelings of guilt and fear (8). In contrast, the world is her oyster to be acquired and pried open.

It is the **COMPARISON** with which Hurston concludes her essay, however, that provides perhaps the most compelling evidence for her claim that distinctions based on race and gender don't control her—and by extension, anyone else. We are each and all, she argues, a mixed bag of essentially similar odds and ends. Empty the bags into a common heap, and each one can be refilled more or less at random "without altering the content of any greatly" (17).

To reduce Hurston's essay to a simple **SUMMARY**, however, is to miss the point of this chapter. The meanings of a densely textured essay like Hurston's are not to be extracted from the text like pulling threads from a tapestry. We can break a complex essay into its constituent parts and patterns, but the full significance and overall structure of the essay derive from the writer's seamless combination of the various elements and **PATTERNS OF WRITING** into a unified whole.

A MODEST PROPOSAL

JONATHAN SWIFT (1667–1745) was born in Ireland and educated at Trinity College, Dublin, where he was censured for breaking the rules of discipline, graduating only by "special grace." He was ordained as a clergyman in the Anglican Church in 1694 and became dean of St. Patrick's Cathedral, Dublin, in 1713. Swift's satires in prose and verse, including *Gulliver's Travels* (1726), addressed three main issues: political relations between England and Ireland; Irish social questions; and matters of church doctrine. Swift's best-known essay was published in 1729 under the full title "A Modest Proposal for Preventing the Children of Poor People in Ireland, from being a Burden to Their Parents or Country, and for Making Them Beneficial to the Publick." Using irony as his weapon, Swift explains his deep contempt for materialism and for logic without compassion.

IT IS A MELANCHOLY OBJECT to those who walk through this great town[1] or 1 travel in the country, when they see the streets, the roads, and cabin doors, crowded with beggars of the female sex, followed by three, four, or six children, all in rags and importuning every passenger for an alms. These mothers, instead of being able to work for their honest livelihood, are forced to employ all their time in strolling to beg sustenance for their helpless infants, who, as they grow up, either turn thieves for want of work, or leave their dear native country to fight for the Pretender in Spain, or sell themselves to the Barbadoes.[2]

I think it is agreed by all parties that this prodigious number of children 2 in the arms, or on the backs, or at the heels of their mothers, and frequently of their fathers, is in the present deplorable state of the kingdom a very great additional grievance; and therefore whoever could find out a fair, cheap, and easy method of making these children sound, useful members of the commonwealth would deserve so well of the public as to have his statue set up for a preserver of the nation.

But my intention is very far from being confined to provide only for the 3 children of professed beggars; it is of a much greater extent, and shall take in the whole number of infants at a certain age who are born of parents in effect as little able to support them as those who demand our charity in the streets.

As to my own part, having turned my thoughts for many years upon this 4 important subject and maturely weighed the several schemes of other projectors,[3] I have always found them grossly mistaken in their computation. It is true, a child just dropped from its dam may be supported by her milk for a solar year, with little other nourishment; at most not above the value of two shillings,[4] which the mother may certainly get, or the value in scraps, by her lawful occupation of begging; and it is exactly at one year old that I propose to provide for them in such a manner as instead of being a charge upon their parents or the parish, or wanting food and raiment for the rest of their lives, they

1. Dublin, capital city of Ireland.
2. That is, sell themselves into indentured servitude to masters in Barbados, an island colony in the West Indies. The pretender to the throne of England was James Francis Edward Stuart (1688–1766), son of the deposed James II.
3. Men whose heads were full of foolish schemes or projects.
4. The British pound sterling was made up of 20 shillings; 5 shillings made a crown.

shall on the contrary contribute to the feeding, and partly to the clothing, of many thousands.

There is likewise another great advantage in my scheme, that it will prevent those voluntary abortions, and that horrid practice of women murdering their bastard children, alas, too frequent among us, sacrificing the poor innocent babes, I doubt, more to avoid the expense than the shame, which would move tears and pity in the most savage and inhuman breast.

The number of souls in this kingdom being usually reckoned one million and a half, of these I calculate there may be about two hundred thousand couple whose wives are breeders; from which number I subtract thirty thousand couples who are able to maintain their own children, although I apprehend there cannot be so many under the present distress of the kingdom; but this being granted, there will remain an hundred and seventy thousand breeders. I again subtract fifty thousand for those women who miscarry, or whose children die by accident or disease within the year. There only remain an hundred and twenty thousand children of poor parents annually born. The question therefore is, how this number shall be reared and provided for, which, as I have already said, under the present situation of affairs, is utterly impossible by all the methods hitherto proposed. For we can neither employ them in handicraft or agriculture; we neither build houses (I mean in the country) nor cultivate land. They can very seldom pick up a livelihood by stealing till they arrive at six years old, except where they are of towardly parts,[5] although I confess they learn the rudiments much earlier, during which time they can however be looked upon only as probationers, as I have been informed by a principal gentleman in the county of Cavan,[6] who protested to me that he never knew above one or two instances under the age of six, even in a part of the kingdom so renowned for the quickest proficiency in that art.

I am assured by our merchants that a boy or a girl before twelve years old is no salable commodity; and even when they come to this age they will not yield above three pounds, or three pounds and half a crown at most on the Exchange; which cannot turn to account either to the parents or the kingdom, the charge of nutriment and rags having been at least four times that value.

5. Having natural ability.
6. A county in northeast Ireland.

I shall now therefore humbly propose my own thoughts, which I hope 8
will not be liable to the least objection.

I have been assured by a very knowing American of my acquaintance 9
in London, that a young healthy child well nursed is at a year old a most
delicious, nourishing, and wholesome food, whether stewed, roasted, baked,
or boiled; and I make no doubt that it will equally serve in a fricassee or a
ragout.

I do therefore humbly offer it to public consideration that of the hundred 10
and twenty thousand children, already computed, twenty thousand may be
reserved for breed, whereof only one fourth part to be males, which is more
than we allow to sheep, black cattle, or swine; and my reason is that these
children are seldom the fruits of marriage, a circumstance not much regarded
by our savages, therefore one male will be sufficient to serve four females. That
the remaining hundred thousand may at a year old be offered in sale to the persons of quality and fortune through the kingdom, always advising the mother
to let them suck plentifully in the last month, so as to render them plump and
fat for a good table. A child will make two dishes at an entertainment for
friends; and when the family dines alone, the fore or hind quarter will make a
reasonable dish, and seasoned with a little pepper or salt will be very good
boiled on the fourth day, especially in winter.

I have reckoned upon a medium that a child just born will weigh twelve 11
pounds, and in a solar year if tolerably nursed increaseth to twenty-eight
pounds.

I grant this food will be somewhat dear, and therefore very proper for 12
landlords, who, as they have already devoured most of the parents, seem to
have the best title to the children.

Infant's flesh will be in season throughout the year, but more plentiful in 13
March, and a little before and after. For we are told by a grave author, an emi-
nent French physician,[7] that fish being a prolific diet, there are more children
born in Roman Catholic countries about nine months after Lent than at any
other season; therefore, reckoning a year after Lent, the markets will be more
glutted than usual, because the number of popish infants is at least three to

---

7. François Rabelais (1494?–1553), French satirist.

one in this kingdom; and therefore it will have one other collateral advantage, by lessening the number of Papists[8] among us.

I have already computed the charge of nursing a beggar's child (in which 14 list I reckon all cottagers, laborers, and four fifths of the farmers) to be about two shillings per annum, rags included; and I believe no gentleman would repine to give ten shillings for the carcass of a good fat child, which, as I have said, will make four dishes of excellent nutritive meat, when he hath only some particular friend or his own family to dine with him. Thus the squire will learn to be a good landlord, and grow popular among the tenants; the mother will have eight shillings net profit, and be fit for work till she produces another child.

Those who are more thrifty (as I must confess the times require) may 15 flay the carcass; the skin of which artificially[9] dressed will make admirable gloves for ladies, and summer boots for fine gentlemen.

As to our city of Dublin, shambles[10] may be appointed for this purpose 16 in the most convenient parts of it, and butchers we may be assured will not be wanting; although I rather recommend buying the children alive, and dressing them hot from the knife as we do roasting pigs.

A very worthy person, a true lover of his country, and whose virtues I 17 highly esteem, was lately pleased in discoursing on this matter to offer a refinement upon my scheme. He said that many gentlemen of this kingdom, having of late destroyed their deer, he conceived that the want of venison might be well supplied by the bodies of young lads and maidens, not exceeding fourteen years of age nor under twelve, so great a number of both sexes in every country being now ready to starve for want of work and service; and these to be disposed of by their parents, if alive, or otherwise by their nearest relations. But with due deference to so excellent a friend and so deserving a patriot, I cannot be altogether in his sentiments; for as to the males, my American acquaintance assured me from frequent experience that their flesh

8. Roman Catholics, called Papists because of their allegiance to the pope. Though Catholics made up the majority of the Irish population in this period, English Protestants controlled the government, and Catholics were subject to discrimination and oppressive policies.
9. Skillfully, artfully.
10. Slaughterhouses.

was generally tough and lean, like that of our schoolboys, by continual exercise, and their taste disagreeable; and to fatten them would not answer the charge. Then as to the females, it would, I think with humble submission, be a loss to the public, because they soon would become breeders themselves: and besides, it is not improbable that some scrupulous people might be apt to censure such a practice (although indeed very unjustly) as a little bordering upon cruelty; which, I confess, hath always been with me the strongest objection against any project, how well 'soever intended.

But in order to justify my friend, he confessed that this expedient was put into his head by the famous Psalmanazar, a native of the island Formosa,[11] who came from thence to London above twenty years ago, and in conversation told my friend that in his country when any young person happened to be put to death, the executioner sold the carcass to persons of quality as a prime dainty; and that in his time the body of a plump girl of fifteen, who was crucified for an attempt to poison the emperor, was sold to his Imperial Majesty's prime minister of state, and other great mandarins of the court, in joints from the gibbet,[12] at four hundred crowns. Neither indeed can I deny that if the same use were made of several plump young girls in this town, who without one single groat[13] to their fortunes cannot stir abroad without a chair, and appear at the playhouse and assemblies in foreign fineries which they never will pay for, the kingdom would not be the worse.

> A single extended example (p. 186) may be sufficient to make your point.

Some persons of a desponding spirit are in great concern about that vast number of poor people who are aged, diseased, or maimed, and I have been desired to employ my thoughts what course may be taken to ease the nation of so grievous an encumbrance. But I am not in the least pain upon that matter, because it is very well known that they are every day dying and rotting by cold and famine, and filth and vermin, as fast as can be reasonably expected. And as to the younger laborers, they are now in almost as hopeful a condition. They cannot get work, and consequently pine away for want of nourishment

---

11. Former name of Taiwan. George Psalmanazar (1679?–1763), a Frenchman, fooled British society for several years by masquerading as a pagan Formosan.
12. A structure for hanging a felon.
13. A British coin of the time, worth the equivalent of four cents.

to a degree that if at any time they are accidentally hired to common labor, they have not strength to perform it; and thus the country and themselves are happily delivered from the evils to come.

I have too long digressed, and therefore shall return to my subject. I   20
think the advantages by the proposal which I have made are obvious and many, as well as of the highest importance.

For first, as I have already observed, it would greatly lessen the number of   21
Papists, with whom we are yearly overrun, being the principal breeders of the nation as well as our most dangerous enemies; and who stay at home on pur-pose to deliver the kingdom to the Pretender, hoping to take their advantage by the absence of so many good Protestants, who have chosen rather to leave their country than stay at home and pay tithes against their conscience to an Episcopal curate.[14]

Secondly, the poorer tenants will have something valuable of their own,   22
which by law may be made liable to distress, and help to pay their landlord's rent, their corn and cattle being already seized and money a thing unknown.

Thirdly, whereas the maintenance of an hundred thousand children,   23
from two years old and upward, cannot be computed at less than ten shillings a piece per annum, the nation's stock will be thereby increased fifty thousand pounds per annum, besides the profit of a new dish introduced to the tables of all gentlemen of fortune in the kingdom who have any refinement in taste. And the money will circulate among ourselves, the goods being entirely of our own growth and manufacture.

Fourthly, the constant breeders, besides the gain of eight shillings ster-   24
ling per annum by the sale of their children, will be rid of the charge of main-taining them after the first year.

Fifthly, this food would likewise bring great custom to taverns, where the   25
vintners will certainly be so prudent as to procure the best receipts for dress-ing it to perfection, and consequently have their houses frequented by all the fine gentlemen, who justly value themselves upon their knowledge in good eating; and a skillful cook, who understands how to oblige his guests, will contrive to make it as expensive as they please.

14. Tithes are taxes or levys, traditionally 10 percent of one's income, paid to the church or other authority. Swift blamed much of Ireland's poverty on large landowners who avoided church tithes by living and spending their money abroad.

Sixthly, this would be a great inducement to marriage, which all wise 26 nations have either encouraged by rewards or enforced by laws and penalties. It would increase the care and tenderness of mothers toward their children, when they were sure of a settlement for life to the poor babes, provided in some sort by the public, to their annual profit instead of expense. We should see an honest emulation among the married women, which of them could bring the fattest child to the market. Men would become as fond of their wifes during the time of their pregnancy as they are now of their mares in foal, their cows in calf, or sows when they are ready to farrow; nor offer to beat or kick them (as is too frequent a practice) for fear of a miscarriage.

Many other advantages might be enumerated. For instance, the addition 27 of some thousand carcasses in our exportation of barreled beef, the propagation of swine's flesh, and improvement in the art of making good bacon, so much wanted among us by the great destruction of pigs, too frequent at our tables, which are no way comparable in taste or magnificence to a well-grown, fat, yearling child, which roasted whole will make a considerable figure at a lord mayor's feast or any other public entertainment. But this and many others I omit, being studious of brevity.

Supposing that one thousand families in this city would be constant 28 customers for infants' flesh, besides others who might have it at merry meetings, particularly weddings and christenings, I compute that Dublin would take off annually about twenty thousand carcasses, and the rest of the kingdom (where probably they will be sold somewhat cheaper) the remaining eighty thousand.

I can think of no one objection that will possibly be raised against this 29 proposal, unless it should be urged that the number of people will be thereby much lessened in the kingdom. This I freely own, and it was indeed one principal design in offering it to the world. I desire the reader will observe, that I calculate my remedy for this one individual kingdom of Ireland and for no other that ever was, is, or I think ever can be upon earth. Therefore let no man talk to me of other expedients:[15] of taxing our absentees at five shillings a pound: of using neither clothes nor household furniture except what is of our own growth and manufacture: of utterly rejecting the materials and instruments

15. The following are all measures that Swift himself proposed in various pamphlets.

that promote foreign luxury: of curing the expensiveness of pride, vanity, idleness, and gaming in our women: of introducing a vein of parsimony, prudence, and temperance: of learning to love our country, in the want of which we differ even from Laplanders and the inhabitants of Topinamboo:[16] of quitting our animosities and factions, nor acting any longer like the Jews, who were murdering one another at the very moment their city[17] was taken: of being a little cautious not to sell our country and conscience for nothing: of teaching landlords to have at least one degree of mercy toward their tenants: lastly, of putting a spirit of honesty, industry, and skill into our shopkeepers; who, if a resolution could now be taken to buy only our native goods, would immediately unite to cheat and exact upon us in the price, the measure, and the goodness, nor could ever yet be brought to make one fair proposal of just dealing, though often and earnestly invited to it.

Therefore I repeat, let no man talk to me of these and the like expedients, till he hath at least some glimpse of hope that there will ever be some hearty and sincere attempt to put them in practice. 30

But as to myself, having been wearied out for many years with offering vain, idle, visionary thoughts, and at length utterly despairing of success, I fortunately fell upon this proposal, which, as it is wholly new, so it hath something solid and real, of no expense and little trouble, full in our own power, and whereby we can incur no danger in disobliging England. For this kind of commodity will not bear exportation, the flesh being of too tender a consistence to admit a long continuance in salt, although perhaps I could name a country[18] which would be glad to eat up our whole nation without it. 31

After all, I am not so violently bent upon my own opinion as to reject any offer proposed by wise men, which shall be found equally innocent, cheap, easy, and effectual. But before something of that kind shall be advanced in contradiction to my scheme, and offering a better, I desire the author or authors will be pleased maturely to consider two points. First, as things now stand, how they will be able to find food and raiment for an hundred thou- 32

16. The British of Swift's time would have considered the inhabitants of Lapland (region in northern Europe) and Topinamboo (area in the jungles of Brazil) uncivilized.
17. Jerusalem, sacked by the Romans in 70 CE.
18. England.

sand useless mouths and backs. And secondly, there being a round million of creatures in human figure throughout this kingdom, whose sole subsistence put into a common stock would leave them in debt two millions of pounds sterling, adding those who are beggars by profession to the bulk of farmers, cottagers, and laborers, with their wives and children who are beggars in effect; I desire those politicians who dislike my overture, and may perhaps be so bold to attempt an answer, that they will first ask the parents of these mortals whether they would not at this day think it a great happiness to have been sold for food at a year old in the manner I prescribe, and thereby have avoided such a perpetual scene of misfortunes as they have since gone through by the oppression of landlords, the impossibility of paying rent without money or trade, the want of common sustenance, with neither house nor clothes to cover them from the inclemencies of the weather, and the most inevitable prospect of entailing the like or greater miseries upon their breed forever.

I profess, in the sincerity of my heart, that I have not the least personal interest in endeavoring to promote this necessary work, having no other motive than the public good of my country, by advancing our trade, providing for infants, relieving the poor, and giving some pleasure to the rich. I have no children by which I can propose to get a single penny; the youngest being nine years old, and my wife past childbearing.

UNDERSTANDING THE ESSAY

1. **IRONY** is sometimes misdefined as saying the opposite of what is meant. Swift, however, is not really arguing that the people of Ireland should *not* eat children. How would you define irony based on this example?

2. How and how well does Swift's use of a *persona* (or stand-in) contribute to his irony? Give specific examples from throughout the text.

3. **SATIRE** is writing that uses irony, humor, and sarcasm to expose and correct wrongdoing. Who are the main wrongdoers in Swift's great satire, and what have they done, in his view?

4. Swift's projector makes a rational argument for cannibalism. Does this mean Swift himself thinks that reason and logic are useless for solving problems in human affairs? Why or why not?

THOMAS JEFFERSON

THE DECLARATION OF INDEPENDENCE

THOMAS JEFFERSON (1743–1826) was the third president of the United States and one of the country's Founding Fathers. A lawyer by training, he was also a philosopher and scholar. Charged with drafting the Declaration of Independence (1776), he was assisted by Benjamin Franklin, John Adams, and the Continental Congress. A model of the rational thinking of the Enlightenment, the Declaration is as much a timeless essay on tyranny and human rights as a legal document announcing the colonies' break with England. Despite his assertion that "all men are created equal," Jefferson owned slaves and opposed the abolition of slavery in the US. The version reprinted here is published on the website of the US National Archives, www.archives.gov.

WHEN IN THE COURSE OF HUMAN EVENTS, it becomes necessary for one people to dissolve the political bands which have connected them with another, and to assume among the powers of the earth, the separate and equal station to which the Laws of Nature and of Nature's God entitle them, a decent respect to the opinions of mankind requires that they should declare the causes which impel them to the separation.

We hold these truths to be self-evident, that all men are created equal, 2 that they are endowed by their Creator with certain unalienable Rights, that among these are Life, Liberty and the pursuit of Happiness. That to secure these rights, Governments are instituted among Men, deriving their just powers from the consent of the governed. That whenever any Form of Government becomes destructive of these ends, it is the Right of the People to alter or to abolish it, and to institute new Government, laying its foundation on such principles and organizing its See p. 477 for arguing from general premises to a specific conclusion. powers in such form, as to them shall seem most likely to effect their Safety and Happiness. Prudence, indeed, will dictate that Governments long established should not be changed for light and transient causes; and accordingly all experience hath shewn, that mankind are more disposed to suffer, while evils are sufferable, than to right themselves by abolishing the forms to which they are accustomed. But when a long train of abuses and usurpations pursuing invariably the same Object evinces a design to reduce them under absolute Despotism, it is their right, it is their duty, to throw off such Government, and to provide new Guards for their future security. Such has been the patient sufferance of these Colonies; and such is now the necessity which constrains them to alter their former Systems of Government. The history of the present King of Great Britain[1] is a history of repeated injuries and usurpations, all having in direct object the establishment of absolute Tyranny over these States. To prove this, let Facts be submitted to a candid world.

He has refused his Assent to Laws, the most wholesome and necessary 3 for the public good.

He has forbidden his Governors to pass Laws of immediate and pressing 4 importance, unless suspended in their operation till his Assent should be obtained; and when so suspended, he has utterly neglected to attend to them.

He has refused to pass other Laws for the accommodation of large districts 5 of people, unless those people would relinquish the right of Representation in the Legislature, a right inestimable to them and formidable to tyrants only.

1. George III (ruled 1760–1820).

He has called together legislative bodies at places unusual, uncomfort- 6 able, and distant from the depository of their public Records, for the sole purpose of fatiguing them into compliance with his measures.

He has dissolved Representative Houses repeatedly, for opposing with 7 manly firmness his invasions on the rights of the people.

He has refused for a long time, after such dissolutions, to cause others to be 8 elected; whereby the Legislative powers, incapable of Annihilation, have returned to the People at large for their exercise; the State remaining in the mean time exposed to all the dangers of invasion from without, and convulsions within.

He has endeavoured to prevent the population of these States; for that 9 purpose obstructing the Laws of Naturalization of Foreigners; refusing to pass others to encourage their migration hither, and raising the conditions of new Appropriations of Lands.

He has obstructed the Administration of Justice, by refusing his Assent 10 to Laws for establishing Judiciary powers.

He has made Judges dependent on his Will alone, for the tenure of their 11 offices, and the amount and payment of their salaries.

He has erected a multitude of New Offices, and sent hither swarms of 12 Officers to harass our people, and eat out their substance.

He has kept among us, in time of peace, Standing Armies without the 13 Consent of our legislatures.

He has affected to render the Military independent of and superior to 14 the Civil power.

He has combined with others to subject us to a jurisdiction foreign to 15 our constitution, and unacknowledged by our laws; giving his Assent to their acts of pretended Legislation:

For Quartering large bodies of armed troops among us: 16

For protecting them, by a mock Trial, from punishment for any Murders 17 which they should commit on the Inhabitants of these States:

For cutting off our Trade with all parts of the world: 18

For imposing Taxes on us without our Consent: 19

For depriving us in many cases, of the benefits of Trial by Jury: 20

For transporting us beyond the Seas to be tried for pretended offenses: 21

For abolishing the free System of English Laws in a neighbouring Province, 22 establishing therein an Arbitrary government, and enlarging its Boundaries so as to render it at once an example and fit instrument for introducing the same absolute rule into these Colonies:

For taking away our Charters, abolishing our most valuable Laws, and altering fundamentally the Forms of our Governments: 23

For suspending our own Legislatures, and declaring themselves invested with power to legislate for us in all cases whatsoever. 24

He has abdicated Government here, by declaring us out of his Protection and waging War against us. 25

He has plundered our seas, ravaged our Coasts, burnt our towns and destroyed the lives of our people. 26

He is at this time transporting large Armies of foreign Mercenaries to compleat the works of death, desolation and tyranny, already begun with circumstances of Cruelty & perfidy scarcely paralleled in the most barbarous ages, and totally unworthy the Head of a civilized nation. 27

He has constrained our fellow Citizens taken Captive on the high Seas to bear Arms against their Country, to become the executioners of their friends and Brethren, or to fall themselves by their Hands. 28

He has excited domestic insurrections amongst us, and has endeavoured to bring on the inhabitants of our frontiers, the merciless Indian Savages, whose known rule of warfare, is an undistinguished destruction of all ages, sexes and conditions. 29

In every stage of these Oppressions We have Petitioned for Redress in the most humble terms: Our repeated Petitions have been answered only by repeated injury. A Prince whose character is thus marked by every act which may define a Tyrant, is unfit to be the ruler of a free people. 30

Nor have We been wanting in attentions to our British brethren. We have warned them from time to time of attempts by their legislature to extend an unwarrantable jurisdiction over us. We have reminded them of the circumstances of our emigration and settlement here. We have appealed to their native justice and magnanimity, and we have conjured them by the ties of our common kindred to disavow these usurpations, which would inevitably interrupt our connections and correspondence. They too have been deaf to the voice of justice and of consanguinity. We must, therefore acquiesce in the necessity, which denounces our Separation, and hold them, as we hold the rest of mankind, Enemies in War, in Peace Friends. 31

We, therefore, the Representatives of the United States of America, in   32
General Congress, Assembled, appealing to the Supreme Judge of the world
for the rectitude of our intentions, do, in the Name, and by Authority of the
good People of these Colonies, solemnly publish and declare, That these United
Colonies are, and of Right ought to be Free and Independent States; that they
are Absolved from all Allegiance to the British Crown, and that all political
connection between them and the State of Great Britain, is and ought to be
totally dissolved; and that as Free and Independent States, they have full Power
to levy War, conclude Peace, contract Alliances, establish Commerce, and to
do all other Acts and Things which Independent States may of right do. And
for the support of this Declaration, with a firm reliance on the protection of
divine Providence, we mutually pledge to each other our Lives, our Fortunes
and our sacred Honor.

UNDERSTANDING THE ESSAY

1. Thomas Jefferson's main **PURPOSE** in the Declaration of Independence is to declare the sovereignty of the United States. How and where does he use **CAUSE AND EFFECT** to help achieve this purpose?

2. How does Jefferson **DEFINE** what it means to be a tyrant? In what way does this definition help him achieve his main purpose?

3. The Declaration of Independence presents a logical **ARGUMENT**. How and where does Jefferson use **INDUCTION** (reasoning from specific instances to a general conclusion) to make the point that King George is indeed a tyrant?

4. Jefferson uses this conclusion about King George as the minor premise of a **DEDUCTIVE** argument (from general principles to specific conclusions). The argument's conclusion is that "these United Colonies are, and of Right ought to be Free and Independent States" (32). What is the major premise of the argument? Explain.

5. Why does Jefferson address his "British brethren" (31)? What **AUDIENCE** does he have in mind, and why would he need to convince them that his cause is just?

6. According to Jefferson and the other signers of the Declaration, what is the purpose of government, and where does a government get its authority? What form of government do they envision for the states, and how well does the Declaration make the case for this form of government? Explain.

AIN'T I A WOMAN?

SOJOURNER TRUTH (c. 1797–1883) is the name assumed by Isabella Baum-free, who was born into slavery in Hurley, New York and freed in 1827. Truth became a speaker for the causes of abolition and women's rights. "Ain't I a Woman?" is the title given to a speech that Truth delivered at the Women's Rights Convention in Akron, Ohio, in 1851. Since the speech was extemporaneous, the versions of it that exist today are composites of her words and the recollections of individuals who witnessed it. The version reprinted here derives from the one published by abolitionist Frances Dana Gage in the *National Anti-Slavery Standard* on May 2, 1863. Gage added the title phrase "Ain't I a Woman?" and many specific details to Truth's plea for equal rights for women and people who are Black.

WELL, CHILDREN, WHERE THERE IS SO MUCH RACKET there must be some- 1
thing out of kilter. I think that 'twixt the negroes of the South and the women at the North, all talking about rights, the white men will be in a fix pretty soon. But what's all this here talking about?

That man over there says that women need to be helped into carriages, and 2
lifted over ditches, and to have the best place everywhere. Nobody ever helps me

into carriages, or over mud-puddles, or gives me any best place! And ain't I a

Using personal experience to make a point is discussed on p. 474.

woman? Look at me! Look at my arm! I have ploughed and planted, and gathered into barns, and no man could head me! And ain't I a woman? I could work as much and eat as much as a man—when I could get it—and bear the lash as well! And ain't I a woman? I have borne thirteen children, and seen most all sold off to slavery, and when I cried out with my mother's grief, none but Jesus heard me! And ain't I a woman?

Then they talk about this thing in the head; what's this they call it? 3 [member of audience whispers, "intellect"] That's it, honey. What's that got to do with women's rights or negroes' rights? If my cup won't hold but a pint, and yours holds a quart, wouldn't you be mean not to let me have my little half measure full?

Then that little man in black there, he says women can't have as much 4 rights as men, 'cause Christ wasn't a woman! Where did your Christ come from? Where did your Christ come from? From God and a woman! Man had nothing to do with Him.

If the first woman God ever made was strong enough to turn the world 5 upside down all alone, these women together ought to be able to turn it back, and get it right side up again! And now they is asking to do it, the men better let them.

Obliged to you for hearing me, and now old Sojourner ain't got nothing 6 more to say.

UNDERSTANDING THE ESSAY

1. What "racket" is Truth referring to in the opening paragraph of her speech? What is "out of kilter" in her view and that of the other women who attended the convention? What solution to this imbalance do they propose?

2. What **EVIDENCE** does Truth offer to support her **CLAIM** that women are equal to men? How sufficient is that evidence to prove her point? Explain.

3. If women want to set the world right again, Truth argues, "the men better let them" (5). Does this part of her **ARGUMENT** appeal mostly to the listener's intellect ("this thing in the head"), emotions, or sense of ethics (3)? Explain.

4. Why does Truth address her **AUDIENCE** as "children" (1)? Is this an effective strategy? Why or why not?

5. Why does Truth draw an **ANALOGY** between "these women" and Eve (5)?

6. The title "Ain't I a Woman?" is also a **RHETORICAL QUESTION**. What is the effect of repeating it four times in this short speech?

HOW IT FEELS
TO BE COLORED ME

ZORA NEALE HURSTON (1891–1960), an anthropologist, folklorist, and writer, was a central figure of the Harlem Renaissance of the 1920s and 1930s. Hurston was born in Notasulga, Alabama, and grew up in Eatonville, Florida, the daughter of a preacher and a seamstress. She received a BA from Barnard College, where she studied anthropology and developed an interest in the folk traditions that would infuse her short stories and novels, such as *Their Eyes Were Watching God* (1937). Just as Hurston was finishing her studies at Barnard, "How It Feels to Be Colored Me" was published in *World Tomorrow* (1928), a magazine founded by the Fellowship of Reconciliation, a religious group devoted to nonviolence. It was later included in *I Love Myself When I Am Laughing . . . and Then Again When I Am Looking Mean and Impressive* (1979), a volume of Hurston's writing edited by the writer Alice Walker.

I AM COLORED but I offer nothing in the way of extenuating circumstances except the fact that I am the only Negro in the United States whose grand-father on the mother's side was not an Indian chief.   1

I remember the very day that I became colored. Up to my thirteenth year   2
I lived in the little Negro town of Eatonville, Florida. It is exclusively a colored town. The only white people I knew passed through the town going to or com-ing from Orlando. The native whites rode dusty horses, the Northern tourists chugged down the sandy village road in automobiles. The town knew the Southerners and never stopped cane chewing[1] when they passed. But the Northerners were something else again. They were peered at cautiously from behind curtains by the timid. The more venturesome would come out on the porch to watch them go past and got just as much pleasure out of the tourists as the tourists got out of the village.

The front porch might seem a daring place for the rest of the town, but it   3
was a gallery seat for me. My favorite place was atop the gate-post. Prosce-nium box for a born first-nighter. Not only did I enjoy the show, but I didn't mind the actors knowing that I liked it. I usually spoke to them in passing. I'd wave at them and when they returned my salute, I would say something like this: "Howdy-do-well-I-thank-you-where-you-goin'?" Usually automobile or the horse paused at this, and after a queer exchange of compliments, I would probably "go a piece of the way" with them, as we say in farthest Flor-ida. If one of my family happened to come to the front in time to see me, of course negotiations would be rudely broken off. But even so, it is clear that I was the first "welcome-to-our-state" Floridian, and I hope the Miami Cham-ber of Commerce will please take notice.

During this period, white people differed from colored to me only in that   4
they rode through town and never lived there. They liked to hear me "speak pieces" and sing and wanted to see me dance the parse-me-la, and gave me generously of their small silver for doing these things, which seemed strange to me for I wanted to do them so much that I needed bribing to stop. Only they didn't know it. The colored people gave no dimes. They deplored any joyful tendencies in me, but I was their Zora nevertheless. I belonged to them, to the nearby hotels, to the county—everybody's Zora.

---

1. Chewing sugarcane.

But changes came in the family when I was thirteen, and I was sent to 5
school in Jacksonville. I left Eatonville, the town of the oleanders,[2] as Zora.
When I disembarked from the river-boat at Jacksonville, she was no more. It
seemed that I had suffered a sea change. I was not Zora of Orange County any
more, I was now a little colored girl. I found it out in certain ways. In my heart as
well as in the mirror, I became a fast brown—warranted not to rub nor run.

But I am not tragically colored. There is no great sorrow dammed up in my soul, 6
nor lurking behind my eyes. I do not mind at all. I do not belong to the sobbing
school of Negrohood who hold that nature somehow has given them a lowdown
dirty deal and whose feelings are all hurt about it. Even in the helter-skelter
skirmish that is my life, I have seen that the world is to the strong regardless
of a little pigmentation more or less. No, I do not weep at the world—I am too
busy sharpening my oyster knife.[3]

Someone is always at my elbow reminding me that I am the grand- 7
daughter of slaves. It fails to register depression with me. Slavery is sixty
years in the past. The operation was successful and the patient is doing well,
thank you. The terrible struggle[4] that made me an American out of a potential slave said "On the line!" The Reconstruction said "Get set!"; and the generation before said "Go!" I am off to a flying start and I must not halt in the
stretch to look behind and weep. Slavery is the price I paid for civilization, and
the choice was not with me. It is a bully adventure and worth all that I have
paid through my ancestors for it. No one on earth ever had a greater chance
for glory. The world to be won and nothing to be lost. It is thrilling to think—
to know that for any act of mine, I shall get twice as much praise or twice as
much blame. It is quite exciting to hold the center of the national stage, with
the spectators not knowing whether to laugh or to weep.

The position of my white neighbor is much more difficult. No brown 8
specter pulls up a chair beside me when I sit down to eat. No dark ghost

2. Fragrant tropical flowers, common in the South.
3. Reference to the idiom "the world is my oyster," meaning that someone feels in control
of the world and able to receive anything it offers.
4. The Civil War. The Reconstruction was the period immediately following the war; one
of its effects was that Northern educators came South to teach newly freed slaves.

thrusts its leg against mine in bed. The game of keeping what one has is never so exciting as the game of getting.

I do not always feel colored. Even now I often achieve the unconscious   9
Zora of Eatonville before the Hegira.[5] I feel most colored when I am thrown against a sharp white background.

For instance at Barnard. "Beside the waters of the Hudson"[6] I feel my   10
race. Among the thousand white persons, I am a dark rock surged upon, and overswept, but through it all, I remain myself. When covered by the waters, I am; and the ebb but reveals me again.

Sometimes it is the other way around. A white person is set down in our midst,   11
but the contrast is just as sharp for me. For instance, when I sit in the drafty basement that is The New World Cabaret with a white person, my color comes. We enter chatting about any little nothing that we have in common and are seated by the jazz waiters. In the abrupt way that jazz orchestras have, this one plunges into a number. It loses no time in circumlocutions, but gets

Figures of speech, p. 85, can help to make your writing vivid.

right down to business. It constricts the thorax and splits the heart with its tempo and narcotic harmonies. This orchestra grows rambunctious, rears on its hind legs and attacks the tonal veil with primitive fury, rending it, clawing it until it breaks through to the jungle beyond. I follow those heathen—follow them exultingly. I dance wildly inside myself; I yell within, I whoop; I shake my assegai[7] above my head, I hurl it true to the mark *yeeeeooww!* I am in the jungle and living in the jungle way. My face is painted red and yellow and my body is painted blue. My pulse is throbbing like a war drum. I want to slaughter something—give pain, give death to what, I do not know. But the piece ends. The men of the orchestra wipe their lips and rest their fingers. I creep back slowly to the veneer we call civilization with the last tone and find the white friend sitting motionless in his seat, smoking calmly.

5. Journey undertaken away from a dangerous situation into a more highly desirable one (literally, the flight of Muhammad from Mecca in 622 CE).
6. Barnard, an American women's college in New York City, located near the Hudson River; i.e., the psalmist's "by the waters of Babylon."
7. South African hunting spear.

"Good music they have here," he remarks, drumming the table with his 12 fingertips.

Music. The great blobs of purple and red emotion have not touched him. 13 He has only heard what I felt. He is far away and I see him but dimly across the ocean and the continent that have fallen between us. He is so pale with his whiteness then and I am *so* colored.

At certain times I have no race, I am *me*. When I set my hat at a certain angle 14 and saunter down Seventh Avenue, Harlem City, feeling as snooty as the lions in front of the Forty-Second Street Library, for instance. So far as my feelings are concerned, Peggy Hopkins Joyce on the Boule Mich[8] with her gorgeous raiment, stately carriage, knees knocking together in a most aristocratic manner, has nothing on me. The cosmic Zora emerges. I belong to no race nor time. I am the eternal feminine with its string of beads.

I have no separate feeling about being an American citizen and colored. I 15 am merely a fragment of the Great Soul that surges within the boundaries. My country, right or wrong.

Sometimes, I feel discriminated against, but it does not make me 16 angry. It merely astonishes me. How *can* any deny themselves the pleasure of my company? It's beyond me.

But in the main, I feel like a brown bag of miscellany propped against a 17 wall. Against a wall in company with other bags, white, red and yellow. Pour out the contents, and there is discovered a jumble of small things priceless and worthless. A first-water diamond, an empty spool, bits of broken glass, lengths of string, a key to a door long since crumbled away, a rusty knife-blade, old shoes saved for a road that never was and never will be, a nail bent under the weight of things too heavy for any nail, a dried flower or two still a little fragrant. In your hand is the brown bag. On the ground before you is the jumble it held—so much like the jumble in the bags, could they be emptied, that all might be dumped in a single heap and the bags refilled without altering the content of any greatly. A bit of colored glass more or less would not matter. Perhaps that is how the Great Stuffer of Bags filled them in the first place—who knows?

8. Peggy Hopkins Joyce (1893–1957), American beauty and fashion-setter of the 1920s; "Boule Mich," Boulevard Saint-Michel, a fashionable Parisian street.

UNDERSTANDING THE ESSAY

1. Zora Neale Hurston's essay originally appeared in a magazine intended for a liberal Christian readership. How and where does she seem to be appealing directly to such an **AUDIENCE**? Point to specific passages in the text.

2. Hurston's essay tells the story of how she "became colored" (2). What happened to bring about this transformation? When and why did she feel her race most deeply?

3. Hurston refers to the front porch of her childhood home in Eatonville as a "gallery" and to the passers-by as "actors" (3). Where else in her essay does she use terms from the theater to describe her experience of race in America? What are some of the implications of such **METAPHORS**?

4. Hurston ends her essay by **COMPARING** the contents of a mixed bag of odds and ends. What is the point of this comparison, and what does it convey about Hurston's sense of personal identity?

GEORGE ORWELL

POLITICS AND THE ENGLISH LANGUAGE

GEORGE ORWELL was the pen name of Eric Arthur Blair (1903–1950), a British novelist and essayist who is perhaps best known for *Animal Farm* (1945) and *Nineteen Eighty-Four* (1949), his political satires on collectivism and dictatorship. Although Orwell was educated at Eton College in Berkshire, England, he was born in Bengal, India, and served in the Indian Imperial Police in Myanmar (then called Burma) from 1922 to 1927, a period captured in his classic essay, "Shooting an Elephant" (1936). Wounded in the Spanish Civil War, Orwell returned to England and settled in Hertfordshire to raise hens and vegetables and to write. The following selection, published in the politically chaotic days immediately after World War II, is from "Politics and the English Language" (1946), a classic and much-discussed essay on the social necessity of responsible writing.

Most people who bother with the matter at all would admit that the English language is in a bad way, but it is generally assumed that we cannot by conscious action do anything about it. Our civilization is decadent and our language—so the argument runs—must inevitably share in the general collapse. It follows that any struggle against the abuse of language is a sentimental archaism, like preferring candles to electric light or hansom cabs to airplanes. Underneath this lies the half-conscious belief that language is a natural growth and not an instrument which we shape for our own purposes.

Now, it is clear that the decline of a language must ultimately have political and economic causes: it is not due simply to the bad influence of this or that individual writer. But an effect can become a cause, reinforcing the original cause and producing the same effect in an intensified form, and so on indefinitely. A man may take to drink because he feels himself to be a failure, and then fail all the more completely because he drinks. It is rather the same thing that is happening to the English language. It becomes ugly and inaccurate because our thoughts are foolish, but the slovenliness of our language makes it easier for us to have foolish thoughts. The point is that the process is reversible. Modern English, especially written English, is full of bad habits which spread by imitation and which can be avoided if one is willing to take the necessary trouble. If one gets rid of these habits one can think more clearly, and to think clearly is a necessary first step toward political regeneration: so that the fight against bad English is not frivolous and is not the exclusive concern of professional writers. I will come back to this presently, and I hope that by that time the meaning of what I have said here will have become clearer. . . .

A mixture of vagueness and sheer incompetence is the most marked characteristic of modern English prose, and especially of any kind of political writing. As soon as certain topics are raised, the concrete melts into the abstract and no one seems able to think of turns of speech that are not hackneyed: prose consists less and less of *words* chosen for the sake of their meaning, and more and more of *phrases* tacked together like the sections of a prefabricated hen-house. . . .

I am going to translate a passage of good English into modern English of the worst sort. Here is a well-known verse from *Ecclesiastes*:

I returned and saw under the sun, that the race is not to the swift, nor the battle to the strong, neither yet bread to the wise, nor yet riches to men of understanding, nor yet favour to men of skill; but time and chance happeneth to them all.

Here it is in modern English:　　　　　　　　　　　　　　　　　　　　　5

Objective consideration of contemporary phenomena compels the conclusion that success or failure in competitive activities exhibits no tendency to be commensurate with innate capacity, but that a considerable element of the unpredictable must invariably be taken into account.

This is a parody, but not a very gross one. . . . It will be seen that I have not　6 made a full translation. The beginning and ending of the sentence follow the original meaning fairly closely, but in the middle the concrete illustrations—race, battle, bread—dissolve into the vague phrase "success or failure in competitive activities." This had to be so, because no modern writer of the kind I am discussing—no one capable of using phrases like "objective consideration of contemporary phenomena"—would ever tabulate his thoughts in that precise and detailed way. The whole tendency of modern prose is away from concreteness. Now analyze these two sentences a little more closely. The first contains forty-nine words but only sixty syllables, and all its words are those of everyday life. The second contains thirty-eight words of ninety syllables: eighteen of its words are from Latin roots, and one from Greek. The first sentence contains six vivid images, and only one phrase ("time and chance") that could be called vague. The second contains not a single fresh, arresting phrase, and in spite of its ninety syllables it gives only a shortened version of the meaning contained in the first. Yet without a doubt it is the second kind of sentence that is gaining ground in modern English. I do not want to exaggerate. This kind of writing is not yet universal, and outcrops of simplicity will occur here and there in the worst-written page. Still, if you or I were told to write a few lines on the uncertainty of human fortunes, we should probably come much nearer to my imaginary sentence than to the one from *Ecclesiastes*.

As I have tried to show, modern writing at its worst does not consist in　7 picking out words for the sake of their meaning and inventing images in order to make the meaning clearer. It consists in gumming together long strips of words which have already been set in order by someone else, and making the results presentable by sheer humbug. The attraction of this way of writing is that it is easy. It is easier—even quicker, once you have the habit—to say *In my opinion it is a not unjustifiable assumption that* than to say *I think*. If you use ready-made phrases, you not only don't have to hunt about for words; you also don't have to bother with the rhythms of your sentences, since these phrases are generally so arranged as to be more or less euphonious. When you are composing in a hurry—when you are dictating to a stenographer, for instance, or making a public speech—it is natural to fall into a pretentious, Latinized style. Tags like *a consideration which we should do well to bear in mind* or *a conclusion to which all of us would readily assent* will save many a sentence from coming down with a bump. By using stale metaphors, similes and idioms, you save much mental effort, at the cost of leaving your meaning vague, not only for your reader but for yourself. This is the significance of mixed metaphors. The sole aim of a metaphor is to call up a visual image. When these images clash—as in *The Fascist octopus has sung its swan song, the jack-boot is thrown into the melting pot*—it can be taken as certain that the writer is not seeing a mental image of the objects he is naming; in other words he is not really thinking. . . . A scrupulous writer, in every sentence that he writes, will ask himself at least four questions, thus: What am I trying to say? What words will express it? What image or idiom will make it clearer? Is this image fresh enough to have an effect? And he will probably ask himself two more: Could I put it more shortly? Have I said anything that is avoidably ugly? But you are not obliged to go to all this trouble. You can shirk it by simply throwing your mind open and letting the ready-made phrases come crowding in. They will construct your sentences for you—even think your thoughts for you, to a certain extent—and at need they will perform the important service of partially concealing your meaning even from yourself. It is at this point that the special connection between politics and the debasement of language becomes clear.

In our time it is broadly true that political writing is bad writing. Where   8 it is not true, it will generally be found that the writer is some kind of rebel, expressing his private opinions and not a "party line." Orthodoxy, of whatever color, seems to demand a lifeless, imitative style. The political dialects to be found in pamphlets, leading articles, manifestos, White Papers and the speeches of under-secretaries do, of course, vary from party to party, but they are all alike in that one almost never finds in them a fresh, vivid, home-made turn of speech. When one watches some tired hack on the platform mechanically repeating the familiar phrases—*bestial atrocities, iron heel, bloodstained tyranny, free peoples of the world, stand shoulder to shoulder*—one often has a curious feeling that one is not watching a live human being but some kind of dummy: a feeling which suddenly becomes stronger at moments when the light catches the speaker's spectacles and turns them into blank discs which seem to have no eyes behind them. And this is not altogether fanciful. A speaker who uses that kind of phraseology has gone some distance toward turning himself into a machine. The appropriate noises are coming out of his larynx, but his brain is not involved as it would be if he were choosing his words for himself. If the speech he is making is one that he is accustomed to make over and over again, he may be almost unconscious of what he is saying, as one is when one utters the responses in church. And this reduced state of consciousness, if not indispensable, is at any rate favorable to political conformity. . . .

I said earlier that the decadence of our language is probably curable. 9
Those who deny this would argue, if they produced an argument at all, that language merely reflects existing social conditions, and that we cannot influence its development by any direct tinkering with words and constructions. So far as the general tone or spirit of a language goes, this may be true, but it is not true in detail. Silly words and expressions have often disappeared, not through any evolutionary process but owing to the conscious action of a minority. . . .

But one can often be in doubt about the effect of a word or a phrase, and 10
one needs rules that one can rely on when instinct fails. I think the following rules will cover most cases:

(i)   Never use a metaphor, simile or other figure of speech which you are used to seeing in print.
(ii) Never use a long word where a short one will do.
(iii) If it is possible to cut a word out, always cut it out.
(iv) Never use the passive where you can use the active.
(v)   Never use a foreign phrase, a scientific word or a jargon word if you can think of an everyday English equivalent.
(vi) Break any of these rules sooner than say anything outright barbarous.

These rules sound elementary, and so they are, but they demand a deep change   11
of attitude in anyone who has grown used to writing in the style now fashionable. One could keep all of them and still write bad English, but one could not
write the kind of stuff that I quoted . . . at the beginning of this article.

I have not here been considering the literary use of language, but merely   12
language as an instrument for expressing and not for concealing or preventing
thought. Stuart Chase[1] and others have come near to claiming that all abstract
words are meaningless, and have used this as a pretext for advocating a kind of
political quietism. Since you don't know what Fascism is, how can you struggle
against Fascism? One need not swallow such absurdities as this, but one ought
to recognize that the present political chaos is connected with the decay of language, and that one can probably bring about some improvement by starting at the
verbal end. If you simplify your English, you are freed from the worst follies of
orthodoxy. You cannot speak any of the necessary dialects, and when you make a
stupid remark its stupidity will be obvious, even to yourself. Political language—
and with variations this is true of all political parties, from Conservatives to
Anarchists—is designed to make lies sound truthful and murder respectable,
and to give an appearance of solidity to pure wind. One cannot change this all in
a moment, but one can at least change one's own habits, and from time to time
one can even, if one jeers loudly enough, send some worn-out and useless
phrase—some *jackboot, Achilles' heel, hotbed, melting pot, acid test, veritable inferno*
or other lump of verbal refuse—into the dustbin where it belongs.

UNDERSTANDING THE ESSAY

1. In this classic essay, George Orwell offers a "defense of the English language."
   Why is such a defense necessary, in his view? What exactly is wrong with "modern English prose," according to Orwell, and what are some of the specific reasons
   that it's in such "a bad way" (3, 1)?

2. Of the many **EXAMPLES** of "bad" English that Orwell gives throughout his essay,
   which ones do you find particularly exemplary—and why?

---

1. Stuart Chase (1888–1985) was an American economist who criticized corporate advertising and advocated for consumer protection. His works include *The Tragedy of Waste*
(1925) and *Your Money's Worth* (1928). [Editor's note]

3. Orwell argues not only that politics and the English language need to be improved but that they *can* be. How? What "conscious action" is he urging readers to undertake (1)? How might such action, according to him, produce a salutary effect not only on language but on "civilization" itself (1)?

4. Orwell is writing long before the rise of social media and the internet. How relevant are his general observations about language and politics to today's flood of "fake news" and "alternative facts"? How about Orwell's specific "rules" for thinking and writing more clearly (11)? Are they still useful, or should they be swept into the "dustbin" (12)? Explain.

THE OTHER AMERICA

MARTIN LUTHER KING JR. (1929–1968) was a Baptist minister and civil rights activist known for his doctrine of nonviolent protest. A graduate of Morehouse College and Crozer Theological Seminary, he was awarded a PhD in theology from Boston University in 1955. That same year, King was selected by the local chapter of the National Association for the Advancement of Colored People (NAACP) to lead a boycott of the segregated bus system in Montgomery, Alabama. The boycott resulted in a Supreme Court ruling banning racial segregation on the city's buses. King used his national stature to speak and demonstrate tirelessly in the cause of civil rights. His efforts culminated in the peaceful march on Washington, DC, in 1963 of more than a quarter-million protesters, to whom he delivered his "I Have a Dream" address. The next year King received the Nobel Peace Prize. He was assassinated on April 4, 1968, in Memphis, Tennessee. In the month before his death, King gave the last of several speeches addressing the inequality of income and opportunity for "many people of various backgrounds." The following selection is from the version of this important (and radical) speech that King delivered on April 16, 1967, at Stanford University.

Members of the faculty and members of the student body of this great institution of learning; ladies and gentlemen.

Now there are several things that one could talk about before such a large, concerned, and enlightened audience. There are so many problems facing our nation and our world, that one could just take off anywhere. But today I would like to talk mainly about the race problems since I'll have to rush right out and go to New York to talk about Vietnam tomorrow. And I've been talking about it a great deal this week and weeks before that.[1]

But I'd like to use a subject from which to speak this afternoon, the Other America.

And I use this subject because there are literally two Americas. One America is beautiful for situation. And, in a sense, this America is overflowing with the milk of prosperity and the honey of opportunity. This America is the habitat of millions of people who have food and material necessities for their bodies; and culture and education for their minds; and freedom and human dignity for their spirits. In this America, millions of people experience every day the opportunity of having life, liberty, and the pursuit of happiness in all of their dimensions. And in this America millions of young people grow up in the sunlight of opportunity.

But tragically and unfortunately, there is another America. This other America has a daily ugliness about it that constantly transforms the ebulliency of hope into the fatigue of despair. In this America millions of work-starved men walk the streets daily in search for jobs that do not exist. In this America millions of people find themselves living in rat-infested, vermin-filled slums. In this America people are poor by the millions. They find themselves perishing on a lonely island of poverty in the midst of a vast ocean of material prosperity.

In a sense, the greatest tragedy of this other America is what it does to little children. Little children in this other America are forced to grow up with clouds of inferiority forming every day in their little mental skies. As we look

1. On April 4, 1967, at Riverside Church in New York City, King had delivered a sermon opposing the Vietnam War, which he feared was drawing funds and support away from the civil rights movement. King would return to the city on April 17 to speak against the war and join a protest march.

at this other America, we see it as an arena of blasted hopes and shattered dreams. Many people of various backgrounds live in this other America. Some are Mexican Americans, some are Puerto Ricans, some are Indians, some happen to be from other groups. Millions of them are Appalachian whites. But probably the largest group in this other America in proportion to its size in the population is the American Negro. . . .

In 1964 the Civil Rights Bill came into being after the Birmingham movement which did a great deal to subpoena the conscience of a large segment of the nation to appear before the judgment seat of morality on the whole question of Civil Rights. After the Selma movement in 1965 we were able to get a Voting Rights Bill.[2] And all of these things represented strides.   7

But we must see that the struggle today is much more difficult. It's more difficult today because we are struggling now for genuine equality. It's much easier to integrate a lunch counter than it is to guarantee a livable income and a good solid job. It's much easier to guarantee the right to vote than it is to guarantee the right to live in sanitary, decent housing conditions. It is much easier to integrate a public park than it is to make genuine, quality, integrated education a reality. And so today we are struggling for something which says we demand genuine equality. . . .   8

Using parallel structures to tie key ideas together is discussed on p. 64.

. . . [R]acism is still alive in American society. And much more widespread than we realized. And we must see racism for what it is. It is a myth of the superior and the inferior race. It is the false and tragic notion that one particular group, one particular race, is responsible for all of the progress, all of the insights in the total flow of history. And the theory that another group or another race is totally depraved, innately impure, and innately inferior.   9

2. In the spring of 1963, King and others led a protest march on Birmingham, Alabama, that directly paved the way for the passage of the Civil Rights Act of 1964. The act was not uniformly enforced, however, leading to further protests and demonstrations. On March 7, 1965, state troopers attacked peaceful participants with tear gas and nightsticks when they refused to turn back during a march from Selma, Alabama, to the state capitol in Montgomery. In response, Congress overwhelmingly passed the landmark Voting Rights Act, which was signed into law on August 6, 1965.

In the final analysis, racism is evil because its ultimate logic is geno- 10
cide.[3] Hitler was a sick and tragic man who carried racism to its logical conclusion. He ended up leading a nation to the point of killing about 6 million
Jews. This is the tragedy of racism because its ultimate logic is genocide. If
one says that I am not good enough to live next door to him; if one says that I
am not good enough to eat at a lunch counter, or to have a good, decent job, or
to go to school with him merely because of my race, he is saying consciously or
unconsciously that I do not deserve to exist.

To use a philosophical analogy here, racism is not based on some empiri- 11
cal generalization; it is based rather on an ontological affirmation. It is not the
assertion that certain people are behind culturally or otherwise because of
environmental conditions. It is the affirmation that the very being of a people
is inferior.[4] And this is the great tragedy of it.

I submit that however unpleasant it is we must honestly see and admit 12
that racism is still deeply rooted all over America. It is still deeply rooted in
the North, and it's still deeply rooted in the South. . . .

In 1875 the nation passed a Civil Rights Bill and refused to enforce it.[5] 13
In 1964 the nation passed a weaker Civil Rights Bill and even to this day, that
bill has not been totally enforced in all of its dimensions. The nation heralded
a new day of concern for the poor, for the poverty stricken, for the disadvantaged. And brought into being a Poverty Bill and at the same time it put such
little money into the program that it was hardly, and still remains hardly, a
good skirmish against poverty.[6] White politicians in suburbs talk eloquently
against open housing, and in the same breath contend that they are not racist.

3. Recognized in international courts of law as a "crime against humanity," the term
"genocide" is defined by the UN Office on Genocide Prevention as any act "committed
with the intent to destroy, in whole or in part, a national, ethnical, racial or religious
group, as such."
4. King is making the philosophical argument that racism has no basis in the study of
actual fact and human experience (empiricism) but is a false, preconceived notion imposed
on the study of being (ontology).
5. The Civil Rights Act of 1875 affirmed "the equality of all men before the law"; the act
was deemed unconstitutional by the US Supreme Court in 1883.
6. The Economic Opportunity Act (or "Poverty Bill") was passed in August 1964. The bill
provided job training, adult education, and small business loans through such federal programs as the Job Corps and Volunteers in Service to America (VISTA).

And all of this, and all of these things, tell us that America has been backlashing on the whole question of basic constitutional and God-given rights for Negroes and other disadvantaged groups for more than 300 years. . . .

Now let me go on to say that if we are to deal with all of the problems 14 that I've talked about, and if we are to bring America to the point that we have one nation, indivisible, with liberty and justice for all, there are certain things that we must do. The job ahead must be massive and positive. We must develop massive action programs all over the United States of America in order to deal with the problems that I have mentioned. . . .

Now there's another notion that gets out, it's around everywhere. It's in 15 the South, it's in the North, it's in California, and all over our nation. It's the notion that legislation can't solve the problem, it can't do anything in this area. And those who project this argument contend that you've got to change the heart and that you can't change the heart through legislation. Now I would be the first one to say that there is real need for a lot of heart changing in our country, and I believe in changing the heart. I preach about it. I believe in the need for conversion in many instances, and regeneration, to use theological terms. And I would be the first to say that if the race problem in America is to be solved, the white person must treat the Negro right, not merely because the law says it, but because it's natural, because it's right, and because the Negro is his brother. And so I realize that if we are to have a truly integrated society, men and women will have to rise to the majestic heights of being obedient to the unenforceable.

See p. 481 for tips on anticipating other points of view.

But after saying this, let me say another thing which gives the other 16 side, and that is that although it may be true that morality cannot be legislated, behavior can be regulated. Even though it may be true that the law cannot change the heart, it can restrain the heartless. Even though it may be true that the law cannot make a man love me, it can restrain him from lynching me. And I think that's pretty important also. And so while the law may not change the hearts of men, it can and it does change the habits of men. And when you begin to change the habits of men, pretty soon the attitudes will be changed; pretty soon the hearts will be changed. And I'm convinced that we still need strong civil rights legislation. And there is a bill before Congress right now to have a national or federal Open Housing Bill. A federal law declaring discrimination in housing unconstitutional. . . .

There is a need for fair housing laws all over our country. And it is tragic 17
indeed that Congress last year allowed this bill to die. And when that bill died
in Congress, a bit of democracy died, a bit of our commitment to justice died.
If it happens again in this session of Congress, a greater degree of our commitment to democratic principles will die. And I can see no more dangerous
trend in our country than the constant developing of predominantly Negro
central cities ringed by white suburbs. This is only inviting social disaster.
And the only way this problem will be solved is by the nation taking a strong
stand, and by state governments taking a strong stand against housing segregation and against discrimination in all of these areas.

Now there's another thing that I'd like to mention as I talk about the 18
massive action program and time will not permit me to go into specific pro-
grammatic action to any great degree. But it must be realized now that the
Negro cannot solve the problems by himself. There again, there are those who
always say to Negroes, *"Why don't you do something for yourself? Why don't you
lift yourselves by your own bootstraps?"* And we hear this over and over
again. . . .

. . . [B]ut it is a cruel jest to say to a bootless man that he oughta lift 19
himself by his own bootstraps. And the fact is that millions of
Negroes, as a result of centuries of denial and neglect, have been left
bootless. They find themselves impoverished aliens in this affluent society. And there is a great deal that the society can and must
do if the Negro is to gain the economic security that he needs.

> An analogy like this
> is a form of com-
> parison often used
> to support an argu-
> ment (p. 324).

Now one of the answers, it seems to me, is a guaranteed annual income, a 20
guaranteed minimum income for all people, and for our families of our country. It seems to me that the Civil Rights movement must now begin to organize for the guaranteed annual income. Begin to organize people all over our
country, and mobilize forces so that we can bring to the attention of our
nation this need, and this is something which I believe will go a long long way
toward dealing with the Negro's economic problem and the economic problem
which many other poor people confront in our nation. Now I said I wasn't
going to talk about Vietnam, but I can't make a speech without mentioning
some of the problems that we face there because I think this war has diverted
attention from civil rights. It has strengthened the forces of reaction in our
country and has brought to the forefront the military-industrial complex that

even President Eisenhower warned us against at one time. And above all, it is destroying human lives. It's destroying the lives of thousands of the young promising men of our nation. It's destroying the lives of little boys and little girls in Vietnam.

But one of the greatest things that this war is doing to us in Civil Rights   21 is that it is allowing the Great Society[7] to be shot down on the battlefields of Vietnam every day. And I submit this afternoon that we can end poverty in the United States. Our nation has the resources to do it. The National Gross Product of America will rise to the astounding figure of some $780 billion this year. We have the resources: The question is whether our nation has the will, and I submit that if we can spend $35 billion a year to fight an ill-considered war in Vietnam, and $20 billion to put a man on the moon, our nation can spend billions of dollars to put God's children on their own two feet right here on earth.

Let me say another thing that's more in the realm of the spirit, I guess,   22 that is that if we are to go on in the days ahead and make true brotherhood a reality, it is necessary for us to realize more than ever before, that the destinies of the Negro and the white man are tied together. Now there are still a lot of people who don't realize this. The racists still don't realize this. But it is a fact now that Negroes and whites are tied together, and we need each other. The Negro needs the white man to save him from his fear. The white man needs the Negro to save him from his guilt. We are tied together in so many ways, our language, our music, our cultural patterns, our material prosperity, and even our food are an amalgam of black and white.

So there can be no separate black path to power and fulfillment that   23 does not intersect white groups. There can be no separate white path to power and fulfillment short of social disaster. It does not recognize the need of sharing that power with black aspirations for freedom and justice. We must come to see now that integration is not merely a romantic or esthetic something where you merely add color to a still predominantly white power structure. Integration must be seen also in political terms where there is shared power,

---

7. In his first inaugural address in January 1964, President Johnson declared an "unconditional war on poverty" in America. The aim of the sweeping program of social legislation that followed this declaration was to establish what he called the "Great Society."

where black men and white men share power together to build a new and a great nation.

In a real sense, we are all caught in an inescapable network of mutuality, tied in a single garment of destiny. John Donne placed it years ago in graphic terms, *"No man is an island entire of itself. Every man is a piece of the continent, a part of the main."* And he goes on toward the end to say, *"Any man's death diminishes me because I'm involved in mankind. Therefore never send to know for whom the bell tolls. It tolls for thee."*[8] And so we are all in the same situation: the salvation of the Negro will mean the salvation of the white man. And the destruction of life and of the ongoing progress of the Negro will be the destruction of the ongoing progress of the nation.

Now let me say finally that we have difficulties ahead but I haven't despaired. Somehow I maintain hope in spite of hope. And I've talked about the difficulties and how hard the problems will be as we tackle them. But I want to close by saying this afternoon, that I still have faith in the future. And I still believe that these problems can be solved. And so I will not join anyone who will say that we still can't develop a coalition of conscience. . . .

And so I can still sing "We Shall Overcome." We shall overcome because the arc of the moral universe is long but it bends toward Justice. We shall overcome because Carlyle is right, *"No lie can live forever."* We shall overcome because William Cullen Bryant is right, *"Truth crushed to earth will rise again."* We shall overcome because James Russell Lowell is right, *"Truth forever on the scaffold, Wrong forever on the throne—Yet that scaffold sways the future."*[9] With this faith, we will be able to hew out of the mountain of despair a stone of hope.

With this faith, we will be able to transform the jangling discourse of our nation into a beautiful symphony of brotherhood. With this faith, we will

24

25

26

27

---

8. John Donne (1572–1631) was an English poet, lawyer, and cleric; his "Meditation 17," from which these lines are taken, appeared in *Devotions upon Emergent Occasions* (1624). The toll of a church bell signaled a death in the parish.
9. King is quoting, respectively, *The French Revolution: A History* (1837), pt. 1, bk. 6, chap. 3, by the Scottish historian and mathematician Thomas Carlyle (1795–1881); "The Battlefield" (1839) by American poet and editor of the *New-York Evening Post*, William Cullen Bryant (1794–1878); and "The Present Crisis" (1845), a poem about slavery by the abolitionist writer James Russell Lowell (1819–1891).

be able to speed up the day when all of God's children, black men and white men, Jews and Gentiles, Protestants and Catholics, will be able to join hands and live together as brothers and sisters, all over this great nation. That will be a great day, that will be a great tomorrow. In the words of the Scripture, to speak symbolically, that will be the day when the morning stars will sing together and the sons of God will shout for joy.

UNDERSTANDING THE SPEECH

1. How does Martin Luther King Jr. **DEFINE** the "two Americas," and what specific qualities and attributes does he assign to each (4)?

2. Why does King think that the struggle "today is much more difficult" for "genuine equality" than it was before the passage of the Civil Rights Act of 1964 (8)?

3. "Racism," King argues, "is still alive in America" (9). What **EVIDENCE** does he offer in support of this claim, and is it sufficient to make the case? Why or why not?

4. According to King, racism is based on a "myth" (9). What is the nature of this myth in his view?

5. One **DEFINITION** of a myth is "a story we no longer (or should no longer) believe in." How and how well does this definition support King's "philosophical" argument against racism in paragraphs 9–11? Explain.

6. Although King addresses the issue of racism, the main target of "The Other America" is the related problem of economic inequality. What specific forms of action does King call for, and which ones are (or are not) most likely to be effective in your view? Explain.

7. King closes his speech on a note of "hope" (25). Is his hopefulness justified? Why or why not?

APPENDIX
USING SOURCES IN YOUR WRITING

W HATEVER your purpose, academic research requires finding sources of information that go well beyond your own immediate knowledge of a subject. If you're examining an issue discussed in one of the selections that appear in this book—the role war memorials play in learning about history or the way technology influences our relationships—it's likely that you will need to consult additional sources. This appendix shows how to find reliable sources, use what you learn in your own writing, and document your sources accurately.

FINDING AND EVALUATING SOURCES

As you do your research, you will encounter a wide range of potential sources—print and online, general and specialized, published and firsthand. You'll need to evaluate these sources carefully, choose the ones that best support your **THESIS**,* and decide how to incorporate each source into your own paper.

Finding Appropriate Sources

The kinds of sources you turn to will depend on your topic. If you're doing research on a literary or historical topic, you might consult scholarly books and articles and standard reference works such as *The Dictionary of American Biography* or the *Literary History of the United States*. If your research is aimed

---

*Words printed in **SMALL CAPITALS** are defined in the Glossary/Index.

at a current issue, you would likely consult newspapers and other periodicals, websites, and recent books.

Check your assignment to see if you are required to use primary or secondary sources—or both. PRIMARY SOURCES are original works, such as historical documents, literary works, eyewitness accounts, diaries, letters, and lab studies, as well as any original field research you do. SECONDARY SOURCES include books and articles, reviews, biographies, and other works that interpret or discuss primary sources. For example, novels and poems are primary sources; articles interpreting them are secondary sources.

Whether a work is considered primary or secondary often depends on your topic and purpose. If you're analyzing a poem, a critic's article analyzing the poem is a secondary source—but if you're investigating the critic's work, the article would be a primary source.

ONLINE SOURCES

You'll probably consider starting your research by searching and browsing the internet. The web offers countless sites sponsored by governments, educational institutions, businesses, and individuals—it's not a bad place to begin. Because it's so vast and dynamic, however, finding useful and reliable information online can be a challenge. There are several good ways to start your search online:

- *Keyword searches. Google, Bing, DuckDuckGo, Yahoo!,* and other search sites scan the web looking for the keywords you specify.

- *Metasearches. Yippy, SurfWax,* and *Dogpile* let you use several search engines simultaneously.

- *Academic searches.* For peer-reviewed academic writing in many disciplines, try *Google Scholar* or *JURN;* for scientific, technical, and medical documents, use *Scirus.*

Although many websites provide authoritative information, keep in mind that web content varies greatly in its stability and reliability: what you see on a site today may be different (or gone) tomorrow. So save or make copies of pages you plan to use, and carefully evaluate what you find. Here are just a few of the many resources available on the web:

- *Indexes, databases, and directories.* Information put together by specialists and grouped by topics can be especially helpful. You may want to consult, for example, the *WWW Virtual Library*, the Directory of Open Access Journals, or databases likely accessible through your library like *JSTOR* and *ProQuest*.

- *News sites.* Many newspapers, magazines, and radio and TV stations have websites that provide both up-to-the-minute information and also archives of older news articles. Through *Google News* and *NewsLink,* for example, you can access current news worldwide, whereas *Google News Archive Search* has files going back to the 1700s.

- *Government sites.* Many government agencies and departments maintain websites where you can find government reports, statistics, legislative information, and other resources. *USA.gov* offers information, services, and other resources from the US government.

- *Digital archives.* These sites collect and organize materials from the past—including drawings, maps, recordings, speeches, and historic documents—often focusing on a particular subject or country. For example, the National Archives and Records Administration and the Library of Congress both archive items relevant to the culture and history of the United States.

- *Discussion lists and forums.* Online mailing lists, newsgroups, discussion groups, and forums let members post and receive messages from other members. To join a discussion with people who may be knowledgeable about your topic, try searching for your topic—for example, "E. B. White discussion forum." Don't take what you read at face value, though; be sure to check out claims and statements of fact to be sure they're accurate.

LIBRARY SOURCES

Because online sources require extra work to ensure they're accurate and reliable, when conducting academic research it's often more efficient to start with your library's website rather than with a *Google* search. Library websites provide access to a range of well-organized and trustworthy resources, including scholarly databases through which you can access authoritative articles that have been screened by librarians or specialists in a particular field. In general, there are three kinds of sources you'll want to consult: reference works, books, and periodicals.

- *Reference works.* The reference section of your school's library is the place to find encyclopedias, dictionaries, atlases, almanacs, bibliographies, and other reference works. Remember, though, that reference works are only a starting point, a place where you can get an overview of your topic or basic facts about it. Some reference works are *general*, such as *The New Encyclopaedia Britannica* or the *Statistical Abstract of the United States.* Others are *specialized*, providing in-depth information on a single field or topic.

- *Books.* The library catalog is your main source for finding books. Most catalogs are computerized and can be accessed through the library's website. You can search by author, title, subject, or keyword. When you click on a specific source, you'll find more bibliographic data about author, title, and publication; the call number (which identifies the book's location on the library's shelves); related subject headings (which may lead to other useful materials in the library)—and more.

- *Periodicals.* To find journal and magazine articles, you'll need to search periodical indexes and databases. Indexes (such as the *New York Times Index*) provide listings of articles organized by topics; databases (such as LexisNexis) provide the full texts. Some databases are available for free, and many others may be accessible at no cost through your library.

SEARCHING ELECTRONICALLY

When you search for subjects online or in library catalogs, indexes, or databases, you'll want to come up with keywords that will lead to the information you need. Specific commands vary among search engines and databases, but most search engines offer "Advanced Search" options that allow you to narrow your search by typing keywords into text boxes labeled as follows:

- All of these words
- The exact phrase

- Any of these words
- None of these words

In addition, you may filter the results to include only full-text articles (articles that are available in full online); only certain domains (such as *.edu*, for educational sites; *.gov*, for government sites; or *.org*, for nonprofit sites); and, in library databases, only scholarly, peer-reviewed sites. Type quotation marks around words to search for an exact phrase: "Twitter revolution" or "Neil Gaiman."

Some databases may require you to limit searches through the use of various symbols or Boolean operators (AND, OR, NOT). See the Advanced Search instructions for help with such symbols, which may be called *field tags*.

If a search turns up too many sources, be more specific ("homeopathy" instead of "medicine"). If your original keywords don't generate good results, try synonyms ("home remedy" instead of "folk medicine"). Keep in mind that searching requires flexibility, both in the words you use and the methods you try.

Evaluating Sources

Searching the *Health Source* database for information on the incidence of meningitis among college students, you find 17 articles. An "exact words" *Google* search yields more than two million. How do you decide which sources to read? The following questions can help you select reliable and useful sources.

- *Is the source relevant?* Look at the title and at any introductory material to see what it covers. Does the source appear to relate directly to your purpose? What will it add to your work?

- *What are the author's credentials?* Has the author written other works on this subject? Is the author known for taking a particular position on it? Do an internet search to see what others say about the author. Do other reliable sources confirm the author's credentials? Do you learn anything else important about the author?

- *What is the stance?* Does the source cover various points of view or advocate only one perspective? Does its title suggest a certain slant? If you're evaluating a website, check to see whether it includes links to sites expressing other perspectives and visit those links to see that they're trustworthy, too.

- **Who is the publisher?** Books published by university presses and articles in scholarly journals are peer-reviewed by experts in the field before being published. Those produced for a general audience don't always undergo such rigorous review and fact-checking. At well-established publishing houses, however, submissions are usually vetted by experienced editors or even editorial boards.

- **If the source is a website, who is the sponsor?** Is the site maintained by an organization, interest group, government agency, or individual? If the site doesn't give this information on its home page, look for clues in the URL domain: *.edu* is used mostly by colleges and universities, *.gov* by government agencies, *.org* by nonprofit organizations, *.mil* by the military, and *.com* by commercial organizations. Be aware that the sponsor may have an agenda—to argue a position, present biased information, or sell a product—and that text on the site does not necessarily undergo rigorous review or fact-checking. Also, don't trust what the site says about itself—do an internet search to see what other reliable sources reveal about the site and its sponsor.

- **What is the level of the material?** Texts written for a general audience might be easier to understand but may not be authoritative enough for academic work. Scholarly texts will be more authoritative but may be harder to comprehend. Don't assume a source is scholarly just because it sounds academic, especially if you turned up the source online.

- **How current is the source?** Check to see when books and articles were published and when websites were last updated. (If a site lists no date, see if links to other sites still work; if not, the site is probably too dated to use.) A recent publication date or updating, however, does not necessarily mean the source is better—some topics require current information whereas others call for older sources.

- **Does the source include other useful information?** Is there a bibliography that might lead you to additional materials? How current or authoritative are the sources it cites? Are the cited sources trustworthy?

Taking Notes

When you find material that will be useful to your argument, take careful notes.

- *Use index cards, a computer file, or a notebook,* labeling each entry with information that will enable you to keep track of where it comes from— author, title, the pages or the URL, and (for online sources) the date of access.

- *Take notes in your own words, and use your own sentence patterns.* If you make a note that is a detailed paraphrase, label it as such so that you'll know to provide appropriate documentation if you use it.

- *If you find wording that you'd like to quote,* enclose the exact words in quotation marks to distinguish your source's words from your own.

- *Label each note with a subject heading* so you can organize your notes easily when constructing an outline for your paper.

INCORPORATING SOURCE MATERIALS INTO YOUR TEXT

There are many ways to incorporate source materials into your own text. Three of the most common are quoting, paraphrasing, and summarizing. Let's look at the differences among these three forms of reference and then consider when to use each one and how to work these references into your text.

Quoting

When you quote someone else's words, you reproduce their language exactly, in quotation marks—though you can add your own words in brackets or omit unnecessary words in the original by using ellipsis marks (. . .). This example from Mary Roach's "How to Know if You Are Dead" uses all of these conventions:

In her analysis of the life-saving role of human cadavers, Mary Roach notes that "a gurney with a [newly deceased] cadaver commands no urgency. It is wheeled by a single person, . . . like a shopping cart" (167).

Paraphrasing

When you paraphrase, you restate information from a source in your own words, using your own sentence structures. Because a paraphrase includes all the main points of the source, it is usually about the same length as the original.

Here is a paragraph from Diane Ackerman's essay "Why Leaves Turn Color in the Fall," followed by two sample paraphrases. The first demonstrates some of the challenges of paraphrasing.

ORIGINAL SOURCE

Where do the colors come from? Sunlight rules most living things with its golden edicts. When the days begin to shorten, soon after the summer solstice on June 21, a tree reconsiders its leaves. All summer it feeds them so they can process sunlight, but in the dog days of summer the tree begins pulling nutrients back into its trunk and roots, pares down, and gradually chokes off its leaves. A corky layer of cells forms at the leaves' slender petioles, then scars over. Undernourished, the leaves stop producing the pigment chlorophyll, and photosynthesis ceases. Animals can migrate, hibernate, or store food to prepare for winter. But where can a tree go? It survives by dropping its leaves, and by the end of autumn only a few fragile threads of fluid-carrying xylem hold leaves to their stems.

UNACCEPTABLE PARAPHRASE

Ackerman tells us where the colors of leaves come from. The amount of sunlight is the trigger, as is true for most living things. At the end of June, as daylight lessens, a tree begins to treat its leaves differently. It feeds them all summer so they can turn sunlight into food, but in

August a tree begins to redirect its food into its trunk and roots, gradually choking the leaves. A corky group of cells develops at the petioles, and a scar forms. By autumn, the leaves don't have enough food, so they stop producing chlorophyll, and photosynthesis also stops. Although animals are able to migrate, hibernate, or stow food for the winter, a tree cannot go anywhere. It survives only by dropping its leaves, and by the time winter comes only a few leaves remain on their stems (257).

This first paraphrase borrows too much of the language of the original or changes it only slightly. It also follows the original sentence structure too closely. The following paraphrase avoids both of these pitfalls.

ACCEPTABLE PARAPHRASE

Ackerman explains why leaves change color. Diminishing sunlight is the main instigator. A tree nourishes its leaves—and encourages photosynthesis—for most of the summer. By August, however, as day-light continues to lessen, a tree starts to reroute its food to the roots and trunk, a process that saves the tree but eventually kills the leaves. In autumn, because the leaves are almost starving, they can neither manufacture chlorophyll to stay green nor carry out photosynthesis. By this time, the base of the petiole, or leaf's stem, has hardened, in preparation for the final drop. Unlike animals, which have many ways to get ready for winter—hiding food ahead of time, moving to a warm climate, sleeping through winter—a tree is immobile. It can make it through the winter only by losing its leaves (257).

Summarizing

Unlike a paraphrase, a SUMMARY does not present all the details in the original source, so it is generally as brief as possible. Summaries may boil down an entire book or essay into a single sentence, or they may take a paragraph or more to present the main ideas. Here, for example, is a summary of the Ackerman paragraph:

In late summer and fall, Ackerman explains, trees put most of their food into their roots and trunk, which causes leaves to change color and die but enables trees to live through the winter (257).

Deciding Whether to Quote, Paraphrase, or Summarize

Follow these rules of thumb to determine whether you should quote a source directly, paraphrase it in detail, or merely summarize the main points:

- *Quote* a text when the exact wording is critical to making your point (or that of an authority you wish to cite) or when the wording itself is part of what you're analyzing.

- *Paraphrase* when the meaning of a text is important to your argument but the original language is not essential or when you're clarifying or interpreting the ideas (not the words) in the text.

- *Summarize* when the main points of the text are important to your argument but the details can be left out in the interest of conciseness.

Using Signal Phrases

When you quote, paraphrase, or summarize a source, identify your source clearly and use a signal phrase ("she says," "he thinks") to distinguish the words and ideas of your source from your own. Consider this example:

> Professor and textbook author Elaine Tyler May claims that many high-school history textbooks are too bland to interest young readers (531).

This sentence summarizes a general position about the effectiveness of certain textbooks ("too bland"), and it attributes that view to a particular authority (Elaine Tyler May), citing her credentials (professor, textbook author) for speaking with CREDIBILITY on the subject. By using the signal phrase "claims that," the sentence also distinguishes the words and ideas of the source from those of the writer.

The verb you use in a signal phrase can be neutral ("says" or "thinks"), or it can indicate your (or your source's) stance toward the subject. In this case, the use of the verb "claims" suggests that what the source says is arguable (or that the writer of the sentence believes it is). The signal verb you choose can influence your reader's understanding of the sentence and of your attitude toward what it says.

ACKNOWLEDGING SOURCES AND AVOIDING PLAGIARISM

As a writer, you must acknowledge any words and ideas that come from others. There are numerous reasons for doing so: to give credit where credit is due, to recognize the various authorities and many perspectives you have considered, to show readers where they can find your sources, and to situate your own arguments in the ongoing academic conversation. Using other people's words and ideas without acknowledgment is plagiarism, a serious academic and ethical offense in the US.

MATERIAL THAT DOESN'T HAVE TO BE ACKNOWLEDGED

- Facts that are common knowledge, such as the name of the current president of the United States
- Well-known statements accompanied by a signal phrase: "As John F. Kennedy said, 'Ask not what your country can do for you; ask what you can do for your country.'"

MATERIAL THAT REQUIRES ACKNOWLEDGMENT

- Direct quotations, paraphrases, and summaries
- Arguable statements and any information that is not commonly known (statistics and other data)
- The personal or professional opinions and assertions of others
- Visuals that you did not create yourself (charts, photographs, and so on)
- Collaborative help you received from others

Plagiarism is (1) using another writer's exact words without quotation marks, (2) using another writer's words or ideas without in-text or other documentation, (3) paraphrasing or summarizing someone else's ideas using language or sentence structure that is close to the original. The following practices will help you avoid plagiarizing:

- *Take careful notes,* clearly labeling quotations and using your own phrasing and sentence structure in paraphrases and summaries.

- *Check all paraphrases and summaries* to be sure they are stated in *your* words and sentence structures—and that you put quotation marks around any of the source's original phrasing.

- *Know what sources you must document,* and identify them both in the text and in a works-cited list.

- *Check to see that all quotations are documented;* it isn't enough just to include quotation marks or indent a block quotation.

- *Be especially careful with online material*—copying source material directly into a document you are writing invites plagiarism. Like other sources, information from the web must be acknowledged.

- *Recognize that plagiarism has consequences.* A scholar's work will be discredited if it too closely resembles the work of another scholar. Journalists who plagiarize lose their jobs, and students sometimes fail courses or are dismissed from school when they are caught cheating—all too often by submitting essays that they have purchased from online "research" sites.

So don't take the chance. If you're having trouble with an assignment, ask your instructor for assistance. Or visit your school's writing center. Writing centers can help with advice on all aspects of your writing, including acknowledging sources and avoiding plagiarism.

DOCUMENTATION

Taken collectively, all the information you provide about sources is your *documentation*. Many organizations and publishers—for example, the American Psychological Association (APA), the University of Chicago Press, and the Council of Science Editors (CSE)—have their own documentation styles. The focus here is on the documentation system of the Modern Language Association (MLA) because it is one of the most common systems used in college courses, especially in the liberal arts.

MLA style has two basic parts: (1) brief in-text documentation for quotations, paraphrases, or summaries and (2) more detailed information for each in-text reference in a list of works cited at the end of the text. See p. 617 for a sample paper with MLA-style citations MLA style requires that each item in your works-cited list include the following "core elements" when they are available: author, title of the source, title of any "container" (MLA's term for a larger work in which the source is found—an anthology, a website, a journal or magazine, a database, even a streaming service like *Netflix*), other contributors, version, volume and issue numbers, publisher, date of publication, and location of source (page numbers, URL, permalink, DOI, etc.). Here is an example of how the two parts work together. Note that you can identify the author either in a signal phrase or in parentheses:

IN-TEXT DOCUMENTATION (WITH AND WITHOUT SIGNAL PHRASE)

As Lester Faigley puts it, "The world has become a bazaar from which to shop for an individual 'lifestyle'" (12).

As one observer suggests, "The world has become a bazaar from which to shop for an individual 'lifestyle'" (Faigley 12).

CORRESPONDING WORKS-CITED REFERENCE

Faigley, Lester. *Fragments of Rationality: Postmodernity and the Subject of Composition.* U of Pittsburgh P, 1992.

MLA IN-TEXT DOCUMENTATION

Brief documentation in your text makes clear to your reader what you took from a source and where within the source you found the information. As you cite each source, you'll need to decide whether or not to name the author in a signal phrase—"as Toni Morrison writes"—or in parentheses—"(Morrison 24)." For either style of reference, try to put the parenthetical documentation at the end of the sentence or as close as possible to the material you've cited without awkwardly interrupting the sentence. When citing a direct quotation (as in no. 1), note that the parenthetical reference comes after the closing quotation marks but before the period at the end of the sentence.

1. AUTHOR NAMED IN A SIGNAL PHRASE

If you mention the author in a signal phrase, put only the page number(s) in parentheses. Do not write "page" or "p."

> McCullough describes John Adams's hands as those of someone used to manual labor (18).

2. AUTHOR NAMED IN PARENTHESES

If you do not mention the author in a signal phrase, put the author's last name in parentheses along with the page number(s). Do not use punctuation between the name and the page number(s).

> Adams is said to have had "the hands of a man accustomed to pruning his own trees, cutting his own hay, and splitting his own firewood" (McCullough 18).

3. AFTER A BLOCK QUOTATION

When quoting more than three lines of poetry, more than four lines of prose, or dialogue between two or more characters from a drama, set off the quotation from the rest of your text, indenting it half an inch (or five spaces) from the left margin. Do not use quotation marks, and place any parenthetical documentation *after* the final punctuation.

> In *Eastward to Tartary,* Kaplan captures ancient and contemporary Antioch:
>
> > At the height of its glory in the Roman-Byzantine age, when it had an amphitheater, public baths, aqueducts, and sewage pipes, half a million people lived in Antioch. Today the population is only 125,000. With sour relations between Turkey and Syria, and unstable politics throughout the Middle East, Antioch is now a backwater—seedy and tumbledown, with relatively few tourists. I found it altogether charming. (123)

4. TWO OR MORE AUTHORS

For a work with two authors, name both, either in a signal phrase or in parentheses.

> Carlson and Ventura's stated goal is to introduce Julio Cortázar, Marjorie Agosín, and other Latin American writers to an audience of English-speaking adolescents (5).

For a work by three or more authors, name the first author followed by "et al.," which means "and others."

> One popular survey of American literature breaks the contents into sixteen thematic groupings (Anderson et al. A19–24).

5. ORGANIZATION OR GOVERNMENT AS AUTHOR

Acknowledge the organization either in a signal phrase or in parentheses. It's acceptable to shorten long names.

The US government can be direct when it wants to be. For example, it sternly warns, "If you are overpaid, we will recover any payments not due you" (Social Security Administration 12).

6. AUTHOR UNKNOWN

If you can't determine an author, use the work's title or a shortened version of the title in the parenthetical reference.

A powerful editorial in last week's paper asserts that healthy liver donor Mike Hurewitz died because of "frightening" faulty postoperative care ("Every Patient's Nightmare").

7. LITERARY WORKS

When referring to literary works that are available in many different editions, give the page numbers from the edition you are using, followed by information that will let readers of any edition locate the text you are citing.

Novels: Give the page and chapter number, separated by a semicolon.

In *Pride and Prejudice*, Mrs. Bennet shows no warmth toward Jane when she returns from Netherfield (105; ch. 12).

Verse plays: Give the act, scene, and line numbers; separate them with periods.

Macbeth continues the vision theme when he says, "Thou hast no speculation in those eyes / Which thou dost glare with" (3.3.96-97).

Poems: Give the part and line numbers (separated by periods). If a poem has only line numbers, use the word "line(s)" in the first reference.

The mere in *Beowulf* is described as "not a pleasant place!" (line 1372). Later, it is called "the awful place" (1378).

8. WORKS CITED TOGETHER

If you cite two or more works in the same parentheses, separate the references with a semicolon.

Critics have looked at both *Pride and Prejudice* and *Frankenstein* from a cultural perspective (Tanner 7; Smith viii).

9. SOURCE QUOTED IN ANOTHER SOURCE

When you are quoting text that you found quoted in another source, use the abbreviation "qtd. in" in the parenthetical reference.

> Charlotte Brontë wrote to G. H. Lewes: "Why do you like Miss Austen
> so very much? I am puzzled on that point" (qtd. in Tanner 7).

10. WORK WITHOUT PAGE NUMBERS

For works without page numbers, including many online sources, identify the source using the author or other information either in a signal phrase or in parentheses. If the source has chapter, paragraph, or section numbers, use them with the abbreviations "ch.," "par.," or "sec."

> Studies show that music training helps children to be better at multi-
> tasking later in life ("Hearing the Music," par. 2).

11. AN ENTIRE WORK OR A ONE-PAGE ARTICLE

If you cite an entire work rather than a part of it, or if you cite a single-page article, there's no need to include page numbers.

> Throughout life, John Adams strove to succeed (McCullough).

MLA LIST OF WORKS CITED

A works-cited list provides full bibliographic information for every source cited in your text. Here's some general advice to help you format your list:

- Start the list on a new page.

- Center the title (Works Cited) one inch from the top of the page.

- Double-space the whole list.

- Begin each entry flush with the left-hand margin, and indent subsequent lines one-half inch or five spaces.

- Alphabetize entries by the author's last name. If a work has no identifiable author, use the first major word of the title (disregard "A," "An," "The").

- If you cite more than one work by a single author, list them all alphabetically by title, and use three hyphens in place of the author's name after the first entry (see no. 4 for an example).

- *Authors:* List the primary author last name first, and include any middle name or initial after the first name.

- *Titles:* Capitalize all principal words in titles and subtitles, including short verbs such as "is" and "are." Do not capitalize "a," "an," "the," "to," or any preposition or conjunction unless they begin a title or subtitle. Italicize book titles, periodical titles, and titles of other long works, but place quotation marks around a chapter of a book, a selection from an anthology, or an article title.

- *Versions:* If you cite a source that's available in more than one version, specify the one you consulted in your works-cited entry. Write ordinal numbers with numerals, and abbreviate "edition": 2nd ed.

- *Numbers:* If you cite a book that's published in multiple volumes, indicate the volume number. Abbreviate "volume," and write the number as a numeral: vol. 2. Indicate any volume and issue numbers of journals, abbreviating both "volume" and "number": vol. 123, no. 4.

- *Publishers:* Write publishers' names in full, but omit business words like "Inc." or "Company." For university presses, use "U" for "University" and "P" for "Press"—Princeton UP, U of California P.

- *Dates:* Whether to give just the year or to include the month and day (or even the time stamp) depends on the source. Give the full date that you find there. If the date is unknown, simply omit it.

  Abbreviate months except for May, June, and July: Jan., Feb., Mar., Apr., Aug., Sept., Oct., Nov., Dec.—for example, 9 Sept. 2020.

  For books, give the year of publication: 1948. If a book lists more than one date, use the most recent one.

  Periodicals may be published annually, monthly, seasonally, weekly, or daily. Give the full date that you find in the periodical: 2020, Apr. 2020, Spring 2020, 16 Apr. 2020.

  For online sources, use the copyright date or the most recent update, giving the full date that you find in the source. If the source does not give a date, use the date of access: Accessed 6 June 2020. And if the source includes the time when it was posted or updated, give the time along with the date: 18 Oct. 2020, 9:20 a.m.

  Because online sources may change or even disappear, the date of access can be important for indicating the exact version you've cited. Some instructors may require this information, so we've included access dates in this chapter's guidelines for specific kinds of sources, but check with your instructor to see if you're required to include this information.

- *Location:* For most print articles and other short works, give a page number or range of pages: p. 24, pp. 24–35. For articles that are not on consecutive pages, give the first page number with a plus sign: pp. 24+.

  Indicate the location of online sources by giving the URL, omitting "http://" or "https://". If a source has a permalink (a stable version of its URL) or a DOI (a digital object identifier, a stable number identifying the location of a source accessed through a database), give that instead.

- *Punctuation:* Some URLs will not fit on one line. MLA does not specify where to break a URL, but we recommend breaking it before a punctuation mark. Do *not* add a hyphen.

  Sometimes you'll need to provide information about more than one work for a single source—for instance, when you cite an article from a periodical that you access through a database. MLA refers to the periodical and database (or any other entity that holds a source) as "containers." Use commas between elements within each container and put a period at the end of each container.

> Semuels, Alana. "The Future Will Be Quiet." *The Atlantic*, Apr. 2016, pp. 19–20. *ProQuest*, search.proquest.com/docview /1777443553?accountid+42654. Accessed 5 Apr. 2016.

Authors and Other Contributors

The following guidelines for citing authors and other contributors apply to all sources you cite: in print, online, or in some other media.

1. ONE AUTHOR

> Anderson, Curtis. *The Long Tail: Why the Future of Business Is Selling Less of More.* Hyperion, 2006.

2. TWO AUTHORS

Follow the order of names on the book's title page. List the second author first name first.

> Lunsford, Andrea, and Lisa Ede. *Singular Texts/Plural Authors: Perspectives on Collaborative Writing.* Southern Illinois UP, 1990.

3. THREE OR MORE AUTHORS

Provide the first author's name, followed by "et al." (Latin for "and others").

> Sebranek, Patrick, et al. *Writers INC: A Guide to Writing, Thinking, and Learning.* Write Source, 1990.

4. MULTIPLE WORKS BY AN AUTHOR

Give the author's name in the first entry, and then use three hyphens in the author slot for each of the subsequent works, listing them alphabetically by the first important word of each title.

Kaplan, Robert D. *The Coming Anarchy: Shattering the Dreams of the Post
Cold War.* Random House, 2000.

---. *Eastward to Tartary: Travels in the Balkans, the Middle East, and the
Caucasus.* Random House, 2000.

5. AUTHOR AND EDITOR OR TRANSLATOR

Austen, Jane. *Emma.* Edited by Stephen M. Parrish, W. W. Norton,
2000.

Dostoevsky, Fyodor. *Crime and Punishment.* Translated by Richard
Pevear and Larissa Volokhonsky, Vintage Books, 1993.

Start with the editor or translator if you are focusing on that contribution
rather than the author's.

Pevear, Richard, and Larissa Volokhonsky, translators. *Crime and
Punishment.* By Fyodor Dostoevsky, Vintage Books, 1993.

6. ORGANIZATION OR GOVERNMENT

Diagram Group. *The Macmillan Visual Desk Reference.* Macmillan, 1993.

For a government publication, give the name of the government first, followed
by the names of any department and agency.

United States, Department of Health and Human Services, National
Institute of Mental Health. *Autism Spectrum Disorders.*
Government Printing Office, 2004.

Articles and Other Short Works

Articles, essays, reviews, and other short works are found in journals,
magazines, newspapers, other periodicals, and books—all of which you may
find in print, online, or in a database. For most short works, you'll need to
provide information about the author, the titles of both the short work and the
longer work, any page numbers, and various kinds of publication information.

7. ARTICLE IN A JOURNAL

PRINT

Cooney, Brian C. "Considering *Robinson Crusoe's* 'Liberty of Conscience'
in an Age of Terror." *College English,* vol. 69, no. 3, Jan. 2007,
pp. 197–215.

ONLINE

> Gleckman, Jason. "Shakespeare as Poet or Playwright? The Player's Speech in *Hamlet*." *Early Modern Literary Studies,* vol. 11, no. 3, Jan. 2006, purl.oclc.org/emls/11-3/glechaml.htm. Accessed 31 Mar. 2020.

8. ARTICLE IN A MAGAZINE

PRINT

> Neyfakh, Leon. "The Future of Getting Arrested." *The Atlantic,* Jan.-Feb. 2015, pp. 26+.

ONLINE

> Khazan, Olga. "Forgetting and Remembering Your First Language." *The Atlantic,* 24 July 2014, www.theatlantic.com/international /archive/2014/07/learning-forgetting-and-remembering-your-first-language/374906/. Accessed 2 Apr. 2020.

9. ARTICLE IN A NEWSPAPER

PRINT

> Saulny, Susan, and Jacques Steinberg. "On College Forms, a Question of Race Can Perplex." *The New York Times,* 14 June 2011, p. A1.

To document a particular edition of a newspaper, list the edition ("late ed.," "natl. ed.," and so on) after the date. If a section of the newspaper is numbered, put that detail after the edition information.

> Burns, John F., and Miguel Helft. "Under Pressure, YouTube Withdraws Muslim Cleric's Videos." *The New York Times,* 4 Nov. 2010, late ed., sec. 1, p. 13.

ONLINE

> Banerjee, Neela. "Proposed Religion-Based Program for Federal Inmates Is Canceled." *The New York Times,* 28 Oct. 2006, www .nytimes.com/2006/10/28/us/28prison.html?_r=0. Accessed 4 Apr. 2020.

10. ARTICLE ACCESSED THROUGH A DATABASE

> Stalter, Sunny. "Subway Ride and Subway System in Hart Crane's 'The Tunnel.'" *Journal of Modern Literature,* vol. 33, no. 2, Jan. 2010,

pp. 70–91. *JSTOR,* doi: 10.2979/jml.2010.33.2.70. Accessed 30
   Mar. 2020.

11. ENTRY IN A REFERENCE WORK

PRINT

Provide the author's name if the entry has one. If there's no author given,
start with the title of the entry.

"California." *The New Columbia Encyclopedia,* edited by William H. Harris
   and Judith S. Levey, 4th ed., Columbia UP, 1975, pp. 423–24.
"Feminism." *Longman Dictionary of American English,* Longman, 1983,
   p. 252.

ONLINE

Document online reference works the same as print ones, adding the URL and
access date after the date of publication.

"Baseball." *The Columbia Electronic Encyclopedia,* edited by Paul Lagassé,
   6th ed., Columbia UP, 2012, www.infoplease.com/encyclopedia.
   Accessed 25 May 2020.

12. EDITORIAL

PRINT

"Gas, Cigarettes Are Safe to Tax." *The Lakeville Journal,* 17 Feb. 2005,
   p. A10. Editorial.

ONLINE

"Keep the Drinking Age at 21." *Chicago Tribune,* 28 Aug. 2008, articles
   .chicagotribune.com/2008-08-26/news/0808250487_1 _binge-
   drinking-drinking-age-alcohol-related-crashes. Accessed 26
   Apr. 2020. Editorial.

13. LETTER TO THE EDITOR

Pinker, Steven. "Language Arts." Letter. *The New Yorker,* 4 June 2012,
   www.newyorker.com/magazine/2012/06/04/language-arts-2.
   Accessed 6 Apr. 2020.

14. REVIEW

PRINT

> Frank, Jeffrey. "Body Count." Review of *The Exception,* by Christian Jungersen. *The New Yorker,* 30 July 2007, pp. 86–87.

If a review has no author or title, start with what's being reviewed:

> Review of *Ways to Disappear,* by Idra Novey. *The New Yorker,* 28 Mar. 2016, p. 79.

ONLINE

> Donadio, Rachel. "Italy's Great, Mysterious Storyteller." Review of *My Brilliant Friend,* by Elena Ferrante. *The New York Review of Books,* 18 Dec. 2014, www.nybooks.com/articles/2014/12/18/italys -great-mysterious-storyteller. Accessed 28 Sept. 2020.

15. ONLINE COMMENT

> Nick. Comment on "The Case for Reparations." *The Atlantic,* 22 May 2014, 3:04 p.m., www.theatlantic.com/business /archive/2014/05/how-to-comment-on-reparations /371422/#article-comments. Accessed 8 May 2015.

Books and Parts of Books

For most books, you'll need to provide information about the author, the title, the publisher, and the year of publication. If you found the book inside a larger volume, a database, or some other work, be sure to specify that as well.

16. BASIC ENTRIES FOR A BOOK

PRINT

> Watson, Brad. *Miss Jane.* W. W. Norton, 2016.

EBOOK

Document an ebook as you would a print book, but add information about the ebook—or the type of ebook if you know it.

Watson, Brad. *Miss Jane.* Ebook, W. W. Norton, 2016.

Watson, Brad. *Miss Jane.* Kindle ed., W. W. Norton, 2016.

IN A DATABASE

Anderson, Sherwood. *Winesburg, Ohio.* B. W. Huebsch, 1919. *Bartleby .com,* www.bartleby.com/156/. Accessed 8 Apr. 2020.

17. ANTHOLOGY

Kitchen, Judith, and Mary Paumier Jones, editors. *In Short: A Collection of Brief Creative Nonfiction.* W. W. Norton, 1996.

18. WORK IN AN ANTHOLOGY

Achebe, Chinua. "Uncle Ben's Choice." *The Seagull Reader: Literature,* edited by Joseph Kelly, W. W. Norton, 2005, pp. 23–27.

TWO OR MORE WORKS FROM ONE ANTHOLOGY

Prepare an entry for each selection by author and title, followed by the anthology editors' last names and the pages of the selection. Then include an entry for the anthology itself (see no. 17).

Hiestand, Emily. "Afternoon Tea." Kitchen and Jones, pp. 65–67.

Ozick, Cynthia. "The Shock of Teapots." Kitchen and Jones, pp. 68–71.

19. MULTIVOLUME WORK

If you cite all the volumes, give the number of volumes after the year of publication.

ALL VOLUMES

Churchill, Winston. *The Second World War.* Houghton Mifflin, 1948–53. 6 vols.

If you cite only one volume, give the number after the title and the total number of volumes after the year of publication.

SINGLE VOLUME

Sandburg, Carl. *Abraham Lincoln: The War Years.* Vol. 2, Harcourt, Brace & World, 1939. 4 vols.

20. GRAPHIC NARRATIVE

> Bechdel, Alison. *Fun Home: A Family Tragicomedy.* Houghton Mifflin,
> 2006.

If the work has both an author and an illustrator, start with the one whose
work is more relevant to your research, and label the role of anyone who's not
an author.

> Pekar, Harvey. *Bob & Harv's Comics.* Illustrated by R. Crumb, Running
> Press, 1996.
> Crumb, R., illustrator. *Bob & Harv's Comics.* By Harvey Pekar, Running
> Press, 1996.

21. EDITION OTHER THAN THE FIRST

> Fowler, H. W. *A Dictionary of Modern English.* 2nd ed., Oxford UP, 1965.

22. REPUBLISHED WORK

Provide the year of original publication after the title, followed by the current
publisher and year of republication.

> Bierce, Ambrose. *Civil War Stories.* 1909. Dover, 1994.

23. FOREWORD, INTRODUCTION, PREFACE, OR AFTERWORD

> Tanner, Tony. Introduction. *Pride and Prejudice,* by Jane Austen,
> Penguin, 1972, pp. 7–46.

24. PUBLISHED LETTER

> White, E. B. Letter to Carol Angell. 28 May 1970. *Letters of E. B. White,*
> edited by Dorothy Lobarno Guth, Harper and Row, 1976, p. 600.

Websites

Many sources are available in multiple media—for example, a print periodical
that is also on the web and contained in digital databases—but some are
published only on websites. This section covers the latter.

25. ENTIRE WEBSITE

Provide the author's name followed by the author's role.

> Zalta, Edward N., principal editor. *Stanford Encyclopedia of Philosophy*.
> Metaphysics Research Lab, Center for the Study of Language,
> Stanford U, 1995–2015, plato.stanford.edu/index.html. Accessed
> 21 Apr. 2020.

PERSONAL WEBSITE

> Heath, Shirley Brice. *Shirley Brice Heath*. 2015, shirleybriceheath.net.
> Accessed 6 June 2020.

26. WORK ON A WEBSITE

Provide the author's name, if any. If there is no author, begin with the title of
the work.

> "Global Minnesota: Immigrants Past and Present." *Immigration History
> Research Center*, U of Minnesota, 2015, cla.umn.edu/ihrc.
> Accessed 25 May 2020.

27. BLOG ENTRY

> Hollmichel, Stefanie. "Bringing Up the Bodies." *So Many Books*, 10
> Feb. 2014, somanybooksblog.com/2014/02/10/bring-up-the
> -bodies/. Accessed 12 Feb. 2020.

If the entry has no title, use "Blog entry" (without quotation marks). Document a whole blog as you would an entire website (no. 25) and a comment on a
blog as you would a comment on an online article (no. 15).

28. WIKI

> "Pi." *Wikipedia*, Wikimedia Foundation, 28 Aug. 2013, en.wikipedia.org
> /wiki/Pi. Accessed 25 Oct. 2020.

Personal Communication and Social Media

29. EMAIL

> Smith, William. "Teaching Grammar—Some Thoughts." Received by
> Richard Bullock, 19 Nov. 2013.

30. POST TO AN ONLINE FORUM

> @somekiryu. "What's the hardest part about writing for you?" *Reddit,* 22 Apr. 2016, redd.it/4fynio.

31. POST ON SOCIAL MEDIA

> @POTUS44 (Barack Obama). "I'm proud of the @NBA for taking a stand against gun violence. Sympathy for victims isn't enough—change requires all of us speaking up." *Twitter,* 23 Dec. 2015, 1:21 p.m., twitter.com/POTUS44/status /679773729749078016. Accessed 20 Apr. 2020.
>
> Black Lives Matter. "Rise and Grind! Did you sign this petition yet? We now have a sign on for ORGANIZATIONS to lend their support." *Facebook,* 23 Oct. 2015, 11:30 a.m., www.facebook.com/Black-LivesMatter/photos/a.294807204023865.1073741829.1802127554 83311/504711973033386/. Accessed 20 Apr. 2020.
>
> @quarterlifepoetry. Illustrated poem about girl at Target. *Instagram,* 22 Jan. 2015, www.instagram.com/p/yLO6fSurRH/. Accessed 20 Apr. 2020.

Audio, Visual, and Other Sources

32. ADVERTISEMENT

PRINT

> Cal Alumni Association. Sports Merchandise ad. *California,* Spring 2016, p. 3.

AUDIO OR VIDEO

> Microsoft. Super Bowl commercial. 28 Jan. 2020. *YouTube,* www .youtube.com/watch?v=_xPn4DXIj5w. Accessed 24 Mar. 2020.

33. ART

ORIGINAL

> Van Gogh, Vincent. *The Potato Eaters.* 1885, Van Gogh Museum, Amsterdam.

REPRODUCTION

> Van Gogh, Vincent. *The Potato Eaters.* 1885. *History of Art: A Survey of the Major Visual Arts from the Dawn of History to the Present Day,* by H. W. Janson, Prentice-Hall/Harry N. Abrams, 1969, p. 508.

ONLINE

> Warhol, Andy. *Self-portrait.* 1979. *J. Paul Getty Museum,* www.getty.edu/art/collection/objects/106971/andy-warhol-self-portrait-american-1979/. Accessed 20 Jan. 2020.

34. CARTOON

PRINT

> Chast, Roz. "The Three Wise Men of Thanksgiving." *The New Yorker,* 1 Dec. 2003, p. 174. Cartoon.

ONLINE

> Munroe, Randall. "Up Goer Five." *xkcd,* 12 Nov. 2012, xkcd.com/1133/. Accessed 22 Apr. 2020. Cartoon.

35. FILM

Name individuals based on the focus of your project—the director, the screenwriter, the cinematographer, or someone else. If your essay focuses on one or more contributors, you may put their names before the title.

> *Breakfast at Tiffany's.* Directed by Blake Edwards, Paramount, 1961.

STREAMING

> *Interstellar.* Directed by Christopher Nolan, Paramount, 2014. *Amazon Prime Video,* www.amazon.com/Interstellar-Matthew-McConaughey/dp/B00TU9UFTS. Accessed 2 May 2020.

36. INTERVIEW

If the interviewer's name is known and relevant to your argument, include it after the word "Interview" or the title: Interview by Stephen Colbert.

BROADCAST

> Gates, Henry Louis, Jr. Interview. *Fresh Air,* NPR, 9 Apr. 2002.

PUBLISHED

Stone, Oliver. Interview. *Esquire,* Nov. 2004, pp. 170-71.

PERSONAL

Roddick, Andy. Personal interview. 17 Aug. 2013.

37. MAP

If the title doesn't make clear it's a map, add a label at the end.

"National Highway System." US Department of Transportation Federal
Highway Administration, www.fhwa.dot.gov/planning/images
/nhs.pdf. Accessed 10 May 2020. Map.

38. MUSICAL SCORE

Stravinsky, Igor. *Petrushka.* 1911. W. W. Norton, 1967.

39. PODCAST

If you accessed a podcast online, give the URL and date of access; if you
accessed it through a service such as *iTunes* or *Spotify,* indicate that instead.

Koenig, Sarah, host. "DUSTWUN." *Serial,* season 2, episode 1, WBEZ,
10 Dec. 2015, serialpodcast.org/season-two/1/dustwun. Accessed
23 Apr. 2020.
Foss, Gilad, author and performer. "Aquaman's Brother-in-Law." *Superhero Temp Agency,* season 1, episode 1, 16 Apr. 2015. *iTunes.*

40. RADIO PROGRAM

Glass, Ira, host. "In Defense of Ignorance." *This American Life,* WBEZ,
22 Apr. 2016, thisamericanlife.org/radio-archives/episode/585/
in-defense-of-ignorance. Accessed 2 May 2020.

41. SOUND RECORDING

ONLINE

Simone, Nina. "To Be Young, Gifted and Black." *Black Gold,* RCA Records, 1969. *Spotify.*

CD

Brown, Greg. "Canned Goods." *The Live One,* Red House, 1995.

42. TV SHOW

Name contributors based on the focus of your project—director, writers, actors, or others. If there's a key contributor, you might include that contributor's name and role before the title of the episode.

> "Stormborn." *Game of Thrones*, written by Bryan Cogman, season 7,
> episode 2, HBO, 23 July 2017.

DVD

> "The Pants Tent." 2003. *Curb Your Enthusiasm: Season One*, performance
> by Larry David, season 1, episode 1, HBO Video, 2006, disc 1.

ONLINE

> "Shadows in the Glass." *Marvel's Daredevil*, season 1, episode 8, Netflix,
> 10 Apr. 2015. *Netflix*, www.netflix.com/watch/80018198.
> Accessed 3 Nov. 2020.

43. VIDEO GAME

> Metzen, Chris, and James Waugh, writers. *StarCraft II: Legacy of the
> Void*. Blizzard Entertainment, 2015. OS X.

SOURCES NOT COVERED BY MLA

To document a source that isn't covered by the MLA guidelines, look for models similar to the source you're citing. Give any information readers will need in order to find the sources themselves—author, title, subtitle, publisher, dates, and any other pertinent information. You might want to try out the documentation information yourself, to be sure it will lead others to your source.

SAMPLE RESEARCH PAPER

The following report was written by Dylan Borchers for a first-year writing course. It's formatted according to the guidelines of the MLA (style.mla.org).

Dylan Borchers
Professor Bullock
English 102, Section 4
4 May 2019

Against the Odds:

Harry S. Truman and the Election of 1948

Just over a week before Election Day in 1948, a *New York Times* article noted "[t]he popular view that Gov. Thomas E. Dewey's election as President is a foregone conclusion" (Egan). This assessment of the race between incumbent Democrat Harry S. Truman and Dewey, his Republican challenger, was echoed a week later when *Life* magazine published a photograph whose caption labeled Dewey "The Next President" (Photo of Truman 37). In a *Newsweek* survey of fifty prominent political writers, each one predicted Truman's defeat, and *Time* correspondents declared that Dewey would carry 39 of the 48 states (Donaldson 210). Nearly every major media outlet across the United States endorsed Dewey and lambasted Truman. As historian Robert H. Ferrell observes, even Truman's wife, Bess, thought he would be beaten (270).

The results of an election are not so easily predicted, as the famous photograph in fig. 1 shows. Not only did Truman win the election, but he won by a significant margin, with 303 electoral votes and 24,179,259 popular votes, compared to Dewey's 189 electoral votes and 21,991,291 popular votes (Donaldson 204–07). In fact, many historians and political analysts argue that Truman would have won by an even greater margin had third-party Progressive candidate Henry A. Wallace not split the Democratic vote in New York State and Dixiecrat Strom Thurmond not won

Fig. 1. President Harry S. Truman holds up an edition of the *Chicago Daily Tribune* that mistakenly announced "Dewey Defeats Truman" (Rollins).

four states in the South (McCullough 711). Although Truman's defeat was heavily predicted, those predictions themselves, Dewey's passiveness as a campaigner, and Truman's zeal turned the tide for a Truman victory.

In the months preceding the election, public opinion polls predicted that Dewey would win by a large margin. Pollster Elmo Roper stopped polling in September, believing there was no reason to continue, given a seemingly inevitable Dewey landslide. Although the margin narrowed as the election drew near, the other pollsters predicted a Dewey win by at least five percent (Donaldson 209). Many historians believe that these predictions aided the president in the long run. First, surveys showing Dewey in the lead may have prompted some of Dewey's supporters to feel overconfident about their candidate's chances and therefore to stay home from the polls on Election Day. Second, these same surveys may have energized Democrats to mount late get-out-the-vote efforts ("1948 Truman-Dewey Election"). Other analysts believe that the overwhelming predictions of a Truman loss also kept at home some Democrats who approved of Truman's policies but saw a Truman loss as inevitable. According to political analyst Samuel Lubell, those Democrats may have saved Dewey from an even greater defeat (Hamby, *Man* 465). Whatever the impact on the voters, the polling numbers had a decided effect on Dewey.

Historians and political analysts alike cite Dewey's overly cautious campaign as one of the main reasons Truman was able to achieve victory. Dewey firmly believed in public opinion polls. With all indications pointing to an easy victory, Dewey and his staff believed that all he had to do was bide his time and make no foolish mistakes. Dewey himself said, "When you're leading, don't talk" (Smith 30). Each of Dewey's speeches was well crafted and well rehearsed. As the leader in the race, he kept his remarks faultlessly positive, with the result that he failed to deliver a solid message or even mention Truman or any of Truman's policies. Eventually, Dewey began to be perceived as aloof and stuffy. One observer compared him to the plastic groom on top of a wedding cake (Hamby, "Harry S. Truman"), and others noted his stiff, cold demeanor (McCullough 671–74).

As his campaign continued, observers noted that Dewey seemed uncomfortable in crowds, unable to connect with ordinary people. And he made a number of blunders. One took place at a train stop when the

Short title given for author with multiple works cited.

Paragraphs indent $\frac{1}{2}$ inch or 5 spaces.

Two works cited within the same sentence.

candidate, commenting on the number of children in the crowd, said he was glad they had been let out of school for his arrival. Unfortunately for Dewey, it was a Saturday ("1948: The Great Truman Surprise"). Such gaffes gave voters the feeling that Dewey was out of touch with the public.

Again and again through the autumn of 1948, Dewey's campaign speeches failed to address the issues, with the candidate declaring that he did not want to "get down in the gutter" (Smith 515). When told by fellow Republicans that he was losing ground, Dewey insisted that his campaign not alter its course. Even *Time* magazine, though it endorsed and praised him, conceded that his speeches were dull (McCullough 696). According to historian Zachary Karabell, they were "notable only for taking place, not for any specific message" (244). Dewey's numbers in the polls slipped in the weeks before the election, but he still held a comfortable lead over Truman. It would take Truman's famous whistle-stop campaign to make the difference.

Few candidates in US history have campaigned for the presidency with more passion and faith than Harry Truman. In the autumn of 1948, he wrote to his sister, "It will be the greatest campaign any President ever made. Win, lose, or draw, people will know where I stand" (91). For thirty-three days, Truman traveled the nation, giving hundreds of speeches from the back of the *Ferdinand Magellan* railroad car. In the same letter, he described the pace: "We made about 140 stops and I spoke over 147 times, shook hands with at least 30,000 and am in good condition to start out again tomorrow for Wilmington, Philadelphia,

Jersey City, Newark, Albany and Buffalo" (91). McCullough writes of Truman's campaign:

> No President in history had ever gone so far in quest of support from the people, or with less cause for the effort, to judge by informed opinion. . . . As a test of his skills and judgment as a professional politician, not to say his stamina and disposition at age sixty-four, it would be like no other experience in his long, often difficult career, as he himself understood perfectly. More than any other event in his public life, or in his presidency thus far, it would reveal the kind of man he was. (655)

He spoke in large cities and small towns, defending his policies and attacking Republicans. As a former farmer and relatively late bloomer, Truman was able to connect with the public. He developed an energetic style, usually speaking from notes rather than from a prepared speech, and often mingled with the crowds that met his train. These crowds grew larger as the campaign progressed. In Chicago, over half a million people lined the streets as he passed, and in St. Paul the crowd numbered over 25,000. When Dewey entered St. Paul two days later, he was greeted by only 7,000 supporters ("1948 Truman-Dewey Election"). Reporters brushed off the large crowds as mere curiosity seekers wanting to see a president (McCullough 682). Yet Truman persisted, even if he often seemed to be the only one who thought he could win. By going directly to the American people and connecting with them, Truman built the momentum needed to surpass Dewey and win the election.

The legacy and lessons of Truman's whistle-stop campaign continue to be studied by political analysts, and

Quotations of more than 4 lines indented $\frac{1}{2}$ inch (5 spaces) and double-spaced.

Parenthetical reference after final punctuation.

politicians today often mimic his campaign methods by scheduling multiple visits to key states, as Truman did. He visited California, Illinois, and Ohio 48 times, compared with 6 visits to those states by Dewey. Political scientist Thomas M. Holbrook concludes that his strategic campaigning in those states and others gave Truman the electoral votes he needed to win (61, 65).

The 1948 election also had an effect on pollsters, who, as Elmo Roper admitted, "couldn't have been more wrong." *Life* magazine's editors concluded that pollsters as well as reporters and commentators were too convinced of a Dewey victory to analyze the polls seriously, especially the opinions of undecided voters (Karabell 256). Pollsters assumed that undecided voters would vote in the same proportion as decided voters—and that turned out to be a false assumption (Karabell 257). In fact, the lopsidedness of the polls might have led voters who supported Truman to call themselves undecided out of an unwillingness to associate themselves with the losing side, further skewing the polls' results (McDonald et al. 152). Such errors led pollsters to change their methods significantly after the 1948 election.

After the election, many political analysts, journalists, and historians concluded that the Truman upset was in fact a victory for the American people, who, the *New Republic* noted, "couldn't be ticketed by the polls, knew its own mind and had picked the rather unlikely but courageous figure of Truman to carry its banner" (T.R.B. 3). How "unlikely" is unclear, however; Truman biographer Alonzo Hamby notes that "polls of scholars consistently rank Truman among the top eight presidents in American history"

Work by 3 or more authors is shortened using "et al."

(*Man* 641). But despite Truman's high standing, and despite the fact that the whistle-stop campaign is now part of our political landscape, politicians have increasingly imitated the style of the Dewey campaign, with its "packaged candidate who ran so as not to lose, who steered clear of controversy, and who made a good show of appearing presidential" (Karabell 266). The election of 1948 shows that voters are not necessarily swayed by polls, but it may have presaged the packaging of candidates by public relations experts, to the detriment of public debate on the issues in future presidential elections.

Works Cited

Donaldson, Gary A. *Truman Defeats Dewey*. UP of Kentucky, 1999.

Egan, Leo. "Talk Is Now Turning to the Dewey Cabinet." *The New York Times*, 20 Oct. 1948, p. 8E, www.nytimes .com/timesmachine/1948/10/26/issue.html. Accessed 18 Apr. 2019.

Ferrell, Robert H. *Harry S. Truman: A Life*. U of Missouri P, 1994.

Hamby, Alonzo L., editor. "Harry S. Truman: Campaigns and Elections." *American President*, Miller Center, U of Virginia, 11 Jan. 2012, millercenter.org/president /biography/truman-campaigns-and-elections. Accessed 17 Mar. 2019.

---. *Man of the People: A Life of Harry S. Truman*. Oxford UP, 1995.

Holbrook, Thomas M. "Did the Whistle-Stop Campaign Matter?" *PS: Political Science and Politics,* vol. 35, no. 1, Mar. 2002, pp. 59–66.

Karabell, Zachary. *The Last Campaign: How Harry Truman Won the 1948 Election*. Alfred A. Knopf, 2000.

McCullough, David. *Truman*. Simon and Schuster, 1992.

McDonald, Daniel G., et al. "The Spiral of Silence in the 1948 Presidential Election." *Communication Research,* vol. 28, no. 2, Apr. 2001, pp. 139–55.

"1948: The Great Truman Surprise." *The Press and the Presidency*, Dept. of Political Science and International Affairs, Kennesaw State U, 29 Oct. 2003, kennesaw .edu/pols.3380/pres/1984.html. Accessed 10 Apr. 2019.

"1948 Truman-Dewey Election." *American Political History*, Eagleton Institute of Politics, Rutgers, State U of New

Jersey, 1995–2012, www.eagleton.rutgers.edu/research /americanhistory/ap_trumandewey.php. Accessed 18 Apr. 2019.

Photo of Truman in San Francisco. "The Next President Travels by Ferry Boat over the Broad Waters of San Francisco Bay." *Life*, 1 Nov. 1948, p. 37. *Google Books*, books.google .com/books?id=ekoEAAAAMBAJ&printsec=frontcover #v=onepage&q&f=false. Accessed 20 Apr. 2018.

Rollins, Byron. "President Truman with *Chicago Daily Tribune* Headline of 'Dewey Defeats Truman.'" Associated Press, 4 Nov. 1948. *Harry S. Truman Library & Museum,* www .trumanlibrary.org/photographs/view.php?id=25248. Accessed 20 Apr. 2019.

Roper, Elmo. "Roper Eats Crow; Seeks Reason for Vote Upset." *Evening Independent,* 6 Nov. 1948, p. 10. *Google News*, news.google.com/newspapers?nid=PZE8UkGerEcC&dat =19481106&printsec=frontpage&hl=en. Accessed 13 Apr. 2019.

Smith, Richard Norton. *Thomas E. Dewey and His Times.* Simon and Schuster, 1982.

T.R.B. "Washington Wire." *The New Republic,* 15 Nov. 1948, pp. 3–4. *EBSCOhost,* search.ebscohost.com/login.aspx ?direct=true&db=tsh&AN=14779640&site=ehost-live. Accessed 20 Apr. 2019.

Truman, Harry S. "Campaigning, Letter, October 5, 1948." *Harry S. Truman,* edited by Robert H. Ferrell, CQ P, 2003, p. 91.

A range of dates is given for web projects developed over a period of time.

Every source used is in the list of works cited.

PERMISSIONS
ACKNOWLEDGMENTS

Ocean Vuong: "Immigrating into English," from *The New Yorker* May 30, 2016. © Ocean Vuong. Reprinted by permission of Condé Nast and Ocean Vuong.

Eric A. Watts: "The Color of Success" first appeared in *The Boston Alumni Monthly*, April 1992. Copyright © 1992 by Eric Watts. Reprinted by permission of the author.

Tim Wendel: "King, Kennedy, and the Power of Words," by Tim Wendel, from *The American Scholar*, Volume 81, No. 4, Autumn 2012. Copyright © 2012 by the author.

Philip Weiss: "How to Get Out of a Locked Trunk." Originally published in *Harper's* magazine. Copyright by Philip Weiss. Reprinted by permission of the author.

E. B. White: "Once More to the Lake" from *One Man's Meat*, Copyright © 1941 by E. B. White. Reprinted by permission of ICM Partners.

Zachary Wood: "Introduction" from *Uncensored: My Life and Uncomfortable Conversations at the Intersection of Black and White America* by Zachary R. Wood, copyright © 2018 Zachary R. Wood. Used by permission of Dutton, an imprint of Penguin Publishing Group, a division of Penguin Random House LLC. All rights reserved.

Nancy Wang Yuen: *Reel Inequality: Hollywood Actors and Racism*. New Brunswick: Rutgers University Press, 2017. Copyright © 2017 by Nancy Wang Yuen. Reprinted by permission of Rutgers University Press.

IMAGES

Page 19: MPI/Getty Images; p. 78: AP Photo/Jose Luis Magana; p. 88: Barbara Joy Cooley; p. 89: Photo by Olivia Feheery; p. 91: Sean Pavone/Alamy Stock Photo; p. 96: Photo by Nancy L. Ford; p. 100: Sam Quinones; p. 107: Ana Cwalinski; p. 112: Photo courtesy of Bancroft Press, publisher of the book *The Miss Dennis School of Writing*; p. 121: Simon Bruty/Sports Illustrated via Getty Images/Getty Images; p. 137: W. W. Norton & Company, Inc.; p. 138: Melissa Unbankes; p. 141: Melissa Unbankes; p. 145: Wilson Special Collections Library, UNC Chapel Hill; p. 154: Ryan Enn Hughes/the New York Times/Redux; p. 160: Paul Grover/Shutterstock; p. 166: Ryan Knighton; p. 172: Leonardo Cendamo/Getty Images; p. 189: WildSnap/Shutterstock; p. 190: Madison

Ogletree; p. 198: Amelia Martin/Shutterstock; p. 201: © Richard Lederer; p. 207: Photo © Michael Kienitz; p. 214: Geraint Lewis/Alamy Stock Photo; p. 216: Hulton Archive/Getty Images; p. 220: James Leynse/Corbis via Getty Images; p. 222: Aaron M. Sprecher via AP; p. 234: Ariella Foss/W. W. Norton & Company, Inc.; p. 241: Gary Gershoff/Getty Images; p. 249: Photo by Dave Allocca/Starpix/Shutterstock; p. 254: Washington University Photographic Services Department Collection, Washington University Libraries, Department of Special Collections; p. 261: Image Press Agency/Alamy Stock Photo; p. 268: ZUMA Press, Inc./Alamy Stock Photo; p. 287: ElenaBs/Alamy Stock Vector; p. 288: The Cornell Daily Sun; p. 292: Photo by Maria Wulf; p. 298: AP Photo/Shiho Fukada; p. 303: Photo courtesy Kim Truett, University of South Carolina; p. 315: Ian Bates Photography; p. 318: Ret Alui/Alamy Stock Photo; p. 332: © We Ride Australia www.weride.org.au; p. 333: Courtesy of Dan Treadway; p. 337 © Alexander Lumans; p. 343: AP Photo; p. 349: Pete Souza/KRT/Newscom; p. 358: Linda A. Cicero/Stanford News Service; p. 365 Alexandra Freltoft; p. 366 (left): Album/Alamy Stock Photo, (right): Photofest; p. 380: Roz Chast/The New Yorker Collection/The Cartoon Bank; p. 381: Matthew Treacy; p.386: Copyright Peter Murphy. Used with permission from the Robert Wood Johnson Foundation; p. 392: Heather Kresge; p. 399: Courtesy of Mike Rose; p. 402: Courtesy of Mike Rose; p. 403: National Archives; p. 406: Courtesy of Mike Rose; p. 411: Mark Woodward; p. 417 (left): WENN Rights Ltd/Alamy Stock Photo; (right): © Philip Friedman; p. 433: john st. advertising; p. 434: courtesy of Elisa Gonzalez; p. 439: Tim Wendel; p. 441: New York World-Telegram and the Sun Newspaper Photograph Collection, Library of Congress; p. 444: www.AlDiazPhoto.com; p. 448: Tony Cenicola/the New York Times/Redux; p. 454: Official Supreme Court photo of Sonia Sotomayor, Public Domain; p. 461: Steven Ferdman/Patrick McMullan via Getty Images; p. 484: Barbara Joy Cooley; p. 489: Evan Agostini/Invision/AP Photo; p. 493: Bob Daemmrich/Alamy Stock Photo; p. 499: Photo by Ashley Rhian; p. 505: Daniel Roland/AFP via Getty Images; p. 511: Erik Jacobs/the New York Times/Redux; p. 516: Photo by Ron Bolander; p. 524: © Kelly Campbell; p. 530: Iain Masterton/Alamy Stock Photo; p. 535 © Jimee Sechinbaatar; p. 546: Granger Collection; p. 556: Granger Collection; p. 561: Photo Researchers, Inc./Alamy Stock Photo; p. 563: Everett Collection Historical/Alamy Stock Photo; p. 569: GL Archive/Alamy Stock Photo; p. 576: Lee Lockwood/Time Life Pictures/Getty Images; p. 618: Bettmann/Getty Images.

GLOSSARY/INDEX

•)——————————————(•

A

Abstract, 58, 77, 82, 86, 180–81, 187 Generally, having to do with essences and ideas: Liberty, truth, and beauty are abstract concepts. Most writers depend upon abstractions to some degree; however, abstractions that are not fleshed out with vivid particulars are unlikely to hold a reader's interest. See also **CONCRETE**.

Addison, Liz, 485

Adichie, Chimamanda Ngozi, 214

Ain't I a Woman? (Truth), 561

All Seven Deadly Sins Committed at Church Bake Sale (The Onion), 196

Allusion, A passing reference to a work, person, place, or event. Allusions are an efficient means of enlarging the scope and implications of a statement. They work best, of course, when they refer to works most readers are likely to know.

Analogy, 480 A **COMPARISON** that explains aspects of something unfamiliar by likening it to something that is more familiar. In **EXPOSITORY** writing, analogies are used as aids to explanation and as organizing devices. In a **PERSUASIVE** essay, a writer may argue that what is true in one case is also true in the similar case that he or she is advancing. An **ARGUMENT** "by analogy" is only as strong as the terms of the analogy are close.

This Glossary/Index defines key terms and concepts and directs you to pages in the book where they are used or discussed. Terms set in **SMALL CAPTIALS** are defined elsewhere in the glossary/index.

Anecdote, 129, 131, 183 A brief **NARRATIVE** or humorous story, often told for the purpose of **EXEMPLIFYING** or explaining a larger point. Anecdotal evidence is proof based on such stories rather than on statistical or scientific inquiry.

Argument, 14, 16–17, 17, 37, 52, 426, 469–83, 545 An argument makes a case or proves a point. It seeks to convince someone to act in a certain way or to believe in the truth or validity of a statement or **CLAIM**. According to traditional definitions of argumentation and persuasion, a writer can convince a reader in one of three ways: by appealing to reason, by appealing to the reader's emotions, or by appealing to the reader's sense of ethics.

Audience, 38, 44–45, 82, 131, 184–85, 229, 281–82, 326, 375, 426–28, 469, 473–74 The people to whom a piece of writing is addressed. Writers are more likely to achieve their purpose in writing if they keep the needs and expectations of their audience in mind throughout the writing process when making choices about topics, **DICTION**, support, and so on. For example, an essay written for athletes that attacks the use of performance-enhancing drugs in sports might emphasize the hazards of taking steroids. On the other hand, an essay with the same **PURPOSE** but written for an audience of sports fans might focus more on the value of fair play and of having heroes who are drug-free.

B

Back of the Bus, The (Mebane), 145

Barrientos, Tanya Maria, 386

Barry, Lynda, 154

633

C

Causal chain, 427 A series of circumstances or events in which one circumstance or event **CAUSES** another, which in turn causes another and so on—all leading to an ultimate **EFFECT**. A row of dominoes on end is a classic example: The fall of one domino causes another to tip over, which in turn pushes over another domino, until the entire row has toppled.

Cause and effect, 37, 52, 72, 128, 423–32 A strategy of **EXPOSITION**. Cause and effect essays analyze why an event occurred and/or trace its consequences. See the introduction to Chapter 12 for further discussion of this strategy.

Claim, 50, 470, 473 The main point that an **ARGU-MENT** is intended to prove or support; a statement that is debatable, that people can disagree with.

Classification, 51, 69, 226–33, 544–45 A strategy of **EXPOSITION** that puts people or things into categories based on their distinguishing characteristics. Strictly speaking, classification assigns individuals to categories ("This coin is a Lincoln cent"), and division separates individuals in a group according to a given trait or traits ("Put the pennies in a box, the nickels in this one, and give me the quarters and half dollars"). Classification is a mode of organizing an essay as well as a means of obtaining knowledge. See Chapter 8 for further discussion of this strategy.

Cliché, A tired expression that has lost its original power to surprise because of overuse: *We'll have to go back to the drawing board. The quarterback turned the tables and saved the day.*

Climax, 15, 128, 133 An aspect of **PLOT** in **NARRA-TIVE** writing. The climax is the moment when the action of a narrative is most intense—the culmination, after which the dramatic tension is released.

Coherence, 34–37 Unity in writing, where each idea is clear and connected to other ideas.

Comparison and contrast, 16, 36–37, 51, 70–71, 322–31, 545 A strategy of **EXPOSITORY** writing that explores the similarities and differences between two persons, places, things, or ideas. See Chapter 10 for a more detailed explanation.

Concrete, 14–15, 58, 77, 82, 86, 180–81, 187 Definite, particular, capable of being perceived directly. Opposed to **ABSTRACT**. *Rose, Mississippi, pinch* are more concrete words than *flower, river, touch. Five-miles-per-hour* is a more concrete idea than *slowness.* It is good practice to make your essays as concrete as possible, even when you are writing on a general topic.

Connotations, The implied meaning of a word; its overtones and associations over and above its literal meaning. The strict meaning of *home,* for example, is "the place where ones lives"; but the word connotes comfort, security, and love.

Credibility, 470, 481, 594 The power (or lack thereof) of any piece of writing to inspire trust and belief in the mind of the reader. A piece of writing is likely to seem more trustworthy—and thus more credible to the reader—if it cites reliable sources, reports facts clearly and accurately, and uses solid evidence to support its claims.

D

Deduction, 469, 477–78 A form of logical reasoning that proceeds from general premises to specific conclusions. See also **SYLLOGISM**.

Definition, 52, 71–72, 131, 229, 371–79 A basic strategy of **EXPOSITORY** writing. Definitions give the essential meaning of something. *Extended* definitions enlarge on that basic meaning by analyzing the qualities, recalling the history, explaining the purpose, or giving **SYNONYMS** of whatever is being defined. See the introduction to Chapter 11 for further discussion of this strategy.

Description, 13–15, 36, 51, 67, 77–87, 544 One of four **PATTERNS**. Description appeals to the senses: it tells how something looks, feels, sounds, smells, or tastes. An *objective* description focuses on verifiable facts and the observable physical details of a subject, whereas a *subjective* description conveys the writer's thoughts and feelings about a subject, in addition to its physical characteristics. See Chapter 5 for further discussion of the descriptive mode.

Desmond, Matthew, 207

Dialogue, 129, 134–35 Direct speech, especially between two or more speakers in a **NARRATIVE,** quoted word for word.

Diction, Word choice. Mark Twain was talking about diction when he said that the difference between the almost right word and the right word is the difference "between the lightning bug and the lightning." *Standard* diction is defined by dictionaries and other authorities as the language taught in schools and used in the national media. *Nonstandard* diction includes words like *ain't* that are generally not used in formal writing. *Slang* includes informal language such as *bonkers* and *weirdo,* or *dough* for money, and *garbage* for nonsense. Slang words often pass quickly into the standard language or just as quickly fade away. *Colloquial diction* is the language of informal speech or writing: *I'm crazy about you, Virginia. Regional* language is that spoken in certain geographic areas—for example, *remuda,* a word for a herd of riding horses, is used in the Southwest. *Obsolete* language includes terms like *pantaloons* and *palfrey* (saddle horse) that were once standard but are no longer used.

Dominant impression, 15, 79, 84–85 In **DESCRIPTIVE** writing, the main impression of a subject that a writer creates through the use of carefully selected details.

Doughty, Caitlin, 268
Dreamland (Quinones), 100
Dude, Where's My Frontal Cortex? (Sapolsky), 358

E

English Is a Crazy Language (Lederer), 201

Etymology, 373–74, 378 A word's history or the practice of tracing such histories. The modern English word *march,* for example, is derived from the French *marcher* ("to walk"), which in turn is derived from the Latin word *marcus* ("a hammer"). The etymological definition of *march* is thus "to walk with a measured tread, like the rhythmic pounding of a hammer." In most dictionaries, the derivation, or etymology, of a word is explained in parentheses or brackets before the first definition is given.

Evidence, 45, 49, 53–55, 469, 474–75, 545 Proof; the facts and figures, examples, expert testimony, personal experience, and other support that a writer provides in order to make a point.

Example, 51, 68–69, 180–88, 425–26 A specific instance of a general group or idea. Among "things that have given males a bad name," for example, humorist Dave Barry cites "violent crime, war, spitting, and ice hockey." See the introduction to Chapter 7 for more on using examples in writing.

Exposition, 13–16 One of the four **PATTERNS OF WRITING.** Expository writing is informative writing. It explains or gives directions. All the items in this glossary are written in the expository mode; and most of the practical prose that you write in the coming years will be—e.g., papers and examinations, job applications, business reports, insurance claims, your last will and testament.

F

Fallacy, 181, 425 See also **LOGICAL FALLACY.**

Family History (Gonzalez), 434

Figures of speech, 10, 85 Colorful words and phrases used in a nonliteral sense. Some common figures of

Logical fallacy, 181, 425, 478–80 An error in logical reasoning. Common logical fallacies include reasoning *post hoc ergo propter hoc; non sequiturs;* begging the question; arguing *ad hominem;* and false analogies. See the introduction to Chapter 13 for further discussion of logical fallacies.

M

Metaphor, 16, 79, 85 A direct **COMPARISON** that identifies one thing with another. See also **FIGURES OF SPEECH.**

Metonymy, 99, 111 A form of verbal association. See also **FIGURES OF SPEECH.**

N

Narration, 13, 15, 36, 51, 68, 127–36, 183, 544 One of the four **PATTERNS OF WRITING.** An account of actions and events that happen to someone or something in a particular place and time. Because narration is essentially storytelling, it is often used in fiction; however, it is also an important element in almost all writing and speaking. The opening of Lincoln's *Gettysburg Address,* for example, is in the narrative mode: "Fourscore and seven years ago our fathers brought forth on this continent a new nation . . ."

Narrator, 86, 127–29, 134, 279 In a **NARRATIVE,** the person who is telling the story. The narrator can participate directly in the events of the story— or serve mainly as an observer reporting on those events.

O

Objective, 77–78, 82 A **DESCRIPTION** that presents its subject impartially.

Onomatopoeia, The use of words that sound like what they refer to: *What's the buzz?* or *The cat purred, the dog barked, and the clock ticked.*

Oxymoron, An apparent contradiction or bringing together of opposites for **RHETORICAL** or humorous effect, as in *eloquent silence* or *mournful optimist.*

P

Patterns of writing, Basic patterns of writing, including **DESCRIPTION, NARRATION, EXPOSITION,** and **ARGUMENTATION.** Description is explained in detail in Chapter 5; narration, in Chapter 6; exposition, in Chapters 7–12; and argumentation, in Chapter 13.

Personification, 79, 85 Assigning human characteristics to inanimate objects or ideas: *Death lurked around the corner.* See also **FIGURES OF SPEECH.**

Topic sentence, 9, 63–64 A sentence, often at the beginning of a paragraph, that states the paragraph's main point. The details in the rest of the paragraph should support the topic sentence.

Transitions, 65–66, 133, 187, 284 Connecting words or phrases—such as *next, by contrast, nevertheless, therefore, on the other hand*—that link sentences, paragraphs, and ideas in a piece of writing.

U

Understatement, A verbal playing down or softening for humorous or ironic effect. See **FIGURES OF SPEECH**.

V

Vantage point, 80, 85–86 In a **DESCRIPTION**, the physical perspective from which a subject is described. See the introduction to Chapter 5 for further discussion of vantage point.

W

Y